Traditional Neighbors, Different Modernities

Bhutan, Sikkim and the Mon Region

Traditional Neighbors, Different Modernities

Bhutan, Sikkim and the Mon Region

Edited by

Seiji Kumagai
Miguel Álvarez Ortega
Françoise Pommaret
Anna Balikci-Denjongpa

Kyoto University Press

TRANS PACIFIC PRESS

Published in 2024 jointly by:

Kyoto University Press
69 Yoshida Konoe-cho
Sakyo-ku, Kyoto 606-8315, Japan
Telephone: +81-75-761-6182
Fax: +81-75-761-6190
Email: sales@kyoto-up.or.jp
Web: http://www.kyoto-up.or.jp

Trans Pacific Press Co., Ltd.
PO Box 8547
#19682
Boston, MA, 02114, United States
Telephone: +1-6178610545
Email: info@transpacificpress.com
Web: http://www.transpacificpress.com

Copyedited by Miriam Riley, Armidale, NSW, Australia
Layout designed and set by Ryo Kuroda, Tsukuba-city, Ibaraki, Japan

Distributors

USA and Canada
Independent Publishers Group (IPG)
814 N. Franklin Street
Chicago, IL 60610, USA
Telephone inquiries: +1-312-337-0747
Order placement: 800-888-4741 (domestic only)
Fax: +1-312-337-5985
Email: frontdesk@ipgbook.com
Web: http://www.ipgbook.com

Europe, Oceania, Middle East and Africa
EUROSPAN
Gray's Inn House,
127 Clerkenwell Road
London, EC1R 5DB
United Kingdom
Telephone: +44-(0)20-7240-0856
Email: info@eurospan.co.uk
Web: https://www.eurospangroup.com/

Japan
For purchase orders in Japan, please contact any distributor in Japan.

China
China Publishers Services Ltd.
718, 7/F., Fortune Commercial Building,
362 Sha Tsui Road, Tsuen Wan, N.T.
Hong Kong
Telephone: +852-2491-1436
Email: edwin@cps-hk.com

Southeast Asia
Alkem Company Pte Ltd.
1, Sunview Road #01-27, Eco-Tech@Sunview
Singapore 627615
Telephone: +65 6265 6666
Email: enquiry@alkem.com.sg

Library of Congress Control Number: 2024908510

ISBN 978-1-920850-23-4 (hardback)
ISBN 978-1-920850-24-1 (paperback)
ISBN 978-1-920850-25-8 (eBook)

Table of Contents

List of Illustrations

Figures

Tables

Photographs

Contributors

Miguel Álvarez Ortega has an academic background in law, linguistics and translation studies. After completing his PhD in contemporary Western philosophy of law, he studied Buddhist philosophy and Tibetan language at the Rangjung Yeshe Institute in Kathmandu, and Sanskrit at Kyoto University. Currently, his main research line deals with Buddhist approaches to law, politics and public ethics with a focus on the Himalayas. He is an associate professor at the Kyoto University Graduate School of Law, where he teaches legal anthropology in East Asia, legal philosophy and religion and law.

Anna Balikci-Denjongpa is Research Coordinator at the Namgyal Institute of Tibetology, Sikkim, and editor of the *Bulletin of Tibetology*. She received her PhD in social anthropology from the School of Oriental and African Studies, University of London, which was published as *Lamas, Shamans and Ancestors: Village Religion in Sikkim* (Brill, 2008). Her research interests center on Sikkim's indigenous cultures, Sikkimese history and the medium of ethnographic films and historic photographs. Together with her team, she completed a dozen ethnographic films on Sikkim's Lepcha and Bhutia communities, which were screened at ethnographic film festivals worldwide. In 2021, she co-authored *The Royal History of Sikkim: A Chronicle of the House of Namgyal* (Serindia, 2021).

Jenny Bentley is a research scholar (PhD Social Anthropology, Zürich University) with fifteen years' fieldwork experience in the South Asian Himalayas. Currently, she is engaged in a research project on Lepcha storytelling, empowerment and language learning in collaboration with the University of Toronto. Further, she contributes to diverse projects with the multi-disciplinary design company Echostream as the ethnographic research head. Her research explores ethno-political and environmental movements, Indigeneity and belonging ritual practice, sacred landscape and youth engagement.

Kikee Doma Bhutia completed her doctoral studies at the Department of Estonian and Comparative Folklore, University of Tartu, Estonia with a dissertation titled *Mythic History, Belief Narratives, and Vernacular Buddhism among the Lhopos of Sikkim* (2016–2022). A graduate of North-Eastern Hill University in Shillong, Meghalaya (India), she holds a master's degree in English language and literature. During her two years as a research assistant (2014–2016), she worked on the translation and compilation of a volume on Bhutia proverbs and sayings at the Namgyal Institute of Tibetology (Gangtok, India). She is currently a research fellow at the Asia Center of the University of Tartu. Her current research interest is identity, geopolitics and political conflicts in the Himalayas.

Dendup Chophel is a postdoctoral fellow at the Centre for Contemporary Buddhist Studies in the University of Copenhagen's Department of Cross-Cultural and Regional Studies. He was a 2023 Early Career Research Fellow of The Robert H. N. Ho Family Foundation Program in Buddhist Studies. He started his career as a policy researcher at the government think-tank organisation, the Centre for Bhutan and GNH Studies, based in Thimphu. He completed his PhD in anthropology at the Australian National University in Canberra.

Pascale Dollfus is a researcher at the CNRS (France). A social anthropologist by training (PhD in 1987, Université Paris Nanterre), she has carried out extended fieldwork research since 1980 in the western Indian Himalayas: in Ladakh with sedentary farmers and nomadic pastoralists; in Spiti, particularly in the Pin valley, working with mediums and other religious specialists; and to a lesser extent in Kinnaur. Since 2010, she has been researching the Shertukpens, a small Tibeto-Burman-speaking population in West-Kameng district (Arunachal Pradesh), in Northeast India, at the opposite end of the Himalayan range. She has penned six books, edited four volumes/journals, and written some eighty articles and book chapters.

Tenzin Dorji is a lecturer at the College of Language and Culture Studies (CLCS), Royal University of Bhutan. He teaches Buddhism, Tibetan and Dzongkha language and literature to graduates and undergraduate students. He served as the dean of research and industrial linkages, and the coordinator of the Research Centre for Buddhist Studies at the CLCS. He has a master's degree in Indo-Tibetan Buddhist philosophy from the Central Institute of Higher Tibetan Studies in Varanasi, India. Dorji has authored seven books and published several research articles in the field of Buddhism, culture and language in various national and international journals.

Marlene Erschbamer is an independent scholar with a PhD in Buddhist studies from the Ludwig-Maximilians-University in Munich and an editor for the Oral History of Tibetan Studies project. Her research interests include the Barawa Kagyu tradition, Sikkim studies and the intersection of religion, nature and culture in the Tibetan Cultural Area.

Lungtaen Gyatso has an MA in Buddhist studies, an MA in Tibetan language and an MA in Sanskrit literature and is currently serving as the president of the College of Language and Culture Studies, Royal University of Bhutan, where he is also the pro-vice chancellor, research and planning. He is a member of the executive faculty of the Royal Institute of Governance and Strategic Studies (RIGSS), Phuentsholing, and the associate faculty of the Bhutan Institute of Wellbeing (BIW), Thimphu. He has been a member of the adjunct faculty of Kathmandu University since 2016. He sits on many decision-making boards and committees, including the National Constitution Drafting Committee. He has co-authored *The Light of My Life* (2001), compiled the *English-Dzongkha Dictionary, Dzongkha-English Dictionary* (2006) and published several articles and book-chapters on philosophy, language, wellbeing and culture.

Ngawang Jamtsho is a researcher and lecturer at the Paro College of Education, Royal University of Bhutan, after spending more than fifteen years as a lecturer at the College of Language and Culture (CLCS). He has an MA in history from Nalanda University (India). He has published several articles in English and Dzongkha and contributed extensively to the Bhutan cultural atlas (http://bhutanculturalatlas.clcs.edu.bt). His research interests are local rituals and lineages.

Seiji Kumagai is a professor at the Institute for the Future of Human Society (IFoHS) and divisional director at Kokoro Research Center. His field of research is Buddhist Madhyamaka and Abhidharma philosophy in India, Tibet and Bhutan, and also that of Bon religion. He has published numerous books and papers on Buddhism and the Himalayas, including *Bhutanese Buddhism and Its Culture* (Vajra Publications, 2014).

Thierry Mathou is both a career diplomat in the French diplomatic service and a scholar of Asian studies. As a diplomat, he held several ambassadorial posts in Asia and Oceania and serves currently as France's ambassador in India. As a scholar, he specialized in Himalayan studies and China-India relations. For the last thirty years, one of his main focuses has been Bhutanese politics and geopolitics. He has written several books and articles on the subject. He holds a PhD in political studies and Asian affairs and is associated with the National Centre for Scientific Research (CNRS) in Paris. He initiated the '*Tashi Gomang* Project'.

Alex McKay has a BA (Hons.) in religious studies and history and a PhD in South Asian history from the London University School of Oriental and African Studies (SOAS). Originally from New Zealand, he is now retired and living in the Australian countryside. He is a former lecturer and research fellow both at SOAS and at the International Institute for Asian Studies in Leiden, the Netherlands. He has edited a number of volumes, most recently co-editing *The Early 20th Century Resurgence of the Tibetan Buddhist World: Studies in Central Asian Buddhism* (University of Amsterdam Press, 2021), with Ishihama Yumiko. In addition, he is the author of four academic monographs, the most recent of which is *The Mandala Kingdom: A History of Buddhist Sikkim, 1815-1947* (Rachna books, 2021), which introduced a considerable amount of new historical material drawn from the Sikkim Palace Archives. He has also contributed around forty-five articles in academic journals, edited volumes and conference proceedings.

Françoise Pommaret, PhD, is a cultural anthropologist, director of Research Emeritus at the CNRS (France) and associate professor at the College of Language and Culture (CLCS, Bhutan). She has been associated with Bhutan in different capacities since 1981 and has published numerous scholarly articles and books on different aspects of Bhutanese culture. She is currently involved in the Bhutan cultural atlas project (http://bhutanculturalatlas.clcs.edu.bt). Her latest book with co-author Stephanie Guyer-Stevens, is *Divine Messengers: The Untold Story of Bhutan Female Shamans* (Shambhala, 2021).

Lobsang Tenpa received his doctoral degree from the University of Leipzig, Germany. His research focuses on the history and cultures of the Tibeto-Himalayan region and its peoples, through a South and Inner Asian studies disciplinary lens. His main publications include: *A Brief History of the Establishment of Buddhism in Monyul: Tawang & West Kameng Districts, Arunachal Pradesh, India* (Govt. of Arunachal Pradesh, 2013); *Himalayan Nature and Tibetan Buddhist Culture in Arunachal Pradesh, India: A Study of Monpa* (Springer, 2015, co-authored); and *An Early History of the Mon Region (India) and Its Relationship with Tibet and Bhutan* (Library of Tibetan Works & Archives, 2018).

Akiko Ueda is an associate professor at the Graduate School of International Development, Nagoya University. Her current research areas include GNH policies, rural development, food security and inequality in Bhutan. Prior to her present position, she was a specially appointed associate professor with the Global Collaboration Centre at Osaka University. Dr Ueda worked previously with the UNDP in the Bhutan Country Office as a coordination officer. She holds a doctorate in development studies from the School of Oriental and African Studies (SOAS), University of London. She is the author of a number of publications, including 'Understanding the Practice of Dual Residence in the Context of Transhumance: A Case from Western Bhutan' in the edited volume, *Bhutanese Buddhism and Its Culture* (Vajra Books, 2014).

Mélanie Vandenhelsken is a research scholar in anthropology (guest researcher at the Institute for Social Anthropology, Austrian Academy of Sciences, and lecturer at the University of Vienna). Her research concerns the interplay of cultural and political dynamics, and the construction of ethnicity and identity, citizenship and borders, with a special focus on the Indian state of Sikkim (eastern Himalayas). She currently carries out research on spatial imagination through rituals in the Sikkim-Nepal borderland. She edited the special issue 'Ancestrality, Migration, Rights and Exclusion: Citizenship in the Indian State of Sikkim', of *Asian Ethnicity* (vol. 22, no. 2, 2021). Her recent publications include the chapter 'Buddhist Studies' in *The Routledge Companion to Northeast India* (2023), and the article '"They turned the deity Yuma into a god!": Religious Reconstructions and Dissensions among the Limbu of Sikkim' (*Ateliers d'Anthropologie,* no. 49, 2021).

Richard W. Whitecross is a qualified, non-practicing lawyer with degrees in history, law and social anthropology. He has conducted qualitative research in the UK, Bhutan, Nepal and India. His doctoral research took a legal anthropological approach and examined everyday understandings of law and state transformation in Bhutan. Richard taught and held several positions at the University of Edinburgh and is now professor of socio-legal studies and head of law at Edinburgh Napier University. Since 2000, Richard has written extensively on the development of Bhutanese law and the Constitution. In 2023, his chapter 'The Zhabdrung's Legacy: Buddhism and Constitutional Transformation in Bhutan' was published in *Buddhism and Comparative Constitutional Law* (Cambridge University Press), edited by T. Ginsburg and B. Schonthal.

Introduction

Traditional Neighbors, Different Modernities in the Southeastern Himalayas – Bhutan, Sikkim and the Mon Region

Seiji Kumagai, Miguel Álvarez Ortega,
Anna Balikci-Denjongpa, Françoise Pommaret and
Lobsang Tenpa

The Himalayas: allure, isolation and contact

When the Himalayas are brought up in conversation, many people may recall Mount Everest, the highest peak in the world. 'Himalaya' originally comes from the Sanskrit word '*himālaya*': '*hima*' means 'snow' and '*ālaya*' means 'storehouse'. Thus, Himalaya poetically refers to the 'snow-covered mountain range'.

The Himalaya is often referred to as the 'roof of the world', having fourteen mountain peaks over 8,000 meters high. Therefore, it has stood as an attractive and challenging wall for Western mountaineers. The mountain range, extending to the east and west of the southern edge of the Tibetan plateau, was a high wall dividing Tibet and South Asia, a steep obstacle for those who tried to enter Tibet from countries to its south and even for Tibetan people traveling south.

Buddhism, a central cultural element associated with the region, was actually introduced into Tibet from India at a very late stage. While Buddhism had already reached Japan by the middle of the sixth century, it was not introduced into Tibet until the beginning of the seventh despite its proximity to India, possibly because of Tibet's lack of political unity before that time.

At the beginning of the seventh century, Songtsen Gampo (Srong btsan sgam po, b. 581, r. 618–649) unified Central Tibet and established the Tibetan Empire. From that period onwards, a relationship with India started to develop across the Himalayan range. Songtsen Gampo, while continuing to foster a relationship with China, sent Tonmi Sambhota (Thon mi saṃbhoṭa) to India in 633 to learn Sanskrit and to create a writing system and grammar for the Tibetan language. Thereafter, Sanskrit Buddhist scriptures started to be translated into Tibetan.

At the end of the eighth century, during the reign of Trisong Detsen (Khri srong lde brtsan, r. 742–797), Indian Buddhist master Śāntarakṣita (ca. 725–788) was invited to Tibet, although his visit achieved little. After staying for six years in the Nepalese slopes of the southern Himalayas, Śāntarakṣita revisited Tibet, this time along with Vajrayāna master Padmasambhāva (eighth century), and founded the Samye (Bsam yas) Monastery, where Mahāyāna Buddhism was transmitted. After the foundation of the Samye Monastery, Śāntarakṣita's disciple Kamalaśīla (ca. 740–795) was invited to Tibet to debate with a Chinese Chan master from Dun Huan (敦煌). The Tibetan tradition insists that Kamalaśīla won the debate, thus explaining how Indian Buddhism became the state religion of the Tibetan Empire.[1]

By that period, the Tibetan Empire had become a military superpower stronger than China. In 763, during the An Lushan Rebellion, the Tibetan Empire attacked the Tang (唐) Empire and occupied its capital Chang An (長安: today's Xi'an), which was inadequately guarded. In 786, the empire conquered Dun Huan (敦煌), establishing its influence over the Silk Road.

The influence of imperial Tibet even reached the southeastern Himalayas, where the 'ancient Mon region', comprising, according to some scholars, present-day southeast Tibet, Sikkim, Bhutan and the 'present Mon region', was part of the administrative structure of the Tibetan Empire.[2] It is thus a sound assumption that there was already a large population in such Himalayan regions, directly and indirectly influenced by Central Tibet. Peddlers and caravans might have crossed over the region on their way to Tibet and India. The lack of political structures alluded to above would explain the lack of written information concerning such ties found in official documents and inscriptions.

---

1 According to Chinese sources, however, their representative won the debate.

2 See Tenpa (2018: 44, n. 83–85); or maps in Ryavec (2015: 44–45, m. 11), and Hazod (2009: 221, m. 2); as well as in Aris (1979: 1–144).

The southeastern Himalayan regions are often overlooked, being sandwiched between and overshadowed by India and China, two mighty powers. It is true that the development of military power in these regions was not significant, implying that they could hardly have had any major external political impact. Even so, the Himalayas as a whole have been an important area for both India and Tibet (China) from the point of view of international relations. In the modern era, the Himalayas became an important strategic area in dealings with Asia, especially for the British Empire.

Southeastern Himalayas: a fascinating Asian crossroad

The particular interest of the southeastern Himalayas lies in its rich and complex development as a contact area, one of intricate multilayered cultural tapestries, a fascinating crossroads among, and therefore influenced by, Central Tibet to its north and India to its south.

The southeastern Himalayan enclaves, such as Bhutan, Sikkim and the Mon region, are adjacent to Southern Tibet, which means that their politics, religion, culture and society have been influenced by Tibet. These regions have been typically regarded as belonging to the Tibetan cultural areas and therefore studied within the framework of Tibetology as frontier areas.

However, we need to note that these regions, separated from Tibet by the Himalayan range, were also influenced by India and Southeast Asia. Actually, Tibetans traditionally called the areas on the Tibetan Plateau north of the Himalayan range 'Pö' (Bod), while the southern fringes of the Himalayas, e.g., territories such as Bhutan and Arunachal Pradesh, were referred to as 'Mon'. Thus, they clearly differentiated the two areas. In the seventeenth century, nations were first established in the current locations of Bhutan and Sikkim, named Druk-yul ('Brug yul) and Drenjong ('Bras ljongs) respectively. Again, this points to a clear separation from Tibet.

Since the nineteenth century, the southern Himalayas have been influenced by British India. Owing to the relatively easy crossing over Sikkim's Nathu La pass into Tibet, Sikkim became an important base allowing entrance from India into the Himalayas and Tibet. However, Sikkim was incorporated into the Republic of India in 1975. The Mon region, under the direct control of the Tibetan government since 1680, became part of British India in 1914, and was fully incorporated into the Republic of India in February 1951. Bhutan is an independent nation member of the SAARC (South Asia Association for Regional Cooperation) and so from an international political point of view it pertains to South Asia. Having been incorporated into India and South Asia, the southeastern Himalayas are currently cut-off from Tibet.

The southeastern Himalayas, although initially belonging to the Tibetan cultural areas, have been influenced by the cultures and politics of the British Empire and India since the nineteenth century. On the other hand, Tibet has been politically controlled and culturally influenced by China since its official annexation in the 1950s. Sinicized Tibet and the Indianized southeastern Himalayas have different characteristics, while to some extent, still belonging to the Tibetan cultural area. Thus, we can more clearly understand the notions of 'Tibetan-ness' and 'Himalayan-ness' by comparing both regions with different external influences.

Bhutan, Sikkim and the Mon region: background, similarities and differences

This book focuses on Bhutan, Sikkim and the Mon region within the context of the southeastern Himalayas. In this regard, it is important to draw from the core idea that these three regions are not only neighbors that once shared a blurred contact zone, but also entities that present both clear sociohistorical similarities and dissimilarities. Even if all three territories developed culturally in multiethnic contexts in which Tibetan groups and their Mahāyāna-Tantric form of Buddhism played a clear central role, their singular identities and political configuration and history are notably divergent.

Sikkim, Bhutan and the Mon region were part of the Tibetan imagination as mythical southern borderlands populated by uncivilized people, but at the same time, they were regarded as a land of hidden religious treasures and therefore as a sacred refuge for royals and monastics in troubled times. It is, therefore, significant that historical accounts from these regions typically date from the seventeenth century onwards, when the Gelukpa school hegemony led to the establishment of the Ganden

Phodrang regime by the fifth Dalai Lama in the wider context of the continued marginalization of other schools and monastic leaders. In that period, Bhutan and Sikkim emerged as 'state' entities after their founding by Tibetan elites, while the Mon region had its relative local independence seriously curtailed by the monastic Gelukpa presence.

Subsequently, all three regions experienced British colonialism, resulting in territorial diminishments, the signing of treaties and later varied modalities of incorporation, *lato sensu,* into the empire (a protectorate in the case of Sikkim; a country guided in external affairs in the case of Bhutan; and a frontier administrative section of Assam province for the Mon region) in the late nineteenth to early twentieth centuries. The British presence also entailed significant socio-demographic fluctuations mainly due to an ever-increasing tide of Nepalese immigration. In 1947, the British Empire collapsed, leading to a period of sociopolitical uncertainties in which its successor, Constituent India, would start a long and complex process of negotiations and political reconfigurations leading to quite different results. Bhutan had its sovereignty recognized by India in 1949 and accessed the United Nations in 1971, while Sikkim came under Indian suzerainty in 1950 and was finally annexed in 1975, when it became the twenty-second state of the Indian Union. The Mon region, which had been subject to an international controversy with China since the delimitation of its frontier in 1914 (the so-called 'McMahon line'), ended up as a part of the newly created State of Arunachal Pradesh in 1972, currently corresponding to the districts of West Kameng and Tawang.

Their current political status is a major and essential diverging feature, but it is obviously not the only one. Historically, Bhutan's origins and character were more bellicose, engaging in different wars with its neighbors, namely Tibet, and even invading Sikkim twice. Sikkim, on the other hand, seems to have been militarily weaker, suffering in the late eighteenth century an invasion by the Gurkha, who controlled parts of the country west of the Teesta River for twenty-eight years. The relationship with the British was also closer in the case of Sikkim. The weight of the religious component of their legitimacy differs as well. Bhutan, founded by a Drukpa Kagyü religious leader Zhabdrung[3] Ngawang Namgyal

3 An honorific title meaning 'at whose feet (one submits)'.

(Zhabs drung Ngag dbang rnam rgyal, b. 1594, d. 1651) who had to flee from Tibet in 1616, was directly ruled by monastic institutions from its inception up to the advent of the Wangchuck dynasty in 1907. Even though the political origins of Sikkim are also associated with Tibetan religious figures, followers of the Nyingma (Rnying ma) school, they did not institute ecclesiastical rule. Rather, a lay lord, Phuntsog Namgyal (Phun tshog rnam rgyal, b. 1604, d. 1670), was endorsed, giving birth to a royal dynasty, the Namgyals, who ruled Sikkim as *chogyals* (dharma kings) up to its merger with India. In the Mon region the rise of the Gelukpa implied a more direct Lhasa administration from 1680 with a corresponding loss of full autonomy for the local rulers (*jo bo*), who claimed to be descendants of the Tibetan aristocracy.

It is also notable that ethno-demographic changes affected these countries differently. The inflow of Nepalese immigrants in Sikkim was so important that by the beginning of the twentieth century they had become the majority (sixty-two percent; currently seventy-five percent), and presently the originally ruling Bodish groups (Bhutia-Lepcha) constitute a meagre minority (less than twenty percent) belonging to the legal minority category of 'Scheduled Tribes'. In the case of Bhutan, two-thirds of the population consists of Tibeto-Burman groups, while Nepalese remain a minority at less than thirty-five percent. The Mon region is arguably the least affected by such migrations, with less than twenty percent of the population of West Kameng and less than five percent in Tawang being Nepalese. The majority of the populations pertain to the Mon group, ethno-culturally akin to some parts of the eastern Bhutan population, or to one of the other four Tibeto-Burman 'Scheduled Tribes' of the districts.

Historical overview and internal diversity

Bhutan

Bhutan is a country situated on the southern slopes of the Himalayas, south of Lhasa. Its land area is 38,400 km^2, a size equivalent to Switzerland or Taiwan. It is adjacent to Tibet (PRC) to the north and the Indian states of Sikkim to the west, Arunachal Pradesh to the east, and West Bengal and Assam to the south. It is thus sandwiched between and influenced by India and Tibet.

The northern parts belong to an alpine zone comprising 7,000 m-class mountains, while the southern parts, standing less than 500 meters above sea level, have a subtropical climate; thus, a wide range of species of animals and plants exist in the country. There is also a notable variety of languages, nineteen of which are officially recognized, and cultures. Although Dzongkha is the national language and English is the medium of instruction, people speak Dzongkha in western Bhutan; Tshangla (or Sharchopkha), Brokpakha and Dzalakha/Dakpakha in eastern Bhutan; Bumthangkha dialects in central and south-central Bhutan; and Nepalese in southern Bhutan, to name just the main linguistic varieties. Certain enclaves, like Laya (in northern Bhutan) and Merak and Sakteng (in eastern Bhutan) as well as the Lhops (in southwestern Bhutan), are usually regarded as particularly distinctive in their folklore, clothing and culture.

Regarding religion, Buddhism is by far the most important in sociological and historical terms, followed by Hinduism. Christianism is still a recent and minority phenomenon, with proselytism prohibited under the law. While being a small country with a population of around 750,000, Bhutan constitutes a major tourist destination, attracting visitors from all over the world with its wide variety of climates, landscapes, languages, cultures and religions.

The early history of Bhutan is still poorly understood and only known through archaeological research, since there is no written information in historical documents prior to the seventh century. Some researchers insist that people have resided in the area of current Bhutan since 2000–1500 BCE.[4]

Central Tibet, north of Bhutan, was first unified by King Songtsen Gampo as an empire at the beginning of the seventh century, and he continued to integrate surrounding regions. Buddhism is said to have been introduced to Tibet from India during the reign of this very king. According to Bhutanese tradition, King Songtsen Gampo is said to have built Buddhist temples in Bhutan, such as Kichu Temple (Skyer chu lha

4 For example, Michel Aris (1979) estimated the date of stone tools found in Bhutan to be 2000–1500 BCE, and used it as the proof for the above date of residence of people in Bhutan. It is important to note that this date has not been confirmed through scientific methods such as radiocarbon dating.

khang) in Paro in western Bhutan and Jampa Temple (Byams pa lha khang) in Bumthang in central Bhutan.

Buddhism declined in Tibet after the collapse of the Tibetan Empire at the end of the ninth century, but it revived when it was reintroduced from India after the eleventh century. Tibetan Buddhist schools seem to have started to send their missionaries to the region currently known as Bhutan in the late tenth century.[5]

Bhutan, situated to the south of Central Tibet, was geographically an ideal missionary destination for Tibetan Buddhist schools. Products such as rice, bamboo and medicinal herbs could be obtained in warm areas in Bhutan, thus constituting attractive places to recruit new local sponsors for Tibetans living on the Tibetan Plateau over 3,500 meters high, which lacked such products.

The four major Tibetan Buddhist schools (Nyingma, Kagyu, Sakya and Geluk) sent missionaries to Bhutan, each of them becoming prevalent in a particular area. The Nyingma school predominated in central and eastern Bhutan; the Drukpa Kagyü school prevailed in western Bhutan; the Geluk school only had a notable presence in certain parts of the eastern edge of Bhutan; and the Sakya school founded some monasteries in western and northern Bhutan, but disappeared from the country in the 1950s.[6] Since before the first half of the seventeenth century, there were also other schools known as the 'Five Groups of Lamas' (bla ma khag lnga), which resisted the monastic leader Zhabdrung Ngawang Namgyal who fled from Tibet and established Bhutan (Drukyul) in the first half of the seventeenth century. At the end of his life, the Zhabdrung appointed a 'regent' (*sde srid*) and a 'chief abbot' (*rje mkhan po*), and entrusted them with political and religious powers respectively. This system continued after the Zhabdrung's death.

While Bhutan had historically maintained an international relationship with Tibetan cultural areas and Nepal, it began to have some contact with the European world through the British Indian Empire only after the eighteenth century.

---

5 See Aris (1979: 149–199).

6 See Kumagai (2014).

In 1851, British India declared the annexation of the Assamese and Bengali Duars (frontier foothill areas) and granted Bhutan a payment of 10,000 rupees (2,400 pounds) per annum in compensation for their loss of territory. Tension increased on both sides, however, and British India finally declared war against Bhutan on 12 November 1864. Bhutan surrendered after a few months, and Bhutan and British India signed the Treaty of Sinchula on 11 November 1865. Bhutan lost its southern territories in the Duars (Assam and Bengal foothill regions), but received 50,000 rupees per year as compensation. The Bhutan military leader in the war was Jigme Namgyal (b. 1825, d. 1881), then the Trongsa governor (*penlop*) and the most powerful man in the country. Acknowledging that Bhutan was in great danger with such a powerful and ambitious neighbor, he decided to avoid conflict with the surrounding countries, and rather concentrated on domestic governance inside Bhutan.

His son Ugyen Wangchuck[7] (b. 1882, d. 1926) was elected as the first king of Bhutan in 1907, thus establishing the Wangchuck dynasty. In 1910, he signed with British India the Treaty of Punakha, which succeeded the Treaty of Sinchula, signed by his father Jigme Namgyal in 1865. Bhutan retained internal autonomy but agreed to allow the British to 'advise' it on foreign affairs.

In the reign of the second king Jigme Wangchuck (b. 1905, d. 1952), the recently independent India and Bhutan signed a Treaty of Peace and Friendship on 8 August 1949, according to which India would not intervene in Bhutanese domestic politics but Bhutan would follow India's advice in foreign affairs. Such an agreement tightened the relationship between the two countries.

The third king Jigme Dorji Wangchuck (b. 1929, d. 1972) was responsible for the modernization and internationalization of Bhutan, which granted him the epithet of 'Father of Modern Bhutan'. After his enthronement in 1952, he established the National Assembly in 1953 and the Royal Advisory Council in 1965, paving the transition from an absolute monarchy to a constitutional monarchy. Bhutan started a series of five-year plans in 1961, and built roads, schools and hospitals with the financial aid of the Indian government. His final political achievement was

7 From the third king on, the spelling changes to 'Wangchuck'.

the entry of Bhutan into the United Nations (21 July 1971), turning Bhutan into a country internationally recognized as an independent state.

After his accession to the throne in 1972, the fourth king Jigme Singye Wangchuck (b. 1955), following in his father's footsteps, continued the opening of Bhutan and accelerated its development. He also had to face an often sensitive international context that seemed to cast shadows over the country's independence. Tibet was incorporated into China in the 1950s; China and India had a frontier conflict over Arunachal Pradesh in 1962; and Sikkim was annexed by India in 1975. In such a complex international scenario, the South Asia Association for Regional Cooperation (SAARC) was founded in 1985 with the participation of Bhutan, which has since then been considered as politically part of South Asia. Historically speaking, therefore, such developments implied a shift in the geopolitical affiliation of the country. Even though southeastern Himalayan countries such as Bhutan are traditionally considered to have received significant influence from Tibet since the foundation of the Tibetan Empire in the seventh century, during the power games between India and China, northern Himalayan countries such as Tibet were incorporated into East Asia (i.e., China), while southern Himalayan countries such as Bhutan were incorporated into South Asia. For Bhutan it meant that cultural relations with Tibet were suddenly cut off by the vagaries of geopolitics.

One of the biggest achievements of the fourth king of Bhutan was the invention of the concept of GNH (Gross National Happiness) in the 1970s: 'Gross National Happiness is more important than Gross National Product'. The concept was further systematized as comprising four pillars, nine domains and thirty-three indicators. GNH surveys have been conducted by the Bhutanese government, especially by the Centre for Bhutan Studies and GNH Research.[8] Also, a specially created GNH Commission has been assessing all proposed public policies in terms of their compliance with the goals pursued under the concept of GNH. The current Constitution of Bhutan (Article 9, Section 2) declares that GNH forms the base of Bhutanese policy.[9]

---

8 The GNH Survey was conducted in 2008, 2010 and 2015.

9 Constitution of the Kingdom of Bhutan, Article 9, Section 2: 'The State shall strive to promote those conditions that will enable the pursuit of Gross National Happiness'.

After his enthronement in 2006, the fifth king Jigme Khesar Namgyel Wangchuck (b. 1980) further advanced the political reforms carried out by his father, the fourth king, who led the democratization process that made his son the first constitutional king upon the ratification of the Constitution of Bhutan in 2008. The legal history prior to the current constitution is traditionally dated back to the premodern monastic rules known as Chayik Chenmo (cha yig chen mo), attributed to the Zhabdrung, and the first modern basic legal code known as Thrimzhung Chenmo (khrim zhung chen mo), composed in 1957. Major political milestones in the reign of the fifth king have been the establishment of direct democratic elections from 2008, and the adoption of a bicameral parliamentary system with the addition of the National Council to the National Assembly. Ever since his enthronement, the fifth king has striven to foster and further improve democracy in this kingdom.

As a result of the historical developments briefly described above, Bhutan is today a diverse and culturally rich country. Bhutan may be divided into three broad cultural regions that correspond to its western, central-eastern and southern parts.

The western part has been mostly influenced by the Drukpa Kagyü school and especially Zhabdrung Ngawang Namgyal, who first founded Simtokha Dzong (monastery-fortress) in Thimphu between 1629 and 1630, Punakha Dzong in Punakha in 1637 and Wangdue Phodrang Dzong in Wangdue Phodrang in 1638. He was therefore responsible for the establishment of the crucial administrative bases in western Bhutan. Since then, the Drukpa Kagyü school has been highly influential in these areas, where locals are usually referred to as 'Ngalops'.

The central and eastern parts of Bhutan have been influenced by the Nyingma school. Tibetan Nyingma scholar-monk Longchenpa (Klong chen rab 'byams pa Dri med 'od zer, b. 1308, d. 1363) visited central Bhutan and established, among others, Tharpaling Monastery and the Shingkhar Temple in Bumthang. The Bhutanese born Pema Lingpa (Padma gling pa, b. 1450, d. 1521), who was regarded as the reincarnation of Longchenpa, contributed to the propagation of the Nyingma school in Bumthang, where he built Tamzhing Monastery in 1501. It is said that Pema Lingpa's influence spread throughout eastern Bhutan and even into the Mon region in current Arunachal Pradesh (India), where his sibling Ogyan Sangpo

(O rgyan bzang po) had founded the monasteries of Ugyenling, Tsokgyeling, etc. Pema Lingpa's grandson Pema Thinley (b. 1564, d. 1642) built the Gangtey Monastery in the Phobjika Valley (Wangdue Phodrang) of the Black Mountains in 1613, which became the westernmost base of the Nyingma school.

The Tibeto-Burman ethno-linguistic group prevalent in eastern Bhutan is known as Sharchop and they speak Tshangla, commonly known as Sharchopkha, but there are other groups in eastern Bhutan who speak an array of Tibeto-Burman languages.

The southern part of Bhutan is characterized by the influence of Nepalese people, termed Lhotshampas, who speak Nepali and mainly follow Hinduism. Most of them moved from eastern Nepal and the Darjeeling region to southern Bhutan at the end of the nineteenth century and the beginning of the twentieth century, a movement encouraged by the British. Following a census in 1988, which showed that many had settled in Bhutan but had no papers, there was political unrest and many left Bhutan for refugee camps in Nepal, before being resettled in Western countries. Those who remained in Bhutan are currently citizens of the country with the same rights as any other Bhutanese.

Sikkim: an overview

Sikkim was an independent Himalayan Buddhist kingdom founded in the 1640s by Tibetan Nyingma lamas and ruled by the Namgyal dynasty, a monarchy claiming Tibetan origin. Sikkim became a British protectorate in 1890 and was integrated into the Union of India in May 1975, simultaneously putting an end to the rule of the Namgyals.

Today, Sikkim is a state of Northeast India bordering the Tibet Autonomous Region of China in the north, Bhutan in the east, Nepal in the west and the Indian state of West Bengal in the south. Sikkim is of great political and strategic importance to India because of the Nathu La pass, which links Sikkim to China's Chumbi Valley, and for its location along several international borders. With a total area of 7,096 km^2, Sikkim lacks flat land and elevations vary from a few hundred meters above sea level to the world's third highest peak, Mount Khangchendzonga, at 8,586 meters. Owing to this altitudinal gradation, Sikkim has an exceptionally rich biodiversity which led to the inscription of the Khangchendzonga National Park as a mixed (nature-culture) World Heritage Site by UNESCO in 2016.

Ethnic composition

The ethnic composition of Sikkim's 650,000 inhabitants is extremely varied considering that it is a tiny state with twenty percent of its territory lying under perpetual snow. The Anthropological Survey of India has documented twenty-five different communities that can be grouped in three main categories: (1) Bhutias and Lepchas, who now represent less than twenty percent of Sikkim's total population; (2) people of Nepalese origin, who represent more than seventy-five percent of the population; and (3) people from the plains of India, who are a small but rapidly growing minority.

The Lepchas have no history of migration and are considered Sikkim's indigenous people. The Bhutias are descendants of inhabitants of the neighboring Himalayan valleys of Chumbi and Ha who were later joined by settlers from Kham Minyak in eastern Tibet. Their descendants call themselves Lhopo (*lho pa* – 'people from the south') but are generally known as Bhutia, Sikkimese or even Denjongpa, the people of Denjong or Dremojong ('Bras mo ljongs – 'the fruitful valley'), as Sikkim used to be known. The great majority of Sikkim's Nepali-speaking people are descendants of immigrants from Nepal who were resettled in an organized manner from the 1860s onwards on agricultural estates in Sikkim's southern belt. A small minority of Sikkimese Limbus, locally referred to as Tsong, are considered indigenous to Sikkim's western region bordering on their own ancient region of Limbuan, today an integral part of eastern Nepal.

Establishment of the kingdom

The kings of Sikkim are believed to descend from a Minyak prince by the name of Guru Tashi who left Kham Minyak in eastern Tibet and came down to Chumbi via Lhasa and Sakya in Central Tibet in what is thought to have been the thirteenth century. Guru Tashi's family gained political authority in the Chumbi Valley, authority that eventually came to include what is known today as Sikkim. Guru Tashi's eldest son, Gye Bumsag, first came to Sikkim with his wife in search of the Lepcha patriarch Thekong Tek. The couple was childless and requested that Thekong Tek perform a ritual so they might be blessed with a male descendant. Upon their return to Chumbi, the couple had three sons who later became the ancestors of a number of Bhutia patrilineal descent groups, including that of the royal family. An oath of blood brotherhood was sworn between the Lepchas and the Tibetans whereby the mountain god Khangchendzonga and all the guardian deities of Sikkim were invoked to stand witness to the pledge of unity between the two communities.

Gye Bumsag's descendant Phuntsog Namgyal was crowned Sikkim's first king in the 1640s by three Tibetan Nyingma lamas: Gyalwa Lhatsun Namkha Jigme (b. 1597, d. 1653), Kahthog Kuntu Zangpo and Ngadag Sempa Chenpo Phuntshog Rigdzin (b. 1591, d. 1656), who came to Sikkim in search of Guru Padmasambhava's blessed refuge valleys known as 'Hidden Lands'. The lamas entered Sikkim from three different directions and converged upon Yuksam where they sought to ensure that the 'Hidden Land' be ruled according to Buddhist law. Invoking a prophesy, Phuntshog Namgyal was invited to Yuksam and enthroned as *chogyal* or 'king who rules according to the Buddhist dharma'. Together, the three pioneer lamas and the first *chogyal* are referred to as the Four Patron Saints.

Between Tibet and British India

From its emergence as a Buddhist kingdom in the seventeenth century until late in the nineteenth century, Sikkim looked to Tibet for political, cultural and religious guidance. The Sikkim *chogyals* sought ladies from the Tibetan aristocracy for matrimony and trade was carried out with Sikkim's northern neighbor rather than with Bengal to the south. This changed with the arrival of British influence in the region following the Anglo-Nepal war of 1814–1816. Spanning the nineteenth century, a series of events and treaties followed each other in rapid succession resulting in the severance of Sikkim's close ties with Tibet and the latter's recognition of Sikkim as a British protectorate. Amongst these events were the restoration of Sikkimese territory west of the Teesta River by the British in 1817 (Treaty of Titalia); the granting of Darjeeling by Sikkim to British India in 1835; the military expedition against Sikkim leading to the 1861 Treaty of Tumlong and British annexation of Sikkim's estates in the Terai; the 1888 Lungthu British military expedition aimed at pushing Tibetans back to the Sikkim-Tibet border along the watershed; the 1889 appointment of a British 'Political Officer Sikkim, Bhutan and Tibet' based in Gangtok; the 1890 convention signed between China and Great Britain recognizing Sikkim as a British protectorate; and eventually, the detention of the *chogyal* at Darjeeling for over three years while the British reorganized Sikkim's administration and initiated its development. The organized settlement of migrants from Nepal, which had begun in the late 1860s, now continued unabated with the blessing of the political officer. Initially resettled on agricultural estates along Sikkim's southern belt, the Nepalese introduced irrigated rice cultivation and greatly contributed to the economic development of the kingdom. Their arrival resulted in such a consequential demographic shift that the indigenous Sikkimese soon found themselves in the minority. Now with a Hindu Nepali-speaking majority, Sikkim's future as part of South Asia was effectively ensured. The eventual 1975 integration of Sikkim into the Union of India was only a natural progression and consequence of these nineteenth century events.

Economy

Agriculture, tourism and hydro-power are now the basis of Sikkim's economy. Sikkim's main crops are terraced rice cultivation, large cardamom, oranges, ginger and tea. Sikkim is one of the world's main producers of cardamom, which was introduced at the end of the nineteenth century and, for several decades, remained the only form of cash revenue for the indigenous farmers. Copper and dolomite mining were initiated in the nineteenth century but eventually abandoned. Tourism greatly expanded from the 1990s followed by the construction of a cascade of dams along the Teesta River and the export of hydro-power to India.

A lucrative trade between Tibet and India was carried out over the mountain passes of Sikkim down to Kalimpong in Bengal from the end of the nineteenth century. The Kalimpong trade was dominated by wool sourced in Tibet but included salt, furs, borax, carpets, silk, yak tails and gold dust. An older local trade with Tibet was carried out over the Nathu La pass down to Gangtok as well as over the passes in northern Sikkim. For example, people from Lachen in North Sikkim took locally grown apples, timber and vegetable dyes to Gyantse and returned with commodities in demand in Sikkim such as salt, barley, carpets, brocades and Tibetan brick tea. All trade over the passes of Sikkim came to an abrupt end in 1962 when, following the Sino-Indian War, the border between Sikkim and Tibet (China) was sealed. The trade through the Nathu La pass was eventually revived in 2006 to a limited extent.

The economic development of Sikkim initiated by the first political officer gained momentum during the reign of the eleventh Chogyal Tashi Namgyal (b. 1893, d. 1963), when the state administration was reorganized and expanded. By 1947, the state council ended the various forms of porterage duty and compulsory unpaid labor on behalf of the state and the landlords. By 1948, they abolished the judicial and magisterial functions of the landlords, and a high court was established in 1955. The landlord system was altogether abolished in 1951, and the first scientific cadastral land survey was commenced the same year. In 1954, the first loans from India were negotiated by the future twelfth Chogyal Palden Thondup Namgyal (b. 1923, b. 1982) to fund three successive economic development plans, which changed the face of Sikkim forever.

Sikkim's integration within the Republic of India

When India gained independence from British rule in 1947, Sikkim's protectorate status was maintained and transferred to the new Indian government, which controlled Sikkim's defense, external relations and strategic communication. Sikkim formally became India's protectorate following the signing of the 1950 Indo-Sikkim Treaty. Eventually, following the birth of political parties, India took control of Sikkim as an associate state in April 1973, and by May 1975, the *chogyal* was deposed and Sikkim declared the twenty-second state of India.

The Mon region (mon yul, in Arunachal Pradesh)

The Mon region (mon yul) refers to a geographical zone comprising the two westernmost districts of Tawang and West Kameng in the state of

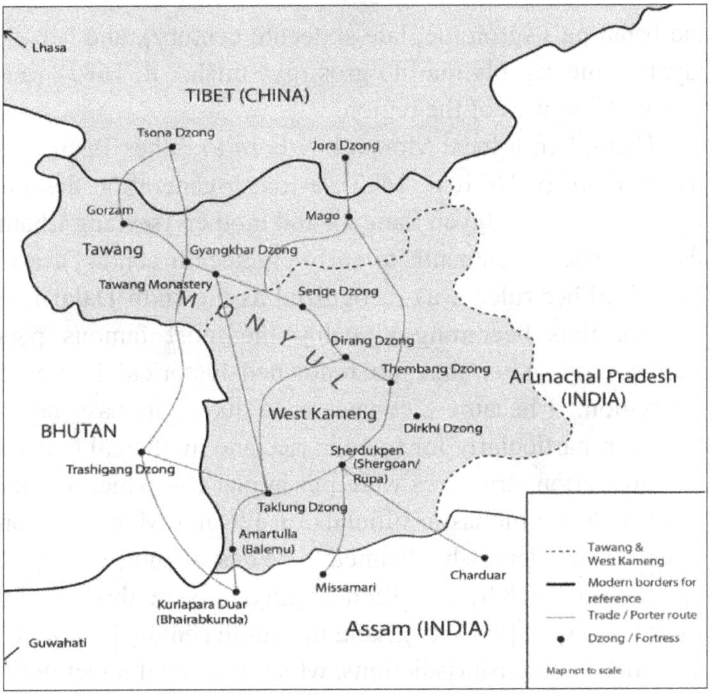

Figure 0.1: The Mon region: Tawang and West Kameng districts Source: Tenpa (2018)

Arunachal Pradesh, India. Mon is a traditional denomination not officially used nowadays. However, it is actually an archaic Tibetan word that refers to a low-lying densely forested region with a narrow valley, and it is still used throughout the Himalayas. The term is commonly applied to both a region and an ethnic group. Therefore, locally, the territory is still lovingly called Monyul and its people Monpa. Within Monpas we find people who speak different languages, along with other ethnic minorities, such as Bugun, Hrusso-Aka, Miji, Sartang and Sherdukpen, among others (cf. Figure 0.1). Historically, a larger picture can be drawn after 1680, when it was formally annexed into the Ganden Phodrang Government of Tibet (1642–1959). Before that, it was merely an unspecific region rarely mentioned in texts, although Pema Lingpa's visits in 1489 and 1507 with his sibling Ogyan Sangpo provided the first account of the region by a historical person. After them, Kunden Sangey Yeshe (kun mdun sangs rgyas ye shes, sixteenth century), Merak Lama Tenpe Donme (me rag bla ma bstan pa'i sgron me, late sixteenth century), and Merak Lama Lodeo Gyatso (me rag bla ma blo gros rgya mtsho, d. 1682) were some of the renowned figures of the region.

Thereafter, a local Monpa boy born to father Tashi Tenzin (bkra shis bstan 'dzin, b. 1651, d. 1697), a fourth-generation descendant of Pema Lingpa's sibling Ugyan Sangpo, and mother Tsewang Lhamo (tshe dbang lha mo, late seventeenth to early eighteenth century), a princess of the local Berkher ruler, was recognized as the sixth Dalai Lama Tsangyang Gyatso, thus becoming arguably the most famous person from the Mon region. After that, no renowned historical figures emerged from the region. It became a contact zone due to its easy passage to Assam, however, particularly for trade in rice and medicinal herbs. Hence, strong administration structures were put in place in which the local clan rulers dealt with the monastic officials of Tawang Monastery on equal terms. Those local rulers, who claimed to be descendants of the Tibetan imperial princes (either Khyikha Rathoe [khyi kha ra thod, eighth century] or Lhase Tsangma [lha sras gtsang ma, ninth century]), enjoyed considerable autonomy in their jurisdictions, which remained intact until 1951.

A significant and little-known example of such autonomy is the signing by local rulers of four treaties with British Indian officials in 1844 and 1853. These agreements seem to have had a considerable effect when the 1914 Simla Agreement established the McMahon Line to include the Mon region, although British India was well aware that the region was being administered by Lhasa. However, in 1938, the Simla Convention was clandestinely inserted in the last (fourteenth) volume of Aitchison's treaties of 1929,[10] and thus the existence of the Simla Convention of 1914 was acknowledged. The Indo-Tibetan border thus came to be known as the McMahon Line and was bilaterally rectified in 1938, and Monyul was renamed as 'Tawang Tract' in official documents. Subsequently, a British Indian army convoy under the direction of Captain Lightfoot reached

10 The Foreign and Political Department entrusted C.U. Aitchison (1832–1896), under-secretary to the Government of India, with a multi-volume compilation entitled: *A Collection of Treaties, Engagements and Sanads Relating to India and Neighbouring Countries.* The fifth edition, which appeared posthumously in 1929–33, included the referred to fourteenth volume.

Tawang on 30 April 1938. However, the convoy did not settle there, and again in 1944 military posts of the Assam Rifles were established at Dirang Dzong and Rupa, but the nature of such 'posts' is not clear. At the same time, in 1946, the 'North-East Frontier Tract' (1919–1946) was renamed as the 'North-East Frontier Agency' (NEFA, 1946–1972), and subsequently Monyul was renamed as the 'Sela Sub Agency' (1946–1954), succeeding the former 'Tawang Tract' (1919–1946). It seems that neither this renaming nor the establishment of 'military posts' had an effective impact on the administration of the region, because British Indian official Imdad Ali reported in the mid-1940s that the local Tibeto-Mon officials were enforcing their own regulations.[11] In February 1951, a column of Assam Rifles led by Major R. Khating annexed Tawang, leading to the return to Lhasa of the last Tibetan monk-official Thubten Choephel (Thub bstan chos 'phel, r. 1949–1951).[12] Within a few weeks, the Mon region was directly administered by the Government of India. Major Khating himself was the first to be appointed as 'assistant political officer' of the 'Sela Sub Agency', and in July 1952 he, representing the Government of India, agreed to maintain the status quo of the sociopolitical systems as well as the privileges of the Tawang Monastery and local rulers.

A few years later, the Sela Sub Agency was renamed after the Kameng River as the 'Kameng Frontier Division' (1954–1980), and a newly formed hill-station called Bomdila became its headquarters. In 1980 it was divided into the West and East Kameng districts, and 'West Kameng' (1980–1984) was further split into the Tawang and West Kameng districts in 1984. At the same time, the region as well as the state was administered by the Ministry of External Affairs (MEA) until 1965, when the Government of India transferred it to the Ministry of Home Affairs (MHA). In 1972, the status of Union Territory of India was conferred under the name of Arunachal Pradesh. It obtained a fully-fledged state status in February 1987, becoming the twenty-fourth state of the Union of India.

Due to its recent convulsive history and ongoing Chinese territorial claims, the Mon region is one of the most restricted territories within the state, which is one of the reasons the region is largely understudied,

11 See Imdad Ali (1946; n.d.).

12 See Khating (1951).

particularly by foreigner researchers. This Mon region presently covers 9,595 km^2 (Tawang: 2,172; West Kameng: 7,422) and has a population of around 134,000 people (Tawang: 49,977; West Kameng: 84,000), of which native tribes represent between seventy and ninety percent. Mainland Indian migrants and undocumented Nepali speakers are estimated to constitute around twenty percent. In its brief history as part of an Indian state, this small region has provided three chief ministers – Pema Khandu Thungan (r. 1975–1979) from the Sherdukpen tribe, Dorjee Khandu (r. 2007–2011) and Pema Khandu (r. 2016–) from the Monpa tribe – as well as a number of state ministers and central government representatives. Both districts, in collaboration with their state government, have established a network of schools, colleges and other educational institutes, and are currently engaged in a steady development process that tries to combine modern infrastructure with traditional foundations and values.

Scholarly background and aim of this book

Even though the Tibetan Plateau has been the object of modern scholarly study since at least the mid-twentieth century, attention to Central Tibet started earlier and has been greater compared to the peripheral regions. Besides scattered references in works with a wider scope and singular ethnographic studies and dictionaries, the southeastern Himalayas began to produce modern standardized academic literature in the late 1970s to early 80s. Chronologically, in this regard, the pioneering work started earlier in Bhutan, with figures such as Michael Aris, and later included Sikkim and even more recently the Mon region. The specialized academic background was settled for these regions in recent decades, mainly by historians and anthropologists, many of whom collaborate in the present volume.

The present volume, thus, does not take place in a scholarly vacuum; neither does it claim to be the first cross-regional approach, yet such comparative enterprises have typically been restricted to a single discipline, namely anthropology.[13] It thus seems necessary to continue academic research in each region both in an individual and relational fashion

13 Huber, ed. (2012).

stressing interdisciplinarity to try to understand the Eastern Himalayas more comprehensively. Such an aim entails addressing:

1. the originality of the southeastern Himalayas as well as the influence received from Tibet (affinity and differences between southeastern Himalayas and Tibet);
2. affinity and differences within the southeastern Himalayas (Bhutan, Sikkim and the Mon region); and
3. the influence on the southeastern Himalayas exerted by the British Empire and India.

Namely, this book aims to clarify the characteristics of the southeastern Himalayas in comparison with Tibet (to the north) and India (to the south), and also the defining features of each region within the Eastern Himalayas.

The contents of this book are as follows: Part 1 – Religion and Culture; Part 2 –Society and Education; and Part 3 – Law and Politics.

The book examines the languages, cultures, society and international relations of the southeastern Himalayas from a wide interdisciplinary point of view. The fact that each chapter of this book draws from humanities and social sciences while omitting the perspective of natural sciences is admittedly a limitation.

Each chapter of this book is an academic article primarily aiming to present new findings and discussions. While being a specialized book, it includes a summary and introduction so that even non-specialists may grasp its general content. The body of each chapter is accessible enough so that researchers from different disciplines can understand it. We expect that the readers will be motivated and challenged to try to comprehend the specialized and cutting-edge contents of this book.

Part 1: Religion and Culture

The first part focuses on religious issues and their wider cultural impact, providing both historical takes and contemporary approaches centered mainly on rituals. Thierry Mathou's article (Chapter 1) links the historical background with contemporary practices. Mathou introduces the history of the traditional portable shrine known as *tashi gomang*. Although it was traditionally used to teach Buddhism to local people in Tibet and the Himalayas, it reached the verge of extinction in Bhutan. Recent attempts to revive its use in Bhutan raise interesting questions concerning religious traditions in a globalized Himalayas and bear importance for understanding Himalayan religious art. The historical take is further examined by Seiji Kumagai's study (Chapter 2), presenting a re-examination of the Drukpa Kagyü school, the state Buddhist school in Bhutan since its inception as a country. Kumagai offers new information on how the founder of the school, Tsangpa Gyare, educated his disciples and how such groups were classified after his death.

The current situation of traditional religious rituals is analyzed in a series of case studies in the three studied regions, pointing to a still vibrant relevance despite the changing and challenging scenarios. The Bhutanese context is represented with Tenzin Dorji's (Chapter 3) detailed analysis of Lha Bon, a three-day local ritual conducted in two villages in central Bhutan every two years. It provides copious information about the contents, schedule and texts used in the ritual. In the case of the Mon region, Pascale Dollfus (Chapter 4) analyses a local ritual performed by the Shertukpen (Sherdupken) tribe in the West Kameng district of Arunachal Pradesh, providing new information and insights on local animistic traditions. Finally, for the Sikkimese context, Kiki Doma Bhutia's article (Chapter 5) addresses the role of ritual healers in daily life by focusing on people living in three villages in North Sikkim. The author's interviews with local healers not only give insight into the contents of healing rituals, but also open a window into their inner experience in their daily lives.

Part 2: Society and Education

This section presents essential keys to unlocking an understanding of the social configuration of these Himalayan regions, covering defining elements such as membership, landscape physicality and education ideals. As for the first element, Himalayan societies cannot be separated from religion, especially Buddhism, which implies that social stratification and lineages are intertwined with religious aspects and institutions. A good example may be found within the Nyingma school, the oldest among the Tibetan Buddhist schools, which spread and had a strong influence in various places in Tibet and its surrounding regions. Within the Nyingma school, Pema Lingpa is regarded as one of the 'five king discoverers of ancient hidden texts or *terma*' (gter ston rgyal po lnga), and is highly respected in central and eastern Bhutan, i.e., his homeland. Françoise Pommaret and Ngawang Jamtsho's article (Chapter 6) clarifies the Jatsawa lineage, which is an offshoot of Pema Lingpa's lineage. The article provides a great example of Himalayan genealogy and clan dynamics in central and eastern Bhutan. This issue of membership bears special relevance considering that Himalayan societies present a complex social configuration in typically multi-ethnic scenarios. In the case of Sikkim, the Limbu are considered among the earliest inhabitants. Mélanie Vandenhelsken's paper (Chapter 7) offers a comprehensive account of Limbu social identity developed in Sikkim and its interaction with nation-state making in the region. The case of the Limbu is particularly interesting, as being present both in Nepal and Sikkim, they have developed a double identity as both indigenous and foreign.

The importance of landscape physicality is stressed in two papers dealing with the environment and its symbolism exemplified, respectively, in the cases of dams and bridges. Thus, Jenny Bentley's paper (Chapter 8) examines the balance between large development projects (construction of dams) and the protection of the environment of sacred places. The article focuses on the case of Dzongu in Sikkim and aims to clarify the conflictive problems between modernity and tradition. Marlene Erschbamer's article (Chapter 9) examines the role of bridges in Sikkim from religious, historical, economic, sociocultural and political aspects. Her article shows that not only were bridges important to render pilgrimage sites more accessible and provide necessary infrastructure for trade, but also that they work as a metaphor signifying that the country of Sikkim itself played a bridging role in connecting India and Tibet from an international political perspective.

Finally, education and what it represents as a social ideal is explored in the final papers of this section. Adopting a wide perspective, Akiko Ueda's article (Chapter 10) examines Bhutanese education according to three levels: the global level, the national level and the grassroots level. At the same time, the article proposes an education-related social classification distinguishing between educated persons who benefit others, and economically and socially successful persons. Her research suggests that the former group is highly appreciated within Bhutanese education and society. A more concrete example of the education goals and ideals prevalent in Bhutan is the case of language instruction. Drawing from the notion that language is an important factor for national identity and sociocultural expression, the Bhutanese government has emphasized the importance of education in Dzongkha, established as the national language in 1971. Continuous efforts in this regard may be observed in the provision of Dzongkha language education for both foreign residents and students. Lungtaen Gyatso's paper (Chapter 11) presents the first methodological project specifically designed to teach Dzongkha to foreign language speakers.

Part 3: Law and Politics

This last section focuses on the legal-political sphere, both domestic and international, and it includes both historical and contemporary approaches. The relationship between these two angles is addressed in the paper on the official representation of legal history in Bhutan and Sikkim by Miguel Álvarez Ortega (Chapter 12). His paper presents an overview of the legal history in both countries to compare it with the narratives developed by the branches of government and local scholars in a context prompted by nation-building needs. An emic angle is also adopted by Dendup Chophel (Chapter 13) in his study of the origins of the Bhutanese State and its bureaucracy, innovatively complementing official documents with folk narratives. The author stresses the importance of state festivals and ceremonies and presents an analysis of the ritual text of a warrior deity (Dralha). This notion of self-representation explored by Álvarez Ortega and Chophel is further developed in Richard Whitecross's paper (Chapter 14), focusing on Bhutan's implementation of the UN Convention on the Rights of the Child. Whitecross explores the initial tensions between the 'traditional values' discourse, prevalent in the early 2000s, and international standards on rights to show a dynamic context whereby the process leading to the 2008 Constitution fostered the 'cultural work necessary for the translation and vernacularization of the principles of the UNCRC'.

As pointed out above, the geographical situation of the southeastern Himalayan regions, sandwiched between India and China (Tibet), has strongly influenced their social and political history. Thus, the interest of Sikkim for colonial Britain, leading to its takeover in 1888/1889, lay mainly in its function as a gateway to Tibet. Alex McKay's article (Chapter 15) addresses the complex history of the international relationships of Sikkim with Britain and Tibet from the end of nineteenth century to the beginning of the twentieth century, focusing especially on three kings and their changing roles: Thubtob Namgyal (r. 1874–1914), Sidkeong Tulku (r. 1914) and Tashi Namgyal (r. 1914–1963). British India also had territorial ambitions on the current region of Arunachal Pradesh state in the middle of the nineteenth century. Lobsang Tenpa's article (Chapter 16) introduces a forgotten extradition agreement signed between British India and Tibet to secure the southern bordering regions between the Mon region and Assam in 1854.

All in all, this three-part collective volume aims to provide an adequate forum for the latest scholarship on the southeast Himalayas, trying to highlight the similarities and differences among the studied entities: Bhutan, Sikkim and the Mon region in Arunachal Pradesh. We hope it may contribute towards keeping academic discussions on a still understudied area vigorous and thriving, while encouraging newcomers to further cultivate their interest in this fascinating part of the world.

Acknowledgments

We would like to express our gratitude to the participants in this volume for their outstanding contributions and their patience throughout the whole publishing journey, which, as is often the case, has taken more than expected. We would also like to thank Tetsuya Suzuki from Kyoto University Press and Miriam Riley from Trans Pacific Press for their kind, thorough and dedicated assistance during the editing and proofreading process.

Our heartfelt appreciation goes to the local institutions and scholars who have supported different research projects upon which much of the content of this book is based, namely Dasho Karma Ura, president of the Centre for Bhutan & GNH Studies, and Lopen Lungtaen Gyatso, president of the College of Language and Culture Studies of the University of Bhutan. Such projects were possible thanks to the funding provided by several MEXT/JSPS KAKENHI research grants: 'A Study of Minority Schools in Bhutanese Buddhism' (22KK0003) and 'A Study on the Drukpa Kagyu School' (20H01183), directed by Seiji Kumagai, as well as 'Philosophical Foundations of the Legal-Political Realm in the Tibeto-sphere' (22K01112), directed by Miguel Álvarez Ortega.

A last word of gratitude goes to Prof. Yasuo Deguchi and Ms. Ayumi Yamamoto from the Institute for the Future of Human Society (IFoHS) of Kyoto University, who provided invaluable technical aid and helped us obtain generous financial support from said institute for the publication of this volume.

Bibliography

Ali, I. (1946). 'Report by the Political Officer, Balipara Frontier Tract, on Tribute other than Monastic Tribute, in Sela Sub-Agency'. In 'File No. 59-NEF (SECRET) 1946', Ministry of External Affairs, Delhi: National Archives.

Ali, I. (n.d.). 'Tour Diary of Mr. Imdad Ali, Political Officer of the Balipara Frontier Tract. 1945–1947', L/PS/12/4200, London: British Library India Office Collection.

Aris, M. (1979). *Bhutan: The Early History of a Himalayan Kingdom*, Warminster: Aris & Phillips Ltd.

Hazod, G. (2009). 'Imperial Central Tibet'. In B. Dotson, *The Old Tibetan Annals: An Annotated Translation of Tibet's First History. With an Annotated Cartographical Documentation by Guntram Hazod*, Vienna: Verlag der ÖAW, pp. 163–269.

Huber, T., ed. (2012). *Origins and Migrations in the Extended Eastern Himalayas*, Leiden: Brill Academic Pub.

Khating, Maj. R. (1951). '[Confidential]. Occupation of Tawang, [and] Earthquake Relief Measures by Major Kathing', File No. 56/51, Shillong: Assam Adviser's Secretariat.

Kumagai, S. (2014). 'History and Current Situation of the Sa skya pa school in Bhutan'. In S. Kumagai, ed., *Bhutanese Buddhism and Its Culture*, Kathmandu: Vajra Publications, pp. 127–139.

Ryavec, K.E. (2015). *A Historical Atlas of Tibet*, Chicago: University of Chicago Press.

Tenpa, L. (2018). *An Early History of the Mon Region (India) and Its Relationship with Tibet and Bhutan*, Dharamsala: Library of Tibetan Works and Archives.

Part I
Religion and Culture

1 *Tashi Gomang*: Preserving a Bhutanese Tradition

Thierry Mathou

Nestled in the heart of the Himalayas between India and China, Bhutan is the only surviving Mahayana Buddhist kingdom in the world. Strong emphasis has thus been laid in the country on the promotion and preservation of its unique culture and religious traditions. The history and significance of *tashi gomang* (*Bkra shis sgo mang*)[1] are particularly relevant in that context.

In the Mahayana tradition, the term *tashi gomang*, which literally means 'one with many auspicious doors', usually designates the third of the eight kinds of *chörten* (*mchod rten*) (stupa) representing the most important events in the life of the historical Buddha. Also known as the Dharma Wheel Stupa, or Choekhor (Chos'khor) *chörten* in Tibetan or Kumbum (Sku'bum; 'one hundred thousand holy images') it commemorates the Buddha's teachings at Deer Park in Sarnath (Varanasi), India. This type of stupa is characterized by a very distinctive design: a square structure featuring a three-dimensional mandala with many tiers and multilayered niches crowded with deities. The most famous *tashi gomang chörten* is the fifteenth century Gyantse (Rgyal rtses) Kumbum *chörten*, in Pelkor Chode (Dpal 'khor chos sde) Monastery in Tibet, an outstanding architectural achievement rising thirty-five meters high with nine stories, seventy-five chapels and 108 cells. 'The *lhakangs* (*lha khang*) (chapels) of the nine levels of the *Kumbum*, decreasing in number at each level, are structured according to the compendium of Sakya (*Sa skya*) tantras called

1 The Wylie system is used to transliterate Tibetan and Dzongkha terms, names of people (when they have a historical dimension) and places. For easy reading the transliteration is only indicated for the most significant terms and only once for each.

Drubthab Kuntu (*Sgrub thabs kun btus*). Each *lhakang* and each level thus create a mandala, and the entire *Kumbum* represents a three-dimensional path to the Buddha's enlightenment in terms of increasingly subtle tantric mandalas'.[2]

Some of the most spectacular examples of *tashi gomang chörtens* to be seen in Tibet are relevant to the religious history of Bhutan. The thirteen-tiered *chörten* built in Ralung (rwa lung) in the Tsang (gtsang) region of Southern Tibet was erected on the relics of the first Gyalwang Drukpa (Rgyal dbang 'brug pa), Drogon Tsangpa Gyare Yeshe Dorje ('Gro mgon Gtsang pa rgya ras yes shes rdo rje) (b. 1161, d. 1211), founder of the Drukpa Kagyü ('Brug pa bka' brgyud) school which became the dominant Buddhist school in Bhutan. Initially built by the first Gyalwang Drukpa's nephew, Wonre Darma Sengge (Dbon ras Dar ma seng ge) (b. 1177, d. 1237), it was destroyed before being rebuilt by Polhané (pho lha nas) (b. 1728, d. 1747) the ruling prince of Tibet, then destroyed again during the Chinese Cultural Revolution. This stupa, which has not been restored since then, was described by Giuseppe Tucci as 'a great isolated *Kumbum*, slightly smaller than the Gyantse one'.[3] It probably inspired Zhabdrung Ngawang Namgyal (zhabs drung ngag dbang rnam rgyal) (b. 1594, d. 1651), the eighteenth abbot of Ralung Monastery, who unified Bhutan and is credited with the fatherhood of the *tashi gomang* tradition in the country. Chung Riwoche Kumbum (gcung ri bo che sku'bum) *chörten* near Lhatse (Lha rtse), southwest of Shigatse (Gzhis ka rtse), is another example of the intertwining between *tashi gomangs* and the religious history of Bhutan. This *chörten* was constructed by Thangtong Gyalpo (Thang stong rgyal po) (b. 1385, d. 1464), also known as Chakzampa, the 'Iron Chain Maker', after his return to Tibet from Bhutan where he is highly revered. In Tibet the tradition of *tashi gomang chörtens* came into full blossom under his influence. Thangtong Gyalpo is believed to have had a vision during a trip to India where he saw a *tashi gomang chörten* that inspired him. 'He visited *Zang(s) Gling* (the Copper-Island) and saw a stupa of the *Tashi Gomang* type. Then the *siddhas* (flying dancers) Shabari and Kukuripa

---

2 Dowman (1988: 270).

3 Tucci (1956).

appeared and gave him instruction in stupa design'.[4] According to his autobiographical notes, he even 'assisted the construction of the first big *Kumbum chörten* in Lhatse, Jonang (*Jo nang*) stupa, in 1354 in his former incarnation. It was also recorded that he was an assistant at the construction of the neighboring Gyang Bumoche *Kumbum* (*Rgyang 'bum moche sku'bum*) as well'.[5] Before entering Bhutan in 1433, he made a stopover at Ralung Monastery. While in Paro (Spa gro) he built the Dumtseg lhakang (zlum brtsegs lha khang) stupa which is believed to be his first creation of a *chörten*. 'This specific stupa includes a representation of the Buddhist system of teaching through pictures for laymen and monks alike. The concept, by which one apprehends Buddhism by watching pictures, while carrying on the circumambulation, was later on introduced at the Chung Riwoche *Kumbun*'[6] which was his final masterpiece. As will be seen below, Thangtong Gyalpo played a prominent role in the development of the *tashi gomang* tradition in Bhutan.

Paradoxically, *tashi gomang chörtens* are rather rare in Bhutan although the symbolism attached to them is very present. For instance, every fourth day of the sixth month in the Bhutanese calendar (around July or August), the Central Monastic Body conducts a special religious ceremony called Namgyal Tongchoe (Rnam gyal stong mchod), in the Trashichho (Bkra shis chos) Dzong (*rdzong*; monastery-fortress) in Thimphu, to celebrate the Buddha's teachings at Deer Park in Sarnath known as Drukpa Tshezhi ('Brug pa tshes zhi) (the first sermon of Lord Buddha), which is considered as one of the most sacred dates in the Buddhist calendar. At this occasion several sacred relics are displayed for the public to receive blessings, including a small *tashi gomang chörten*.

In Bhutan the term *tashi gomang* is more frequently used to designate this kind of miniature portable shrine whose design is based on that of the eponymous stupa. These multi-tiered movable shrines feature dozens of small doors that open to reveal hundreds of painted images and niches containing statues of Buddhist deities and were once carried around by wandering bards, known as *manips* (*bla ma Nipa-s*), to confer the Buddhist

---

4 De Montmollin (1992: 606).

5 Gerner (2007: 37).

6 Gerner (2007: 36).

teachings on the masses at public gatherings, especially in remote rural areas. In Bhutan they are considered an indigenous tradition. Different factors have led to the gradual disappearance of the tradition. Yet *tashi gomangs* have recently been declared a national treasure of Bhutan and different initiatives have been taken to promote their cultural and religious significance. The present paper will cover the subject from a number of different perspectives: the 'Tashi Gomang Project', an initiative set up to record, conserve and revive the tradition; the Tibetan connection of the tradition; its Bhutanese origin in connection with the role played by Zhabdrung Ngawang Namgyal, the founding father of Bhutan; a tentative classification of *tashi gomangs* based on current knowledge; a description of the role of *manips*; and eventually an evocation of the current status of the tradition. Conceived as a general introduction to the knowledge of *tashi gomangs*, this chapter aims to both develop the awareness of the general public regarding the relevance of the tradition and to inspire fields in the academic community to study its significance regarding the knowledge of Buddhism, its dissemination in Bhutan, the history of the kingdom and its sociocultural heritage.

The 'Tashi Gomang Project': preserving a national treasure of Bhutan

Twenty years ago, regular visitors to Bhutan had a good chance of seeing *manips* displaying miniature shrines known as *tashi gomangs* during *tshechus* (*tshes bcu*) (religious festivals) or in populated public areas like the weekend market or the memorial *chörten* in Thimphu on auspicious days. This opportunity has dwindled considerably over the years. Most *tashi gomangs* have been locked away in *dzongs* and temples, sometimes for decades. Nowadays they are rarely displayed in public. Although most Bhutanese have heard about them or remember having seen one, few of them really know about the vanishing tradition. The possibilities of seeing a *tashi gomang* in a foreign museum are equally rare. An example can be viewed in the city of Neuchâtel (Switzerland), where the Museum of Ethnography keeps it as the masterpiece of its Bhutanese collection initiated in 1968 by the third king of Bhutan. This piece is not an antiquity but a new altar specially commissioned for the museum where it was exported after being made in Bhutan in the late 1980s with the authorization of the fourth king of Bhutan and under the patronage of Lyonpo[7] Sangye Penjor, then Minister for Social Services. This endeavor was the first attempt, although limited in its scope, to revive the *tashi gomang* tradition. For this occasion, a team of skilled craftsmen comprising a carpenter, a painter, a sculptor and a silversmith was formed under the direction of a well-known religious publisher Mr. Kunzang Tobgyel in association with the oldest *manip* known at that time whose grandfather, Thang Ugyen Tshering, was known in Bhutan as the last professional builder of *tashi gomangs*. In addition to the shrine kept in the Neuchâtel museum and two other items identified respectively at the Tibet House Museum in New Delhi and at the National Museum in Liverpool,[8] there have been only four occasions in recent years where this rare object has been displayed out of its usual context. The first was a temporary exhibition (*Tashi Gomang of Bhutan: Asian Concept of the Cosmos*) which took place at Laforet Museum, Harajukuin, Tokyo, Japan from 22 November to 12 December 1982. Four *tashi gomangs* were sent to Japan for this occasion by the Ministry of Communications and Tourism of Bhutan. Two *manips* respectively known as Kiba and Thayba participated in the event. The second occasion was the display of a *tashi gomang* from Sinphu Monastery (Sin phu dgon pa) (in Trongsa province) in Paris at the Cité de la Musique in October 2005 during a festival featuring dance, music and chants from the Himalayas. The third occasion was the presentation of a *tashi gomang* in 2008 in the USA during an exhibition, *Bhutan: Land of the Thunder Dragon*, organized by the Smithsonian Folklife Festival.[9] A Bhutanese Buddhist 'spiritual singer', Yeshi Wangchuk, chanted prayers at this occasion. Eventually a temporary exhibition titled *Once Upon Many Times: Legends and Myths in Himalayan Art* organized at the Rubin Museum in New York from 16 September 2011 to 30 January 2012, featured, among others objects, a

---

7 *Lyonpo* is an honorary title given to ministers or equivalent officials. A *lyonpo* wears a ceremonial orange scarf.

8 The *tashi gomang* kept in New Delhi is registered as coming from Tibet. The one in Liverpool is referenced as coming from Bhutan through the Harry Geoffrey Beasley collection.

9 Cadaval, et al. (2016).

tashi gomang lent by a private collector. No academic has ever conducted comprehensive research on the tradition. Even the number of *tashi gomangs* kept in Bhutan was unknown, as was the number of *manips*. No census had ever been carried out in this regard. Only two short academic papers have been devoted to *tashi gomangs*, one by Yoshiro Imaeda and Doffu Drukpa published in 1982[10] on the occasion of the Tokyo exhibition, and one by Marceline de Montmollin published in 1987[11] concerning the *tashi gomang* kept in Neuchâtel. It therefore felt urgent to launch an initiative to preserve this unique tradition, especially when my research led me to realize that there were only two surviving *manips*, whose very advanced age made the duty of conservation all the more necessary.

From November 2016 to February 2017, a remarkable exhibition was shown at the Royal Textile Academy (RTA) in Thimphu. Titled *Tashi Gomang: A National Treasure of Bhutan*, this landmark exhibition, featuring no less than twenty-nine *tashi gomangs*, was organized in the context of the celebration of the 400th anniversary of the arrival to Bhutan of Zhabdrung Ngawang Namgyal, who is credited with introducing the tradition in Bhutan, and in connection with the 'Tashi Gomang Project', which was launched under the Royal Patronage of Her Majesty the Royal Grandmother Ashi Kesang Choeden Wangchuck. This project, which I had the honour of initiating in 2015,[12] was set up to record, conserve and revive the tradition.

The first phase of this two-year long project consisted of an identification and inventory process. It was generally believed that there were around twenty *tashi gomangs* in the country, assuming that most of the twenty regions (*dzongkhags*; *rdzong khag*), especially those with a fortress founded by Zhabdrung Ngawang Namgyal or a prominent monastery (*goempa*; *dgon pa*) or temple (*lha khang*), could have at least one. In 1982,

10 Imaeda and Drukpa (1982).

11 De Montmollin (1992: 606).

12 The project was conducted, under the royal patronage and in cooperation with my good friend Tshering Tashi, with the support of the Central Monastic Body, the Department of Culture of the Ministry of Home and Cultural Affairs, and Princess Ashi Kesang Choeden Wangchuck, executive director of the Thangka Conservation and Restoration Centre in Thimphu.

Yoshiro Imaeda and Doffu Drukpa wrote: 'there are approximately 25 *Tashi Gomangs* in Bhutan'. In 2015, one of the two *manips* we interviewed for the project suggested the number of twenty-three.[13] During the implementation of the project we have been able to locate thirty-six *tashi gomangs* in Bhutan,[14] all of which are antiques except one. According to the survey conducted by the Tangka Conservation Center and completed by our findings, only twelve out of the current twenty *dzongkhags* house at least one *tashi gomang*. Some have up to five. This is not surprising assuming there were only nine provinces in ancient Bhutan. Most of the shrines are concentrated in five provinces that were at the center of ancient Bhutan religiously, politically and geographically: Thimphu (Thim phu) (five), Punakha (Spu na kha) (four), Wangdue Phodrang (Dbang 'dus Pho brang) (five), Trongsa (Krong gsar) (five) and Bumthang (Bum thang) (five). Paro, another province with high historical significance, has two items. Three have been identified in the border province of Haa (Has) from where the tradition could have been exported into the neighboring Chumbi valley in Tibet where the presence of *tashi gomangs* was observed at the beginning of the twentieth century. Three have also been identified in the northeastern province of Lhuentse (Lhun rtse). This distribution could suggest a pattern for the initial prevalence of the tradition which started in Punakha. Although the survey has been conducted with the support of the Central Monastic Body, this count is probably provisional. There might be other *tashi gomangs* in Bhutan, possibly under private custody (even though an individual should not own such a shrine) or in secret sealed locations as suggested by the shrine discovered inside a partially open

---

13 Interview of *manip* Kunzang Tenzi conducted by Tshering Tashi in the presence of the author, in Thimphu in April 2015. According to him, eight *dzongs* were supposed to host a *tashi gomang*: Bumthang, Dagana, Lhuentse, Paro, Punakha, Trashigang, Trongsa and Wangdue Phodrang. He also mentioned several monasteries and even *tulkus* (*sprul sku*) (prominent reincarnations) as custodians of *tashi gomangs*.

14 The table presented at the end of the chapter lists the thirty-three *tashi gomangs* formally identified under the project. Since the organization of the RTA exhibition, three other *tashi gomangs* have been reported to me. Because I have not been able to see and identify them yet, they are marked with an asterisk.

chörten in the province of Haa.[15] This count also excludes *tashi gomangs* kept abroad, especially in private collections as this object is very rare in museums as noted above. Given this scarcity, the project was conceived as a documentary mission and was greatly facilitated by the exhibition organized at the RTA. Thousands of pictures have been taken to keep visual records. Experts from the Department of Culture, Ministry of Home and Cultural Affairs, which plays a central role in conserving, protecting, developing and promoting tangible and intangible cultural heritage in Bhutan, have been invited to draw sketches.

The second objective of the project was to ensure the conservation of *tashi gomangs* and to promote manufacturing techniques. Although the altars listed under the project had been carefully stored, they are often very old. The fact that they used to be carried from one place to another and that they are very fragile objects, which can be easily dismantled if not properly handled, explains why some needed restoration. As a result, the *tashi gomangs* brought to Thimphu for the exhibition were cleaned and repaired as necessary. This process, which was conducted by qualified craftsmen under the supervision of monks from the Thangka Conservation and Restoration Centre, mainly involved precision carpentry, carving, silversmithing and painting. It concerned not only the shrines themselves but also the boxes used for their transportation as they are sometimes genuine pieces of art. After the exhibition, *tashi gomangs* were returned to their caretakers in a better state of conservation. Considering that the making of a *tashi gomang* involves nine of the thirteen traditional types of arts and crafts registered in Bhutan, the project was also an opportunity to promote manufacturing techniques. As already mentioned, the last *tashi gomang* manufactured in Bhutan was made in the late 1980s for Neuchâtel Museum of Ethnography. Following the presentation of our project, the prime minister of Bhutan took the initiative to propose the manufacturing of a new item to commemorate the sixtieth birthday of the fourth king. The new shrine was commissioned by the present king and manufactured by qualified craftsmen under the supervision of Mr. Lam Kezang Chhoephel, CEO of the Agency for the Promotion of Indigenous Crafts (APIC).[16] It

---

15 Some *chörtens* house precious relics.

16 Created in 2011, APIC is a government agency under the Ministry of Economic

Photo 1.1: *Tashi gomang* (Zangtopalri type), Punakha, Bhutan, seventeenth century
Notes: Closed and opened. Wood, brass, silver, gold-plated, semi-precious stones, glass beads and clay statues, 13" (l) x 13" (w) x 24" (h). Exhibited in 2016 at the Royal Textile Academy (RTA), Thimphu, Bhutan, *Tashi Gomang, A National Treasure of Bhutan*, Exhibition Catalogue (courtesy of RTA, Department of Culture, Ministry of Home and Cultural Affairs, Royal Government of Bhutan).

took a team of ten – three carpenters, three silversmiths, two painters and two coordinators – six months to build the altar which has 144 doors and contains 150 miniatures. The team used the *tashi gomang* enshrined in Paro Dzong as the prototype. The new altar was presented to the fourth king in November 2015. An unfinished prototype is also kept at APIC. Although the last professional maker of *tashi gomangs* passed away more than one hundred years ago, this initiative demonstrated that Bhutan still has highly talented craftsmen skilled enough to build this unique piece of Himalayan arts and crafts.

The specificity of the *tashi gomang* tradition lies as much in the object itself as in the rites surrounding its use. This is why the third pillar of the project concerned the *manips* themselves. Realizing that there were only two surviving professional *manips* who knew the complete ritual,

Affairs. It is responsible for the execution of crafts and related initiatives under the Accelerating Socio-Economic Development project, with the support of other relevant agencies of the Royal Government of Bhutan.

Photo 1.2:
Lam *manips* displaying *tashi gomangs* during religious festivals (1): Paro *tshechu*, Paro, Bhutan, 1983
Source: Photographed by Brian and Felicity Shaw.

Photo 1.3:
Lam *manips* displaying *tashi gomangs* during religious festivals (2): Punakha *dromche*, Punakha, Bhutan, 1981
Source: Photographed by Brian and Felicity Shaw.

Kunzang Tenzi and Kinley, respectively seventy-two and eighty-five years old when we started the project, was the trigger of the Tashi Gomang Project.[17] It gave a sense of urgency to the overall enterprise. Should these two survivors have passed away without an initiative to record and transmit their knowledge, the tradition could have disappeared. In that context different initiatives have been taken. The two *manips* have been interviewed, recorded and filmed. A pilot project has been launched in cooperation with Sinphu Monastery, in Trongsa province, where four young *gomchens* (*sgom chen*) (lay practitioners) have been trained as

17 There are also a few 'non-professional' *manips* who have not been involved in this activity on a regular basis but who know about the tradition.

manips. The first training session was organized at the monastery in May 2016 in the presence of Kunzang Tenzi. A *tashi gomang* trust fund has been set up in Thimphu to finance this initiative.

Eventually, in order to develop the awareness of the general public regarding the relevance of the tradition, several initiatives were undertaken by different stakeholders: a theatrical performance on *tashi gomangs* was held during the opening of the exhibition at the RTA; the *Bhutan Post* edited commemorative stamps about *tashi gomangs*; and documentaries about the tradition were shot. Thanks to the mobilization of all, the project has achieved the objectives it has set for itself and has contributed to the valorization of the tradition. From an academic point of view, it would be particularly opportune to extend it with an in-depth research project. Many aspects of this unique tradition are worth studying in detail: the iconography, the classification of *tashi gomangs*, the building techniques, the rites, chants and social practices involved in their transportation and display, and the geographical spread of the tradition. Such research would prove very useful for the knowledge of Buddhism, its dissemination in Bhutan, the history of the kingdom and its sociocultural heritage. Following are some general guidelines about the above aspects.

Tashi gomang: an indigenous Bhutanese tradition with Tibetan connections?

The concept of mobile shrines sometimes referred to as 'god-boxes' carried by travelling priests exists in many cultures and religions. 'Some of the boxes resemble diminutive temples: their pair of hinged doors open to reveal the deity inside, just as the doors of a real temple sanctuary are thrown open for worshippers to experience ceremonial viewing'.[18] 'Portable altars were used in ancient Egypt during the Ptolemaic dynasty (305–30 BC) to transport deities within and outside temples'.[19] They were carried by priests. Similar objects have been recorded throughout the history of Christianity. As far as Buddhism is concerned, pilgrimages have always

18 Lyons (2003: 253–254).

19 The Smithsonian's National Museum of Asian Art: Freer Gallery of Art Egyptian collection. http://www.asia.si.edu/collections

been associated with 'portable cult objects' including miniature altars. The transfer of sacred items through 'visual Buddhism' has been essential for the transmission of Buddhist texts throughout Asia. Peripatetic picture-showmen using boxlike devices with panels have also been mentioned in early Buddhist literature. The presence of portable shrines in Khotan, one of the major centers on the Silk Road, has been well documented. They featured images of the Buddha or bodhisattvas. 'Executed in stone, wood, or metal [...], portables shrines were originally in the form of a diptych or triptych, which through hinged leafs could be folded when carried [...]. Their function was not attached to a fixed place [a worship space in a temple, a monastery or a domestic altar] but was expressly meant for travelling'.[20] The concept of wooden foldable shrines may have been inspired by stone portable altars from ancient northwest India. Still vivid in Rajasthan is the tradition of *kaavad*, a portable shrine with multiple doors that fold into themselves. The object itself and its carrier are probably the closest to the *tashi gomang* tradition outside Bhutan. 'The *Kaavadiya Bhat* (storyteller) journeys with his brightly painted wooden box to the homes of his patrons, to recite their genealogies and regale them with the stories of the pantheon of deities painted on the shrine. It is a tradition that binds communities in common memory and mythology'.[21] Other examples of portable shrines can be found in India, like the *biman* from Orissa made for pilgrims returning from Puri during the Ratha Yatra Hindu festival. In Andhra Pradesh, masked storytellers tell legends painted on the side of a wooden box before opening its front doors to display a deity. Quite different is the Japanese *mikoshi*, a divine palanquin, which Shinto followers use as a vehicle to transport a deity during a festival (*matsuri*) or between two temples. Portable shrines are also common throughout the Himalayan region. Yet most of them are prayer or amulet boxes (Tibetan: *ga'u*) meant for individual usage contrary to *tashi gomangs*, which were used by practitioners to preach to their listeners. Mostly made from metal in a repoussé style of construction, with intricate designs, auspicious symbols and mantras inscribed on their outer surface, *ga'u* are used by travelers as a personal protection to help ward off negative energy and

20 Forte (2015: 151–185).

21 Sabnami (2014).

attract blessings. They are worn on a cord around the neck and can contain all sorts of sacred objects: a religious image or statue, relics, a folded-up scroll of mantras, healing stones and even consecrated medicine.

As far as *tashi gomang* miniature shrines are concerned, their presence has been attested in ancient Tibet but their origin still needs clarification. Several Tibetans in exile have been quoted as remembering seeing in different parts of Tibet multi-doored portable altars displayed by wandering priests. In an interesting description of the social life in Lhasa at the beginning of the twentieth century, Jamyang Norbu writes:

> [I]n Lhasa, especially during the Monlam [smon lam chen mo] (Great Prayer) Festival and also during the Saga Dawa festival [sa ga zla ba dus chen] commemorating the Enlightenment of the Lord Buddha, the sides of the Lingkor [gling skor] (Outer Circuit) road were jammed with a variety of mendicant as [well as] the *Lama Mane* [*manip*], who recited the lives of saints using *thangkas* as visual aid. The *Tashi Gomang* did much the same but with elaborate miniature temples behind whose many doors and windows were tiny statuettes of saints and deities.[22]

Charles Bell, who was the British political officer in Sikkim around the same period, even took pictures of *tashi gomangs* on his way to Lhasa in 1920.[23] According to a Tibetan lama quoted by Marceline de Montmollin, ‘the first Tibetan shrines of that kind were invented by Nyangrel Nyima Ozer (myang ral nyi ma ’od zer) (1124/1136-1192/1204) and entrusted by him to educated people for teaching purposes’.[24] A major figure in renaissance Tibet, the latter was a reincarnation of the Dharma King Thrisong Detsen (Khri-srong lDe btsan) and the first of the five great *tertön* (*gter ston*) (treasure revealer) in the Nyingma (Rnying ma) tradition. Yet

22 Norbu (2015: 243).

23 See Charles Bell Collection: Album 9, National Museum Liverpool, UK and Mathou (2016: 37). The first two pictures show a *tashi gomang* and a *manip* carrying the shrine in its box. They were taken on the way to Lhasa, possibly in Chumbi valley, in November 1920. Another photo shows two people, of whom at least one is a *manip* who is pointing at a *thangka* with a *tashi gomang* at his feet. It was taken between November 1920 and October 1921.

24 De Montmollin (1992: 606).

to our knowledge there are no references in his known biographies about *tashi gomang*.

Another way to identify the presence of *tashi gomangs* in ancient Tibet would be to focus on the origin and activity of *manips*. Tashi Tsering, director of the Amnye Machen Institute in Dharamsala, who has studied the origin of the *manip* tradition, also called *buchen* (*bu chen*) or *lochen* (*lo chen*) depending on the region in Tibet, has found out there were *manips* all over the Ü and Tsang regions in ancient Tibet. 'Some of the most famous and well-coordinated ones were from two serkyimpa[25] (*ser kyim pa*) (lay) monasteries in Gyangkar (*rgyal mkhar*)', in Rinpung (Rin spungs) county, Shigatse. 'One group was required to perform opera, while the other traditionally served as manip [...]. Among the manips there were two types: one which used a thangka as a visual aid in telling their stories and the other which used a special type of image, actually a stupa, known as Tashi Gomang'.[26]

Tashi Tsering even mentions different styles of *tashi gomangs* being present in Tibet prior to 1959: 'those modeled after Zangdopelri (*Zangs mdog dpal ri*), the Potala, Mount Tsari and Mount Kailash'. This tradition, however, has disappeared. When he inquired into the present *manip* tradition, as it was supposed to exist in ancient Gyangkar, Tashi Tsering 'did not uncover anything about storytellers who still used Tashi Gomang images'.[27] The *buchen* tradition has also been reported in the valley of Spiti in Himachal Pradesh. Although no reference is made to *tashi gomangs* in that case, Tashi Tsering notices that they seemed linked to a monastery that followed the Nyingma traditions of the Bhutanese *tertön* Pemalingma (Pad ma Gling pa, b. 1450, d. 1521) from Bumthang, which gives an interesting indication about Bhutanese influence far from the country. For Michael Aris who studied ancient Tibet and Bhutan, the tradition of *tashi gomang* was somehow specific to the latter even if he did not provide any evidence: 'Tibetan bards, by contrast [to Bhutanese], used to hang up scroll paintings to illustrate their stories [...]. The Tibetan

25 The term *serkyimpa* refers to practitioners who wear yellow (*ser*) monastic clothing but live as householders (*kyimpa*).

26 Tsering (2011: 82).

27 Tsering (2011: 91).

prototype of the Bhutanese Tashi Gomang was probably an object called a jo-'kor, a distinctive emblem of the Tibetan manip to which offerings were also made on behalf of the deceased relatives'.[28]

At this stage we must make reference to the origin of *manips* and its possible implication for *tashi gomangs*, which raises the question of the influence of Thangtong Gyalpo 'who is credited by Tibetan oral tradition as the founder of the manip tradition, usually called buchen'.[29] As already mentioned, this saint who was born in Tibet and travelled to Bhutan has played a major role in the development of *tashi gomang chörtens*. Yet, as noted by Marceline de Montmollin, it is 'not quite clear whether besides erecting the large and famous Tashi Gomang chörten at Riwoche, he created as well portable shrines of the same type'.[30] Since this remark was made, research has progressed. Tashi Tsering has studied different biographies of the saint. According to one of them, 'The Awe-Inspiring Ocean (Tibetan: Ngo mtshar rgya mtsho), Thangtong Gyalpo gave buchen Shakya dpal bzang and eight others, a Tashi Gomang image and a letter with his seal' from which Tashi Tsering concludes 'we can glean that manips carried Tashi Gomang images'.[31] Yet there is no description of those images. As noticed by Tashi Tsering himself: Thangtong Gyalpo's biographies 'say nothing specific about his instituting the traditions of manip storytellers using thangkas as visual aids, or carrying the Tashi Gomang images'. Therefore, if the presence of *tashi gomang* portable shrines has been mentioned in Tibet, with possible origins in the fifteenth century, further research is needed to confirm the tradition was around at that period or even at an earlier date. What seems obvious is that the *tashi gomang* tradition may have disappeared in Tibet as no ethnographic records have been made about the tradition before or after 1959. As mentioned by Tashi Tsering: 'in Tibet, there are virtually no more examples of the *tashi gomang* images used in *manip* storytelling'. The only item known to be referenced as coming from Tibet is the miniature shrine that has been kept at the Tibet House Museum in New Delhi since the mid-1960s.

28 Aris (1994: 147).

29 Tsering (2011: 82).

30 De Montmollin (1992: 606).

31 Tsering (2011: 91).

In the absence of documented Tibetan evidence, we have no indication about its exact origin, the context in which it was used or the involved rituals. Although its structure is roughly similar to *tashi gomangs* found in Bhutan, its design is far less sophisticated, which could mean it may have been copied from the tradition originating in Bhutan. Therefore, although the Tibetan connection is attested, more substantive indications are needed to trace its origin. At this stage, the conclusion proposed by Marceline de Montmollin in the early 1990s is still valid: 'whatever its primary origin, this tradition may have been attested at one time in both Tibet and Bhutan but while it was being gradually substituted in Tibet by the use of thangka (wood being there particularly scarce), it grew its own roots in Bhutan [...]. In that view, the exclusivity claimed by the Bhutanese does not look unfounded'.[32]

Zhabdrung Ngawang Namgyal: the founding father of the tradition

As in Tibet, there is no known written record about the *tashi gomang* tradition in Bhutan. However, the oral tradition provides an alternative literature which gives precious indications. There are several stories[33]

32 De Montmollin (1992: 606).

33 One of these stories attributes the origin of *tashi gomang* to a *gomchen* named Drangsong (*drang srong*) living in a mythical place. Following are the two successive phases of this legend as narrated by one of the two surviving *manips*: 'Gomchen Drangsong was a man, who had gained a sense of detachment from all things worldly, like anger, jealousy and attachment to materials. His name Drangsong literally means detached and was derived from his character. Gomchen Drangsong had a daughter, Kandum Zhugkinim. As a test, the king of Tagzhinor asked [for] her hand in marriage. Goemchen [*sic*] Drangsong told the king that, if he refused, it would destroy all that he'd worked and strived for. Saying so, he handed over his daughter to the king. A huge celebration followed and the daughter was taken away. The moment his daughter left him Drangsong was overcome with emotion. He climbed a hill to see his daughter leave. As they disappeared into the distance, he climbed a tree to get a better view, but he fell and died. When Drangsong died, out of his body, the precious Tashi Gomang emerged'. The story then goes on to explain how *tashi gomang* came from heaven to earth: 'It was a time of greed. There was no religion or faith. Evil was rampant. Buddha wanted to eradicate greed, anger, ignorance and arrogance, and

about the origin of *tashi gomang* in Bhutan. It is impossible to verify their authenticity as they proceed both from Buddhist parables and legends, and ancient folktales. These stories are closely associated with the history of the Drukpa Kagyü school, the dominant religious tradition in the country. As there are no similar stories in the oral tradition in Tibet, at least according to currently known records, this may confirm the hypothesis that the *tashi gomang* tradition grew its own roots in Bhutan as a component of the local Drukpa Kagyü legacy. Before telling the most popular of these stories, contextualization is needed. As described by Marc Dujardin,

> [T]he responsibility for the conceptualization of and materialization of Buddhist stock ideas in the form of a distinct architectural practice can be traced to a trinity of key actors, referred to as the patron, the ritual master and the master-builder. The higher the political and religious rank of the trinity, the more advanced the level is at which this peculiar play architecture "do-thinking" takes place, and the more impact it may have on the architectural actualization in all of Bhutan.[34]

This observation can be applied to *tashi gomang*, a miniaturized architectural work involving its own trinity: the patron who commissions its building (the Zhabdrung, then the king); the care-taking institution or individual (a monastery or a designated *trulku* [*sprul sku*]), and eventually the *manip* who is responsible for keeping it; and the master-builder who is entrusted with its construction.

As far as the patron is concerned, Zhabdrung Ngawang Namgyal (b. 1594, d. 1651) often appears as the central figure of those stories. It is not

---

make people feel the presence of god and goodness. To start with an appropriate preaching in Varanasi, Lord Buddha visited heaven, where he met Tegor, the king of the gods, who had five khandums [wrathful female *bardo* deities]. The five khandums instructed Buddha to visit gomchen Drangsong, who lived in a village of a god called Tshangchen. A powerful and sacred religious instrument called Tashi Gomang, derived from Drangsong's own body, was there. Buddha was told that it would help subdue every evil and, as he preached, if the Tashi Gomang could fly to Varanasi, it would help spread religion. Back in Varanasi, as Buddha preached, the Tashi Gomang flew down from heaven'. (http://acrossbhutan.blogspot.fr/2011/04/blessing-in-box.html)

34 Dujardin (2000: 165).

surprising as he was both an heir to the throne of the Druk Monastery in Ralung and the founder of Bhutan as a nation-state. Ngawang Namgyal, who became the greatest figure in the history of the country, was a great religious and political ruler. From an early age he was groomed to succeed his grandfather Mipham Choegyal (Mi pham chos rgyal) on the throne of Ralung. He studied religion and art and became skilled in the art of painting and sculpture, which is relevant to the tradition of *tashi gomang*. Recognized as the incarnation of the great Drukpa scholar Kuenkhyen Pema Karpo (Kun mkhyen Pad ma dkar po, b. 1527, d. 1592), who himself was the reincarnation of the founder of the Drukpa Kagyü school, Tsangpa Gyare Yeshey (Gtsang pa rgya ras ye shes rdo rje), he became the eighteenth prince-abbot of Ralung at the early age of twelve years old. Following a dispute with the Tsang Desi (Gtsang sde srid) (temporal ruler) he decided to leave Tibet. One day he had a vision of the protective deities Yeshey Goenpo (ye shes mGon po) (Mahakala) and Palden Lhamo (Dpal ldan lha mo) (Mahakali) offering him the valleys of Bhutan. In 1616 at the age of twenty-three, he left Ralung for Bhutan where his forefathers had built numerous monasteries and had many followers. While in Bhutan he repelled several Tibetan invasions, created a unique national identity, set up a dual system of government, both spiritual and temporal, gave Bhutan its first codification of laws, and built several *dzongs*. Eventually, after a long retreat, he passed away twenty-five years after his arrival from Tibet. The *dzongs* that still exist today are a unique feature of Bhutan.

The most important is Punakha Dzong, which is the second key 'actor' in the original *tashi gomang* trinity. Although it is only the second oldest and largest monastery-fortress in Bhutan, it can be considered as the mother of all *dzongs* because it was built under the command of the Zhabdrung to house the precious relics he brought from Ralung, the most sacred being *Rangjung Kharsapani*, a self-created image of Avalokiteshvara (Chenrezig) made from the vertebra of Tsangpa Gyare (Gtsang pa rgya ras), the founder of the Drukpa school at the time of his cremation in Tibet. Built to accommodate up to 600 monks, the *dzong* became the seat of the Central Monastic Body (Zhung Dratshang: gzhung grwa tshang). After his death, the embalmed body of Zhabdrung Ngawang Namgyal was placed in the main chapel of the *dzong*, the *machen* (*Ma chen*) (preserved body) *lhakhang*, where it is still kept today together with the relics of Tsangpa

Gyare and the *kudung* (*sku gdung*) (catafalque) containing the remains of the Buddhist Saint Pema Lingpa (b. 1450, d. 1521). The most precious *tashi gomang* believed to have been manufactured under the command of the Zhabdrung in the course of the construction of the *dzong* was kept there. Every year, the Central Monastic Body used to carry it when shifting its winter and summer residences between Punakha Dzong and Trachhicho Dzong in Thimphu respectively. The reference to Punakha Dzong in the stories about *tashi gomangs* gives indications not only about the religious significance of the tradition but also about the date of its origin, as the building of the fortress started during the Fire Ox year 1637.[35]

Last but not least, stories about the creation of both Punakha Dzong and the first *tashi gomang* portable shrine, which are closely intertwined, tell us about the master-builder who had the responsibility of designing and building the structure. This role fell to a master carpenter known as Trulbi-zow Baleb (Sprul pa's bzo ba Pa le pa) or simply Zow (bzo ba) (master craftsman) Balep (also translated as Zowo Balingpa), a man from Palip (Balingka; Pa le pa), a small village in Punakha valley. According to a local source translated by Michael Aris and published by Marc Dujardin:

> An expert in carpentry called "The Emanation Craftsman Balingpa" came forth at the time when Zhabdrung Rinpoche was building the *dzong* of Punakha. He constructed fortresses, houses and the other buildings by adding as appropriate a multiplicity of beautifying elements in the ancient designs still being used in building constructions. And so there

35 In 1651 the Zhabdrung entered into strict retreat in the *dzong* and was never to reappear. In the meantime, Bhutan resisted attacks from the Tibetans who tried to steal *Rangjung Kharsapani* in vain. Although Punakha ceased to be the seat of government in 1955, when the capital was transferred to Thimphu, the *dzong* has kept its high status under the monarchy. The lineage of the royal family goes back to Zhabdrung Ngawang Namgyal. On 17 December 1907, the former Trongsa *penlop* (governor) Ugyen Wangchuck was enthroned there as the first hereditary king of Bhutan. The royal weddings of the fourth king, H.M. Jigme Singye Wangchuck and of the present H.M. King Jigme Khesar Namgyel Wangchuck, took place in the *dzong* respectively on 31 October 1988 and on 13 October 2011. Punakha Dzong is also the place where the investiture ceremony of the Je Khenpo (Rje Mkhan-po), the head-abbot of the Drukpa Kagyü school, is performed.

(later) arose the expert woodworkers of Bhutan who are renowned to the lineage of the master craftsman Balingpa.[36]

Although Aris argues that the term 'Emanation craftsman' (*Trulbi zow*) is to be understood more as a eulogy rather than indicating he was a reincarnation, Zow Balep is generally presented as a *trulku*, the 'incarnation of the divine craftsman Vishvakarma'[37] ('The all-accomplishing, maker of all, all-doer, the divine architect'), described in the *Mahabharata* as 'the lord of the arts, the carpenter of the gods, and the most eminent of artisans',[38] a Hindu deity who is believed to be the 'Principal Architect of the Universe' and the presiding god of all architects and craftsmen. Although Vishvakarma is an alien deity, he is also venerated by Buddhists and all Bhutanese master-builders and craftsmen feel associated with his tradition. 'The idea of belonging to the important lineage associated with the mythical figure of Vishvakarma provides ritual meaning to the praxeology of cultural transfer from the most senior master-builder of the King to the local village carpenter'.[39]

Whatever was his true nature, Zow Balep had acquired a high reputation[40] and was definitely a great master of arts and crafts (*zo rig slob dpon*). However, some doubts have been expressed by the Bhutanese regarding his capacity to mastermind the manufacturing of his masterpieces. According to the history of Bhutan as taught in local schools, 'he (the Zhabdrung) sent somebody to call him (Balip) to build the *dzong*. Although this man was intelligent, his mind could not grasp what the Zhabdrung exactly wanted. He could not conceive his great project so the Zhabdrung guided him magically to the paradise of Guru Rinpoche, the Zangdopelri and showed him this place'.[41] As noticed by Dujardin: 'this passage suggests a potentially "challenging" relationship

36 Dujardin (2000: 166, 180).

37 Lamsam and Wangchuck (2012).

38 http://hinduism.about.com/od/godsgosdesses/p/vishwakarma.htm

39 Dujardin (2000: 166).

40 Zhongar Dzong in Mongar (Mong sgar) is also attributed to Zow Balep. The fortress is believed to have been built at a site where the master saw a white bowl.

41 Pommaret (1988), as quoted by Dujardin (2000: 167, 180).

between the patron and the master-builder (in the sense of who is guiding the process of architectural design and construction). The master-builder's primary role is to merge his profound knowledge of Buddhist iconography [...] with the practical and spiritual objectives of the patron in the form of an architectural synthesis'.[42]

Now that we have described the context and know more about the 'trinity', it is time to tell the story. The following is a synthesis of the oral tradition as told by Kuenza Tenzi, one of the last two surviving *manips* in Bhutan,[43] and of narratives recorded in different contemporary printed materials.[44]

Ngawang Namgyal was residing at Puna *lhakhang*, also called Dzongchung (rdzong chung; little fortress), a small temple built during the fourteenth century by the Indian saint Vanaratna, known in Bhutan as Ngagi Rinchen (Ngag gi rin chen), at the confluence of Pho Chhu (male) and Mo Chhu (female), the two rivers flowing in Punakha. It had been twenty-one years since he came to Bhutan. Eight years have passed since the construction of his first *dzong* at Semtokha (Sems rtogs kha) at the lower end of Thimphu valley. He was contemplating building a large fortress to fulfill a prediction made in the eighth century by Guru Ugyen Rinpoche (Padmasambhava) who had predicted that 'between the two rivers, a Drukpa fortress would be established by someone named Namgyal who would come to [reside] on the trunk of the mountain which resembled a haughty elephant'.[45] Ngawang Namgyal was forty-three years old in 1637 when he started building the *dzong* just in front of Dzongchung. Several magical events happened. Wood and stones were offered by local deities. The protecting deity of Tsachaphu village had timber floating down

42 Dujardin (2000: 167).

43 Kuenza Tenzi was interviewed in May 2015 in the presence of the author. The interview was conducted by Tshering Tashi who gave a synthesis in a preliminary unpublished paper presented on 22 June 2016 at the fourteenth Seminar of the International Association for Tibetan Studies (IATS) held in Bergen, Norway: 'The *Tashi Gomang*: Portable Shrines of Bhutan'. http://www.iats.info

44 Imaeda and Drukpa (1982); De Montmollin (1992: 605–606); Gayleg (2008); Phuntsho (2013: 230); Zangpo (2016: 37–41); Tendrel (2016); Across Bhutan Blog (2011).

45 Phuntsho (2013: 230).

the Pho Chhu so it could be delivered easily.[46] The protecting deity of Norbugang (nor bus gang), a neighboring village (located today in Talog [rta log] gewog), together with a female deity, Dorichum, the Lady of Stones, revealed a quarry in the neighborhood by causing a landslide, but evil forces were also at work. At night they would demolish the structures built during the daytime. The Zhabdrung had already been confronted by such adversity.

In such a situation he would enter into a state of meditation to find the proper solution. While he was meditating, a *dakini* (sky dancer) known as Dechen Gyem (Bde chen gyem) appeared to him. She told him that using a *tashi gomang* was the solution to subdue the evil forces and build the *dzong*. After seeing the vision, the Zhabdrung summoned the best carpenters. None of them had seen or even heard of *tashi gomangs*. Without a prototype, completing the task seemed impossible. Fortunately, the Zhabdrung was informed about a man living in Balep, a neighboring village. He was known as Trulku (reincarnation) Zow Balep and was believed to be the incarnation of the divine craftsman Vishvakarma. Although still young, he had acquired a great reputation as being a fine architect, a skilled sculptor and a master in miniature art. When the Zhabdrung summoned him, Zow Balep came to his court with a bucket of milk and a basket of red berries. The Zhabdrung was very pleased with these gifts which he considered highly auspicious: the milk which had turned into curd was a sign that the Buddha dharma would flourish like pure milk, meaning that the *dzong* would be built, while the red berries heralded the growth of the red-robed monastic community to be installed in the *dzong* where the sangha would flourish like the berries.

The Zhabdrung made Zow Balep sleep beside him for three consecutive nights. Through his spiritual powers he took him in his dreams. On the second night he entrusted the protecting deities, Yeshey Goenpo and Palden Lhamo, to take the dreaming consciousness of Zow Balep to Ralung Monastery, the main seat of the Drukpa Kagyü school in Tibet. On the third night he visited Zangtopelri, the copper-colored mountain paradise of Padmasambhava, in order to see the architectural designs of the site. On the morning of the fourth day, the Zhabdrung

46 *Bhutan Times* Ltd. (2007: 51).

asked Zow Balep to recount his dream. Based on his descriptions, he then asked the master to build a replica of the *tashi gomang chörten* he saw in Ralung in a miniature version. Zow Balep first made a prototype out of a radish. As the Zhabdrung was satisfied with his skill he told him to carve it out of wood.[47] When the structure of the *tashi gomang* was built the Zhabdrung added his own touch. He was capable of instantly carving Buddhist figures with his thumb. A few years later he would demonstrate this exceptional ability by making 100,000 *tsha-tsha* (miniature images molded in clay), each of them bearing 115 deities.[48] As far as the *tashi gomang* was concerned, he imprinted several Buddhist figures on clay molds which were then installed in the miniature shrine. The following day, he summoned the best painters to decorate the wooden structure. The last craftsmen to be called were the blacksmiths who were asked to make engravings to decorate the *tashi gomang* which was completed within four days. A vajra (Tibetan: *dorje, rdo rje*; 'thunderbolt') made by a legendary blacksmith was put inside the *tashi gomang* as its major sacred relic. The Zhabdrung personally presided over the consecration of the shrine which was later installed in the *utse* (*dbu rtse*) (tower) of Punakha Dzong. Upon completion of the *tashi gomang*, the building of the *dzong* resumed swiftly. The pace even doubled as the former evil forces joined in to support the construction activity. People came from all over Bhutan to help the Zhabdrung and Zow Balep to build the *dzong*. Everyone worked hard and the *dzong* which came to be known as Pungthang Dewa Chenpo Phodrang (spung thang bde ba chen po'i pho sbrang) (The Palace of Great Bliss) was built very quickly. As part of its inauguration ceremony several relics including the *Rangjung Kharsapani* were put in the different temples of the *dzong*. The *tashi gomang* made by Zow Balep was among those relics. The Zhabdrung was so happy with Zow Balep's achievement that he gave him the title of Trülpe (sprul pa'i) (emanation being) Zowor divine craftsman, an indication that could confirm Michael Aris' argument that Balep might not have been a *trulku*. Punakha Dzong became the primary fortress from where the Zhabdrung solidified his political and

47 In some accounts, it is mentioned that the model of the portable shrine equally served as the model for the construction of Punakha Dzong itself.

48 Dargye (2001: 141).

secular dominance. Every year, to this day, during the Punakha Drubchen (grub chen) and *tshechu* (festivals), the construction of the *dzong* is re-enacted.[49] The Zhabdrung thought that *tashi gomangs* could be used as an instrument for preaching the teachings of the Buddha to the masses on the occasion of public gatherings, especially in remote rural areas. Therefore, he is believed to have commissioned the making of several other miniature portable shrines. Later on, similar shrines were made in different monasteries for the benefit of the people.

Although this story clearly attributes the first *tashi gomang* to the instigation of Zhabdrung Ngawang Namgyal, other accounts reported by Marceline de Montmollin claim that the real instigator was his second successor in line and mind reincarnation, Jigme Drakpa (Jigs med grags pa, b. 1791, d. 1831), the fourth Zhabdrung, who was also the first Bhutanese Zhabdrung. According to some informants the shrine believed to be the oldest in Bhutan is said to be sealed in the monastery of Talo in Punakha valley. Founded over a century after the death of the first Zhabdrung in 1651, this monastery became the seat of Jigme Drakpa around 1807. This story, however, does not contradict the latter. Punakha Dzong was ravaged by fire and had to be partially reconstructed in 1750. As noticed by de Montmollin, the original *tashi gomang* kept in the *utse* may have been destroyed in the blaze. 'No other shrine was constructed until the reign of the Fourth Zhabdrung. Therefore, both the First and the Fourth Zhabdrung have played a major role in the diffusion of *Tashi Gomang* in

49 Re-enacting occurs on the eleventh day of the first month of the Bhutanese calendar during the second day of the *tshechu*. It comprises five main scenes involving mask dances, music and songs: 1. The Zhabdrung is shown prophesying the building of a *dzong* and giving orders to Zow Balep; 2. A dance describes the building of the *dzong*; 3. An enactment showing the building by Zow Balep and his co-workers is presented; 4. A dance portraying the building of the *dzong* called 'Om Sala Mani' is performed, and the visit by the Zhabdrung at the construction site is then described; 5. Eventually comes the consecration ceremony of the *dzong* where Zow Balep, other craftsmen and the public are shown presenting scarves. Later there is also a scene showing the moment where the governors along with people from different parts of the country are offering white scarves in thankfullness to the Zhabdrung followed by a performance of the dance called '*tashi gomang*'.

(https://www.windhorsetours.com/wind/pdf/20090612112543_Punakha%20Drubchen%20and%20Tsechu%20details.pdf)

Bhutan: Ngawang Namgyal introduced the tradition and Jigme Drakpa ensured its revival'.[50] If the original *tashi gomang* made by Zow Balep was effectively destroyed by fire, the shrine currently kept by the Central Monastic Body could be a replacement for which the origin is unclear. It is interesting to notice that this specific *tashi gomang* holds an image of the first Zhabdrung and the only known image of Zow Balep himself.

A highly symbolical jewel of Buddhist arts and crafts

A *tashi gomang* is both a remarkable example of miniature art and a tridimensional mandala involving complex symbolism. As noted by Dujardin: 'in Buddhism, the contribution to the realization of a spatial environment complying with Buddhist ideas about life and after-life is considered a deed of virtue, irrespective of one's rank, position or talent'. This is verified with *tashi gomangs*. All those involved in the process of building and using a portable shrine are made 'spiritually better': 'the initiator and patron for his enlightened idea, devotion and sponsorship; the master-carpenter (*zorig lopon* or *zow*) for his profound expertise of iconometric building and artisanal craftsmanship; the Buddhist monk for his wisdom, talent of meditation and astrological knowledge [we can add the *manip* there]; (…) and the users for being blessed with yet another earthly place that is spiritually ordered'.[51] A *tashi gomang* usually measures between fifty and sixty cm in height and about thirty cm in width and has a maximum of 108 doors. Each item traditionally comes with a special document, a kind of license, bearing the seals of the highest religious authorities and describing the conditions under which it can be used. Since the demise of the Zhabdrung system, only the king has the power to commission a *tashi gomang*. When not in use, the shrine is stored in a wood transportation box that is often painted and decorated with brass ornaments. Two leather straps are fastened to the box so that the *manip* can carry it on his back. The *tashi gomang* is carefully wrapped in several layers of five-colored brocade inside the box. Only the *manip* is supposed to remove the cloth and unfold the shrine. He

50 De Montmollin (1992: 606).

51 Dujardin (2000: 159).

first pulls out its four corners, which causes the *tashi gomang* to open into the shape of a swastika, revealing the multiple miniature doors that conceal the minuscule niches. The shrine is then mounted on top of its box and can be rotated clockwise. With the help of a special stick, the *manip* opens the doors to expose the deities inhabiting the niches and chants the appropriate prayers. He usually raises his left hand to his ear 'in the classical attitude of divine inspiration turning his prayer-wheel with the other'.[52] According to popular belief, the *tashi gomang* is 'an amalgamation of sacred *nye* (*gnas*: holy sites), brought together by Buddha for the benefit of the people. Looking at the *tashi gomang* is believed to be equivalent to seeing all the sacred *nye*, which would cleanse all sins'.[53] It is usually admitted that there are four types of *tashi gomangs* in Bhutan. Each kind corresponds to a particular realm in the Buddhist cosmogony. However, different classifications have been proposed. The most commonly recognized in Bhutan are as follows:

- The Zangtopalri Phodrang (Zangs mdog dpal ri Pho brang) type corresponds to the Copper Colored-Mountain Palace also described as the Heavenly Palace of Padmasambhava (pad ma 'byung gnas) situated in the Ngyayab ling (rna yab gling) 'Fan Tail' Island in the south-west of Jambudvipa (Dzambuling, 'dzam bu gling), 'Rose-Apple Tree' Continent, south of Mount Meru. It is dedicated to Padmasambhava.
- The Dewachen gi shingkham (Bde ba can [blissful land] gyi zhing khams) type corresponds to the Sukhavati or Western Paradise (Dewachen in Dzongkha). It is dedicated to Buddha Amitabha known as Oepamey ('Od dpag med) in Bhutan.
- The Ngoenpargawa (mNgon par dga' ba) type, 'delightful', corresponds to Abhirati (Mngon par dga' ba), the mountain island believed to be the realm of Buddha of the East Akshobhya (Mikoedpa/Mitrugpa, mi bskyod pa/mi 'khrugs pa).

---

52 De Montmollin (1992: 607).

53 Across Bhutan Blog (2011).

- The Riwotala (Ri po ta la) type corresponds to Mount Potalaka (brilliance) which is the mythical realm of bodhisattva Avalokiteshvara (Chenrezig, spyan ras gzigs), to whom it is dedicated.

Yoshiro Imaeda and Doffu Drukpa have proposed a slightly different classification.[54] Lam Kezang Chhoephel, CEO of the Agency for the Promotion of Indigenous Crafts (APIC), has even heard about a version with five types.[55] According to our findings, it seems that classifications have largely depended on the *manip*'s interpretations. Codification is not as strict as it could be. There is not necessarily a distinct shape and structure for each type of *tashi gomang*. However, the way the Buddha families and associated deities have been arranged in the shrine according to a direction or a specific realm of the Buddhist cosmogony is the dominant pattern that helps categorize *tashi gomangs*. A comprehensive study of the iconography of the different *tashi gomangs* is needed to formulate a definitive view on their classification. Preliminary contributions already exist that show interesting patterns.[56] While most of the *tashi gomang*s are square shaped (Zangtopalri and Namgyal), some are round shaped. The number of stories is different from one to another (for example Zangtopalri has three while Namgyal has only two). In some cases, the four sides

---

54 This classification is as follows: the Zangtopalri Phodrang type (same as previous classification); the Dewachen gi shingkham type (same as previous classification); the Jang Shambhala (Byang Shambha la) type corresponds to the Paradise to the North mentioned in the Kalacakra (wheel of time) tantra – it is the realm ruled over by Jampa (byams pa) (Maitreya), the future Buddha; and the Namgyal (rNam ryal) stupa type or 'all-victorious' stupa corresponds to one of the eight kinds of stupas that symbolizes the Buddha's agreement to extend his life by three months, after one of his followers had pleaded with him not to pass away. See Imaeda and Drukpa (1982: 12).

55 This classification is as follows: Shar Chhog Ngoenpargawa (East), dedicated to Buddha Dorje Sempa (rdo rje sems dpa') (Akshobya) (same as the first classification); Lho Chhog Palden Zepa (South), dedicated to Buddha Rinchhen Jungney (rin chen 'byung gnas) (Ratnasambhava); Nup Chhog Dewachen (West) dedicated to Buddha Oepame ('Od dPag Med) (Amitabha) (same as the two previous classifications); Jaang Chhog Layrab Zog (North), dedicated to Buddha Dhoyon Duba (don yo dru pa) (Amogasiddhi); Eue Chhog Toogpu Kod (Centre), dedicated to Buddha Nampar Nangdze (rnam par snang mdzad) (Vairocana).

56 Imaeda and Dukpa have proposed a description of the Zangtokpalri and Namgyal types. De Montmollin has also described the Zangtopalri type.

which correspond to the four directions are similar, except for a specific detail like the presence of a tablet on one side in the case of Namgyal. The roof of the *tashi gomang* is usually mounted with an ornamental pinnacle. When the *tashi gomang* is displayed a lotus flower often appears on its top. When pulled with a thread a figurine pops up in the center of the flower. It most often represents Guru Ugyen Rinpoche. Although *tashi gomangs* are all hard wooden nail-less objects, some are metal plated. They all contain a central axis, but their structure may differ. In some cases, a chapel has been carved at the base to house one or even two main deities. The number of folding panels, doors, clay images (*tsha tsha*), statues and paintings also varies. The pantheon represented in each type of *tashi gomang* is diverse. Ornamental features like turquoise and coral sets, painted auspicious symbols and engraved scriptures also constitute elements of differentiation.

The making of a *tashi gomang* required highly talented artists. The country's most senior master-craftsmen entrusted with the task of technically implementing what had been decided by the highest level of patronage are traditionally referred to as *zorig* (various arts and crafts) *lopons* (masters). The making of a *tashi gomang* involves no less than nine of the thirteen traditional arts and crafts (*zorig chusum*) of Bhutan, five relating to the religious tradition (painting, sculpture, carving, bronze-casting, embroidery and appliqué) and four to the secular tradition (weaving, carpentry, gold- and silver-smithery, and blacksmithery).[57] There are few records about the master-craftsmen who were able to make *tashi gomangs*. While Zow Balep is considered the first master-craftsman to have made such a shrine, the tradition apparently disappeared at the end

57 The thirteen traditional arts and crafts include *thagzo* (*thags bzo*; weaving), *tshazo* (*tshar bzo*; bamboo weaving), *shazo* (*shags bzo*; wood turning), *lhazo* (*lha bzo*; painting), *shingzo* (*shing bzo*; carpentry), *dozo* (*rdo bzo*; masonry), *phazo* (*spar bzo*; wood carving), *jimzo* (*'jim bzo*; clay work), *lugzo* (*blug bzo*; bronze casting), *garzo* (*mgar bzo*; blacksmithing), *troezo* (*spros bzo*; ornament making, gold- and silver-smithery), *dezo* (*'dal bzo*; paper making), and *tshemzo* (*tshem bzo*; embroidery). The classification between religious and secular arts and crafts was probably codified in the late seventeenth century in the context of the dual system of government established by Zhabdrung Ngawang Namgyal. See Dorji (2015: 195).

of the nineteenth century when Thang Ugyen Tshering, a man believed to be the last professional builder of *tashi gomang*, passed away.[58] However, highly skilled artists could still make *tashi gomang* after this demise, even if it was not their specialty. One of these highly talented artists was no less than the maternal great-grandfather of the present king of Bhutan. Born Kuenga Gyelshen in the Haa region, he came to be known as Tsham Go Seb (the meditator in yellow garb, because he had a penchant for yellow attire) after spending six and a half years in rigorous meditation. His life has been briefly recorded by one of his granddaughters, H.M. the Queen Ashi Dorji Wangmo Wangchuck (consort of the fourth king, H.M. Jigme Singye Wangchuck) who highlighted his achievement in a book about her father where Tsham Go Seb is described in a chapter titled 'The Patriarch of the Family and Master of Miniature Art'.[59] From this precious account we learn that he was very knowledgeable about Buddhism. He was one of the disciples of Chogley Yeshey Ngodrup (b. 1851, d. 1917), the fifth speech reincarnation of Zhabdrung Ngawang Namgyal.[60] 'He contributed his expertise as an artist and idol-maker at several places'. Among several achievements, 'he made a beautiful miniature altar complete with minute idols. This unique and portable chapel can still be seen in Kuengachholing (Kun dga' chos gling) (monastery in Paro)'. Chogley Yeshey Ngodrup (Phyogs las ye shes dngos grub), who himself had artistic talents, and Tsham Go Seb 'used to have an exercise to determine who could write in microscopic letters twelve lines of *Meldon Drugay* (text of prayer) on their thumb-nail. Chogley [who was said to have been able to draw an image of Avalokitesvara on a single grain of barley[61]] could fit the text written in a circular formation. But [Tsham Go Seb] wrote it in straight lines and still had a line and a half to spare'. This talent, which has given him the reputation of a 'master of miniature art', was indeed vital to the construction of miniature shrines such as *tashi gomangs*.

---

58 De Montmollin (1992: 608).

59 Wangchuck (1999: 75–79).

60 Chogley Yeshey Ngodrup was also the fifty-seventh and last Druk Desi, the secular ruler of Bhutan before the introduction of the monarchy. From 1915 until his death in 1917 he was also in office as Bhutan's fifty-third Je Khenpo (head-abbot).

61 http://treasuryoflives.org.biographies/view/Yeshe-Ngodrup/8397

An instrument of worship and propitiation used by wandering bards to propagate Buddhism

Although they were initially carried by ordained priests, responsibility for the *tashi gomang* was later placed in the hands of the lay practitioners known as *lam manips* (*bla ma Nipa-s*), or simply *manips* (*ma Nipa-s*), those 'who chant prayers' (*maNi*). Also known by other names depending on the region in the Tibetan world, they have been roaming through the countryside since ancient times. Some were using *thangkas* in support of their teachings. Others preferred a prayer wheel under a canopy with hanging bells as observed in northern and eastern Kham. Interesting studies have been made on the status of *manips* in different regions of Tibet.[62] In Bhutan, *manips* have always been known to carry portable shrines. They are a category of *gomchens*[63] although they are ranked higher in the monastic hierarchy. Their red ceremonial scarves have more folds than the usual ones and they are allowed to wear *dralham* (*drag lham*) (traditional leather and silk boots) contrary to other *gomchens*. They are free to live either in a monastery or in a village. They are permitted to marry and raise a family. The overall tradition of *gomchen* is anterior to *manip*. It was started in Bhutan during the eighth century when Guru Rinpoche, who was himself a lay practitioner, introduced Buddhism into the country. The first 'official' *gomchen* was his assistant Haminatha from central Bhutan.[64] Although they are not ordained priests, *manips* are highly knowledgeable about Buddhism. There are two ways to become a *manip*: the first is to study individually as an apprentice under the guidance of an older reliable *manip*, and the second is to receive training in a monastic school.

Traditionally, *manips* would go from village to village and even from house to house, chanting mantras and spiritual songs of devotion and realization. Initially, *tashi gomangs* were closely associated with the propagation of the Drukpa Kagyü tradition in the country. *Manips* were also involved in *tshechus* and took the opportunity of mass gatherings like weekend markets to display their shrines. While displaying his shrine – of which he was the caretaker and not the owner – the *manip*

---

62 Tsering (2011: 81); Pommaret (1989: 22–23).

63 In Tibet it means meditators while in Bhutan it refers simply to lay practitioners.

64 Tashi (2005: 211–241).

would chant prayers. 'Four prayers are based on the repetitive mantra "*Om mani Padma hûm*". Others are dedicated to the All-compassionate Avalokitesvara, to Yama (the Lord of Death), to the Lake Dhanakosa related with Padmasambhava's miraculous birth, to the Paradise of Padmasambhava. These prayers are mainly chanted for the soul of the dead person'.[65] 'The ornaments belonging to the deceased are offered to the *Tashi Gomang* for the benefit of his soul and to procure him salvation from Hell'.[66] Although some of those prayers have been recorded and categorized,[67] further research is needed to know if they vary according to the type of *tashi gomang*. The overall ritual needs to be studied in a comprehensive manner. According to the memories of a *manip*, the arrival of a *tashi gomang* in a village followed a specific protocol:

> [P]eople in the villages helped carry the *Tashi Gomang* to other villages. *Tashi Gomangs* were kept at the *letshen's* (messenger) house. The *letshens* used to inform the people about the arrival of the *Tashi Gomang* in the village. People were called to come to his house to recite *mani* at night. The *letshen* provided meals to the *manip* who recited *mani* and blew the conch shell once they reached the *letshen's* house. Reciting the *mani* and blowing of the conch shell announced the *Tashi Gomang*'s presence. But *letshens* still had to personally go and inform the people owing to the rugged terrain of the country.[68]

The arrival of a *manip* in a village was 'an excuse to stop work for several days and to gather at the house where he was lodged'.[69] As described by a Bhutanese woman who witnessed a genuine *tashi gomang* ceremony when she was a young girl:

> [C]urious children (would) gather around to take a peek at the miniature statues within the miniature doors and windows, the elders would

65 De Montmollin (1992: 607).

66 Imaeda and Drukpa (1982: 13).

67 Imaeda and Drukpa have proposed a tentative list.

68 *Kuensel*, the national newspaper of Bhutan.

69 Aris (1994: 147).

> prostrate, sit around and sing the prayers devoted to Chenrizig. The monks would lead the elders in paying homage. Villagers would offer grains [called *Soelnyom Choendru*] to the bearers of the box, and woven belts and *namzha* (clothes to drape the relic) to the *chörten.* In the villages, it was customary for residents to invite the group and the sacred relic at their home for a day. It was believed good fortune and blessings would visit the house and its members. With each house wanting to host the relic, it would take days or weeks for the *manips* to start their journey to another place.[70]

Through their activity, *manips* generated revenue for their monasteries as 'spiritual tax collectors'. According to a contemporary record 'around the 3rd King's time [r. 1952–1972], when the barter trade was converted to currency,[71] the [annual] collection [per *tashi gomang*] was valued at Ngultrum 500. In 2011, most reliquaries collected Ngultrum 2000-3000 per year from *ngendhar* (donations) and the rest could be kept by the carrying custodian to cover his own expenses'.[72] Usually *manips* would come out from their summer retreat or residence at the beginning of October when the monsoon was over. They preferred to travel after the harvest season because it was easier to move around without confronting heavy rains and landslides, and because people were more inclined to offer donations in kind, especially rice, but also butter and cheese.

In ancient times *tashi gomangs* were a significant source of revenue in remote areas for their custodian monasteries which had their shrines travel throughout the country four or five times a year to collect donations. The *manips* could take their share to cover their needs for food and other necessities.

The discontinuation in 1996 of the *woola* (*'u la*) system (beneficiary labor contribution),[73] a form of taxation involving free compulsory labor for the benefit of the community, also had an impact. In ancient times

70 Across Bhutan Blog (2011).

71 The economy started to be monetized in the 1960s with the use of the Indian rupee. The national currency (ngultrum) was created in 1974.

72 Wangchuck (2011).

73 Ura (2005).

woola (a word of Mongol origin) provided a fixed workforce to undertake specific tasks for the religious government. 'Such compulsory *corvée* included the transport of government loads'. Thanks to this system, which helped 'support the monk communities which in turn conferred spiritual blessings and protection on the public',[74] *manips* were able to get temporary assistants who could help them carry the shrine for free. Without this aid and with the necessity of earning a decent salary while negotiating rising commodity prices, becoming a *manip* has become a challenge members of the younger generations no longer want to face.

Other factors also led to the gradual disappearance of the tradition. *Tashi gomangs* have attracted the greed of thieves willing to smuggle them out of the country to sell them to foreign collectors. *Manips* have thus become increasingly reluctant to travel without proper security and the shrines have been kept in hidden places. Although Buddhism is still deeply entrenched in the lives of the Bhutanese, the development of modern education, waning interest and an inability to adapt to the lifestyle of a religious practitioner, even a lay-person, the improvement in transportation allowing people who live in remote areas to receive blessings in *dzongs* and monasteries as often as they wish, the decline of the oral tradition in the age of television, mobile phones and the internet and the challenge for young people to carry a fifty lb *tashi gomang* on their back in rugged terrain without a decent salary have all led to the gradual disappearance of the tradition. For the same reason that monastic schools across the country have been recording a drop in enrollment since the 1960s, becoming a *manip* has become less attractive.

Nowadays the tradition of *manips* carrying *tashi gomangs* and traveling throughout the country to display them has vanished. The two surviving professional *manips* only display their shrines at the memorial *chörten* in Thimphu on auspicious days or at the weekend market. *Tashi gomangs* can also be seen occasionally during special ceremonies like the annual Drukpa Tshezhi (celebration of the first sermon of Lord Buddha) in Thimphu. Sometimes the display is even more exceptional as was the case in June 2016 during the Kurjey *tshechu* in Bumthang when a *tashi*

74 Aris (1994: 32).

gomang which was said not to have been displayed for public viewing for about 400 years was shown.

Our Tashi Gomang Project has contributed to the preservation of the tradition. Now designated a 'national treasure', *tashi gomangs* fulfil three main functions. First, they remain an instrument of practice: the Central Monastic Body uses them to perform certain rituals, and new *manips* will be able to ensure the continuity of the tradition at the grassroots level. Although the display of a *tashi gomang* has become a rarity, it is still considered highly auspicious to have the opportunity to see one. Second, their iconography offers a valuable and fairly comprehensive view of the historical development of Buddhism in Bhutan. Last but not least, *tashi gomangs* represent a concentration of a unique artistic and artisanal expertise which makes Bhutan so special.

Table 1.1: *Tashi gomangs* kept in Bhutan[1]

Province (*dzongkhag*)	**Location** (*dzong* [fortress], *goempa* [monastery], *lhakang* [temple], *chörten* [stupa])	***Tashi Gomangs***	
		Number at each location	**Number in each province**
Bumthang	**Choedrak** (chos grags) **Goempa** A monastery located in Chhume (chu smad) valley, where Guru Rinpoche (Padmasambhava) is said to have meditated. The first settlement in this place is attributed to the Drukpa Kagyupa master, Lorepa (lo ras pa) in 1234.	**1**	**5**
	Lamei (la ma'i) **Goempa** Located in Chhoekhor (chos 'khor), built in the 19th century, formerly a royal residence, the building now houses the Ugyen Wangchuck Institute for Conservation and Environment.	**1**	
	Petseling (pad tshal gling) **Goempa** Located in Chhoekhor, this Nyingma monastery was established in 1769 by the first Petseling Tulku, Drubthob Namgyal Lhendup (grubthob rnamrgyal lhun gru). It remains the seat of the incarnation lineage.	**1**	
	Wangdu Choling (Dbang 'dus chos gling) **Palace** Located in Chhoekhor, this palace was built in 1857 on the site of the battle camp of Trongsa Penlop Jigme Namgyal (Jigs med rnam rgyal), father of the first king, who was born there. Both the first and second kings adopted this place as their summer residence.	**1**	
	Zangtopelri Lhakang Built with the support of H.M. Ashi Kesang Choden Wangchuck, queen mother of the fourth king and patron of the Tashi Gomang Project, this new temple, close to Kurje (sku rjes) lhakang, was consecrated in 2008.	**1**	
Dagana	**Dagana Dzong** (Dar dkar na rdzong) This fortress was built in the 17th century under the command of Zhabdrung Ngawang Namgyal. The *tashi gomang* is kept in its main *lhakang*. Zhabdrung Jigme Chogyal (Jigs med bsod rgyal; b. 1862, d. 1904) the fifth incarnation of Zhabdrung Ngawang Namgyal, is said to have constructed this *tashi gomang* in the 18th century.	**1**	**1**

Province (*dzongkhag*)	Location (*dzong* [fortress], *goempa* [monastery], *lhakang* [temple], *chörten* [stupa])	*Tashi Gomangs*	
		Number at each location	**Number in each province**
Haa	**Lungkhar** (Rlung khar) **Lhakhang** This private temple, built during the 20th century, is located in Uesu (Dbus su) *gewog* (*rged 'og*; village block).	**1**	**3**
	Yangthang Goempa This community temple located in Bji (Sbyis) *gewog* was founded in the 18th century by Phurpai Neljorpa Thinley Jamtsho. It was renovated after it sustained extensive damage due to the 2011 earthquake.	**1**	
	Concealed inside a *chörten* Located in Dungchoe village, Uesu *gewog*, this *chörten* is partially destroyed. The presence of the *tashi gomang*, which has been brought to Thimphu for restoration, would have been unnoticed otherwise.	**1**	
Lhuntse	**Lhuntse Dzong** (Lhun rtse rdzong) This fortress was established by Pema Lingpa's son during the 16th century. The *tashi gomang* is kept in the Mitrukpa *lhakang*. Tenzin Chogyal (bstan 'dzin Bsod-rgyal; b. 1700, d. 1767), the 10th Je Khenpo (r. 1755–1762), is credited for its construction.	**1**	**3**
	Goempa Karpo (Dgon pa dkar po) Established during the 18th century by Choying Rangdrol (Chos dbyings rang grol), a famous treasure revealer, this monastery is a replica of Petseling Goempa in Bumthang.	**1**	
	Nyalamdung (Nya lam gdung) **Lhakhang** Nyalamdung village is located in Khoma (*Mkho ma*) *gewog*.	**1***	
Mongar	**Mongar Dzong (**Mong sgar rdzong) This fortress was built in the 1930s during the reign of the second king. The *tashi gomang* is kept in its main *lhakang*. It is said to have been brought from Zhongar (Zhong sgar) Dzong. Zhongar Dzongpon Tenzin (Zhong sgar rjong dpon bstan 'dzin), the brother of Zhabdrung Jigme Chogyal ('Jigs med chos rgyal; b. 1862, d. 1904), the fifth mind incarnation of Zhabdrung Ngawang Namgyal, is credited for the construction of this *tashi gomang*.	**1**	**1**
Paro	**Dongkala** (Dong kha la) **Lhakang** (Founded in the 14th century by Terton Tshering Dorje (Gter ston Tshe ring rdo rje), this temple, located in Shaba (shar pa) *gewog* was severely damaged by an earthquake in September 2011.	**1**	**2**
	Rinpung Dzong (Rin-spungs rdzong) This fortress was built in 1646 under the command of Zhabdrung Ngawang Namgyal.	**1**	

Province (*dzongkhag*)	Location (*dzong* [fortress], *goempa* [monastery], *lhakang* [temple], *chörten* [stupa])	*Tashi Gomangs*	
		Number at each location	**Number in each province**
Punakha	**Dompala** (Dom pa la) **Goempa** The powerful deity Palden Lhamo (Dpal ldan lha mo) is believed to reside in the main temple of this monastery located in Lingmukha (gling mu kha) *gewog*.	**1**	**4**
	Seoula (Se'u la) **Goempa** Located in Chhubu (Chus bug) *gewog*, this monastery was founded in 1732 by Buddhist master and artist Jamgön Ngawang Thinley ('Jam mgon Ngag dbang 'Phrin las). The *tashi gomang* kept in this location is said to have been built during the same period.	**1**	
	Talog (Rta log) **Goempa** Located in Talog *gewog*, this monastery is the seat of the mind reincarnation of Zhabdrung Ngawang Namgyal. Its annual festival is very popular. One of the *tashi gomangs* kept in this location is believed to be the most ancient in Bhutan.	**2**	
Thimphu	**Lingkana** (Glin kha na) **Palace** Located below Tashichho Dzong, the Garden Palace is the residence of the present king.	**1**	**5**
	Tango (Rta mgo) **Goempa** The highest center of Buddhist learning in the country, this monastery was founded by the 'Divine madman' Drukpa Kunley ('Brug pa kun legs) in the 15th century. Zhabdrung Ngawang Namgyal meditated in its cave. The *tashi gomang* kept in this location is said to have been commissioned by Pelden Singye (Dpal ldan sings rgyas; b. 1856, d. 1921) who served as the 52nd (r. 1912–1915) and 55th (r. 1918–1919) Je Khenpo or chief abbot of Bhutan.	**1**	
	Tashichho Dzong Built in 1641 under the command of the first Zhabdrung, this fortress houses the throne room and offices of the king, the cabinet secretariat and the ministries of home affairs and finance. It also houses the office of the Je Khenpo and serves as the summer residence of the Central Monastic Body.	**1**	
	Thadra (Tha brag) **Goempa** Founded in 1731 by Tsulag Gyatsho (Gtsugs lag rgya mtsho), this monastery, located at an altitude of 3,270 meters, can be reached after two hours of uphill hiking from the RBA headquarters in Lungtenphu.	**1**	
	Samteling (Bsam gtan gling) **Palace (Royal Cottage)** The royal residence of the fourth king.	**12**	
Trashigang	**Trasgigang Dzong (**Bkra shis sgang rdzong) One of the largest *dzongs* in Bhutan, this fortress was built in 1659. Its construction was prophesied by Ngawang Namgyal.	**1***	**1**

Province (*dzongkhag*)	Location (*dzong* [fortress], *goempa* [monastery], *lhakang* [temple], *chörten* [stupa])	*Tashi Gomangs*	
		Number at each location	**Number in each province**
Trashi Yangtse	**Trashi Yangtse Dzong** (Bkra shis g-yang tse rdzong) This fortress was initially built in the ninth century. It was later abandoned and fell into ruins when the Tibetans attacked. In the 15th century, Pema Lingpa chanced upon the ruin during one of his visits and decided to rebuild it.	**1***	**1**
Trongsa	**Drangla** (Drang la) **Goempa** Located in Drangla village, Tangsibi (Stang si sbis) *gewog*, this private temple also known as Drangla Lhakhang Nyingpa (Drang la lha khang rnying ma) was probably founded during the time of Terton Dorji Lingpa (Rdo rje gling pa, b. 1346, d. 1405) or during that of his spiritual son, Chogden Gonpo (Mchog ldan mgon po), also a disciple of Terton Pema Lingpa (b. 1450, d. 1521).	**1**	**5**
	Trongsa Dzong (Krong gsar rdzong) This is the largest fortress in Bhutan built in 1647 by Minjur Tempa, Trongsa *penlop* and future third Desi. The *tashi gomang* is kept in Chenrezig *lhakang*.	**2**	
	Nyala (Nya la) **Goempa** Located in Tangsibi *gewog*, this monastery affiliated to the Peling Nyingma tradition was built in the 15th century where a horrendous demoness was supposedly subdued.	**13**	
	Sinphu (Srin phu) **Goempa** Located in Nubi (Nu sbis) *gewog*, this monastery was founded in the 15th century by Terton Dorji Lingpa's (Rdo rje gling pa) grandson. The *tashi gomang* kept in this location is taken out in public for people to seek blessing once every three years.	**1**	

Province (*dzongkhag*)	Location (*dzong* [fortress], *goempa* [monastery], *lhakang* [temple], *chörten* [stupa])	*Tashi Gomangs*	
		Number at each location	Number in each province
Wangdiphodrang	**Dangchu** (Dwangs chu) **Lhakang** This monastery is located in Dangchu *gewog*.	1	5
	Gangteng (Sgang steng) **Goempa** This monastery, located above Phobjikha (Phob sbyis kha) valley, was established in 1613 by Gangteng Tulku Rigdzin Pema Tinley (Sgang steng sprul sku rig 'dzin padma 'Phrin las; b. 1564, d. 1642), the grandson and mind reincarnation of Pema Lingpa.	1	
	Pag-ga Goempa This monastery is located in Sephu (sras phug) *gewog*.	1	
	Rabgatse (Rab dga' rtse) **Lhakang** Known as Duetsidrak, this temple located in Sephu *gewog* is believed to be one of Guru Rinpoche's *drubney* (place of meditation) during the eighth century.	1	
	Nyinzergang Lhakang (Nyi zer sgang lha khang) Located in Rubesa (Rus sbis) *gewog*, this monastery was founded during the 13th century by Terton Wugpa Lingpa (wug pa gling pa) from Tibet. The place is once said to have been afflicted by epilepsy caused by evil spirits. The *terton* subdued the spirits and freed the people from the disease. The *tashi gomang* kept in this location is said to have been constructed under the initiative of Dogyen Thinley Rabgay, one of the longest serving students of Tenzin Chogyal, the 10th Je Khenpo (r. 1755–1762).	1	
TOTAL			36

Notes:

1. This list was compiled from a survey conducted by the Thangka Conservation Center with the support of the Central Monastic Body. Since the organization of the exhibition in Thimphu, three other *tashi gomangs* have been reported to me. Because I have not been able to see and identify them yet, they are marked with an asterisk.
2. The *tashi gomang* registered in this location was designed after that kept in Rinpung Dzong (Paro). It was manufactured in 2015 and presented to the fourth king as a gift on the occasion of his 60th birthday.
3. The *tashi gomang* registered in this location is currently kept in a private house in Thimphu under the custody of Lam Manip Kunzang Tenzing.

Bibliography

Across Bhutan Blog (2011). *Blessing in a Box*, 24 April, accessed at http://acrossbhutan.blogspot.fr/2011/04/blessing-in-box.html

Aris, M. (1994). *The Raven Crown: The Origin of Buddhist Monarchy in Bhutan*, London: Serindia Publications.

Bell, C. (1910). *Collection: Album 9*, National Museum Liverpool, UK.

Bhutan Times Ltd. (2007). *Dzongs of Bhutan: Fortresses of the Dragon Kingdom*, Thimphu: Bhutan Times Publication.

Cadaval, O., S. Kim and D. Baird N'Diaye, eds. (2016). *Curatorial Conversations: Cultural Representations and the Smithsonian Folklife Festival*, Mississippi: University Press of Mississippi.

Dargye, Y. (2001). *History of the Drukpa Kagyud School in Bhutan (12th to 17th Century A.D.)*, Thimphu: Omega Traders.

De Montmollin, M. (1992). 'bKra shis sgo mang of Bhutan: On a Specific Tradition of Shrines and Its Prolongation in the Museum of Ethnography in Neuchâtel', *Tibetan Studies: Proceedings of the 5th Seminar of the International Association for Tibetan Studies, Narita, 1989*, Narita: Naritasan Shinshoji, vol. 2, pp. 605–615.

Dorji, J., ed. (2015). *Intangible Cultural Heritage of Bhutan, Research & Media Division*, Thimphu: National Library & Archives of Bhutan.

Dowman, K. (1988). *The Power-places of Central Tibet: The Pilgrim's Guide*, London/New York: Routledge & Kegan Paul.

Dujardin, M. (2000). 'From Living to Propelling Monument: The Monastery-Fortress (dzong) as Vehicle of Cultural Transfer in Contemporary Bhutan', *Journal of Bhutan Studies*, vol. 2, no. 2, pp. 151–181.

Forte, E. (2015). 'A Journey « to the Land on the Other Side »: Buddhist Pilgrimage and Travelling Objects from the Oasis of Khotan'. In P. McAllister, C. Scherrer-Schaub and H. Krasser, eds., *Cultural Flows across the Western Himalayas*, Vienna: VÖAW, pp. 151–185.

Gayleg, K. (2008). 'Punakha Dzong: The Symbol of Bhutan's Living Architectural Heritage'. In F. Rennie and R. Mason, eds., *Bhutan Ways of Knowing*, Charlotte: Information Age Publishing, pp. 200–230.

Gerner, M. (2007). *Chakzampa Thangtong Gyalpo: Architect, Philosopher and Iron Chain Bridge Builder* (Translated from German by Gregor Verhufen), Thimphu: Centre for Bhutan Studies.

Imaeda, Y. and D. Drukpa (1982). *Bhûtan no Tashi goman/Tashigomang of Bhutan: Asian Concepts of the Cosmos Exhibition*, Tokyo: Laforet Museum.

Lamsam, S. and K.C. Wangchuck. (2012). *Zangdok Palri: The Lotus Light Palace of Guru Rinpoche*, Bangkok: Gatshel Publishing.

Lyons, T. (2003). 'Folk Painting and Painted God-Boxes'. In P. Claus, S. Diamond and M. Margaret, eds., *South Asian Folklore: An Encyclopedia*, New York: Routledge, pp. 215–218, 253–254.

Mathou, T. (2016). 'Tashi Gomang: The Tradition of Miniature Portable Shrines in Bhutan'. In *Tashi Gomang, A National Treasure of Bhutan, Exhibition Catalogue*, Thimphu: Royal Textile Academy, pp. 33–64.

Norbu, J. (2015). 'The Lhasa Ripper: A Preliminary Investigation into the "Dark Underbelly" of Social Life in the Holy City', *Revue d'Etudes Tibétaines*, vol. 31, pp. 233–250.

Phuntsho, K. (2013). *The History of Bhutan*, London: Random House.

Pommaret, F. (1988). *History of Bhutan: Handbook for Teachers*, Thimphu: Department of Education, Royal Government of Bhutan.

Pommaret, F. (1989). *Les das log, « revenants de la mort » dans le monde tibétain: sources littéraires et tradition vivante*, Paris: CNRS Editions.

Sabnami, N. (2014). *Kaavad Tradition of Rajasthan: A Portable Pilgrimage*, New Delhi: Niyogi Books.

Tashi, K.P. (2005). 'The Positive Impact on Gomchen Tradition on Achieving and Maintaining Gross National Happiness'. In *Rethinking Development: Proceedings of the Second International Conference on Gross National Happiness*, Thimphu: Center for Bhutan Studies, pp. 211–241.

Tendrel (2016). *Zhabdrung Ngawang Namgyal and the Creation of the Nation State of Bhutan*, Thimphu: TENDREL Initiatives – Institute of Management Studies.

Tsering, T. (2011). 'Preliminary Notes on the Origin of the Blama Nipa Storytellers and Their Fate in Exile Today'. In P. Sutherland and T. Tsering, eds., *Disciples of a Crazy Saint: The Buchen of Spiti*, Oxford: Pitt Rivers Museum, pp. 79–107.

Tucci, G. (1956). *To Lhasa and Beyond: Diary of the Expedition to Tibet in the Year 1948*, Rome: Istituto Poligrafico Dello Stato.

Ura, K. (2005). *Beneficial Labor Contribution (Woola)*, Thimphu: CBS, Monograph.

Wangchuck, D.W. (1999). *Of Rainbows and Clouds: The Life of Yab Ugyen Dorji as Told to His Daughter*, London: Serindia Publications.

Wangchuck, K.C.T. (2011). 'Tashi Gomang-All Auspicious Many Doors', personal blog, Thimphu, 20 November, accessed at http://babykctw.blogspot.fr/2011/11/tashi-gomang-all-auspicious-many-doors.html

Zangpo, N. (2016). 'Tashi Gomang: Miniature Temple Worth Hundred Temples', *TASHI DELEK*, vol. 17, iss. 2, March/April, pp. 37–41.

2 The Founder and Disciples of the Drukpa Kagyü School: Re-Examination of the Three Sub-Schools of Drukpa Kagyü

Seiji Kumagai

Introduction

Since the introduction of Buddhism to Tibet at the beginning of the seventh century, it has strongly influenced Tibetan culture and society. After the Sakya school achieved governmental control of Tibet under the protection of the Chinese Yuen dynasty in the thirteenth century, various Tibetan Buddhist schools have been influential politically, as well as spiritually, in Tibet. The Kagyü school, one of the four surviving main schools of Tibetan Buddhism, produced the largest number of sub-schools in that tradition. Within that school, the Karma Kagyü school (Karma bka' brgyud) became the most prominent sub-school both religiously and politically. The second largest sub-school in terms of the number of adherents is currently the Drukpa Kagyü school ('Brug pa bka' brgyud), which has been the state Buddhist school in Bhutan (Druk-yul; 'Brug yul) since the establishment of the country by the seventeenth head abbot Zhabdrung Ngawang Namgyal (Zhabs drung Ngag dbang rnam rgyal, b. 1594, d. 1651).

The founder of the Drukpa Kagyü school is Tsangpa Gyare (Gtsang pa rgya ras Ye shes rdo rje, b. 1161, d. 1211). Thorough research on this figure is crucial in order to fully comprehend this particular school, while access to primary sources has been difficult until very recently. Responding to this need, this paper examines his biographies and collected works.[1]

1 Regarding Tsangpa Gyare's biographies and the historical annals that refer to him, see Kumagai (2018a; 2018b; 2020). Concerning his collected works, see Kumagai et al. (2012).

Tsangpa Gyare's disciples, as well as the founder himself, have not yet been systematically studied. Traditionally, the Drukpa Kagyü school is said to have split into three sub-schools: the 'Upper Drukpa Kagyü school' (Stod 'brug), the 'Lower Drukpa Kagyü school' (Smad 'brug) and the 'Middle Drukpa Kagyü school' (Bar 'brug). However, the term 'Middle Drukpa Kagyü school' is not found in the oldest groups mentioned in Buddhist dharma annals. How can such classification be re-examined from historical points of view?

This chapter aims to focus on Tsangpa Gyare's disciples, investigate the actual characteristics of his direct disciples and re-examine the classification of them in relation to the 'First, Middle and Last Great Disciples' and the 'Upper, Lower and Middle Drukpa Kagyü schools'.

Outline of the Drukpa Kagyü school

Mapping Tsangpa Gyare within the Kagyü school

Below is a list of Tsangpa Gyare's lineage of masters and disciples. The Drukpa Kagyü school is one of the sub-schools of the Dagpo Kagyü school (Dwags po bka' brgyud), founded by Gampopa.

1. Marpa Chökyi Lodrö (Mar pa Chos kyi blo gros, b. 1012, d. 1097)
2. Milarepa (Mi la ras pa, b. 1052, d. 1135)
3. Gampopa Sonam Rinchen (Sgam po pa Bsod nams rin chen or Dwags po lha rje, b. 1079, d. 1153)
4. Phagmo Drupa Dorje Gyalpo (Phag mo gru pa Rdo rje rgyal po, b. 1110, d. 1170)
5. Ling Repa Pema Dorje (Gling ras pa Padma rdo rje, b. 1128, d. 1188)
6. Tsangpa Gyare Yeshe Dorje (b. 1161, d. 1211)

Abbotship of the Ralung and Druk monasteries

The Ralung Monastery (Ra lung dgon pa) and the Druk Monastery ('Brug gi dgon pa) became head monasteries of the Drukpa Kagyü school. The list of head abbots of both monasteries, all belonging to the Gya (rGya) clan up to Zhabdrung Ngawang Namgyal, reads as follows.[2]

1. Tsangpa Gyare Yeshe Dorje (b. 1161, d. 1211)
2. Darma Senge Sangye Wonre (Darma seng ge Sangs rgyas dbon ras, b. 1177, d. 1237)
3. Shönnu Senge (Gzhon nu seng ge, b. 1200, d. 1266)
4. Nyima Senge (Nyi ma seng ge, b. 1251, d. 1287)
5. Pökyapa Senge Rinchen (Spos skya pa Seng ge rin chen, b. 1258, d. 1313)
6. Senge Gyalpo (Seng ge rgyal po, b. 1289, d. 1326)
7. Kunga Senge (Kun dga' seng ge, b. 1314, d. 1347)
8. Lodrö Senge (Blo gros seng ge, b. 1345, d. 1390)
9. Sherab Senge (Shes rab seng ge, b. 1371, d. 1392)
10. Yeshe Rinchen (Ye shes rin chen, b. 1364, d. 1415)
11. Namkha Pelzang (Nam mkha' dpal bzang, b. 1398, d. 1425)
12. Sherab Zangpo (Shes rab bzang po, b. 1400, d. 1438)
13. Gyalwangje Kunga Penjor (Rgyal dbang rje Kun dga' dpal 'byor, b. 1428, d. 1476)
14. Ngawang Chögyal (Nga dbang chos rgyal, b. 1465, d. 1540)
15. Ngawang Tenpe Gyaltsen (Ngag dbang Bstan pa'i rgyal mtshan, b. 1506, d. 1538)
16. Mipham Chökyi Gyalpo (Mi pham Chos kyi rgyal po, b. 1543, d. 1604)

---

2 This paper follows Imaeda (2011: 206–208) regarding the number of head abbots. Other scholars use a different system. For example, Karma Phuntsho (2013: 212) omits Namkha Pelzang but adds Mipham Tenpe Nyima (Mi pham Bstan pa'i nyi ma, b. 1567, d. 1619) after Mipham Chökyi Gyalpo, that is, he regards Zhabdrung Ngawang Namgyal as the seventeenth abbot while he considers Gyalwangje Kunga Penjor as the twelfth.

17. Zhabdrung Ngawang Namgyal (b. 1594, d. 1651)
18. Paksam Wangpo (Dpag bsam dbang po, b. 1593, d. 1641)
19. Mipham Wangpo Ngagkyi Wangchuk (Mi pham dbang po Ngag gi dbang phyug, b. 1641, d. 1717)
20. Kagyü Trinle Shingta (Dkar brgyud 'Phrin las shing rta, b. 1718, d. 1766)
21. Kunzig Chökyi Nangwa (Kun gzigs Chos kyi snang ba, b. 1768, d. 1822)
22. Jigme Mingyur Wanggi Gyalpo ('Jigs med Mi 'gyur dbang gi rgyal po, b. 1823, d. 1883)
23. Mipham Chökyi Wangpo (Mi pham Chos kyi dbang po, b. 1884, d. 1930)
24. Tenzin Khyenrab Gelek Wangpo (Bstan 'dzin mkhyen rab Dge legs dbang po, b. 1931, d. 1960)
25. Jigme Pema Wangchen ('Jigs med Padma dbang chen, b. 1963, d.?)

The lineage of Tsangpa Gyare's reincarnation

Tsangpa Gyare's reincarnation was identified more than 200 years after his death. His subsequent reincarnations followed without interruption. After the death of Pema Karpo (Padma dkar po, b. 1527, d. 1592), conflicts occurred between two of his reincarnation candidates: Paksam Wangpo and Zhabdrung Ngawang Namgyal. The regent of the Tsang region recognized the former, while the latter finally moved from Tibet to what is now called Bhutan in 1616. Thus, the Drukpa Kagyü school was split into two: the Northern Drukpa Kagyü school and the Southern Drukpa Kagyü school.

Outline of the life of Tsangpa Gyare

Tsangpa Gyare is said to have been born in 1161 in Saral (Sa ral) in Khule (Khu le) at the bottom of the Hawo Kangzang mountain (Ha 'o

1. Tsangpa Gyare Yeshe Dorje (b. 1161, d. 1211): 1st abbot of the Drukpa Kagyü school
2. Gyalwangje Kunga Penjor (b. 1428, d. 1476): 13th abbot of the Drukpa Kagyü school
3. Jamyang Chökyi Drakpa (b. 1478, d. 1523)
4. Pema Karpo (b. 1527, d. 1592)

Northern Drukpa Kagyü school*

5. Paksam Wangpo (b. 1593, d. 1641)
6. Mipham Wangpo Ngagkyi Wangchuk (b. 1641, d. 1717)
7. Kagyü Trinle Shingta (b. 1718, d. 1766)
8. Kunzig Chökyi Nangwa (b. 1768, d. 1822)
9. Jigme Mingyur Wanggi Gyalpo (b. 1823, d. 1883)
10. Mipham Chökyi Wangpo (b. 1884, d. 1930)
11. Tenzin Khyenrab Gelek Wangpo (b. 1931, d. 1960)
12. Jigme Pema Wangchen (b. 1963)

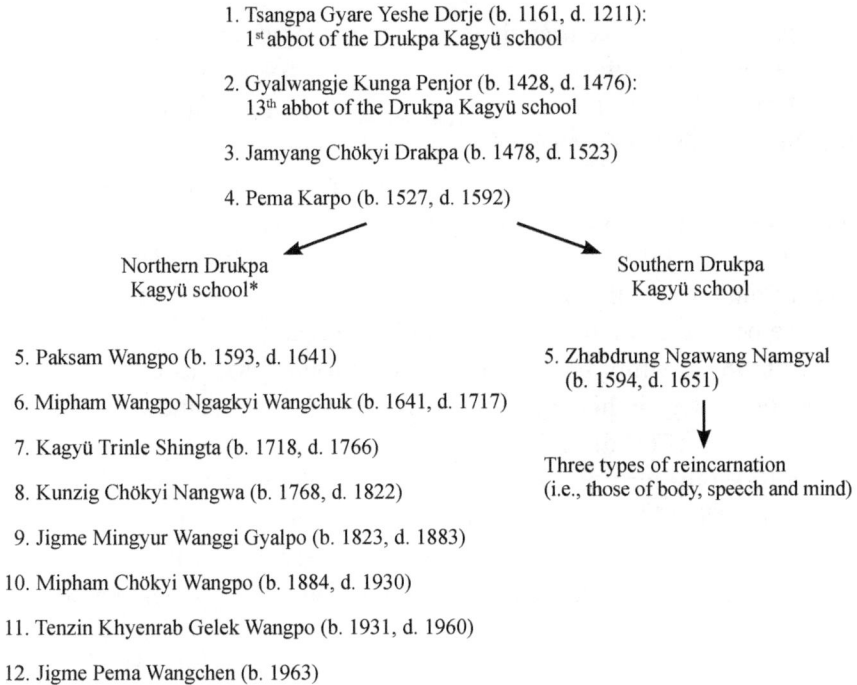

Southern Drukpa Kagyü school

5. Zhabdrung Ngawang Namgyal (b. 1594, d. 1651)

Three types of reincarnation (i.e., those of body, speech and mind)

Figure 2.1: The lineage of Tsangpa Gyare's reincarnation
Note: *See Ardussi (1977: 548).

gangs bzang) in the upper Nyang area (Myang stod) of the Eastern Tsang (Gtsang) region in Central Tibet.

He became a novice monk under the direction of his master Tathangpa (Rta thang pa) in around 1172 (age twelve).[3] He was given the dharma name Sherab Dutsi Korlo (Shes rab bdud rtsi 'khor lo). Thereafter he learned both Sūtrayāna and Vajrayāna Buddhism. His high skills in Sūtrayāna philosophy were proved in the episode in which he won a debate with his master Ling Repa.[4]

Some time between the years 1181 and 1183 (age twenty-one to thirty-three), he became a disciple of his root master (*gtsa ba'i bla ma*) Ling Repa, from whom he learned mainly Vajrayāna Buddhism, rituals and

3 See Kumagai (2018a: 24).

4 On the debate with Ling Repa, see Kumagai (2018a: 25–26).

meditation.[5] He concentrated on meditation practice after Ling Repa's death in 1188 (age twenty-eight).

He became a fully ordained monk in 1193 (age thirty-three) under the direction of lamas Zhang (Zhang G-yu brag pa Brtson 'gru brags pa, b. 1122, d. 1193) and Zepa (Bzad pa), and he received the dharma name Yeshe Dorje (Ye shes rdo rje).

He first founded the Longdol Monastery in 1189, 1193 or 1194 (age twenty-nine, thirty-three or thirty-four).[6] The Longdol Monastery seems to have been a location for his meditation retreat.

In 1196 (age thirty-six), he founded the Ralung Monastery, which was a clan monastery in his home place.[7] After that, he became very active in the education of his disciples.

In 1205 (age forty-five), he founded the Druk Monastery near Nyethang in Central Tibet.[8] He seems to have become well-known by that time.

Tsangpa Gyare passed away in 1211 (age fifty-one) in the Druk Monastery. It is said that hundreds of thousands of followers gathered at his funeral.[9]

Disciples of Tsangpa Gyare

Number of Tsangpa Gyare's disciples

As described in the *Lho rong chos 'byung* and the *Pad dkar chos 'byung*, Tsangpa Gyare had 2,800 disciples, indicating that he successfully produced and educated many intelligent disciples.[10] Tsangpa Gyare's biographies and dharma annals mention that he had few disciples early

---

5 Regarding the study with Ling Repa, see Kumagai (2018a: 26–27).

6 On the foundation of the Longdol Monastery, see Kumagai (2018a: 27–28).

7 Regarding the foundation of the Ralung Monastery, see Kumagai (2018a: 28).

8 On the foundation of the Druk Monastery, see Kumagai (2018a: 29).

9 Regarding the death of Tsangpa Gyare, see Kumagai (2018a: 29).

10 *Lho rong chos 'byung* (664.1–2): *chos brgyud 'dzin pa'i sras ni / spyir chos rje la bu chen ngo mtshar can nyis stong brgyad brgya byon pa'i nang nas /* (Concerning the dharma lineage holders [of the Drukpa Kagyü school], generally speaking, there appeared 2,800 excellent and great disciples of the dharma master [Tsangpa Gyare].)

on, but had tens of thousands of disciples and followers by his later years. How did he gather such a large number of disciples?

After his master, Ling Repa, passed away when Tsangpa Gyare was twenty-eight years old (in 1188), he started making pilgrimages to sacred places such as Tsari and Karchu for meditation retreat with several disciples and dharma friends who came from Loro (Lo ro) and other places.

Within several years of his completion of full ordination at the age of thirty-three (in 1193), Tsangpa Gyare founded the Longdol Monastery and the Ralung Monastery, and gradually increased his number of disciples. His first chief disciple was Pariwa Yeshe Gönpo (Spa ri ba Ye shes mgon po). When Tsangpa Gyare came to see Lama Zhang to receive full ordination, Lama Zhang's disciple Pariwa had strong respect for Tsangpa Gyare, and in the end Zhang allowed him to become Tsangpa Gyare's disciple. After Pariwa, the number of Tsangpa Gyare's disciples increased to several hundred before the construction of the Druk Monastery.

When he founded the Druk Monastery at age forty-five (in 1205), Lorepa and Götshangpa became Tsangpa Gyare's newest two great disciples. Thereafter, the number of his disciples rapidly grew to become thousands or even tens of thousands according to his biographies.

Tsangpa Gyare founded the Ralung Monastery at age thirty-six (in 1196) at a location in the Tsang region,[11] but it was far from Lhasa. On the other hand, the Druk Monastery, founded near Lhasa and Nyethang, played an important role in the recruitment of novice monks from many areas of Tibet.

The following sections introduce Tsangpa Gyare's chief disciples.

Senior disciples and followers

Before his full ordination, Tsangpa Gyare was accompanied by several disciples and followers when he visited sacred places for meditation retreats. They were Tsangpa Gyare's important attendants in his younger days, but they did not become leaders like the great disciples mentioned later. Those who have been identified by name are as follows: Yarre (Dbyar ras), Kunga Tashi (Kun dga' bkra shis), Rikngag (Rig sngags),

11 Regarding the foundation of the Ralung Monastery, see Kumagai (2018a: 28).

Tönrin (Ston rin), Terkhungpa (Gter khung pa), Gompagar (Bsgom pa 'gar), Yegönpa (Ye mgon pa) and Kelden (Skal ldan) – both from Loro (Lo ro ba) – Jobo Yeshe (Jo bo ye shes), Lodrowa (Lo gro ba), Chargom (Byar sgom), Sherab Yeshe (She rab ye shes), Kungadra (Kun dga' sgra), and Kyechok (Skyes mchog), who was a practitioner of emptiness meditation (*zhig po*). Tsangpa Gyare's brothers Jotsul (Jo tshul) and Gompa (Sgom pa) often invited him to their places.

After his full ordination, Tsangpa Gyare received many disciples. Among them, who were his chief disciples?

Tsangpa Gyare's 'Four Real Disciples'

In his biography of Tsangpa Gyare, Gyalthangpa Dechen Dorje (Rgyal thang pa Bde chen rdo rje, b. thirteenth century, d.?) presents a peculiar classification of Tsangpa Gyare's disciples absent from other texts.[12] He refers to the four masters, Lorepa, Melungpa (Me lung pa), Götshangpa and Darma Senge, as 'Tsangpa Gyare's Four Real Disciples' (Gtsang pa don gyi bu bzhi). Among the four, he regards Darma Senge as the only real disciple to maintain Tsangpa Gyare's lineage. This is the oldest attested classification.

The First, Middle and Last Great Disciples

Dharma annals enumerate five or six of Tsangpa Gyare's chief disciples after his full ordination and classify them into three: First, Middle and Last Great Disciples.

- First Great Disciples (dang por che ba): Pariwa Yeshe Gönpo (Spa ri ba Ye shes mgon po) and Kyangmokhapa (Rkyang mo kha pa).
- Middle Great Disciples (bar du che ba): Gyayagpa (Rgya yags pa) and Dremowa Sangyebum ('Bras mo ba Sangs rgyas 'bum).
- Last Great Disciples (tha mar che ba): Lorepa Wangchug Tsöndu (Lo ras pa Dbang phyug brtson 'grus, b. 1187, d. 1250) and Götshangpa Gönpo Dorje (Rgod tshang pa Mgon po rdo rje, b. 1189, d. 1258).

---

12 *Chos rje 'gro ba'i mgon po gtsang pa rgya ras kyi rnam par thar ba* (A34.5–6; P521.5–6).

It is important to note that Gyayagpa is not attested in the *Lho rong chos 'byung*, the oldest dharma annal referred to in this chapter. The *Lho rong chos 'byung*, the *Deb ther sngon po*, Tsangpa Gyare's biography composed by Pema Karpo, the *Pekar chos 'byung*, and the *Lho 'brug chos 'byung* are precious texts that contain rare information about the First and Middle Great Disciples, while the lives of the Last Great Disciples, Lorepa and Götshangpa, are explained in detail as founders of the Lower and Upper Drukpa Kagyü schools in their biographies and many dharma annals.

Pariwa Yeshe Gönpo (Spa ri ba Ye shes mgon po)

Pariwa is explained in the *Lho rong chos 'byung*, *Deb ther sngon po*, in Tsangpa Gyare's biography composed by Pema Karpo, and in the *Pekar chos 'byung* and *Lho 'brug chos 'byung.*[13] Tsangpa Gyare met him at age thirty-three (1193) just after receiving full ordination from Lama Zhang, when Pariwa was a torma maker (*gtor bshoms pa*) for the lama. Tsangpa Gyare and Pariwa appreciated one other, thus Lama Zhang came to order him to become a disciple of Tsangpa Gyare. Pariwa was also called Pari Khyenpe Ngadak (Pa ri ba Mkhyen pa'i mnga' bdag; 'knowledgeable person' in Pari). He founded the Pari Changchupling Monastery (Spa ri byang chub gling). His dharma lineage is known as that of the 'senior disciples' (*bu rgan*).

Kyangmokhapa (Rkyang mo kha pa)

Kyangmokhapa is also described in the five key texts mentioned above.[14] Tsangpa Gyare met him during his three-year meditation retreat that began during the winter of 1193.

---

13 *Lho rong 'chos byung* (664.6–15); *Deb ther sngon po* (585.4–6); *'Gro ba'i mgon po gtsang pa rgya ras pa'i rnam par thar pa ngo mtshar dad pa'i rlabs phreng* (D61.6–62.6; K58.10–59.7); *Chos 'byung bstan pa'i padma rgyas pa'i nyin byed* (582.1–2); *Lho 'brug chos byung* (105.10–14).

14 *Lho rong 'chos byung* (664.16–19); *Deb ther sngon po* (585.6–7); *'Gro ba'i mgon po gtsang pa rgya ras pa'i rnam par thar pa ngo mtshar dad pa'i rlabs phreng* (D64.5–65.2; K61.7–15); *Chos 'byung bstan pa'i padma rgyas pa'i nyin byed* (582.2–3); *Lho 'brug chos byung* (105.14–106.3).

Scholar monks (*dge bshes*) in the Dewachen Monastery (Bde ba can) in Nyethang (Snye thang) became jealous of Tsangpa Gyare, and so sent a scholar monk called Kyangmokhapa who had mastered linguistics, logics and the Tripitaka scriptures in order to win a debate with Tsangpa Gyare and thus force him to go to another place. However, Kyangmokhapa lost the debate and acquired faith in Tsangpa Gyare upon reading his treatises. He learned sutras and treatises and received oral instructions, acquiring both common and supreme accomplishments. He later founded the Kyangmokha Monastery (Rkyang mo kha) in Phur (Phur).

Gyayagpa (Rgya yags pa)

Gyayagpa is discussed in the *Deb ther sngon po*, Tsangpa Gyare's biography composed by Pema Karpo, as well as in the *Pekar chos 'byung* and *Lho 'brug chos 'byung*.[15] Tsangpa Gyare met him at least one year after he met Kyangmokhapa, some time between 1194 and 1197. He was called Gyayagpa ('he who offered 100 presents'; brgya yags pa) because he devoted 100 dharma friends to Tsangpa Gyare. Gyayagpa was also called the 'great accomplished scholar' (mkhas grub chen po). He founded the Gyayag Monastery (Rgya yags) in Phur (Phur) in Zarpo (Zar po), Dra (Gra), and the Ganden Monastery (Dga' ldan) in Drog ('Brog). His dharma lineage is called the Gyayag Kagyü (Rgya yags bka' brgyud).

Dremowa Sangyebum ('Bras mo ba Sangs rgyas 'bum)

Dremowa is the author of one of Tsangpa Gyare's biographies. In its colophon, he is referred to by another name, 'Geshey Dremowa Sangyebum Dremo Jotsun' (dge ba'i bshes gnyen Sangs rgyas 'bum 'Bras mo jo btsun).[16] He may have already been a scholar monk (*geshey*) from the Kadampa school before becoming a disciple of Tsangpa Gyare. Dremowa

15 There is no reference to Gyayagpa in the *Lho rong chos byung*. *Deb ther sngon po* (585.7–586.1); *'Gro ba'i mgon po gtsang pa rgya ras pa'i rnam par thar pa ngo mtshar dad pa'i rlabs phreng* (D66.4–5; K63.2–6); *Chos 'byung bstan pa'i padma rgyas pa'i nyin byed* (582.3–4); *Lho 'brug chos byung* (106.3–7).

16 *Chos rje gtsang pa rgya ras kyi rnam thar* (P452.2–3; T431.6–7).

is discussed in the five key texts.[17] He met Tsangpa Gyare some time after 1201 (age forty-one). He founded the Dremowa Monastery ('Bras mo ba) in Upper Nyang (Nyang stod).

Lorepa Wangchug Tsöndu (Lo ras pa Dbang phyug brtson 'grus, b. 1187, d. 1250)[18]

Lorepa was born in 1187 in a place called Trakchen (Grags chen) in Shung (gZhung). His father was named Näljor (rNal 'byor) and his mother Mesa Kyide (Me gza' skyid de). He was called Lorepa ('cotton-cloth yogin from Lo region'; Lo ras pa) because he belonged to the clan of Lonang (Lo nang). At age sixteen (in 1202), he first met Tsangpa Gyare when he visited Shung and developed a sense of devotion towards him. At age eighteen (in 1204), he ran away from home to live in the Kyormolung Monastery (Skyor mo lung) of the Kadampa school near Nyethang. He became a monk under the abbot Belti (Sbal ti, b. 1129, d. 1215), and received his dharma name Wangchug Tsöndü (Dbang phyug brtson 'grus).

Lorepa's relatives tried to bring him back to their hometown, but he ran away from them and came to the place of Tsangpa Gyare. After his full ordination, he studied monastic discipline, Hevajra, Mahāmāyā, Dohā and Cakrasaṃvara among other subjects. Lorepa made seven promises: 1) not to return to his hometown; 2) not to go down the mountain; 3) to always sit up during meditation; 4) to avoid entering laypeople's houses; 5) to wear only cotton garments; 6) to refrain from conversation; and 7) to continue the ritual of 100 Tormas (Gtor ma rgya rtsa) for the hungry ghosts (*preta*).

After Tsangpa Gyare passed away in 1211 when Lorepa was twenty-five years old, he visited several sacred places such as Jomodrosa (Jo mo gro sa), Jomogang (Jo mo gangs) and Semodo (Se mo do) for meditation retreat and ascetic practices. He founded small hermitages and

---

17 *Lho rong 'chos byung* (664.20–21); *Deb ther sngon po* (586.2); *'Gro ba'i mgon po gtsang pa rgya ras pa'i rnam par thar pa ngo mtshar dad pa'i rlabs phreng* (D78.3–4; K73.18–74.3); *Chos 'byung bstan pa'i padma rgyas pa'i nyin byed* (582.4–5); *Lho 'brug chos byung* (106.7–10).

18 Regarding the life of Lorepa, see *Lho rong chos 'byung* (665.4–691.3) and *Deb ther sngon po* (587.5–591.2).

monasteries such as Chumik Karmo (Chu mig dkar mo), Shingkam (Shing skam), Chakchil (Lcags spyil) and Uri (Dbu ri). During his stay in the Uri Monastery, he had around 1,000 disciples, thus he was also called Uripa (Dbu ri pa). He founded the Karpo Chulung Monastery (Dkar po chos lung) at age fifty-five (1241) and had around 10,000 disciples. He finally moved to Bumthang (Bum thang) in what is now central Bhutan, where he founded the Tharpaling Monastery (Thar pa gling) and finally passed away at age sixty-four (in 1250).

Götshangpa Gönpo Dorje (Rgod tshang pa Mgon po rdo rje, b. 1189, d. 1258)[19]

Götshangpa was born in 1189 in a place called Luchunggi Tra (Lu chung gi khra) in Lhodrak (Lho 'brag). His father was known as Chuchäl Möndrak (Chu chal mon grags) and his mother Sukmo Pälgyän (Zug mo dpal rgyan). He was given the names Gönpopäl (Dgon po dpal)[20] and Miyönpapäl (Mi yon pa dpal).[21]

In his childhood, Götshangpa studied and mastered subjects such as 'stages of the path' (*lam rim*), Madhyamaka philosophy and Bodhicāryāvatāra. When he went to a party in his hometown, he listened to songs celebrating Tsangpa Gyare sung by singers from the Tsang region, and acquired a deep respect for him.

Götshangpa visited Ralung at age nineteen (in 1207), became a monk under Tsangpa Gyare, and received his dharma name Gönpo Dorje (Mgon po rdo rje). He received oral instructions on the Four Yogas (rnal 'byor bzhi), Sahaja Yoga (lhan cig skyes sbyor) and (the six types of) equal taste (ro snyoms). He visited the Druk Monastery and practiced Guru Yoga (Bla sgrub). He visited Central Tibet and met famous masters such as Drigungpa Jikten Gönpo ('Bri gung 'Jig rten mgon po, b. 1143, d. 1217).

From the year after Tsangpa Gyare's death (in 1212), he visited sacred places such as Karchu (dkar chu) in Lhodrak, Mount Kaisash (Gangs

---

19 Regarding the life of Götshangpa, see *Lho rong chos 'byung* (691.4–700.15) and *Deb ther sngon po* (593.6–599.4).

20 See Roerich (1949: 680).

21 See *Deb ther sngon po* (594.1).

Ti se), Kashmir (Kha che'i yul) and Jālandhara (Dza landha ra) to engage in meditation retreat. After practicing meditation retreat for a number of years in several sacred places, he finally received full ordination from Wonre Darma Senge, the second abbot of the Drukpa Kagyü school.

In his late life, Götshangpa founded many monasteries such as the Tendro Monastery (Steng gro), the Kudra Monastery (Skud dra), the Changling Monastery (Byang gling), the Dechenteng Monastery (Bde chen stengs) and the Bardrok Dorjeling Monastery (Bar 'brog rdo rje gling), where thousands of contemplative monks were produced.

Götshangpa's chief disciples (*thugs kyi sras*) included Yangönpa (Yang dgon pa, b. 1213, d. 1258), Ugyänpa (U rgyan pa, b. 1230, d. 1309), Changlingwa (Byang gling ba), Neringpa (Ne rings pa, b. 1225, d. 1281), Phuriwa (Phu ri ba), Bari Chikarwa (Ba ri Spyil dkar ba, b. 1228, d. 1300), Madunpa (Ma dun pa), Shiche Gönpo (Zhi byed mgon po), Sangye Tromre (Sangs rgyas khrom ras), Pelkyer Shingrepa (Dpal skyer shing ras pa), Shākya Repa (Sakya ras pa) and Darre ('Dar ras).

Other chief disciples

In his *Lho rong chos 'byung*, Tatsak Tsewangyäl states that among the 2,800 great disciples of Tsangpa Gyare, thirteen of them had the ability to control their mind and had visualization ability, and 101 benefitted others and sentient beings.[22]

In his biography of Tsangpa Gyare, Pema Karpo provides the following classification of Tsangpa Gyare's disciples after his explanation of the First, Middle and Last Great Disciples:[23]

- Three Yogins (rnal 'byor pa gsum): Gaye (dGa' yes), Joye (Jo yes) and Deye (Bde yes)
- Three Cotton-Cloth Yogins (ras pa gsum): Yakre (G-yag ras), Drenre ('Gran ras) and Lire (Li ras)

22 *Lho rong chos 'byung* (664.1–3).

23 *'Gro ba'i mgon po gtsang pa rgya ras pa'i rnam par thar pa ngo mtshar dad pa'i rlabs phreng* (D105.3–5).

- Four Practitioners of Emptiness Meditation (zhig po bzhi): Reshik (Ras zhig), Shangshik (Shangs zhig), Shikpo Kunchok Senge (Zhig po Dkon mchog seng ge) and Shikpo Kyechok (Zhig po Skyes mchog)
- Three Excellent Ones (dam pa gsum): Dampa Terkhungpa (Dam pa Gter khung pa), Dampa Pagowa (Dam pa Spa sgo ba) and Dampa Kodrakpa (Dam pa Ko brag pa).

Interestingly, in his dharma annal, Pema Karpo enumerated Three Cotton-Cloth Yogins, Three Yogins and 'Three' Practitioners of Emptiness Meditation, thus the number of the latter differs from that in the dharma annal.[24] The Thukän also follows the numbers included in Pema Karpo's dharma annal.[25]

Martön (Mar ston)

Martön was not a direct disciple of Tsangpa Gyare, but a senior monk who played a key role in the expansion of the Drukpa Kagyü school during Tsangpa Gyare's later years. Martön is discussed in the biography of Tsangpa Gyare composed by Martön himself, and also in that composed by Dremowa.[26] In both biographies, Martön is first referred to when Tsangpa Gyare was between forty-one and forty-four years old (between 1201 and 1204), thus he seems to have met Tsangpa Gyare just before the foundation of the Druk Monastery in 1205. Martön's titles were Geshey (dge bshes) and Ācārya (slob dpon), indicating that he may have belonged to the Kadam school.

---

24 *Pad dkar chos 'byung* (581.3–4): *de la slob ma dang por che ba spa rkyang gnyis / bar du che ba rgya 'bras gnyis / mtha' mar che ba lo rgod gnyis / gzhan ras pa gsum / rnal 'byor gsum / gzhig po gzum sogs dbu che gdugs theg pa nyis stong brgyad brgyad byung ba'i.*

25 *Thu'u bkwan grub mtha'* (129.2–3): *gzhan ras pa gsum / rnal 'byor gsum / zhig po gsum sogs mang du byung* (Three cotton-cloth yogins, three yogins, and three practitioners of emptiness meditation also appeared.)

26 *Chos rje 'gro ba'i mgon po gtsang pa rgyal sras kyi rnam par thar ba* (435.6, 437.4–438.6); *Chos rje gtsang pa rgya ras kyi rnam thar* (P433.5; T413.6–7).

In around 1204, Martön invited Tsangpa Gyare to Upper Nyang (Myang stod) and presented him with many offerings. After the foundation of the Druk Monastery, Tsangpa Gyare said 'Thanks to Martön's connection, great ones entered the tradition [of the Drukpa Kagyü school] from other [schools and places]',[27] suggesting that Martön may have sent a lot of novice monks to Tsangpa Gyare'. Tsangpa Gyare also asked Martön to help his nephew Darma Senge with his practice by offering him several pieces of advice, so they may have had a dharma-brother relationship rather than one of master and disciple.[28]

Martön thus seems to have contributed to the recruitement and education of novice monks of the Drukpa Kagyü school. A comtemplative master called Nyerkhungpa also seems to have contributed to such recruitment and education.[29]

27 *Chos rje 'gro ba'i mgon po gtsang pa rgyal sras kyi rnam par thar ba* (437.4): *phyogs nas byon pa'i mi chen srol du tshud pa 'di / Mar ston gyi rten 'brel yin gsungs /* ([Tsangpa Gyare] said: 'Great persons came from [other] places and entered [Drukpa Kagyü's] tradition thanks to Martun'.)

28 *Chos rje 'gro ba'i mgon po gtsang pa rgyal sras kyi rnam par thar ba* (437.4–438.6).

29 *Chos rje 'gro ba'i mgon po gtsang pa rgyal sras kyi rnam par thar ba* (437.3): *de'i dus su rin po che'i zhal nas / bsgom pa gnyer khung pa 'dis nga'i 'khor mang po zhig srol du tshud phan par byung gsungs /* (At that time, Rinpoche [Tsangpa Gyare] said: 'The meditator Nyerkhungpa made many disciples enter into [Drukpa Kagyü's] tradition and made profits'.)

Classification of the Drukpa Kagyü school

The following sections examine the classification of the Drukpa Kagyü school in each period.

Classification of the Drukpa Kagyü school in the *Lho rong chos 'byung* (composed in 1446)

Tatshag Tshewangyel (Rta tshag Tshe dbang rgyal, b. fifteenth century), in his *Lho rong chos 'byung* (composed in 1446), classified Tsangpa Gyare's chief disciples into three according to generations:[30]

- First Great Disciples (dang por che ba): Pa[riwa Yeshe Gönpo] and Kyang[mokhapa]
- Middle Great Disciples (bar du che ba): Dre[mowa Sangyebum]
- Last Great Disciples (tha mar che ba): Lo[repa Wangchug Tsöndu] and Gö[tshangpa Gönpo Dorje].

We need to note that Gyayagpa was not included in the subcategory of 'Middle Great Disciples' in the *Lho rong chos 'byung*. The 'Last Great Disciples' were further subdivided into Götshangpa's 'Upper Drukpa Kagyü school' (Stod 'brug) and Lorepa's 'Lower Drukpa Kagyü school' (Smad 'brug).[31] On the other hand, we need to note that the subcategory of 'Middle Drukpa Kagyü school' (Bar 'brug) is not attested in the *Lho rong chos 'byung*.

---

30 *Lho rong chos 'byung* (664: 5–6): *de dag las kyang dang por che ba spa rkyang gnyis / bar du che ba 'bras mo ba / tha mar che ba lo rgod gnyis zhes pa'i*. (Among them, the first great [disciples] are Pa[riwa Yeshe Gönpo] and Kyang[mo Khapa]; the middle great [disciple] is Dre[mowa Sangyebum]; the last great [disciples] are Lo[repa Wangchug Tsöndu] and Gö[tshangpa Gönpo Dorje].)

31 *Lho rong chos 'byung* (665: 1–3): *tha mar che ba lo rgod gnyis zhes bya ba 'di ni / 'gro don yang shin tu che ste / lo ras nas brgyud pa la smad 'brug dang / rgod tshang nas brgyud pa stod 'brug zer /* (The two last great [disciples] Lo[repa] and Gö[tshangpa] largely profit sentient beings. The lineage of Lore[pa] is called the Lower Drukpa Kagyü school; the lineage of Götshang[pa] is called the Upper Drukpa Kagyü school.)

The *Lho rong chos 'byung* recounts that thirteen disciples could control their minds and appearances therein, and 101 disciples benefited others and sentient beings. This information is, however, not attested in subsequent dharma annals.[32]

Classification of the Drukpa Kagyü school in the *Deb ther sngon po* (composed in 1478)

Gö Lotsawa Zhönnupel ('Gos lo twa wa Gzhon nu dpal, b. 1392, d. 1481), in his *Deb ther sngon po* (composed in 1478), classified Tsangpa Gyare's chief disciples into three groups according to generations:[33]

- First Great Disciples (dang por che ba): Pa[riwa Yeshe Gönpo] and Kyang[mokhapa]
- Middle Great Disciples (bar du che ba): Gya[yagpa] and Dre[mowa Sangyebum]
- Last Great Disciples (tha mar che ba): Lo[repa Wangchug Tsöndu] and Gö[tshangpa Gönpo Dorje].

Gö Lotsawa added Gyayagpa, not mentioned in the *Lho rong chos 'byung*, in the subcategory of 'Middle Great Disciples'.

The 'Last Great Disciples' were further subdivided into Götshangpa's 'Upper Drukpa Kagyü school' (Stod 'brug) and Lorepa's 'Lower Drukpa Kagyü school' (Smad 'brug) as well as in the *Lho rong chos 'byung*.[34] On

---

32 *Lho rong chos 'byung* (664: 2–4): *snang sems dar dbang thob pa bcu gsum / gzhan phan 'gro don byed pa brgya phrag gcig byon pa'i nang na*. (There were thirteen [disciples] who could control appearance and mind, and 101 [disciples] who could benefit other sentient beings. Among them…)

33 *Deb ther sngon po* (585.3–4): *'dis gzhan don rgya cher bskyangs pa'i slob ma'i mchog ni / dang por che ba spa rkyang gnyis / bar du che ba rgya 'bras gnyis / tha mar che ba lo rgod gnyis / shes bya'o //* ([Tsangpa Gyare's] excellent disciples who continued largely beneficial activities for other beings are: the first two great [disciples] Pa[riwa Yeshe Gönpo] and Kyang[mo Khapa]; the middle two great [disciples] Gya[yagpa] and Dre[mowa Sangyebum]; and the last great [disciples] Lo[repa Wangchug Tsöndu] and Gö[tshangpa Gönpo Dorje].)

34 *Deb ther sngon po* (593.5–6): *de ltar lo ras pas brgyud pa rnams la smad 'brug dang / rgod tshang pa nas brgyud pa rnams la stod 'brug grags pas / 'brug skor*

the other hand, we need to note that the subcategory of 'Middle Drukpa Kagyü school' (Bar 'brug) is not attested in the *Deb ther sngon po*. Gö Lotsawa said that the 'Upper Drukpa Kagyü school', whose monks mastered Mahāmudrā, came to have the largest number of disciples.[35] The school might have been given the title 'Upper' due to its popularity.

On the other hand, Gö Lotsawa said that two of the First Great Disciples and two of the Middle Great Disciples had the capacity to benefit sentient beings, but their biographies have not been found[36] and seem to have been lost in an early period.

Classification of the Drukpa Kagyü school in the *Pad dkar chos 'byung* (composed in 1575)

Pema Karpo, in his *Pad dkar chos 'byung* (composed in 1575), classified Tsangpa Gyare's chief disciples into three according to generations:[37]

---

gzhan thams cad de gnyis kyi gseb tu thim pa lta bur gyur to // (Those belonging to Lorepa's lineage were called the Lower Drukpa Kagyü school, and those belonging to Götshangpa's lineage were called the Upper Drukpa Kagyü school. All of the others belonging to the Drukpa Kagyü cycle are incorporated into the two [sub-schools].)

35 *Deb ther sngon po* (613.6): *'brug pa'i brgyud 'dzin pas khrid chen brgyad la gtso bor byed pa yin zhes gsung ba ltar gdams ngag gi gtso bo cha gnyis su gyur pa'i / 'brug skor la ni phyag rgya chen po'i rtogs pa can shin du mang bar byon /* ([Ugyenpa Rinchenpel (U rgyan pa Rin chen dpal, b. 1229/1230, d. 1309)] said 'The holders of the lineage of the Drukpa Kagyü school strongly emphasize the eight types of great instruction'. In this manner, [the Upper Drukpa Kagyü school] produced the largest number [of disciples] who comprehended the Great Seal within the Drukpa Kagyü tradition which was divided into two sub-schools regarding principal oral instructions.) See Roerich (1996: 702).

36 *Deb ther sngon po* (587.4–5): *thog ma dang bar du che ba bzhi po la 'gro ba'i don spyod nus pa kho nar nges mod kyi / rnam par thar pa ni gsal bar ma mthong ngo //* (The first and middle great [disciples], the four, had the ability to benefit sentient beings, but their biographies are not found.) See Roerich (1996: 672).

37 *Pad dkar chos 'byung* (581.3–4): *de la slob ma dang por che ba spa rkyang gnyis / bar du che ba rgya 'bras gnyis / mtha' mar che ba lo rgod gnyis / gzhan ras pa gsum / rnal 'byor gsum / gzhig po gsum sogs dbu che gdugs theg pa nyis stong brgyad brgyad byung ba'i.* ([Tsangpa Gyare] had the first two great disciples: Pa[riwa Yeshe Gönpo] and Kyang[mo Khapa]; the middle two great [disciples]: Gya[yagpa] and Dre[mowa Sangyebum]; and the last two great [disciples]:

- First Great Disciples (dang por che ba): Pa[riwa Yeshe Gönpo] and Kyang[mokhapa]
- Middle Great Disciples (bar du che ba): Gya[yagpa] and Dre[mowa Sangyebum]
- Last Great Disciples (tha mar che ba): Lo[repa Wangchug Tsöndu] and Gö[tshangpa Gönpo Dorje]

Pema Karpo regarded Götshangpa and Lorepa as the founders of the 'Upper Drukpa Kagyü school' and the 'Lower Drukpa Kagyü school' respectively. They are also mentioned in the *Lho rong chos 'byung* and *Deb ther sngon po*.

He further classified the first two disciples and the two middle disciples within the subcategory of 'Middle Drukpa Kagyü school' (Bar 'brug).[38]

He enumerated Cotton-Cloth Yogins (ras pa), Three Yogins (rnal 'byor), and Three Practitioners of Emptiness Meditation (zhig po) belonging to the Middle Drukpa Kagyü school. The Three Cotton-Cloth Yogins are Yakre (G-yag ras), Lire (Li ras) and Drenre ('Gran ras);[39] the Three Yogins are Jobo Yeshe (Jo[bo] ye [she]s), Gabo Yeshe (Dga' [bo] ye [she]s) and Dewa Yeshe (Bde [ba] ye [she]s).[40] Especially, Jobo Yeshe was the editor of Tsangpa Gyare's teachings (*bka'i sdud pa po*) and the founder of the Trarganden Monastery (Grar dga' ldan).[41] He seems to have been a close disciple of Tsangpa Gyare, as he is often mentioned in Tsangpa Gyare's biographies.

Lo[repa Wangchug Tsöndu] and Gö[tshangpa Gönpo Dorje]. There were another 2,800 great disciples such as three cotton-cloth yogins, three yogins and three practitioners of emptiness meditation.)

38 *Pad dkar chos 'byung* (583.3–4): *de dag la sogs pa nyis stong brgyad brgya'i slob rgyun la bu chung brgyud / gnyis ka bsdoms pa la bar 'brug ces grags so //* (The lineage of such 2,800 disciples, integrated with the lineage of small disciples, is known as the Middle Drukpa Kagyü school.)

After this explanation of the Middle Drukpa Kagyü school, Lorepa's Lower Drukpa Kagyü school and Götshangpa's Upper Drukpa Kagyü school are explained differently.

39 *Pad dkar chos 'byung* (582.5–6).

40 *Pad dkar chos 'byung* (583.2–3).

41 *Pad dkar chos 'byung* (583.3).

This section proved that the *Pad dkar chos 'byung* is the oldest dharma annal, among those treated in this paper, to use the term 'Middle Drukpa Kagyü school'. Pema Karpo's classification of the Drukpa Kagyü school seems to have been followed by later historians.

Classification of the Drukpa Kagyü school in the *Thu'u bkwan grub mtha'* (composed in 1801)

The third Thukän (Thu'u bkwan) Lobsang Chökyi Nyima (Blo bzang chos kyi nyi ma, b. 1737, d. 1802), in his doxography *Thu'u bkwan grub mtha'*, classified Tsangpa Gyare's chief disciples into three according to generations:[42]

- First Great Disciples (dang por che ba): Pa[riwa Yeshe Gönpo] and Kyang[mokhapa]
- Middle Great Disciples (bar du che ba): Gya[yagpa] and Dre[mowa Sangyebum]
- Last Great Disciples (tha mar che ba): Lo[repa Wangchug Tsöndu] and Gö[tshangpa Gönpo Dorje].

The Thukän said that Tsangpa Gyare produced many disciples such as the Three Cotton-Cloth Yogins, Three Yogins and Three Practitioners of Emptiness Meditation.[43]

The Thukän also postulated the three subdivisions: Upper, Middle and Lower Drukpa Kagyü schools. However, he provided a different explana-

42 *Thu'u bkwan grub mtha'* (129.1–2): *slob ma mang du byung ba'i gtso bo ni / dang por che ba spa rkyang gnyis / bar du che ba rgya 'bras gnyis / tha mar che ba lo rgod gnyis /* (Principle [disciples] among many produced disciples, the first two great [disciples] are Pa[riwa Yeshe Gönpo] and Kyang[mo Khapa]; the middle two great [disciples] are Gya[yagpa] and Dre[mowa Sangyebum]; and the last two great disciples are Lo[repa Wangchug Tsöndu] and Gö[tshangpa Gönpo Dorje].)

43 *Thu'u bkwan grub mtha'* (129.2–3): *gzhan ras pa gsum / rnyal 'byor gsum / zhig po gsum sogs mang du byung /* (There appeared many other disciples such as three cotton-cloth yogins, three yogins and three practitioners of emptiness meditation.)

tion about the Middle Drukpa Kagyü school from Pema Karpo's. As seen above, Pema Karpo classified the First and Middle Disciples and disciples other than the last two as the Middle Drukpa Kagyü school. On the other hand, the Thukän categorized the lineage of Darma Senge, comprising chief abbots of the Drukpa Kagyü school, as the Middle Drukpa Kagyü school.[44] The Thukän describes the Upper Drukpa Kagyü school as 'stars in the sky' (*gnam gyi skar ma*) and the Lower Drukpa Kagyü school as 'plants on the ground' (*sa'i rtsi shing*).[45] The Upper, Middle and Lower Drukpa Kagyü schools seem to have still been active in the period of the Thukän.[46]

Classification of the Drukpa Kagyü school in the *Lho 'brug chos 'byung* (composed in 1972)

Bhutanese Dharma King and historian Gendun Rinchen (Dge dun rin chen, b. 1926, d. 1997), in his *Lho 'brug chos 'byung*, classified Tsangpa Gyare's chief disciples into three according to generations:[47]

---

44 *Thu'u bkwan grub mtha'* (129.4–11): *gdan sar dbon ras dar ma seng ge bzhugs shing / de nas dbon brgyud rim par byon pa las ... de rnams la bar 'brug ces grags so //* (In the head monastery, Wonre Darma Senge resided. From him there appeared the lineage of Won[re Darma Senge] in order ... They are known as the Middle Drukpa Kagyü school.)

45 *Thu'u bkwan grub mtha'* (131.10–12): *de ltar lo ras nas brgyud pa la smad 'brug dang / rgod tshang dpon slob nas brgyud pa la stod 'brug zer zhing kha skad la stod 'brug gnam gyi skar ma / smad 'brug sa'i rtsi shing zhes mang ba'i tshad du grags so //* (In that manner, the lineage from Lorepa is called the Lower Drukpa Kagyü school and the lineage of Götshangpa is called the Upper Drukpa Kagyü school. According to many oral transmissions, the Upper Drukpa Kagyü school is explained as 'the stars in the sky' and the Lower Drukpa Kagyü school is explained as 'the plants on the ground'.)

46 *Thu'u bkwan grub mtha'* (130.12–14): *'brug pa stod smad bar gsum sogs da lta'i dus su yang dar rgyas bzang zhing chos rgyun rnams kyang phal cher ma chad tsam yod 'dra'o //* (It seems that the three Drukpa Kagyü schools of Upper, Lower and Middle are still widely active and their dharma lineages almost continue.)

47 *Lho 'brug chos 'byung* (105.9–10): *'di la slob ma dang por che ba spa rkyang gnyis / bar du che ba brgya 'bras gnyis / tha mar che ba lo rgod gnyis so //* (Among them, the first two great [disciples] are Pa[riwa Yeshe Gönpo] and Kyang[mo Khapa]; the middle two great [disciples] are Gya[yagpa] and Dre[mowa Sangyebum];

- First Great Disciples (dang por che ba): Pa[riwa Yeshe Gönpo] and Kyang[mokhapa]
- Middle Great Disciples (bar du che ba): Gya[yagpa] and Dre[mowa Sangyebum]
- Last Great Disciples (tha mar che ba): Lo[repa Wangchug Tsöndu] and Gö[tshangpa Gönpo Dorje].

Gendun Rinchen also postulated the classification of Upper, Middle and Lower Drukpa Kagyü schools. Like Pema Karpo, he regarded the First and Middle Great Disciples and their lineages to be the Middle Drukpa Kagyü school, unlike the Thukän, who regarded Darma Senge's lineage as the Middle Drukpa Kagyü school.

Gendun Rinchen counted 2,800 followers, including the First and Middle Great Disciples, as part of the 'Middle Drukpa Kagyü school'. This figure includes the Three Cotton-Cloth Yogins such as Yakre (G-yag ras); Three Yogins such as Jobo Yeshe (Jo [bo] ye[shes]); Practitioners of Emptiness Meditation such as Könchok Senge (Dkon mchog seng ge); and Three Great Ones (*dam pa*) such as Terkhungpa (Gter khungs pa).[48]

Gendun Rinchen describes the Middle Drukpa Kagyü school as 'that which is like sky and ground, filled with the dusts illuminated by sunlight' (*nyi zer gyi rdul gyis gnas sa 'gengs*),[49] the Lower Drukpa Kagyü school as 'that which is like the ground' (*sa yi dreg pa tsam*),[50] and the Upper Drukpa Kagyü school as 'that which is like a star in the sky' (*gnam gyi skar ma tsam*).[51]

and the last two great disciples are Lo[repa Wangchug Tsöndu] and Gö[tshangpa Gönpo Dorje].)

48 *Lho 'brug chos 'byung* (106.10–107.4).

49 *Lho 'brug chos 'byung* (107.3).

50 *Lho 'brug chos 'byung* (109.3).

51 *Lho 'brug chos 'byung* (111.3–4).

Conclusion

This chapter focused on Tsangpa Gyare's disciples, investigating the actual conditions of his direct disciples and re-examining their classification and that of the Drukpa Kagyü school.

Tsangpa Gyare was accompanied by several disciples and dharma friends when he visited sacred places to practice meditation retreat from the age of twenty-eight (when his master Ling Repa passed away) to thirty-three (when he received full ordination). After his full ordination, he started to comprehensively educate his disciples. He first founded the Longdol Monastery and thereafter the Ralung Monastery, thus preparing monastic educational facilities to teach large numbers of novice monks. From the time he founded the Druk Monastery in Central Tibet (age forty-five) until his death (age fifty-one), he is said to have educated up to tens of thousands of disciples.

The oldest classification of Tsangpa Gyare's disciples is found in the biography of Tsangpa Gyare composed by Gyalthangpa in the thirteenth century. Gyalthangpa identified the four masters Lorepa, Melungpa (Me lung pa), Götshangpa and Darma Senge as 'Tsangpa Gyare's Four Real Disciples' (Gtsang pa don gyi bu bzhi).

In the period of the *Lho rong chos 'byung* (composed in 1446) and *Deb ther sngon po* (composed between 1476 and 1478), we can already notice the use of the threefold subdivision according to generations: First, Middle and Last Great Disciples. Both dharma annals also gave the following subdivisions: the 'Upper Drukpa Kagyü school' (Stod 'brug) of Götshangpa and the 'Lower Drukpa Kagyü school' (Smad 'brug) of Lorepa.

The oldest text among those treated in this chapter, which offered the subdivision 'Middle Drukpa Kagyü school', is *Pad dkar chos 'byung*. Pema Karpo classified the first two great disciples (i.e., Pariwa and Kyangmokhapa), the middle two great disciples (i.e., Gyayagpa and Dremowa Sangyebum) and their followers into the 'Middle Drukpa Kagyü school'. The three-fold classification of Upper, Middle and Lower Drukpa Kagyü schools has often been used without any academic rigor, especially from a historical point of view, but it is important to note that the classification is relatively new.

After Pema Karpo, the classification of Upper, Middle and Lower Drukpa Kagyü schools became widespread, but their characterizations are not necessarily identical. The Thukän classified the lineage of Darma Senge into the Middle Drukpa Kagyü school but he did not regard the First and Middle Great Disciples as belonging to that school. Like Pema Karpo (and unlike the Thukän), Gendun Rinchen, in his *Lho 'brug chos 'byung*, regarded the First and Middle Great Disciples as part of the Middle Drukpa Kagyü school. Thus, the Thukän's interpretation of the Middle Drukpa Kagyü school was not followed by later Drukpa Kagyü historians.

Although not addressed in this article, it is important to keep in mind the subdivision into the Northern (or Tibetan) Drukpa Kagyü school and the Southern Drukpa Kagyü school. Needless to say, such subdivision was produced after the Zhabdrung left Tibet to establish himself in Bhutan (in 1616).

Finally, this chapter examines the reason for the postulation of various subdivisions within the Drukpa Kagyü school.

The subdivision into the Northern Drukpa Kagyü school and the Southern Drukpa Kagyü school was suggested because of the conflict between the two candidates for the reincarnation of Pema Karpo: Paksam Wangpo and Zhabdrung Ngawang Namgyal. It was thus produced due to internal political factors. The subdivision into First, Middle and Last Great Disciples was postulated according to the length of their religious careers. Namely, it was produced because of their generational gap.

What about the subdivision of Upper, Middle and Lower Drukpa Kagyü schools? The lineages of the two most famous disciples, Götshangpa and Lorepa, were respectively regarded as the Upper and Lower Drukpa Kagyü schools. At the time of Pema Karpo (i.e., in the sixteenth century), they might have needed to allocate disciples other than Götshangpa and Lorepa into a particular sub-school, therefore postulating the category of Middle Drukpa Kagyü school.

Since the period of its founder, the Drukpa Kagyü school has continued to develop and produce a large number of capable disciples. As a result, this large-scale school has gradually been split and classified into several sub-schools over time.

Bibliography

Primary Sources

Chos rje 'gro ba'i mgon po gtsang pa rgya ras kyi rnam par thar ba by rGyal thang pa bDe chen rdo rje (b. 13th c.).

Anonymous edition: *Chos rje 'gro ba'i mgon po gtsang pa rgya ras kyi rnam par thar ba.* TBRC's Work Number: W1KG2849.

Palampur edition: *Chos rje rin po che gtsang pa ye shes rdo rje'i rnam par thar pa.* In *Dkar brgyud gser 'phren: A Thirteenth Century Collection of Verse Hagiographies of the Succession of Eminent Masters of the 'Brug-pa dKar-brgyud-pa Tradition.* Palampur: Sungrab Nyamso Gyunphel Parkhang, 1973, pp. 485–525. TBRC's Work Number: 23436.

Chos rje 'gro ba'i mgon po gtsang pa rgyal sras kyi rnam par thar ba by Mar ston (b. 12th c.)

Dehradun edition: *Chos rje 'gro ba'i mgon po gtsang pa rgyal sras kyi rnam par thar ba.* In *Bka' brgyud gser phreng chen mo: Biographies of Eminent Gurus in the Transmission Lineage of Teachings of the 'Ba'-ra dkar-brgyud-pa sect.* Dehradun (Published by Ngawang gyaltsen and Ngawang lungtok), 1970, vol. 1 (Ka), pp. 412–451. TBRC's Work Number: W19231.

Chos rje gtsang pa rgya ras kyi rnam thar by Sangs rgyas 'bum 'Bras mo jo btsun (b. 12th c.)

Palampur edition: *Gtsang pa rgya ras kyi rnam thar.* In *Rwa lung dkar brgyud gser 'phreng: Brief Lives of the Successive Masters in the Transmission Lineage of the Bar 'Brug-pa Dkar-brgyud-pa of Rwa-lun* (4 vols.). Palampur: Sungrab Nyamso Gyunphel Parkhang, 1975–1978, vol. 1, pp. 397–452. TBRC's Work Number: 19222. (Reproduced from a set of prints from the 1771–1772 Spuns-than xylographic blocks.)

Thimphu edition: *Chos rje gtsang pa rgya ras kyi rnam thar.* In *Dkar brgyud gser gyi 'phren ba: A Collection of Biographical Materials on the Lives of the Masters of the Rwa-lun Tradition of the 'Brug-pa dkar-brgyud-pa Tradition in Tibet and Bhutan* (3 vols.). Thimphu: Tango Monastic Community, 1982, vol. 1, pp. 379–431. TBRC's Work Number: 23861.

Chos rje rin po che gtsang pa rgya ras pa'i rnam thar mgur 'bum dang bcas pa in Lo ras pa dBang phyug brtson 'grus (1187–1250).

Leh edition: *Chos rje rin po che gtsang pa rgya ras pa'i rnam thar mgur 'bum dang bcas pa.* In *Dkar brgyud ser 'phreng: A Golden Rosary of Lives of Eminent Gurus.* Leh (Published by Sonam W. Tashigang), 1970, pp. 270–293. TBRC's Work Number: 30123.

Deb ther sngon po (*Bod kyi yul du chos dang chos smra ba ji ltar byung ba'i rim pa*). Compiled by 'Gos lo twa wa gzhon nu dpal (b. 1392, d. 1481) between 1476 and 1478. Ed. Chandra (1974).

'Gro ba'i mgon po gtsang pa rgya ras pa'i rnam par thar pa ngo mtshar dad pa'i rlabs phreng by Padma dkar po Nga dbang nor bu (b. 1527, d. 1592).

Darjeeling edition: *'Gro ba'i mgon po gtsang pa rgya ras pa'i rnam par thar pa ngo mtshar dad pa'i rlabs phreng*. Darjeeling: Kargyud Sungrab Nyamso Khang, 1973–1974. TBRC's Work Number: W10736, vol. 3.

Kathmandu edition: *'Gro ba'i mgon po gtsang pa rgya ras pa'i rnam par thar pa ngo mtshar dad pa'i rlabs phreng*. Kathmandu: Gam po pa library, 2007/2013. TBRC's Work Number: W1KG15852.

Lho 'brug chos 'bhung (*Lho phyogs nags mo'i ljongs kyi chos 'byung*). Compiled by Dge 'dun Rin chen (b. 1926, d. 1997) in 1972. Thimphu: KMT Publisher, 2004.

Lho rong chos 'byung (*Dam pa'i chos kyi byung ba'i legs bshad lho rong chos 'byung*). Compiled by rTa tshag Tshe dbang rgyal (b. 15th c.) in 1446. Lhasa: Bod ljongs bod yig dpe rnying dpe skrun khang, 1994.

Lho'i chos 'byung (*Lho'i chos 'byung 'phro mthud 'jam mgon smon mtha'i 'phreng ba*). Compiled by bsTan 'dzin chos rgyal (b.?, d. 1761) in 1759. Thimphu: KMT Publisher, 2004.

Pad dkhar chos 'byung (*Chos 'byung bstan pa'i Padma rgyas pas'i nyin byed*). Compiled by Padma dkar po Nga dbang nor bu (b. 1527, d. 1592) in 1581. In *Tibetan Chronicle of Padma-dkar-po* (Śata-piṭaka Series, Indo-Asian Literatures Volume 75). Edited by Lokesh Chandra, 1–619. New Delhi: International Academy of Indian Culture, 1968.

Thu'u bkwan grub mtha' (*Grub mtha' thams cad kyi khungs dang 'dod tshul ston pa legs bshad shel gyi me long*). Compiled by Thu'u bkwan Blo bzang chos kyi nyi ma (b. 1737, d. 1802) in 1802. Gansu: Kun su'i mi rigs dpe krun khang, 1984.

Secondary Sources

Ardussi, J. (1977). *Bhutan Before the British – A Historical Study* (PhD dissertation, Australian National University).

Aris, M. (1979). *Bhutan: The Early History of a Himalayan Kingdom*, Warminster: Aris & Phillips Ltd.

Baillie, L.M. (1999). 'Father Estevao Cacella's Report on Bhutan in 1627', *Journal of Bhutan Studies*, vol. 1, no. 1, pp. 1–35.

Chandra, L. (1974). *The Blue Annals*, New Delhi: International Academy of Indian Culture.

Imaeda, Y. (2011). *Histoire médiévale du Bhoutan*, Tokyo: Toyo Bunko.

Karma Phuntsho (2013). *History of Bhutan*, Noida/London: Random House India.

Kumagai, S. (2014). 'History and Current Situation of the Sa skya pa school in Bhutan'. In S. Kumagai, ed., *Bhutanese Buddhism and Its Culture*, Kathmandu: Vajra Publications, pp. 127–139.

Kumagai, S. (2018a). 'Introduction to the Biographies of Tsangpa Gyare (1161-1211), Founder of the Drukpa Kagyu School'. In S. Kumagai, ed., *Buddhism, Culture and Society in Bhutan*, Kathmandu: Vajra Publications, pp. 9–34.

Kumagai, S. (2018b). 'A Report on Some Physical Evidences and Oral Transmission about Tsangpa Gyare (1161-1211) Collected at the Ralung Monastery and the Druk Monastery in Tibet'. In *Vajrayana Buddhism in the Modern World: Proceedings of the Second Vajrayana Conference, 28-30 March 2018, Thimphu*, Thimphu: Centre for Bhutan Studies & GNH Research, pp. 34–48.

Kumagai, S. (2020). 'Life and Works of Tsangpa Gyare (1161-1211), Founder of the Drukpa Kagyü School'. In *Oxford Research Encyclopedia of Religion*, Oxford University Press.

Kumagai, S., G. Thupten and A. Yasuda (2012). 'Introduction to the Collected Works of the Founder of the *Drukpa Kagyu* (*'Brug pa bKa' brgyud*) School: Tsangpa Gyare (gTsang pa rgya ras, 1161-1211)'. In K. Ura and D. Chophel, eds., *Buddhism without Borders: Proceedings of the International Conference on Globalized Buddhism, Bumthang, Bhutan May 21-23, 2012*, Thimphu: Centre for Bhutan Studies, pp. 36–52.

Martin, D. (1979). 'Gling-ras-pa and the Founding of the 'Brug-pa School', *The Tibet Society Bulletin*, vol. 13, pp. 56–69.

Miller, W.B. (2005). 'The Vagrant Poet and the Reluctant Scholar: A Study of the Balance of Iconoclasm and Civility in the Biographical Accounts of Two Founders of the 'Brug pa bKa' brgyud Lineages', *The Journal of the International Association of Buddhist Studies*, vol. 28, no. 2, pp. 369–410.

Miller, W.B. (2006). ''Brug pa'i lo rgyus zur tsam: An Analysis of a Thirteenth Century Tibetan Buddhist Lineage History', *Tibet Journal*, vol. 31, no. 3, pp. 17–42.

Roerich, G., trans. (1996). *The Blue Annals* (2nd ed.), Delhi: Motilal Banarsidas.

3 Lha Bon: Invoking Yultsen, an Ancient Ritual Offering and Cultural Belief of Central Bhutan[1]

Tenzin Dorji

Introduction

In Bhutan, local rituals are conducted annually under different names according to region, but their common purpose is to ward off evil influences and bring prosperity to the community.[2] Among them is Lha Bon (lHa bon),[3] an indigenous ritual practiced by the people of Taktse and Yuesa under Drakteng Gewog community center in Trongsa, Bhutan. It is an invocation and offering calling the local spirit or tutelary male deity Dorje Dragtsan (rDo rje drag btsan), the aquatic deity Menmo Tashi Wangzom (sman mo bkra shis dbang 'dzoms), the great Bon deity Ode Gungyal (O de gung rgyal) and others for three days to protect community members and their crops and cattle, to ward off obstacles for a year and to ensure prosperity.

The practice of Lha Bon helps to bring together villagers from distant places, inculcate cultural values in the younger generation, preserve the environment through implanting beliefs about local deities residing on trees and in water, and resolve people's predicaments and obstacles for a year. Therefore, it is beneficial in that it helps to create a harmonious community. However, the practice has declined in the villages of Chendebji,

---

1 This paper was delivered at the 15th Seminar of the International Association of Tibetan Studies (IATS), INALCO, Paris, France on 8 July 2019. I would like to thank the organizers for giving me this opportunity.

2 Pommaret (2014: 114).

3 The Tibetan and Dzongkha terms have been transcribed for easy reading and the Wylie transliteration is given at the first occurrence of each term.

Figure 3.1: Map showing the locations where Lha Bon is practiced

Tangsibji and Tshangkha in the Trongsa district. Even at Taktse and Yuesa, the practice is in decline as there are fewer young people taking an interest in their ancestors' ancient rituals. If Lha Bon disappears, the tangible and intangible cultural values related to this ritual will be lost forever.[4] What is Lha Bon and how is it performed? This paper aims to discuss the meaning of Lha Bon and the process of its performance over three days.

The rationale of Lha Bon

Across the Himalayan region and particularly in Bhutan, there are numerous practices that involve ancient ritual offerings. Among them, Lha Bon is observed by Yuesa and Taktse villages in the Trongsa district as a community ritual that runs over three consecutive days on alternate years from the eleventh to the thirteenth day of the eleventh month of the lunar calendar.

There are five different kinds of annual ancient ritual offerings practiced by the two villages. Lha Bon is one of the essential practices among them. During the event, villagers make invocations and give offerings to their village tutelary deity Dorje Dragtsan, Menmo Tashi Wangzom and

4 See Dondup (2018: 82).

other deities. Further, they appease the local deity, the *naga* (*klu*) and the earth-owning spirit (*sa bdag*) that resides at their village. Concurrently, they make an offering to Ode Gungyal, the primary lord of the nine lords of cyclic existence[5] who pervades the whole of Tibet according to Bon (pre-Buddhist religious practices) tradition. Lha Bon is mainly performed to avoid epidemics, to ward off yearly obstacles and to usher in the auspiciousness of sublime prosperity.

There is no clear record of the origins of Lha Bon. However, before Buddhism in Bhutan, people appealed to and appeased the local spirits and Menmo to aid the living and the ill in different regions and villages. Moreover, holders of Bon performed peaceful and wrathful rituals to appease the gods of rock, water and mountain. It is possible that Bon beliefs came to prevail in this way at Taktse and Yuesa in succession.

The meaning and purpose of Lha Bon

The term 'Lha Bon' is made of two components: '*lha*' means local deities while '*bon*' refers to the act of recitation. Lha Bon thus means making offerings to and invoking local deities.

Firstly, *lha* are worldly gods such as local deities and the great lord Ode Gungyal, who assist people in their present life. According to Chogyal Namkhai Norbu, '*bon*' is an archaic Tibetan term and currently connotes 'to recite words of expression'. In the ancient literature, the term *gyer*, which means 'ritual chant', is used in place of *bon*.[6] The etymology of the word suggests that in the past, Bonpo (practitioners of Bon) treated all kinds of human ailments through mantra recitation and practiced

---

5 Nine lords of cyclic existence (སྲིད་པའི་ལྷ་རབས་དགུ་): 1. great lord father Ode gung gyal (O de gung rgyal); 2. son Yarlha shampo (Yar lha sham po); 3. Nyan chen thang lha (gNyan chen thang lha) of the north; 4. Gatoe jowo jogs chen (sGa stod jo bo sgyogs chen); 5. Ma chen pom ra (rMa chen spom ra) of the east; 6. Jowo yulgyel (Jo bo g.yul rgyal); 7. Kyishoe Zhoelha Chugpo (Kyi shoe zhoe lha chug po); 8. Shelkar jowo tagoe (Shel dkar jo bo rta rgod); and 9. Nyoejin Gangwa Zangpo (Nyoe jin gang wa zang po). According to the Dung dkar blo bzang phrin las (2002: 2070), the nine lords of cyclic existence came into existence along with the birth of Tibet as a protector according to the exegetical tradition of Bon.

6 Norbu (2019).

subjugation activities such as casting away evil spirits. This is how the word '*bon*' came into use, according to Chogyal Namkhai Norbu. As a result, even in a practice, words are recited to invoke and make an offering to the local deities.

Lha Bon is equivalent to Lha Sol or Lha Choed. According to Pommaret, different regions use different nomenclatures for ancient rituals.[7] As a result, she refers to them in English as 'community rituals'. There is a degree of difference in the practices associated with Lha Bon, Kar phud (kar phud), Roop (rup), Goleng (go leng) and Phcha (phyva). Nonetheless, all ancient rituals, which involved offering rituals to the local deities, are alike. The central tutelary deity in the regions of Bumthang and Kheng is Ode Gungyal who came from Central Tibet, Samye.[8] Therefore, the local officiant, called the *phajo*, who leads the ritual, invokes Ode Gungyal through the visualization of his trip from Tibet to Bhutan.

Secondly, Lha Bon also refers to Bonpo, the officiant who leads the practice and communicates between local deities and people. In Gortshom village under Lhuntse district in Bhutan, the term Lha Bon is pronounced 'Ha Bon' and refers to the person who performs prayers and gives offerings to the local deities. The Ha Bon is a Bon practitioner who carries on the practice in accordance with the local custom.[9] During Bumthang Yag Lha (g.Yag lha), the offering specialist is known as *lhapon* (*lHa dpon*), while in Kheng Wamling the Bonpo performs the Khar Phud (mKhar phud) and in Kheng Buli the Gung Lha (Gung lha) rituals. In the case in Yuesa and Taktse villages, the officiant is known as the *phajo*.

The purpose as per the Lha Bon text is as follows:

> སྐུའི་དོན་དུ་ལྷ་དར་དཀར་པོ་བཙུགས། །གསུང་གི་དོན་དུ་ཛ་ལྷ་ཛ་གསེར་ཛ་རྡུང་། །ཐུགས་ཀྱི་དོན་དུ་མར་ཚང་གསུ་ཏུང་ཅན་དུ་དྲངས། །བོན་ལྷ་བོན་བཙན་བོན་མཛོད།། (ལྷ་བོན་དཔེ་ཆ། དཔར་ལོ་མེད། ཤོག་གྲངས་༢༩-༢༥)
>
> Bon rituals like Lha Bon [lha bon] and Tsan Bon [btsan bon] should be performed by erecting the flag of the deity [*lha dar*] for the health of the body.

7 Pommaret (2014: 114).

8 Pommaret (2014: 116).

9 Choden (2004: 3).

> Beating the drums of the deity made from gold for the health of speech.
>
> Likewise, offering the beverage decorated with everlasting signs made from butter for the health of mind. (From the prayer text *lha bon* [n.d.], pp. 24–25)

Is Lha Sol (lha gsol) a Bon traditional offering?

In Bhutan, all kinds of pre-Buddhist practices are termed 'Bon'. According to Choden, Lha Sol is a Bon religious practice. The Bon religion takes two forms: Bon Kar (white Bon; Bon dkar), whose adherents do not engage in animal sacrifices; and Bon Nag (black Bon; Bon nag), whose adherents engage in animal sacrifices.[10] However, according to Pommaret, Bon Kar and Bon Nag are terms used by Buddhists rather than by Bonpos themselves.[11] Indeed, I have not been able to find these words in old Bon texts. It appears that the division into Bon Kar and Bon Nag in Bhutan is part of oral tradition.

The great treasure revealer Dorje Lingpa (rDo rje gling pa, b. 1346, d. 1405) said, 'There is no difference between Buddhism and Bon' (bon chos dbyer med), which refers to the oneness of Bon and Buddhism.[12] Nonetheless, the Bon called Bonchoe (Bon chos), which is common in Bhutan, is not related to Buddhism, but refers to a system of practices and beliefs. Phuntsho wrote that the word '*bon*' has two different meanings in Tibet and Bhutan: one label refers to the Bon beliefs in Tibet before the introduction of Buddhism and the other to the 'organized' Bon religious school Yundrung Bon (g.Yung drung bon), which appeared after the tenth century and is close to the Nyingmapa (rnying ma pa) school.[13]

Karmay explains that Lha Sol also falls under the first four vehicles of Yungdrung Bon.[14] Hence, there is no issue with recognizing Lha Sol and Lha Bon as Bon offering practices. Moreover, in the case under discussion here, during Lha Bon, the prime lord of the nine lords of cyclic existence,

10 Tashi (2004: 3).

11 Pommaret (2014: 114).

12 Pommaret (2014: 113).

13 Karma (2013: 134–136).

14 Karmay (2009: 141).

Ode Gungyal, is worshipped with an offering. He is the most important god related to the sacred mountains of Bon.[15]

Even the term 'Bonpo', the officiant who leads the Lha Sol, suggests that it is part of the Bon tradition. In addition, all the diverse forms of offering in Bhutan are popularly known as Bonchö. Therefore, Lha Sol and Lha Bon are linked to Bon beliefs.

Preparation of Lha Bon

Collection of provisions

Provisions are collected for Lha Bon on the tenth day of the eleventh month of the lunar calendar. In the past, the provisions were only collected from *khyalp* (taxpayers; *khral pa*) of Taktse and Yuesa. However, today, they are gathered from every household in Taktse and Yuesa in the form of rice, chili, ghee, cheese, eggs and alcohol according to standard measurements and handed to the village head (see Photo 3.1). In the past, when the local deity was welcomed to the village from his abode once every three years, an ox or a cow was sacrificed as ritual meat for offering, as well as to feed the crowd. However, in the 1980s, such practice was discontinued, and meat is now bought from the market with money collected from the villagers.

Preparing the *lhachim (lha kyim)* (the deity home) and the large prayer flag

Men from every household assemble on the tenth day at nine o'clock in the morning at the usual ritual ground where Lha Bon is held. They pitch three tents and prepare a hearth. The first tent houses the ritual offerings,

15 The mountain of south Yolga as clearly identified in the *Monlam Grand Tibetan Dictionary* (mountain of Yar lha sham po of yar klungs phu). The mountains of gnyan chen thang lha on the south side of gnam mtsho etc. are nine mountains from which, according to a Tibetan exegetical saying, the nine protectors of Tibet were said to have emerged when Tibet was formed. Therefore, since these nine local deities reside on mountains, the names of the local deities and those of the mountains are the same.

Photo 3.1: Collecting provisions from villagers

Photo 3.2: Preparing the *dongtse thramo*, the top of the deities' flags

the second tent provides shelter for guests and villagers, and the third tent is a store room for provisions.

The *phajo*, the one who leads the practice, enters the tent that represents the home of the deity, and prepares a religious vessel made from bamboo and wool to be placed at the top of a large prayer flag (གདོང་རྩེ་ཁྲ་མོ་ ; *gdong stse khramo*). In the afternoon, elderly ladies come to help clean and card the wool in the tent that houses the deity. The *phajo* then starts to weave three vases made of bamboo and wool (see Photo 3.2). During this time, he is served lunch and tea from the home of the village head.

Main event of Lha Bon

First day

Although Lha Bon is alternately performed at Taktse and Yuesa, a grand ceremony is organized every three years in which the male tutelary deity or local spirit, Dorje Dragtsan, is ushered into the home of the deity from his sacred abode.

The *phajo* leads the musicians, dancers and villagers at eight in the morning on a walk of up to four hours to the sacred site called Pholha Dzong (Pho lha rdzong), home of the male tutelary deity. There, the *phajo* begins to prepare a ritual cake, and people prepare to hoist five-colored flags and burn incense (see Photo 3.3). Then the *phajo* starts the invocation and offering ceremony (see Photo 3.4).

After the libation and offering of incense, at lunch time the musicians, dancers and villagers make the first offering of food and cooked egg from their packed lunch (see Photo 3.5). Lunch is served to the *phajo* from the food offering and the village head cooks the ritual meat from the provisions provided by the villagers. After the preparation of the offering, the invocation and offering ritual begins. At its completion, dancers and musicians dance continuously and synchronously and leave the sacred site of the local deity in procession.

The local deities Dorje Dragtsan and Menmo Tashi Wangzom are ushered to the home of deities and welcomed by attendants such as the lord, chamberlain, manager and steed[16] carrying pictures of the two deities (see Photo 3.6).

ཡུལ་བཙན་རྡོ་རྗེ་བྲག་བཙན་སྤྱན་འདྲེན་གྱི་ཚིག་ནི།

ཀྱཻ༔ ཕུན་ཚོགས་བདེ་ཆེན་ལྷ་ཡི་ཡུལ་ལྗོངས་འདིར། །སྨན་དང་མེ་ཏོག་བྲག་དཀར་འབབ་ཆུ་དང་། །མཛེས་པའི་རི་ཀླུང་སྣ་ཚོགས་ཆོས་ཀྱི་གླིང་། །འཛིན་སྐྱོང་སྤྲེལ་བའི་སྲུང་མ་མཐུ་རྩལ་ཅན། །མ་རུང་འདུལ་ཕྱིར་དྲག་པོའི་སྐུར་སྟོན་པ། །བཙན་རྒོད་ཆེན་པོ་རྡོ་རྗེ་དྲག་ལྡན་པ། །འཁོར་དུ་སྨན་བཙུན་རུ་འདྲེན་སྡེ་བཞི་དང་། །ལྷ་ཀླུ་བདུད་བཙན་གཉན་གྱི་ཚོགས་ཐམས་ཅད། །དབྱངས་སྙན་གདུང་དབྱངས་ལྡན་པས་ཕྱོད་བོད་ན། །མྱུར་བར་རྫུ་འཕྲུལ་ལྡན་པས་འདིར་གཤེགས་ཤིག། བཛྲ་ས་མ་ཡ་ཛཿ (ལྷ་གསོལ་དཔེ་ཆ། དཔར་ལོ་མེད། ཤོག་གྲངས་ ༧)

16 In the past, these roles were appointed on request to those who seemed capable. However, today, youths volunteer to take on these roles in the belief that they will become leaders if they serve as attendants to the local deities.

Photo 3.3:
Preparing the smoke prayer

Photo 3.4:
The *phajo* engaged in invocation and offering

The verse inviting Yultsen Dorje Dragtsan

Oh! In land of the sublime bliss of heaven,

Medicines, flowers, waterfall of white caves

And striking hill and rivers; the land of Dharma.

The custodian of management, the almighty,

To tame unfits, the ferocious form,

The great Tsan god Dorje Dragdenpa,

Surrounded by four groups of Mentsuen,

Photo 3.5:
Musician and dancers offering the first share of food

Photo 3.6:
Ushering the local deities to the village

And the assemblies of god, naga, demon and spirit,

If you are called with endowed song of longing grief and melody

Having the magical power of fastness, come here Varjasamayajrah.

(From the prayer text of *lha gsol* [n.d.], p. 1)

ཡུལ་བཙན་རྡོ་རྗེ་བྲག་བཙན་ལ་བསྟོད་པའི་ཚིག་ནི།

ཀྱཻ༔ བསྟན་པ་བསྲུང་བའི་མཐུ་རྩལ་ཅན། །བཙན་རྒོད་རྡོ་རྗེ་དྲག་པོ་རྩལ། །སྐུ་ལ་རྡོ་རྗེ་རྨོག་ཁྲབ་གསོལ། །སྐུ་མདོག་པདྨ་རཱ་གའི་ཞལ། །སྤྱང་མིག་དགྲ་བོའི་སྲོག་ལ་གཟིར། །སྨྲ་ར་ཨག་ཚོམ་མེ་ལྟར་འབར། །ཕྱག་གཡས་རྡུ་དར་མཁའ་ལ་འཕྱར། །གཡོན་པར་འདོད་འབྱུང་ནོར་བུ་འཛིན། །གློག་ལས་མགྱོགས་པའི་རྟ་དམར་ཆིབས། །བཙན་དམག་འབུམ་སྡེའི་ཚོགས་དང་བཅས། །སྐད་ཅིག་ཙམ་གྱིས་སྟོང་གསུམ་འཁོར། །མཐུ་སྟོབས་རྫུ་འཕྲུལ་བསམ་མི་ཁྱབ།།

དེ་ལྟའི་གནས་སྲུང་ཆེན་པོ་ལ། །བདག་གིས་མཆོད་པ་བསྟོད་ལགས་ན། །རྣལ་འབྱོར་བསམ་པའི་དོན་ཐམས་ཅད། མ་ལུས་འགྲུབ་པར་མཛད་དུ་གསོལ།། (ལྷ་གསོལ་དཔེ་ཆ། དཔར་ལོ་མེད། ཤོག་གྲངས་ ༧)

Yultsen Dorje Dragtsan's expression of honor

Oh! The almighty, who protects the Dharma,

The great Tsan god Dorje Dragpo tsal.

The body festooned with utmost armour and helmet,

The visage like the color of Pema raga

Angry eye thrust to the life of the enemy

Moustache and beard burns like a fire

Right hand holds the division banner

Left hand holds the jewel

Rides a steed faster than lightening

With an army of thousands of *tsan*

In the three realms be wandered in a second

Power and magic are numerous.

To the great protector of the place

If we offer and honor well

All the hopes of the people

Will be entirely fulfilled.

(From the prayer text of *lha gsol* [n.d.], p. 7)

སྨན་མོ་བཀྲ་ཤིས་དབང་འཛོམས་སྤྱན་འདྲེན་གྱི་ཚིག་ནི།

ཀྱཻ༔ གཡང་ཆགས་ས་འཛིན་ནོར་བུས་གཏམས་པའི་ཞིང་། །སྤྲང་ལྗོངས་ནེའུ་གསིང་མེ་ཏོག་སྣ་ཚོགས་བཀྲ། །ཡོངས་འདུའི་ལྗོན་པའི་ཚལ་གྱིས་རབ་བསྐོར་ཞིང་། །རབ་དཀར་རྒྱ་འཛིན་བླ་རེ་ཕུབ་པའི་འོག །གདུང་གི་བ་གམ་བརྩེགས་པའི་ཕོ་བྲང་དབུས། །མཛེས་སྡུག་ཀུན་གྱི་ཕུལ་ཕྱིན་སྨན་བཙུན་ཆེ། །དེ་རིང་དམ་ལྡན་བུ་ཡིས་གནས་མཆོག་འདིར། གདུང་བས་སྤྱན་འདྲེན་དགྱེས་པའི་ཚུལ་གྱིས་གཤེགས། །གཞན་ཡང་འཁོར་དུ་གཏོགས་པའི་ལྷ་མ་སྲིན། །ཐམས་

Photo 3.7: Statue of Yultsen

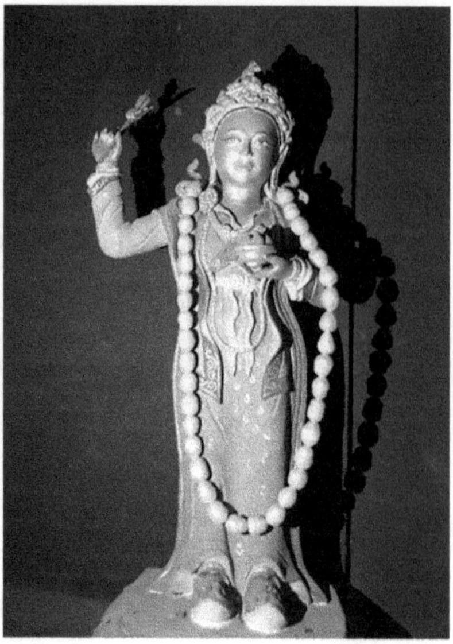

Photo 3.8: Statue of Menmo

ཅད་མིང་དང་མཚན་ནས་མ་འཐོན་ཀྱང་། །རང་རང་དཔུང་གིས་བསྐོར་ནས་གནས་འདི་རུ། །སྒྱུར་བར་བྱོན་ཅིག་
བཛྲ་ས་མ་ཛཿ (ལྷ་གསོལ་དཔེ་ཆ། དཔར་ལོ་མེད། ཤོག་གྲངས་ ༢)

The verse inviting Menmo Tashi Wangzom

Oh! The jewel heaven of prosperity

The meadow of variegated flowers,

Encircled fully by divine woods,

Below the canopy of white cloud

Inside the beams of the domed palace

The eminent of all beauty, Mentsuen,

Today, at my supreme place

Affectionately I invite and come merrily.

All peripheral non-human spirits

Even if the names are missed

At the place with your retinue

Come quickly Vajrasamajrah.

(From the prayer text of *lha gsol* [n.d.], p. 2)

The physical appearance of Yultsen and Menmo is clear through the praise.

སྨན་མོ་བཀྲ་ཤིས་དབང་འཛོམས་ལ་བསྟོད་པའི་ཚིག་ནི།

ཀྱཻ༔ འགྲོ་ལ་ཕན་བདེ་སྟོལ་བའི་སྨན་བཙུན་མོ། །ཁྱོད་ནི་བཅུ་དྲུག་ལོན་པའི་ལང་ཚོ་ཅན། །སྐུ་མདོག་དཀར་ལ་ཞལ་བཟང་ཤིན་ཏུ་འཛུམ། །མཐོང་བས་བདེ་བ་མཆོག་སྟེར་མ་ལ་བསྟོད། །ཕྱག་གཡས་མདའ་དར་གཡོན་པར་ནོར་གཞོང་འཛིན། །པདྨའི་བཀའ་རྟགས་ཀྱི་ཏོར་ནོར་བུས་མཚོན། །ཞབས་གཉིས་བཞེངས་སྟབས་ཚུལ་གྱིས་སྐྱེ་འགྲོ་ལ། །ཚེ་དང་བསོད་ནམས་དཔལ་སྟོལ་མ་ལ་བསྟོད། །ཟ་འོག་རིན་ཐང་བྲལ་བའི་ན་བཟའ་བགྲུབས། །རིན་ཆེན་སྣ་ཚོགས་རྒྱན་གྱིས་ཀུན་ནས་བརྒྱན། །ཚུ་སྐྱེས་ཕྲེང་བ་གསར་པ་ཐོད་དུ་བཅིངས། །འཁོར་ཚོགས་རྒྱ་མཚོའི་དབུས་ན་འཁྱིད་ལ་བསྟོད།། (ལྷ་གསོལ་དཔེ་ཆ། དཔར་ལོ་མེད། ཤོག་གྲངས་ ༨)

Menmo Tashi Wangzom's expression of honor

Oh! Mentsuen, the benefactor,

You are a youthful sixteen

White, fair face and smiling expression.

Praise to the great peace giver.

Arrow of long life in the right hand

Jeweled box in the left hand

Jewel on crown marks the lotus

Two feet in standing posture

Praise to the glorifier of life

She is adorned by glossy silk clothes

Along with varied ornaments

And a lotus rosary around the head,

Praise to you sitting amidst your retinue.

(From the prayer text of *lha gsol* [n.d.], p. 8; see Photo 3.9)

Photo 3.9: Images of Yultsen and Menmo

When the participants return to the *lhachim* at around three o'clock in the afternoon from the abode of the deity, the *phajo* begins preparing the ritual cakes from barley and butter. The cakes are arranged on the altar from the back row towards the front as follows: thirteen *lha shoe* (ལྷ་བཤོས་; *lha bshos*), thirteen *tsan shoe* (བཙན་བཤོས་; *btsan bshos*), thirteen *lo khor* (ལོ་འཁོར་ ; *lo 'khor*), thirteen *men shoe* (སྨན་བཤོས་; *sman bshos*), and thirteen *be kha* (spelling not clear), representing the Thirteen Deities of Existence (སྲིད་པའི་ལྷ་རབས་བཅུ་གསུམ་; srid pa'i lha rabs bcu gsum; see Photo 3.10). From the left to the right side of the altar, ritual cakes are arranged to represent the great deity of Jowo Dursing (ཇོ་བོ་དུར་ཤིང་; Jowo dur shing), Mutsan Dorje Drajom (དམུ་བཙན་རྡོ་རྗེ་དགྲ་འཇོམས་ ; dMu btsan rdo rje dgra 'joms), Khyung Due (ཁྱུང་བདུད་ ; Khyung bdud), Yultsen Dorje Dragtsan (ཡུལ་བཙན་རྡོ་རྗེ་བྲག་བཙན་; Yul btsan rdo rje drag btsan), Menmo Tashi Wangzom (སྨན་མོ་བཀྲ་ཤིས་དབང་འཛོམས་; sManmo bkrashi dbang 'dzom) and Zhidag (གཞི་བདག་ ; bzhi bdag) respectively (see Photo 3.11). One *bre* (བྲེ་ ; 'bre) of paddy rice[17] is collected from each tax-

17 One *bre* is roughly equal to ½ kg, but it is not a standardized measure, and instead varies according to the area, valley, etc.

Photo 3.10: Ritual cakes representing the Thirteen Deities of Existence

Photo 3.11: Ritual offerings on the altar of lachim

payer household and spread beneath the ritual cakes as a base (གཏོར་གདན་; *gtor gdan*). It will become the property of the *phajo* at the end of Lha Bon.

After completing the ritual cakes, the religious vessel tops made the previous day are installed on three flags,[18] as the members from every

18 In the past, the central prayer flag, *mendor*, was brought by the villagers on the rotation roster from the neighboring forest, while the other two prayer flags were brought by the villagers not on the rotation. These prayer flags are hoisted on divine trees called *sersho*. Three men go to the forest, wearing their ceremonial scarf (*kabney*). They do not cut the tree directly. Firstly, they walk around the tree three times and hit it three times with their sword. Then, they sing 'Shomo alay', put their *kabney* on their heads, join hands keeping the tree in the center and walk around it while singing the song of auspicious rainfall ('Tashi char phab'), preceded by whistles and shouts. In this manner, they cut the tree, says

Photo 3.12: Deities' flags, *dongtse thramo*

ye boem household (ཡས་བོནམ་; *yas bonm*: households not on rotation to conduct the practice) assemble at the place where the flags are hoisted.

The three flags with religious vessel (བུམ་པ་) tops are known as *dongtse thramo* (see Photo 3.12). According to Dondup, the three flags with tops made of wool and bamboo, which represent the three great gods, are hoisted and the ritual offering starts.[19] However, the names of the three great gods are not mentioned.

In the Lha Bon held in Taktse and Yuesa, the three flags should symbolize the three great gods, but instead two of the prayer flags signify the male tutelary deity and the middle one signifies Menmo (*phajo*, personal communication, 19 November 2018).

The *phajo* then consecrates the prayer flags by burning incense and the first offering of *bang chang* (*sbang chang*: fermented alcohol) brought by villagers is carried out as libation and the remaining is given to the *phajo* and *ye boem*. After this, the *ye boem* sing a song to harken auspicious

---

Choegyal, the uncle of the present *phajo*. However, when he became aware of this practice, it was no longer a *sersho* tree but a *domseng* tree which was felled in the same manner, and the song 'Shomu alay' is no longer sung. Today, the tree is directly brought from the woods without the aforementioned steps (Ap Norbu from Taktse, personal communication, 16/11/2019). The tree is brought with its bark intact, and in the evening of the first day, the bark is removed and the tree hoisted.

19 Dondup (2018: 79).

Photo 3.13:
Ye boem blessing the village households at night

Photo 3.14:
Lha Bon's *phag* cham

rainfall known as 'Tashi char phab' (བཀྲ་ཤིས་ཆར་ཕབ་; bkra shis char phab). Then, they break for the evening meal.

After dinner, the *phajo* starts the ritual offering at the home of the deity while the *ye boem* visit every household wishing wellness in song till dawn. The owners of the household believe that the local deities bless them in the form of the *ye boem*. Therefore, they welcome them cordially and offer them alcoholic beverages (*bang chang*) (see Photo 3.13). Throughout the night, the *phajo* performs the ritual and there is a male dance called *phag cham* (ཕག་འཆམ་; *phag 'cham*) and a female dance at intervals. The male dancers perform without masks, wear a five-colored silk cloth on their torso and their head is covered by a scarf. The leader and last dancers hold cymbals in their hands while the other dancers have drums (see Photo 3.14).

Photo 3.15: Villagers gathering for lunch

Photo 3.16: Participation in singing and dancing

Second day

People gather on the field of the home of the deity in their best attire, and various dances are performed one after another. While the *phajo* performs the ritual offering, villagers make dough effigies of animals either from wheat or rice flour and take them into the home of the deity. Villagers believe that the deities will bless their dough effigies. People of both villages merrily eat lunch on the ground near the home of the deity and sing and dance till dusk (see Photo 3.15, 3.16). Likewise, from the provisions of the crowd, many pieces of flat bread are made from cooked rice and sanctified at the home of the deity by the *phajo*. Then, it is shared in every household as a blessing. Towards dusk, through visualization, Yultsen, Menmo and other local deities are seen departing for their respective residences by the *phajo* (see Photo 3.17). In the evening, after the ritual offering, villagers also leave to return home.

Photo 3.17: The *phajo* seeing off the deities to their residences

Third day

People in their villages visit other households singing and dancing. House owners welcome them jovially and offer them food and alcohol. The day ends at around five o'clock in the evening.

Community benefits of Lha Bon

What are the benefits of the Lha Bon ritual to the society and community? This research identified six beneficial aspects as follows:

1. It promotes community vitality by fostering social relations among communities and increasing bonds between parents and children, siblings and relatives as many people gather from various places during the event.

2. It encourages social relations and builds healthy bonds within and between families.

3. It inculcates the value of culture in youth through the performance of tangible and intangible cultural elements.

4. It helps protect and preserve the natural environment through the belief that local deities reside in the meadows, forests, hills, caves and water.

5. It ensures peace in the community as the tradition fulfills the people's wishes and wards off adverse circumstances.
6. It provides a platform for elders to instill in the youth the indispensable cultural and traditional knowledge bound in this community ritual.

Threats to the continuation of Lha Bon

In the past, Lha Bon was practiced at Tangsibji, Tsangkha, Langthel and Namther villages in the Trongsa district. However, today, it is only practiced at Taktse, Yuesa and a few other villages. This is because many villages primarily focus on Buddhism, and Lha Bon is part of the Bon tradition. Moreover, some assert that their annual home-based ritual has superseded the need to practice Lha Bon. Some also report that it is difficult to hire a *phajo* from other villages as they have no *phajo* of their own. Therefore, the practice in these places has gradually declined. Even though Yuesa and Taktse continue to conduct the tradition annually, there are less villagers taking part in the practice than in the past.

Conclusion

The three-day tradition of Lha Bon upholds the culture of libation and incense offering, and prayer flags are hoisted in honor of local deities. Although Lha Bon is still alternately performed at Taktse and Yuesa every year, a major ceremony is celebrated only once every three years.

The male tutelary deity or local spirit Dorje Dragtsan, the aquatic deity Menmo Tashi Wangzom and other deities are invited to the village from their sacred abode in the mountain and appeased so that they bless the villages with domestic prosperity, sufficient food, warm clothes, luck and power. Due to these blessings, it is believed that the rain will fall on time, crops will yield well and obstacles will be suppressed. In this way, Lha Bon ushers in a harmonious social and economic life.

In the past, Lha Bon used to be practiced at several communities in the Trongsa district but this practice has declined. Even at Yuesa and Taktse communities, fewer villagers take part in the ritual these days. Some villagers now primarily focus on Buddhist rituals and some believe that their annual Buddhist ritual (ལོ་ཆོག ; *lo chog*) carried out at home will supersede Lha Bon. We can see here, like in many Himalayan communities, the influence of Buddhism working to eradicate the ancient local customs.

To my knowledge, though Lha Bon is a Bon tradition, it has nothing to do with animal sacrifice or activities that would harm any community or the natural environment; instead, it focuses on keeping the value of participation and sharing in the local community. For example, the *ye boem*, who embody the deities, visit every household wishing them happiness in song and dance until dawn, and this creates a social gathering platform for all of the villagers.

Conversely, the Buddhist annual ritual takes place in individual homes. Therefore, it offers no opportunity for social gathering in this way and the local deities, which are important for the villagers' everyday activities, are forgotten.

In villages where Bon and Buddhist rituals once coexisted, today an opposition has been created and it is breaking the traditional community bond embodied by the local deities and ultimately the cultural landscape.

Acknowledgements

I would like to acknowledge Phajo Pema Gyaltshen for answering all the questions related to Lha Bon, Azhang Norbu for helping me to write the song of Lha Bon, and Taktse Tshogpa Rinzin, Ap Tandin Yeshey, Aum Kelzang and Chimi and Sangay Dema for their support of my research. Furthermore, I would like to extend my heartfelt gratitude to Dr. Françoise Pommaret for helping me correct the meanings and references, lecturers Jigme Dorji and Sonam Wangchuk for supporting me to write this paper in English, and Lopon Singye Samdrup and Yeshi Lhuendup for helping me to obtain documents. Lastly, I would like to wholeheartedly acknowledge my family and supporters for continually backing me in my research endeavors.

Bibliography

Choden, T. (2004). 'Ha: The Bon Festival of Gortshom Village'. In *Wayo Wayo: Voices from the Past*, Thimphu: Centre for Bhutan Studies, pp. 1–23.

Dondup, P. (2018). 'Tshang kha lha bon'. In Chorten Tshering, et al., eds., *'Bruggi lam srol dang mtha' skor gnas stangs*, Paro: The National Museum of Bhutan, pp. 71–86.

Karmay, S.G. (2009). 'A General Introduction to the History and Doctrines of Bon'. In S.G. Karmay, ed., *The Arrow and the Spindle, Studies in History, Myths, Ritual and Beliefs in Tibet* (revised edition), Kathmandu: Mandala Book Point, pp. 104–156.

Norbu, C.G. (2016). *'Gziyi phrengba'*, accessed 21 October 2023 at d.bus tsang rig zod https://utsangculture.com/?p=474

Phuntsho, K. (2013). *The History of Bhutan*, Haryana: Random House India.

Pommaret, F. (2014). 'Bon in Bhutan. What Is in the Name?' In S. Kumagai, ed. *Bhutanese Buddhism and Its Culture*, Kathmandu: Vajra Publications, pp. 113–126.

Thinley, D.L. (2002). *Dungkar Tshigzod Chenmo,* Krung goi bod rigpa dpe skun khang.

4 'Soul Retrieval' (*yung luba*): A Shertukpen Healing Ritual

Pascale Dollfus

Rituals for recapturing 'lost soul(s)' and for bringing them back are well known throughout Tibet and the Himalayan regions. A few studies are based on textual materials, such as the pioneering work of Ferdinand D. Lessing,[1] who studied the Chinese translation of a text composed by an eighteenth-century Tibetan scholar. Other research compares texts with their interpretation in present-day rituals,[2] and some provides ethnographic data, especially among populations in which there is no written tradition, as is the case of the Shertukpens.[3] This paper presents an overview of a healing ritual called *ayung luba*, 'soul(s) retrieval', which is performed by *zizi*, local priests and healers. It attempts to discuss the concept of *ayung* (or *yung*) – 'shadow (of human being), image, reflection, soul, self-conscience (when you wake up after a dream)'[4] – by comparing it with the ambiguous Tibetan term '*bla*' used in a similar context in Tibet and the related Himalayan regions.

---

1 Ferdinand D. Lessing (1951).

2 Karmay (1998); Ramble (2009).

3 See among others, in Bhutan (Schrempf 2015a, 2015b; Dorji 2004); in Nepal among the Tamangs (Holmberg 1984), the Gurungs (McHugh 1989, 1997), the Kulungs (Schlemmer 2011, 2015), the Yolmo Sherpas (Desjarlais 1989, 1992), in Mustang (Ramble 2009); among Assam tribes (Fürer-Haimendorf 1952); and on the edge of the Tibetan plateau, among the Nakhi (Lakhi, Stuart and Roche 2009) and the Mosuo (Rock 1959) living in the provinces of Sichuan and Yunnan, China. Similar practices are prevalent in Mongolia and Buryatia (Bawden 1962; Hamayon 2013; Ruhlmann 2009, 2010, 2013) and in Southeast Asia (Porée-Maspero 1951; Tambiah 1985).

4 Jacquesson (2015: 183).

This paper is the result of nine winters among the Shertukpens (West Kameng district, Arunachal Pradesh, India) between 2010 and 2019, following a one-month 'exploratory tour' of the whole western area in February 2010. Most of the information given here comes either from direct observation or from conversations with Shertukpens, individually or in groups, either directly or after they had asked questions of others. It is therefore impossible, most of the time, to assign a particular piece of information to a particular person; all ethnographers in the field are familiar with these realities.

At this point in my introduction, I think it useful to point out an intellectual perspective that may go unnoticed by some younger authors. Both in general anthropology and in the field of Himalayan studies, most French (and foreign) researchers would not dare to raise theoretical issues without first describing facts and contexts and of course try to form a sympathetic description of what local people do and experience. All experienced scholars around the world know well that this requires long and patient stays among local people, making sure that what we may have understood is accepted by informants. This practice avoids unnecessary jargon and intellectual manias that claim to 'explain the world' in supposedly universal vocabulary. It goes without saying that *describing facts and contexts* requires analytical vocabularies, technical choices and categories. This makes descriptive ethnography always a theoretical work. The point here is never erase the descriptive attitude.

The Shertukpen language is not a written language and has been the subject of very few publications. The Tibetologists will no doubt recognize terms that sound familiar – but of course the similarity of words never implies the equivalence of concepts.

I observed this healing ritual and its preparation in January 2014 in Rupa, the main settlement of Shertukpen society, located at the confluence of the rivers Ziding and Dinik at 1,450 meters above sea level. Known as Thük, 'the village', by Shertukpens, nowadays it is no longer a village but a small town with a population of 3,800, a third of whom belong to the Shertukpen ethnic group. After the 1962 'Chinese aggression', the Indian Army occupied a large part of the nearby land, installed numerous camps and organized the road network. A bazaar was set up on a wasteland described as being 'full of cactus'. The opening of motorable roads allowed the transportation of new materials, especially building materials such as cement, iron rods and plastic pipes, but also furniture (chairs, sofas, beds, etc.). At the end of the 1940s,[5] there were thirty-three traditional houses in Rupa, all stone houses (*dadcha'yam*), and *pangthüng yam*, houses with a stone basement, wooden plank walls for the living story and a cane-walled attic. Nowadays, very few of these old traditional houses still exist amid the new world of concrete, most of them having been destroyed, rebuilt or left uninhabited. However, Shertukpen society is still close-knit and has a strong identity: it has kept its own language, its customary laws and traditional institutions.[6]

The social and ritual context

Shertukpens – the term they use when talking with outsiders (or sometimes among themselves)[7] – are a small population (about 4,000), speaking a Tibeto-Burmese language and living in the western part of Arunachal Pradesh in the north-eastern corner of India. Bhutan is 30 km away to the west as the crow flies and the Chinese (Tibetan) border 70 km due north, about 250 km by road, after passing Tawang Monastery. Their name reflects the two components of the community: the people of Tukpen,[8] as

5 As F. Jacquesson (2020) notes: 'This chronology is fixed, because two important events took place just after: the 1950 great earthquake (with no real destruction in Old Rupa), and the 1952-1953 Yuser [an important quarter of Rupa] Great Fire when nearly all old houses in Yuser quarter were burnt down'.

6 See Zaman and Bodhprakash (2016).

7 As Jacquesson (2016) remarks, 'Shertukpen people between themselves use the self-designation *Mö* (*Mẽ/Mõ*), which means "our people", "us". About somebody else, one Shertukpen can ask another one: "he is *Mö?*" = "Is he one of us?". The problem is that, since it is a self-designation, you cannot use it if you are not a Shertukpen!'

8 The etymology of Tukpen is still not clear. For some informants, Thuk comes from Thong, the name of the upper class of Shertukpens; for others, Thuk is another way of pronouncing *thük*, 'village', Rupa being the first village to have been built by Shertukpens, i.e. 'the village par excellence'. In British records, Shertukpens have been variously referred to as Charduar/Chardwar Bhutias, Rooprai Gaon (i.e. Rupa) and Sher Gaon Bhutias, Thebengia Bhutias, Bhutia Roop Roe Gya, Extra-Bhutias, Mombas of Rupa and Shergaon, and so on. One of the first British

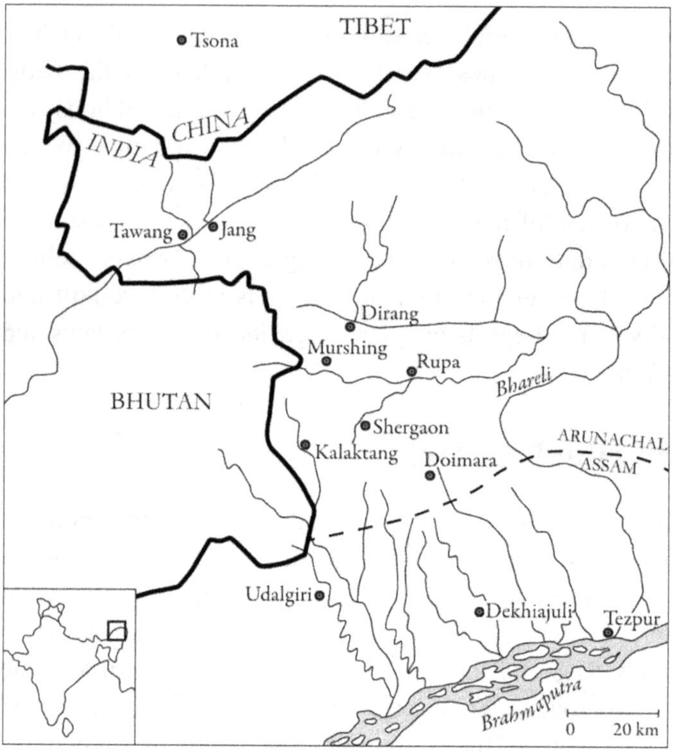

Figure 4.1: The Shertukpen country and its two main centers: Shergaon and Rupa

the inhabitants called the little town of Rupa and its surrounding villages, and the people of Sẽ/Ser/Sher thük, i.e. Shergaon, a large isolated village situated approximately 20 km to the west (see Figure 4.1). They occupy a rather large territory that stretches from the plains bordering Assam in the south to the valley and hills that range from 1,500 to 2,000 meters above sea level in the north, through which most of their villages are scattered.

For neighbors, they have the small Bugun (Khowa) population that lives on the left bank of the Tenga River to the northeast; the Akas (Hrusso) and the Mijis to the east; the Boros and the Assamese people to the south;

nationals to use the ethnonym Sherdukpen/Shertukpen was R.S. Kennedy, who wrote with Captain G.A. Nevill *Report on the Aka Promenade 1913-1914* (British Library Mss Eur157/324(i)). In Tibetan texts, the term gSher-stug-spen (gSher-stug-span/Sher-bstug-span) is used.

and several Monpa subgroups[9] that form a chain along the Bhutanese border up to the Tawang region to the north and west.

People used to practice farming and herding, as well as hunting, fishing, gathering and trade. Before winter, a two-day walk through the forest used to lead the whole community to the foothills where they would trade with the local people. After three months spent in bamboo huts in temporary camps situated at the confluence of two rivers, the population would walk back to the villages bringing not only produce from Assam (*endi* silk made from the moth *Samia cynthia*, brass and copper utensils, rice and betel nuts) but also dried fish and wild game collected during their stay in the jungle. In the 1970s, the Public Distribution System was introduced, an Indian food security system providing the whole population with subsidized rice, wheat, sugar and kerosene; moreover, the timber operation allowed selling timber from the forests and improved some Shertukpen families' revenue. Going to Assam for food was no longer necessary. Winter migrations therefore came to an end. Nevertheless, Shertukpens have maintained links with the people in the plains, and every winter, about a dozen men go down to fetch areca nuts that are essential for Khiksaba celebrations, a winter festival attended by all for the wellbeing of the entire Shertukpen community.[10]

With the emergence of a market system and modern schooling, people have had to adapt their livelihoods: today, many Shertukpens hold government jobs or other types of perennial employment, while others work as contractors or grow cash crops such as tomatoes, kiwis and apples, which have replaced the maize, buckwheat and finger millet that used to be cultivated as staples.

Shertukpen society is a highly hierarchized and patriarchal society. Descent is patrilineal and marriage patrilocal. The father, as head

9 The ethnonym Monpa/Mönba poses many problems (geographical, political, identity-related) that have been identified and analyzed, in particular by Pommaret (1999); Bodt (2012); and Tenpa (2018). Here Monpa refers to the populations centered in the districts of Tawang and West Kameng: Tawang Monpas, also known as Upper Monpas, Dirang or Central Monpas, Murshing and Kalaktang or Lower Monpas.

10 For a detailed account of the Khiksaba festival, see Dollfus and Jacquesson (2013).

of the family, is held in high esteem. His will takes precedence over every important decision. It is impossible for a son, even if he is fifty to sixty years old, to stand up in public when his father is present, and *a fortiori* to contradict him. Property is divided equally between sons. Daughters do not inherit any landed or immovable property from their fathers. Women do not have the right to raise their voices, participate in or attend village council meetings, while men are appointed to all the important decision-making positions. The role of village headman (*thük akhao*) is only assigned to men belonging to the upper class. Indeed, local society is divided into two classes, each of which comprises several exogamous clans.

The Thongs, who consider themselves the descendants of a Tibetan prince, Asu Japtong, form the elite and own most of the land, whether cultivated or not. Most of them live in the town of Rupa and the semi-urban settlement of Shergaon. The Chhaos, on the other hand, mostly reside in remote villages and hamlets. Described either as old-time inhabitants of the land or as the progeny of warriors, porters and servants who made up Asu Japtong's retinue, they used to till the fields, harvest the crops, look after the cattle, collect the honey, cut grass and gather wood in the forest and so on for their Thong patrons. Conversely, the latter are under a moral obligation to come to the Chhaos' assistance if they encounter any difficulty: illness, financial problems and so forth. Although marriage between Thongs and Chhaos is avoided or even formally forbidden, when it comes to 'brother clans',[11] there is no ban on commensality. Over the last few decades, the situation has gradually evolved. Chhaos no longer serve Thongs by carrying out agricultural tasks, herding or grass- and wood-cutting. Today this work is done by Nepalese day laborers. Despite these changes, Chhaos are still expected to carry out menial tasks and ceremonial duties for Thongs, especially at funerals. The latter are not allowed to touch dead bodies: it is the Chhaos who wash the corpse, wrap it in a cloth and carry it for the last rites, receiving compensation in kind for their work. Today, belonging to a class still determines a person's

---

11 Each Thong clan is linked to a Chhao clan. These related clans regard each other as 'brother clans' and support each other in every possible manner. On Shertukpen social stratification, see Megegee (2017).

social and ceremonial activities. This governs marriage, funerals and most religious rituals. Certain functions or roles are reserved exclusively for one group or even for a specific clan. For example, village headmen are chosen from Thong clans, whereas community and household priests, *khikzizi* and *zizi*, come from the Chhaos class, the former belonging only to Dingla and Megẽji clans.

Shertukpens are listed as Buddhists in the Census of India. The propagator of Buddhism is said to have been a Gelukpa monk named Kezang Donyoe Tenzin,[12] who came from Tawang to Rupa in the 1740s to settle a dispute. During his stay, he promoted Buddhism and instigated the construction of the first Buddhist temple. Indeed, prayer flags, prayer walls and *stūpas* are present in the landscape. Though Buddhist temples can be found in the main villages, temple caretakers still come from outside the community, for the most part from among Monpas or natives of Bhutan. A Bhutanese Nyingmapa priest lives in Rupa with his wife and children. Although a growing number of Shertukpens have Buddhist names and call upon Buddhist practitioners for funerals, their knowledge of Buddhism and its practices are, generally speaking, very basic. To sum up, the Buddhization process is far from being complete among Shertukpens who, loath to be subjected to the rules of the Buddhist clergy,[13] still govern according to their own customary laws. They have maintained their own religion (referred to as Bon or Bonist by some authors[14]), which addresses the question of the multitude of non-human entities that inhabit elements of the landscape: mountains, forests, rocks, rivers, caves and so forth.

12 Kezang Donyoe Tenzin (Tib. sKal bzang don yod bstan dzin) is a reincarnation of Merak Lama Lobzang Tenpai Drönme (Tib. Lo bzang bstan pai sgron me) (b. 1475, d. 1542?) who introduced the Gelukpa school to Tawang and its region. See Tenpa (2018).

13 On this topic, see Scott (2009).

14 Throughout eastern Bhutan and the neighboring western part of Arunachal Pradesh, 'Bon' and its derivatives are used as a blanket term to designate a wide range of non-Buddhist ritual specialists and their practices. For a short review of Bon and Shamanism, see Kvaerne (2009); for a criticism of Bon 'shamans', see Bjerken (2004).

Lo, probably a lexical loan from the Tibetan '*lha*' (deity; god; divinity),[15] are described as good or potentially benevolent deities. They comprise two different groups, the *phu* and the *do*, which together are referred to as *phu-do*, for example *phu-do saba*, 'honoring the *phu* and the *do*'; *phu-do sõba*, 'chanting (for) the *phu* and the *do*', and so on. The *phu* reside in the mountains, often on their summits. The ancestral (and clan) gods (*khik*/*khit*) belong to this category.[16] Some are of a rather calm temperament; others are impetuous and prompt to react. Interestingly, in this male-dominated society, female deities are regarded as more ferocious and powerful than their male counterparts. They are thirsty for meat and blood and are not content with offerings of only flowers and fruits. The *do* inhabit the lower part of the mountains, including gorges and rivers.[17] They are harmless and even friendly towards humans if they are shown respect, but can turn dangerous when they feel threatened.

Dȭ are evil spirits or demons. Permanently hostile towards humans, they live on wasteland and in inhospitable places where the black water of rivers floods the land and where cacti grow. In fact, these plants, once very common in Rupa, are called *dȭ -bozao,* 'demon's thorns'.

In addition to *phu-do* and *dȭ*, which are described mainly according to where they live and their actions, there exist about a dozen strange creatures, portrayed according to their physical features, costumes and attributes. They include: *grephu*, a kind of half monkey, half man who lives in the snow-clad mountains; *zegma*(*t*), witches who like to play dice at night; *sinchopi*, who live along rivers where they fish at night and look like goblins, wearing a pointy hat and holding a stick; *thebrangmu*, female spirits who are reported to have impressive milk-filled breasts which trip them up when they run; and *bising/mising*, spirits of dead persons that have not yet attained rebirth and appear here and there like ghosts

---

15 For example, *loyak* < Tib. *Lha-g.yag* (sacrificial bovine presented to the deity), *lochang* < Tib. *Lha-chang*, (sacrificial beer for the deity), *loblang* < Tib. *Lha-brang* (ritual shelter for hosting the deity), and so on.

16 On the word *khik/khit*, see Huber (2015).

17 It is interesting to note that while, to my knowledge, there are no deities or spirits with these names in the myriad of those listed in the Tibetan world, *phu* in Tibetan means the upper part of a sloping valley, higher ground, while *mdo* (pronounced *do*) designates its lower part, the confluence of two rivers.

changing their size and shape at will. Practical jokers, *bising/mising* hide objects, pop up where they are not expected, and at night come to sleep on your chest, causing you to struggle for air. All these non-human beings are the subject of stories based on personal encounters or, most often, are reported back by a third party: 'it is said that …'. Interaction between humans and non-humans (deities, spirits, monsters and other creatures) occurs usually through disorder and adversity: disease, accident, unnatural death, poor harvests, flooding or other calamities. Indeed, 'misfortune is the primary means through which spirits manifest themselves, the most obvious and the common one', as Schlemmer reports about the Kulungs, a Tibeto-Burman population living in eastern Nepal.[18] For better or for worse, humans have to coexist with these non-human entities. Three local religious experts – *khikzizi, zizi* and *raoma* – are in charge of smoothing out any difficulties in cohabitation. Schematically speaking, the boundaries between their respective areas of expertise are to a large extent porous:

- *khikzizi* – selected by the village council (*blu*), they specialize in maintaining good relations with the ancestral deities (*khik/khit*). They carry out all the community rituals. During Khiksaba, they have an exhausting and nonstop part to play; they are not only the organizers and the ritual specialists of the festival but also the community's leading authority. *Khikzizi* apprentices prepare for their future appointment very early on, at about ten to twelve years of age, by moving in with the *khikzizi* they are to succeed.
- *zizi* – household priest-cum-healer and diviner. They perform ceremonies for individuals, their household, their clan or sub-clan, and for a geographical group of households. Present in each hamlet and village until about twenty years ago, their number has drastically declined in recent years. Furthermore, though people remember some cases of women *zizi* in the past, today all *zizi* are men.[19]

18 Schlemmer (2009).

19 About women *zizi*, see Sharma (2013: 76).

- *raoma* (or *raomat*) – regarded as 'super *zizi*'. They are called upon when the summoned *zizis* recognize that the matter at hand is beyond their expertise. They are not just an intercessor. Like shamans, they go into a trance and travel long distances to meet deities and spirits. They talk to them, tease them, trick them and even fight them, helped in their battles by spiritual warriors. One of the most famous *raoma* of all time was a woman, Ayo Lule. No one can say exactly when she lived, some say 150 years ago, but all Shertukpens know of her existence and can name a place related to her or recount an anecdote about her.

Although there is no ban regarding social status or clan, most *zizis* and *raomas* – if not all of them – belong to the Chhaos stratum. And, as already mentioned, *khikzizi* are selected from only two Chhao clans: Dingla and Megẽji.

All three religious experts are householders with a spouse and children. They work the land like their kinsfolk, including ploughing or cutting wood. Their activities as priest, diviner, astrologer, healer or shaman come in addition to this. In the case of the *yung lungba* ritual, it is usually a *zizi* household priest who is called upon, and only in the second instance a *raoma.*[20]

The *zizi*, a priest-cum-diviner and healer

Zizi define themselves as intercessors between humans and local spirits and deities. To describe their function, they use the expression 'intermediate man' (*achung jiring*), which refers to men playing the role of matchmaker when a marriage is taking place. The office of *zizi* is not hereditary and is not a chosen profession. How do you become a *zizi* without wanting to and, I might add, even when you don't wish to? Indeed, unlike *khikzizi* who are selected by the village council within specific clans, *zizi* are chosen by *lo* deities and usually begin by acting as though possessed. This divine election, recounted in the following terms, 'one day, a deity catches you, he enters into you through the fontanel', manifests itself in strange behavior:

20 On these three religious specialists, see Dollfus (2019).

trembling, immense fatigue, the impression of no longer controlling one's own body. It is very difficult, if not impossible, to actively resist.

On this subject, Dorjee refers to the case of one of his peers who was 'caught' by a deity while he was studying at university in Itanagar, Arunachal Pradesh's state capital. One day, he was suddenly seized by fits of trembling. He did not want to become a *zizi* and, above all, to be subjected to the lifelong diet imposed by the function: a garlic- and onion-free diet and, depending on which deity puts his/her grasp on you, no eggs, chicken, fish or meat other than local game.[21] But every time Dorjee's peer ate a forbidden food product, he was seized with trembling and an immense tiredness overcame him. This very unpleasant situation – onion and garlic are ingredients widely used these days in Indian cooking, especially among the younger generation – lasted several years, until the divinity finally let him go and no longer bothered him. However, some deities are more persistent and uncompromising, and to resist them can lead to death. Chhumbi, a thirty-six-year-old *zizi*, confided in me as follows: on the verge of dying after a long illness that no treatment could cure, he ended up giving in to the will of the deity who had chosen him to be his intercessor.

As people told me, the deity literally owns the person they have chosen as their intermediary. The person is one of their belongings in the same way as the mountain goats or elephants that live in their kingdom. The term used, *spu'*, is the same as the one used for the owner of a cow, a car or any other material property.

The *zizi* does not undergo any formal training but is initiated into his art by visions and dreams during which he is told about certain medicines, herbs, jewels, protective charms, etc. to be found in a particular place in the forest, the hills, river, etc., but also how to perform rituals. They are practitioners not only of periodic rituals to clan deities that are carried out during the waxing moon to bring the household health and good fortune, but also of protection rites requested by a household before one of its members sets out on a journey, whether for business, pilgrimage, studying, etc. Until very recently, *zizi* used to attribute names to new-born babies

21 *Zizi* must observe these food taboos throughout their lives to maintain their state of purity and health.

when determining their horoscope. They looked at babies and, according to the impression the infant produced, gave them jolly names, often with an unflattering meaning to avert the attention of malignant spirits. For example, they would name a boy Botrö ('like a lump of clay'), Dzumbo ('chief idiot'), Hogro ('voracious') or Chhumbi ('blackish'), and a girl Ahamu ('with a yellow [complexion]'), Brongkomu ('with straight hair') or Sipi ('with small eyes'). As diviners, *zizi* are consulted before any major decision such as the opportunity of setting up a business, but also to find the culprits, whether supernatural beings or more pragmatically thieves, who have stolen wood from the forest or a cow from pasturelands. As healers, *zizi* perform many exorcism rituals to respond to attacks that have been made on those who come to consult them: 'stone throwing' (*lung than-khan*), 'arrow throwing' (*mik than-khan*), 'stomachache' (*siring nu-khan*), 'evil eye' (*kharam*) or 'soul loss' (*yung likpa*), etc. As exorcists, *zizi* can in turn attack or, at the very least, 'return the poison', *duk kepa*, or 'return the curse', *nyan kepa*, that has been cast on their clients, to the aggressors – and always at a higher level.

Whatever the case, *zizi* are helped by their *armu*, spiritual wives sent by their tutelar deities who have chosen them to advise and to guide them, and, if need be, by spirit warriors and guards (*mokphẽ*) to defend and fight alongside them. In fact, even if the *zizi* does not enter a trance state when performing rituals, his powers are directly linked to those of the deity that patronizes him or, literally, that 'is stuck to him', *pek-khan*.

Tibetan theories concerning *bla*, 'soul', and the Shertukpen concept of *yung*

Since F.D. Lessing, who in 1951 was the first to devote an entire article to the Tibetan concept of 'soul', several scholars have addressed this issue in Tibetan and related Himalayan societies. Theoretically, Buddhism does not recognize the existence of such an entity in living beings. Contrary to Hinduism or Jainism, the Saṃsāra doctrine of Buddhism asserts that while beings undergo endless rebirth cycles, no soul transmigrates from one lifetime to another. Established in Tibet during the eighth century, the new religion never succeeded, however, in completely stamping out the notion of 'soul', *bla* in Tibetan, that was present in early beliefs. Over the centuries, it was gradually assimilated and integrated into popular rituals, such as *bla bslu*, 'the ransom of the soul', *bla bod* or *bla 'gugs*, 'the calling of the soul', even if it contradicted Buddhism's fundamental doctrine of no soul (no-self).[22] In Tibetan textual sources, *bla* is considered the most important of the three physiological principles, which also include 'respiratory breath' (Tib. *dbugs*) and 'vital force' (Tib. *srog*), as well as of the three intellectual principles that comprise 'thought' (Tib. *yid*) and 'mind' (Tib. *sems*).[23] When a person dies, *bla*, *yid* and *sems* are separated and this causes great mental turmoil for the deceased person. In medical treaties, however, as C. Millard[24] points out, there is some confusion as to what exactly *bla* conveys. For instance, in the second volume of the Four Medical Tantras (*Rgyu bzhi*) compiled in the ninth century, in one place the *bla* appears as a 'soul' that can leave the body, and in another it appears as vital energy or a life force, thus similar in meaning to the Tibetan word *srog*, that revolves around the body according to the lunar cycle. Indeed, in the system drawing its authority from the Kālacakra tantra, 'the soul resides (*bla-gnas*) in the middle of the sole of the foot (left foot for men, right for women) on the thirtieth and first of each month (at new moon). Then it rises higher each day, in the shape of a letter of the alphabet, to reside at the top of the head on the fifteenth and sixteenth (at full moon), and return afresh to initial position'.[25] *Bla* is accordingly a mobile soul, but it always needs a support. It can take up residence, temporarily at least, in various objects outside the body: in a tree (*bla shing*), a mountain (*bla ri*), a lake (*bla mtsho*), a rock or a boulder (*bla rdo*), a precious stone such as a turquoise (*bla g.yu*) or an animal, etc. Such objects can also be the 'dwellings of the soul' or the 'seats of the life' of a group of people or a country. Even the gods and demons have their external 'soul' or 'life'. In Lhasa for example, Marpo-ri (Tib. dmar-po ri), the hill on which the Potala stands, is the soul-mountain of Avalokiteshvara (Tib. Spyan-ras-gzigs), the bodhisattva that embodies the compassion of all Buddhas.

---

22 For a summary of *bla* rituals in Tibetan and related Himalayan societies, see Gerke (2007).

23 Karmay (1998: 311).

24 Millard (1997).

25 Stein (1972: 226–227). See also Gerke (2007: 197–198); Millard (2007).

We consequently have to accept the fact that there is not a single but multiple Tibetan ideas of *bla* that cannot be reduced to a common denominator. This multiplicity is reflected in Tibetan-English dictionaries by a wide variety of translations. *Bla* means: 'soul, life; according to oral explanations: 1. strength, power, vitality; 2. blessings, power of blessings; 3. an object with which a person's life is ominously connected';[26] 'life-force/supreme, life energy, vital principle, energy [the basis/support of life force and life span], vital basis',[27] etc. On the other hand, other Tibetan words are also translated as 'soul': *nyam(s)*, hon. *thugs* or *thugs nyams* = 'soul, mind, spirit'; *yid/sems*, hon. *thugs* = 'soul, mind, especially the powers of perception, volition and imagination'; *sems-kyi-nyid* = 'the essence of the soul'; *shes/rnam-shes* = 'soul or spirit separate from the body, soul of departed, consciousness [principle]'; *srog* = 'life, life-force, vital essence, heart, soul'. (The *srog* like the *bla* can take up residence in inanimate objects.)

In popular belief, the *bla* is considered essential for the welfare and integrity of human life. It is connected to life itself, but a person can live, temporarily at least, after the *bla* has left the body. However, a person whose 'soul' has been captured by gods or demons becomes sick.

While Tibetans and related Himalayan communities, such the Yolmo Sherpas in Helambu or the people of Lubra in Mustang, believe in only one 'soul', *bla*, many other populations inhabiting the Himalayan high mountains, middle mountains and foothills share the concept of a plurality of 'souls'. In northeast Bhutan, for example, the number of 'souls' or 'life-forces' – known as *yong* in Tshangla, *phla/phra* in the Dakpa language, *srog* and *bla* in Dzongkha and Tibetan – can vary from three to seven, nine or fifteen, depending on which healer is asked.[28] In Nepal, the western Tamangs attribute nine 'shadow-souls', *pla*, to every person: these are associated with consciousness and emotion. At the time of death, lamas separate the nine *pla* from the body and conjoin them into a unitary soul that is reborn. On the other hand, *so* ('life-force') dies with the body.[29]

26 Jäschke (1881: 383).

27 *Rangjung Yeshe Dictionary* (2003: 1864).

28 Schrempf (2015a: 5 *et seq.*)

29 Holmberg (1984).

In Gurung beliefs, the body, an aggregate of elements – earth, water, fire and air – is made alive by the presence of a set of 'souls', *plah* (nine for men and seven for women).[30] For Kulungs, a Tibeto-Burman speaking population inhabiting eastern Nepal and influenced both by Hinduism and to a lesser extent by Buddhism, it is obvious that there are multiple souls (*law*) even if they do not all agree on their number (the number most frequently given is eight, which evokes totality). The Kulungs' discourse fluctuates between the idea of a collection of different souls and the idea of a single fragmented principle – an ambiguity that is reinforced by the limited use of the plural in the Kulung language.[31] In addition, as noted by E. Porée-Maspero,

> [B]elief in the plurality of souls [...] must be even more frequent than it appears when reading texts on this subject, since the European writer tends to speak of only one soul, even when several are involved, and the observer may not always have sought to know whether it was a single or multiple phenomenon when the language of those with whom he was dealing did not bear the mark of the plural.[32]

Among Shertukpens, both humans and animals are said to have several 'souls', *ayung*. A person is thus believed to have 'seven souls' (*ayung sit*) or 'twelve souls' (*ayung sinik*). Once again, there is no general consensus regarding the number, but everyone agrees that men and women, old people and newborn babies, have the same number of 'souls'. These souls, which are born at the same time as the individual, are considered to be essential to life, although no one is aware of or able to control them. One of these 'souls' remembers the person's past life after the latter's rebirth and in some cases even prompts the reborn child to talk about its former existence. Another stays at home and watches over the person's belongings. A third one accompanies the person when they go outside to work. A fourth one, known as *ding jagkhanpo* ('the grave's watchman'),

30 McHugh (1989, 1996).

31 Schlemmer (2011, 2015).

32 Porée-Maspero (1951: 156).

watches over a person's grave:[33] this *ayung* is the shadow of a person's body and never undergoes rebirth, remaining the shadow of a person's bones even after their death. It is said that when somebody is seriously ill this 'shadow soul' goes out and looks for a suitable grave for them.

By their multiplicity, the names and the functions attributed to some of them, the *ayung* evoke the *law* ('souls') of the Kulungs. Among them,

> [T]here is a soul named *hisulaw-himulaw* that gives strength to move. Another *karulaw-botolaw*, "the soul of the workplace and shoulders", enables a person to accomplish hard work. Another, *gnalilaw*, has a beautiful face, and is smiling, radiant and attractive. Another, *sayolaw*, "the soul of the top of the head", is the principle that gives an individual importance, respectability, superiority over others (if this soul disappears, a person lowers their head in shame).[34]

On the other hand, the Shertukpen *ayung* are in some ways also evocative of *'go ba'i lha*, 'guiding deities' that are an integral part of Tibetan popular religion. G. Tucci observes that *'go ba'i lha* appear in groups of five, seven, thirteen and twenty-one, and posits that they had as their origin 'protective souls, before they changed into protective gods on whom depend the bodily integrity of the individual'.[35] Like *ayung*, these 'personal protective gods' are said to be born with the individual, to reside in their body and to protect various facets of their existence. One of them stands at the side of a person after their death, at the time of judgement.

---

33 Until the 1940s, the Shertukpens disposed of the dead bodies in *Bo: lok* (*bo:* = 'face, mask'; *lok* = 'slope'), a hill slope bearing caves. Corpses, attached in a sitting position, were put on the benches if Thong, at their feet if Chhaos. Today, dead bodies are burnt or buried according to the lama's prescription whatever their status.

34 Schlemmer (2015). 'Il est une âme qui donne la force de bouger (*hisulaw-himulaw*). Elle est proche de celle qui permet d'accomplir les travaux pénibles (*karulaw-botolaw*, 'âme des lieux de travail et des épaules'). Une autre (*gnalilaw*) dote d'un beau visage, souriant, rayonnant, attirant. Une autre, l'âme du haut de la tête (*sayolaw*), est le principe qui confère à un individu de l'importance, de la respectabilité, de la supériorité sur les autres (si cette âme disparaît, on va la tête baissée, avec honte)'.

35 Tucci (1980: 193). See also Samuel (1993: 438–439); Dotson (2017).

Yung are described as mobile, vulnerable and impressionable. They can easily fly out of the body. Fright, a sudden physical shock or intense emotion are all states that prompt a *yung* to flee and thus eventually to be seduced or captured by a passing spirit or deity. Hence the person becomes physically weak and sick. Shertukpens describe the symptoms of 'soul(s) loss', *ayung likpa* (*likpa* = 'to be left behind, to stray behind'), as a lack of appetite, general weakness, loss of consciousness, disturbing dreams, insomnia, and other ailments that cannot be cured with Ayurvedic or Western medicine.[36] They believe the local ritual specialists *zizi* and *raoma* to be more effective than lamas in such cases. Indeed, if not dealt with, the loss of a soul may lead to serious illness.

Babies and young children (*nünü*) are particularly vulnerable to the 'loss of *yung*' (*yung likpa*). People therefore have to take great care with young children. As a preventive measure, whenever the latter are taken out of the house, they are fitted with a protective necklace that is slung diagonally across their upper body. These necklaces, known as *nünü riũ* ('amulet for babies and young children') are made of a 50-cm-long string covered in green or red felt onto which various things are sewn on either side of a small pocket containing a piece of the child's umbilical cord. These objects include offensive weapons said to ward off evil spirits and even to kill them, but also items that ensure that *yung* remain with the baby. The first of these include a piece of *bẽ/bȭ* – a tuberous rhizome like wild ginger – potent with the *zizi*'s spell, a piece of poisonous aconite root sealed in a cloth pouch, the dried leg of an eagle (or owl), the dried snout of a wild boar, the rattling tail of a porcupine, the head of a red hornet and a tiny knife. Among the second ones are the tail of a flying squirrel highly appreciated by *yung* for its exceptional softness; large seashells and small snail shells in which the *yung* can hide when a spirit is lurking nearby; or a small bell, the ringing of which indicates where the baby is at all times and invites the *yung* to follow them (see Photo 4.1).

---

36 The same symptoms are described by R. Desjarlais (1989) among the Yolmo Sherpas, a group in north central Nepal. By contrast, among the Tibetan refugees of Dhorpatan, a village in an east-west valley south of the Dhaulagri mountain, symptoms described by C. Millard (2007) were much more varied: mental illness, sore throat and fever, and pains moving around to different locations in the body.

Photo 4.1: *Nünü riũ*, an amulet for babies and young children

Likewise, when a baby sneezes, the mother or any other woman playfully shouts in time to the baby's sneezes: '*Tsering O!*' ('May you live a long life!' in Tibetan) and then at the next sneeze or smothered sneeze, she yells gleefully, '*Tashi. O!*' ('Good luck!' in Tibetan) both to bring back the 'soul' that might have wandered away from the child when it sneezed and as a long-life blessing.

Social attention may restore a fleeing soul. When someone accidentally scares another person, startling them, the former should whisper four times towards the person's chest or head violently to either side for fear that their case be further aggravated. In fact, each individual has 'fire' (*wangba*) in each of their shoulders and water in their chin, and any sudden movement due to fear or surprise could open the floodgates. This could cause the water in the chin to flow over the fire in either shoulder and, by extinguishing the fire, make the person even more vulnerable. Similarly, among Gurungs, 'if a person slips on a path, others will respond by laying their hands on the person's head and shoulders saying "*shah, shah*" to protect the victim of this minor shock from *phla* ("soul") loss'.[37]

37 McHugh (1989: 79).

The ritual performance

In January 2014, I was in Rupa and went to visit my friend Jamchhu. The next-door neighbor had called upon a *zizi* to perform a healing ceremony for his four-year-old daughter Sangge Dema, better known by the nickname Tutu. She had been running a high fever, which left her half-unconscious about twice a month. She had been taken to hospital in Rupa where the doctors had diagnosed epilepsy and prescribed treatment. When medicine had failed to cure her, her father had consulted a *zizi* to find out the origin of the illness and a way of improving his daughter's state of health. The priest had concluded that one of her *yung* had escaped. A ritual therefore had to be performed in order to restore it. It was around 8 am and *zizi* Pema Megẽji, a grey-haired man is in his fifties, had just arrived. The one-day ceremony was about to begin. The family asked me if I would like to stay and attend it. I readily accepted.

The 'soul-retrieval' ritual (*yung lungba*) is not usually performed in isolation but combined with a long-life ritual (*chhe sogshing sõba*). It is therefore more efficacious, so *zizi* Pema Megẽji maintained. It is worth noting that parts of one ritual alternated with those of another to the extent that it was not always obvious which ritual was actually being performed.

The first part of the ceremony – the identification of the *yung*'s location and the agent responsible – took place outside of the house, in a field where tomatoes had been picked a few months earlier. Pema Megẽji lit a fumigation of juniper wood and leaves, *posi*, to purify the place and to please the gods, and then set up the altar towards the forest in the south where the most dangerous divinities and spirits live. First, he erected a 'life-force tree' (*sogshing hing*), a small pine tree with two white flags (*phõ*) on the upper part of its trunk and five small squares of colored cloth on the first branches. He then hung a garland made of flattened winged seeds of *nampaling* (*Oroxylum indicum*[38]), used as a substitute for a flower

38 *Oroxylum indicum* is a species of a flowering plant that belongs to the family *Bignoniaceae* and is native to the Himalayan foothills. It is commonly called 'midnight horror', 'broken bones' or 'tree of Damocles'. The tree, which can grow 18 meters high, is a night-bloomer and its flowers are adapted to natural pollination by bats. The flowers form enormous seed pods – fruits – up to 1.5 meters long that hang down from bare branches, resembling swords. The long fruits curve downward and resemble the wings of a large bird or dangling sickles

offering, and 'a lead-rope' made of different colored wool whose other end lay in a little basket among balls of wool (*hang lom*). This rope links the human world to the world of spirits and makes communication possible between the latter and the priest: 'It works like a mobile phone', Pema Megẽji explained to me. He then set up a low wooden table covered with a green cloth that served as an altar and on this he carefully lined up the following objects: a piece of juniper wood from which he occasionally tore off large splinters to fuel the incense burner placed on the ground to his left; two pieces of a cloth sheet – one red and one white – to be used as garments by his spiritual helpers; an Assamese brass vase (*loto*) holding the stem of a plant used as a sprinkler; a metal measuring container (*bre*) filled with uncooked rice in which three incense sticks were planted and an orange-colored dice was placed; a silver bowl marked with the twelve animals of the zodiac (*nying*), its entire brim decorated with *nampaling* 'flowers', and containing water; a libation earthen pot (*khanda*); and two small bowls (*bati*) placed on a brass plate, one containing 'solid beer' – that is to say the grains left after extracting beer (*phok-mu*) – and the other filled with soaked rice. The contents of both bowls swelled over the brim, forming a peak shape; the offerings to deities are first and foremost beverages and food. Prior to the retrieval process, Pema had to find out the direction in which the soul had been stolen and who had taken it. While *raoma* travel into otherworldly realms in a possession-like state, *zizi* simply use divination devices and 'see'. As Yeshi Dorji explained, a *zizi*'s female helpers and divine wives guide him from outside, whereas *raoma*'s *armu* enter him every time he performs a ritual.

In his everyday clothes, but having cleansed himself and taken off his shoes, Pema draped a ceremonial scarf around his neck and sat on a mat in front of the altar (see Photo 4.2).

Then, closing his eyes, he began to sing incantations, punctuating them with libations and oblations of rice. One of his spiritual wives (*armu*) made sure his eyes were closed throughout this part of the ritual, so 'as to focus deeply on it and not even let the eyes flicker for a nano-second'. The

---

or swords in the night, giving the name 'tree of Damocles'. The seeds are round with papery wings.

Photo 4.2:
Pema Megẽji in front of the altar, and the rope linking the human world to the world of deities and spirits

same *armu* also relieves the *zizi* of any natural urge to urinate or defecate, which, by distracting him, may compromise the success of the ritual.[39]

Pema Megẽji sang in an obscure and archaic language that has very little in common with the modern Shertukpen language and is unintelligible, especially to the young generation. After a while, he took the orange-colored dice placed on the grains of rice and, after bringing it up to his forehead, he threw it three times. The second and third throws have to be identical to confirm the first result. The same number came out three times in a row: 3. This is the first clue. The priest then took out of the small bag he carried around his neck two new objects known as *pu-cho mu-cho*, 'men's and women's ornaments' and gave them to his spiritual helpers. He put a dagger with a decorative silver handle and a sheath (*tshongtho*) on the piece of white cloth intended for his *mokphẽ* (male guard and warrior), and he laid a necklace of semi-precious stones (*khik namkör*) and a silver hook (*z°rok*) with which Shertukpen women fasten

39 Thongchi and Thongchi (2019: 2).

their shawls on the piece of red cloth destined for his *armu*. He carried on chanting, looking carefully at the water in the silver bowl placed in front of him to see if the escaped 'soul' had returned. Nothing so far. Once again, he put his hand in his bag but this time it came out holding a small box containing some divination tools: cowrie shells and small dice. He threw these, repeating each gesture three times. Finally, he located the lost *yung*. It was with Jumu Wangsing, an important mountain deity (*phu*) who lives in the forest, not the sparse cold forest of mountain pines, but the hot, dangerous jungle down in the plains.[40] The eldest of a large number of sisters, she is reputed to have a short temper and to demand libations of rice or maize beer (*phok*) and bloody sacrifices, especially of sheep and white roosters. Pema talked to her for a long time and finally got her to release Tutu's *yung*. He thanked her with various offerings. He then looked once again into the water, moving it around with the tip of his knife to see if the *yung* had already come back. However, it was not the case. He carried on negotiating with Jumu Wangsing, pausing from time to time to see if the soul was there. He looked once again into the water. The 'soul' – a tiny, triangular brown particle – had come back. The *zizi* seized the 'soul' gently with the tip of his knife so as not to scare it. He laid it on a piece of cotton fabric on which he had blown some kind of *mantra*. Then he enclosed it in the soft cotton wad and placed it in a white ceremonial scarf, which he knotted carefully. Often, so people told me, the *ayung* appears in the form of a tiny white spider that disappears once reinstated in the body of the sick person. Interestingly, similar beliefs about spiders, insects or other small flying animals acting as mediators or messengers are shared among Tibeto-Burman speaking populations across the Eastern Himalayas and southwest China.[41] In both northeast Bhutan and in the adjacent Mon-yul corridor in Arunachal Pradesh, the 'soul' is returned to the patient via a spider that acts as a go-between. Furthermore, in the

---

40 A local mountain goddess, called Ama Jomo, is quoted by M. Schrempf (2015b) as the main protective deity of a female healer in eastern Bhutan. Ama Jomo's palace is located on Mount Kunka (Kun mkhar) in the pastoralist area of Merak (Me rag)/Sakteng (Sag steng) on the border area with Arunachal Pradesh.

41 For examples, see Schrempf (2015a: 13).

Tshangla language, the word for soul (which could also be translated as 'life-principle') is *yong*, while *yong-dama* ('female soul animal') is the term for spider. Similarly, in Khomakha, a dialect of the Dzala language spoken in the neighboring valley of Khoma (Lhuntse district), 'the words *phra* or *phla* can be used for both "soul" or "consciousness" as well as spider'.[42]

Having completed the negotiations and having secured the return of the lost *yung*, *zizi* Pema Megẽji cut the path that connected him to the realm of gods and spirits, and offered the upper part decorated with 'flowers' and still attached to the pine tree in thanks to Jumu Wangsing, keeping the lower part for his young patient as a protective item. The divination session had lasted more than two and a half hours. The *zizi* had successfully managed to establish direct contact with the deities and the spirits and asked them questions for which he read the answers by examining the position of the cowry shells or grains of rice he had thrown and the number on the dice. This process is repeated until the desired result is achieved.[43] The *zizi*'s tasks involves divination aimed at influencing the by definition random outcome of the ritual (see Photo 4.3).

42 Schrempf (2015a: 2). In Shertukpen language, a spider is called *presung*. Elsewhere in Bhutan, spiders act as harbingers. Tandin Dorji (2004) reports that in western Bhutan a spider needs to be found whatever the case. If not, the ritual has to be repeated. 'If the spider is black, it indicates that the "soul" has been brought back from a malignant spirit *bdud* and the white spider from that of a *dman* (pronounced *mem*), both a different class of malignant spirits'. See also Schrempf (2015b).

43 The process is well known among ritual healers: see among others Hamayon (1992). Spectator of a Bonpo soul-retrieval ritual performed in Mustang (Nepal), C. Ramble (2009: 218–219) remarks: 'It is a commonplace in the arena of Tibetan Studies that ritual performance is not just an exact reproduction of textual prescriptions. […] Perhaps the most spectacular liberty taken by Lama Tshultrim [the Bonpo priest] concerned the game of dice. [The text] *sTong rgyung* specifies that a failure on the part of the patient to win at least one of the three rounds is "very bad" (*shin tu rgan*). In fact what the lama effectively did was to change the rules of the game in the patient's favour, by declaring that one winning throw out of six was good enough'.

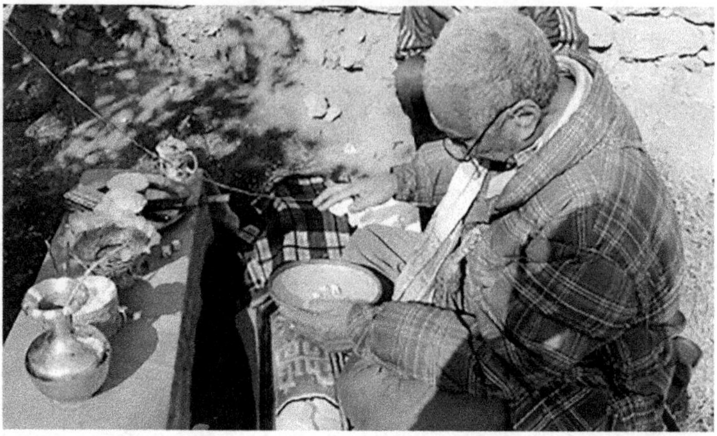

Photo 4.3: *Zizi* Pema Megẽji making divination with cowry shells

Once the 'soul' had been retrieved, the *zizi* went indoors to give it back to Tutu. The little girl had been washed from head to toe and dressed in clean clothes. She sat on her mother's lap beside the *zizi*. The latter began to chant a long litany, invocating all the deities to bless the ailing child with long life, and wrapped the multicolored protective thread (*hang ehek oho*[44]) he had kept from the gods' rope around Tutu's bare torso, lacing it in a very complicated path with numerous changes in direction (see Photo 4.4).

He knotted the white scarf that contained the recovered 'soul' across the little girl's chest. She had to keep it on day and night for three days, the time for the 'soul' to find its way and its place within the body. Then he knotted two other pieces of this multicolored thread around each of her wrists as protective bracelets (*phu-do hang*). In the meantime, the women of the clan and from the neighborhood had been invited for lunch. The elder women had settled in a room next to the one where *zizi* Pema Megẽji, Tutu and her mother were sitting, whereas the younger women stayed outside. Two young men in their twenties did their best to serve the assembly. Respecting the order of age, they brought each woman tea

44 *Hang ehek oho*, literally 'red and blue thread(s)': threads of various colors twined together and tied by the *zizi* around people's wrists and necks as amulets at the end of a ceremony, after rendering them potent with magical spells.

Photo 4.4: Pema Megẽji knotting the scarf containing the recovered 'soul' and different protective threads across Tutu's chest

and local beer to drink, then a dish of fried vegetables and fish with plenty of chili called *kaji*, which had first been consecrated by the *zizi* and also offered as oblation to the *lo* deities. The women finished their meal. They had been careful to leave a little food in their plates and drink in their cups. These leftovers, regarded as direct blessings, were collected from everyone into two separate bowls. They were offered to the little girl to eat and drink so that she could reintegrate with her clan, her neighborhood and more broadly, Shertukpen society. Before leaving, each woman placed a ceremonial scarf around Tutu's neck as a gesture to welcome the *yung* back home and as a blessing for the little girl. Finally, the *zizi* blew sacred utterances, which are believed to have magical powers, over a handful of rice and threw it at Tutu. Then he made her breathe incense and holy water. His work was now done. Tutu was strong again. The little girl was reunited with all her *yung*, blessed with long life, placed under the protection of her clan's tutelary deity and consolidated in her status as a member of the community. Nevertheless, while the retrieved *yung* settled down properly, she still had to be careful by, for example, not taking a bath. The priest also enjoined her family to observe *yam hiba* ('prohibit *hiba* [from entering] a house *yam*'), a confinement ritual. No outsider should be allowed to enter the house for the next three days. A wooden cross made of Nutgali tree (*Rhus semialata*), a wood believed to be the most potent repellent of *kharam*, 'curse',[45] was erected near the entrance to the house in order to let people know about the *yam hiba*. When the sick person is not a child, the *zizi* may also proscribe the former from doing any work or taking anything in their hands, except for eating food, for at least three days. This way of forbidding the use of hands for anything other than food is called *ik hiba*, 'prohibition (*hiba*) to serve with one's hands (*ik*)'. As evening fell, Pema Megẽji was offered a remuneration (*tangrap*) for the rituals he had performed. It usually consists of both cash and payment in kind: money is given wrapped in a ceremonial scarf; payment in kind consists of a winnowing basket full of uncooked rice, grains of corn and other cereals. However, before accepting the remuneration, the *zizi* had to thank his faithful allies – *armu* and *mokphẽ* – with songs and offerings of alcohol and food so that they returned home on a full stomach.

The combination of rituals that *zizi* Pema Megẽji performed on 15 January 2014 was regarded has having a successful outcome. A year later when I met Tutu, she was a healthy, happy child who no longer suffered from a high fever and febrile convulsions.

Conclusion

Rituals for calling the 'soul' or recapturing a wandering or lost 'soul' are well known among Tibetan and Tibeto-Burman populations throughout the Himalayas and are well documented. Shertukpens adhere to the same overall procedure that is followed in all healing rituals: the healer first diagnoses the patient as having a strayed or stolen 'soul(s)' as the cause of their problem; he then identifies the location of the 'soul(s)' and/or the agent responsible; he retrieves the 'soul' by recalling it and offering gifts and substitutes to the captor; and finally, he resolves the matter by reuniting the patient with their 'soul(s)'.[46] However, here, there is no question of a 'ransom': a practice that holds a prominent place among Buddhist and Bon rituals.[47] The *bla* may be seduced and taken hostage

---

45 *Karam*: 'bad eye', a type of curse, that can affect a person's health, their crops and cattle.

46 Schrempf (2005a).

47 Karmay (1998); Ramble (2009); Tucci (1980).

by all sorts of gods and demons, hence the idea of buying it back (Tib. *bla bslu*) with a ransom (Tib. *bla glud*), usually a figure modelled out of dough and resembling the sick person. After establishing in whose hands the 'soul' has fallen, the exorcist asks the captor to accept offerings while he implores the 'soul' to take up abode successively in various supports – thigh-bone, dice, turquoise, coral, wood and so forth. According to G. Tucci, the exorcist ultimately declares that the figure offered as a ransom (Tib. *glud*) is not lifeless or a dead thing but a living creature, and he invites the one who has robbed the 'soul' to release it from its bonds and to accept the *glud* in its place.[48]

Nothing of the sort is to be found in the Shertukpen *yung luba* ritual: if the captor readily releases the *yung*, he is thanked with offerings and gifts in exchange for his good will. However, if he is reluctant and refuses to set the 'soul' free, war is declared. The *zizi* sends his acolytes: *armu* as strategists and *mokphẽ* as guards and warriors. They confront the captor, vanquish him, and forcefully release the captured *yung*. If all fails, a *raoma*, regarded as a super *zizi*, takes over. In a trance, he travels to where the enemy is, sometimes travelling hundreds of kilometers on different mounts – bird, horse, elephant or even crocodile. Then, face to face with him/her, helped by his spiritual wives and his personal warriors (*mokphẽ*), the *raoma* fights until he secures victory and until the surrender or even death of the captor. The *raoma* carries three weapons: a metal claw fitted with a long chain, known as a *chakphor*, which he throws into every corner to capture malevolent beings; a small dagger with a silver sheath, *chhongtho*; and a *phurpa*, a ceremonial peg dagger with three side blades to transfix or to nail and thus kill any troublesome evil spirit once and for all.

Although the way Shertukpens conceive of the soul and treat its loss shows many similarities with the very diverse rituals performed by Tibeto-Burman speaking populations throughout the Himalayas, thus forging links over a vast geographical area extending north beyond the Tibetan plateau to Mongolia and southwards, to Cambodia and the Malay peninsula, it seems futile to me to attempt to sort them into, on the one hand, those who subscribe to an old collection of shamanic beliefs and, on

48 Tucci (1980: 191).

the other hand, those that would have come from Tibetan Buddhism, or to want to oppose the *zizi* to the lama. In fact, in the absence of any written document, it seems impossible to deduce the historical development of the conception of *ayung* and associated rituals. The ethnography reveals that people quite freely alternate between the *zizi* and the lama, using their services according to their own needs. While lamas 'who read from books' are called upon for death-oriented rites, *zizi* 'who speak from their mouths' helped by their spiritual wives and warriors, perform healing rites and life-reviving rituals.

Bibliography

Bawden, C.R. (1962). 'Calling the Soul: A Mongolian Litany', *The Bulletin of the School of Oriental and African Studies*, vol. 25, nos. 1/3, pp. 81–103.

Bjerken, Z. (2004). 'Exorcising the Illusion of Bon "Shamans": A Critical Genealogy of Shamanism in Tibetan Religions', *Revue d'Etudes Tibétaines*, vol. 6, pp. 4–59.

Bodt, T.A. (2012). *The New Lamp Clarifying the History, Peoples, Languages and Traditions of Eastern Bhutan and Eastern Mon*, Wageningen: Monpasang Publications.

Desjarlais, R. (1989). 'Sadness, Soul Loss and Healing Among the Yolmo Sherpa', *Himalaya, the Journal of the Association for Nepal and Himalayan Studies*, vol. 9, iss. 2.

Desjarlais, R. (1992). *Body and Emotion: The Aesthetics of Illness and Healing in the Himalayas*, Philadelphia: University of Pennsylvania press.

Dollfus, P. (2019). 'Sherdukpen: Local Religion: Pantheon and Priests'. In M. Carrin, ed., *Brill's Encyclopedia of the Religions of the Indigenous People of South Asia Online*, Leiden/Boston: Brill, pp. 683–692.

Dollfus, P. and F. Jacquesson (2013). *Khiksaba: A Festival in Sherdukpen Country (Arunachal Pradesh, North-East India)*, Guwahati: Spectrum Publication.

Dorji, T. (2004). 'The Spider, the Piglet and the Vital Principle: A Popular Ritual for Restoring the *sRog*'. In K. Ura and S. Kinga, eds., *The Spider and the Piglet: Proceedings of the First Seminar on Bhutan Studies*, Thimphu: Centre for Bhutan Studies, pp. 598–607.

Dotson, B. (2017). 'On "Personal Protective Deities" (*'go ba'i lha*) and the Old Tibetan Verb *'go*', *Bulletin of the School of Oriental and African Studies*, vol. 80, no. 3, pp. 525–545.

Fürer-Haimendorf, C. von (1952). 'The After-Life in Indian Tribal Belief', *The Journal of the Royal Anthropological Institute of Great Britain and Ireland*, vol. 83, no. 1, pp. 37–49.

Gerke, B. (2007). 'Engaging the Subtle Body: Re-approaching *Bla* Rituals in the Himalaya'. In M. Schrempf, ed., *Proceedings of the Tenth Seminar of the IATS, 2003. Volume 10: Soundings in Tibetan Medicine*, Leiden: Brill, pp. 189–212.

Hamayon, R. (1992). 'Le chamane 'joue' et gagne, ou L'action rituelle chamanique, sur la base de matériaux sibériens'. *Destins des rituels. Revue du Collège de psychanalystes* vol. 41, pp. 65–78.

Hamayon, R. (2013). 'Shamanism and the Hunters of the Siberian Forest: Soul, Life, Force, Spirit'. In G. Harvey, ed., *The Handbook of Contemporary Animism*, London: Routledge, pp. 284–293.

Holmberg, D. (1984). 'Ritual Paradoxes in Nepal. Comparative Perspectives on Tamang Religion', *The Journal of Asian Studies*, vol. 43, no. 4, pp. 697–722.

Huber, T. (2015). 'An Obscure Word for "Ancestral Deity" in Some East Bodish and Neighbouring Himalayan Languages and Qiang: Ethnographic Records towards a Hypothesis'. In M.W. Post, S. Morey and S. DeLancey, eds., *Language and Culture in Northeast India and Beyond*, Canberra: Asia-Pacific Linguistics, pp. 162–181.

Jacquesson, F. (2015). *An Introduction to Sherdukpen Language*, Bochum: Univeritätsverlag Dr. N. Brockmeyer, Diversitas Linguarum.

Jacquesson, F. (2016). 'A Note on Names, Ethics and Sherdukpens', accessed at https://shs.hal.science/halshs-04065987v1

Jacquesson, F. (2020). 'Sherdukpen Rupa, from Village to Township', accessed at https://shs.hal.science/halshs-04065987v1

Jäschke, H.A. (1881). *Tibetan-English Dictionary, with Special Reference to the Prevailing Dialects*, London: Secretary for State for India in Council.

Karmay, S.G. (1998). 'The Soul and the Turquoise: A Ritual for Recalling the *bla*'. In S.G. Karmay, ed., *The Arrow and the Spindle: Studies in History, Myths, Rituals and Beliefs in Tibet*, Kathmandu: Mandala Book Point, pp. 318–330.

Kvaerne, P. (2009). 'Bon and Shamanism', *East and West*, vol. 59, no. 1/4, pp. 19–24.

Lakhi, L., Stuart, C.K. and G. Roche (2009). 'Calling Back the Lost na53 mʑi53 Tibetan Soul', *Asian Highlands Perspectives*, vol. 1, pp. 65–115.

Lessing, F.D. (1951). 'Calling the Soul: A Lamaist Ritual'. In W.J. Fischel, ed., *Semitic and Oriental Studies*, Berkeley and Los Angeles: University of California Press, pp. 263–284.

Megegee, R. (2017). *Stratification and Social Change among Tribals. An Anthropological Study among the Sherdukpens of Arunachal Pradesh*, Delhi-Jaipur: Rawat Publication.

McHugh, E.L. (1989). 'Concepts of the Person among the Gurungs of Nepal', *American Ethnologist*, vol. 16, no. 1, pp. 75–86.

McHugh, E.L. (1997). 'Reconstituting the Self in a Tibetan Tradition: Models of Death and the Practices of Mourning in the Himalayas'. In H. Krasser et al., eds., *Tibetan Studies: Proceedings of the 7th Seminar of the International Association for Tibetan Studies: Graz 1995*, Wien: Verlag der Österreichischen Akademie der Wissenschaften, vol. 2.

Millard, C. (2007). 'Tibetan Medicine and the Classification and Treatment of Mental Illness'. In M. Schrempf, ed., *Proceedings of the Tenth Seminar of the IATS, 2003. Volume 10: Soundings in Tibetan Medicine*, Leiden: Brill, pp. 247–283.

Pommaret, F. (1999). 'The Monpa Revisited: In Search of Mon'. In T. Huber, ed., *Sacred Spaces and Powerful Places in Tibetan Culture. A Collection of Essays*, Dharamsala: Library of Tibetan Works and Archives, pp. 51–54.

Porée-Maspero, E. (1951). 'La cérémonie de l'appel des esprits vitaux chez les Cambodgiens', *Bulletin de l'Ecole française d'Extrême-Orient*, vol. 45, no. 1, pp. 145–183.

Ramble, C. (1982). 'Status and Death: Mortuary Rites and Attitudes to the Body in a Tibetan Village', *Kailash*, vol. 9, pp. 333–359.

Ramble, C. (2009). 'Playing Dice with the Devil: Two Bonpo Soul-retrieval Texts and Their Interpretation in Mustang, Nepal', *East and West*, vol. 59, no. 1, pp. 205–232.

Rangjung, Y. (2003). *Tibetan-English Dictionary of Buddhist Culture* (version 3), Kathmandu: Rangjung Yeshe Publications.

Rock, J. (1959). 'Contributions to the Shamanism of the Tibetan-Chinese Borderland', *Anthropos*, vol. 54, no. 5, pp. 796–817.

Ruhlmann, S. (2009). 'L'enterrement chez les Mongols contemporains : le cercueil, la tombe et la yourte miniature du mort', *Études mongoles et sibériennes, centrasiatiques et tibétaines*, vol. 40, https://doi.org/10.4000/emscat.1521

Ruhlmann, S. (2010). 'Les rites de naissance chez les Mongols Halh. La fermeture/ouverture des corps, des nourritures et du social'. In D. Aigle, I. Charleux, V. Goossaert and R. Hamayon, eds., *Miscellanea Asiatica, Mélanges en l'honneur de Françoise Aubin*, Monumenta Serica Monographs Series LXI, pp. 225–247.

Ruhlmann, S. (2013). 'Quand les âmes errantes des morts se déplacent accrochées aux poils et aux plumes des animaux sauvages. La vie post mortem des âmes en Mongolie contemporaine'. In K. Buffetrille et al., eds., *D'une anthropologie du chamanisme vers une anthropologie du croire. Hommage à l'œuvre de Roberte Hamayon*, Paris: Centre d'études mongoles et sibériennes / Ecole Pratique des Hautes Etudes, pp. 283–302.

Samuel, G. (1993). *Civilized Shamans: Buddhism in Tibetan Societies*, Washington, D.C./ London: Smithsonian Institution Press.

Schlemmer, G. (2010). 'Jeux d'esprits. Ce que sont les esprits pour les Kulung', *Archives de Sciences Sociales des Religions*, vol. 145, pp. 93–108.

Schlemmer, G. (2011). 'La politique des morts. Ancêtres, mauvais morts et modalités d'actions chez les Kulung Rai, une population de l'Himalaya'. In A. Bouchy and M. Ikezawa, eds., *La mort collective et le politique. Constructions mémorielles et ritualisations*, Tokyo: Institut des sciences humaines et sociales de l'Université de Tokyo, pp. 295–303.

Schlemmer, G. (2015). 'L'incomplétude des âmes. Collecter et lister dans les rituels des Kulung du Népal: des formes de préscience?' DOI: 10.13140/RG.2.1.3559.8881

Schrempf, M. (2015a). 'Spider, Soul and Healing in Eastern Bhutan'. In H. Havnevik and C. Ramble, eds., *Festschrift for Per Kvaerne*, Oslo: The Institute for Comparative Research in Human Culture, pp. 481–497.

Schrempf, M. (2015b). 'Becoming a Female Ritual Healer in East Bhutan', *Revue d'Etudes Tibétaines*, vol. 34, pp. 189–213.

Scott, J.C. (2009). *The Art of Not Being Governed: An Anarchist History of Upland Southeast Asia*, New Haven: Yale University Press.

Sharma, A. (2013). *The Sher Thuk Pens of Arunachal Pradesh: a Narrative of Cultural Heritage and Folklore*, New-Delhi: The Indian National Trust for Art and Culture Heritage (INTACH) and Aryan Books International.

Stein, R.A. (1972). *Tibetan Civilization* (trans. J.E. Stapleton Driver), London: Faber and Faber.

Tambiah, S.J. (1985). 'The Galactic Polity in Southeast Asia'. In S.J. Tambiah, ed., *Culture, Thought and Social Action. An Anthropological Perspective*, Cambridge MA: Harvard University Press, pp. 3–31.

Tenpa, L. (2018). *An Early History of the Mon Region (India) and Its Relationship with Tibet and Bhutan*, Dharamsala: Library of Tibetan Works and Archives.

Thongchi, Y.D. Jr and P.N. Thongchi (2019). *Shertukpen, Zizih Customs and Beliefs*, Guwahati: Spectrum Publication.

Tucci, G. (1980). *The Tibetan Religions*, London/Henley: Routledge and Kegan Paul.

5 Interpretive Shifts, Discourse on Possession and Reified Institutional Truths of Reincarnation Claims in Contemporary Sikkim

Kikee Doma Bhutia

Introduction

The presence of spirits, deities and non-human entities and the human possession by these deities are intrinsic to everyday life in large parts of the Himalayas. Well before I began exploring this theme academically, I observed exorcisms and rituals, witnessed cures, and took part in overnight rituals myself. While there are multiple academic works on spirit possession and trance in the Himalayas, this article primarily concerns itself with the different forms and interpretations of possession, and the frequently told and retold tales of possession in the Himalayan region of Sikkim. Usually, the forms of possession discussed in places across the Himalayas include 'voluntary and involuntary possession'[1] or 'solicited and unsolicited possessions'.[2] Whenever a person suffers from uncontrollable shivers, speaks in an unknown language, falls to the ground and starts to act 'crazy', multiple explanations are offered. Few of such explanations describe the experience as an 'illness', caused by the wrath or revenge of spirits or deities over delayed offerings, or perhaps due to the disturbance caused in the abode of the spirits because of *drib* or pollution and noise. At other times, such an experience serves as a step toward recognition as a *nejum* or *rnal 'byor ma* (shaman or ritual specialist). Recently, a third

1 Fisher (1989: 5).

2 Lewis (1971: 35). For further discussion on the difference between the 'voluntary and involuntary' and 'solicited and unsolicited' forms of possession, see Oesterreich (1922), Lewis (1971) and Hitchcock and Jones (1976).

alternative has arisen; especially among young women or others around them, the experience of possession can be cited as evidence that she is a *khandromas*,[3] a female divinity often considered as the reincarnation or an emanation of a Buddhist deity belonging to certain monasteries (in cases presented in this article from Tibet and Bhutan). Such an interpretation is not welcomed by most of the community members, which leads to a sense of shock and dislocation faced by the young women. One of the reasons behind such suspicions, I argue, is the effects of the underlying breakage in the existing indigenous practices and the growing institutional Buddhist prestige and popularity in Sikkim. Earlier, indigenous and Buddhist practices had undergone mutual forms of assimilation and integration,[4] but with the increase in immigration and multiplying communities and their differences, numerous beliefs, manifestations and interpretations have surfaced.

Ruled once by a Buddhist dynasty, Sikkim has undergone a drastic demographic shift. According to the 1981 census, the Nepali population multiplied to fifty-one percent, in the process reducing the indigenous Bhutias and Lepchas to the minority community in the region.[5] Such gradual process of change was quickened further with immigration from Tibet and other settlers from different parts of India, resulting in a radical ethnic mix influencing the religious and cultural life in Sikkim. In this

---

3 In order to maintain the original meaning of the term, I use *mkha' 'gro ma*, the Tibetan official term in the Wylie transliteration. For most of the Bhutia, Nepali and Lepcha vernacular and colloquial language cited here, I use phonological transcription to avoid skewing concepts specific to the region of Sikkim toward an orthodox Tibetan interpretation.

4 I address the exceptions to this rule – indigenous practices that were demonized – in another article titled 'Death by Poisoning: Cautionary Narratives and Inter-Ethnic Accusations in Contemporary Sikkim' (Bhutia 2021). Earlier probes into the lama-shaman relation in Sikkim, Nepal and among Bhutias, Gurungs and Sherpas were conducted by Balikci (2008), Ortner (1995), Mumford (1990) and Paul (1976).

5 Bhasin (2002: 5). Demographically Sikkim is a multi-ethnic state, consisting of Lepchas (Rong), also considered the original inhabitants of Sikkim, Bhutias (Lhopos), who have migrated from regions of Tibet and Bhutan, and Nepali, who immigrated during different periods of time from Nepal. Therefore, the language they speak is also mixed and most of my informants are bilingual and in some cases multi-lingual.

context, this article applies folkloristic perspectives to critically examine within the ethnically mixed population and reflect on an emergent vernacular Buddhism, in which institutional approval of new spiritual manifestations and practices is actively pursued. Young self-proclaimed *khandromas* emphasize that they are the 'reincarnation' and 'emanations' of Buddhist deities and adorn themselves in maroon and yellow monastic robes. Earlier, their performances of spirit possession, deity invocation, healing rituals and divination were undisputedly categorized as pre-Buddhist practices under the *pawos/nejums*[6] heading. Now, they try to break away from existing traditions and weave themselves into the prevailing Buddhist institutional practices. In this environment, where the demography is radically mixed, their position is further jeopardized due to multiple explanations from different community groups.

This article first explores the politics of plurality in this contested environment through the debate and pervasive criticism surrounding young women who claim *khandromas* status. Drawing on their life narratives as told by *khandromas* themselves, or in the 'memorates' of those surrounding them,[7] I contextualize the vernacular practices as interpretations of emanation and reincarnation reimagined through the emic perspective of the young *khandromas*. With such an experience, the *khandromas* enter into a sort of liminality where their position in the community is jeopardized with the handful of devotees who seek their advice on the one hand and the larger village community who discard them as 'fake', 'acting' or 'seeking attention' on the other.

This article thus brings out narratives about the young *khandromas* who seek social acceptance from the village they belong to and investigates the challenges and forms of ostracism they face during the process. I provide first-hand information[8] on how the difficulty lies not in their acceptance

6 *Pawos* and *nejums* are Lhopo (Bhutia) words to identify the ritual specialist, shaman, mediator, healer and indigenous healing practitioner. Usually, the *pawos* and *nejums* are chosen by the spirits or sometimes they inherit the tradition from their ancestors. The elaborate process of identifying and initiating *pawos* and *nejums* are discussed in Balikci (2008).

7 Honko (1964: 6).

8 Sources of the case studies include data from my fieldwork, collected between 2017 and 2019.

but in the experience that they go through individually. I outline my argument in light of two strong traditions – pre-Buddhist and institutional Buddhism – prevalent in the region.

My initial interest in the *khandromas* was triggered by observing Doma (twenty-three years old) who constantly suffered from uncontrollable bouts of possession in my natal village, populated mainly by Bhutia (known as Lhopo). This suggests my personal proximity to Doma by way of 'embodied experiences'[9] of belonging to the same village. Initially she was acknowledged as 'special' by her fellow villagers, but her inconsistency and irresolution including her temporary conversion to Christianity[10] led to a brief expulsion from the community and a general disbelief in her practice. The second *khandroma* I discuss is Dolma Rani – also known as Lashang Dolma Tamang. She was nineteen years old at the time of my study and resides in Pakyong village in the eastern part of Sikkim. The eldest of three siblings, she went viral across Sikkim in 2018 when a family member posted a video of her on social media that showed her being possessed. Soon, the enthusiasm gave way to unfriendly scrutiny as to her motives and mental health, both from her village community and online followers. Both these cases lead me to discuss the change and continuity surrounding pre-Buddhist traditions and institutional Buddhist practices in the village in terms of religious and personal beliefs. Before I venture into the complications within social and spiritual/supernatural trajectories, I first draw on various interpretations of *khandromas* already present in academic discussions.

What are *khandromas*?

In Tibetan and wider Himalayan Buddhism, the *mkha' 'gro ma* are highly institutionalized, often synonymously considered as *ḍākinī* and *yoginī*.

9 Csordas (1990: 5).

10 The Christians in Sikkim constitute 6.7 percent of the population, according to the 2001 census. In Doma's village there are three families who converted to Christianity in the 2000s. They were free to participate in village events such as weddings and funerals, however, when excommunicating Doma, the village authority (head monk) also made an unwritten rule that prohibited Christians in the village from taking part in any events in the village.

Scholars have offered varied definitions as well as interpretations, but the terms are usually translated as 'sky-dancer' or 'sky-enjoyer'. In this chapter, for clarity purposes I use *mkha' 'gro ma* for a better understanding and to differentiate between the existing *mkha' 'gro ma* tradition in Buddhism and *khandromas* as the emerging young girls claiming reincarnation. The most common understanding of the *mkha' 'gro ma* depicts them as 'a wrathful or semi-wrathful female *yidam*'.[11] Waddell, in turn, referred to them as 'goddesses with magical powers'.[12] Das in his *Tibetan Dictionary* defined *mkha' 'gro ma* as 'a class, mainly of female spirits, akin to [...] witches, but not necessarily ugly or deformed'.[13] He explained that there are two types of such beings: 'those who are still in the world and [those] that have passed out of the world [...] known as "the goddesses of wisdom" (*ye shes kyi mkha' 'gro ma*)'. In another interpretation they are referred to as great divine beings such as Yeshe Tsogyal (Ye shes mtsho rgyal) and Mandarava (Mandāravā)[14] – both known as great *yoginīs* and consorts of Guru Rinpoche.[15] Adopting this idea, there are *mkha' 'gro ma*, which fit into the latter category of worldly beings.[16] Lama Topden (sixty-two years old), one of my main interlocutors, explained to me that 'The greatest of *mkha' 'gro mas* are the consorts of Guru Rinpoche, but there are other "hybrid beings" who live among us to provide us protection and prophecies. They are human in the form of a divine being. They can perform magic and [are] referred to as the highest form of Buddhist deity'. According to him, such incarnations can be born only once in a century. Other kinds of *mkha' 'gro mas* are a group of female lay-religious practitioners that include elderly

11 See 'Glossaries' appended to *The Life of Marpa the Translator* (Chögyam Trungpa Rinpoche 1982) and *The Rain of the Wisdom* (Chögyam Trungpa Rinpoche 1980). Both of these texts were translated by the Nalanda Translation Committee under the direction of Chögyam Trungpa Rinpoche.

12 Waddell (1972: 180).

13 Das (1970: 180).

14 There are two translations of the life of the Yeshe Tsogyal: Dowman (1996) and Tarthang Tulku's translation. On Mandarava, see Chonam and Sangye (1998).

15 Guru Rinpoche is also known as Guru Padmasambhava and the Second Buddha. He is known for discovering Sikkim and introducing the form of Buddhism that is today known as Himalayan and Tibetan Buddhism.

16 Das (1970: 181).

women living a religious life without being formally initiated as nuns. Lastly, female partners (consorts) of male religious practitioners are called *sang yum* (*gsang yum*) or *khandro* (*mkha' 'gro*) (Pommaret 2015: 116).[17] Lama Topden continued, 'The mother of so and so Rinpoche and *trulkus* are therefore *khandroma* as well. Without any doubt, in some cases even sisters and nieces can be considered as one. They are *khandroma* just because of who they are. They do not have to perform. A real *khandroma* doesn't need to perform'. Within the established Buddhist belief, *mkha' 'gro ma* holds a rigid position which makes the recognition of the self-proclaiming *khandromas* challenging.

For example, in Nepal on 22 January 2020, a girl from the western part of Sikkim was enthroned as *khandroma* and it was celebrated all over Sikkim. I quote from the page of a website, *Buddhistdoor Global*, titled 'Khandro Tashi Chotso enthroned as Tulku in India':

> Khandro Tashi Chotso was born in Yuksom, western Sikkim. Her great-uncle was His Eminence Domang Yangthang Tulku Rinpoche (1929-2016), a highly revered Nyingma lama who was born in Sikkim, studied in Domang Monastery in Tibet, and, after 22 years in prison during the Chinese invasions, returned to Sikkim. Several years ago, Khandro Tashi Chotso was recognized as the reincarnation of Khandro Kunzang Chodron [regarded as an emanation of Vajravarahi] by Lama Akhyuk Rinpoche (1927-2011), one of the Tibet's most renowned meditation masters of recent times, who founded Yachen Gar Monastery. It is Yangthang Tulku Rinpoche's wish that his grandniece be enthroned as a recognized incarnation and serve the Dharma […].

Most of these interpretations imply *mkha' 'gro ma* is a divine being rather than a human. In cases when they are human, then usually they are someone related to a divine male or somebody in a human form with divine qualities.

The young *khandromas* that I have interviewed express that they face criticism due to their inability to show institutional affiliation and further because they have no divine connection. Often the village authority

17 Pommaret (2015: 116).

discards them as invalid because of their inability to solidify their position further. Below is a passage from my interview with Jigmi Lama.

> Q. Did you hear that there is a girl in – so and so – village who gets possessed by spirits and deities. During one of such possessions, she claimed that she is a *khandroma*. I heard that she is the reincarnation of Tāra,[18] therefore calls herself Dolma Rani. What do you think about it?
>
> A. All these girls calling themselves *khandroma* is purely suffering. The reason behind such pain is caused by *sdé* [evil spirits] who are trying to fool the masses.
>
> Q. But I also hear that they are offering divination and performing healing rituals. They are very effective.
>
> A. It is all a misunderstanding. Tell me one thing, if they are the real *khandroma* and incarnation of Dolma then don't you think, people from their monastery must be looking for them. Where are they? Why no monastery claims them? They should have been searched and initiated, if they are truly the incarnation of the Buddhist deities and belong to a monastery that they say they are from.

On the other hand, Doma mentioned to me that '*khandromas* are like *trulkus*' – explained problematically because *trulku* (*trulkus*, *sprul sku*) are often reincarnations of spiritual leaders and figures. One of the prominent examples is H.H. Dalai Lama and many more recognized by him. It is 'the idea that an eminent person may, after his death, be reincarnated in

18 Tārā (also Drolma) is known as a female bodhisattva and an important goddess in both Buddhism and Hinduism. She represents the female aspect of the universe, which gives birth to warmth, compassion and relief from bad karma as experienced by ordinary beings. She engenders profound sympathy for all living beings, but also acts to relieve suffering wherever she can. Amongst the various schools of Buddhism twenty-one Tārās are recognized in total. There is a dispute among scholars regarding the origin of the Tārā figure as a Buddhist or Hindu deity. For further reading, see Stephen Beyer's *The Cult of Tārā* (1978) and also H.H. Dalai Lama's 'Worlds in Harmony: Dialogues on Compassionate Action' (1998).

a young boy in order to continue his beneficent labor of guidance'[19] and often as reincarnations of spiritual leaders and figures, successors of an already established lineage.

The term carries an elusive sense; it is contested, fluid and open to interpretation. In such light, the intention of this article is not to review or incorporate different definitions and meanings but first and foremost to explore the new interpretation provided by the *khandromas* that I interviewed.

According to institutionalized Buddhism, the position of the *mkha' 'gro ma* is strict and clear. Firstly, they are divine beings; secondly, they could be the consorts or cohorts of religious practitioners; and thirdly, the relatives of the *trulku* and Rinpoche are acknowledged as one. The *khandromas* presented here are not considered divine beings, nor consorts/cohorts and relatives to the religious lineage holder. As the result of this, the process of acceptance and inclusion into the community becomes difficult. I will present in the proceeding sections how the processes of acceptance of *khandromas* are driven through a series of tests. Devoid of institutional affiliations and not backed by religious authorities such as *trulkus* and Rinpoches, the ordinary emerging *khandromas* and their test of authenticity and acceptance gets harder. In addition, their numerous forms of spirit possession and ritual parade categorizes them into the pre-existing belief of *pawos/nejums*, which are still strongly prevalent in the different parts of Sikkim.

Khandromas and their personal experience narratives: case studies

All ethnographic and folkloristic data presented here are the embodied experiences[20] of the *khandromas* and their key eyewitnesses.

---

19 Maraini (2000: 127).

20 Kirshenblatt-Gimblett (1989); Csordas (1990).

Case study of Doma

Doma has long suffered from repeated bouts of *chyi sey* ('to go crazy/ mad'). She would often get possessed by different spirits and subsequently speak in different languages, sometimes including Tibetan. She told me: 'My *sungmo* [protectress/deity] is actually from the monastery in Lhasa'. She emphasized that she is a slave to the deity and that she does what the deity wants her to do. Her body was therefore a vessel for a deity[21] to come and perform healings and assume responsibility for the wellbeing of the community and people seeking help. She continued,

> I started to get possessed when I was twelve years old. When I got possessed, I couldn't recognize my own house, parents and relatives. Seeing me suffer, my mother took me to Gyaltsab Rinpoche. He suggested that I should become a nun. So, I agreed, and my decision was praised and celebrated by the villagers. I became a constant visitor at the *mani lhagang* [village monastery] and together with other *mani aam* [village women who collectively on occasion visit the monastery for meditation and chanting mantras], I partook in village-level religious events and rituals. I adorned myself with a maroon robe and shaved my head. It was four years ago that I became a nun and actively participated, together with other monks of the village in rituals, funeral rites and other religious functions. Within these couple of years, I attended a nunnery in the western part of Sikkim. I felt like I was getting better. But one day, it started again. It was horrible, and I still remember. I ate eggs for dinner, and it seems the vegetables had garlic in them. I started to shiver intensely that night. Seeing me, my roommate ran away, but two other nuns helped me. They told me later that they thought I was going to die and started to offer prayers for me. Later I was taken to Geyzing hospital. My feet were paralyzed. I couldn't walk even. From Geyzing hospital, they referred me to Gangtok hospital. I was barely breathing, and I was given oxygen. Suddenly, on the way to Gangtok hospital, halfway, it seems I got possessed and started to cry and scream. My mother was

21 These deities differed in each case. Doma's deity is a *sungmo*, a protectress of a monastery in Lhasa. She didn't tell me the name as she said 'The deity will feel offended for revealing the secret knowledge that only I am entitled to'.

> with me by that time, she panicked and brought me back home to the village. But I was getting worse and worse. I don't remember any of it, my mother filled me in later. When I was possessed, I could see men dressed in monk robes. I don't remember it clearly who the person was, but I was very scared. Seeing my condition, my neighbor who was the only Christian family in the village suggested that I was tortured by some devil. Aju Pintso [neighbor] suggested that I should become a Christian and then I can be cured. In the hope of getting better, I disrobed and converted to Christianity. After that, everything changed.

Her decision to disrobe was frowned upon by the villagers and conversion to Christianity added oil to the flames, making the villagers bitter. The upset villagers ex-communicated the family and other Christian families in the village from participating in any social occasions, including funerals and weddings. Even after her conversion to Christianity and against the backdrop of village discontentment, her possession continued. On realizing that conversion couldn't cure her, she wanted to return to being a Buddhist. Her mother had to apologize in front of the entire village. Even though now she had rejoined the village community, the negative attitude of the villagers towards her did not change. Instead, now she was the 'drama queen' and considered a 'liar' by the villagers who had lost faith in her. On this, Amchung who is fifty-six years old, neighbor to Doma, and one of the *mani aam* of the village shared with me that when Doma became a nun, she was very happy: 'Even though I didn't have enough money, I went to offer her *khada* [traditional scarf] and I offered 200 rupees as offerings in praise of her becoming a nun. But it turned out that she was just lying'.

This was the initial period of Doma's possession when she suffered from uncontrollably strong seizures. Her mother thought she was sick and took her to multiple hospitals and ritual specialists to cure her. One day, her sister-in-law narrated to me, 'Doma became so strong that she literally pushed away four strong men who were holding her. It was very scary to watch her, gaining so much strength and remembering nothing of it once she was normal'.

Continuing her constant possession periods, and her mother's search for someone or something to cure her, Doma said,

> It's been two years since I disrobed. I am back in my village, and I still continued to suffer. The entire village community accused me of acting. But one day also during my possession period, it seems I was in a trance and through the power of my divination I revealed that I know a person who can help me in the eastern part of Sikkim. I seem to have told them his name and where he resides. You know I have no memory of it, but my mother and aunt began to look for him and they found Barapathing *pawo*.[22] It was only after I met him, then it all started to make sense. [...] You know what, I was suffering because I didn't have proper guidance. The main cause behind all these possessions was a deity wanting to contact my body and trying to turn me into her vessel. When Barapathing *pawo* came, he helped me. When my mother and aunt invited him home to see me, I got possessed and during that time he asked about me, "Who are you? Where did you come from? What do you want?" I do not recall these dialogues but later my mother told me. It seems, I uttered in trance state I belong to a monastery in Lhasa, Tibet. I am not a *nejum*, but a *khandroma*. You know *khandromas* are different than *nejum*. I am more monastic. My deity is not *yul lha gzhi bdag* but a *sungmo* of a monastery in Lhasa.

According to Doma,

> We are like *bharchey shyi-chuk* which means we can make the ill-luck disappear. I am a servant, and my body is a vessel for the deity to embrace and help fight and cure illnesses and bad luck and clear obstacles. Let's say you want me to perform divination, then I need to invoke my deity to come and perform divination. I should fully embrace and accept her. There is a particular *lha* (deity) – of whom I cannot speak with you – I should let her come onto me. Then I can perform divination. But it is not possible for me to perform being me then I am like you [human]. I need to invoke the deity and to do so I need to wear my robe, my headgear, sit on the throne and then only – only then – the deity can be summoned or invoked. I need to invoke them with mantras and *chum-*

22 Barapathing is the name of the place and a ritual specialist who lives there is referred to as Barapathing *pawo*.

> *dü* [rice offering]. I cannot tell you exactly what and how, but after the throwing of the rice and chanting of the mantras the deities come over my body. Today, many devotees from neighboring villages and also sometimes from Gangtok come to my door, when they are sick, when they need help and I provide them assistance with the help of my deity. (Interviewed on 19 November 2017.)

Case study of Dolma Rani

During my second field-visit to Sikkim, one morning in 2018 a Facebook post emerged on my newsfeed about a girl who was fifteen years old being possessed by spirits and performing a possession ritual in the eastern part of Sikkim. The next day, I got the contact number of her father and arranged a meeting hoping to speak to her. Upon reaching her home, twenty-eight km away from Gangtok, I saw Dolma Rani adorned in her maroon and yellow robes seated in her throne, meditating (see Photo 5.1).

Dolma Rani smiled and agreed to recount her experience and said,

> When I was a kid, I used to eat a lot of meat. My body always reacted, sometimes, I would get rashes and other times my tongue and teeth would get taut. Sometime after that I quit eating meat and chose to eat egg over them. But even with eggs, my heart would start to ache. These reactions were very serious that I would even miss school. Earlier, my mother took me to a *jhakri* [Nepali ritual specialist], and they told me that I am inflicted by some *murkhutta* [skeleton or spirit of the dead]. We offered elaborate rituals, but I didn't get better.
>
> It happened, one day at school, my teacher told me to read a Nepali text. While reading the text in front of the class, I started to mumble different words and began speaking in an unknown language. Nobody understood what I was saying, and I was shivering and sweating profusely. After that incident, I started to get sick often and due to which I would miss school and fail. I decided to change school. In my new school, students were expected to wear black school uniforms. I didn't know at that time that black color would affect me as well. One day, during school hours, my friend suggested that she would trim my

hair and help me get rid of the split ends. This was the day when I came to know that I have something wrong with my body, that I am not a normal girl. She started to trim my hair and my entire body started to shiver again and my cheeks turned red. My friend, scared, drenched me in water. They thought maybe I was hungry, so they also gave me some *momos*. But it so happened that the *momos* had garlic in it and it affected me more. After even a bite of *momo* I felt unconscious. When I was unconscious, I could see I was surrounded by monks and that they were carrying *radung* and *gyaling*. I saw I was surrounded by monasteries, big ones. I was in almost a comatose state, but I was seeing things and people. I was even trying to communicate. I felt, somewhere I was speaking in Tibetan language, but I didn't know what I was saying. My mother was called to school and she was panicky and scared. We had a neighbor there [pointing straight], he is a *tsampo* [meditation master] and seeing my condition he suggested I should be taken to the Chorten Monastery in Deorali, Gangtok. I was taken there, and I met Trulku Tome Rinpoche. Upon his audience, he suggested that I should avoid unclean food, meat and that I should recite mantras of the goddess Dolma (Tārā). He then blessed me with *thi* [pure/blessed water]. For some time, I felt better, but my possession continues. Usually after the audience with Rinpoche, whenever I get possessed, I would chant Tārā mantra and I would start to feel better, but it didn't stop completely. One day during such possession, I had told mother that I have a guru, who is in a monastery at Kalimpong.[23] My mother took me to the monastery and upon meeting my *guruji*,[24] it was then there when I found out that I am a *khandroma*, Dolma Rani, a reincarnation and that my deity is Tārā.

Q. Are you possessed by the deity or are you the deity?

A. Even I was confused for a long time. But my *guruji* told me that I am capable of invoking *deuta* [god/deity]. I can speak in a different

---

23 Kalimpong is a small town in West Bengal, India.

24 *Guruji* means teacher. Dolma Rani refrained from telling me who her *guruji* was, saying she is not allowed to reveal secrets of the people involved in the process.

Photo 5.1: Dolma Rani, 29 May 2018

> language and it is called *deu bhasa* [God's language]. When I close my eyes and invoke the *deuta*, it comes. I cannot tell you what I invoke otherwise the deity will feel like I am going against her and that I am not to be trusted. I do not remember what I do when I am taken over by the deity. My body is here but I feel like I am not controlling it. I am like a vessel for the deity to come and do her job [healing]. When people are sick, and they do not know where to seek help, they come to me. Sometimes, I feel like the deity is my mother and other times like a friend. But the deity never comes in her real form, to me she appears like a little kid and sometimes like a monk.

Her mother had told me earlier that they had a patient/client visit them because their son was under the influence of bad spirits and Dolma Rani had cured him. Dolma Rani's fame increased due to her social media indulgences which brought to surface scrutiny from people all over. The comments consisted of people remarking *Om tare tu tare tu re suha* (*Om Tare Tuttāre Ture Svāhā*) (Tārā mantra) showing support and devotion, but also speculation blaming her for seeking attention and having mental health issues. The people in her vicinity were partly annoyed due to the flow of people gathering at her door. Some of them even considered her an 'actress' (said by a shopkeeper).

According to Doma, she is a *khandroma* because she is a 'body' or a 'vessel' for the deity to enter and perform healing rituals whereas in the case of Dolma Rani, the deity appears outside of her in different forms, appearance and bodies. In both cases, there are uses of different items which play an important role, as well as wearing robes, sitting on a throne, and putting on headgear. Both of them agree that they are humans chosen by divine beings to become mediums. The argument made by the reputed monks from different parts of Sikkim goes strongly against the belief that *khandromas* are some kind of medium or divine being, therefore the paradigm of 'acting' and 'just being' becomes relevant. Lama Jigmi adds that a 'Goddess like Tārā is a *yeshe kyi lha* which means, they are liberated, and enlightened ones, and therefore cannot reincarnate into a mere human body'.

When I asked them both about the unacceptance and the scrutiny that they have received from the community members in their respective places, Doma answered with considerable apprehension,

> My mother gave birth to me and raised me. I never thought I would become *khandroma*. Nor did I choose to become like this. Everyone is born into something. I have no enjoyment. I don't even go out. At this very moment, I can only pray that nobody suffers like me in the coming generation. I wish they won't be born like me. It is very hard. Fight for yourself and fight with all. It is tiring.

Dolma Rani too echoed similar sentiments:

> So many of my friends accused me of acting and pretending to be sick. But let's think properly. Why would I act? I am fifteen years old which means this is my time to have fun and go out. So many girls of my age play on mobiles. Why would I choose to sit in this throne from morning till evening, offering divinations and curing illnesses? All this is only because my *deuta* [god, deity, *lha*] wants me to do it. I will only say that if they don't want to believe in me, then they are free to do so. But just because they do not believe doesn't give them [the] right to judge me. I didn't choose to become like this. I am doing what I am asked to do. That's all! (Interviewed on 15 June 2018.)

Change and continuity in the socio-religious setting

According to institutionalized Buddhist belief, rationalized by Lama Jigmi, '*khandromas* are the highest form of female deities and they should not act but just be'. He further elucidated that their suffering is because of the dichotomy of someone 'acting' rather than just 'being'. This is reflective of the pre-Buddhist beliefs that still have a strong hold in the minds of the people. In this section I focus on two main questions: from what kind of pre-existing beliefs are the *khandromas* trying to distance themselves, and why do they struggle to gain social support for being *khandromas*?

Buddhism, even though familiarized in Sikkim in the eighth century by Guru Rinpoche, didn't flourish or establish itself until the state formation of its kingdom. In the seventeenth century, three Tibetan lamas – Lhatsun Chenpo, Karthok Rikzin Chenpo and Ngadak Sempa Chenpo, otherwise known as the Three Patron Saints of Sikkim – hailing from three different directions met at Norbugang, Yuksom in west Sikkim and decided to establish a Buddhist monarchy. This culminated in the crowning of the first spiritual and temporal king of Sikkim, named the *chogyal*.[25] Following this event, the three lamas along with the king worked towards bolstering Buddhism by setting up multiple monasteries across Sikkim, seeking to establish Buddhism as the national religion. Thus, through its royal patronage, Buddhism became popular and spread all across Sikkim. The spread of Buddhism not only involved the conversion of people, but also the process of converting the deities inhabiting the land into Dharma Protectors (Chos Kyong sung ma). Together with the local ritual specialists belonging to different communities and lamas, they were adept at devising new and improved techniques to deal with the local deities and subjugate them.[26] Data collected from Tibet, Nepal and Mongolia shows examples wherein spirit mediums (shamans) and monks/oracles (lamas) have been portrayed as rivals;[27] often in similar cases where one is needing to tame or domesticate the other[28] or lamas are functioning as

---

25 Title of the Sikkimese kings. From Tibetan *chos*, Dharma and *rgyal po*, king, or the one who rules according to religion (Balikci 2008: 378).

26 DeCaroli (2004); Balikci (2008).

27 Mumford (1989).

28 Day (1990); Bellezza (2005).

substitutes for original shamans.[29] In the context of Sikkim, Anna Balikci writes in her book *Lamas, Shamans and Ancestor: The Village Religion of Sikkim*, 'The *pawo* (*dpa' bo*) and the *nejum* (*rnal 'byor ma*), the male and female shamans of the Sikkimese Lhopo, have remained independent of the Buddhist establishment and, for the most part, were neither suppressed nor greatly influenced by the lamas'.[30] This argument in terms of the *khandromas* case might have some loopholes. Due to strong pre-existing beliefs and institutionalized Buddhist set rules, the *khandromas* are subjected to scrutiny and are often ostracized in their practices and not recognized. This ostracism is also partly due to, according to a monk, the fact that 'they are the victims of spirits tortured for their wrong deeds' (Jigmi Lama, seventy years old). The 'wrong deeds' presumably include defying normative dictations of the community and the institutional – in this case Buddhism. The 'wrong deeds' imply their performance of spirit possessions and trance. Additionally, the 'wrong deeds' could also include conversion to Christianity as in Doma's case and social media displays of possession rituals as in Dolma Rani's case. In the two different cases presented, while unknown to each other, both suffer from the same kind of 'illness' or 'illnesses', leading them to become either recognized or self-professed as *khandromas*. One of the prominent themes argues that they do not belong to pre-Buddhist tradition (*pawos/nejums*), but rather they trace their origins to the monastery and monastic institution (*mkha' 'gro*). These negotiations and gradual attempts at integration have been at play for decades. Essentially, this involves representatives of different faiths, as Bellezza writes, 'a variety of religious specialists, both male, and female, who through distinctive ritual techniques "call down the gods", embody the spirits, reveal truths and give advice to the local community.'[31]More specifically, Bellezza continues, when possessed by the deities, the mediums 'heal sick people and livestock, exorcise evil spirits, bring good fortune to those struck by bad luck, and predict the outcome of the future events'. The ability to become possessed and perform healings has subjected the

---

29 Heissig (1953).

30 Balikci (2008: 3).

31 Bellezza (2005: 1).

khandromas to claims they are *nejums*. Their own testimony that when in trance they are *khandromas* rather than *nejums* is rejected.

In Sikkim today, the belief in spirit-mediums and spirit possession is endangered but has not entirely disappeared. The reasons include, first, the increasing popularity of Buddhist institutional practices and rituals; and second, rarity in the number of ritual practitioners who are recognized and are capable of performing healing rituals. Moreover, these few practitioners are not easily accessible and 'inviting them every time and the ritual proceedings are far more expensive than the Buddhist rituals' (Aju Pintso, fifty-four years old).[32] The reason for the discrepancy in the divisive treatment of *khandromas*, as most of the interlocutors explained, is partly because the practices are clearly pre-Buddhist. To build along these lines I would like to present an interview excerpt conducted with Doma's neighbor Amchung in the winter of 2018 after Doma had claimed herself as a *khandroma*.[33]

Q: So, I hear Doma is a *nejum*?

A: No, not *nejum*, she considers herself *khandroma*, at least that's what I hear. But if you ask me, I doubt her claims of being anything.

Q: Why is it so?

A: It is better not to have too many *nejums* or *khandromas* like her. It is better to have more reincarnations of lamas like *rinpoches* and *trulkus*.[34]

---

32 The conversations around 'expensive rituals' were common among the Christian convert locals. Some said that Buddhist rituals are expensive, and others said that the reason behind such costs includes inviting both lamas and shamans to perform the rituals as they occur side by side in most cases.

33 The claims of being *khandroma* were very new. *Nejums* are usually mediators and ritual specialists, whereas *khandromas* are higher in status and they are closer to the institution of Buddhism due to the emanation related to the Buddhist deities.

34 *Trulkus*, *sprul sku* generally refers to spiritual leaders and figures, successors of the already established lineages. They are also known as bodhisattvas or Buddhas. On *rinpoches* and *trulkus* there are many academic works available. See for instance: Aziz (1976); Bärlocher (1982); Gyatso (1991); Brauen (2005); Chayet (1985); Diemberger (2007); *Unmistaken Child* (2009: Documentary movie); and

Q: Why is it bad to have more *nejums* and *khandromas*?

A: You see, then the *sdé* increases too. If the number of people who can feed them increases, then the number of those spirits who eat them increases too, *sdé* will not sleep then. If there are no *pawos* and *nejums*, then they can sleep, no one will feed them, no one can mediate their desires and demands and their hope for food (offerings) will disappear too. If we have more *rinpoches* and *trulkus* then even obstacles will be cleared. It is more of a blessing.

According to Amchung, the majority of *pawos* and *nejums* are subjected to awakening the sleeping/resting spirits and deities by invoking and making offerings to them through spirit possessions and ritual performances. Aju (sixty-seven years old), from the same village, warned me, '*ssshhhh*, don't wake them, don't speak about them. Let them sleep and let them remain silent'. There is an emphasis on how the spirit mediums are subjected to interfere in the abode of the deities and awaken them.

(Not) finding a path and failed initiation

In the experience of the *khandromas* whom I have interviewed, they deem themselves to be stuck in *bhalethule* ('in-between' in Bhutia language or *lhokay*); *bato napayera* (literally translated as '[not] finding a path' or 'in between stage' in Nepali). In the timespan between one's recognition by a teacher and the moment one properly practices one's craft by performing healing rituals, divinations and propitiations (annually), *khandromas* find themselves stuck in 'liminality'. This liminality, I argue, is caused by the hardship in adapting oneself to the already existing tradition. The inability to grasp their position during the possession situates them in an 'in-between' stage where they cannot understand where they belong. Victor Turner, in his *Liminality and Communitas*, began to explore the concept of 'liminality' by describing particular individuals as 'neither here nor there', 'betwixt and between' the positions assigned to them and arrayed by law, custom, convention and ceremony in various life stages.[35] He points out that

---

Baratz (2009). Also, see Germano and Gyatso (2000) and Wylie (1978).

35 Turner (1969: 95).

liminality can be seen in many areas when there is a 'release from normal constraints, making possible the deconstruction of the "uninteresting" construction of common sense, the "meaningfulness of ordinary life"'.[36] He calls this attribute of liminality or of liminal personae 'threshold people', which is ambiguous, within which the conditions and network of classification of a person are jeopardized into a position of uncertainty where one's status is not secured. Even though the spirit mediums like *pawos/nejums* have always been liminal, the *khandromas*, to overcome their liminality, carve for themselves certain 'rites of passage'[37] which would 'accompany their every change of place, state, social position and age'.[38] Such passages include (failed) Christian conversion; associating with the institutionalized tradition; searching for an authorization of their liminal status in Buddhist tradition; and acknowledging themselves as *khandroma* (instead of *nejum*) to seek recognition and reaggregation in the community.

Van Gennep in his work *The Rites of Passage*[39] describes 'rites of passage' as having a three-part structure: separation, liminal period and re-assimilation. In the case of pre-Buddhist beliefs and among *pawos/nejums*, traditionally the 'rites of passage' could be passed through 'initiations' and installations conducted by the senior and experienced *pawos/nejums*. In above presented data, this 'rite of passage' is somewhat provided initially – in Doma's case by Barapathing *pawo* and in Dolma Rani's case by her *guruji* from Kalimpong. Such initiations include the ritual performance of initiation and invocation when the deities are summoned and tied to the healer. Traditionally, the initiations would solidify their liminal positions and elevate their status in the community as official ritual performer. But in both cases under discussion here, these initiations failed. In both cases, the senior ritual healers were able to recognize that the young women were 'special' and had acquired the power to mediate but that they were not at the same level as the senior ritual healer. In cases like these, the senior ritual healer understands that the person is a 'mediator' but not

36 Turner (1969: 95).

37 Van Gennep (1909); Turner (1969); Honko (1964).

38 Turner (1969: 94).

39 Van Gennep (1909).

nejums – rather *khandromas*, which require extra assertion in terms of framing and congealing their distinctive position, which they failed to do in these cases. In a section entitled 'Initiation Ritual', Balikci narrates the story of the failed initiation of a *nejum* in Tingchim village in Sikkim. She writes, '[…] Yeshe Gonpo failed to take possession of her as head of all *pho lha mo lha*, and instead, she kept repeating in trance that she wasn't a *nejum* but a *khandro* (*mkha' 'gro*), a manifestation of the celestial female deity of Buddhism'.[40] Later, in a discussion of the *pawo* of Lachung, she writes that '[…] he concluded from the deities manifesting themselves through her that she was of different tradition and for this reason, the *pawo* could not help her any further in becoming a successful *nejum*'.[41]

This aspect of 'different tradition' or the emphasis on 'requiring extra assertion' plays a major role that deciphers an eclectic mix of pre-existing beliefs and institutional Buddhism; therefore, I consider it as an emergent vernacular form of Buddhism. Within such grounds, the *khandromas* find themselves 'liminal' between these two strong traditions. It is not only the two strong traditions that need to accept and recognize them but also the community. As Doma says, 'I am just a lost servant in search of my master and recognition as *khandromas* from my community'.

In such a situation, for Doma even after the realization that she is *khandroma*, she remains in a liminal stage where she has become a bridge or a link between the human and non-human realms. This suggests that the liminality is not something that can be overcome but is rather a shift in practices one must accept and adjust to permanently. By the time my fieldwork had ended, the villagers had still refused to accept Doma as a full-fledged functioning *khandroma*. This refusal adds complexity to Doma's position as a community member. She remained 'liminal' both before and after becoming an (almost) initiated *khandroma* because her position can only be firmly settled after the acceptance or recognition from the community. In another sequence of events, Dolma Rani sought approval from the community through narrating a vision, or a future that is interpreted through her dreams: 'I mostly see monasteries in my dreams – a river where leaves fall off a tree – floating – bridges and beyond a bridge

40 Balikci (2008: 156).

41 Balikci (2008: 156).

I see a monastery. I see a monastery in Bhutan called Tashigang. I want to go there. I want to take refuge and retreats. I hope one day, I will be able to do so. At the moment, I still need to make sure that the community understand and accept that I am the reincarnation Dolma Rani'.

For the village community, on the other hand, the *khandromas*' position is often subjected to doubts and disbelief, which are further strengthened when the representative of the institutionalized tradition does not allow such 'transitions' to occur by adhering to the 'traditional' definition of *khandroma*. When devotees flock to their doors from neighboring locales to seek their advice and healing, *khandromas* are hopeful of gaining recognition within their own community in the near future. Dichen, Doma's relative, recollects 'Many people come to seek her divination from Phodong, Ramthang and even from Gangtok. She is becoming stronger day by day'. Even Dolma Rani's mother exclaimed, 'We have many devotees, from different backgrounds coming to see her. You need to make an appointment next time you come. Even today, someone is coming right after you leave. They are from Gangtok'.

This suggests that the ritual healer cannot achieve installation into the community merely through self-realization. Neither can they achieve it through the acceptance of a deity as their protector nor through initiation by a master. Inclusion into the communal hierarchy by the villagers and the community is important. It must involve collective community recognition of the *khandroma* and thereby result in elevating them to the position of a village ritual specialist – other than *nejums* – within the local social hierarchy. It is this social elevation to the position of ritual specialist and the acceptance of liminality from the community that amount to a 'rite of passage', confirming that *khandroma* refers to a social status rather than a spiritual entity.

Motifs in the vernacular *khandromas* tradition

This section seeks to explore continuities in narrative tropes and motifs in the presented case studies in a table above.

As I talk about possession and *khandromas*' personal experiences, the narratives of possession share similarities and tropes. This begins with multiple involuntary bouts of possession and is aimed at seeking

Table 5.1: Narrative tropes and motifs of possession

	Doma	Dolma Rani
1st phase	• Uncontrolled possessions • Meat/garlic • Changes in language (speaking in Tibetan) • Strength to throw four men holding her • Role of a mother	• Uncontrolled possessions • Meat and garlic • Changes in language (speaking in *Deo bhasa*) • Black colour • Trimming the hair • Role of a mother
2nd phase	• Seeking *rinpoche/bongthing* • Accused of acting/drama queen	• Seeking *trulkus/rinpoche* • Accused of acting/seeking attention
3rd phase	• Dreams and visions • Servant of the deity • Healer/prophetess	• Dreams and visions • Mediator/vessel of the deity • Healer

communal acceptance. The involvement of the authorities in both cases and accusations of 'acting' subjected the young women to further distancing from recognition. Additionally, the strong role of their mothers who are particularly subjected to the retelling of their experiences corresponds to their liminal status. The retelling is a means of consolidating their story and is geared towards shaping popular imagination. When I visited Dolma Rani, her mother was the first person who spelled out to me the possession experiences and suffering journeys of her daughter. Such retelling helps *khandromas* to relive their experiences and forge a connection between themselves and the events that happened to them which they most often fail to remember. Oftentimes the *khandromas*' memories are blurred and spaced when the trance occurs, but these gaps are later filled by family members, especially mothers, who are witness to their bouts of possession. Mothers' roles are not only confined to retelling: they are the closest to the *khandromas* in understanding them and therefore helping them in the proceeding steps. They also play an important part in validating the clients/devotees visiting them by hosting them and translating the results of the illnesses. In Doma's case, the conversion to Christianity, and in Dolma Rani's case, social media played a pivotal role in them being scrutinized by the spectators. It is also important to highlight that the devotees who flock to their doors are 'outsiders' while the communities they seek validation from are their village community. In both cases, we also find a discourse on social realities, such as ethnic, communal and religious differences. Doma is a Lhopo in a Lhopo-dominated village (eighty-two Bhutia Buddhist houses in total) and therefore she was easily accepted in the beginning, but later due to her conversion, doubts arose. She occasionally retreats to the basement of her house and performs meditation and other Buddhist rituals such as chanting mantras and making offerings to deities. Dolma Rani, on the other hand, belongs to the minority community (Tamang). The small town she comes from is a community formed by a variety of different ethnic backgrounds. The majority are Nepalese, but they live side by side with Indian merchants, Bhutias and Lepchas. I consider her a minority because even though Tamang and Sherpas are a sub-tribe of the Nepali community, they are Buddhist in their religious affiliation. The Tamang families living in the locality also constitute a small minority compared to the dominant Nepalese and Indian (Hindu) community – thereby rendering them a minority amongst other minorities.

'Kunchok sum has descended one step down'

This section is dedicated to one of the leitmotifs common among almost all the participants in the interview process. The theme of 'Kunchok sum (Triple Gem) descending one step down' forms a level of consistency among both the *khandromas* and their spectators. Since their village communities disregard their bouts of possession as acting and seeking attention, the *khandromas* find other means of validation. Any form of small recognition whether from the outside community or from any higher authorities from different backgrounds is considered as a proof of Kunchok sum trying to help them. They use the phrase and interpret it as a form of their genuine suffering and genuine practices. Doma exclaimed to me, 'Kunchok sum has descended one step down and it is true. Sooner or later, the villagers have to accept me because sooner or later they will realize that I am true'. Doma is hopeful that one day villagers will accept her as an active member and realize the power she inhabits.

On the other hand, for the villagers, this same phrase is interpreted to be the equivalent of 'time will tell' – now that Kunchok sum has descended one step down, they cannot lie for much longer. For the spectators, the phrase stands for patience for a time when the truth will be revealed, and it will be proven that the *khandromas* are 'fake'. To elaborate, Laden Ama, an elderly village woman from Doma's village, narrated to me a particular possession event that happened to Doma in the village recently. Doma had a client (a woman) from a nearby village, seeking her assistance because her husband was suffering from an illness. This illness was in the form of possession and Doma's divination explained that he was under the influence of an evil spirit and needed to appease the spirit. Harking back to one such experience witnessed by Laden Ama, she narrates that, at one point, Doma became possessed by the 'spirit of the dead' who belonged to her oldest son who had died four years earlier. Doma cried out and said, 'Sherap [pseudonym for Laden Ama's second son], I didn't receive proper *gyo* [death ritual offering].[42] Will you please offer a ritual for me?' Spitting in anger, the old lady exclaimed, 'How dare she? My son, if his soul came back and got a chance to interact with us. Do you think, he will say that he didn't receive a proper ritual? Won't he be happy to see us? Won't he ask us about our wellbeing? She is a liar. I tell you, it will be possible for her to lie or pretend only for a short time, as Kunchok sum has descended one step down'.

Kunchok sum is interpreted as the Triple Gem, consisting of three components: Senge, Chö and Gedun (Buddha, Dharma [the law] and Sangha [the religious community] according to institutionalized Buddhism). The fact that the *khandromas* seek social acceptance and not a spiritual resurgence shows that institutional approval is more important than spiritual awakening. In the local context, 'Kunchok sum has descended one step down' is a form of proverbial saying, which is usually used as a curse in the form of wishing something bad will happen to someone else in future. In earlier times, people could do wrong and get away with it, but these days wrong deeds cannot remain hidden for long.

In another local context, it could also be used as a form of appreciation when justice is done, or when a kind of reward is bestowed. Kunzang, a

42 *Gyo* is a death ritual offered to bring peace to the dead and allow them to find their path. It doesn't only function as a death ritual but also in a social context: if a family member of the deceased is not able to perform a proper *gyo*, it often brings shame to the family. It is considered as a bridge between the living and the dead.

villager, returned from her pilgrimage to Bodh Gaya, Bihar. She received an audience with H.H. Dalai Lama and upon her return claimed that she was now able to meet her god and that she believed Kunchok sum had descended one step lower and that it is true.

Being close enough to be able to meet one's gods and the fact that nothing truly remains hidden for long are some of the explanations of the saying that were narrated to me. In this article, all such interpretations are played out in different circumstances. Kunchok sum here breaks away from the established idea and provides a literal and figurative metaphor in reference to the religious and local village authority involved in the acceptance and rejection of the *khandromas.* It implies a form of hope that one day God will help *khandromas* establish themselves in the form of communal acceptance and conversely that the community seeking the truth will expose them as false.

It was used by the villagers to show their disbelief and by the *khandromas* to indicate their authenticity. The belief in reincarnation which began in the thirteenth century in Tibet gradually achieved enormous success and was adopted by nearly every Buddhist school in that country. In fact, almost every significant monastery is headed by a reincarnated *trulku* (phantom body / boddhisattva). The *khandromas,* claiming they are like *trulkus,* are often subjected to certain pressure from the community to prove their credibility by performing miracles or healing people. This performance of possession therefore can be seen as removed from the local cultural knowledge yet influenced by it to some extent. The challenges faced by the emerging *khandromas* highlight to some degree the problem of disintegrating tradition and the social exclusion and hardship of gaining social authority in the context of emerging beliefs and at the same time conforming to the established traditions.

Conclusion

In this article, I have discussed the problems and challenges faced by the *khandromas* in constituting and reinforcing the new interpretation of reincarnation into the institutionalized Buddhist tradition, far removed from the pre-existing practices of spirit possession and trance by *pawos and nejums*. The case study evidence shows the shifting and blurred boundaries surrounding the discourse, doctrines and reformulation of reified institutional truths. The *khandromas* are trying to escape the folds of pre-Buddhist traditions and are trying to gain acceptance within high Buddhism for better visibility and respect. The challenge to be included, which depends upon the acceptance of the institutional authorities, is discussed through the changing interpretation of the Kunchok sum. In all these cases, the community and institutional recognition are posing a threat to the *khandroma* as an entity and as a community member. Living in a close-knit community where the role of the lamas, shamans and deities are explained through illnesses and placation, the silence and disbelief surrounding the *khandromas* are examples of the purgatorial space (the emergent practices) between pre-existing beliefs and institutionalized Buddhist beliefs. The purgatorial space, I argue here, is the tussle between the agency of power divided between the lamas, shamans and existing official institutional narratives and the local narratives and interpretations of them. Even though those of the pre-Buddhist faith have converted to Buddhism and the deities of the land were subjugated, the process of subjugation was done only partially, as shown in these case studies. Total conversion to Buddhism must have faced multiple challenges, due to remoteness from the monastic institutions and the royal palace, the existing syncretism due to the immigration of Tibetan Buddhist reincarnates, local narratives of resistance and Sikkim related lamas and shamans.

Acknowledgements

This research was supported by the Dora Plus Sub-Activity 1.2, which is funded by the European Regional Development Fund and implemented by the Archimedes Foundation. I am grateful to Tingchim villagers and Dolma Rani's family for sharing their knowledge with me. I further thank my supervisor Ülo Valk as well as Dorothy Noyes, Anna Balicki

Denjongpa and Marc Henri Deroche for their feedback on a draft of this paper. I am also grateful to Seiji Kumagai, Françoise Pommaret, Miguel Alvarez Ortega, and other members of the 'Religion, History and Culture in Bhutan, Sikkim and Arunachal: Towards the Establishment of Eastern Himalayan Studies' panel held at the conference of the International Association of Tibetan Studies (IATS), Paris 2019, for their support and constructive comments.

Bibliography

Aziz, B. (1976). 'Reincarnation Reconsidered: Or the Reincarnated Lama as Shaman'. In J.T. Hitchcock and R.L. Jones, eds., *Spirit Possession in the Nepal Himalayas*, New Delhi: Vikas Publishing House, pp. 343–360.

Balikci, A. (2002). 'Kangchendzönga: Secular and Buddhist Perceptions of the Mountain Deity of Sikkim Among the Lhopos', *Bulletin of Tibetology*, vol. 38, no. 2, Gangtok: Namgyal Institute of Tibetology, pp. 5–37.

Balikci, A. (2008). *Lamas, Shamans and Ancestors: Village Religion in Sikkim*, Leiden: Brill.

Bärlocher, D. (1982). *Testimonies of Tibetan Tulkus: A Research Among Reincarnate Buddhist Masters in Exile*, Zurich: Tibet-Institute.

Bellezza, J.V. (2005). *Spirit-Mediums, Sacred Mountains and Related Bon Textual Traditions in Upper Tibet: Calling Down the Gods*, Leiden/Boston: Brill.

Bessenger, S.M. (2017). '"I am a god, I am a god, I am definitely a god": Deity Emanation and the Legitimization of Sönam Peldren', *Revue d'Etudes Tibétaines*, no. 38, pp. 84–103.

Beyer, S. (1978). *Cult of Tara: Magic and Ritual in Tibet*, Berkeley: University of California Press.

Bhasin, V. (2002). 'Ethnic Relation Among the People of Sikkim', *Journal of Social Sciences*, vol 6., no. 1, pp. 1–20.

Bhutia, K.D. (2021). 'Death by Poisoning: Cautionary Narratives and Inter-Ethnic Accusation in Contemporary Sikkim'. *Journal of Ethnology and Folkloristics*, vol. 15, no. 1, pp. 65–84.

Brauen, M., ed. (2005). *The Dalai Lamas: A Visual History*, Chicago: Serindia.

Buyers, C. (2002). *The Namgyal Dynasty: Brief History*, accessed 14 May 2008 at https://www.royalark.net/India/sikkim4.htm

Chayet, A. (1985). 'Women and Reincarnation in Tibet: The Case of Gung ru mKha' 'gro ma'. In A. Cadonna and E. Bianchi, eds., *Facets of Tibetan Religious Tradition and Contacts with Neighbouring Cultural Areas*, Firenze: Olschki Editore.

Chögyam Trungpa Rinpoche (1980). *The Rain of Wisdom*, Nalanda Translation Committee, Shambhala: Prajna Press.

Chögyam Trungpa Rinpoche (1982). *The Life of the Marpa: The Translator*, Nalanda Translation Committee, Shambhala: Prajna Press.

Chonam, L. and K. Sangye (1998). *The Lives and Liberation of Princess Mandarava: The Indian Consort of Padmashambhava*, Boston: Wisdom Publication.

Csordas, T.J. (1990). 'Embodiment as a Paradigm for Anthropology', *Ethnos*, vol. 18, pp. 5–47.

Dalai Lama, H.H. (1992). *Worlds in Harmony: Dialogue on Compassionate Action*, Berkeley: Parallax Press.

Das, S.C. (1970). *A Tibetan English Dictionary*, New Delhi: Motilal Banarsidass.

Diemberger, H. (1991). 'Lhakama [lha-bka'-ma] and khandroma [mkha- 'gro-ma]: The Sacred Ladies of Beyul Khenbalung [sbas-yul-mkhan-pa-lung]'. In E. Steinkellner, ed., *Tibetan History and Language*, Vienna: Arbeitskreis für Tibetische und Buddhistische Studien, pp. 137–154.

Diemberger, H. (2007). *When a Woman Becomes a Religious Dynasty*, New York: Columbia.

Dowman, K. (1996). *Sky Dancer: The Secret Life and Songs of Lady Yeshe Tsogyel*, Ithaca: Snow Lion Publication.

Fisher, W.T. (1989). 'Retold Tales: Towards an Understanding of Spirit Possession in Central Nepal', *Himalaya*, vol. 9, no. 2, pp. 1–16.

Gergan, M.D. (2014). 'Precarity and Possibility: On being Young and Indigenous in Sikkim, India', *Himalaya*, vol. 34, no. 2, pp. 67–80.

Germano, D. and J. Gyatso (2000). 'Longchenpa and the Possession of the Dakinis'. In D.G. White, ed., *Freedom in Exile: The Autobiography of the Dalai Lama*, Princeton: Princeton University Press.

Ghosh, M. (1980). *Development of Buddhist Iconography in Eastern India: A Study of Tārā, Prajñās of Five Tathāgatas and Bhrikitī*, New Delhi: Munshiram Manoharlal.

Gyatso, T. (Dalai Lama XIV) (1991). *Freedom in Exile: The Autobiography of the Dalai Lama*, San Francisco: Harper Perennial.

Hitchcock, J.T. and R. Jones, eds. (1976). *Spirit Possession in the Nepal Himalayas*, Warminster: Aris and Phillips, Ltd.

Honko, L. (1964). 'Memorates and the Study of Folk Beliefs', *Journal of the Folklore Institute*, vol. 1, no. 1/2, pp. 5–19.

Karmay, S.G. (1998). *The Arrow and the Spindle: Studies in History, Myths, Rituals, and Beliefs in Tibet*, Kathmandu: Mandala.

Kirshenblatt-Gimblett, B. (1989). 'Authoring Lives', *Journal of Folklore Research*, vol. 26, no. 2.

Klasanova, L. (2020). 'Khandro Tashi Chotso Enthroned as Tulku in India', *Buddhist Door Global*, accessed on 18 July 2021 at https://www.buddhistdoor.net/news/khandro-tashi-chotso-enthroned-as-tulku-in-india/

Kratz, N. (1977). 'Anima and mKha' 'gro-ma: A Critical Comparative Study of Jung and Tibetan Buddhism', *The Tibet Journal*, vol. 2, no. 3, pp. 13–43.

Lewis, I.M. (1971). *Ecstatic Religion: An Anthropological Study of Spirit Possession and Shamanism*, Baltimore: Penguin Books.

Little, K. (2009). 'Deep Ecology, Dams, and Dzonguland Lepchas Protest Narratives about Their Threatened Land', *The Trumpeter*, vol. 25, no. 1, pp. 34–64.

Miklos, A. (director) and A. Co (writer) (2013). *Daughters of Dolma*, documentary film, 67 minutes, UK, Hungary, Nepal: Alive Mind Cinema.

Mumford, S.R. (1989). *Himalayan Dialogue: Tibetan Lamas and Gurung Shamans in Nepal*, Madison: The University of Wisconsin Press.

Nati Baratz (2009). *Unmistaken Child.* Bstan 'dzin rgya mtsho (Dalai Lama XIV), Lama Konchog. Oscilloscope Laboratory. DVD.

Oesterreich, T.K. (1930). *Possession, Demoniacal and Other: Among Primitive Races, in Antiquity, the Middle Ages, and Modem Times*, Routledge: London.

Ortner, S.B. (1995). 'The Case of Disappearing Shamans, or No Individualism, No Relationalism', *Ethos*, vol. 23, no. 3, pp. 355–390.

Pang Lhabsol (1989). *Souvenir*, Sikkim Tribal Youth Association, Gangto: Sikkim.

Paul, R.A. (1976). 'Some Observations on Sherpa Shamanism'. In J.T. Hitchcock and R.L. Jones, eds., *Spirit Possession in the Nepal Himalaya*, Warminster: Aris and Phillips, pp. 141–151.

Pommaret, F. (2015). 'Empowering Religious Women Practitioners in Contemporary Bhutan', *Revue d'Etudes Tibétaines*, no. 34, pp. 115–138.

Schaefer, L. (1995). 'A Sikkim Awakening', *Himal Himalayan Magazine*, vol. 5, pp. 8–16.

Schrempf, M. (2015). 'Becoming a Female Ritual Healer in Eastern Bhutan', *Revue d'Etudes Tibétaines*, vol. 34, pp. 189–213.

Tsering, T. (1994). 'Introductory Notes on Biographical Sketches of Six Incarnations of Gungru Khandroma', *G.yu mtsho*, vol. 1, pp. 27–47.

Tulku, T. (1983). *Mother of Knowledge: The Enlightenment of Yeshe mTsho-rgyal*, Berkeley: Dharma Publishing.

Turner, V. (1985). *On the Edge of the Bush: Anthropology as Experience*, Tucson: University of Arizona Press.

Turner, V. (1969). *The Ritual Process: Structure and Anti-Structure*, Chicago: Aldine Pub. Co.

Valk, Ü. (2001). *The Black Gentleman: Manifestations of Devil in Estonian Folk Religion*, FF Communications, Helsinki: Suomalainen Tiedeakatemia.

Van Gennep, A. (1909). *The Rites of Passage* (trans. M.B. Vizedom and G.L. Caffee), London: Routledge and Kegan Paul.

Vitebsky, P. (2001 [1995]). *Shamanism*, Norman: University of Oklahoma Press.

Von Sydow, C.W. (1934). 'Geography and Folk-Tale Ecotypes', *Béaloideas*, vol. 4, pp. 244–265.

Waddel, A. (1972 [1895]), *Tibetan Buddhism*, London: Allen & Co Ltd.

Whitehead, N.L. (2002). *Dark Shamans: Kanaima and the Poetics of Violent Death*, Durham: Duke University Press.

Wylie, T. (1978). 'Reincarnation: A Political Innovation'. In L. Ligeti, ed., *Proceedings of the Csoma de Koros Memorial Symposium*, Budapest: Akademiai Kiado, pp. 579–586.

Part II
Society and Education

6 The Jatsawa Lineage in Trongsa and Their Links to the Religious Noble Families of Central and Eastern Bhutan

Françoise Pommaret and Ngawang Jamtsho[1]

This paper explores the history and role of the Jatsawa (Brag gi rtsa ba/ Byag gi rtsa ba)[2] lineage and the links between southern Trongsa, Bumthang and eastern Bhutan based on an examination of written sources and interview data.[3] We are very much aware that this paper gives only a partial view of the extended Jatsawa genealogy, but we hope that it contributes to record, even imperfectly, a part of the history of Bhutan. This study is an attempt to document the information that is still alive in the memory of a few elders and lineage descendants who are today scattered all over Bhutan (Trongsa, Gelephu, Punakha, Thimphu, Dagana, Trashigang, Paro, Bumthang, Lhuntse and Pemagatshel). Many personalities in contemporary Bhutan can claim their ancestry to Jatsawa.[4]

---

1 This research was made possible by a grant from the Wenner-Gren Foundation in the framework of the IDG programme to CLCS, Royal University of Bhutan.

2 Brag gi rtsa ba is the classical spelling while Byag gi rtsa ba is the Dzongkha spelling reflecting the pronunciation.

3 Pommaret has extensively covered in several articles the religious, social and economic interdependence between the regions of Bumthang, Kurtoe, Trongsa and Zhemgang (see bibliography). Ngawang Jamtsho has been researching Trongsa and Zhemgang for the Bhutan Cultural Atlas (https://bca.clcs.edu.bt/) and visited the Jatsawa (Brag gi rtsa ba) ruined mansion during a trip in early 2017. He also published an article on Jatsawa in Dzongkha in 2020.

4 Lyonpo Om Pradhan writes about his wife's ancestry in the preface of his book, *The Roar of the Dragon* (2012):

'The great great grand father of my wife Jigme Wangmo was Trongsa Dronyer Hyonchung [*sic*] who was "the Trongsa Penlop Jigme Namgyal's most reliable official and confidante, serving in the capacities of both Trongsa Dronyer

It also aims to explore the links between the noble religious families, Chöje (chos rje), and their importance in Bhutan.

However, given the space restriction and the complexity of Bhutanese genealogies, we present here a summary of our work which will be enriched by further research in the future.

Bhutanese society of central Bhutan was characterized by powerful lineages that claimed their origin, among others, to the great religious figure Pema Lingpa (Padma gling pa) (b. 1450, d. 1521). From the early sixteenth century, besides religious prestige, these lineages called 'Chöje' attained political and economic powers through a series of alliances either with the previous local nobility, or amongst themselves. These powers largely extended beyond Bumthang to reach eastern Bhutan as well as Trongsa and Zhemgang in central Bhutan. When the Wangchuck dynasty ascended to the throne in 1907, as it hailed from central Bhutan, it used this network of lineages to govern central and eastern Bhutan.[5]

The origins of the Jatsawa lineage and Chöje

Trongsa is located in central Bhutan and was the historical location of the Wangchuck dynasty and was an important administrative center for the eight eastern districts of Bhutan before the advent of the monarchy. The mansion at Jatsawa, which gave its name to the lineage, is located below a cliff above Dandung village under Langthel 'block' in the Trongsa district.

---

and Zimpon. In one of the battles […] Hyonchung was fatally wounded and passed away in the arms of Jigme Namgyal". Hyonchung's family continued to serve Jigme Namgyal till his death, and were also appointed to the position of Zhongar Dzongpon, popularly known for generations as "Zhongaps" governors of the eastern province of Zhongar.

On Dec 17, 1907 Zhongar dzongpon Dorji Paljore, Jigme Wangmo's grandfather, was one of the 47 signatories of the famous genja or agreement that installed Trongsa Penlop Ugyen Wangchuck as the first hereditary king of Bhutan. This position of Zhongar Dzongpon was done away with shortly after the passing away of the last Dzongpon Dasho Kunzang Wangdi at the time of the 3rd King. However the descendants of the Zhongap family continued to be appointed to important positions – one of the most prominent among them being Gyaldron Thinley who was the chief official in the 3rd King's court'.

5 Pommaret (2018).

Jatsawa is a forty-three km drive from Trongsa town and a further one-hour steep walk from the mansion and temple of Tatsherla (Rta 'tsher la).[6]

The late Dasho Lama Sangnag mentioned Jatsawa in his work.[7] Moreover, in the last ten years, several people – Rinchen Dorji, Lama Tashi Wangdi and Lama Kezang Choepel – have written short texts in Dzongkha on this lineage but they have not yet been published. Their work is based on Dasho Lama Sangnag's book supplemented with personal notes and they were kind enough to lend us their texts. Recently, Dasho Sangye Dorji published a book on all the temporal rulers of Bhutan.[8] He briefly mentions Jatsawa in the chapter on the second temporal ruler but also refers to Dasho Lama Sangnag.

The Jatsawa lineage is an offshoot of Tertön (gter ston) Pema Lingpa's (b. 1450, d. 1521) lineage. As is often the case in Bhutan when dealing with Pema Lingpa's descendants, we had to go back to the origin of Pema Lingpa's lineage in Bumthang and interview several elders of religious noble families.[9] This led us to conduct more interviews in Trongsa and Thimphu and made us realize the importance of this lineage and its ramifications in terms of alliances and power extending as far as eastern Bhutan.[10]

At the same time, historical texts mentioning this lineage are very few except the *Smyos rabs* by Dasho Lama Sangnag (1983, reprint 2005), which describes the genealogies of Pema Lingpa's descendants.

The Jatsawa lineage originally stems from two main religious and historical figures:

1. Thugse Dawa Gyaltshen (Thug sras Zla ba rgyal mtshan, b. 1499, d. 1587), Pema Lingpa's son, who travelled from Bumthang to

6 See the website of the Bhutan Cultural Atlas: https://bca.clcs.edu.bt/

7 Lama Sangnag (2005, vol. 3).

8 Dasho Sangay Dorji (2017: 45–59).

9 Karma Phuntsho (2013: 170) writes 'Pema Lingpa's family, since his time, emerged as a leading class of religious aristocrats and gave rise to the largest network of religious nobilities in Bhutan, many of whom intermarried with the existing religious Chöje and secular Dung, Khoche and Pönche elites'.

10 Interviews with Sumthrang Chöje in Sumthrang (2017), Aum Drondon, great

northern Trongsa and settled partially at Gagar (Dga' gar).[11] His son Kunga Gyaltshen (Kun dga' rgyal mtshan) went to Tatsherla (Rta tsher la), south of Trongsa and started the lineage of the Tatsherla Chöje in the late sixteenth century.[12] He used to spend the winter there and the summer at Namphur (Gnam phur) in Bumthang Chume (Chu smad).[13] Kunga Gyaltshen's younger son, Pema Tenzin, became the Tatsherla Chöje.[14]

2. Tenzin Drukda (Bstan 'dzin 'brug grags, b. 1602, d. 1667), the second temporal ruler of Bhutan (Sde srid). The Jatsawa mansion is said to have been founded by Rigyal Wangpo (Rig rgyal dbang po) who was the grandson of Tenzin Drukda, himself the son of Yab Tenpai Nyima (Bstan pa'i nyi ma, b. 1567, d. 1619) from the Drukpa Kagyü school who was also the father of the Zhabdrung Ngawang Namgyal (Zhabs drung Ngag dbang rnam rgyal, b. 1594, d. 1651) who founded the state of Bhutan in the seventeenth century.

The second temporal ruler (*desi*) Tenzin Drukdra was brought up at Ralung (Rva lung) Monastery in Central Tibet and was close to his elder half-brother Zhabdrung Ngawang Namgyal. It is said that the half-brothers looked very much alike. What really interest us here, however, is the second *desi*'s filiation. As already mentioned, his father was Yab Tenpey Nyima, a hierarch of the Drukpa school of the Gya (Rgya) lineage. His mother was from Yuling village above today's Trongsa.[15] However, another tradition says that his mother was a religious woman who met Yab Tenpey Nyima at Dungkar in Dungsam (today Pemagatshel), where her brother-in-law was the lama. She went back to Trongsa with Yab Tenpey

granddaughter of Honchung in Koishala (2018), Lama Tashi Wangdi in Langthel (2018), Lyonpo Sonam Tobgay in Thimphu (2019), Lam Kesang Choephel in Thimphu (2019), and others who wish to remain anonymous.

11 See the website of the Bhutan Cultural Atlas: https://bca.clcs.edu.bt/

12 Dasho Lama Sangnag (2005, vol. 3: 96).

13 Department of Culture (2014: 257–258).

14 Dasho Lama Sangnag (2005, vol. 3: 99–100).

15 Karma Phuntsho (2013: 261) and Gedun Rinchen (2004: 229, 383).

Nyima and settled at Yuling.[16] To further complicate the issue, the place where Dungkar Temple is located is also called Yuling.[17] In this version of events, the lady was the youngest daughter of Pema Gyamtsho, the Kheri Chöje in Dungsam considered to belong to the twenty-ninth generation of the Nyoe (Smyos) clan and descending from Kunga Wangpo's son, one of Pema Lingpa's sons.[18]

Therefore, the second *desi*, Tenzin Drukdra, embodied two prestigious lineages, the Gya of the Drukpa and Pema Lingpa's Nyoe. Tenzin Drukdra had one son in eastern Bhutan before he went to Ralung: Sonam Dargay at Dungkar Gonpa in Dungsam (eastern Bhutan).[19]

In turn, Sonam Dargay had two sons. The elder, Nyida Wangpo, settled at Chungkhar in Dungsam while the younger, Rigyal Wangpo, is at the origin of the Jatsawa Chöje lineage.[20] Dasho Lama Sangnag mentioned the Tatsherla Chöje Riwang Gyalpo,[21] who had a son called Dargye.

Jatsawa is often considered as an offshoot of Tatsherla, located one hour's walk above it. It is said that Jatsawa was a side house (*zur*) of Tatsherla.[22] However, the foundation of Jatsawa is unclear and nor has it been established how Rigyal Wangpo came to this area of Trongsa from eastern Bhutan. He might have come to Tatsherla as the *mag pa* (husband) of a lady descending from Kunga Gyaltshen, Pema Lingpa's grandson. However, this assumption needs to be verified.

In an unpublished clarification at the end of Lama Tashi Wangdi's manuscript, Rinchen Dorji makes it clear that he is well aware of the complexity surrounding the origin of the Jatsawa lineage:

---

16 Oral Communication, Lyonpo Sonam Tobgye, 21 April 2019.

17 Dasho Lama Sangnag (2005, vol. 3: 14).

18 Dasho Lama Sangnag (2005, vol. 3: 15). Kheri was one of the seats of Kunga Wangpo, Pema Lingpa's son.

19 Dasho Lama Sangnag (2005, vol. 3: 16). It is said that Dungsam Dungkar was founded by Yab Tenpay Nima, the Zhabdrung's father (2018: 115).

20 Rinchen Dorji (2010) in Lama Tashi Wangdi (unpublished ms.: 6) and in Lama Kesang (2018, unpublished ms.: 7).

21 Dasho Lama Sangnag (2005, vol. 3: 102). 'Riwang' could be a typo for 'Rigyal'.

22 Dasho Lama Sangnag (2005, vol. 3: 102).

> These days, people provide a variety of background justifications about the origin of the Jatsawa noble family. Some have mistakenly written documents which may cause misunderstanding in the near future. There are different versions on the advent of the Jatsawa noble family. Some people have mentioned that it initially originated from the Tatsherla Chöje as a secondary lineage and settlement, and some mentioned that it was separated from the Kyetsel lineage. There are also some people who say that Jatsawa is related to the Langthel Zhelngo of Trongsa, the Chungkhar religious noble family of Pemagatshel in eastern Bhutan, or the Kungacholing and Samtencholing religious noble families of Bumthang. Furthermore, some people have noted that the current structure of the Jatsawa mansion was initially built by the Zhongar Dzongpön Dorji Penjor, who was the eldest son of Dronyer Honchung. However, although the Jatsawa lineage had strong linkages with all those religious noble families of different regions through internal marriage practice, it does not trace its origins from any of these lineages; it is a separate lineage from all of them.[23]

In spite of Rinchen Wangdi's words of caution, it seems clear that the Jatsawa lineage can claim two prestigious religious ancestries: the Gya (rGya) house of Druk Ralung ('Brug Rva lung) and Pema Lingpa's Nyoe (sMyos) lineage.

---

23 Ngawang Jamtsho's translation from Rinchen Wangdi's text. Wylie transliteration from Dzongkha:

Dogs sel

Brag rtsar chos rje's skor da ras nangspar khungs sna tshogs skyel mi dang/La lo gis yig thog lu yang nor ba sbe bkod de go ba brda log 'gy ni gi nyen kha 'dug//

La lo gis 'bad ba cin Brag rtsa ba'i mi brgyud 'di Rta 'tsher la chos rje rje las zur pa sbe 'thon te 'gyo 'gyowa yin pa'i skor las bkod de 'dug/La lo gis 'bad ba cin skyid tshal las brgyud brgyud pa yinm sbe slab yin pas/la lo gis Glang thil zhal ngo/ La lo gis Khyung mkhar chos rje/ La lo gis Kun dga' chos gling gdung/ La lo gis Bsam gtan gling chos rje yinpa'i khungs tshu bkod pa ma tshad Bra rtsar gyi khyim yang Gzhong sgar pa A rgyas kyis bzo bzow yinm sbe phyi 'gyur sbe bkod de mgo 'thoms ni gi nyen kha 'dug//

Jatsawa Honchung and his descendants

In the second half of the nineteenth century, the Jatsawa lineage emerged as an important player in Bhutan's political landscape producing Honchung, its most powerful member.

The second Desi Tenzin Drukdra's grandson was Rigyal Wangpo or Riwang Gyalpo and his son was Dargye. Dargye's son[24] Kunzang from Jatsawa was appointed as the Dungsam region manager (*sa srung pa*). Unfortunately, it has been so far impossible to identify Kunzang's spouse.

Kunzang's son is said to have been Honchung, who reportedly took over from his father as the Dungsam region manager. He also commanded the garrison at Deothang (Dewangiri for the British). He was then promoted to the position of Trongsa chamberlain (*dronyer*) by the Trongsa Penlop Jigme Namgyal as appreciation for his bravery during the 1864–1865 war with the British. Therefore, Honchung moved back to Trongsa with his wife and a large retinue. He initiated the renovation work at Jatsawa mansion and turned it into a three-story central tower (*dbu rtse*) surrounded by a two-story enclosure (*shag skor*).[25] However, as Jatsawa was an offshoot of Tatsherla, Honchung is sometimes called Tatsherla Chöje[26] and sometimes Jatsawa Chöje.

It is interesting to note that Honchung is a nickname meaning 'fresh youth'. Honchung's real name does not seem to have been recorded, which is a little odd. Moreover, his supposed father Kunzang is not really remembered in the family oral tradition. Lastly, his son Tshewang Paljor, who became state chamberlain (*zhung dronyer*) at Punakha, was about fifty at the time of Ugyen Wangchuck's coronation in 1907. Although generation and age gaps are sometimes a little confusing in Bhutanese

---

De 'badwa las Brag rtsar chos rje skor las thad kar du ha go dgop 'di yang ma gzhi gong lu bkod mi tshi dang gcig khar 'brel ba yod dgo mi 'di ga ra dang gcig khar gnyen phar dang tshur lhags yod ni 'di gis mi gcig sbe song mi de bden rung/ Brag rtsar chos rje 'di de tshu las brgyud pa men par rigs rus rang so so yin//

24 Dasho Lama Sangnag (2005, vol. 3: 103).

25 Lama Tashi Wangdi (unpublished ms.: 6).

26 Dasho Lama Sangnag (2005, vol. 3: 17), but Lama Tashi Wangdi (unpublished ms.: 6) calls Honchung the Jatsawa Chöje.

families, we would suggest that there is no space for a generation between Dargye and Honchung. In this case could Kunzang and Honchung in fact be the same person, and Honchung Dargye's son? Of course, this is a hypothesis which would have to be verified.[27]

Honchung married Lungten Gyalmo from the Bangtsho Chöje/ Chungkhar Chöje lineage[28] in Dungsam descending from Kunga Wangpo, Pema Lingpa's son as well as from the Tibetan prince Lhase Tsangma's son Pel Thongley.[29] The families who are descendants of Prince Tsangma are called Khoche (Kho che) in eastern Bhutan and intermarried with the Chöje families.

Honchung and Lungtaen Gyalmo had five children: Tshewang Paljor,[30] Dorji Paljor, Drolma, Sonam Paljor and Phurpa Dorje.[31]

The second eldest son Dorji Paljor married Tenzin Gyalmo, the Chungkhar Chöje Gyaltshen Wangdu's daughter, who was related to his wife Lungtaen Gyalmo (cross-cousins) and became the Zhongar (gZhong

27 For this hypothesis, I am indebted to one of my informants who knows his family lineage well but wishes to remain anonymous.

28 Lungten Gyalmo was from the Bangtsho Chöje lineage according to several informants but Dasho Lama Sangnag (2005, vol. 3: 17, 103) writes that she was from the Chungkhar Chöje lineage.

We have not carried out extensive research on these two lineages but these places, as well as Kheri, are geographically close to each other (today in Zobel 'block' of Pemagatshel district) and intermarriages were taking place. This Dungsam Bangtsho is not to be mistaken for the Kurtoe Bangtsho although the families were related (Dasho Lama Sangnag 2005, vol. 3: 31–35). For further research see Dasho Lama Sangnag (2005, vol. 3).

29 *Bhutan Observer* (16–23 September 2011: 5) 'Dungsam's own son recalls the region's past glory' and *rGyal rigs* (2009: 29, 35).

30 Tshewang Paljor was the state chamberlain in Punakha and his descendants are now settled in that area. He played a role as the chair of the cabinet (*lhengye zhungtsog*) that endorsed the recommendation of Kazi Ugyen Dorji to institute a monarchy with Gongsar Ugyen Wangchuck as the first hereditary king. His role was particularly significant in the power vacuum as the Zhabdrung reincarnate had not been installed and Choglay Yeshey Ngodrup as the last *desi* had left his post vacant. This fact is established by the order of the signatories of the Genja of 1907 in which Tshewang Paljor's seal is just after those of the ecclesiastical representatives. His brother Dorji Paljor's seal is also on the document, so there are two signatories from the family of Jatsawa on this historic document.

31 It is not certain that Phurpa Dorje was Lungtaen Gyalmo's son.

sgar) Dzong governor – Zhongar Dzong being the most important administrative center covering the whole of eastern Bhutan at that time.[32] Dorji Paljor was nicknamed 'Zhongarpa Agye'. It is possible that this important appointment was due to the family's close relations with Ugyen Wangchuck and the fact that Tshewang Paljor, his elder brother, was the Punakha state chamberlain.

Dorji Paljor and Tenzin Gyalmo had five children who became important figures in Bhutan: the Dagana governor Rigzin Dorji, the Zhongar Dzong governor Kunzang Wangdi who finally settled in Chungkhar where his mother was from; the Khengkhar sub-governor Tandin Gyamtsho; Tshomo who married the Bumthang Buli Trulku Agya Rinpoche Khachab Namkha Dorji; and Zangmo who married into the Bumthang Samtenling Chöje lineage.

The links between Tatsherla/Jatsawa in Trongsa and Dungsam in southeast Bhutan were well established by that point.

Jatsawa in contemporary Bhutan

In 1953, serfdom was abolished by the third king and over the next ten years large land holdings were dismantled and the land was redistributed. This bold agricultural reform impacted most of the Chöje families of central and eastern Bhutan. It drastically changed their lives. New taxes and the land regulation reforms considerably impoverished them and they were suddenly deprived of manpower and land holdings. Many could not maintain their mansions and many had to find a new way to make a living.

The Jatsawa family still living in Jatsawa slowly abandoned their mansion in the mountain and came down to the valley of Mangdechu near the villages of Dangdung and Koshila, which in the 1980s had better access to modern facilities (education, health services, electricity, water supply and roads). The Jatsawa mansion is now in ruins and desolated among thick bushes.

---

32 Lyonpo Om Pradhan (2012: preface), and Kunzang Thinley (2009: 132–149).

Table 6.1: Jatsawa alliances

Some examples of Jatsawa alliances with religious noble families from central Bhutan: Trongsa, Bumthang and Kurtoe (Lhuntse)	**Some examples of Jatsawa alliances with religious noble families from Eastern Bhutan: Trashigang, Zhongar (Mongar) and Dungsam (Pemagatshel)**
Honchung's daughter Drolma inherited Jatsawa and married Namgay from the Taktserla lineage	Dorji Paljor, second eldest son of Honchung, married Tenzin Gyalmo, daughter of Gyaltshen Wangdu from the Chungkhar Chöje lineage, Dungsam (Pemagatshel)
Drolma's daughter Paldon inherited Jatsawa and married Dorji from the Taktserla lineage (her cousin)	Paldon's daughter, Lemo from Jatsawa, married Thinley Tobgay (Sey Dopola / Tashigangpa) Dzongpon of Trashigang, originally from Kurtoe Dungkar
Drolma's youngest son Goley married Lemo from Tatsherla (his cousin) and moved to Tatsherla as magpa	Jatsawa Honchung married Lungtaen Drolma from Dungsam
Kunzang Wangdi, Honchung's grandson, first married Koencho from the Kurtoe Ney lineage in Lhuntse, then married Kunzang Choden and Dechen Zangmo, the two daughters of the Kurtoe Gyarey Zhelngo in Lhuntse	
Tatsherla Goley's daughter, Pema Zangmo, married Bumthang Chume Uru Ugyen	
Kunzang Wangdi's son, Gyeldron Thinley Dorji, from Kurtoe Ney married two half-sisters: Rinzin, daughter of the Zangling Chöje from Bumthang Choekhor Toe and Karma Lhatshog, the daughter of Paro Ponlop Kusho Tshering Penjor	
Dorji Tshomo, Kunzang Wangdi's sister, married Agya Lama Buli Tulku (b. 1883, d. 1941) of Dorji Lingpa's lineage in Bumthang. Their son was Agya lama Zhenphen Drodul Dorji Tenzin Rinpoche (b. 1921, d. 2005).	
Zangmo, Kunzang Wangdi's younger sister, married into the Bumthang Samtenling Chöje lineage (Kunkhyen Lonchen's lineage and Pema Lingpa's lineage)	

Many contemporary influential Bhutanese can trace their origin back to Jatsawa as that lineage concluded many alliances with other Chöje families of central and eastern Bhutan, themselves descending from the other sons of Pema Lingpa, or with the Khoche families claiming to descend from the Tibetan prince Lhase Tsangma who settled in eastern Bhutan after his arrival from Tibet in the ninth century.

Besides its value as a source for the study of memory and ways of remembering the past, this study of the Jatsawa lineage sheds light on the complex and often fascinating strategic interactions and alliances among the religious noble families of central and eastern Bhutan. It shows that they used religious and political strategies to concentrate power in the hands of families with prestigious ancestors, a topic discussed in our earlier works.[33]

Three main patterns or models of transmission of property and status can be identified:

1. Land and household possessions. The eldest daughter usually kept the ancestral home while the younger daughters were given away as a *mna'ma* (spouse who went to live at her husband's place) to the heirs of religious lineages.

2. The transmission of a prestigious administrative post from father to elder son. The other sons went either to the monastery or as a *mag pa* (spouse who went to live at his wife's place) to another lineage.

3. Marital alliances and kinship between cross-cousins[34] or in related lineages were used in order to maintain the *rigs gtsang* (pure lineage), but this can also be understood as a strategy to keep land, wealth and prestigious religious ascendancy within a family or lineage and as a way to acquire political and economic power.

From a forgotten ruin in the mountain, with the assistance of texts and oral history, we were able to partially reconstruct and document the lineage of Jatsawa which played an important role in the political history of Bhutan[35] and whose descendants are still preeminent figures today.

---

33 Pommaret (2016, 2017, 2018).

34 Among the Chöje families, one of the preferred alliances was amongst cross-cousins, which means the daughter/son of the father's sister or mother's brother. Parallel cousins (daughter/son of the father's brother or mother's sister) were considered as brothers and sisters and therefore not permitted to marry.

35 Offshoots of this lineage are still to be studied in Punakha, Trongsa and Dagana.

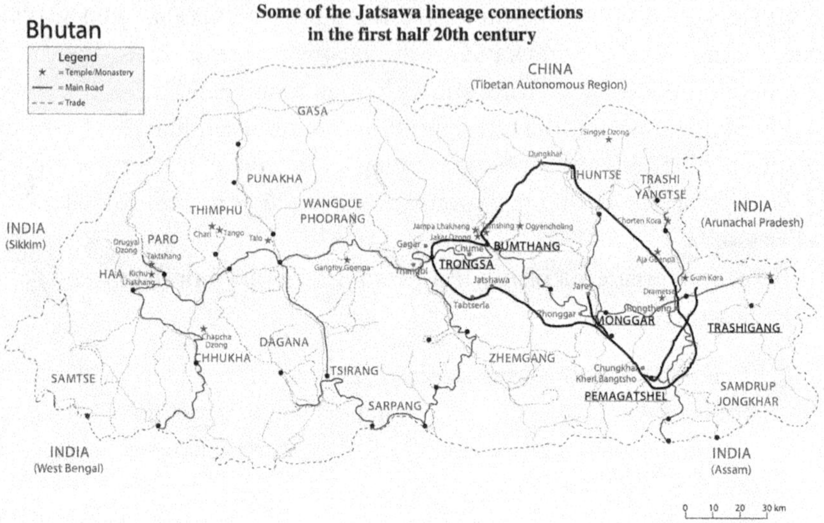

Figure 6.1: Some of the Jatsawa lineage connections in the first half of the twentieth century

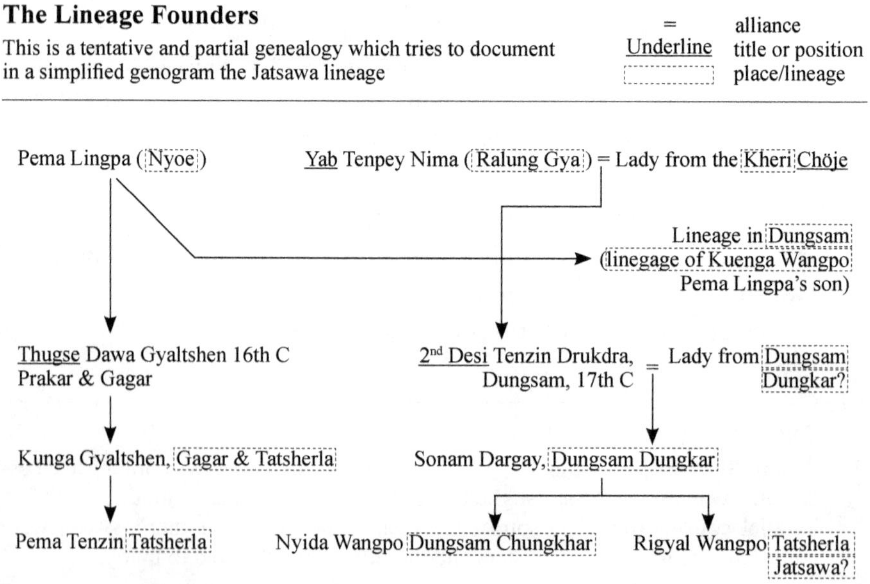

Figure 6.2: Partial genealogy presenting a simplified genogram of the Jatsawa lineage

Simplified and Partial Genealogy mid 19th to mid 20th century

= alliance
Underline title or position
[dashed box] place/lineage

Jatsawa Rigyal Wangpo
→ Dar gye

Jatsawa **Kunzang** (Dungsam governor /Sasungpa) = ?? unknown

'Agye' Honchung = **Lungten Drolma** from Bangtsho Chöje, connected to Chungkhar and Kheri Chöje later

Dungsam governor
later Trongsa Dronyer under Jigme Namgyal

They had 5 children: Tshewang Paljor Zhung Dronyer in Punakha, Dorji Paljor, Drolma, Sonam Paljor Nabji Dungpa and Nyerchen Phurpa Dorji (with whom we will not deal here).

→ **Drolma** inherits Jatsawa = *magpa* Namgay from Tatsherla

→ Jatsawa Goley went to Tatsherla as *magpa* = Lemo (Tatsherla)
Descendants are today Tatsherla Chöje

→ Peldon inherits Jatsawa = Dorji (Tatsherla) went to Jatsawa as *magpa*

Jatsawa Lemo = Thinley Tobgay (d.1961)/Sey Dopola Tashigang Dzongpon from Kurtoe Dungkar by his father Sonam Tshering). He settled in Rongthong, Trashigang and married four times.

→ **Dorji Paljor** 9th Zhongar Dzongpon = **Tenzin Gyalmo**, daughter of Gyaltshen Wangdu from Chungkhar, Lhasey Tsangma's lineage

→ 1 - Rinzin Dorji became the Governor of Daga dzong

→ 2 - Tandin Gyamtsho became the Dy administrator (*drungpa*) of Khenkhar (south of Zhongar and north of Dungsam)

→ 3 - Kunzang Wangdi 10th Zhongar Dzongpon
He settled in Chungkhar where his mother was from and married thrice

= 1 Koencho (Kurtoe Ney Chukmo)

Choden (inherits the Ney mansion) Gyaldron Thinley Dorji (born in Kurtoe Ney Pema Chholing). Served the 2nd and 3rd king) = 2 half sisters, Rigzin, daughter of Bumthang Zangling Chöje (Pemalingpa lineage) & Karma Lhatshog, daughter of Paro Penlop Kusho Tshering Penjor

= 2 Kunzang Choden

= 3 Dechen Zangmo, Kunzang Choden's sister
(both daughters of Kurtoe Gyarey Shelngo).
They went to live in Chungkhar and had 8 children.

→ 4 - Dorji Tshomo = Bumthang Buli Tulku

→ 5 - Zangmo = Bumthang Samtenling Chöje

Figure 6.3: Simplified and partial genealogy (mid-nineteenth to mid-twentieth century)

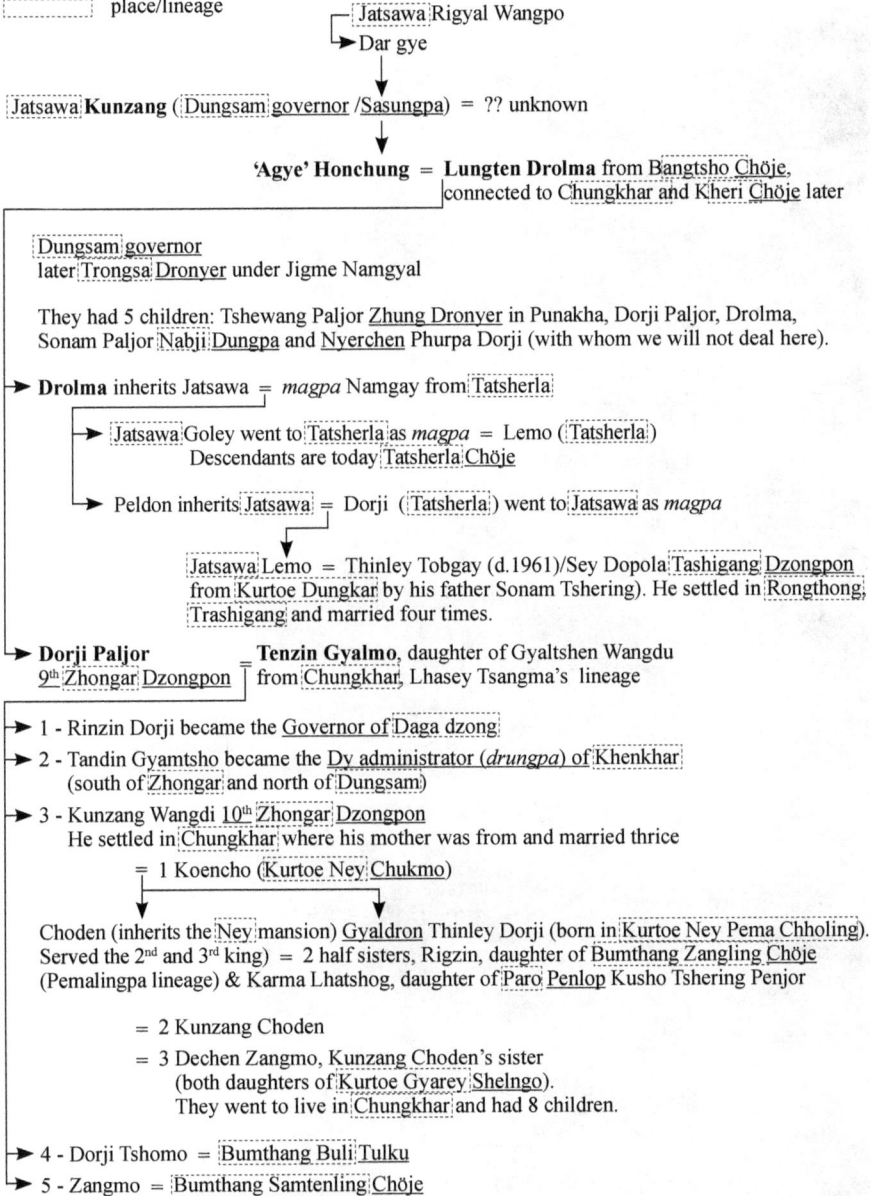

Photo 6.1: The site of Jatsawa (2017)

Source: Ngawang Jamtsho and Françoise Pommaret.

Photo 6.2: The Jatsawa ruins (1)

Source: Ngawang Jamtsho and Françoise Pommaret.

Photo 6.3: The Jatsawa ruins (2)

Source: Ngawang Jamtsho and Françoise Pommaret.

Photo 6.4: Tatsherla Mansion and temple (1)
Source: Ngawang Jamtsho and Françoise Pommaret.

Photo 6.5: Tatsherla Mansion and temple (2)
Source: Ngawang Jamtsho and Françoise Pommaret.

Bibliography

Aris, M. (2009). *Sources for the History of Bhutan*, : New-Delhi: Motilal. First published in 1986 in Wien by Universität Wien. (Here called *rGyal rigs*.)

Dasho Lama Sangnag (Drag shos Bla ma gSang sngags) (2005 [1983]). *'Brug gi smyos rabs yang gsal me long*, vol. 3, Thimphu: KMT.

Dasho Sangay Dorji (Drag shos Sangs rgyas rdo rje) (2017). *'Brug gi sDe srid khri rabs rim byon gyi mdzad rnam deb ther dpyod ldan dgyes pa'i do shal*, Thimphu: CBS.

Department of Culture, Ministry of Home and Culture, Bhutan (2014). *gNas yig kun phan lam ston. Zhal sgang dang Krong gsar rdzong khag*, Thimphu.

Dorji Phuntsho (2016). *Sey Dhopola: The Last Trashigangpa (in Bhutan)*, unpublished manuscript.

Gedun Rinchen (69th Je Khenpo) (2004). *dPal ldan 'Brug pa'i gdul zhing lho phyogs nags mo'i ljongs kyi chos 'byung blo gsar (lHo 'Brug Chos 'byung)*, Thimphu: KMT.

Jatshon Mebar ('Ja mtshon Me 'bar) (2015). *Thugs sras Zla ba rgyal mtshan gyi rnam thar. The Biography of Thugse Dawa Gyaltshen*, Karma Phuntsho and Dorji Gyaltshen, eds., Thimphu: Shejun.

Karma Phuntsho (2013). *The History of Bhutan*, India: Random House.

Kunzang Thinley (2009). 'Founding of Zhongar (Mongar) Dzong'. In *Fortress of the Dragon. Proceedings of the 4th Colloquium*, Paro: National Museum of Bhutan, pp. 131–160.

Lam Kesang Chophel (2018). *Krong gsar Byag gi rtsa ba'I mi brgyud skor las phra zhing phraba sbe rgyus cha med rung pha mes rgan rim tshu gi kha rgyun dang zhib 'tshel pa'i zin bris lu gzhi bzhag thog ma 'ongs bu rgyud kyi lam ston chung ku gcig bkod pa*, Thimphu: unpublished Dzongkha document.

Lama Tashi Wangdi (2016?). *Byag gi rtsa ba'i mi brgyud skor las rgyas shing rgyas par rgyus cha med rung rang gis shes mi mgron gnyer Hon cungib uu gzhis gsum rtsa ba'imi brgyud gyr gzhi gzhag ste mdor bsdus*, Langthel: unpublished Dzongkha document.

Lyonpo Om Pradhan (2012). *Bhutan. The Roar of the Thunder Dragon*, Thimphu: K Media.

National Land Commission (2018). *Nye. Religious, Cultural and Historical Atlas of Bhutan*, Thimphu: National Land Commission.

Ngawang Jamtsho (2020). 'Sde srid 'Jigs med rnam rgyal gyi mgron gnyer Hon cung gi pha khyim Krong gsar Byag rtsa ba'i byung rabs', *Brug gi Lam srol*, vol. 1, Taktse: CLCS, pp. 54–65.

Pommaret, F. (2012). 'Ogyen Choling: The Story of a Himalayan Estate'. In K. Choden and D.C. Roder, eds., *Ogyen Choling. A Manor in Central Bhutan*, Thimphu: Riyang Publications, pp. 31–36.

Pommaret, F. (2015). 'Men Have Titles, Women Have Property. Note on the History of Wangdu Choling, Bumthang, Bhutan'. In H. Havnevik and C. Ramble, eds., *From Bhakti to Bon. Festschrift for Per Kvaerne*, Oslo: The Institute for Comparative Research in Human Culture, pp. 395–408.

Pommaret, F. (2016). 'Alliances and Power in Central Bhutan: A Narrative of Religion, Prestige and Wealth (mid 19th–mid 20th centuries)', *Bulletin of Tibetology*, special issue, 'The Dragon and the Hidden Land: Social and Historical Studies of Sikkim and Bhutan', vol. 45, no. 2 and vol. 46, no. 1, pp. 49–66.

Pommaret, F. (2017). 'Tracing Yarlung in South-central Bhutan. Myths, Migrations and Society: The Community of Ngangla Trong in Lower Kheng', *Bulletin of Tibetology*, vol. 50, nos. 1 and 2, pp. 17–52.

Pommaret, F. (2018). 'The Bumthang Web. A Story of Interdependence: Myths, Alliances, Religion and Power in Bhutan'. In S. Kumagai, ed., *Buddhism, Culture and Society in Bhutan*, Proceedings of the 14th IATS, Kathmandu: Vajra, pp. 149–170.

Websites

Bhutan Cultural Atlas website

https://bca.clcs.edu.bt/2014/07/tatsherla-nagtshang-rta-tsher-la-snag-tshang/

https://bca.clcs.edu.bt/2015/10/gagar-lhakhang-2/

7 Bordering between Sikkim and Nepal: The Making of the Limbu as a Borderland People[1]

Mélanie Vandenhelsken

Introduction

The Limbu community's ancestral territory stretches roughly between the rivers Arun, in Nepal, and Teesta, in Sikkim.[2] It was divided into two parts by the border that separates eastern Nepal from the Indian state of Sikkim and that was established by two treaties: one between the East India Company and the Nepali rulers (Treaty of Sugauli, 1816), and the other between the East India Company and Sikkim (Treaty of Titalia, 1817). Today, a number of Limbu intellectuals in Sikkim claim, 'We have our own culture,

---

1 This research was funded by the FWF Project 'Trans-Border Religion: Re-composing Limbu rituals in the Nepal–Sikkim borderlands' (P29805), hosted by the Centre for Interdisciplinary Research and Documentation of Inner and South Asian Cultural History (CIRDIS), University of Vienna, Austria. I thank Prem Chhetri (CIRDIS, University of Vienna) for his translation of the Nepali texts used in this article into English, as well as for his assistance in the exploration of archival documents. I also thank Dr. Buddhi L. Subba (Khamdhak), assistant professor, Nar Bahadur Bhandari College, East Sikkim, for the invaluable information and numerous references he provided for this article.

2 Limbu (often Limboo in Sikkim), also known as *subbā*, and, in Sikkim, *Tsong*; autonym: Yakthungba. The Limbu language belongs to the Bodic branch of the Tibeto-Burman language family (van Driem 1987; Ebert 1994). There are altogether about 700,000 Limbus, mostly residing in north-east Nepal, between the Arun and Mechi rivers (387,300 in Nepal, which represents 1.46 percent of the country's total population: Central Bureau of Statistics *Census 2011*). There are 56,650 Limbus in the Indian state of Sikkim (DESME 2006: 32), including 34,292 Limbu speakers (Linguistic Survey of India Sikkim Part-I 2001). There are also Limbus in West Bengal (particularly in Darjeeling and Kalimpong), Assam and Nagaland, as well as in the Middle East, South East Asia, Europe and the United States.

religion, language and script; we have everything'. The Limbu also feel the need to reassert their indigeneity in Sikkim. These assertions are firstly a reaction to the questioning of the indigeneity of the community in certain political speeches and actions: In the Sikkimese-Tibetan historiography that narrates the early days of the kingdom of Sikkim, the Limbu were one of the three communities (with the Lepcha and Bhutia) that formed the kingdom of Sikkim; in 1663, their representatives recognized the Bhutia Phuntsog Namgyal as their common ruler in western Sikkim.[3] The Limbu were consequently described as one of the 'three races living in Sikkim'.[4] However, in the first census of Sikkim carried out during its colonization (1888–1918), they were included into the groups of 'more or less allied' ethnic communities.[5] Shortly after, when the colonists established the first laws differentiating the 'natives' from the 'settlers' in Sikkim – as in other parts of north-east India – Limbu were not included in the first category and had to pay the same taxes as Nepali 'settlers', which were different than that of the 'natives', then reduced to the Lepcha and the Bhutia.[6]

The Limbu's assertions concerning their cultural 'capital', homogeneity and their indigeneity in Sikkim also reflect a conformity of ethnic 'identities' with state representations of ethnicity, which ethnic leaders perceive as necessary to get 'recognition' by the state, in particular as a Scheduled Tribe (ST), and be involved in decision making.[7] Indigeneity is not part of the official criteria for being listed as an ST, and is not clearly defined in official papers.[8] However, state officials in Delhi consider it obvious that only 'indigenous' groups can be STs.

In the case of borderland communities such as the Limbu, compliance with state classifications implies demonstrating the presence of the community before the establishment of the border and, simultaneously,

---

3 Mullard (2011: 140).

4 The Lho Mon Tsong gsum: Namgyal and Dolma (1908: 23), section 'Pedigree of Sikkim Kazis'.

5 *Gazetteer of Sikhim* (1894: 27).

6 See Vandenhelsken (2016, 2021).

7 On these processes in the region at large, see Shneiderman (2015: 12–13) and Middleton (2016).

8 Middleton (2015: 9).

within the present-day national territory. The need to conform to state classifications also leads ethnic leaders to assert that Sikkimese Limbu are culturally different from Nepali Limbu, and in particular, less influenced by Hinduism. At the same time, cultural homogeneity within the community must also be demonstrated. These paradoxical assertions show first the influence of a state-centric concept of ethnicity and territory on ethnic leaders, or of 'territorialization'. Territorialization is here understood as a process – and territory as 'the effect of networked socio-technical interventions rather than an a priori attribute of the state'[9] – that includes the delimitation of a state territory as a means of controlling people within it. It entails a concept of the 'isomorphy' of culture, ethnicity and state territory, that is to say, the fiction that national, regional and village boundaries 'Enclose cultures and regulate cultural exchange'.[10] In this frame, borderland people's connections to two states, like dual citizenship, 'breaks with the segmentary logic of the classic nation-state, according to which one could belong to only one state at a time'.[11] As concerns the Limbu, being indigenous and having connections through common ethnicity with the other side of the border are considered as contradictory. Limbu leaders' assertions highlight, secondly, the 'transfer' of the geo-political border within a cross-border community,[12] in other words, the production of the border by that community through its internal cultural division.

In this chapter, I argue that the present day 'identity' of the Limbu community in Sikkim – I approach 'identity' as both collective-self-perception and perception by others, and as socially constructed – is largely determined by processes of 'territorialization' taking place in the region since the early nineteenth century. In other words, the questioning of Limbu indigeneity by the state, as well as the need felt by Limbu leaders to prove this wrong by asserting the geographic and cultural 'isomorphy' of the Limbu with the national territory of Sikkim, are part of processes of

9 Reeves (2014: 241).

10 Gupta and Fergusson (1992: 19).

11 Sejersen (2008: 524).

12 Schimanski and Wolfe (2010).

bordering, defined as the process of the construction of borders,[13] which is part of state-making.

By revisiting the history of the Singalila border, this article aims to demonstrate that while the physical demarcation of the border has been a slow, contested and incomplete process, the demarcation occurred through the division of the Limbu people: this division of the Limbu community, and its spatial fixation, thus played a central role in the realization or 'performance' of the border, and of territorialization.

Rather than giving definitive answers, I highlight questions related to, on the one hand, the transformations of the concept of a trans-local Limbu community, and, on the other hand, its linking to a specific territory from the eighteenth century to the nineteenth century.

'Limbuness' before the Gurkha conquests

The emergence of ethnic consciousness in the meaning of a sense of belonging to a supra-local community linked by close but also distant kinship ties, a common culture and a shared memory – which is central today to political life in the region – is a recent phenomenon in Sikkim and Darjeeling.[14] What enabled this emergence still needs to be explored in greater depth, and this raises questions in particular because of the longstanding migrations and high levels of mobility in the region at large, including Nepal. This leads us to ask how ethnic communities have come to be associated with a particular territory, while also being characterized by a set of definable 'cultural traits'. Ethnic consciousness is, indeed, also conditioned by the definition of clearly identifiable cultural-ethnic boundaries, and the concept of community formed through a common and unique culture took its present day form of measurable 'object' in the early phase of anthropology, which shaped colonial knowledge in the region.[15] Here, I examine together the association of an ethnic community to the state territory and its definition in terms of a group sharing an identifiable

13 Kolossov and Scott (2013: 3).

14 On this question, see among others Chalmers (2003); Dhakal (2009); Sharma (2016); Chettri (2017).

15 Cohn (1987).

common and distinct culture – as fixing people into governable categories and to a specific territory were narrowly entangled during colonization in the region[16] like in other parts of north-east India[17] – focusing on specific historical moments relevant to these processes. This leads us to question not the attachment to a community nor the existence of specific cultural practices, but the processes of their combined territorial and cultural 'fixation', which has led to the consideration of mobility, multiple affiliations and cultural exchanges as anomalies, whereas these were (and still are) constructive elements of cultural and social dynamics.

Schlemmer[18] has highlighted the complexity of the question of the conditions for the emergence of a 'Kirant' ethnic consciousness in Nepal.[19] The multiple layers of identity, combining kinship (household, lineage, clan) and locality (village, valley), linguistic diversity, the possibility of shifting from one ethnic community to another enabled by ritual practices[20] as well as numerous migrations and the divisions of kinship units they allowed, raise particular concerns about the conditions of emergence of 'supra-local' communities such as the Rai and Limbu.[21]

Warner argued that the ethnic communities of Sikkim (Limbu and Lepcha) were involved – sometimes forcibly – in the state's efforts to define a territory.[22] Differentiating the communities was part of this effort, as it also divided them. She also writes that 'several key documents indicate that Kiranti social organization revolved around loosely defined obligations and rights and that group membership was determined by community acceptance or rejection rather than a strictly territorial or ethnic basis'.[23] As concerns the Rai under Vijaypur's jurisdiction before

---

16 Warner (2014).

17 Baruah (2013).

18 Schlemmer (2010).

19 The ethnic label 'Kirant' includes several smaller ethnic entities, whose number varies depending on sources, but most often incorporates the numerous Rai groups and the Limbu (about the Kirant, see Gaenszle [2000: 4–12]).

20 Vansittart (1896: 129).

21 Vansittart (1896: 129).

22 Warner (2014: 160–161).

23 Warner (2014: 166).

the Gurkha conquests (see details about these conquests below), taxes were levied per family, and the boundaries of the land were not recorded but depended upon local negotiation, though the boundaries of the region under Vijaypur were defined (between the Arun and Kankayi rivers).[24] Warner then draws on Chemjong's writings about the Limbu to show that the ritual adoption of a person from another ethnicity into the community was possible.[25] In her opinion: 'the adoption ceremony represent[s] cultural and political arrangements for attracting and maintaining manpower in a fluid frontier region where state power was not firmly wedded to territory'.[26] Though Chemjong's information should be handled with care as he generally does not allow for precisely identifying his sources and neglects contextualization, the ritual adoption into the community in the past is asserted by Limbu in Sikkim today. In brief, this information suggests that 'fixing' the communities (notably the Limbu and the Lepcha) to the state territory has been a concern of the Sikkim state since its foundation in the late seventeenth century, that it was likely not done through cultural objectification and that it took place in a context of fluid linkages between belonging and territory.

As concerns the Limbu in Sikkim, their descriptions from the early days of the Sikkim kingdom firstly highlight, indeed, the malleability of their external ascriptions: the term 'Mön', used today to specifically designate the Lepcha, also included the Limbu.[27] Assimilation of Lepcha and Limbu also appears in Namgyal and Dolma's *History of Sikkim*,[28] for example when the clan Sanyit-bho is firstly described as Lepcha, and then as Tsong (i.e., the name given to the Limbu by the Bhutia in Sikkim). Thus, Mön and Tsong have possibly been malleable categories that referred to a social status in comparison to that of the Bhutia, rather than to clearly identified ethnic communities.[29]

---

24 Warner (2014: 167); Forbes (1999).

25 Warner (2014: 167).

26 Warner (2014: 168).

27 Mullard (2011: 62, n. 24, 86, n. 49, and 154)

28 Namgyal and Dolma (1908 annex: 21).

29 On the people called Monpa in Bhutan and references on this ethnonym in the Tibetan cultural area, see Pommaret (1999).

Archival documents collected in Nepal by the scholar-administrator Brian Houghton Hodgson (1801–1894),[30] dating from the early or mid-eighteenth century, hint at a sense of 'trans-local' community among the Limbu prior to the Gurkha conquests. This early form of ethnic consciousness appears in documents attributed to Srijanga Thebe (also called Teyongshi, i.e., 'reincarnation'), the early-eighteenth-century Limbu leader to whom the invention of the 'Srijanga script' is attributed.[31] Srijanga was assassinated in 1741 in Sikkim by Buddhist lamas likely because he wrote '[…] books in which the deities of the indigenous Limbu pantheon figured at least as prominently as Buddhist doctrine'.[32] Texts whose date of writing is estimated to lie between the early and the mid-eighteenth century, and possibly written by Srijanga, include an alphabet book and his 'teachings'.[33] The latter include texts on moral teachings and traditional sayings (called *Mundhum sāplā*), on cosmology (called *lakṣmī sāṃlo*), as well as sayings of the Limbu (also known as *lakṣmī sāṃlo*).[34] The ethnonym used by Srijanga is not Limbu, however, but Yakthung (IPA: yɔk-dhuŋ). A section of the *Mundhum sāplā*, in Limbu, reads as follows:

---

30 On Hodgson's life and contribution to Himalayan studies, see Hunter (1896); Pels (1999); Pradhan (2001); Waterhouse (2004).

31 This script is used today by Limbu in Sikkim and Nepal to write their language. On Srijanga, see also among others Vansittart (1896); *Gazetteer of Sikhim* (1989: 37); Sprigg (1959: 591); T.B. Subba (1999: 243); J.R. Subba (1999); van Driem (2001: 674–675); Dhungel (2006); Mullard (2011); Gaenszle (2013).

32 van Driem (2001: 675); Dhungel (2006).

33 These three texts are included in MSS EUR HODGSON/86 of the Papers of Brian H. Hodgson 1821–1856, Oriental and India Office Collection (hereafter OIOC); see the section '86 The Limbu texts on ethics and morality, including so-called Lakṣmīsāṃlo 1746': http://catalogue2.socanth.cam.ac.uk:8080/exist/servlet/db/Hodgson/hodgson.xq.

34 Vansittart (1896: 141–144) gives a translation of 'wise sayings' attributed to Srijanga, from an original document lent to him by 'Mr Paul' in Darjeeling – actually Alfred Wallis Paul (1847–1912), Deputy Commissioner in Darjeeling 1881–1896. These 'wise sayings' concern duties of husband and wife toward each other, means to domesticate animals, obedience to the elders, hygiene, prevention of envy, murder and theft, and advocating respect for the poor, and they also mention sacred books and rebirth after death.

Photo 7.1: Movable types of Kirant letters made by the Yakthung Songjumbho of Kalimpong in the 1990s Source: Mélanie Vandenhelsken (12 May 2019).

> *Yɔk-dhuŋ-le niŋ-wa hop-tero*
> The Limbu lack "knowledge"[35]
> *Yɔk-dhuŋ-sok nirum*
> We need a Limbu script[36]

This highlights simply the existence of a concept of a community called Yakthumba, and the possibility of enhancing its 'knowledge' or 'education' through a script, which suggests the idea of a community formed by its common language. The other texts attributed to Srijanga suggest the existence of sayings and a cosmology specifically Yakthumba.

The size of this community to which Srijanga Thebe refers is, however, unknown. Srijanga was born in 1704 in Yangwarok,[37] today in the Taplejung district, which was one of the Limbu chiefdoms allied to Sikkim[38] – the others were the chiefdoms of Tambar (in today's Taplejung

35 The Limbu term '*nigwa*' means 'mind', 'mental state', 'brain power' and 'wisdom' (Kainla 2010: 231), and, according to Sikkimese Limbu scholar Buddhi L. Subba Khamdhak, can here be translated as 'idea' or 'knowledge', in the sense of 'education'.

36 OIOC, MSS EUR HODGSON/86, pp. 8 and 12. Transliteration and translation from Limbu by Buddhi L. Subba (Khamdhak).

37 Chemjong (2003 [1948]: 3).

38 Chemjong (2003 [1948]: 162).

district), Ilam, Phakphok (today in Ilam district) and Darjeeling.[39] This was, however, only a part of the 'ten Limbu kingdoms' that constituted the whole 'Limbuan'. The concept of Limbuan formed by ten 'kingdoms' appears nevertheless to be an ancient one. They are mentioned in the 'Limbu Vamsavali' (i.e., local chronicle) quoted by Vansittart,[40] which narrates how ten brothers and three priests coming from Benares settled in the eastern Himalayas and founded the Limbu chiefdoms and community (some of the brothers firstly went to Lhasa, and then joined the others who had directly gone to the eastern Himalayas). But, because they were oppressed, the Limbu people chased the kings, and elected in their place ten 'chiefs', *hang*. Then, they fixed the boundaries of their 'territory': to the Tibet border in the north, to 'Mades' (the plain) in the south, the Arun River to the west, and the Mechi River to the east. 'After this division of the country [into ten principalities] the Limbu remained rulers of their country until the Gurkhas waged war against them'.[41]

Vansittart does not provide any information about this text, and Pradhan points out the Indo-Aryan influence of Vansittart's narrative illustrated by the names of the principalities.[42] The narrative also highlights the intellectual debates in Nepal about the origins of the 'Kiratas', which, in broad strokes, concern the relations of the eastern Himalayas 'Kirant' or 'Kirat' with the Kiratas of ancient India and the Kathmandu valley, with the 'Aryans', and with the so-called 'Mongoloid' groups that migrated from the east.[43] This debate gained momentum in India during British colonization.[44]

Nevertheless, the forts of some of the Limbu principalities are still visible in Nepal today, and their history is conveyed through oral history, and in Chemjong's accounts.[45] Pradhan supposes that the latter based his

39 Chemjong does not give his source.

40 Vansittart (1896: 139).

41 Vansittart (1896: 141).

42 Pradhan (2009 [1991]: 55–56).

43 See Singh (1990) for a detailed discussion on these points.

44 Singh (1990: 7)

45 Chemjong (2003 [1948]).

account on the Limbu oral tradition, i.e., the *mundhum*.[46] Today, the ten Limbu chiefdoms represent the Limbu territory or Limbuan as well as the wholeness of the Limbu community.

Secondly, the role of land ownership in 'fixing' Limbu people to the territory and in making ethnic boundaries more rigid is to be examined. In the aftermath of the Gurkha conquests of Limbuan, a system of communal land ownership known as '*kipat*' was established, which is discussed further below.[47] Before the Gurkha conquests, a form of land ownership likely existed in Middle and Far Kirant.[48] In a context where the Sen army was composed of men from the hills, Hamilton mentions land grants in the hills given to military commanders by Sena rulers.[49] He also describes the Kirat (Khambus or Rais) and the Limbu separately, suggesting, as Pradhan notes, 'that the process of eroding tribal lands in the Middle Kirat or Khambuan was largely completed under the Senas'.[50] Additionally, we know that land grants were not given to non-Kirant groups;[51] however, they were given to individuals who had no right to levy taxes or, probably, to transmit land to their descendants,[52] in contrast with the *kipat* lands set up later, which were under the control of segments of the Limbu clans.[53] Sagant mentions a tenure system named (lb.) *thok sing thang sing* that would have prevailed before the Gurkha conquests.[54] This appellation is very likely the same as '*tangsing kok sing*', used in present-day Sikkim, which refers to the founding ancestor of a village (these ancestors have mostly a ritual function). This suggests that the *thok sing thang sing* was a

---

46 Pradhan (2009 [1991]: 56).

47 The *kipat* system was a communal system of land tenure in the sense that an individual could obtain rights to land by virtue of his membership of a localized clan that was part of the Limbu community (Caplan 1970: 3, 28).

48 See Hamilton (1819); Pradhan (2009: 89); Sagant (1996: 123).

49 Hamilton (1819: 148).

50 Pradhan (2009: 89).

51 Pradhan (2009: 89).

52 See Hamilton (1819: 148); Pradhan (2009: 81–91).

53 Sagant (1996: 123); about the *kipat* land system, see also Regmi (1965); Caplan (1970); Forbes (1999).

54 Sagant (1996: 123).

system of land rights given to the first settler and subsequently transmitted within his lineage or clan. Later, under the *kipat* system, rights to occupy particular areas of land were derived by virtue of being 'first settlers'.[55] Thus, possibly, the *thok sing thang sing* mentioned by Sagant was an old form of land tenure, which was continued in the *kipat* system.

Possibly, the relations of the Limbu with the Sen kingdoms in the plains played a role both in the political organization of the Limbu, and in the emergence of Limbu ethnic consciousness. Schlemmer[56] shows how the varying use of the ethnonyms Rai and Khambu within the Rai community follows the division of the Sen kingdoms along the Arun River; this territorial division gradually became a marker of ethnic differentiation.[57] Possibly, the differentiation between Rai and Limbu emerged from the division of the Sen kingdoms as well: in the first half of the eighteenth century, the demarcation between the Sen kingdoms of Chaudandi and Vijaypur was the Kosi River, which prolonged the Arun in the south.[58] This followed an earlier division along the same line in the seventeenth century.[59] Baburam Acharya explains that the ministers (*chautara*) of Vijaypur were appointed exclusively from among the Limbus, though their title was 'Rai' as well, whereas in Chaudandi 'The local Khambus were given the responsibility of defending that region'.[60] We can propose the hypothesis that the division between 'Khambu' and 'Limbu', similar to that between people identifying themselves as Khambu or Rai, followed the prolongation in the north of the line of division between the 'Raya' of Chaudandi and the 'Raya' of Vijaypur.

---

55 See Caplan (1970: 25).

56 Schlemmer (2010, 2018).

57 Schlemmer (2010: 11–12).

58 Either in 1735, which is the date of the foundation of the kingdom of Chaudandi according to Kamaljung Rai and Indradev Rai (2014: 51–54) (Hemkarṇasenko sāmrājyvidī haikam nistej pārna [...] Hemkarṇasenkā bhāī Jagatsenlāī san 1735 mā navarājya Caudaṇḍīko sthāpanā garī tyas rājyako rāja tulyāe) or in 1753 (Acharya 1973: 81).

59 Pradhan (2009: 75)

60 Acharya (1973: 81, 83).

The label 'Limbu' probably appeared in the context of the Gurkha conquests in the eighteenth century (see details about these conquests below) and was likely instrumental in the formation of the pan-local community. According to van Driem,[61] it is a Nepali term taken from one of the Rai languages (in particular, the Dumi Rai used the term 'Li?mbi'), and it very unlikely derives from one of the Limbu autonyms. This is also the opinion of a number of Limbu intellectuals in Sikkim and Kalimpong. Therefore, possibly, the term 'Limbu' was popularized by the Gurkha during the conquests in the eighteenth century. There are several other hypotheses about the origins of the term that J.R. Subba[62] recalls: 'Limbuwan', designating the land of the Limbu, would derive from *li* (bow) *ābu* (to shoot) *bān* (past tense), i.e., the 'land conquered by bow and arrow';[63] and 'Limbu' could derive from the name of either the Limbu king Lilimhang of Suswaden or his great grandson Limbukhang. Others argue that it comes from 'Limbusringam', which is the Sanskritized version of 'Lumbasumba' i.e., Khanchenjunga,[64] or from the Limbu verb '*lingba*', 'to grow by itself'.[65]

The oldest known written occurrence of the term is in a letter from King Prithvi Narayan Shah issued in April 1774 to 'Limbus and Rais', who were from the easternmost part of the Kirant territory, Pallo Kirant.[66]

61 van Driem (1993: 4).

62 Subba (1999: 80).

63 Buddhi L. Subba Khamdhak considers this interpretation to be dubious as the word literally means 'having shot the bow' (personal information).

64 Kandangwa (1990).

65 Kaila (1992: 23). On the possible origins of the term 'Limbu', see also C. Subba (1995: 22); Chemjong (2003 [1948]); Mabohang and Dhungel (1990).

66 Anonymous (1974a: 81–84). The north-eastern part of Nepal, known as the region inhabited by people called 'Kirant', was divided in three parts defined by their distance from the Kathmandu valley: Close Kirant (Wallo Kirant), Middle Kirant (Majh Kirant) and Far Kirant (Pallo Kirant). The view that the term 'Limbu' was used for the first time in this document is supported by Mabuhang (2019). According to him, when the Limbus came in contact for the first time with the Gurkha conquerors, they introduced themselves with the names of their ancestors, 'Susuva Lilim Yakthuṅhāṅ', from which the Gurkha retained only 'Lilim', from which 'Limbū' derives. I am grateful to Prem Chettri (CIRDIS, University of Vienna, FWF) for having brought this article to my attention.

As Schlemmer shows, there is a fluctuating use of the term 'Rai' in the letters from Prithvi Narayan Shah to Kirant leaders from this period, and, in particular, Rai and 'Subba' are not always differentiated; however, 'Between the end of the eighteenth and the middle of the nineteenth century, the use of the term "Rai" became more precise and designated above all the chiefs of the Middle Kirant (while those of the Far Kirant would take the title of Subba)'.[67] In a royal order of August 1774 (Nepali month śrāvaṇ 22),[68] following the conquest of Vijaypur by the Gurkha, Limbu and Rai are clearly distinguished:

> *[...] śrī śrīsun rāī śrīkum rāī śrījaṅ rāī aru sabai gairhā limbu rāīke [...]*
>
> Shun Rai, Kum Rai, Jang Rai, and all Limbu and Rai
>
> *[...] tā̃mbā̃ patra bācāko tasali muluki lālmohor bādhī māthī lekhinye limbu kul bhailāī diñyu [...]*
>
> I promise to abide to this "national" agreement written on a copper plate to the above-mentioned Limbu brotherhood.[69]

This suggests that whereas 'Rai' and 'Subba' designated political offices and statuses as well as land rights prerogatives that were sometimes used interchangeably,[70] 'Limbu' seems, since its emergence, to have designated members of an ethnic community as perceived by the Gurkhas. From the second half of the eighteenth century, the Gurkha conquest of the 'Far Kirant', present-day north-eastern Nepal, was instrumental in the

---

67 Schlemmer (2010: 49).

68 This document is dated śrāvaṇ 22 in Chemjong (2003 [1948]: 207) and Laoti (2005: 175), but śrāvaṇ 12 in Anonymous (1974a: 85); the former date is commonly accepted among Limbus today.

69 The original document is published in Laoti (2005: 215), as well as in http://theveergorkha.blogspot.com/2013/03/history-of-gorkha-limbuwan-treaty-of.html. The transcription in present-day Nepalese is given in Laoti (2005: 175), and a transliteration in Latin characters in Chemjong (2003 [1948]: 207); the translation can be found in Anonymous (1974a: 85) and Chemjong (2003 [1948]: 207).

70 Regarding 'Subba', see the previous section; the term 'Rai' derives from 'Ray', the title given to a Kirant minister in the sixteenth-century kingdom in Morang; 'Ray' then remained the title of the Kirant chief minister (*chautariya*) in the Sen kingdoms in present south-eastern Nepal (see Hamilton [1819: 133]; Schlemmer [2010: 41–48]).

formation of Limbu ethnicity as well as in the division of the community between Nepali and Sikkimese Limbu, as we shall now see.

Limbu ethnicity and loyalty during the Gurkha conquests

In an account of the Gorkhā conquest written in 1846 by Jobhānsing Phāgo Liṃbu, and translated by I.S. Chemjong, the emergence of a division among Limbus is described. A section of Chemjong's *History and Culture of the Kirat People* includes almost the entire text, which the author calls the 'Kirat manuscript'.[71] In brief, Jobhānsing Phāgo Liṃbu describes the three phases of the Gurkha invasion of the Kirant region, firstly that of 'the land of Khambu kings', which was conquered in 1773. The Gurkha army then crossed the Arun to attack the Limbu. On the other side, the 'officers of the Limbu forces were Sangbot Ray, Tesakpa, Kangka Ray and Kangso Ray',[72] who drove the enemy back from their land, but battles continued for three years in the region between Chainpur and Dumja. The third invasion of Far Kirant started from Chainpur. The news of this attack reached the Sikkimese Palace, and

> the Sikkimese King then declared war against the Gurkhas [...]. The Limbus of Yangwarok district of Limbuwan,[73] having claimed their nationality as Sikkimese, joined the Lepcha and Bhutia forces of Sikkim. But by this time, the Gurkhas made a treaty with the Limbus; and for some time, the Limbu–Gurkha war came to an end.[74]

---

71 Chemjong (2003 [1948]: 191–204). See I.S. Chemjong's translation (British Library MSS Eur. D537) of the original document (in Limbu), MSS EUR HODGSON/85, fol.129 (Pradhan [2009: 130] also refers to this document). I am grateful to Bairagi Kainla and Boyd Michailovsky for their respective copies of the document. For other accounts of the Gurkha conquests of east Nepal and Sikkim, see Namgyal and Dolma (1908); *Gazetteer of Sikhim* (1894); Pradhan (2009).

72 Phāgo Liṃbu/Chemjong (1843/1962: 1).

73 According to Chemjong (2003 [1948]), Yangwarok was the only part of Limbuan left to Sikkim after 1774.

74 Phāgo Liṃbu/Chemjong (1843/1962: 3).

After this treaty, the Gurkha king made a regiment of the Limbus,[75] which contributed to the conquest of West Nepal, and retributed them: In east Nepal, Limbus got two pieces of land as Jagir near Bijaipur. These were called Panambari and Guwabari Moujas. In Chainpur, their lands were at Suna Khani, Budhisero, Kokoliyawa and Nimana Piti. They were given to these Limbus with the autonomous right to a flag called the Nishana and a kettle drum accompanied by a written document called the Lall Mohor.[76]

According to Jobhānsing Phāgo Liṃbu, the Limbus of Yanwarok then induced the Sikkimese to attack Chainpur. The Sikkimese were defeated and went back to Sikkim, pursued by the Gurkhas till Ilam. There, 'the Sikkimese had reached their country. So the Gurkhas occupied the land of Phakphok and Ilam'.[77] Finally,

> From that time the Limbus were divided into two groups. Those Limbus who fought for the Gurkhas were called the Gurkha Limbus (in Sikkim they are called Khor-Chong [actually Gor Tsong]) and those Limbus who fought against the Gurkhas were called E-Chong [Ü Tsong, Tib. *yul* i.e. 'country'] or the Sikkimese Limbus.[78] Thus, the Sikkimese Limbus left their Native land and emigrated to Sikkim.[79]

Similar events, and the division they created among the Limbu, are also reported in other historical accounts though differently: According to Pradhan, in preparation for the conquest in the east, Prithvi Narayan Shah

75 Pradhan doubts, however, that Limbus were recruited into the regular army (2009: 142), but a conscription order of July 1791 suggests that there were Limbus among regular soldiers during the war with Tibet: 'From King Ran Bahadur Shah to Subha Kirtiman Singh: (The adult members) of every family of Subhas of the 22 clans [Nep. *Thar*] as well as of (other) functionaries [Nep. *pagaṛi*], soldiers, and (common) subjects in Limbuwan shall assemble in your presence along with arms… and leave for the front. We hereby sanction allowances to them from the revenues of the territories conquered in Bhot' (Anonymous 1970: 267).

76 Vansittart defined a 'Lalmohar' as 'a commission sealed with a red seal' (1896: 142 fn.).

77 Phāgo Liṃbu/Chemjong (1843/1962: 6).

78 I am grateful to Anna Balikci-Denjongpa for the Tibetan signification of these names.

79 Phāgo Liṃbu/Chemjong (1843/1962: 6).

endeavored to 'create a rift' in the Kirant camp.[80] In April 1774, he wrote to several Kirant chiefs, whom he addressed by their names, as well as to 'other Limbus and Rais' to promise them protection; he also drew a distinction between them and the '90,000 Rais' to whom the promise did not apply.[81] According to Pradhan, these chiefs were those of Athrai, Pachthar and Chaubis Thum respectively,[82] whereas the 'others' were from other parts of Limbuan.[83] The chiefs accepted the truce, and after the Gurkha army crossed the Tamar River in August–September 1774, Prithvi Narayan Shah confirmed their rights.[84] The order of 1774 granted to the Limbu the status of vassals rather than subjects, of 'younger brothers rather than serfs'.[85] According to Baburam Acharya (1973), after July 1774, the Limbu chiefs 'of the area from Islingwa to Changthapu in the Limbuwan region bordering Sikkim accepted Prithvi Narayan Shah's suzerainty'.

Jobhānsing Phāgo Liṃbu also describes a battle between Sikkimese and Gurkha Limbus at Sapido in 1792. Later, after Sikkimese forces were pushed away from Chainpur, the Gurkhas killed Limbus who were still supporting the Sikkimese. Consequently, 32,000 Limbu people left for Sikkim, Bhutan and Assam.

The events that followed the invasion of Sikkim by the Gurkhas in 1788 were also instrumental to the elaboration of the representation of the Limbu in Sikkim in the centuries to come. The Gurkha took control of the administration up to the Teesta from 1789.[86] According to the *History of Sikkim*, after the Gurkha invasion of Tashi Lhunpo in 1791 and up until 1792, Sikkimese troops pushed back the Gurkha with the help of Tibetans; the leaders of the troops included Limbus such as 'Tsong Ashadeva, Dzar-sha-mookha, Sho-na-hang and Yongyong-hang'.[87] The Chinese and Sikkimese's advances caused the Kirant to revolt against the

80 Pradhan (2009: 130).

81 Anonymous (1974a: 83).

82 Pradhan (2009: 130).

83 Pradhan (2009: 134).

84 Anonymous (1974b: 84); Pradhan (2009: 131–134).

85 Sagant (1978: 81–87).

86 Pradhan (2009: 146).

87 *History of Sikkim* (1908: 50).

Gurkhas.[88] The rebellion in Kirant was suppressed by the Gurkhas with severity, which resulted in emigration and the depopulation of villages. A large number of Limbus then left for Sikkim, Bhutan and Assam.[89]

In brief, the Limbu community was divided by the war. Today, the names Gor Tsong and Ü-Tsong are still used in Sikkim to differentiate Limbu from Nepal and from Sikkim. This denotes not only a difference of national belonging but also of religion, as Hinduism was introduced among the Limbu in Nepal and Buddhism was the state religion in Sikkim. This division has been influential in the classification of the Limbu in Sikkim, which in turn had consequences in their access to political representation. It seems, however, to have been ignored by John Claude White in his framing of the land revenue system after 1889: then, taxpayers were divided into two groups, the Bhutia-Lepcha and the 'Paharia' (or 'Nepalese'), which included the Limbu; each group paid a different amount of land taxes.[90] All Limbu in Sikkim, whether from Nepal or Sikkim, were then included in the category of recent migrants from Nepal. This administrative categorization had important consequences when the access to citizenship in Sikkim in 1961 was defined as a right stemming from the old settlement in the kingdom. The Sikkimese ruling elite, however, continued distinguishing the Limbu from Nepal and the Limbu from Sikkim: at the end of the nineteenth century, the term 'Gor Tsong' was used by the Sikkimese to refer to Limbus from Nepal who had illegally settled in Sikkim in 1870.[91] When the administration of Sikkim was modernized from the 1940s, the government also organized specific political representation for the 'Tsong' among the Limbu, which implicitly referred to the 'Sikkimese Limbu'.[92]

Jobhānsing Phāgo Liṃbu's historical account above sheds light on the primary reason for this division: the division between 'Gurkha Limbu' and 'Limbu from the country' (Sikkim) was initially not a territorial and

88 Pradhan (2009: 141–151).

89 Pradhan (2009: 141–151); Vansittart (1896: 141); Chemjong ([1948] 2003); see also Campbell (1840: 597).

90 Sikkim Administrative Report 1912–13.

91 I am grateful to Anna Balikci-Denjongpa for this information.

92 See Vandenhelsken (2016).

cultural division, but rather based on loyalty to either the Gurkha or the Sikkimese rulers. They were supporters of both camps on both sides, and as the battle front between Sikkim and Nepal did not coincide with former political alliances, Limbu had to migrate: as Jobhānsing Phāgo writes, 'Sikkimese Limbus left their Native land and emigrated to Sikkim'.[93] A letter from the Tibetan government to the Sikkimese rulers following the Tibet-Nepal war of 1791 suggests that Limbus in Sikkim supported the Gurkhas, and paid a heavy price for it: 'Fighting in a good cause, you have extricated your sacred land from the enemy's hands and driven him out with great slaughter of those traitorous people (Tsongs) who were originally your own subjects'.[94]

The alignment of loyalty with the new territorial organization in the region caused large scale migrations and severe violence. As van Driem has shown, 'acts of resistance against the alien government were to continue in eastern Nepal into the XIXth century', and extremely violent methods of coercion were used by the Gurkha army (and probably by the Sikkimese as well, as we have seen above) against the Limbu.[95]

The division of loyalty among Limbu thus preceded the establishment of the border between Nepal and Sikkim through the treaties of Sugauli in 1816 and Titalia in 1817, which also fixed the division of their territory between Sikkim and Nepal. It also preceded the differentiation between Sikkimese and Nepali Limbu stemming from the introduction of means of integration into the sociopolitical order among Nepali Limbu, i.e., the *kipat* system and the Hindu laws and practices.

Fixing the Limbu division in the territory

This section focuses on the period between 1788, when the Gurkhas crossed the Mechi River towards the east and took control over the territory up to the Teesta River – considered by the Sikkimese rulers as their own – and the late 1830s, when border disputes between Nepal and Sikkim were settled. It shows that this half-century of construction of the

---

93 Phāgo Liṃbu/Chemjong (1843/1962: 6).

94 Namgyal and Dolma (1908: 51).

95 van Driem (2001, vol. 2: 601–605).

border between Nepal and Sikkim played a part in giving Limbu ethnicity its present-day form, while also prolonging pre-colonial forms of political territorialization based on alliances and loyalties.

This period was marked by the formation of Nepal from the territories conquered by the Gurkhas, and the emergence of the control of these territories by the new Nepali state. In the east of Nepal, the *kipat* communal system of land tenure allowed incorporating the Limbu headmen into the governing structure of the kingdom.[96] Land tenure was here a stake of state-making: it maintained the tribal tenurial customs on their ancestral land, through placing them under Gurkha suzerainty,[97] while also giving the Limbu a large degree of autonomy, allowing them at times to challenge the state's authority.[98] The transformation of the *kipat* system by the Nepali state, until its end in the 1990s, highlights the gradual increase of control over, and the integration of the Limbu into, political and religious Nepali governance. When the state controlled the territory through local chiefs, defining clear territorial and ethnic boundaries was not necessary, though, as we shall see now, as the *kipat* was granted on the basis of membership to the Limbu community, it reinforced group identity in relation to the land, but differently than from the nineteenth century onwards. At the turn of the twentieth century, when the land became scarce, the Limbu kin groups 'have been compelled to define their criteria of membership more rigidly in order to defend their interests', and outsiders were no more absorbed into the kinship and land systems.[99] However, at the end of the Anglo-Gurkha war, which allowed the implementation of the colonial concept of territory in the region,[100] and is the period on which the next section focuses, the *kipat* system was still young.

96 Burghart (1984).

97 Burghart (1984).

98 Forbes (1999).

99 Caplan (1970: 24, 45).

100 Michael (2012).

Kipat *in its early days, and ethnic differentiation*

From 1774, after the Gurkha conquered Pallo Kirant, the government granted '*kipat*' lands to the Limbus. The royal order of August 1774 (Nepali month śrāvaṇ 22) states:

> Take care of the lands as you did when it was being ruled over by your own chieftains. Enjoy the land from generation to generation as long as it remains in existence […]. In case we confiscate your land, may our ancestral gods destroy our kingdom. We hereby inscribe this pledge on a copper plate and also issue this royal order and hand it over to our Limbu brethren.[101]

According to Schlemmer:

> This state acknowledgement of the collective possession of *kipaṭ* had a double effect. First, the land-tenure system shifted from an oral rule conceived on a local scale (addressed to surrounding communities sharing the same land-ownership rules), to a legitimation based on a legal, written, unified law imposed by a State. Secondly, this new tenure system may also have reinforced group identity in relation to the land. Being part of a group became the legal criterion for land access and this was enshrined in the state law.[102]

Possibly, *kipat* were granted to groups under the Limbu chiefs (*hang*) known to the Sen kings; however, these chiefs were known by place names, and not by any kinship ties.[103] Then, as the term 'Rai' came specifically to name the chiefs of the middle Kirant,[104] the term 'Limbu' came to name *kipat*-holders in far Kirant. This strengthened the differentiation between Limbu and Rai in Pallo Kirant, which still endures in people's narratives in Nepal today despite the abolition of the *kipat* system in this region. For example, Nar Bir Kerung, former Subba of the village of Chitre, located at

101 Anonymous (1974a: 85).

102 Schlemmer (2018: 7); see also Caplan (2004 [1970]: 4).

103 Pradhan (2009: 128).

104 Schlemmer (2010: 48).

the east of Phidim near the Sikkim border, recalled in 2017 that, in the past in the valley, only Limbu had this form of land ownership whereas Rai had all obtained their lands from Limbus.[105]

Did the *kipat* system also reinforce the differentiation between Nepali and Sikkimese Limbu? After 1817, possibly. However, between 1788 and 1817, Gurkha were settled in the western part of present-day Sikkim. This was mainly a military presence, and the administration of the land was given to a local Lepcha (see below for details). However, Limbu tax collectors were appointed, who had similar functions to the 'Subba' in Far Kirant.[106] The descendants of one of the Limbu *mandals* (i.e., tax collectors) of Sombaria (West Sikkim) reported that his ancestor had been given a '*subbāṅgī*' or order by the Gurkhas conferring on him the title of Subba.[107] Since that time, the family explained, they had observed the Hindu practice of sacrificing goats for Dassera (they stopped this practice in 2013) 'to show their loyalty to the Hindu rulers'.[108] All Limbu and Gurung *karbaris* (i.e., assistant tax collectors) and *mandals* in the regions of Soreng, Tharpu and Darap used to practice this Dassera sacrifice. The power to collect taxes of the above-mentioned Sombaria Limbu *mandal*'s family was continued by the Sikkimese king as shown by a contract in Tibetan still in the possession of its descendants and dating likely from 1873.[109]

In the early eighteenth century in Sikkim, the various functions related to tax collection were distributed differently by the rulers according to

105 Interview carried out by Prem Chettri in Chitre, Memeng Rural Municipality, East Nepal, 10 September 2017.

106 Hamilton reports that Subbas in this region collected custom duties, but he also explains that he could not learn all the specifics (1819: 156).

107 Unlike in other parts of Nepal under the Shah, the *subbāṅgī* in east Nepal and Sikkim does not seem to have been a tax (Dabarl 'Charan' 1986: 116) but an order conferring the position of Subba (Sundas 2017: 562). Vansittart defined the 'Sobangji' as 'a rank [that] corresponds practically on a small scale to a Deputy Commissioner [chief district officer]' (1896: 142 fn). On *subbāṅgī*, see also J.R. Subba (1999: 86).

108 Sombaria *mandal* family member interviewed by Buddhi L. Khamdhak and myself in Sombaria, 18 November 2018.

109 The descendants of the *mandal* were shown this document and provided information to Buddhi L. Khamdhak and I in Sombaria, 18 November 2018. The

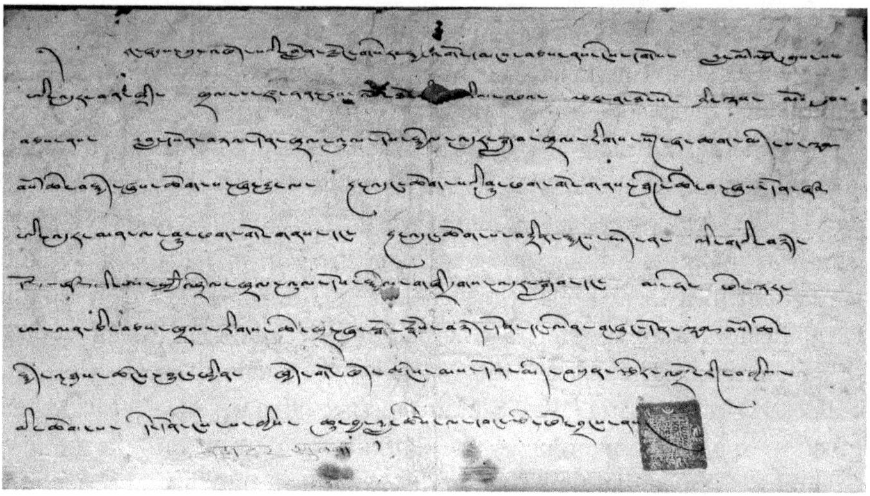

Photo 7.2: Order of appointment of Limbu Nembang tax collectors in Sombaria with the Sikkim king's seal, 1873

Source: Document in the possession of the family in Sombaria; photo taken by Mélanie Vandenhelsken.

ethnicity, and this distribution highlighted as well as reified the Bhutia's hierarchization of the three ethnic communities of Sikkim. There were, however, overlaps between ethnicities, and the criterion of clan status combined with ethnicity to form the hierarchy.[110] Some of the functions were attributed to several groups, and others to only one group. For example, the function of *tasa* (i.e., tax collector, Tib. *rta sa*)[111] was exclusively granted to Lepcha and Limbu, and *subba*, only to the Limbu.[112]

In Rimbi, Shu Phang, one of the Limbu signatories of the 1663 Lho Mön Tsong Sum treaty, was a tax collector (*tasa*). A document dated 1779 mentions that the function and rank of tax collector over the agricultural tenants had been conferred on a Limbu man called Domikpa by the second

document was translated by Tsering Drongshar and Tsewang Gyatso, IKGA-Austrian Academy of Sciences, Vienna. It was issued in the Tumlong palace in the water bird year, very likely corresponding to 1873.

110 Vandenhelsken and Khamdhak (2021: 241).

111 See Mullard and Wongchuk (2010: 5).

112 Vandenhelsken and Khamdhak (2021).

chogyal of Sikkim, Tenzung Namgyal (1670–1700) in Daley (identified by Limbus today as Bhara Khelay, near Soreng); the document confirms that Domikpa's descendants are still in charge of tax collection.[113] In 1845 there were Limbu *tasa* in Zamdong and Namchi.[114] The case of the Subba of Sombaria therefore shows that the Gurkhas had taken over the nomination of (at least one) tax collector during the period of their settlement in present-day West Sikkim (1788–1816). However, it is unclear at this point whether a system similar to the *kipat* was then implemented between the Mechi and Teesta rivers between 1788 and 1816/17, and in particular, if ethnicity was involved in the attributions of the functions related to tax collection, and if the Lepcha rulers of West Sikkim on behalf of the Gurkhas maintained or transformed the previous tax collection system.

The territorialization of the division of the Limbu has been a slow process. Although the border and the process of national integration differentiated Limbu in Sikkim from those in Nepal, even after 1817 the border remained unsettled, with border disputes continuing until 1836. During these two decades, the loyalty within the Limbu community to both powers continued to shift, as we shall now see.

Fluctuating border, mobile loyalty and 'itinerant territoriality'[115]

The old western border of Sikkim was 'uncertain'[116] or not definite,[117] but was also considered by 'native authorities' from Sikkim as being the Kankai, which flowed north to south and crossed Ilam.[118] Whereas the entire Morung belonged to Vijaypur, Sikkim possessed a tract of land between the Mahananda River (the river now traversing Siliguri) and the

113 See PD/ I.I /002 in Mullard and Wongchuk (2010: 15). The full translation of this document is displayed on the cover of A.B. Subba (2016). See also Mullard (2015).

114 PD/1.1/013 in Mullard and Wongchuk (2010: 19).

115 Mbembe (2001).

116 Hamilton (1820, vol. 2: 720).

117 Pradhan (2009: 78).

118 Hamilton (1820, vol. 2: 720).

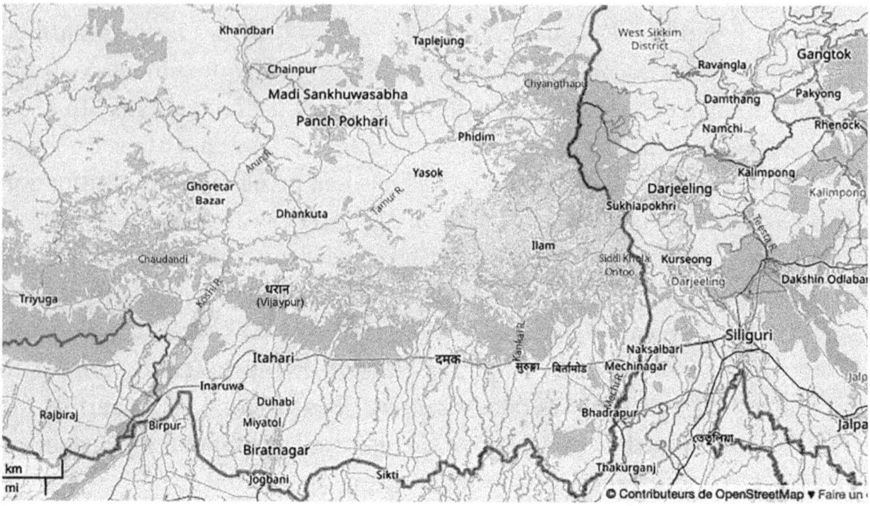

Figure 7.1: Map of the study area

Teesta.[119] However, there is a discrepancy between the Sikkimese and Nepali sources: according to Baburam Acharya,[120] the Teesta formed the eastern boundary of Morung. Pradhan mentions a document dated from 1774 that also highlights the view of the Teesta being the eastern boundary of the Sena kingdoms:

> If Sikkim remains quiet even after the occupation of Chyangthapu and Islimba, if it does not break the truce and come to fight, do cross the Kankai very cautiously. But if Sikkim is offended by our occupation of Chyangthapu and Islimba and breaks the peace, don't evacuate the plains. You must quickly advance up to the Tista which forms of the border of Hindupati [Makwampur].[121]

Sikkim ceded Ilam to Nepal in September 1774.[122] However, as we shall see below, some landlords in Ilam continued paying taxes to both Nepal

119 Hamilton (1820, vol. 2: 720).

120 Baburam Acharya (1973).

121 Pradhan (2009: 134).

122 Acharya (1973).

and Sikkim until 1826. From the Sikkimese point of view, a treaty in 1775 fixed the boundary with Nepal, 'from Shango-chu, in the higher hills, Shangdijong, Malliayan and called in Tibetan the Lha-chu and in Hindi called the Kanika [Kankai] River. East of these was fixed and settled as Sikkim Territory'.[123] Pradhan argues that this treaty merely concerned trade between Tibet and Nepal and doubts that it concerned the boundary between Sikkim and Nepal, adding that Sikkimese claims over Limbuan and Morung were likely unjustifiable.[124] He nevertheless states that 'In the east, the promise given to Sikkim in 1775 remained operative for thirteen years'.[125] The *History of Sikkim* states, however, that between 1775 and 1779 the Sikkimese and Gurkha armies fought a number of battles between the Arun and the Teesta: at Tob-Jong and Illam in 1775; Relling, Karmi and Chakung in 1775 as well; Chainpur in 1776 (or 1787 according to the *Gazetteer of Sikhim*[126]; Pradhan questions both dates[127]); and at Namchi in 1779. Furthermore, the Gurkha army advanced as far as Chongthang Jong (Tsang thang[128]), and the Sikkimese up to the Arun during the same period.

There is a consensus that the Gurkha invasion of Sikkim was in 1788. The Gurkha then took control of the area up to the eastern bank of the Teesta. However, they probably only maintained a military presence in two stations – in Nagri-dzong, in present-day Darjeeling district, and probably in or around Rabdentse.[129] The collection of taxes and civil gov-

123 Namgyal and Dolma (1908: 46).

124 Pradhan (2009: 131–143).

125 Pradhan (2009: 142).

126 *Gazetteer of Sikhim* (1894).

127 Pradhan (2009: 142, 149).

128 I am thankful to Anna Balikci-Denjongpa for the identification of this place name.

129 Namgyal and Dolma's *History of Sikkim* suggests that a Gurkha army commander was stationed in Rabdentse at least for some time after the capture of the palace: 'These lay and Lama representatives proceeded as far as Namchi and Chakung, and they summoned the Gurkha leader Joharsingh from Rabdentse, and told him that as long as they did not get a communication from Nepal, he must vacate Rabdentse and retire to Bijapur, and he did so for a time' (p. 72 of my copy). Hamilton (1819: 123) writes 'there were Gurkhalese troops at Sikim and Darjiling, the two chief places in the district', and we know that in Hamilton's writing, 'Sikim' refers to the place where the Sikkimese king used to live, i.e. Rabdentse, and not to the country (see about this Risley in the *Gazetteer of*

ernment was soon given back to a Sikkimese Lepcha, Yug Kunda, who in 1808 paid a fixed annual sum to the Subba of Chainpur.[130] In 1805, Yug Kunda was responsible for territory and tax revenue for both Sikkim (everything east of the Mechi) and Nepal (parts of Chainpur and Vijaypur as well as parts of Ilam).[131] The Subba of Chainpur moved to Nagri, and until 1846 he shared the administration of some territories with the Sikkimese government.[132]

The region between the Kankai and the Mechi was not the only one whose administrators paid taxes to both Sikkim and Nepal: Wallungchu, taken by the Gurkhas in 1775,[133] paid taxes to both states in 1848.[134] These areas were both shared and disputed spaces, controlled not by the states but by local leaders.[135]

The treaty of 1792 between Nepal and Tibet, after the Gurkhas had been pushed away from Sikkim, and those of 1816 (Sugauli) and 1817 (Titalia), further highlighted the disagreements between Nepal and Sikkim over the location of the border. According to the Sikkimese, Sikkim was not represented in the negotiation between Tibet and the Gurkhas, and:

> The Gurkhas falsely represented to the Tunthang, who did not know the former boundaries of Sikkim, that Sikkim's boundary comprised of Teesta below and Singalila above, and they made it appear as if they had restored the Pemionchi and lower parts of Sikkim, where they had

Sikhim, 1894: 40).

130 Hamilton (1819: 123); Pradhan (2009: 141–147); Mullard (2013); *Gazetteer of Sikhim* (1894: 19).

131 Mullard (2013).

132 Pradhan (2009: 148).

133 Pradhan (2009: 140).

134 J.D. Hooker (1980 [1855], vol I: 205); Steinmann (1991).

135 Mullard (2013). This included for example Ilam which, according to Hodgson, during the quarter-century following the conquest, was administered separately by its own military authorities (Hodgson [1880: 201] quoted in Caplan [1970: 14]). On the administration of Ilam during this period, see also Mullard (2013).

> once been masters of [*sic*] a time, but from which the Sikkimites had expelled them.[136]

Despite the treaty, Sikkimese complained that the Gurkhas had again sent raiding parties into Sikkim. When the Anglo-Nepal war ended, the Sikkim ruler requested of the British that:

> At the least, our boundaries ought to be Singli-La on the top and Manchi river at the foot. The Morang Terai territories are bounded on the west by Kanika and the Teesta on the East. The top forests extended up to Timar Choten formerly, but the Arun River constituted our real natural boundary.[137]

However, 'The 1816 Sugauli Treaty signed between Nepal and the English fixed the Mechi river as Nepal's eastern boundary';[138] it was firstly ceded to the company, and then restored to Sikkim by the treaty of Titalia in 1817.[139]

Border disputes between Sikkim and Nepal occurred in several instances after the signature of the treaty of Titalia, as in 1826.[140] As K.L. Pradhan explains, one of these disputes concerned a tract of land called Kopilashi, located between the old and new branches of the Mechi River:

> The last important boundary to be settled was between Nepal and Sikkim. This portion was clearly demarcated by the river Mechi, but the problem soon arose as the river was divided itself into two branches before entering into India. Capt. B. Latter, the political agent in Sikkim [*sic*] held that the old Mechi should be confirmed as the boundary. It was not clear in 1817, because Resident Gardner was reluctant to add that any discussion of this sort would create trouble, because the Treaty of Sagauli did not clarify whether old or new Mechi would be [the]

136 Namgyal and Dolma (1908: 51).

137 Namgyal and Yeshe Dolma (1908: 51–59).

138 Shrestha (1976: 50).

139 Pradhan (2009: 156).

140 Pradhan (2009: 158).

> boundary and it would be impossible to satisfy the Darbar on this point. The matter was kept pending till 1830 when it gave rise to a serious and prolonged dispute, and finally settled in Nepal's favor in 1839.[141]

Another dispute concerned a ridge called 'Oontoo' (or Unthoo) in the Ilam area (this dispute is also known as the Siddi Khola dispute), located between two streams that join to form the Mechi River: 'The western river was called Mechi by Sikkimites and Siddhi by the Gurkhas; and the eastern stream was entitled by Sikkimites as Kanchi and Mechi by the Nepalese'. Investigations conducted by British officers concluded in 1839 that the eastern stream was the Mechi as well as the border between Nepal and Sikkim, and thus, that the tract between both rivers, 'Oontoo', belonged to Nepal.[142]

While the border between Nepal and Sikkim was contested,[143] Limbus were 'in-between', 'not to be trusted',[144] and were asked to spy on the other side.[145] The reports about the part taken by Limbu during the Gurkha conquests also show that Limbu sub-groups changed sides during the war; the categorization as Gor Tsong and Ü Tsong thus remained fluid for some time. The length of the period during which the border remained disputed accentuated the marginalization of the Limbu in Sikkim, already stemming from the suspicion that they were continuing to support the enemy.

At the end of the nineteenth century in the frame of British expansion and domination, 'nationalist narratives [...] sought to create historical

---

141 K.L. Pradhan (2012: 69). Capt. B. Latter was actually not a political agent in Sikkim but in charge of diplomatic contacts with Sikkim (see Bray [2012]).

142 Ramakant (1968: 131–139). See also the *Gazetteer of Sikhim* (1894: 19); Pinn (1990); Sprigg (1995: 89). The original documents concerning this dispute are held at the British Library: IOR/F/4/1813/74755.

143 Michael (2012) shows that, more than having been contested, the Anglo-Nepali border in general moved depending on tenurial relationship. This form of indirect and mobile sovereignty of the state confused the East India Company, which conceived the exercise of state sovereignty within a territory having contiguous and fixed borders.

144 Anonymous (1971: 279).

145 Anonymous (1982: 60).

legitimacy for the existence of the Sikkimese nation and in particular the royal family through the appropriation of [Buddhist] religious symbolism'.[146] Then exclusive boundaries were drawn, physically and symbolically, between Nepal and Sikkim, settlers and natives, and Hindu and Buddhist, reducing the Sikkimese 'natives' to the Bhutias and Lepchas. As 'apprehensive territoriality'[147] settled – in a context where bordering between Nepal and Sikkim not only remained disputed, but also opened the door to colonial domination – it became an anomaly to be both from Nepal and Sikkim.

Conclusion

This chapter has shed light on the immediate effects of the Singalila/Mechi border on borderland people in the eighteenth and early nineteenth centuries, in particular on how the border was 'transferred' into the Limbu community in the early phase of modern state-making in the region. It shows firstly that the pre-colonial attachment of the Limbu to the territory differed from their situation after the establishment of the border in that it coexisted with other forms of belonging, which, for example, allowed passages between ethnicities, and because it was fluid as political power and control of the land were also fluid.

Secondly, it shows that the perpetuation of the division of the Limbu into two groups is an outcome of the passage between a form of membership based on alliances and a national membership based on belonging to a territory,[148] which durably fixed people to a national territory from the early nineteenth century in the region. Unlike groups forced to move across borders when they are settled or redefined, Limbu became 'borderland people' without moving, because their territory had been redefined according to the new nation-states and the colonial territorial ordering. In other words, they became a borderland people as a result of

146 Mullard (2011: 59).

147 van Schendel (2013).

148 Gellner (2013).

the shift from the government of people to the government of territory, which commonly characterizes nation-state making.[149]

Subsequently, the divided and shifting loyalty of the Limbu during the Gurkha conquests was fixed in the territory by the settlement of the border, and became a determinant of their integration into the states of both Nepal and Sikkim when, later in the nineteenth century, political rulers endeavored to assimilate the state and the nation. At that point, what had been a circumstantial and fluid division within the community became a marker that determined both their social identity and the conception of their ethnic boundaries. In particular, after the mid-nineteenth century, when the ethnic balance in Sikkim changed as part of colonial expansion and the distinction between 'native' and 'settlers' became a criterion for the definition of the Sikkimese 'nation' and suzerainty, the division of the Limbu territory and their membership of two states challenged the historical narrative that legitimized the Sikkimese rulers' political power. Additionally, their ability as a transborder community to cross that border as well as to 'belong' to both states kept them under suspicion from both sides. And it highlighted the fragility of this border, thus challenging the Sikkimese rulers' determination to affirm its existence.

Thirdly, we also saw in this chapter evidence that the cultural and religious distinction within both parts of the Limbu community as well as the questioning of Limbu indigeneity in Sikkim are outcomes of the border, and are part of processes of state-making and of bordering: political factors – not cultural – determined the distinction between the two sub-groups within the Limbu community, as well as shaping Limbu social identity in Sikkim. A sense of shared community and language had been evident before the Gurkha conquests, but it allowed for the adoption of outsiders, as we have seen. The division of the Limbu into those loyal to the Gurkhas and those loyal to Sikkim (Gor Tsong and Ü Tsong) in any case preceded the introduction of Hinduism among the Limbu in Nepal in the early nineteenth century.[150]

Today, the Hindu influence on the Nepali Limbu, contrasting with the Sikkimese Limbu who lived in a Buddhist kingdom (without, however,

149 Wilson and Donnan (1998: 8); van Schendel (2013).

150 Pradhan (2009: 181–185).

generally having converted to Buddhism), is viewed as the main cultural difference between the sub-groups. As a way to smooth their relations with the Hindu kingdom, in the early nineteenth century, Limbu were exempted from some of these religious laws;[151] others, however, were enforced with just as much violence as elsewhere,[152] and Hinduism gradually made its way into Limbu territory through the settlement of a large number of Hindus,[153] although the memory of Limbu resistance to Hinduism was expressed in ritual practices up until the 1960s.[154] The *kipat* system established another important difference between Sikkimese and Nepalese Limbu, but this occurred later as well.

Finally, this chapter shows that the Limbu community's links with the other side of the border do not call into question its indigeneity, since their indigeneity predates the border. What has not been discussed in this work is the people's response to state-making in their region, although the classification in Gor Tsong and Ü Tsong is reported by a Limbu writer and could have been an endo-classification, which suggests a certain level of adaptation if not to the state's territorialization, at least to the new organization of power in the region. Little information is available on this subject, and more research on this topic would be a substantial contribution to the knowledge about the Limbu and state-making in this region.

151 Pradhan (2009: 184).

152 Pradhan (2009: 185).

153 See Caplan (1970); Sagant (1996).

154 See in particular Sagant (1996: pt. 1, ch 1, and pt. 2).

Bibliography

Acharya, B. (1973). 'Annexation of the Sen Kingdoms', *Regmi Research Series*, Year 5, no. 5, pp. 81–85.

Anonymous (1970). 'On the Nepal-Tibet War, 1791', *Regmi Research Series*, Year 2, no. 11, pp. 261–271.

Anonymous (1971). 'Nepal, Sikkim and the East India Company 1793', *Regmi Research Series*, Year 3, no. 12, pp. 271–279.

Anonymous (1974a). 'Notes on the Kipat System-I. Letter to Jang Rai and Others', *Regmi Research Series*, Year 6, no. 5, p. 83.

Anonymous (1974b). 'Notes on the Kipat System-I. Another Letter to Jang Rai and Others', *Regmi Research Series*, Year 6, no. 5, p. 84.

Anonymous (1982). 'Remission of Jhara Obligations (A.D. 1811–17). Royal Order to the Limbus and Rais of Yangrup 1811', *Regmi Research Series*, Year 14, no. 1–4, p. 60.

Baruah, S. (2013). 'Politics of Territoriality: Indigeneity, Itinerancy and Rights in North-East India'. In J. Smadja, ed., *Territorial Changes and Territorial Restructurings in the Himalayas*, New-Delhi: Adroit Publishers and Paris: Centre for Himalayan Studies, pp. 69–83.

Bray, J. (2012). 'Captain Barré Latter and British Engagement with Sikkim during the 1811–1816 Nepal War'. In A. Balicki-Denjongpa and A. McKay, eds., *Buddhist Himalaya: Studies in Religion, History and Culture. Volume II: The Sikkim Papers*, Gangtok: Namgyal Institute of Tibetology, pp. 71–93.

Burghart, R. (1984). 'The Formation of the Concept of Nation-State in Nepal', *The Journal of Asian Studies*, vol. 44, no. 1, pp. 101–125.

Campbell, A. (1840). 'Note on Limboos and Other Hill Tribes', *Journal of the Asiatic Society of Bengal*, pt. 1, pp. 491–615.

Caplan, L. (1970). *Land and Social Change in East Nepal: A Study of Hindu-Tribal Relations*, London: Routledge & Kegan Paul Limited.

Central Bureau of Statistics (2012). *National Population and Housing Census 2011*, Kathmandu: National Planning Commission Secretariat, Government of Nepal.

Chalmers, R. (2003). 'The Quest for Ekrupata: Unity, Uniformity and the Delineation of the Nepali Community in Darjeeling'. In A.C. Sinha and T.B. Subba, eds., *The Nepalis in Northeast India. A Community in Search of Indian Identity*, New Delhi: Indus Publishing Company, pp. 331–360.

Chemjong, I.S. (2003 [1948]). *History and Culture of the Kirat People. Part I-II*, Lalitpur: Kirat Yakhtung Chumlung.

Cohn, B. (1987). *An Anthropologist among the Historians and Other Essays*, Delhi: Oxford University Press.

Dabarl 'Charan', S. P. (1986). 'Gorkhali Rule in Kumaun', *Regmi Research Series*, Year 18, no. 8, pp. 111–116.

DESME (Department of Economics, Statistics, Monitoring and Evaluation). (2006). *State Socio Economic Census 2006*, Gangtok: Government of Sikkim.

Dhakal, R.P. (2009). 'The Urge to Belong: An Identity in Waiting'. In T.B. Subba, A.C. Sinha, G.S. Nepal and D.R. Nepal, eds., *Indian Nepalis. Issues and Perspectives*, New-Delhi: Concept Publishing Company, pp. 141–167.

Dhungel, R. (2006). 'The Long-Ago Fight for Kirant Identity', *Himal South Asian*, vol. 19, no. 7, pp. 51–56. http://www.himalmag.com/2006/october/essay.htm

Ebert, K. (1994). *The Structure of Kiranti Languages: Comparative Grammar and Texts*, Zürich: Seminar für Allgemeine Sprachwissenschaft.

Forbes, A.A. (1999). 'Mapping Power: Disputing Claims to Kipat Lands in Northeastern Nepal', *American Ethnologist*, vol. 26, no. 1, pp. 114–138.

Gaenszle, M. (2000). *Origins and Migrations: Kinship, Mythology and Ethnic Identity among the Mewahang Rai of East Nepal*, Kathmandu: Mandala Book Point & The Mountain Institute.

Gaenszle, M. (2013). 'The Power of Script: Phalgunanda's Role in the Formation of Kiranti Ethnicity'. In V. Arora and N. Jayaram, eds., *Routeing Democracy in the Himalayas: Experiments and Experiences*, New Delhi: Routledge, pp. 51–73.

Gazetteer of Sikhim (1989 [1894]). Gangtok: Sikkim Nature Conservation Foundation.

Hamilton, F. (1819). *An Account of the Kingdom of Nepal: And of the Territories Annexed to this Dominion by the House of Gorkha*, Edinburgh: Archibald Constable and Company.

Hamilton, W. (1820). *Geographical, Statistical and Historical Description of Hindostan and the Adjacent Countries*, London: John Murray.

Hunter, W.W. (1896). *Life of Brian Houghton Hodgson, British Resident at the Court of Nepal*, London: John Murray.

Kainla, V. (1992). *Limbū Bhāṣā ra Sāhityako Samkśpta Pricaya. A Brief Introduction to Limbu Language and Literature*, Kathmandu: Nepal Rajakīya Prjñā Prtisṣṭhān.

Kainla, V. (2010 [2067 B.S.]). *Limbu-Nepali-English Dictionary*, Kathmandu: Nepal Pragya Pratishthat.

Kandangwa, K. (1990). 'Raiharu Kahiledekhi Limbu bhae?', *Chhahara Weekly*, vol. 10, no. 10 (7 June).

Kolossov, V. and J. Scott (2013). 'Selected Conceptual Issues in Border Studies', *Belgeo 1*, DOI: https://doi.org/10.4000/belgeo.10532

Laoti, Y. (2005). *Adivasi Limbu Jatika Sangkshita Paritsaya* (A brief account on indigenous Limbu), Kathmandu: Dil Bahadur Laoti.

Linguistic Survey of India, 2001, Sikkim part 1 (2009). Language Division, Office of the Registrar General, India.

Mabohang, S.P. Bahadur Limbu, and B.N. Dhungel (1990). *Sankshipta Nepal Itihas*, Kathmandu: Kirata Publication.

Mbembe, A. (2001). 'At the Edge of the World: Boundaries, Territoriality, and Sovereignty in Africa'. In A. Appadurai, ed., *Globalization*, Durham/London: Duke University Press.

Michael, A.B. (2012). *Statemaking and Territory in South Asia. Lessons from the Anglo-Gorkha War (1814-1816)*, London: Anthem Press.

Middleton, T. (2016). *The Demands of Recognition. State Anthropology and Ethnopolitics in Darjeeling*, Stanford: Stanford University Press.

Mullard, S. (2011). *Opening the Hidden Land: State Formation and the Construction of Sikkimese History*, Leiden: Brill.

Mullard, S. (2013). 'Recapturing Runaways, or Administration through Contract: The 1830 Covenant (Gan rgya) on Kotapa Tax Exiles and Sikkimese Border Regions'. In C. Ramble, P. Schwieger and A. Travers, eds., *Studies in the Social History of Tibetan Societies: Tibetans who Escaped the Historian's Net*, Kathmandu: Vajra Books, pp. 171–208.

Mullard, S. and H. Wongchuk (2010). *Royal Records: A Catalogue of the Sikkimese Palace Archive*, Andiast: International Institute for Tibetan and Buddhist Studies.

Namgyal, T. and Y. Dolma (1908). *History of Sikkim*, English translation, unpublished manuscript.

Pels, P. (1999). 'From Texts to Bodies: Brian Houghton Hodgson and the Emergence of Ethnology in India'. In J. Breman and A. Shimizu, eds., *Anthropology and Colonialism in Asia and Oceania*, Surrey: Curzon Press, pp. 65–92.

Phago Limbu, J. / I.S. Chemjong (trans.) (1843 / 1962). *Limbu History* (Trans.: *Free Translation of the Limbu History*). MSS EUR HODGSON/85, fol.129. Trans.: MSS Eur. D537.

Pinn, F. (1990). *The Road of Destiny. Darjeeling Letters 1839*, Calcutta: Oxford University Press.

Pommaret, F. (1999). 'The Mon pa Revisited: In Search of Mon'. In T. Huber, ed., *Sacred Spaces and Powerful Places in Tibetan Culture*, Dharamsala: Tibetan Library of Works and Archives, pp. 51–73.

Pradhan, K. ([1991] 2009). *The Gorkha Conquests. The Process and Consequences of the Unification of Nepal, with Particular References to Eastern Nepal*, Kathmandu: Himal Books.

Pradhan, K.L. (2001). *Brian Hodgson at the Kathmandu Residency 1821–1843*, Guwahati: Spectrum Publications.

Pradhan, K.L. (2012). *Thapa Politics in Nepal. With Special Reference to Bhim Sen Thapa (1801–1839)*, New Delhi: Concept Publishing Company.

Ramakant (1968). *Indo-Nepalese Relations 1811–77*, Delhi: S. Chand and Co.

Reeves, M. (2014). 'Roads of Hope and Dislocation: Infrastructure and the Remaking of Territory at a Central Asian Border', *Ab Imperio*, vol. 2, pp. 235–257, https://doi.org/10.1353/imp.2014.0032

Regmi, M.C. (1965). *Land Tenure and Taxation in Nepal. Volume 3. The Jagir, Rakam, and Kipat Tenure Systems*, Berkeley: University of California, Institute of International Studies.

Regmi, M.C. (1995). *Kings and Political Leaders of the Gorkhali Empire 1761–1814*, Hyderabad: Orient Longman.

Sagant, P. (1978). 'Ampleur et profondeur historique des migrations népalaises', *L'Ethnographie*, vol. 77, no. 78, pp. 91–119.

Sagant, P. (1996). *The Dozing Shaman. The Limbus of Eastern Nepal*, Delhi: Oxford University Press.

Schlemmer, G. (2010). 'Rai, Khambu, Subba, Kirant, etc.: Ethnic Labels or Political and Land Tenure Categories? Logics of Identification of an Ensemble of Populations in Nepal'. In C. Culas and F. Robinne, eds., *Inter-Ethnic Dynamics in Asia Considering the Other through Ethnonyms, Territories and Rituals*, London and New York: Routledge, pp. 41–56.

Schlemmer, G. (2018). 'Enshrining Space: Shrines, Public Space and Hinduization among the Kulung of Nepal', *South Asia Multidisciplinary Academic Journal*, vol. 18, DOI: https://doi.org/10.4000/samaj.4603

Sharma, J. (2016). 'Producing Himalayan Darjeeling: Mobile People and Mountain Encounters', *Himalaya, the Journal of the Association for Nepal and Himalayan Studies*, vol. 35, no. 2, article 12, http://digitalcommons.macalester.edu/himalaya/vol35/iss2/12

Shneiderman, S. (2015). *Rituals of Ethnicity: Thangmi Identities Between Nepal and India*, Philadelphia: University of Pennsylvania Press.

Shrestha, S.L. (1976). 'Some Old Taxes of Jhapa District', *Regmi Research Series*, Year 8, no. 3, pp. 51–52.

Singh, G.P. (1990). *The Kiratas in Ancient India*, Delhi: Gian Publishing House.

Sprigg, R.K. (1959). 'Limbu Books in the Kiranti Script', *Akten des Vierundzwangzigsten Internationalen Orientalisten Krongresses. Munich 26 August – 4 September*, pp. 591–592, http://eprints.soas.ac.uk/16711/1/Sprigg%201959%20Limbu%20script.pdf

Sprigg, R.K. (1995). '1826: An End of an Era in the Social and Political History of Sikkim', *The Bulletin of Tibetology*, vol. 19, no. 2, pp. 88–92.

Steinmann, B. (1991). 'The Political and Diplomatic Role of a Tibetan Village Chieftain (go-ba) on the Nepalese Frontier'. In E. Steinkellner, ed., *Wiener Studien zur Tibetologie und Buddhismuskunde 26: Tibetan History and Language*, Vienna: Arbeitskreis für Tibetische und Buddhistische Studien, pp. 467–486.

Subba, C. (1995). *The Culture and Religion of Limbus*, Kathmandu: K.B. Subba.

Subba, J.R. (1999). *The Limboos of the Eastern Himalayas*, Gangtok: Sikkim Yakdhung Mundhum Saplopa.

Subba, T.B. (1999). *Politics of Culture: A Study of Three Kirata Communities in the Eastern Himalayas*, Chennai: Orient Longman.

Sundas, B. (2020). 'The Process of State Formation and Its Impact on Social Formation in Eastern Nepal and Sikkim, 16th-19th Centuries'. In S.K. Chaudhuri, S. Maiti and C.K. Lepcha, eds., *The Cultural Heritage of Sikkim*, London/New York: Routledge, pp. 51–69.

van Driem, G. (1987). *A Grammar of Limbu*, Berlin: Mouton de Gruyter.

van Driem, G. (1993). *A Grammar of Dumi*, Berlin/New York: Mouton de Gruyter.

van Driem, G. (2001). *Languages of the Himalayas. An Ethnolinguistic Handbook of the Greater Himalayan Region*, Leiden: Brill.

van Schendel, W. (2013). 'Making the Most of "Sensitive" Borders'. In D.N. Gellner, ed., *Borderland Lives in Northern South Asia*, Durham/London: Duke University Press, pp. 266–271.

Vandenhelsken, M. (2016). 'Politics of Ethnicity amongst the Limbu in Sikkim: Literary Development, Religious Reforms and the Making of the Community', *Irish Journal of Anthropology*, Special Issue, 'Emerging Adivasi and Indigenous Studies II – Identity Assertions and Symbolic Re-appropriations in India' (edited by L. Guzy and M. Carrin), vol. 19, no. 2, pp. 61–83.

Vandenhelsken, M. (2021). 'The 1961 Sikkim Subject Regulation and "Indirect Rule" in Sikkim: Ancestrality, Land Property and Unequal Citizenship', *Asian Ethnicity*, vol. 22, no. 2, pp. 254–271, DOI: 10.1080/14631369.2020.1801338

Vandenhelsken, M. and B.L. Khamdhak (2021). 'Loyalty, Resistance, Subalterneity: A History of Limbu "Participation" in Sikkim', *Asian Ethnicity*, vol. 22, no. 2, pp. 235–253, DOI: 10.1080/14631369.2020.1763777

Vansittart, E. (1896). *Notes on Nepal*, Calcutta: Office of the Superintendent of Government Printing.

Warner, C. (2014). *Shifting States: Mobile Subjects, Markets, and Sovereignty in the India-Nepal Borderland, 1780-1930* (PhD dissertation, University of Washington).

Waterhouse, D.M. (2004). *The Origins of Himalayan Studies. Brian Houghton Hodgson in Nepal and Darjeeling 1820–1858*, London and New York: Routledge.

Wilson, T.M. and H. Donnan, eds. (1998). *Border Identities. Nation and State at International Frontiers*, Cambridge: Cambridge University Press.

8 Negotiating Sacred Himalayan Landscape: Contested Knowledge Production on Environment, Dams and the Deities' Wrath in Sikkim

Jenny Bentley[1]

> Endless bio-diversity. Mountains are our guardians. Rivers, our identity, our pride. Let the rivers run freely. #riversforlife.[2]

Since the Affected Citizens of Teesta (ACT) ignited the protest movement against dam construction along the river Teesta in the Indian state of Sikkim with a hunger strike (2006–2009) seventeen years ago, its members have repeatedly drawn attention to the dangers of building such large-scale development projects.[3] They point out the importance of the rivers, the

---

1 This chapter is based on research conducted during my doctoral research, funded by the *Janggen Poehn Stiftung* and the *Forschungskredit der Universität Zürich.* I would like to thank Prof. Seiji Kumagai and Dr. Anna Balikci-Denjongpa for including my research in the Bhutan-Sikkim panel at the IATS 2019. I am indebted to the people of Dzongu for sharing their knowledge with me. Special reference goes to the Lepcha religious specialists, among others Netuk Lepcha and Kinchok Lepcha, and the anti-dam activists, including Dawa Lepcha, Gyatso Lepcha, Tenzing Gyatso Lepcha and Tseten Lepcha. My work would not have been possible without Kachyo Lepcha, who conducted the ethnographic research together with me and spent many days discussing, translating, and questioning our findings. I thank Amelie Huber, Mabel Gergan and the anonymous reviewer for their extremely valuable comments and suggestions on earlier versions of this article. Last, but not least, I am grateful to Ben Young for proof reading. All remaining mistakes are my own.

2 Examples of slogans on protest posters, 20 June 2020, fourteenth anniversary of the hunger strike.

3 On the history of protest against dams in the Teesta River in Sikkim, see Lepcha (2012, 2020). For accounts of the anti-dam movement, see Arora (2007, 2008, 2009, 2014); Chettri (2017); Dutta (2007); Joshi, Platteeuw and Teoh (2018),

region's biodiversity and the function of the mountain deities. According to the Government of Sikkim, sixteen hydroelectric power projects are either ongoing or completed in the small Indian state, while seventeen have been cancelled and six are under litigation.[4] The activists[5] opposed the dams due to their negative environmental impact in this fragile and seismically active Himalayan region, known for its rich biodiversity and partly protected by the Kanchenjunga National Park, since 2016 a mixed UNESCO heritage site, and the Kanchenjunga Biosphere Reserve. Additionally, several of the dams were planned and in part constructed in or bordering on Dzongu, a historically protected region for the local Lepcha community, a Tibeto-Burman speaking group accepted as among the Indigenous inhabitants of Sikkim.[6]

In the past decade, repeatedly severe landslides have occurred that the affected people ascribed to the destabilizing effects that the dam constructions have on the fragile Himalayan region by for instance blasting tunnels or incorrectly disposing of debris.[7] Incidents that occurred in Dzongu in 2020 serve as an example: a flash flood destroyed sixteen houses in Passingdang village and a landslide above the Teesta V hydroelectric project (HEP) left debris piled up on the dam and affected the villages of Jang and Aapdara. While locals asserted the landslide could have been avoided if National Hydroelectric Power Corporation Ltd. (NHPC) had

---

Huber and Joshi (2015); Little (2008, 2009, 2010a, 2010b, 2012, 2013); McDuie-Ra (2011); Subba (2014); Wangchuck (2007).

4 Government of Sikkim (2019a).

5 In Sikkim and the Darjeeling hills 'activist' is not a frequent self-denomination. Usually the term 'social workers' is used, implying their sacrifice for the welfare of the society around them and distinguishing them from politicians, a category of people that 'common knowledge' holds to be selfish, shrewd and working for their own benefits. I have retained the term 'activist', adapting the local terminology to global usage, so as to enable a conversation larger than the local context. Currently, ACT members prefer the term 'pro-river' rather than anti-dam. Here, I keep the term 'anti-dam activist' as it was the one used during my fieldwork.

6 The Indigenous reserve is protected by the 'Old Laws', meaning legal documents deriving from before 1975, when the kingdom of Sikkim became part of India. See Bentley (2020) on the legal history of Dzongu.

7 Dsouza (2022); see also Bhutia et al. (2016); Lepcha et al. (2018: 55).

implemented proper protective measures,[8] in a public Facebook post, ACT general secretary, Gyatso Lepcha, pointed out an adit for the Panan HEP at the source of the flash flood.[9] Further, he questioned the transparency and seriousness of reports on dam safety.[10] Then, on 4 October 2023, the worst-case scenario happened: Heavy rains caused the South Lhonak glacial lake to breach its banks. When the glacier lake outburst flood (GLOF) hit the dam reservoir in Chungtang in North Sikkim, the Sikkim Urja Limited's Teesta Stage III hydropower project broke. It was the first complete breakthrough of a major dam in India. The flood caused massive destruction along the riverbanks in Sikkim and West Bengal: it washed away bridges, roads and houses, affecting around 22,000 people and taking more than 100 lives.[11] Leading scientists as well as ACT general secretary Gyatso Lepcha doubted the 'naturalness' of the disaster and put forward the negligence of the various actors involved on multiple fronts as the primary cause.[12]

Immediately after the disaster, topics such as mountain fragility, climate change and GLOF, lack of technological preparedness and corruption in dam construction dominated the public debate on dams[13] – in stark contrast to the prior discussion on dams. Previously more public attention went to the ethnic lines of arguments also – but not exclusively – put forward by the anti-dam activists. As ACT general secretary Gyatso Lepcha remarked in 2020, 'basically not just the fragile mountain but even deities aren't happy either'.[14] The activists that went on hunger strike in 2007 were primarily residents of Dzongu, thus all members of the Lepcha community, and wanted to safeguard its sanctity and its people.[15] Dzongu and its rivers are tied to the lifecycle of the Lepcha community

---

8 SANDRP (2020). The company did not publicly react to the allegations made by the villagers (*Sikkim Express* 2020).

9 Gyatso Lepcha (29 June 2020).

10 Gyatso Lepcha (27 June 2020).

11 Ellis-Petersen (2023).

12 Sehgal (2023); *Sikkim Chronicle* (2023).

13 EastMojo (2023).

14 Gyatso Lepcha (29 June 2020).

15 See the ACT webpage for their own description of their cause: www.actsikkim.com.

from origin to marriage and death.[16] Building on this importance, the activists revitalized Dzongu as the 'last bastion of the Lepcha',[17] a notion common among educated Lepcha and put to paper by Arthur Foning, a famous Lepcha author.[18] Dzongu became reframed as a holy land for all Lepcha.[19] Sacred connections to ancestral lands and the deities embedded therein became a part of the dam protest – much like, for example, the earth beings in the protest against mines in the Andes.[20] However, in the public imagination, the anti-dam protest was a Lepcha protest to protect their ancestral lands, and as a consequence it became understood as an ethnic issue. Much has already been written on the framing of the anti-dam movement as an ethnic environmental discourse revolving around the Indigenous Lepcha and their knowledge of the sacred landscape.[21] Several scholars note that this prevented mobilization taking place beyond the Lepcha community and, together with the regional focus on Dzongu, hampered the interaction with affected people from other dam sites.

In this article, I deconstruct the dominant ethnic environmentalism discourse and highlight the contested and fragmented knowledges concerning the implementation of large development projects, environmental risk and sacred landscapes that interact and interlace in Dzongu and the Lepcha community at the heights of the anti-dam protest.[22] In my

16 Bentley (2020); Lepcha (2007); Staff Reporter (2008); Tamsang (2008).

17 Lepcha (2007).

18 Foning (1987).

19 Bentley (2020/21).

20 De la Cadena (2010).

21 Arora (2007, 2008); Bentley (2020, 2020/21); Chettri (2017); Little (2008, 2009, 2013); Subba (2011); Wangchuck (2007).

22 I draw on ethnographic material collected during fieldwork I conducted in Sikkim from 2006 to 2013, as well as a follow-up trip in 2019. In 2019, the ruling Sikkim Democratic Front (SDF) lost the elections; the SDF president Pawan Chamling had been the chief minister since 1994. An alliance between Sikkim Krantikari Morcha (SKM) and BJP has unsettled the political landscape in Sikkim. These drastic political changes and their implications are not included in the paper, as they are still unfolding at the time of writing. While in 2014 one of the leading anti-dam activists had contested the Dzongu MLA elections for SKM and brought the scrapping of the dam projects into the party manifesto, in 2019 the party was silent about their stance on development projects. It remains

analysis, disaster acts as a heightened moment to unravel such interlaced knowledge production based on examples of the 2011 Sikkim earthquake and drawing parallels to the 2023 Teesta flood. Following Campbell,[23] I analyze knowledge production, exchange and assemblage to conceptualize the diverse experiences and agency, power struggles and inequalities involved in the environmental discourse grounded in the anti-dam protest in Dzongu. I maintain that we need to include in the analytical framework the multitude of knowledges, the ontologies they are embedded in and the power negotiations that take place around them. Actors in Sikkim and Dzongu, be they activists, pro-dam supporters, government agents or local people, translate and activate various sets of knowledges: from Indigenous knowledge on sacred landscape, via technical and environmental-risk-related knowledge, to the non-ethnicized local knowledge on the impact of dams on their surrounding environment.

These diverse assemblages of knowledge shape different approaches to seeing the world and making sense of large infrastructure projects. Importantly, aligned with Theriault, I conceptualize that the assembling of knowledges brings 'competing ontological assumptions and world-making practices into mutually transformative encounters with one another'.[24] Such processes of assemblage are tied into power inequalities and are visible as struggles over knowledge legitimacy. Publicly contested assemblages can reproduce a dominant discourse, but at the same time may create spaces to build resistance against it and open new spaces of 'survivance', defined as survival on one's own terms, beyond dominance and victimhood.[25] A careful analysis of the modalities of knowledge production on (sacred) environment and infrastructure projects, I argue, unravels positionings in a context of power asymmetries and divisive politics and helps us understand environmental action or inaction, as suggested by Huber et al.[26]

---

to be seen what stance the new ruling government will take on dams and the protection of the environment.

23 Campbell (2011).

24 Theriault (2017: 116).

25 Vizenor (1994); Tuck (2009).

26 Huber et al. (2017).

In doing so, I distance myself from an ethnic understanding of social action that reproduces 'essentialist views of identity, indigeneity and place', as also criticized by Dukpa et al.[27] In order to deconstruct the reading of anti-dam protest as something 'ethnically' Lepcha, I study the assembled knowledges and negotiations over development projects in that very community, giving a different perspective and theoretical framework. Essentially, I am interested in the role of Indigenous knowledge in these contested assemblages, with particular focus on environmental fragility and risk management, in which I see the key to understanding the resistance to and support for dams in Dzongu. The Lepcha reserve was a focal region of fieldwork for my PhD thesis. My research on the attachments to the current and historical landscape activated in the community rituals strongly influences my approach.[28] For these reasons, I concentrate on Dzongu, even though it is not the only place with large-scale dam projects and protest against them, while I acknowledge the importance of also including responses to and narratives on dams in other affected regions as described by Chettri, Huber and Joshi and Dukpa et al.[29]

The article is structured into eight short sections. The first section details my theoretical approach. In the second section I outline the state-driven knowledge politics on larger infrastructure projects in Sikkim that rely on strategic uncertainty and ignorance to downplay risks. I particularly highlight the brokerage of compensation and the patron–clientele relations. Then, in a third section, I describe how anti-dam activists challenged the existing knowledge politics when they started the protest movement in mid 2000. As new knowledge brokers they brought into

27 Dukpa et al. (2018: 70).

28 I use a mixed-methods approach. During long-term residence in Sikkim, I conducted interviews, informal conversations and participant observation in everyday situations as well as during rituals and public events. In addition, I performed a content analysis of newspaper reports and social media posts and drew on secondary literature. All the notes from participatory observation and interview recordings/transcripts are with the author.

29 Chettri (2017); Huber and Joshi (2015). See Dukpa et al. (2019) for a discussion of the protest in the Northern Sikkim regions of Lachen and Lachung, while Dukpa et al. (2018) examines modes of resistance and approval in Chungtang, a region located just outside of Dzongu, on the way to Lachen and Lachung.

existence alternative avenues of knowledge production. The fourth section highlights the contestations over legitimate knowledge, which followed these new modes of brokerage, and the emergence of the politics of fear in Dzongu. The fifth section uses the example of a devastating earthquake in 2011 to discuss how disaster can change the power dynamics in the knowledge production on large infrastructure projects and draws parallels to the devastating flood in 2023. In the sixth section I explain the impact of disaster by carefully analyzing the epistemological conceptualization of and interactions with sacred space in Dzongu. Importantly, in a seventh section, I include knowledge on how natural disasters can be mitigated through a local epistemology that shapes interactions with development projects. The eighth section explains the difference between the activists' framing of Dzongu's sacred landscape and the modalities of ancestral knowledge that were invigorated in the aftermath of the earthquake. I discuss the interethnic modalities of the Indigenous epistemology in order to open up comparison with other Indigenous groups of the Himalayas.

The conclusion highlights that more analytical emphasis on various contested 'way[s] of observing, discussing, and making sense of new information'[30] could enrich the discussion on environmental protest in Sikkim and the larger Himalayan zone, as it enables us as researchers to question a politicized local reading of anti-dam protest as ethnically motivated or anti-national. While the 'content' of the knowledge is undisputedly important, my contribution is to lay open the several modalities of knowledge production that contribute to multiple contested understandings of dams, sacred space and risk mitigation.

Knowledge production, experts, ontologies and power: a theoretical framework

With regard to environmental knowledge, Lidskog points out that 'citizens seem to have no choice but to trust experts in order to achieve a healthy and safe life'.[31] But who is the expert? The environmental scientist paid

30 Berkes (2009: 153).

31 Lidskog (2010: 70).

by the dam developer, the activist researcher or the Indigenous religious specialist? And what kind of knowledge do these experts disseminate?

While the modernist discourse theorizes expert knowledge as being opposed to Indigenous knowledge, I rely on more recent approaches that conceptualize knowledge productions in relation to other knowledges.[32] Scientific expert knowledge would be defined as knowledge produced by scientists and people formally trained in a tertiary educational institution in their respective fields, such as engineers, seismologists, geologists and so forth. In the context of development, such knowledge is generally associated with the deployment of technologies.[33] Scientific knowledge is often disseminated along channels that are beyond the reach of residents in the areas affected by large infrastructural projects – and this is certainly the case in Sikkim, where few have access to scientific journals or the specific education needed to comprehend the way data is presented therein.

Consequently, lay people become dependent on the actors who transfer the scientific knowledge to them, such as government agents, developers, journalists or activists. Brokers are crucial in processing knowledge.[34] Knowledge is produced and exchanged in specific sites and over specific channels, and in the case of protest and development these could be public hearings, protest rallies, newspapers, social media or informal conversations in private settings. Thus, much expert knowledge reaches the public reassembled. This process of localization is tied to power relations that can be exploitative or liberating depending on the type of knowledge and the positioning of the individuals within the larger power network.[35]

---

32 Berkes (2009: 153). There is significant literature on the relation between scientific and Indigenous knowledge, including with regard to development: see for example Agrawal (1995, 2002); Briggs (2005); Green (2008); Yeh (2016). For the local context, see Huber et al. (2017).

33 Akena (2012: 604).

34 Kloster and van Leynseele (2018); Collier and Ong (2005).

35 Turnbull (2009); Haraway (1998); Akena (2012: 602); Adorno (2002); see also Huber et al. (2017).

In addition – and this is crucial to my argument here – the process of localization translates between ontologies, defined as ways of formulating and enacting reality. Before I return to this point, however, I must more clearly define my understanding of Indigenous knowledge. I use the terminology 'Indigenous knowledge' in this article purposefully. In doing so, I am well aware that any definition of Indigenous knowledge needs to take into account the fact that the denomination of specific local knowledge as 'Indigenous' is crucially tied to local and international political relations and acknowledgements of historic positioning, which makes the distinction between 'local' and 'indigenous' knowledge blurry and contested.[36] It is important to take this into consideration with regard to local ethnic politics and access to resources and rights.

As I am more interested in the modalities rather than the 'content' of knowledge production, I understand Indigenous knowledge as a 'way of observing, discussing, and making sense of new information', or in short as 'ways of knowing',[37] which – and this is important – build on interactions with land and relations between generations.[38] Thus, it is produced in interaction between people and place, while also incorporating past interactions of people and place.[39] As such it is not so much the content that makes Indigenous knowledge unique, as the procedures or 'processes for acquisition and transmission'[40] that are associated with it.

Based on his work with First Nations in Canada, Houde introduces a helpful distinction between the 'faces' of what he defines as 'traditional ecological knowledge': 1. factual observation, classifications and system dynamics; 2. management systems; 3. factual knowledge regarding past and current uses of the environment; 4. ethics and values; 5. traditional ecological knowledge as a vector for cultural identity; and 6. cosmology.[41] This clear framework, I suggest, is helpful to analyze the modalities of

---

36 Baruah (2020); Karlsson (2000, 2013); Li (2000); Subba and Karlsson (2006); van Schendel (2011).

37 Berkes (2009: 153).

38 Berkes (2009); Berkes and Berkes (2009); Berkes, Colding and Folke (2000).

39 Basso (1996); Escobar (2001).

40 Berkes (2009: 153).

41 Houde (2007).

Indigenous knowledge beyond the sacredness of landscape, which is an important undertaking considering the reductionist representation of Indigenous knowledge in the Sikkimese political context. At the same time, the last face in Houde's conceptualization, 'cosmology', is inseparable from the others. To this, I make the important addition that cosmology is inseparable from all the other qualities when Indigenous knowledge is grounded in Indigenous ontologies.

Here, I draw on what Escobar has termed the ontological turn,[42] arguing that brokers translate more than knowledge: they in fact translate between the different ontologies according to which the knowledge has been produced and thereby also engage in a mutually transformative process. So when Houde suggests that the inseparability of what he calls cosmology poses a challenge for modernist discourses on risk management, I argue that this is because scientific expert knowledge on ecological resource management is based on a modernist ontology that makes a distinction between nature and culture (and would define Indigenous cosmology as culture!), a distinction that clashes with the conceptualization of the environment according to Indigenous ontologies. Thus, I argue that research on knowledge production in and around anti-dam protest in Dzongu challenges us as researchers to question our own conceptualizations and address core questions raised in the discussion on decolonizing research on Indigenous people.[43]

With regard to Indigenous knowledge, I introduce the theoretical distinction between knowledge systems based on Indigenous ontology, which I will call Indigenous epistemology, and knowledge framed by calling upon Indigeneity as a political resource. The latter is a political positioning 'which draws upon historically sedimented practices, landscapes and repertoires of meaning and emerges through particular patterns of engagement'.[44] I suggest that both formulations of Indigenous knowledge draw to a certain extent on the same sources and relations but derive from different ontologies. In the Indian context, Indigeneity as a political position formulates Indigenous knowledge according to

42 Escobar (2007).

43 Blaser (2012); Denzin and Lincoln (2008); Smith (2012); Yeh (2016).

44 Li (2000: 150).

the parameters of a modernist and colonially rooted culturalist ontology. This is necessary, because capitalizing on 'culture' is the only way for Indigenous people to assert rights in the present-day political system.[45] Here, I suggest, following Broines,[46] that a clear analytical distinction should be drawn between the practices of making and shaping reality and the practices of belonging that are based on one specific way of formulating the world. We need to distinguish between *what* knowledge is, *how* it is translated and assembled and *which* power relations inflect the process.

Knowledge of the dominant: patronage, uncertainty and risk management

The Sikkimese government and the longstanding ruling party, the Sikkim Democratic Front (SDF) (1994–2019), promoted dams as an environment- and climate-friendly way of generating energy, emphasizing in particular the use of run-of-the-river-dams as more ecologically sustainable than reservoir dams. In this way, the state government aligned the large infrastructure projects with their international image as a green, organic state.[47] The Sikkimese state drew upon two additional discourses to justify the necessity of dams, both commonly disseminated by government agents in India. First, the hydropower projects were styled as symbols of modernity, bringing development to remote regions through managing and manipulating nature – in this case through reaping the wealth of the rivers.[48] Second, due to the Indian need for electricity, dam implementation became an 'act of national sacrifice', a discourse common to development projects

45 Povinelli (2011); De la Cadena (2010); Hirtz (2003); Karlsson (2013).

46 Broines (2013).

47 See Ahlers et al. (2015) and Huber and Joshi (2015) on the promotion of dams as an environmentally friendly alternative. In 2003 the Sikkim government launched an action plan to go fully organic and went on to win an 'Oscar for best policies' conferred by the Food and Agriculture Organisation of the UN (Government of Sikkim 2019b; FAO 2018), alongside other awards for environmental protection. Environmentalism was combined with beautification in 'The Green Mission', launched in 2006 (Government of Sikkim 2018), and a 'State Action Plan on Climate Change' was published in 2014 (Government of Sikkim 2014).

48 Huber and Joshi (2015); Drew (2018); Escobar (1995).

in Indian borderlands.[49] The government formed by Sikkim Krantikari Morcha (SKM) in 2019 did not significantly change the discourse.

The knowledge bound up with these dominant state discourses was brought into Dzongu by various established brokers – local politicians, government officials, dam company officials and some executive members of the Mutanchi Lom Aal Shezum (MLAS; a prominent NGO in Dzongu) – but rarely scientists. A significant number of these brokers were Lepcha, and some were residents of Dzongu. Many held powerful positions within Sikkimese society and were recognized as 'educated resource people'. Through their positions, their levels of education and their financial and political backing by ruling party and state, they had a significant amount of power – they were *thulo manchhe*, translated from Nepali as 'big people', a local expression referring to political leaders, public servants and other people with both political and economic leverage. The public's relationship to them was shaped by a considerable degree of faith and trust on the one hand, as well as widespread fear on the other. The latter was instilled through state repression or threats directed at people who dissent from the state-backed agenda.

This state-dominated brokerage created spaces of strategic ignorance and manufactured scientific uncertainty to conceal risks.[50] The powerful players in knowledge production negated, downplayed or brushed aside environmental concerns, or framed the impact on the environment as limited to the period of construction.[51] To them, this was a bankable risk.[52] State-dominated brokers actively participated in facilitation, defined as the process of enabling powerful actors to reap private gains from environmental projects in vulnerable locations.[53] As a consequence, it became difficult, if not impossible, for there to be informed knowledge

---

49 Drew (2018).

50 Huber (2019); Lord (2019); Butler and Rest (2017); see Frickel (2008); Boelens, Shah and Bruins (2019); and McGoey (2012) on strategic ignorance and knowledge gaps.

51 Huber (2019); Huber and Joshi (2015); Gergan (2019).

52 On Nepal, see Butler and Rest (2017).

53 Huber et al. (2017); Collins (2008: 22).

exchange on the realistic risk to environment and livelihoods, mitigation measures, and accountability.

Against this backdrop, for many affected people the only way forward was to negotiate benefits with the developers and the state in order to compensate for any potential negative effects of the dams on their immediate livelihood.[54] In Sikkim, as in India and other South Asian states, state services are not taken for granted, but are part of the bargain for livelihoods that depends on political favoritism.[55] Interactions between the brokers and the affected people followed established channels of patronage and clientelism. In this way, 'affectedness' became a new means to achieve recognition and increase one's bargaining power.[56] The affected people thus claimed agency in the context of fragmented knowledge. Their actions gave them a sense of being in charge of their own fate, as well as the hope of reducing their marginality and maybe even improving their material means and social status – even if this meant increasing their vulnerability with regard to environmental risks. Accordingly, to acquire security or even status according to the parameters of a modern capitalist ontology, the villagers portrayed themselves as damaged.[57]

---

54 See Government of Sikkim (2017) for minutes of a public hearing between developers, the state and the public to get an impression of the interactions.

55 Huber and Joshi (2015); Chettri (2013, 2017b). See Huber and Joshi (2013) on the manufacturing of popular consent; Huber (2019) for a description of the long-term effects of Teesta V HEP in Sikkim; and McDuie-Ra (2011) on pro-dam actors' negotiations. See Lord (2016) for a detailed analysis of the financialization of benefits with regard to the border regions of Nepal. See Pfaff-Czarnecka (2008) for a conceptualization of distributional coalitions in Nepal; Wenner (2015) on the legitimizing of political authority through patronage in the Darjeeling hills, and Wenner (2018) on morals and political conduct to contextualize the described patronage and clientele relations in the wider Himalayan region. Finally, see Gupta (2005) and Corbridge et al. (2005) on the state, corruption, governmentality and poverty in India.

56 Lord (2016: 146–147).

57 See Tuck (2009) on damage narrative.

The new knowledge brokers

With the anti-dam protests, another set of players became active in Dzongu, shaking the foundations of the established patterns of patronage and knowledge brokerage. These new players were from Dzongu; many were young and had been educated outside the Indigenous reserve. Most anti-dam protesters did not have political leverage or patronage. While some did come from historically influential families, they were not the typical *thulo manchhe*. Even though the opposition parties immediately tried to tie the protest to their agenda – something from which ACT initially clearly distanced itself – there was no financial support as such, nor political patronage. The protestors could not give the people immediate benefits or offer alternative income; on the contrary, their actions brought government sanctions upon them and their family members, such as transfers of those holding government jobs to undesired positions or to remote areas in other districts – according to the ACT general secretary a situation of victimization upheld till date during the SKM government.[58]

The anti-dam protestors contested the expert knowledge of the developers and the government-led actors, who downplayed the risk of dams and created uncertainty. They became brokers of an alternative discourse on environmental knowledge, climate change and development that included both Indigenous and scientific knowledge. The anti-dam protestors transferred knowledge from experts – scientists and activists – to Dzongu, providing evidence of the negative environmental impact of dams and the complicating influences of climate change.[59] Their counter-discourse was fed by interactions with members of national and international civil society organizations, some of them leading anti-dam activists from other parts of India, as well as researchers and journalists. These actors played an important role in training, coordinating and funding the anti-dam activists in Sikkim. They brought alternative knowledge reservoirs and solidarity, which energized the local activists and strengthened their confidence and self-understanding with regard to

58 Gyatso Lepcha (16 October 2023); Little (2009); Joshi and Huber (2015).

59 For the scientific literature on the negative impact of dams, see Bhushal (2015); Grumbine and Pandit (2013); Palmer et al. (2008); Shah (2013); and Vagholikar and Das (2010).

pushing forward alternative forms of knowledge, in opposition to leading state actors, on the environmental impact of dams.

As Gergan points out, prior to the construction of dams and the anti-dam protests, Dzongu was a place where the precarity of the vulnerable landscape and the harsh living conditions formed the experiences and everyday lives of the residents.[60] The roads are barely drivable, landslides regularly cut off connectivity, and power cuts are common, to mention just some of the quotidian difficulties. Leading activists from Dzongu had their own personal experiences of the terrain and the changes occurring, and some had seen the impact of dam construction. The anti-dam activists interacted with people in the affected areas, collecting information and sharing concerns and know-how. Their interactions and knowledge exchanges were concentrated on learning from affected people about the impact on livelihoods and environment: collecting local knowledge on sinking lands, houses that had been damaged due to nearby construction, drying fields, and so forth. They documented any disregard of regulations by the developers or the government, whether in the proceedings themselves or the non-implementation of promises made to the affected people.[61]

In the regions where the dam constructions had not yet started, the activists spoke about their concerns. In the initial stages of the anti-dam movement, youth from Dzongu walked from one village to the next, going house to house, interacting with the residents, sharing experiences of other affected areas, and raising awareness about the issue.[62] In this way the activists shared knowledge of the environmental impact beyond the dam sites. Additionally, they acquired and transferred knowledge on the technical aspects of dam construction, legal procedures, the rights of affected people, developers' obligations towards the affected people and possible environmental impacts. In order to do this, the activists drew on their newly gained national and international environmentalist networks.

---

60 Gergan (2014).

61 See ACT (2006b); http://www.actsikkim.com/violations.html.

62 See Drew on other *padyatras* (walking journeys), which go from village to village to raise awareness about issues in anti-dam movements in India (Drew 2018: 154–155).

Working together with environmental organizations and lawyers, several of them filed court cases related to the implementation of various dam projects, some of which are still pending. In this way, the anti-dam activists also became a force to check if the developers' promises to the people were actually being put into practice.

Contested legitimacy, fear and the fragmentation of Dzongu

The anti-dam protests changed the dynamics of knowledge brokerage in the region. This initiated a struggle over who was the legitimate provider of knowledge when it came to the environmental risk of the dam projects. Many senior resource people felt threatened by this young force and their vocal dissent.[63] It created a new situation in which 'the educated people' did not share the same opinion and, more importantly, openly contested the others' knowledge, especially on the environmental impact of the dams. The villagers found this hard to navigate, particularly in the context of uncertainty created by state actors, as described above. The trustworthiness of the experts or institutions, or moreover the trust individuals had in the respective expert or institution, became vital[64] – trust being a necessity for defining knowledge as legitimate and for the assertion of knowledge-claims over others. Different agents – the state, the activists and the religious specialists called in Lepcha language *búngthíng* or *mun* – were involved in accrediting the produced knowledge with legitimacy through their social, religious or political positionings.[65] Thus knowledge production involved struggles over ownership and authority.

Besides the questions of legitimacy and knowledge, fear was also a crucial factor in preventing the villagers openly debating the pros and cons of infrastructural projects and arriving at an informed opinion. Creating such an alternative knowledge base was dangerous. State representatives and developers repressed complaints and expressions of grievances, framing such exchanges of knowledge as against the government or even

63 Personal conversations, Dzongu, 2011.

64 Lidskog (2010: 81).

65 Akena (2012); Huber et al. (2017).

anti-national.[66] The strict government sanctions against the anti-dam protests had initiated a dynamic of fear and confrontation. The factions severed ties, and avenues of knowledge exchange were destroyed. It became very difficult to remain neutral towards the implementation of large dams in the reserve area, or to get access to knowledge, without taking sides. Very few individuals were able to navigate the divide, opening avenues of knowledge exchange.

The pro-dam versus anti-dam division increasingly hardened, and as a result people stopped talking with each other; neither side would listen to any argumentation by the other. As already mentioned, in Dzongu, like in other parts of Sikkim and India, there is huge dependency on the state. The villagers were economically reliant on ruling party members as patrons, often expressed through the distribution of goods such as food, seeds, livestock and other supplies; and for those not or not entirely occupied with agriculture, the government was the main employer.[67] In a context where dissidence is sanctioned, sharing knowledge with activists could be perceived as co-conspiring, which could threaten vital channels of income and lead to social exclusion. The developers profited from this situation since anyone who voiced criticism of their actions or the proceedings more widely was categorized as anti-dam and anti-government, a perception that many people sought to avoid. Hence, few people pushed to hold the developers accountable.[68] Many residents of Dzongu remained silent. A phrase I often heard was: 'I am uneducated, how would I know what is best?'

The impact of the earthquake upon the politics of knowledge

The described stalemate between pro- and anti-dam actors was quite literarily shaken open, when on 18 September 2011, an earthquake of magnitude 6.9 on the Richter scale hit the Sikkim Himalayas. North Sikkim was the most affected region, and there was devastation throughout

66 Personal conversations; Huber (2019: 16).

67 Huber and Joshi (2015); Gergan (2014).

68 See also Huber and Joshi (2015).

the dam sites on the Teesta River. The earthquake left several villagers in Dzongu dead. Massive landslides had torn down the steep valleys of the north, destroying roads and covering half of the village of Bey close to the Panang HEP site. There were rumors of a significant death toll among the laborers in the dam sites of Teesta HEP III, and although the figures were never officially confirmed, they nevertheless saturated the public perception with the fragility and the hazardous potential of the dam – at least for a certain time after the incident. The destruction fed the public fear that the dams had induced this seismic event, even though geologists and scientists rejected this possibility.[69]

The 2011 earthquake made the Sikkimese people experience the fragility of their landscape, and thus perceive the risks of large-scale infrastructure projects. This had an ongoing impact on knowledge production and exchange regarding dams and the fragile Himalayan ecosystem. The pro-dam stance of the state government and the ruling party remained unchanged; however, a growing section of the larger Sikkimese public began to caution about building dams in unpredictable ecosystems, amongst them government servants and leading politicians from North Sikkim. Some significant local brokers shifted camp. In 2015, the Dzongu MLA, together with the elected *panchayats*, public servants and members of the public boycotted a public hearing of the planned Teesta IV HEP and jointly opposed the implementation of all forms of hydroelectric power projects in Dzongu.[70] This was astonishing, because, until just a year beforehand, as the Minister of the Electric, Power and Labour Department, the Dzongu MLA had been vehemently pro-dam.

In 2017, again, the same MLA together with 450 locals, including members of ACT, decided to approach the state government to demand that the Teesta River between the Stage III powerhouse in Singhik and the Stage V dam in Dikchu remained without dams. The MLA stated that the dam had been 'a persistent worry for him ever since he learned of details after a visit to Delhi', while the North Zilla Adhakshya called his prior support of the dams a mistake.[71] At the same time, the Sikkim Lepcha

69 See also Gergan (2020).

70 ACT (2015).

71 Bhutia (2017).

Association, another influential pro-dam actor in past years, issued a press release supporting the protest against Teesta Stage IV HEP as it would 'hamper the fragile environment'.[72] The executive members 'endorsed that the aggrieved voices of the people of Dzongu are genuine and their plea must be taken seriously by the public of North Sikkim, the project developers, the Government, and the people of Sikkim to safeguard the future from the harmful impact on the ecology & environmental changes'.[73]

While the struggle against the implementation of large-scale dams continued, the change in stance by leading political figures from the Lepcha community lent a new credibility and trustworthiness to the knowledge of a precarious environment and the disastrous impact of dams promoted by the activists and their allied environmental experts. At the same time, leading anti-dam protestors became the driving force for alternative income-generating activities in Dzongu, such as organic farming and eco-tourism. Through these activities, they promoted environmental knowledge while making a living for themselves. This was crucially important, because their success undermined the traditional power of patronage and clientele relations and showed that generating a livelihood was possible beyond the hand-outs of amenities and services based on political dependencies. It gave hope that despite the government sanctions for dissidence – i.e. being cut off from government amenities – an economically and socially viable life was still possible.

The altered perception regarding dams ignited by the earthquake, however, was not dominant and long-lasting enough to impact realpolitik and the government continued to push the implementation of dam projects along the Teesta – such as Panang HEP and NHPC Teesta Stage IV HEP in Dzongu. Just one week before the 4 October 2023 flashflood and dam breach the government issued a corrigendum to the notification No. 51/LR&DMD/ACQ/GOS, dated 31 December 2021, regarding the land acquisition for NHPC Teesta Stage IV HEP (Government of Sikkim 2023). In the aftermath of disaster yet again the outlook (temporarily?) changed. For example, Sikkim Forest and Environment Minister Karma Loday Bhutia was quick to state that no more dams should be built in

72 Summit Report (2017).

73 Summit Report (2017).

Chungtang,[74] and Chief Minister P.S. Golay pledged to leave the decision to the people if Teesta Stage IV HEP should be constructed or not.[75] However, considering the experiences after the 2011 earthquake it remains doubtful if the flashflood and dam breach will trigger a lasting shift in government policies regarding large-scale hydroelectric projects.

Natural disasters and the wrath of the deities

What, then, did the earthquake trigger? Why did it help the anti-dam movement gain wider support in the Lepcha community? Why did certain influential brokers change their position on dams in Dzongu? A look at Lepcha religious tradition and its understanding of natural disasters can help answer these questions.

It had been a long time since people in the region had experienced such a severe earthquake and had lost loved ones in a large-scale natural disaster. The incident enhanced the sense of being at the mercy of nature – a dependency etched into the local religious knowledge and everyday practices. Lepcha religious epistemology can be described as managing and also manipulating nature, albeit according to a logic completely different to that conceptualized in the discourses on development or on environmental protection. It builds on a reciprocal relationship between self, society, the other-than-human beings and the natural landscape, which regularly requires negotiation to ensure prosperity, health and welfare. Within the Indigenous epistemology, knowledge about the risks of the fragile environment has been passed down over generations. Ritual practice is the chosen mechanism for balancing and mitigating risk. Religious practices and knowledge production adapt and transform together with the environment, as well as with historical developments and political incidents.[76]

In Dzongu, the villages organize annual protective rituals to which every permanent household contributes offerings. The *búngthíng* summons

74 Dhungel (2023).

75 Gurung (2023).

76 See for example Bentley (2020) for the transformative effect of the Sikkimese kingdom and concurrent wars on the ritual cycle of Dzongu as well as the

the supreme mountain deity residing in Mount Kangchendzonga, called the holy Kóngchen king (Ne Kóngchen pano) in Lepcha, the guardian deities of the locality, called the protectors/owners of land and water (*lyáng dók* úng *dók*), and other divine beings.[77] The local deities reside in hillocks, water sources, rivers, bamboo groves, rocks, etc., and are intrinsically associated with specific narratives of the place, often linked to certain clans, tying ancestry to the immediate landscape. The divine beings are presented with offerings, and in return are requested to protect the village from harm (diseases, social unrest, natural disaster, etc.). Within the ontological framework guiding this ritual practice, the body, the social fabric and the natural surrounding are not perceived as separate, but all are vulnerable to the same impairments from which divine protection is required.

Events or experiences in the aftermath of the annual rituals give insight into the ritual efficacy of garnering divine protection. Villagers perceive the ritual as successful – meaning the deities are satisfied with the offering, the religious specialist performed the ritual correctly and included all necessary ritual acts and deities – if nothing extraordinary happens in the community until the following year, when the next ritual is due. The ritual and environmental knowledge of the religious specialists, ergo their professional expertise, are the main influencers of ritual success. In contrast, if an incident does occur, such as a landslide, a hailstorm that destroys the harvest, or a disease, the local explanation is that the deities are displeased and did not fulfil their side of the contract: they did not protect the village space. Local epistemology explains the causes of earthquakes similarly. The earthquake king, a divine being called Matli pano in Lepcha, causes earthquakes by moving. It is in the power of Ne Kóngchen pano and the guardian deities of the locality to pin Matli pano down and prevent his movement. Consequently, if earthquakes happen, the deities have not fulfilled their obligation of protection to the people – an indication that they are angered and dissatisfied with the offerings given to them.

---

creation of an annual ritual in the aftermath of a devastating landslide in Panang in the mid-nineteenth century.

77 See Bentley (2011, 2012, 2020) for more information on the rituals in Dzongu.

ACT did not issue any statements after the earthquake that associated the natural disaster with the large-scale dam projects and the disturbance of the divine. The activists distanced themselves from such speculation, while engaging in the rebuilding of Dzongu. A leading activist told me they did not want to 'use it for their benefits' – by 'it' he meant the earthquake and the suffering of the Dzongu residents.[78] However, the 'easy resolution'[79] that the dams had angered the deities still circulated among activists and prevailed in the minds of the people. In 2007, for example, four laborers involved in works related to the Panang hydroelectric project died in a flash flood. SAFE, a coalition of NGOs supporting the protest, publicly framed this as the wrath of the deities about the sale of the land, as the signing-over occurred on the same day as the flash flood. Anti-dam protestors warned the government and the pro-dam supporters that the continuance of the projects would 'further annoy and anger the ruling deities and eventually spell a total disaster wiping out the entire Lepcha race of Dzongu'.[80] The statement hit a nerve, as it activated relations to the local landscape that are crucial to the Indigenous epistemology and it deeply offended the villagers who had sold their land, who saw themselves as defamed for being greedy and having brought divine punishment on the region.[81]

The force of the natural disaster triggered fear among the residents of Dzongu that the deities were indeed angry, a fear that runs deep and goes beyond political affiliations. This fear is grounded in a lived relationship with more-than-human beings that have agency and influence their wellbeing. The relationship is formulated by ancestrally transmitted Indigenous knowledge, enacted regularly in rituals, and reformulated through lived experiences such as disaster. The earthquake can be read as the failure of all the mechanisms that Lepcha religious tradition has to offer in order to keep the deities satisfied and ensure prosperity. Here, it is important to add that the brokers who changed their stance did not oppose all dams in Sikkim, but merely wanted to prevent the constructions

78 Personal conversation, Dzongu (2011).

79 Gergan (2016: 6).

80 NOW Report (2007: 2).

81 Wangchuk (2007: 48).

of more dams in Dzongu, the place where the earthquake caused most destruction and the deities were most feared.

Local epistemology, agency and development

In this logic, the destruction of the landscape, and therefore of the local protective deities' abodes, in the name of development, angers the deities or at least prevents them from performing their protective duties. This in turn has a detrimental impact on the prosperity of the residents. So, why did not all Dzongu residents protest against the destruction of the landscape by dams? Why did they risk the consequences of the potential anger of the deities, the loss of their protection and a subsequent loss in prosperity?

Several deities' abodes have been destroyed in recent years. For example, preliminary works on the Panang HEP drained a sacred lake referred to as King Dâthyep; due to the construction of a road to Petong village, Sungtóng hill, home to a local guardian deity, was likewise blasted away.[82] Development projects shape and alter places;[83] this, however, does not necessarily directly translate into environmental action or protest against the respective invasive project, as Dukpa et al. and McDuie-Ra point out.[84] There are several reasons for this.[85] Primarily, residents in remote and precarious landscapes in the Himalayas often welcome development projects, such as roads or electricity lines, that benefit them directly and make their lives easier. The power dynamics and knowledge productions aligned with the development discourse in Sikkim, described in the previous sections, further explain the positioning of people affected by large infrastructural projects.

I argue that an additional form of reasoning is at work here, however, one that is grounded in Lepcha religious epistemology itself. When Gergan interviewed Dzongu residents in the aftermath of the earthquake, her interview partners perceived the hydropower projects as defiling

82 Interview, Pentong (2010); Bentley (2020).

83 Drew (2018); Gidwani (2002).

84 Dukpa et al. (2018); McDuie-Ra (2011).

85 McDuie-Ra (2011).

the sacred landscape, but she cautions that most non-activists are 'less certain of the spiritual cause and effect'.[86] A chain of causation between defiling or destroying the sacred landscape, disturbing the deities and incurring their immediate wrath is not given in Lepcha religious tradition, because the ritualized interaction between residents and the embedded divine beings can also be about managing risk. The deities are angered by noise, destruction and pollution, but when the disturbance is inevitable, ritualized interaction can mitigate that anger. The culprits apologize for any destruction – ritually 'owning up' to the negative impact – and ask for protection despite it. This becomes clear, for example, at the end of every community ritual: the religious specialist gives the last offering to the supernatural beings in the ritual place and apologizes for the disturbance the ritual has caused them.[87] Other examples would be killing animals or building houses, all requiring ritual interactions to restore cosmic order.

In this context, ritual practice becomes a tool to mitigate the negative effects of actions that have defiled the abodes of supernatural beings and potentially incited their wrath. Consequently, along this logic development projects can begin with the performance of a ritual, as happened with the initial drillings for the Panan HEP in Dzongu. Ceremonial as it might be, for people involved in the projects and living within the religious epistemology described above, the ritual performance is meant to appease the deities and ensure their continuing holistic protection of body, society and environment, despite the destruction or disturbance due to the development projects.[88] The reciprocity in the relationship with the benevolent or malevolent divine beings, and thus with the landscape they are embedded in, is negotiated and interpreted differently depending on the situation and the actor.

---

86 Gergan (2016: 5, 6).

87 Recitations, Lingthem religious specialist (2010).

88 Similar ritual interactions are performed by indigenous people in other parts of the world too in order to mitigate the invasion of development or resource extraction projects within the realm of the divine beings (see for example Bolay [2014] for gold extraction in Guinea). In contrast, in Lachen a ritual was performed binding the humans to an oath to stop the large-scale development projects from scarring the landscape and disturbing the deities. These examples underline the power of ritual.

Subsequently, one adequate reaction to disaster would be ritual practice as an attempt to satisfy the divine beings and restore the cosmic order. After the 2011 earthquake the demand for rituals in Dzongu was high, particularly because religious specialists and other elders cited the neglect of ritual practice as a reason for the earthquake. A senior religious specialist pointed out that the selective and devastating destruction of certain localities, such as Bey village, while others such as neighboring Pentong village remained basically unharmed, was a consequence of the affected residents no longer performing the annual community rituals.[89] The religious specialists had so many requests to perform rituals for the local guardian deities they didn't know how to fit them all into their schedules.[90]

The ritualized and ancestrally transmitted relationship with divine beings, embedded in the landscape, forms ways of seeing the world through interaction and negotiation. The interactive process between human, other-than-human and space within which knowledge is produced is thus not straightforward, because ritual action can influence the outcome, for example by averting the deities' wrath. This gives the people a form of agency faced with the fragility of the Himalayan landscape and the precarity of their livelihoods.[91] Which directionality this agency takes up depends on several contemporary factors, builds on past interactions and is negotiated within the respective community. In contrast to Dzongu, for example, in the high-altitude North Sikkimese village of Lachen a ritual was performed binding the residents to an oath to stop the large-scale development projects from scarring the landscape and disturbing its sanctity,[92] using ritual agency as a strong tool to prevent the implementation of dams within the village vicinity. This example underlines the power of ritual in shaping current-day interactions of humans, place and the supernatural. My point is that Indigenous knowledge – encapsulated in the religious tradition – can be interpreted as the transmitted art of negotiating a living in a precarious and fragile environment. How it affects

89 Interview, Pentong, 2011.

90 Interview, Lingya, 2011.

91 See also Bentley (2009, 2014).

92 Dukpa et al. (2019: 16).

peoples' opinions on development projects and environmental destruction varies, due to the multitude of potential interactions with the divine beings, landscape and their respective sentiments. In summary, multiple interpretations and activities result from the close association with sacred landscape within the Lepcha community.

Processes of protest and essentialized Indigenous knowledge

How does the interaction with the landscape and the divine beings embedded therein, as described in the last two sections, differ from the activists' framing of Dzongu as a holy land of the Lepcha?

Here, I recall the distinction I made between Indigenous epistemology and Indigeneity as a political positioning. In their struggles for recognition, activists formulate their attachments to sacred landscape according to the parameters of modernist culturalist ontology. In this, the logic of constituting and understanding self derives from the colonial categorization of people into tribes and castes equipped with fixed attributes and a catalogue of cultural traits. As I have argued elsewhere, anti-dam activists also criticize the dominant modalities activated in defining the ethnic Lepcha in Sikkim, which require their self-depicting as damaged (as seen, for example, in the need to be 'primitive'), and align themselves instead with a global discourse of indigeneity. It is particularly in the rejection of the 'damage narrative'[93] that the Indigenous peoples' sacred connection to nature regains importance.[94] Nevertheless, to constitute themselves as a political group, the anti-dam activists emphasize the Lepchas' primordial 'firstness' in relation to territory when articulating attachments to a sacred landscape. Hence, the activists' framing of the sacred landscape and ancestral knowledge production is bound into a process of naturalization of political differences along the lines of cultural specificities and ethnic belonging.[95] Thereby, Indigenous knowledge on sacred landscapes is designated as a product owned by one ethnic group. Through this process, the rights over

---

93 See Tuck (2009) on this concept.

94 Bentley (2020/21).

95 Arora (2014); Chettri (2017b); Gergan (2016); Middleton (2016); Subba (2014).

natural resources and territory become perceived as privileges of this one group[96] – and a privilege reserved for the humans, while the divine lose their agency to speak. Traditional ecological knowledge as a vector of cultural identity, as defined by Houde and mentioned in the introduction, becomes overtly highlighted, while other aspects fall into its shadow.

It is this framing that Chettri refers to when she points out that 'ethnic environmentalism'[97] denies agency to people who lack this ancient connection to land. I agree with her assessment to the extent that in Sikkim, and to a certain extent in the academic writing about it, the anti-dam protest was understood as such. It was a 'Lepcha thing',[98] exclusive to and reduced to an ethnic group, despite the outspoken pro-dam actors in the Lepcha community[99] and the anti-dam stance of members of the Lachenpa and Lachungpa communities.[100] This was certainly because the protection of the sacred landscape of Dzongu dominated the public discourse on anti-dam movements during the time when the hunger strike was going on in the capital of Gangtok between 2007 and 2009. In this way, in its public framing, the anti-dam protests unraveled along the lines of the pre-existing inequities between ethnic groups, and in particular their legal statuses with regard to locality.[101] To do the activists justice, executive members of ACT did interact with affected people of other areas such as Lachen or West Sikkim, regardless of ethnicity, a fact that is often forgotten in the ethnic framing of the movement. One example occurred when the ACT activists engaged in the renewed protest against dams on Rathong chu

---

96 Baviskar (2005).

97 Chettri (2017).

98 Little (2010b: 121); Wangchuk (2007).

99 McDuie-Ra (2011).

100 Dukpa et al. (2019).

101 Dukpa, Joshi and Boelens (2018) look into why – despite being located in 'indigenous heartland' – the Teesta Stage III dam in Chungtang, North Sikkim, was built without any significant protest. They analyze the legal, social and emotional attachments of various residents to the place, as well as their respective agency with regard to the development project (Dukpa et al. 2018). Elsewhere, I discuss the importance of regional citizenship in the success and failure of activating attachments to sacred territory in Indigenous rights movements among the Lepcha community (Bentley 2020/21).

in 2012.[102] Similarly, they continuously put forward environmental and technical knowledge exchanges concerning dams, as I have elaborated in the third section. In the aftermath of the 4 October 2023 flashflood and dam breach ACT strongly voiced their expertise on the legal procedures and assessments required for the building of dam projects, technical details such as spillways for excess water, environmental-risk-related issues such as GLOF and climate change, and so forth.[103]

The formulation of issues along ethnic lines is state-driven and inherent to the way politics functions in Sikkim, as Vandenhelsken points out;[104] it is not a process observed merely with the mobilizations around environmental issues. Ethnic demands that are intertwined with claims to ancient territorial belonging are the prime way of accessing resources in Sikkim. Therefore, it is not surprising that the anti-dam protestors publicly aligned their environmental demands with claims to indigeneity. Demarcating one type of knowledge on landscape as Indigenous while not acknowledging others is part and parcel of the political and historical process of shaping indigeneity that is tied to the political dynamics of ethnicity, territorial belonging and nation-building. However, this distinction does not say anything about the modalities of knowledge production processes themselves.

Lepcha religious tradition, on which the framing of the sacred Lepcha landscape builds, contains unique myths and practices revolving around a multitude of divine beings, ancestral lineages and places. However, the Indigenous epistemology and the ritual mitigation of environmental hazards – as I have elaborated above – exist in interaction and are not solely and exclusively practiced by the Lepcha community. The religious epistemologies of many other communities in the Himalayan region, such as the Bhutia, Limbu, Rai, Newar and Magar, build upon similar interactions between people, divine beings and place – albeit in their

102 Huber and Joshi (2015).

103 *Sikkim Chronicle* (16 October 2023).

104 Vandenhelsken (2020/21); see Chettri (2013); Middleton (2016); Shneiderman (2014); and Vandenhelsken (2010/11) for insights into the ethno-politics of the Sikkim Darjeeling region.

own distinctive ways and with their own ancestors and histories.[105] These interactions between people, the environment and the embedded divine thus do not follow the ethnic borders formed by the ethno-politics of the past century, but are constituents of Himalayan shamanic ontologies. The close link between sacred landscape and prosperity, for example, has been associated with the pre-Buddhist shamanic fabric of the Himalayas.[106]

These similar epistemologies allow relations and interactions over ethnic boundaries. In everyday practice, embedded divine beings, ritual elements as well as the office of the religious specialist transcend ethnic boundaries.[107] These deities or the religious office remain associated with the original ancestral transmission lineage they come from. Here, ethnic difference is not naturalized or used to 'other', but becomes a part of practice, of the transmitted art of negotiating a living in a precarious and fragile environment.

---

105 See Oppitz (2017); also Allen (1972); Hirsch (1995); Ramble (1996); Bickel and Gaenszle (1999); Gingrich (1996); Bickel (1997); Blondeau and Steinkeller (1996); Gaenszle (1999); Höfer (1999); Macdonald (1997); Steinmann (1996).

106 Karmay (1993).

107 The examples here are multiple. Evil spirits of Lepcha religious tradition – residing in specific places – can when disturbed also make a non-Lepcha person sick. Then, the affected person would seek help from a Lepcha religious specialist. Community rituals can also include deities from other religious traditions. As an example, a Limbu village in West Sikkim regularly performs a ritual they call Hik fát to a Lepcha deity. The Lhopo (Bhutia) of Tingchim perform rituals to Lenji Anyo, the Lepcha deity who owns the cardamom plants and the lands they are on (Balikci 2008: 210). The hills are full of stories of how Lepcha religious specialists sent evil curses. These curses occurred within the Lepcha community as well as beyond these ethnic boundaries, affecting people of other communities (see also Balikci 2008: 99, 104, 194). Here, again, the only way to mitigate the negative effects is to perform regular ritual sacrifice to specific supernatural beings. Moreover, through inter-community marriage entire lineages of religious specialists have crossed over between the ethnic groups. Today there are many Lepcha *yabas/yama* or *biswas*, religious specialists considered to come from Bhutia and the Limbu religious traditions respectively (see Balikci [2008: 226] for examples in the Lhopo community).

Conclusion

This article analyzed various modalities of knowledge production with regard to the implementation of hydro projects and environmental hazards, assembled and negotiated in and around Dzongu in the past years. One of the most important achievements of the anti-dam activists – besides the scrapping of four hydroelectric projects in Dzongu – was the continuous articulation of alternative knowledge on environmental impacts and climate change. Thereby, they undermined the power hierarchies and patron-client relations that the Sikkimese state and its (often) Lepcha agents have established in interaction with affected people, which more often than not ignored the affected peoples' knowledge and rights. As knowledge brokers, the activists opened new channels for communicating grievances, challenged inequities and the marginality of affected people with regard to powerful brokers, developers and the state, and framed alternative futurities.[108] The protest movement took the experience of the precarious Himalayan landscape seriously by listening to villagers and processing both Indigenous knowledge and local experiential knowledge. And they aroused hopes that the villagers could gain the means to survive and prosper on their own terms. Fear of retribution, and the delegitimation of the activists' knowledge, made this process difficult, drawn-out and contested. To conclude, I should stress that a significant amount of knowledge production and exchange initiated by the anti-dam activists was unrelated to ethnicity or ethnic belonging.

Regarding the sanctity of the landscape, anti-dam activists and the public discourse on the dam protest promoted an essentialized framing of sacred Lepcha landscape according to the existing logic of a politics based on ethnic and cultural particularism. The only public activist voice that was given space to speak in the political environment of Sikkim was the ethnic one. Attachments to sacred landscape were reduced to attachments to territory defined in a way that bypassed Indigenous epistemology, through historically rooted current social and legal definitions of what being local is in Sikkim. As such, rights to recognition and agency were

108 See Gergan and Curley (2021) on environmentalism, Indigenous youth and decolonial futurities with reference to the anti-dam activists in Dzongu.

tied to the positioning of the Lepcha as hereditary Sikkimese citizens.[109] A multi-faceted self-definition of indigeneity became reduced to claims to firstness and concerns about immigration. This reproduced existing inequities regarding access to resources, particularly to land, and various forms of injustice, including environmental.[110] Therefore, claiming rights in the current ethno-political Sikkimese context – similar to other parts of Northeast India – requires more than activating what Tuck calls the 'damage narrative'; it additionally requires people to constitute the attachment of self and sacred landscape according to a modernist culturalist ontology.

Consequently, a multitude of other modalities of Indigenous knowledge production failed to enter the public discourse on dams or become politically viable tools. For instance, neither the reciprocity in people's relationship with the environment and the deities inhabiting the landscape, nor the fluidity with which deities transcend ethnic groups, nor ritual risk-mitigation practices, gained any public salience as a result of the protest. As I have shown with regard to the earthquake, it is specifically the Indigenous epistemology which is lived through this interactive relationship that triggered a new consciousness about the risks involved in dams among significant power players after the earthquake. Indigenous epistemologies, or 'way[s] of observing, discussing, and making sense of new information',[111] hold the potential to expand the knowledge production on environmental issues and reconceptualize the possible interactions between people and environment. Similarly, in the aftermath of the 4 October 2023 flood and dam breach, in the public expressions of anti-dam activists as well as other citizens of Sikkim, River Teesta regained agency. Referred to in her female manifestation, she 'can't be tamed' or 'she has freed herself' are recurring comments.[112] Once again,

109 Bentley (2020/21).

110 See Lord (2016) on a discussion of the contradictory concept 'local' and its capitalization in hydro projects in Nepal; see Forbes (1998) on the importance of being local; see Shneiderman (2015) and De Sales (2011) on the concept of village and belonging.

111 Berkes (2009: 153).

112 A video made by Denmit Lepcha (2021), circulated since the 4 October 2023 flood and dam breach, captures these sentiments. Similarly, a poem posted on

disaster has heightened interaction with nature and its more-than-human beings along Indigenous epistemologies.

Importantly, Indigenous epistemologies and practices have the potential to transcend ethnic boundaries – something also felt in the aftermath of disaster. While interactions between human and more-than-human beings were not always constructive – such as the curses shamans direct at neighbors – they demonstrate that the non-porous boundaries between Himalayan communities as formulated in ethnic politics do not represent the reality of lived Indigenous knowledge systems or support survival and livelihood in a fragile mountain region. Including local knowledge as formulated within Indigenous ontologies in political demands could be fruitful in imagining self, community, rights and opportunities beyond the logic of the processes of othering and categorizing people – processes that were formed by colonial history, and that today are cultivated in strategies for affirmative action. Considering that members of multiple ethnic and caste communities have been affected by the 2023 flood and dam breach, it will be interesting to analyze if the discourse on dams and affectedness moves beyond the ethnic Lepcha lens.

How can knowledge formulated through Indigenous ontologies become a political resource without needing an earthquake or a flood to trigger an innate fear response and a subsequent rethink, as it did with the influential Lepcha leaders? Does Indigenous knowledge always have to be reformulated to become a resource in struggles to protect the rights of marginalized communities against the exploitation of resources and ancestral landscapes by powerful political and economic players? If so, can Indigenous knowledge be reformulated beyond cultural particularism to become salient in a modern globalized world? Rather than searching for radical differences between modern/scientific and Indigenous ontologies, or conceptualizing ontologies as constituting other worlds,[113] I suggest that it would be fruitful for anthropology to study how members of Indigenous communities translate between different knowledges and ontologies, focusing on the reflexivity, the contestations and power inequalities, but

---

Instagram by Valley Notes on 5 October 2023 addressing the mother Teesta, describes her as seeking her freedom and sweeping her children away.

113 Blaser (2013).

also on the constructive bridging of difference and creative assemblages in the process. From an engaged anthropological standpoint, such research could contribute to (re)framing ecological co-management or participant action research projects.

Bibliography

Adorno, T.W. (2002). 'Lecture Four: Society is Not Definable'. In C. Gödde, ed., *Introduction to Sociology*, Palo Alto: Stanford University Press, pp. 27–35.

Agrawal, A. (1995). 'Dismantling the Divide Between Indigenous and Scientific Knowledge', *Development and Change*, vol. 26, pp. 413–439.

Agrawal, A. (2002). 'Indigenous Knowledge and the Politics of Classification', *International Social Science Journal*, vol. 173, pp. 287–297.

Ahlers, R., J. Budds, D. Joshi, V. Merme and M. Zwarteveen (2015). 'Framing Hydropower as Green Energy: Assessing Drivers, Risks and Tensions in the Eastern Himalayas', *Earth System Dynamics*, vol. 6, pp. 195–204.

Akena, F.R. (2012). 'Critical Analysis of the Production of Western Knowledge and Its Implications for Indigenous Knowledge and Decolonization', *Journal of Black Studies*, vol. 43, no. 6, pp. 599–619.

Allen, N. (1972). 'The Vertical Dimension in Thulung Classification', *Journal of the Anthropological Society of Oxford*, vol. 3, pp. 81–94.

Arora, V. (2007). 'Unheard Voices of Protest in Sikkim', *Economic and Political Weekly*, vol. 42, no. 31, pp. 3451–3454.

Arora, V. (2008). 'Gandhigiri in Sikkim', *Economic and Political Weekly*, vol. 43, no. 38, pp. 27–28.

Arora, V. (2009). '"They are all set to dam(n) our future": Contested Development through Hydel Power in Democratic Sikkim', *Sociological Bulletin*, January-April, vol. 58, no. 1, pp. 94–114.

Arora, V. (2014). 'Weepingsikkim.blogspot.com. Reconfiguring Lepcha Belonging with Cyber-belonging'. In G. Toffin and J. Pfaff-Czarnecka, eds., *Facing Globalization in the Himalayas: Belonging and the Politics of the Self*, New Delhi: Sage Publications, pp. 344–370.

Balikci, A. (2008). *Lamas, Shamans and Ancestors. Village Religion in Sikkim*, Leiden: Brill.

Baruah, S. (2020). *In the Name of the Nation. India and Its Northeast*, Stanford: Stanford University Press.

Basso, K.H. (1996). 'Wisdom Sits in Places'. In S. Feld and K.H. Basso, eds., *Senses of Place*, Santa Fe: School of American Research, pp. 53–90.

Baviskar, A. (2005). 'Adivasi Encounters with Hindu Nationalism in MP', *Economic and Political Weekly*, vol. 40, no. 48, pp. 5105–5113.

Bentley, J. (2009). 'Narrations of Contest: Competition among Representatives of Lepcha Belief and Guru Rinpoche in Sikkim', *Bulletin of Tibetology*, vol. 45, no. 1, pp. 135–160.

Bentley, J. (2011). 'Sátáp Rum Fát and Chirim: Shamanic Rituals of the Lepcha in Dzongu', *Thoughts & Pen*, vol. 1, no. 1, pp. 1–12.

Bentley, J. (2012). 'Shamanic Practice in a Hidden Himalaya Valley', *Passage*, pp. 18–19.

Bentley, J. (2014). 'The King's Ritual and the Religious Power of the Untamed', *Bulletin of Tibetology*, vol. 50, nos. 1 and 2, pp. 133–152.

Bentley, J. (2020). *Guardians of the Land and Water. Rituals, Vulnerability, and Indigenous Belonging among the Himalayan Lepcha.* (PhD dissertation, University of Zurich.) Forthcoming publication with Seismo: Zurich (2024).

Bentley, J. (2020/21). 'Protectors of the Land and Water: Citizenship, Territory, and Vulnerability among the Lepcha of Sikkim and West Bengal', *Asian Ethnicity*, Special Issue, 'Ancestrality, Migration, Rights and Exclusion: Citizenship in the Indian State of Sikkim' (edited by M. Vandenhelsken), vol. 22, no. 2, pp. 330–352.

Berkes, F. (2009). 'Indigenous Ways of Knowing and the Study of Environmental Change', *Journal of the Royal Society of New Zealand*, vol. 39, no. 4, pp. 151–156.

Berkes, F. and M.K. Berkes (2009). 'Ecological Complexity, Fuzzy Logic, and Holism in Indigenous Knowledge', *Futures*, vol. 41, pp. 6–12.

Berkes F., J. Colding and C. Folke (2000). 'Rediscovery of Traditional Ecological Knowledge as Adaptive Management', *Ecological Applications*, vol. 10, no. 5, pp. 1251–1262.

Bhushal, R. (2015). 'Nepal's Hydropower Output Falling Due to Climate Change, Developers Claim', *thethirdpole.net*, 20 July.

Bhutia, U., K. Lepcha and E.K. Santha (2016). 'When Gods' Abode Dissented: Mantam Landslide in North Sikkim', *Economic & Political Weekly*, vol. 51, no. 36.

Bickel, B. (1997). 'Spatial Operations in Deities, Cognition, and Culture: Where to Orient Oneself in Behare'. In J. Nuyts and E. Pederson, eds., *Language and Conceptualization*, Cambridge: Cambridge University Press, pp. 46–83.

Bickel, B. and M. Gaenszle, eds. (1999). *Himalayan Space. Cultural Horizons and Practices*, Zürich: Völkerkundemuseum Zürich.

Blaser, M. (2012). 'Ontology and Indigeneity: On the Political Ontology of Heterogeneous Assemblages', *Cultural Geographies*, pp. 1–10.

Blaser, M. (2013). 'Ontological Conflicts and the Stories of People in Spite of Europe. Towards a Conversation on Political Ontology', *Current Anthropology*, vol. 54, no. 5, pp. 547–568.

Blondeau, A.-M. and E. Steinkeller, eds. (1996). *Reflections of the Mountain. Essays on the History and Social Meaning of the Mountain Cult in Tibet and the Himalaya*, Wien: Verlag der Österreichischen Akademie der Wissenschaften.

Boelens, R., E. Shah and B. Bruins (2019). 'Contested Knowledges: Large Dams and Mega-Hydraulic Development', *Water*, vol. 11, no. 416, pp. 1–27, https://doi.org/10.3390/w11030416.

Bolay, M. (2014). 'When Miners Become "Foreigners": Competing Categorizations within Gold Mining Spaces in Guinea', *Resources Policy*, vol. 40, pp. 117–127.

Briggs, J. (2005). 'The Use of Indigenous Knowledge in Development: Problems and Challenges', *Progress in Development Studies*, vol. 5, no. 2, pp. 99–114.

Briones, C. (2013). 'Comments on M. Blaser'. *Current Anthropology*, vol. 54, no. 5, pp. 559–560.

Butler, C. and M. Rest (2017). 'Calculating Risk, Denying Uncertainty: Seismicity and Hydropower Development in Nepal', *Himalaya*, vol. 37, no. 2, pp. 15–25.

Campbell, B. (2011). 'Beyond Cultural Models of the Environment: Linking Subjectivities of Dwelling and Power'. In A. Guneratne, ed., *Culture and Environment in the Himalaya*, New Delhi: Routledge, pp. 188–203.

Chettri, M. (2013). 'Choosing the Gorkha: At the Crossroads of Class and Ethnicity in the Darjeeling Hills', *Asian Ethnicity*, vol. 14, no. 3, pp. 293–308.

Chettri, M. (2017a). 'Ethnic Environmentalism in the Eastern Himalaya', *Economic and Political Weekly*, LII, pp. 34–40.

Chettri, M. (2017b). *Ethnicity and Democracy in the Eastern Himalayan Borderland: Constructing Democracy*, Amsterdam: Amsterdam University Press.

Collier, S.J. and A. Ong (2005). 'Global Assemblages, Anthropological Problems'. In A. Ong and S.J. Collier, eds., *Global Assemblages: Technology, Politics, and Ethics as Anthropological Problems*, Malden/Oxford/Victoria: Blackwell Publishers, pp. 3–21.

Collins, T. (2008). 'The Political Ecology of Hazard Vulnerability: Marginalization, Facilitation and the Production of Differential Risk to Urban Wildfires in Arizona's White Mountains', *Journal of Political Ecology*, vol. 15, pp. 21–43.

Corbridge, S., G. Williams, M. Srivastava and R. Veron (2005). *Seeing the State: Governance and Governmentality in India*, Cambridge: Cambridge University Press.

Denzin, N.K. and Y.S. Lincoln. (2008). 'Introduction: Critical Methodologies and Indigenous Inquiry'. In N.K. Denzin, Y.S. Lincoln and L.T. Smith, eds., *Handbook of Critical and Indigenous Methodologies*, Thousand Oaks: Sage Publications, pp. 1–20.

De la Cadena, M. (2010). 'Indigenous Cosmopolitics in the Andes: Conceptual Reflections Beyond "Politics"', *Cultural Anthropology*, vol. 25, no. 2, pp. 334–370.

De Sales, A. (2011). 'Hamro Gaon: Practices of Belonging in Rural Nepal'. In J. Pfaff-Czarnecka and G. Toffin, eds., *The Politics of Belonging in the Himalayas: Local Attachments and Boundary Dynamics, Governance, Conflict, and Civic Action 4*, New Delhi: Sage Publication, pp. 3–24.

Drew, G. (2018). 'Contested Modernities: Place, Subjectivity, and Himalayan Dam Infrastructures'. In S. Yü and J. Michaud, eds., *Trans-Himalayan Borderlands. Livelihoods, Territorialities, Modernities*, Amsterdam: Amsterdam University Press, pp. 147–166.

Dukpa, R.D., D. Joshi and R. Boelens (2018). 'Hydropower Development and the Meaning of Place. Multi-ethnic Hydropower Struggles in Sikkim, India', *Geoforum*, vol. 89, pp. 60–72.

Dukpa, R.D., D. Joshi and R. Boelens (2019). 'Contesting Hydropower Dams in the Eastern Himalaya: The Cultural Politics of Identity, Territory and Self-Governance Institutions in Sikkim, India', *Water*, vol. 11, no. 3, 412, pp. 1–23, https://doi.org/10.3390/w11030412.

Dutta, S. (2007). 'Lepcha v Hydropower. Do Gangtok and New Delhi Policy Makers View the Lepcha Ancestral Homeland as Sacrosanct or Not? The Answer Can Be Both', *Himal*, September.

Escobar, A. (1995). *Encountering Development: The Making and Unmaking of the Third World*, Princeton: Princeton University Press.

Escobar, A. (2001). 'Culture Sits in Places: Reflections on Globalism and Subaltern Strategies of Localization', *Political Geography*, vol. 20, pp. 139–174.

Escobar, A. (2007). 'The "Ontological Turn" in Social Theory: A Commentary on "Human Geography without Scale", by Sallie Marston, John Paul Jones II and Keith Woodward', *Transactions of the Institute of British Geographers*, vol. 32, no. 1, pp. 106–111.

Foning, A.R. (1987). *Lepcha, My Vanishing Tribe*, Kalimpong: Chyu-Pandi Farm.

Forbes, A.A. (1998). 'Sacred Geography on the Cultural Borders of Tibet'. In A.-M. Blondeau, ed., *Tibetan Mountain Deities, Their Cults and Representations. Papers Presented at a Panel of the 7th Seminar of the International Association for Tibetan Studies, Graz 1995*, Wien: Verlag der Österreichischen Akademie der Wissenschaften, pp. 111–122.

Frickel, S. (2008). 'On Missing New Orleans: Lost Knowledge and Knowledge Gaps in an Urban Hazardscape', *Environmental History*, vol. 13, pp. 643–650.

Gaenszle, M. (1999). 'Travelling Up - Travelling Down: The Vertical Dimension in Mewahang Rai Ritual Journeys'. In M. Gaenszle and B. Bickel, eds., *Himalayan Space. Cultural Horizons and Practices*, Zürich: Völkerkundemuseum Zürich, pp. 135–166.

Gergan, M.D. (2014). 'Precarity and Possibility: On Being Young and Indigenous in Sikkim, India', *Himalaya*, vol. 34, no. 2, pp. 67–80.

Gergan, M.D. (2016). 'Living with Earthquakes and Angry Deities at the Himalayan Borderlands', *Annals American Association of Geographers*, vol. 107, pp. 490–498.

Gergan, M.D. (2019). 'Geological Surprises: State Rationality and Himalayan Hydropower in India', *Roadsides. Infrastructural Times*, Collection no. 001, pp. 35–42.

Gergan. M.D. and A. Curley (2021). 'Indigenous Youth and Decolonial Futures: Energy and Environmentalism among the Dine in the Navajo Nation and the Lepchas of Sikkim, India', *Antipode*, vol. 55, no. 3, pp. 749–769.

Gidwani, V. (2002). 'The Unbearable Modernity of "Development"? Canal Irrigation and Development Planning in Western India', *Planning in Progress*, vol. 58, no. 1, pp. 1–80.

Gingrich, A. (1996). 'Hierarchical Merging and Horizontal Distinction - A Comparative Perspective on Tibetan Mountain Cults'. In A.-M. Blondeau and E. Steinkellner, eds., *Reflections of the Mountain. Essays on the History and Social Meaning of the Mountain Cult in Tibet and the Himalaya*, Wien: Verlag der Österreichischen Akademie der Wissenschaften, pp. 233–260.

Green, L.J.F. (2008). '"Indigenous Knowledge" and "Science": Reframing the Debate on Knowledge Diversity', *Archaeologies: Journal of the World Archaeological Congress*, vol. 4, no. 1, pp. 144–163.

Grumbine, R.E. and M. Pandit (2013). 'Threats from India's Himalaya Dams', *Science*, vol. 339, no. 6115, pp. 36–37.

Gupta, A. (2005). 'Narratives of Corruption: Anthropological and Fictional Accounts of the Indian State', *Ethnography*, vol. 6, no. 1, pp. 6–34.

Haraway, D. (1998). 'Situated Knowledges: The Science Question in Feminism and the Privilege of Partial Perspective', *Feminist Studies*, vol. 14, pp. 575–599.

Hirsch, E. (1995). 'Introduction: Landscape: Between Place and Space'. In E. Hirsch and M. O'Hanlon, eds., *The Anthropology of Landscape. Perspectives on Place and Space*, Oxford: Clarendon Press, pp. 1–30.

Hirtz, F. (2003). 'It Takes Modern Means to be Traditional: On Recognizing Indigenous Cultural Communities in the Philippines', *Development and Change*, vol. 34, pp. 887–914.

Höfer, A. (1996). 'Nomen est numen: Notes on the Verbal Journey in Some Western Oral Ritual Texts'. In B. Bickel and M. Gaenszle, eds., *Himalayan Space. Cultural Horizons and Practices*, Zürich: Völkerkundemuseum Zürich, pp. 205–244.

Houde, N. (2007). 'The Six Faces of Traditional Ecological Knowledge: Challenges for Canadian Co-Management Arrangements', *Ecology and Society*, vol. 12, pp. 34–50.

Huber, A. (2019). 'Hydropower in the Himalayan Hazardscape: Strategic Ignorance and the Production of Unequal Risk', *Water*, vol. 11, pp. 414–437.

Huber, A. and D. Joshi (2013). 'Hydropower in Sikkim. Coercion and Emergent Socio-Environmental Justice'. In P.J. Das, C. Mahanta, K.J. Joy, S. Paranjape and S. Vispute, eds., *Water Conflicts in Northeast India: A Compendium of Case Studies*, Pune: Forum for Policy Dialogue on Water Conflicts, pp. 102–110.

Huber, A. and D. Joshi (2015). 'Hydropower, Anti-Politics, and the Opening of New Political Spaces in the Eastern Himalayas', *World Development*, vol. 76, pp. 13–25

Huber, A., S. Gorostiza, P. Kotsila, M.J. Beltrán and M. Armiero (2017). 'Beyond "Socially Constructed" Disasters: Re-Politicizing the Debate on Large Dams through a Political Ecology of Risk', *Capitalism Nature Socialism*, vol. 28, no. 3, pp. 48–68.

Joshi, D., J. Platteeuw and J. Teoh (2018). 'The Consensual Politics of Development: A Case Study of Hydropower Development in the Eastern Himalayan Region of India', *New Nepal Journal of Social Science and Public Policy*, vol. 51, no. 1, pp. 1–23.

Karlsson, B.G. (2003). 'Anthropology and the "Indigenous slot". Claims to and Debates about Indigenous Peoples' Status in India', *Critique of Anthropology*, vol. 24, no. 4, pp. 402–423.

Karlsson, B.G. (2013). 'The Social Life of Categories: Affirmative Action and Trajectories of Indigenous', *Focaal*, vol. 65, pp. 33–41.

Karmay, S. (1993). 'The Wind-Horse and Well-Being of Man'. In C. Ramble and M. Brauen, eds., *Anthropology of Tibet and the Himalayas, Proceedings of the International Seminar of the IATS, 1990*, Zürich: Ethnographical Museum of the University of Zürich, pp. 150–157.

Klosters, M. and Y. van Leynseele (2018). 'Brokers as Assemblers: Studying Development through the Lens of Brokerage', *Ethnos*, vol. 83, pp. 803–813.

Lepcha, D. (2012). 'Affected Citizens of Teesta (ACT) Fighting the Goliaths'. In D.T. Bhutia, ed., *Independent People's Tribunal on Dams, Environment and Displacement*, New Delhi: Human Rights Law Network, pp. 79–82.

Lepcha, G. (2007). 'Dzongu, the Last Bastion of the Lepchas', *King Gaeboo Achyok*, pp. 23–25.

Lepcha, K. (2020). *The Teesta Hydro Power Projects: A Historical Analysis of the Protest Movement in North Sikkim (1964-2011)* (PhD dissertation, University of Sikkim.)

Lepcha, T., G. Lepcha and S. Wagh (2018). 'Undermining Cultural Values: An Indigenous Perspective on the Khanchendzonga Nomination', *World Heritage Watch Report*, pp. 52–56.

Li, T.M. (2000). 'Articulating Indigenous Identity in Indonesia: Resource Politics and the Tribal Slot', *Comparative Studies in Society and History*, vol. 42, pp. 149–179.

Lidskog, R. (2008). 'Scientised Citizens and Democratised Science. Re-Assessing the Expert-Lay Divide', *Journal of Risk Research*, vol. 11, no. 1, pp. 69–86.

Little, K. (2008). 'Lepcha Narratives of Their Threatened Sacred Landscapes', *Transforming Cultures eJournal*, vol. 3, no. 1, pp. 227–255.

Little, K. (2009). 'Deep Ecology, Dams, and Dzonguland. Lepchas Protest Narratives about Their Threatened Land', *The Trumpeter*, vol. 25, no. 1, pp. 34–64.

Little, K. (2010a). 'Democracy Reigns Supreme in Sikkim? A Long March and a Short Visit Strains Democracy from Lepcha Marchers in Sikkim', *Australian Humanities Review*, vol. 48, pp. 109–129.

Little, K. (2010b). 'From the Villages to the Cities. The Battlegrounds for Lepcha Protests', *Transforming Cultures eJournal*, vol. 5, no. 1, pp. 84–111.

Little, K. (2012). 'Sanctity, Environment and Protest: A Lepcha Tale'. In D.T. Bhutia, ed., *Independent People's Tribunal on Dams, Environment and Displacement*, New Delhi: Human Rights Law Network, pp. 83–94.

Little, K. (2013). *Stories of the Lepcha. Narratives from a Contested Land* (PhD dissertation, the University of Technology, Sydney).

Lord, A. (2016). 'Citizens of a Hydropower Nation: Territory and Agency at the Frontiers of Hydropower Development in Nepal: Nepalese Hydropower Development', *Economic Anthropology*, vol. 3, no. 1, pp. 145–160.

Lord, A. (2019). 'Speculation and Seismicity: Reconfiguring the Hydropower Future in Post-Earthquake Nepal'. In F. Menga and E. Swyngedouw, eds., *Water, Technology, and the Nation-State*, Milton Park: Routledge, pp. 167–199.

Macdonald, A.W. (1997). *Maṇḍala and Landscape. Emerging Perceptions in Buddhist Studies*, vol. 6, New Delhi: D.K. Printworld.

McDuie-Ra, D. (2011). 'The Dilemmas of Pro-Development Actors: Viewing State-Ethnic Minority Relations and Intra-Ethnic Dynamics through Contentious Development Projects', *Asian Ethnicity*, vol. 12, no. 1, pp. 77–100.

McGoey, L. (2012). 'Strategic Unknowns: Towards a Sociology of Ignorance', *Economy and Society*, vol. 41, no. 1, pp. 1–16.

Middleton, T. (2016). *The Demands of Recognition: State Anthropology and Ethnopolitics in Darjeeling*, Stanford: Stanford University Press.

Oppitz, M. (2017). 'Analogies, Variations, Chance: Comparing Local Shamanisms', *Shaman*, vol. 25, nos. 1–2, pp. 61–91.

Palmer, M.A., C.A.R. Liermann, C. Nilsson, M. Förke, J. Alcamo, P.S. Lake and N. Bond (2008). 'Climate Change and the World's River Basins: Anticipating Management Options', *Frontiers in Ecology and the Environment*, vol. 6, no. 2, pp. 81–89.

Pfaff-Czarnecka, J. (2008). 'Distributional Coalitions in Nepal: An Essay on Democratization, Capture, and (Lack of) Confidence'. In D.N. Gellner and K. Hatchethu, eds., *Local Democracy in South Asia: Microprocesses of Democratization in Nepal and Its Neighbours*, New Delhi: Sage Publications, pp. 71–104.

Povinelli, E. (2011). *Economics of Abandonment: Social Belonging and Endurance in Late Liberalism*, Durham: Duke University Press.

Ramble, C. (1996). 'Patterns of Places'. In A.-M. Blondeau and E. Steinkellner, eds., *Reflections of the Mountain. Essays on the History and Social Meaning of the Mountain Cult in Tibet and the Himalaya*, Wien: Verlag der Österreichischen Akademie der Wissenschaften, pp. 141–156.

Shah, M. (2013). 'Water: Towards a Paradigm Shift in the Twelfth Plan', *Economic and Political Weekly*, vol. 48, no. 3, pp. 40–52.

Shneiderman, S. (2014). 'Reframing Ethnicity: Academic Tropes, Recognition beyond Politics, and Ritualized Action between Nepal and India', *American Anthropologist*, vol. 116, no. 2, pp. 279–295.

Shneiderman, S. (2015). 'Regionalism, Mobility and "the Village" as a Set of Social Relations: Himalayan Reflections on a South Asian Theme', *Critique of Anthropology*, vol. 35, no. 3, pp. 318–337.

Smith, L.T. (2012). *Decolonizing Methodologies: Research and Indigenous Peoples*, London: Zed Books.

Staff Reporter (2008). 'Four Hydel Electric Power Projects in Dzongu Scrapped', *Aachuley*, vol. 12, no. 3, p. 14.

Steinmann, B. (1996). 'Mountain Deities: The Invisible Body of Society: A Comparative Study of the Representations of Mountains by the Tamang and the Thami of Nepal, the Lepcha and Bothia of Sikkim'. In A.-M. Blondeau and E. Steinkellner, eds., *Reflections of the Mountain. Essays on the History and Social Meaning of the Mountain Cult in Tibet and the Himalaya*, Wien: Verlag der Österreichischen Akademie der Wissenschaften, pp. 179–218.

Steinmann, B. (1998). 'The Opening of the sBas Yul 'Bras Mo'i Gshongs According to the Chronicles of the Rulers of Sikkim. Pilgrimage as a Metaphorical Model of the Submission of Foreign Populations'. In A. McKay, ed., *Pilgrimage in Tibet*, New York: Routledge, pp. 117–142.

Subba, T.B. (2014). 'Power Projects, Protests, and Problematics of Belonging in Dzongu, Sikkim'. In G. Toffin and J. Pfaff-Czarnecka, eds., *Facing Globalization in the Himalayas: Belonging and the Politics of the Self*, New Delhi: Sage Publications, pp. 326–343.

Tamsang, L. (2008). 'A Short Account of the Indigenous Lepchas' Pilgrimage to Dzongu, North Sikkim', *Aachuley*, vol. 12, no. 3, pp. 46–51.

Theriault, N. (2017). 'A Forest of Dreams: Ontological Multiplicity and the Fantasies of Environmental Government in the Philippines, *Political Geography*, vol. 58, pp. 114–127.

Tuck, E. (2009). 'Sụspending Damage: A Letter to Communities', *Harvard Educational Review*, vol. 79, no. 3, pp. 409–427.

Turnbull, D. (2009). 'Introduction: Futures for Indigenous Knowledges', *Futures*, Special Issue, 'Futures of Indigenous Knowledges' (edited by D. Turnbull), vol. 41, no. 1, pp. 1–5.

Vagholikar, N. and P.J. Das (2010). *Damming Northeast India*, Pune: Kalpavriksh, Aaranyak, and Action Aid India.

Van Schendel, W. (2011). 'The Dangers of Belonging. Tribes, Indigenous Peoples and Homelands in South Asia'. In D.J. Rycroft and S. Dasgupta, eds., *The Politics of Belonging in India. Becoming Adivasis*, London/New York: Routledge, pp. 19–43.

Vandenhelsken, M. (2010/11). 'Reification of Ethnicity in Sikkim: "Tribalism" in Progress', *Bulletin of Tibetology*, vol. 45, no. 2 and vol. 46, no. 1, pp. 161–194.

Vandenhelsken, M. (2020/21). 'Ancestrality, Migration, Rights and Exclusion: Citizenship in the Indian State of Sikkim. Introduction to the Special Issue', *Asian Ethnicity*, Special Issue, 'Ancestrality, Migration, Rights and Exclusion: Citizenship in the Indian State of Sikkim' (edited by M. Vandenhelsken), vol. 22, no. 2, pp. 213–234.

Vizenor, G. (1994). *Manifest Manners: Post-Indian Warriors of Survivance*, Middleton: Wesleyan University Press.

Wangchuck, P. (2007). 'Lepchas and Their Hydel Protest', *Bulletin of Tibetology*, vol. 43, nos. 1 and 2, pp. 33–58.

Wenner, M. (2015). 'Legitimisation through Patronage? Strategies for Political Control beyond Ethno-Regional Claims in Darjeeling, India', *Geoforum*, vol. 66, pp. 234–243.

Wenner, M. (2018). '"Breaking Bad" or being Good? Moral Conflict and Political Conduct in Darjeeling/India', *Contemporary South Asia*, vol. 26, no. 1, pp. 2–17.

Yeh, E.T. (2016). 'How Can Experience of Local Residents Be "Knowledge"? Challenges in Interdisciplinary Climate Change Research', *Area*, vol. 48, no. 1, pp. 34–40.

Primary Sources

ACT (2015). Press release, 13 May.

ACT (2006a). 'Teesta Hydro Electro Power Projects Sikkim, India. Peoples' Perspective', unpublished.

ACT and T. Lepcha (2006b). 'Stop the Grant of Environmental Clearance for the Teesta Hydro Electric Power Project, Stage III', 8 June.

ACT (n.d.) 'Violations at Teesta Stage V', http://www.actsikkim.com/violations.html, accessed 29 June 2023.

Government of Sikkim (2014). *Sikkim State Action Plan on Climate Change (2012-2030)*, Gangtok: Government of Sikkim.

Government of Sikkim (2017). *Public Hearing Report of 25 MW Rahi Kyoung Hydro Electric Power Project, Upper Dzongu, North Sikkim*, Gangtok: Department of Forest, Environment and Wildlife Management.

Government of Sikkim (2018). 'State Green Mission. A Unique Innovative Environment Programme Launched in Sikkim'. In Forests, Environment and Wildlife Management Department, ed., *Chapter II: Schemes and Policies Implemented from 1995-96 till 2010-11*, Gangtok: Government of Sikkim.

Government of Sikkim (2019a). 'Hydel Project Status. Gangtok: Energy and Power Department', accessed 29 June 2023 at https://power.sikkim.gov.in/status-of-ongoing-andor-completed-schemes/

Government of Sikkim (2019b). 'Sikkim Organic Mission. Framing of Action Plan 2003', accessed 11 December 2019 at https://www.sikkimorganicmission.gov.in/towards-organic-sikkim/action-plan-2003/

Government of Sikkim (2023). Corrigendum No. 358-III/LR&DMD/ACQ/GOS, dated 27 September 2023. Government Gazette No. 323, dated 28 September 2023.

Lepcha, D. (2021). Spoken word poem 'Damn your dams'. International Rivers, 21 March 2021 accessed 19 October 2023 at https://www.youtube.com/watch?v=Xy2LHGB4S2Y

Valley Notes (2023). Aamu Teesta (Mother), Instagram, 5 October 2023, accessed 19 October 2023 at https://www.instagram.com/p/CyAJlO5R-jr/?igshid=MzRlODBiNWFlZA==

Newspapers

Bhutia, W. (2017). 'Right-Bankers Want Teesta to Be Allowed Its Last Stretch of Free-Flowing Run. Save Dzongu Committee Reiterates Position against Stage-IV, Will Approach CM with Petition', *Summit Times*, 3 July 2017.

Dhungel, P. (2023). 'There should be no dam in Chungthang: Sikkim Environment Minister', *EastMojo*, 9 October 2023, accessed 19 October 2023 at https://www.eastmojo.com/sikkim/2023/10/09/there-should-be-no-dam-in-chungthang-sikkim-environment-minister/

Dsouza, A. (2022). Landslides: Large Hydropower worsening the disaster for the Lepcha's of Dzongu. *International Rivers*, 4 February 2022, accessed 19 October 2023 at https://www.internationalrivers.org/news/landslides-large-hydropower-worsening-the-disaster-for-the-lepchas-of-dzongu/

EastMojo (2023). Development at what cost? The Sikkim conundrum. *East Mojo*, 5 October 2023, accessed 19 October 2023 at https://www.youtube.com/watch?v=Eggi466ro9Q

Ellis-Petersen, H. (2023). 'India floods: 14 killed and 102 missing after lake overflows and highways washed away', *The Guardian*, 5 October, accessed 19 October 2023 at https://www.theguardian.com/world/2023/oct/05/india-floods-death-toll-lhonak-lake-injuries-missing-sikkim

FAO (2018). 'Sikkim, India's First "Fully Organic" State Wins FAO's Future Policy Gold Award', accessed 29 June 2023 at http://www.fao.org/india/news/detail-events/en/c/1157760/

Gurung, B. (2023). 'Will act as per people's decision: CM on Teesta-IV Dzongu HEP project', *Sikkim Express*, 18 October 2023, accessed 19 October 2023 at http://epaper.sikkimexpress.com/date/2023-10-18/.

NOW Report (2007). 'SAFE Sees Divine Warning in Rongyong Chu Flash Flood, Warns Lepchas against Angering Ruling Deities', *NOW!* 20 August 2007, vol. 6, no. 189, p. 2.

SANDRP (2020). 'Landslide in Sikkim Damages NHPC's Teesta V Dam Project', *SANDRP*, 27 June 2020, accessed 29 June 2023 at https://sandrp.in/2020/06/27/landslide-on-nhpcs-teesta-v-project-in-sikkim-damages-the-dam/

SE Report (2020). 'No Damage to Teesta V Dam at Dikchu: NHPC', *Sikkim Express*, 29 June 2020, accessed 29 June 2023 at http://www.sikkimexpress.com/news-details/no-damage-to-teesta-v-dam-at-dikchu-nhpc.

Sehgal, R. (2023). 'After Sikkim Disaster…There Should be no More Hydro Projects in the Himalayas', *Newsclick*, 16 October 2023, accessed 19 October 2023 at https://www.newsclick.in/after-sikkim-disasterthere-should-be-no-more-hydro-projects-himalayas

Sikkim Chronicle (2023). '"Teesta Stage III Dam, a mistake government must acknowledge": Gyatso Lepcha', *Sikkim Chronicle*, 16 October 2023, accessed 19 October 2023 at https://fb.watch/nMINGFQ9oC/

Summit Report (2017). 'Lepcha Association supports anti-Stage IV voices', *Summit Times*, 8 June 2017, p. 2.

9 Religious Connections, Economic Obstacles and Personal Fates: Contextualizing the Roles of Bridges in Sikkim (Himalayas)

Marlene Erschbamer*

Even if no bridge over the river exists,
there is no alternative but to cross [it].[1]
(Tibetan proverb)

In Sikkim, an Indian state in the Himalayas, the torrents regularly washed – and still wash – away bridges and thus disconnect communities. Over the last centuries, such incidents have been recorded by Tibetan Buddhist personages as well as by Westerners who traveled to this remote region in the Himalayas. For example, during his expedition through North Sikkim in June 1849, British Joseph D. Hooker (b. 1817, d. 1911) recorded that

---

* This study is a follow up of two postdoctoral projects, 'Glorious Riceland, Gateway to Tibet. Northern Sikkim in Tibetan and Western Travel Reports' and 'Element Water – Source of Life. Rituals, Myths, and Tradition in a Buddhist Society in the Himalaya', both sponsored by the Bavarian Gender Equality Grant (BGF) and the women's representative, Ludwig-Maximilians-University (LMU) Munich. I sincerely thank Prof. Seiji Kumagai and Dr. Anna Balikci-Denjongpa for organising the Bhutan-Sikkim panel at IATS 2019 and for including my research in their proceedings. Thanks are also due to the anonymous reviewers of this paper for their valuable input.

1 See *Bod kyi gtam dpe phyogs bsgrigs* (2004: 128): *Chu la zam pa med na // brgal ba las 'os med //.* See also Cüppers and Sørensen (1998: 88) and Richardus (1989: 61). Tibetans occasionally reached hardly wadable rivers. For adventurous reports on crossing the Kyichu or Lhasa River in Tibet, which is a tributary of the Brahmaputra River and one that has frequently flooded Lhasa, see Sørensen and Hazod (2007: 497 n.159).

Photo 9.1: Bridge over torrent, 1936
Source: Richard Nicholson Collection, Namgyal Institute of Tibetology.

'a snow bridge [...] was carried away by the daily swelling river, while the continued bad weather prevented any excursions for days together'.[2] Exactly 170 years later, in June 2019, the Sikkimese newspaper *Sikkim Express* headlined '13 villages marooned: Mantam footbridge, road washed away'.[3] Hence, bridges being carried away by thundering rivers have not lost their relevance. Since the Himalayan rivers are turbulent and dangerous, it is doubtful, if the initially mentioned Tibetan proverb is to be taken literally, that people should walk through the wild rivers of North Sikkim in the absence of any bridge.

Once a Buddhist kingdom tied culturally, religiously and politically with Tibet, Sikkim has been frequently visited by Tibetan Buddhist personages. Apart from bringing their respective Buddhist teachings and traditions with them, these masters also helped locals in providing them with infrastructure. Among others, they built bridges. As Samuel noted, '[b]ridge-building is not as unusual an activity for a Tibetan lama as it

2 See Hooker (1854: 57–58).

3 See Gurung (2019). Mantam is a village in Upper Dzongu, North Sikkim. About 4,000 villagers were isolated after this bridge collapsed.

might seem at first sight. The biographies of many Tibetan lamas recount their role in promoting public works of various kinds'.[4] The most famous Tibetan engineer was Tangtong Gyelpo (Thang stong rgyal po, b. 1361/5, d. 1480/6 or b. 1385, d. 1464), who, among other achievements, constructed numerous iron bridges in Tibet and Bhutan. As Schaeffer pointed out, '[t]hese iron-link bridges were his "service" to the Tibetan people. They connected communities and helped people across natural barriers. They formed crucial links in trade routes'.[5] Even more, these constructions influenced the Western way of building suspension bridges.[6] In the course of many centuries, various Tibetan Buddhist personages traveled to Sikkim and some of them were also involved in bridge-building activities. By doing so, they helped connect local communities, making pilgrimage sites more accessible and providing necessary infrastructure for trade.

Sikkim is a state of many bridges, which are of different types, including cantilever bridges, suspension bridges, cane bridges and simple temporary bridges. They are either made of R.C.C. (reinforced cement concrete), steel, timber or bamboo.[7] In general, bridges are important for connecting two sides of a river and for crossing a current safely. Besides this literal importance, the image of a bridge can be a symbol or a metaphor. Regarding Sikkim, the image of a bridge could symbolize cultural or religious bridging between different groups within and across the state, a barrier that is simultaneously a connection between regions, kingdoms and states in the Himalayas, or an aid to the exchange of ideas and economic

4 See Samuel (1993: 518).

5 See Schaeffer (2013: 485).

6 See Gerner (2007: 120). Besides, Tangtong Gyelpo was also responsible for erecting shrines and statues to protect from diseases, invasions and natural disasters, among others, at Lhasa, an area that frequently suffered from floods; see Sørensen and Hazod (2007: 486–487). For further reading on the 'iron-bridge man' (*chakzampa*, *lcags zam pa*) Tangtong Gyelpo, see also Gerner (2007), Kalmus (2015: 20–32, including numerous photographs) and Stearns (2007). For Tangtong Gyelpo's activities in Bhutan, see Phuntsho (2013: 177–180). Scotsman George Bogle (b. 1746, d. 1781), who visited Bhutan and Tibet in 1774–75 to establish diplomatic relations for the British, mentioned several bridges in his reports; see Markham (1876: 20–22, 214–215, 271).

7 For the different types of bridges in the Himalayas, see Gerner (2007: 49–69).

goods. And, as discussed below, bridges could also represent symbols of personal fate and places of freedom, once they were successfully crossed.

Besides the existing literature on bridges in Tibet and Bhutan, there is a general lack of available research on the religious, historical, economic, sociocultural and political facets of bridges in Sikkim. Accordingly, the aim of this study is to analyze and contextualize the roles of bridges in Sikkim, a region in the Himalayas where heavy rains are frequent, bridges regularly wash away and, consequently, people are cut off from each other. The following aspects shall be addressed.

1. Religious connections: Various Tibetan Buddhist personages were involved in bridge-building activities in Sikkim. By doing so, they helped locals and, at the same time, pilgrims and traders also benefited from these activities.

2. Economic obstacles: Bridges include economic aspects. Some important trade routes that connected the Indian subcontinent with the Tibetan capital Lhasa led through Sikkim. These routes became the subject of political and military incidents, including invasions of the Gurkhas and missions led by the British. On the one hand, Sikkim was regarded as a bridge in the Himalayas that connected one side of the Himalayas with the other. On the other hand, the crossing of rivers and thus the building of bridges was perceived as an urgent matter that could decide the success or failure of economic and political missions. Besides, Western mountaineers seeking adventure and glory explored the Sikkimese Himalayas. The lack of bridges was a serious obstacle. In other words, the existence of bridges was decisive for their progress and success.

3. Personal fates: Two instances shall be presented that stylize bridges as places of personal fate and as symbols of freedom. First, the practice of throwing accused people over a bridge into the violent river was once used as a supernatural adjudication in North Sikkim. Second, a North Sikkimese bridge became the temporary destination for a Tibetan refugee while seeking exile in the twentieth century.

Figure 9.1: Map of places mentioned in the paper
Source: Tiles © Esri – USGS, Esri, TANA, DeLorme, and NPS. Map by author.

Finally, this study will be completed by examining a selected list of Tibetan Buddhist personages who visited Sikkim prior to 1959 and who were, to some extent, involved in providing infrastructure (see Addendum).

Religious connections: Buddhist masters and bridges in Sikkim

Starting with the legendary Guru Rinpoche in the eighth century, various Buddhist personages, whether on pilgrimage or in search of a safe place to practice, have traveled from Tibet to Sikkim. They metaphorically built bridges in the Himalayas by spreading their teachings and connecting places on both sides of the mountain range, but they were also literally involved in building activities. In the following, some of these personages that mentioned Sikkimese bridges in their writings will be set in context.

Bridges to a hidden land: Guru Rinpoche and Buddhist treasure revealers

According to legendary accounts, Guru Rinpoche – or 'precious master', as Padmasambhava, the lotus-born tantric master, is respectfully called in Sikkim – visited Sikkim during the eighth century. His followers, members of the Nyingma tradition (Rnying ma pa), which is the most widespread Tibetan Buddhist tradition in Sikkim, still venerate him as the Second Buddha. In Sikkim, it is said that he had tamed supernatural entities, discovered precious Buddhist treasures and prepared the whole land for the Buddhist doctrine. By doing so, he 'built' the first bridge for Buddhist practitioners, who would arrive and practice in Sikkim centuries later.

The first Tibetan master to recognize Sikkim as a sacred hidden land that had been blessed by Guru Rinpoche was Rindzin Gödemchen (Rig 'dzin rgod ldem chen, b. 1337, d. 1408). Being an early treasure revealer (*tertön*, *gter ston*), he discovered some of the sacred treasures hidden by Guru Rinpoche. In one treasure text, the *Pilgrimage Guide to the Hidden Land of Drémoshong*,[8] Rindzin Gödemchen mentioned what would be necessary to reach this sacred land. Among others, he notes that one should lay bridges to 'heal' dangerous paths.[9]

During the fourteenth century, the treasure revealer Sanggyé Lingpa (Sangs rgyas gling pa, b. 1340, d. 1396) mentioned the advantages of building bridges for locals after having seen that Sikkim is a land with a considerable amount of water. The importance of maintaining and establishing bridges was emphasized in different passages.[10]

Similarly, Péma Lingpa (Padma gling pa, b. 1450, d. 1521),[11] an important religious figure in Bhutan who also revealed a guidebook (*néyik*, *gnas yig*) to the hidden land of Drémoshong, advised that bridges

---

8 Drémoshong, meaning 'the hidden fruitful valley', was an early Tibetan name for present-day Sikkim.

9 See *Sbas yul 'bras mo ljongs kyi lam yig* (*Pilgrimage Guide to the Hidden Land of Drémoshong*; 2008: 164).

10 See *'Bras ljongs gnas yig zur phyug* (2008: 196–197, 211, 220, 235).

11 One of his aunts was the consort of the above-mentioned famous bridge builder Tangtong Gyelpo; see Maki (2011).

should be built in Sikkim. For example, he suggested a bridge be built at the southern door to make the journey a success and to allow entry to this hidden land from that direction.[12] In another passage, he depicted the western part of the valley of Drémoshong, describing a river where a bridge should be constructed.[13] Furthermore, he mentioned that this sacred hidden land shall be reached by crossing iron or wooden bridges.[14]

Bridges for a Buddhist kingdom: Buddhist masters in Sikkim

Eventually, in the seventeenth century, the land was ritually opened by three Tibetan Buddhist masters of the Nyingma tradition of Tibetan Buddhism. They enthroned the first Buddhist king of Sikkim, a lineage that became known as the Namgyal dynasty. Together, these four protagonists, the three Tibetan masters and the first Sikkimese king, are called 'the four yogis who are brothers'.[15] Metaphorically, they built a new bridge to Sikkim, which made this young Buddhist kingdom a place of refuge and practice for Tibetan Buddhists as well as a pilgrimage site.[16]

Lhatsün Namkha Jikmé (Lha btsun chen po Nam mkha' jigs med, b. 1597, d. 1650), a great Dzokchen (rdzogs chen) master and one of the three Tibetan Buddhist masters who ritually opened Sikkim, wrote the Nésöl (*gnas gsol*) text, which is still the most important Buddhist ritual text in Sikkim. Lhatsün Namkha Jikmé mentioned, among others, how to overcome natural obstacles. For example, he advised building a bridge if one had to cross a river.[17] During the decades and centuries that followed, various Buddhist personages arrived from Tibet and some of them built bridges along their routes in Sikkim.

---

12 See *Sbas yul 'bras mo gshongs kyi gnas yig* (2008: 259).

13 See *Sbas yul 'bras mo gshongs kyi gnas yig* (2008: 267).

14 See *Sbas yul 'bras mo gshongs kyi gnas yig* (2008: 248).

15 See Ehrhard (2005: 11) and Mullard (2011a: 53).

16 On the deteriorating situation in Central Tibet that led to the remembering of the prophecies of Guru Rinpoche to go to the supreme hidden land in the South, namely to Sikkim, see Ehrhard (2005: 18). On the creation of Sikkim as a pilgrimage site, see Steinmann (1998).

17 See *'Bras ljongs gnas gsol* (2000: 32b.2–3).

Shortly after the ritual opening of Sikkim, the first Tibetan master belonging to the Barawa Kagyü tradition ('Ba' ra ba Bka' brgyud pa) of Tibetan Buddhism, Könchok Gyeltsen (Dkon mchog rgyal mtshan, b. 1601, d. 1687), arrived. Prior to this, he had been active in Bhutan, but, since he had been among the five groups of lamas that had been thrown out of Bhutan, Könchok Gyeltsen started concentrating his activities in Sikkim. There, he was involved in building bridges and repairing roads and thus he helped locals, traders and pilgrims by providing them with infrastructure.[18]

Several decades later, in 1724, the so-called 'care-free yogin' (*jatang*, *bya btang*), Sönam Chödzin (Bsod nams chos 'dzin, b. 1668), followed in the footsteps of his teacher Sönam Tendzin (Bsod nams bstan 'dzin, b. 1639, d. 1694), who is the throne-holder of the Tibetan Sakya monastery Tsédong (Rtse gdong), and stayed in Sikkim from 1692 to 1694. Sönam Chödzin traveled to Lachung, Chungthang and Lachen in North Sikkim, where he erected village prayer halls, roads and bridges and thus provided locals with infrastructure.[19] Furthermore, he described various episodes wherein he referred to heavy rains, dangerous bridges and difficult paths in North Sikkim. For example, on the way from Tibet to the village of Lachung in North Sikkim, his party arrived at a river that was extremely loud with floodwater that was turbulent like a storm. Because of that, the accompanying yaks trembled as if they were being brought to slaughter and thus they were not able to cross the bridge and had to return.[20] Sometime later, as Sönam Chödzin was traveling from Lachung to Chungthang, his party had to cross a bridge. Suddenly, at the end of the

---

18 See *Dkon mchog rgyal mtshan gyi rnam thar* (1970: 117). On the five groups of lamas that had to leave Bhutan, see Ardussi (1977: 218–220), Kumagai (2014: 128–129) and Phuntsho (2013: 227, 235). For further reading on the Barawa Kagyü tradition in Sikkim, see, among others, Erschbamer (2013, 2017). Already in the 1510s, a Barawa master named Namkha Gyeltsen (Nam mkha' rgyal mtshan, 'Ba' ra ba Sprul sku, b. 1466, d. 1540) visited present-day Sikkim. Both Namkha Gyeltsen and Könchok Gyeltsen stood in the same transmission lineage; see Ehrhard (2009).

19 See Erschbamer (2015: 57; 2019: 7).

20 See *Mthong thos yid kyi dga' ston* (38a.5–38b.2). For further reading on Sönam Chödzin, see Ehrhard (2015: 138–142) and Erschbamer (2015: 57; 2019: 7–8).

Photo 9.2: Yaks crossing a bridge, 1936
Source: Richard Nicholson Collection, Namgyal Institute of Tibetology.

bridge, one of his three companions fell into the river because of a water demon (*dréchu, 'dre chu*). Luckily, he was unhurt.[21] Then, the party set out from Chungthang to Lachen, but before they were able to reach the village of Lachen, new bridges had to be erected. All in all, Sönam Chödzin described the construction of three larger and three smaller bridges. He further mentioned many bridges that were dangerous to cross and, more generally, paths that were difficult to traverse.[22]

Similar to Sönam Chödzin's account, the British explorer and professor of Tibetan, Laurence A. Waddell (b. 1854, d. 1938), mentioned bridges that were destroyed and bridges that were dangerous to cross in his book *Among the Himalayas* (1900). He provided illustrative insights into the behavior of Himalayan people when they were crossing a difficult bridge. He gave the following account describing his journey to North Sikkim:

> As we reached the bridge, our men sent up a loud shout, calling on the malignant water-spirit to let us cross in safety. And certainly, it looked

21 See *Mthong thos yid kyi dga' ston* (40b.3–4).

22 See *Mthong thos yid kyi dga' ston* (44a.4–44b.2).

Figure 9.2:
Crossing a Torrent by a Rickety Cane-Bridge
Source: Waddell (1900: ii).

> as if special prayers for our safety were really required, for the bridge, dangerous at all times, was a mere ragged skeleton of itself and slippery with green slime.[23]

While Waddell and his party proceeded safely, the Tibetan Sönam Chödzin and his party had not been so lucky: They attributed the incident on the bridge to a water demon that negatively affected their journey.

A Sikkimese lama on bridges

The picture of a bridge was used in a different setting by the Sikkimese Trinlé Gyatso ('Phrin las rgya mtsho, seventeenth/eighteenth century)[24]

---

23 See Waddell (1900: 123).

24 Trinlé Gyatso, born at Rinchenpung (Rin chen spungs) south of Tashiding (Bkra shis sdings), was a Nyingma master who belonged to the Ngadak (Mnga' bdag) tradition. He frequently traveled to Bhutan and Nepal as well as Tibet. In addition,

in his autobiography and in the songs that he intoned as instructions (*lapja*, *bslab bya*) for his disciples, which together were published in 1983. Although his autobiography comprises only twenty-four folios, he repeatedly included passages that described heavy rainfalls and floods that obstructed his journeys.[25] Furthermore, he described how he came to a swift mountain stream, which he was not able to cross, leading him to ponder how joyful it would have been if there had have been a bridge.[26] He not only described observations and experiences depicting heavy rainfalls and bridges but he also used the image of a bridge in an allegory: 'Like the sun that illuminates all four continents [i.e. the whole world], similarly, a lamp escorts in darkness, boats and bridges [lead across] large rivers'.[27] While he was at the Southern Cave in Sikkim, he depicted how a footbridge had been carried away by the river and how the assembled people were frightened as a result.[28] Since this happened regularly in the Himalayas, he had undoubtedly experienced such an incident before. Altogether, his descriptions of heavy rains, floods and bridges lead to the conclusion that these themes bothered him frequently and, most likely, also his contemporaries in Sikkim and the Himalayas.

Besides these Buddhist masters from Tibet and Sikkim, who recognized the importance of bridges, others interested in economic relations with Tibet were also aware of the relevance of bridges in this part of the Himalayas.

Economic obstacles: Sikkim as a bridge to Tibet

While most Tibetans reached Sikkim from the north, various Westerners traveled to this remote Himalayan region via the south, from the Indian

---

he used to practice at the Southern Cave in Sikkim, which was once blessed by Guru Rinpoche. He studied, among others, under Terdak Lingpa (Gter bdag gling pa, b. 1646, d. 1714); see *Gtsug nor sprul pa'i rnal 'byor mched bzhi brgyud* (2002: 241–244) and *'Phrin las rgya mtsho'gsung rnam* (1983: 1–47).

25 See *'Phrin las rgya mtsho'gsung rnam* (1983: 34.5–37.1).

26 See *'Phrin las rgya mtsho'gsung rnam* (1983: 21.5).

27 See *'Phrin las rgya mtsho'gsung rnam* (1983: 45.3–4).

28 See *'Phrin las rgya mtsho'gsung rnam* (1983: 192.4–5).

subcontinent. They described various episodes in their records where they mentioned the condition of bridges, the construction of bridges or other situations involving bridges. Hence, they cared about bridges, which could be decisive for the success or failure of their respective missions. Further, the British mountaineer Douglas W. Freshfield (b. 1845, d. 1934) compared Sikkim itself to a bridge in the Himalayas, which connected British India with Tibet, and regarded Sikkim as economically and politically important.[29]

Besides the British, for whom Sikkim was a kind of a bridge or buffer zone in the Himalayas, neighboring authorities also recognized this significant aspect of Sikkim. Consequently, they have tried to gain influence in this part of the Himalayas. For example, during the eighteenth century, the Gurkhas were extending their territory and invaded Sikkim several times. Since the Sikkimese opened a new trade route with Tibet leading through the Chumbi valley in 1784, the traders could avoid Nepalese taxes, which displeased the Gurkhas, who strove for a trade monopoly in the Himalayas. The Manchu were also aware of the importance of Sikkim from a strategic point of view. In 1790–1791, the Manchu Amban Baotai (in Tibet from 26 September 1790 to 17 October 1791) urged the Sikkimese to reinforce their borders with Nepal, since a Gurkha invasion of Tibet via Sikkim was feared. As a result of the wars with the Gurkhas, the Sikkimese frontiers were drawn anew: parts of the Chumbi valley that initially belonged to the Sikkimese kingdom were annexed to Tibet by the Manchu in 1792.[30]

Afterwards, Sikkim remained an important connecting bridge in the Himalayas. The Ganden Phodrang (Dga' ldan pho brang, r. 1642–1959),

---

29 See Freshfield (1903: 16).

30 See Erschbamer (2018: 129–133) and Mullard (2014). Ever since the two Himalayan states Sikkim and Bhutan were founded in the seventeenth century, the Chumbi valley, nestled between Tibet, Sikkim and Bhutan, has been the subject of conflicts; see Ardussi (2011: 35–38). On the Chumbi valley, the political officer of Sikkim, John C. White (1853–1918), noted in his records that '[a]ccording to local tradition, Chumbi itself came into the possession of the Sikhim Raja a little more than a hundred years ago as the dower of a Tibetan wife […]. I tried to trace the previous history of the valley, but I could find no one with any knowledge of or interest in the subject' (White 1909: 111). However, the Chumbi valley was

the Buddhist government of the Dalai Lamas, was aware of this and sent Tibetan masters to Sikkim to perform rituals meant to secure the border regions. For example, Rindzin Péma Wanggyel Dorjé (Rig dzin Padma dbang rgyal rdo rje, b. 1779, d. 1841) was assigned this duty in the 1830s.[31]

Bridge-building by the British

Nearly at the same time, the British and Russian empires struggled for supremacy in Central and South Asia. Sikkim was an important strategic point for the British that bridged the Himalayas during this so-called 'Great Game'. The British wanted to open a new trade route that connected British India with Lhasa. Since there had been trade disputes between the British and the Qing, this development displeased the latter. As a result, the Qing exerted leverage on Tibet to prevent British interference in that country, and this led to disputes around the Sikkimese border with Tibet, known as the Sikkim-Gampa disputes.[32] Mullard showed that during 'this particular period of Tibetan and Sikkimese relations the border between the two countries was an area of real political concern particularly after the rise of British interest in the Himalaya'.[33] For the British, as pointed out by McKay, 'Sikkim seemed the ideal route to Lhasa'.[34]

In order to explore trade routes with Tibet, John W. Edgar (b. 1839, d. 1902), deputy commissioner of Darjeeling, toured through Sikkim in 1873. He concluded that the absence of bridges was the biggest impediment

---

regarded as part of the Sikkimese kingdom up to the late eighteenth century. Furthermore, the Sikkimese kings even had their summer palace there from the 1780s to 1888. They were allowed to sojourn in the Chumbi valley after the official annexation to Tibet in 1792. On the borders in the Chumbi valley, see also *Gzhis rtse'i lo rgyus* (2005: 95–97). Besides the invasions of the Gurkhas, the Bhutanese also invaded parts of Sikkim during the reigns of the third Sikkimese king, Chakdor Namgyal (Phyag rdor rnam rgyal, b. 1686, d. 1717, r. 1700–1717), and the fourth Sikkimese king, Gyurmé Namgyal ('Gyur med rnam rgyal, b. 1707, d. 1733, r. 1717–1733); see, among others, Basnet (1974: 18–21), Phuntsho (2013: 310) and *Kun gsal me long* (2003: 125–146).

31 See Ehrhard (2008: 15).

32 See Mullard and Wongchuk (2010) and Mullard (2012).

33 See Mullard (2012: 155).

34 See McKay (2009/2010: 45).

to trade, ranking this even higher than any possible counteraction by the Lhasa-based Amban, the representative of China's Qing emperor, or by the Tibetans themselves. He identified the construction of bridges to be the most urgent matter before being able to proceed with the planned trade with Tibet. Furthermore, he was convinced that if the British 'are unwilling to spend the few thousand rupees required for these all-important bridges, we can scarcely take credit for doing all that we may fairly be asked to do for the development of the trade with Thibet'.[35]

In 1884, still in search of possible trade routes through Sikkim, the British Colman Macaulay (b. 1849, d. 1890) crossed the Lachen valley. Similar to Edgar's account, he reported that by expanding the necessary infrastructure, trade could be initiated. He gave the following account on a possible trade route via the Lachen valley in North Sikkim:

> But though they [i.e. people from Lachen] have constant communication with Tibet by the Kongra Lama pass, they are cut off from Sikkim and Darjeeling for five months of the year owing to the destruction of their temporary bridges and the submersion of the track in places by the rise of the river […]. But I cannot doubt that the road would have an important effect in opening up Lower Sikkim and the rich and healthy Lachen and Lachung valleys. I have already referred to what the Jongpen said regarding the obstructions which he is now ordered to place in the way of trade through Kambajong. But if these can be removed, there can be no doubt that a large trade would pass down by the Lachen valley were a proper road available.[36]

Macaulay tried to convince the Sikkimese authorities, the ninth Sikkimese king, Tutop Namgyal (Mthu stobs rnam rgyal, b. 1860, d. 1914; r. 1874–1914), as well as the Phodang Lama and his brother, the Kangsa Dewan, to open a permanent trade route through the Lachen valley by constructing roads and bridges. Furthermore, he assured that the British would pay

35 See Edgar (1874: 82).

36 See Macaulay (1885: 103–104).

for these constructions and the Sikkimese would only have to provide laborers and rest houses.[37]

Indeed, the most important trade routes from India to Tibet through Sikkim were either via the Chumbi valley, which was part of the Sikkimese kingdom up to 1792, or via the Lachen and Lachung valleys. As shown by Ehrhard, 'sacred sites in Himalayan regions are often to be found in the vicinity of a trade route'.[38] Chungthang, a village in North Sikkim, is one such example. It was once blessed by Guru Rinpoche, who had a rest on a stone in Chungthang on his way back to Tibet. There, he left his footprints, he produced drinking water for the locals and threw away some rice, which is why rice is supposed to be able to grow there. This spot, known as Guru Nédo (Gu ru Gnas rdo), the rock where Guru Rinpoche rested, became an important Buddhist pilgrimage site. Various Tibetan Buddhist masters reached Sikkim along a trade route in the very north and, consequently, passed Chungthang, where they visited Guru Nédo, the monastery of Chungthang, or both of them.[39]

In 1900, Captain O'Connor (b. 1870, d. 1943) published the book *Routes in Sikkim*, wherein he described in detail roads, bridges and camp possibilities, focusing on the routes that lead to the border areas. On the North Sikkimese village of Chungthang, he noted the following:

> From the bridge there is a steep ascent to the monastery of Chungthang (6 miles). There is enough ground below the monastery to camp 2,000 or 3,000 men. Some of the ground, however, is damp, and it might be unhealthy. The upper storey of the monastery has been made into a rest-

---

37 See Arora (2013), Macaulay (1885: 9–15, 103–104) and Singh (1988: 207).

38 See Ehrhard (2008: 22).

39 Besides the already mentioned Barawa Kagyü master Könchok Gyeltsen and the 'care-free yogin' Sönam Chödzin, various Lhatsün Trülku, for example the third Lhatsün Trülku Jikmé Pawo or the forth Lhatsün Trülku Künzang Jikmé Gyatso, traveled along this route and visited Chungthang and its sacred places; see *'Jigs med dpa' bo'i bka' 'bum* (1983: 482.3–483.2), *Gtsug nor sprul pa'i rnal 'byor mched bzhi brgyud* (2002: 187–188) and *'Bras ljongs dgon sde'i lo rgyus* (2008: 152–153). The Lhatsün Trülku is the incarnation lineage of the Nyingma master Lhatsün Namkha Jikmé, one of those who ritually opened Sikkim for the Buddhist doctrine in the seventeenth century.

Figure 9.3: *Cane-Bridge Below Chungthang* Source: Hooker (1854: 21).

> house. 3 rooms. Chungthang, standing at the junction of the Lachen and Lachung valleys, is of some strategical importance, as it bars all ingress from the northern frontier of Sikkim. There are only some five houses. In its present condition the road is far too narrow for pack transport.[40]

Chungthang not only lies at the confluence of two rivers which proceed as Teesta, the main river of the region, but also at the spot where two trade routes with Tibet met. Tibetans used the route through the Lachen valley during winter, since in that season the rivers were not as violent and thus the route was less dangerous. In summer, the yak caravans had to cross the Donkia La and they came down the Lachung valley. But, as explained by Freshfield, because of the 'absence of permanent bridges'[41] and the wild river itself, the route through the Lachen valley remained less attractive.

In 1903, a British party consisting of Francis Younghusband (b. 1863, d. 1942), John Claude White (b. 1853, d. 1918) and Captain O'Connor,

40 See O'Connor (1900: 48); see also McKay (1997). Mountaineer Sir Douglas Freshfield explored different mountains in North Sikkim in 1899. He gave a similar description of Chungthang and its strategical importance; see Freshfield (1903: 87).

41 See Freshfield (1904: 86).

among others, reached Chungthang. They proceeded through the Lachen valley up to Thangu in North Sikkim and from there to the nearby Gampa Dzong (Gamp pa rdzong) in Tibet to discuss trade and frontier matters.[42] This party was accompanied by Mr. Dover, who was the British engineer in Sikkim and thus responsible for the necessary trade infrastructure.[43] Younghusband noted that Dover 'had made such excellent rough roads and bridges'.[44] Thus, Edgar's suggestion to construct bridges to develop trade with Tibet was taken seriously. However, no agreement was achieved by Younghusband, White and O'Connor regarding the trade and frontier matters, which eventually led to a British invasion of Tibet via the Chumbi valley.[45]

Nonetheless, the aforementioned Great Game seems to have continued in the twentieth and twenty-first centuries, even though the opponents have changed. The importance of Chungthang as a strategical point has not changed over the years. Thus, the recent construction of infrastructure in North Sikkim is not only to connect locals and to help the economy but also to satisfy military needs.[46] Even more, the whole region has been transformed in aesthetic, economic, sociocultural and religious ways, resulting from the presence of military forces and migrant laborers that work, for example, for the Border Roads Organisation.[47]

Bridges as obstacles in mountaineering expeditions

While the above descriptions addressed political and economic matters of infrastructure, several mountaineers explored the Himalayas in search of adventure and glory. They described the challenge of crossing torrents and

42 See Younghusband (1910).

43 See also Freshfield (1903: 242).

44 See Younghusband (1910: 116).

45 For the Anglo-Sikkim war of 1861, see McKay (2009/2010); for the British invasion of Tibet in 1903–04, see McKay (1997; 2012). On various Westerners on missions in North Sikkim, see Erschbamer (2015).

46 See Walcott (2010: 74).

47 The Border Roads Organisation is responsible for constructing roads thus 'to ensure swift and easy passage to army vehicles'; see Chettri (2017: 39).

Photo 9.3: Repairing a bridge over Zemu Chu, 1936
Source: Richard Nicholson Collection, Namgyal Institute of Tibetology.

bridges in North Sikkim from their adventurous point of view. Alexander M. Kellas (1868–1921), for example, characterized the crossing of rivers and bridges as 'the most sporting incidents of Himalayan travel'.[48]

This description matches reports of an expedition that was led to Northern Sikkim to explore the Zemu Glacier in 1936. Based on the written accounts of the different expedition members, the local porters crossed the swinging or half-destroyed bridges without considerable problems. But for the Westerners, this was an uncomfortable and unnerving experience.[49]

Hettie Dyhrenfurth (b. 1892, d. 1972), the only woman who was part of an international expedition to the Khangchendzonga Mountain Range in 1930 and the only female voice in this study, provided a vivid description of bridges in North Sikkim. From the Lhonak valley in North Sikkim the Western explorers traveled through the Lachen valley on their way to Gangtok. On the way to Lachen, they crossed several smaller streams by jumping from one side to the other, while for the broader rivers, they had to wade through them. Dyhrenfurth's description is reminiscent of the

48 See Kellas (1913: 139).

49 See Chapman (1945: 54) and Roaf (2001: 176–177). On this expedition and their experience in the Lachen valley, see also Erschbamer (2015: 62).

Tibetan proverb mentioned at the beginning of the paper that one should go through a river, if there is no bridge. However, in one spot, Hettie was forced to return because the river was too turbulent and dangerous to cross, and she had to search for a better place to wade across. In the meantime, still in the Lachen valley, the party was hindered by tremendous downpours that caused numerous landslides, which in turn tore away bridges. The only way to proceed was to walk over breakneck emergency bamboo bridges, balancing on tree trunks. At one bridge they came across an amusing information board: 'Take care not to sleep on this bridge!', an idea that made them shudder. Of course, that board meant 'not to slip'. Indeed, they had to be careful not to slip on these temporary bridges, which were wet because of the rain. Finally, when the whole party reached Gangtok, they were invited by the eleventh Sikkimese monarch, Tashi Namgyal (b. 1893, d. 1963; r. 1914–1963), and had dinner in his palace.[50]

Moreover, records exist of dramatic incidents involving bridges in Sikkim. These occurrences represent additional aspects of bridges: Sikkimese bridges that turned into sites of personal fate as well as symbols of freedom.

Personal fate: bridges as symbols of freedom

In the following, two examples that stylize bridges as symbols of freedom will be set in context. The first is a bridge in North Sikkim that was depicted as a supernatural adjudication by a British national. The second is another bridge in North Sikkim that became a Tibetan refugee's symbol of freedom.

50 See G. Dyhrenfurth (1942: 172–176) and H. Dyhrenfurth (1931: 53–59). The book by Hettie Dyhrenfurth contains different photographs from their expedition: among others, one of Hoerlin, another expedition member, showing an 'adventurous bridge', as Hettie named it. Besides, the Earl of Ronaldshay (b. 1876, d. 1961) compared the construction of a North Sikkimese bridge to a spider building its web and he spoke about the 'whole gamut of emotions to be derived from bridges'; see Dundas (1923: 144–146). For other Westerners, who referred to their experience with Sikkimese bridges in their reports, see, among others, Brown (1934), Gawler (1873, including drawings of different bridges), Temple (1887) and White (1909).

Supernatural adjudication

David Macdonald (b. 1870/3, d. 1962), British trade agent in Yadong (Sharsingma, Shar gsing ma) and Gyantsé (Rgyal rtse) from 1909 to 1924, described a bridge in North Sikkim, where the accused were thrown into the river. If they drowned, they were regarded as guilty, but if they were to survive, it was taken as proof of their innocence.

> The Chungtang monastery is passed a mile before reaching the bungalow, the road crossing the Lachen River a little to the south of the rest house. From this bridge, in bygone days, criminals were thrown into the river below, as a kind of trial by ordeal. If drowned, they were guilty ; if they emerged alive, their innocence was presumed.[51]

Hence, this particular bridge was regarded as a form of supernatural adjudication. The above-mentioned Younghusband was fascinated by the energy of the Teesta River, which also flowed under this bridge: 'With a force and tumult that nothing could withstand it comes swirling down the valley. Before its rushing impetuosity everything would be swept away'.[52] Furthermore, the mountaineer Frederick Chapman (b. 1907, d. 1971), who toured around North Sikkim in the 1930s, reported on dangerous bridges and noted on the rivers in the Lachen valley that '[n]o one who fell into one of these torrents would have a hope of getting out alive'.[53] Together, these descriptions raise the question, how would a person ever be able to survive and thus be assumed to be innocent? And, how would this act of cruelty ever be questioned since it stood under the umbrella of supernatural adjudication?

In this context, the described bridge became the symbol of a crossroad for the accused: They were being regarded as either guilty or innocent and, consequently, it was a place of either surviving or dying. However, the chances of surviving and thus of being regarded as innocent can be assumed minimal at best. Nonetheless, up to the 1870s, the abbots of Chungthang Monastery have held jurisdiction over the valleys of Lachen

51 See Macdonald (1943: 96).

52 See Younghusband (1921: 16).

53 See Chapman (1945: 55).

and Lachung. Does this imply that a Buddhist lama was responsible for such a jurisdiction, a thoroughly non-Buddhist practice? At least, Larip Dechan, the last Chungthang lama with jurisdiction in North Sikkim, was known for his cruelty and tyranny.[54]

Destination for refugees

Bridges also became a destination for refugees and thus symbols of freedom. In 1960, the Tibetan Khyusar Ngödrup Penden (Khyu gsar dngos grub dpal ldan, b.1940), a native from Panam (Pa snam) county in Western Tibet, fled from Tibet to seek exile in India. In 2017, his autobiography was published as part of the oral history project of the Library of Tibetan Works & Archives, which aims to preserve first-hand knowledge of Tibetans from all stratums of society. This Tibetan refugee wanted to stay at Lachung but he was informed that each and every Tibetan refugee had to first cross the bridge at Chungthang and stay there for some time. Eventually, he was allowed to return to Lachung, where he was involved in road constructions for about two years.[55] Thus, the bridge at Chungthang became his destination in seeking exile as well as a symbol of freedom.

Conclusion

From the first contact with Buddhism in the eighth century up to the twenty-first century, bridges played a notable role in Sikkim, both literally and metaphorically. First, bridges had to be erected in order to reach the prophesied sacred hidden land and thus to introduce Buddhism in Sikkim. Over the course of many centuries, various Tibetan Buddhist masters arrived in Sikkim and were involved in bridge-building activities. They described the torrents and bridges in North Sikkim that were both difficult and dangerous to cross. Westerners also traveled to this remote region in the Himalayas and frequently referred to the importance of bridges for economic matters. Furthermore, since Sikkim lies in a strategic position in

54 See Erschbamer (2015: 60), Erschbamer (2019: 11), Freshfield (1903: 87) and Macaulay (1885: 50–51).

55 See *Mi ser dkyus ma zhig gi lo rgyus* (2017: 197–204).

the Himalayas, it has been considered itself a bridge that connects different parts of the mountain range. This becomes evident at different stages in history whenever political opponents (the Qing, British, Russian empires as well as Gurkhas, Bhutanese and Tibetans) were trying to extend their influence and, in some cases, were even trying to gain supremacy in this part of the world. Besides this, bridges became places of personal fates and symbols of freedom: Certain bridges in North Sikkim were used to decide on the future life of the accused and refugees. Finally, bridges connect people and villages; they symbolize the possibility of exchanging goods, news and ideas. Hence, bridges occupy crucial roles in the Himalayas from religious, historical, economic, sociocultural and political perspectives, and thus their relevance should not be underestimated.

Addendum

Here follows an overview of selected Tibetan Buddhist personages who visited Sikkim before 1959. Most of them belonged to the Nyingma tradition of Tibetan Buddhism. However, members of other traditions, for example Sakyapa or Kagyüpa (Barawa, Drukpa and Karma Kagyü), also visited and acted in Sikkim. Several of these personages arrived in Sikkim as a result of political tensions or wars in their home regions. In such times, the prophesied hidden lands were remembered as safe places to stay and practice Buddha-dharma. Besides bringing along their teachings, some of these personages were involved in providing locals with different kinds of infrastructure, as discussed above.

NB: The legendary visit of Guru Rinpoche during the eighth century is not included.[56] Whenever possible, literature in Western languages shall be provided. For Tibetans or scholars who prefer reading Tibetan primary sources, the indicated secondary sources include the relevant references.

56 For lists of venerated Buddhist masters who arrived in Sikkim from 1959 onwards see Gyatso (2005: 52–54) and *Deng rabs ris med bla ma skyes chen dam pa* (2012: 27–31).

Table 9.1: Selected Tibetan Buddhist personages who visited Sikkim before 1959

	Name	Dates	Notes	Selected References
1	Rindzin Gödemchen (Rig 'dzin rgod ldem chen)	1337–1408	Discovered Sikkim as a hidden land, probably the first Tibetan lama in Sikkim.	Balikci (2008: 88); Boord (2003); Khenpo Lha Tshering (2002: 13–18); Valentine (2016); Vandenhelsken (2006: 66, 73)
2	Sönam Gyeltsen, Katokpa (Kaḥ thog pa Bsod nams rgyal mtshan)	1466–1540	Opened the western gate to Sikkim during the end of the 15th century.	Ehrhard (2003, 2007); Khenpo Lha Tsering (2002: 20–22)
3	Namkha Gyeltsen, Barawa Trülku (Nam mkha' rgyal mtshan, 'Ba' ra ba Sprul sku)	1466–1540	Incarnation of Gyeltsen Pelzang (Rgyal mtshan dpal bzang, b. 1310, d. 1391), the founding father of the Barawa tradition. In the 1510s, he visited places where Guru Rinpoche had once stayed, among others, present-day Sikkim.	Erschbamer (2017: 99)
4	Ngari Rindzin Lekden Dorjé (Mnga' ris rig 'dzin legs ldan rdo rje)	n.a.	Involved in preparing Sikkim for Buddhist doctrine.	Khenpo Lha Tsering (2002: 23–26)
5	Püntsok Rindzin, Ngadak Sempa Chenpo (Mnga' bdag Sems dpa' chen po Phun tshogs rig 'dzin)	1592–1656	One of the Tibetan masters who ritually opened Sikkim and enthroned the first Buddhist ruler (*chögyel*, *chos rgyal*) of Sikkim.	Ehrhard (2005); Khenpo Lha Tsering (2002: 37–51); Mullard (2011b: 89–113); Vandenhelsken (2006: 73–76)
6	Namkha Jikmé, Lhatsün Chenpo (Lha btsun chen po Nam mkha' jigs med)	1597–1653	One of the Tibetan masters who ritually opened Sikkim and enthroned the first Buddhist ruler of Sikkim.	Khenpo Lha Tsering (2002: 65–143); Lachung Rinpoche (2008: 157–163); Mullard (2011b: 115–138); Steinmann (2004); Vandenhelsken (2006: 76–79)
7	Küntu Zangpo, Katokpa (Kaḥ thog pa Kun tu bzang po)	n.a.	One of the Tibetan masters who ritually opened Sikkim and enthroned the first Buddhist ruler of Sikkim.	Khenpo Lha Tsering (2002: 231–236); Mullard (2011b: 44–46)
8	Rindzin Lhündrup (Rig 'dzin lhun grub)	d. 1650	Nephew or brother of Namkha Jikmé; first in line of the Pelri Trülku (Dpal ri Sprul sku) of Sikkim.	Deroche (2013: 90, n. 44); Ehrhard (2008: 9, 11–12)

	Name	Dates	Notes	Selected References
9	Chöying Lhündrup (Chos dbyings lhun grub)	d. 1684	Nephew of Namkha Jikmé; stayed in contact with the Fifth Dalai Lama; was involved in recognising Lhatsün Trülku; resided in Sikkim.	Ehrhard (2008: 9–12); Khenpo Lha Tsering (2002: 139)
10	Könchok Gyeltsen (Dkon mchog rgyal mtshan)	1601–1687	Established Barawa tradition, i.e. subbranch of Drukpa Kagyü, in Sikkim; met the first Buddhist ruler Püntsok Namgyal (Phun tshog rnam rgyal).	Ardussi (2011: 36); Dzigar Khenchen Trinlé Dorjé (2013: 198–200); Ehrhard (2009: 196); Erschbamer (2013, 2017)
11	Lachen Dréshokpa Dorjé (Bla chen Bres gshogs pa rdo rje)	1602–1687/9	Arrived in Sikkim soon after opening to study under Ngadak Sempa Chenpo (1592–1656).	Erschbamer (2015: 57, n. 31); Péma Trinlé (1972: 383.2–4)
12	Orgyen Pelzang (O rgyan dpal bzang)	1617–1677	From kingdom of Lobo (Glo bo), present-day Mustang in Northern Nepal; stayed at Tashiding in 1646; refused request of Sikkimese king to remain in Sikkim at Lektsé (Legs rtse; present-day Lingzey?).	Ehrhard (2005; 2013a: 221)
13	Sönam Tendzin (Bsod nams bstan 'dzin)	1639–1694	Throne-holder of Sakya monastery Tsédong; disciple of the above-mentioned Lachen Dréshokpa Dorjé; traveled to North Sikkim in 1692, where he passed away in 1694.	Ehrhard (2015: 138); Erschbamer (2015: 57; 2019: 7)
14	Ngakwang Künzang Jikmé Mikyö Dorjé, 2nd Lhatsün Trülku (Ngag dbang kun bzang 'Jigs med mi bskyod rdo rje)	b. 1656	Born in Bhutan.	Ehrhard (2008: 5–6); Khenpo Lha Tsering (2002: 143–145); Lachung Rinpoche (2008: 163)
15	Rinchen Tenpé Seljé, Barawa Trülku (Rin chen bstan pa'i gsal byed)	1658–1696	In 1687, he traveled from Tibet to Chungthang in North Sikkim to perform funeral rituals for his teacher, the Barawa master Könchok Gyeltsen.	Dzigar Khenchen Trinlé Dorjé (2013: 200–202); Ehrhard (2009: 196); Erschbamer (2013: 30; 2017: 136–137, 149–150)
16	Sönam Chödzin (Bsod nams chos 'dzin)	b. 1668	Disciple of Sönam Tendzin; traveled to North Sikkim in 1724; construction of bridges, roads and village prayer halls in Lachung, Chungthang and Lachen.	Ehrhard (2015: 138–142, 148–154); Erschbamer (2015: 57; 2019: 7–8)

	Name	Dates	Notes	Selected References
17	Jikmé Pawo, 3rd Lhatsün Trülku ('Jigs med dpa' bo)	1682–1735	Incarnation of Namkha Jikmé; was invited by the Sikkimese king; became important religious and political personage in Sikkim.	Khenpo Lha Tsering (2002: 147–185); Lachung Rinpoche (2008: 164); Mullard (2011b: 165–187); Vandenhelsken (2006: 79–82)
18	Lama Dorjé Lingpa (Bla ma Rdo rje gling pa)	n.a.	Nyingma Lama from Mindröling; fled from the Dzungars and arrived in Sikkim in 1717; met Jikmé Pawo in the monastery of Sangngak Chöling; proceeded to Bhutan.	Khenpo Lha Tsering (2002: 246–247); Samten Gyatso (2008: 143–144)
19	Rindzin Longyang (Rig 'dzin klong yangs)	1686–1756	Nyingma Lama and son of Tertön Dorjé Lingpa with whom he left Tibet and went to Sikkim in 1717; met Jikmé Pawo in the monastery of Sangngak Chöling; founded Doling Monastery in South Sikkim.	Khenpo Lha Tsering (2002: 248–250); Samten Gyatso (2008: 144–146); Tashi Tsering (2008: 62–66)
20	Jétsün Migyur Pelgyi Drönma (Rje btsun Mi 'gyur dpal gyi sgron ma)	1699–1769	Daughter of Rindzin Terdak Lingpa (Rig 'dzin Gter bdag gling pa); taught the Tibetan ruling prince Polhané (Mi dbang Pho lha nas Bsod nams stobs rgyas, 1689–1747); escaped Dzungar armies and arrived in Sikkim in 1718; welcomed by the 4th king Gyurmé Namgyal (b. 1707, d. 1733) and Jikmé Pawo.	Ehrhard (2008: 6; 2013b: 370); Bhutia (2014); Mullard (2011b: 168–170); Samten Gyatso (2008: 127–128)
21	Künzang Jikmé Gyatso, 4th Lhatsün Trülku (Kun bzang 'jigs med rgya mtsho)	n.a.	Born in Walung; was invited by Sikkimese king.	Ehrhard (2008: 7); Lachung Rinpoche (2008: 164); Khenpo Lha Tsering (2002: 187–195); Samten Gyatso (2008: 152–156)
22	Péma Déchen Gyatso, 5th Lhatsün Trülku (Padma bde chen rgya mtsho)	n.a.	Born in Tsang; was invited by the Sikkimese king. Established Yanggang Monastery in South Sikkim.	Khenpo Lha Tsering (2002: 194–195); Lachung Rinpoche (2008: 164)
23	Jétsün Künga Chönyi, 6th Lhatsün Trülku (Rje btsun Kun dga' chos nyid)	n.a.	Was born in Sakya.	Lachung Rinpoche (2008: 164)

	Name	Dates	Notes	Selected References
24	Péma Ömbar, Tödraknak Lama (Stod brag nag bla ma Padma 'od 'bar)	d. 1776	Erected small wooden heritage in Thangu, North Sikkim; took Sikkimese wife; showed his magical power as locals wanted to punish the couple for their relationship.	Erschbamer (2015: 50–51)
25	Rindzin Chöying Dorjé (Rig 'dzin chos dbyings rdo rje)	1772–1838	Master of the Barawa Kagyü tradition; provided different teachings for the Sikkimese king Tsukpü Namgyal (gTsug phud rnam rgyal, 1785–1863) and his family in the Chumbi valley between 1828 and 1837.	Ehrhard (2009: 201); Erschbamer (2017: 173; 2018)
26	Rindzin Péma Wanggyel Dorjé, 4th Pelri Trülku (Rig 'dzin Padma dbang rgyal rdo rje, Dpal ri Sprul sku)	1779–1841	Arrived at Sikkim during late 1830s; preceptor to King Tsukpü Namgyal (Gtsug phud rnam rgyal, 1785–1863); performed rituals to protect Tibetan borders as ordered by Ganden Phodrang.	Ehrhard (2008: 15)
27	Künzang Ngédön Longyang (Kun bzang nges don klong yangs)	b. 1804	Disciple of Rindzin Péma Wanggyel Dorjé, who invited him to Sikkim to act as priest of the Sikkimese king.	Ehrhard (2008: 15)
28	Orgyen Tendzin (Shar khum bu'i bla ma O rgyan bstan 'dzin)	19th c.	Stayed some time at Lachen Monastery in North Sikkim.	Erschbamer (2015: 53)
29	Gönpo Namgyal (Mgon po rnam rgyal)	19th c.	Disciple of Orgyen Tendzin; established new Lachen Monastery in North Sikkim in 1896.	Erschbamer (2015: 54)
30	Sungrap Gyatso (Gsung rab rgya mtsho)	19th–20th c.	Arrived from Khams to North Sikkim; established Lachen Mani Lhakhang.	Erschbamer (2015: 58)
31	Chaktak Rinpoche (Lcags thag Rin po che)	19th c.–1958	Built many Buddhist reliquary shrines (*chörten, mchod rten*) in Sikkim; took Lepcha wife.	Vandenhelsken (2006: 84–86; 2008)

	Name	Dates	Notes	Selected References
32	Tendzin Gyeltsen (Bstan 'dzin rgyal mtshan)	1894–1977	Drukpa lama; native from Khunu in Himachal Pradesh (India); in his youth, he went to Sikkim to study under Orgyen Tendzin (O rgyan bstan 'dzin); he served at Trashilhünpo and became a famous scholar.	Dzigar Khenchen Trinlé Dorjé (2013: 510); Jackson (2003: 63–64)
33	Khandro Péma Déchen (Mkha' gro Padma bde chen)	1923–2006	Arrived in Sikkim in 1946; stationed at Lachung with her husband Trülzhik Rinpoché ('Khrul zhig rin po che, 1897–1952)	Vandenhelsken (2006: 86–89)

Bibliography

Primary sources

Dékyi Zangmo (Bde skyid bzang mo, b.20th c.), ed. (2005). *Gzhis rtse'i lo rgyus rig gnas dpyad gzhi'i rgyus cha bdams bsgrigs*, vol. I, Lhasa: Bod ljongs mi dmangs dpe skrun khang [= *Gzhis rtse'i lo rgyus*].

Dzigar Khenchen Trinlé Dorjé ('Dzi sgar mkhan chen Phrin las rdo rje, b. 1971). (2013). *Don brgyud dpal ldan 'brug pa'i mkhas grub bla ma rgya mtsho'rnam thar legs bshad nor bu'i gter mdzod*, vol. I, Kathmandu: Khenpo Shedup Tenzin [= *Rnam thar legs bshad nor bu*].

Géshé Lhakdor (Dge bshes Lhag rdor, b. 20th c.), ed. (2017). *Bod gzhung dga' ldan pho brang pa chen po'i gzhung rgyug mi ser dkyus ma zhig gi lo rgyus*, Oral History Series 41, Dharamsala: Library of Tibetan Works and Archives [= *Mi ser dkyus ma zhig gi lo rgyus*].

Horkhang Sönam Pembar (Hor khang Bsod nams dpal 'bar, 1919–1994), ed. (2004). *Bod kyi gtam dpe phyogs bsgrigs*, Lhasa: Bod ljongs mi dmangs dpe skrun khang [= *Bod kyi gtam dpe phyogs bsgrigs*].

Jikmé Pawo ('Jigs med dpa' bo, b. 1682, d. 1735). (1983). *Rdzogs chen rig 'dzin 'jigs med dpa' bo'i bka' 'bum mthon grol chen mo*, Gangtok: Dzongsar Khyentse Labrang, BDRC bdr:W21558 [= *'Jigs med dpa' bo'i bka' 'bum*].

Khenpo Chöwang (Mkhan po Chos dbang, b. 20th c.). (2003). *Sbas yul 'bras mo ljongs kyi chos srid dang 'brel ba'i rgyal rabs lo rgyus bden don kun gsal me long*, Gangtok: Namgyal Institute of Tibetology [= *Kun gsal me long*].

Khenpo Lha Tsering (Mkhan po Lha tshe ring, b. 20th c.). (2002). *Mkha' spyod 'bras mo ljongs kyi gtsug nor sprul pa'i rnal 'byor mched bzhi brgyud 'dzin dang bcas pa'i byung ba brjod pa blo gsar gzhon nu'i dga' ston*, Gangtok: Khenpo L. Tsering [= *Gtsug nor sprul pa'i rnal 'byor mched bzhi brgyud*].

Lachung Rinpoche (La chung rin po che 'Jigs med rnam rgyal, b. 20th c.). (2008). 'Rgyal ba lha btsun chen po'i mdzad rnam rags bsdus su bkod pa rig 'dzin dgongs rgyan'. In Tashi Tsering and Tenpa Nyima, eds., *Buddhist Himalaya: Studies in Religion, History and Culture*, vol. III: The Tibetan Papers, Gangtok: Namgyal Institute of Tibetology, pp. 157–166 [= *Lha btsun chen po'i mdzad rnam*].

Lhatsün Namkha Jikmé (Lha btsun Nam kha' 'jigs med, b. 1597, d. 1650). (2000). ''Bras ljongs gnas gsol'. In Rig 'dzin srog sgrub, ed., *Rdzogs pa chen po rig dzin srog sgrub kyi chos skor*, Delhi: Chos spyod dpar skrun khang, BDRC bdr:MW13779 [= *'Bras ljongs gnas gsol*].

Péma Lingpa (Padma gling pa, b. 1450, d. 1521). (2008). 'Klong gsal gyi skor las / om : sbas yul 'bras mo gshongs kyi gnas yig'. In Tashi Tsering Josayma (Jo sras bkra shis tshe ring), ed., *Mkha' spyod 'bras mo ljongs kyi gnas yig phyogs bsdebs*, Gangtok/ Dharamsala: Namgyal Institute of Tibetology/Amnye Machen Institute, pp. 237–276 [= *Sbas yul 'bras mo gshongs kyi gnas yig*].

Péma Trinlé (Pad ma 'phrin las, b. 1641, d. 1717). (1972). 'Lha chen bres gshongs pa chos rgyal rdo rje'i rnam thar', *bKa' ma mdo dbang gi bla ma brgyud pa'i rnam thar*, Leh: Tashigangpa, fol. 379-388, BDRC bdr:MW21523 [= *Chos rgyal rdo rje'i rnam thar*].

Rinchen Tenpé Seljé (Rin chen bstan pa' gsal byed, b. 1658, d. 1696). (1970). 'Grub thob chen po dkon mchog rgyal mtshan gyi rnam thar mdor bsdus ngo mtshar bdud rtsi'i chu rgyun zhes bya ba', *Bka' brgyud gser phreng chen mo*, vol. III, Dehradun: Ngagwang Gyaltsen and Ngagwang Lungtok [= *Dkon mchog rgyal mtshan gyi rnam thar*].

Rindzin Gödemchen (Rig 'dzin rgod ldem chen, b. 1337, d. 1408). (2008). 'Sbas yul 'bras mo ljongs kyi lam yig le'u drug pa lde mig 'khrul gyi dgu skor bdog go' (Pilgrimage Guide to the Hidden Land of Drémoshong). In Tashi Tsering Josayma (Jo sras bkra shis tshe ring), ed., *Mkha' spyod 'bras mo ljongs kyi gnas yig phyogs bsdebs*, Gangtok/ Dharamsala: Namgyal Institute of Tibetology/Amnye Machen Institute, pp. 139–165 [= *Sbas yul 'bras mo ljongs kyi lam yig*].

Samten Gyatso (A tsar ya Bsam gtan rgya mtsho Leb ca, b. 20th c.). (2008). *'Bras ljongs dgon sde'i lo rgyus gsar bzhad chu skyes bung ba'i rol mtsho*, Gangtok: Namgyal Institute of Tibetology [= *'Bras ljongs dgon sde'i lo rgyus*].

Sanggyé Lingpa (Sangs rgyas gling pa, b. 1340, d. 1396). (2008). 'Bla ma dgongs pa 'dus pa las / ma 'ongs lung bstan gsang ba'i dkar chag bkod pa zhes pa las 'bras ljongs gnas yig zur phyug'. In Tashi Tsering Josayma (Jo sras bkra shis tshe ring), ed., *Mkha' spyod 'bras mo ljongs kyi gnas yig phyogs bsdebs*, Gangtok/Dharamsala: Namgyal Institute of Tibetology/Amnye Machen Institute, pp. 166–236 [= *'Bras ljongs gnas yig zur phyug*].

Sönam Chödzin (Bsod nams chos 'dzin, b. 1668). (n.d.). *Bstan 'gro spyi dang rang gzhan phan dbe ba rnams / mthong thos yid kyis [kyi] dga' bston [ston]*, Manuscript, 117 fols., NGMPP reel-nos. AT 145/28-146/1 [= *Mthong thos yid kyi dga' ston*].

Tashi Tsering Josayma (Jo sras bkra shis tshe ring, b. 20th c.), ed. (2008). *'Bras ljongs nang dgon sde khag gcig gi chags rabs yig cha*, Gangtok/Dharamsala: Namgyal Institute of Tibetology/Amnye Machen Institute [= *'Bras ljongs nang dgon*].

Trinlé Gyatso ('Phrin las rgya mtsho, b. 17th/18th c.). (1983). *'Phrin las rgya mtsho'i gsung rnam*, Gangtok: Pema Wangchen, BDRC bdr:MW23561 [= *'Phrin las rgya mtsho'i gsung rnam*].

Tsultsem Gyatso Acharya (Ātsārya Tshul khrims rgya mtsho, b. 20th c.). (2012). *Sbas yul 'bras mo ljongs su deng rabs ris med bla ma skyes chen dam pa rnams kyis mdzad pa phyag ris ji bskyangs kyi rnam thar shin tu bsdus pa blo gsar padom 'dzum pa'i nyi zer*, Gangtok: Namgyal Institute of Tibetology [= *Deng rabs ris med bla ma skyes chen dam pa*].

Secondary sources

Ardussi, J. (1977). *Bhutan before the British: A Historical Study* (PhD dissertation, Australian National University, http://hdl.handle.net/1885/11280.)

Ardussi, J. (2011). 'Sikkim and Bhutan in the Crosscurrents of Seventeenth and Eighteenth Century Tibetan History'. In A. Balikci-Denjongpa and A. McKay, eds., *Buddhist Himalaya: Studies in Religion, History and Culture*, vol. II: The Sikkim Papers, Gangtok: Namgyal Institute of Tibetology, pp. 29–42.

Arora, V. (2013). 'Routeing the Commodities of the Empire through Sikkim (1817–1906)'. In J. Curry-Machado, ed., *Global Histories, Imperial Commodities, Local Interactions*, London: Palgrave Macmillan, pp. 15–37.

Balikci, A. (2008). *Lamas, Shamans and Ancestors: Village Religion in Sikkim*, Leiden: Brill.

Basnet, L.B. (1974). *Sikkim: A Short Political History*, New Delhi: S. Chand & Co.

Bhutia, K.D. (2014). 'The Importance of Jetsun Mingyur Paldron in the Development of Sikkimese Buddhism'. In K.L. Tsomo, ed., *Eminent Buddhist Women*, Albany: State University of New York Press, pp. 153–158.

Boord, M. (2003). 'A Pilgrim's Guide to the Hidden Land of Sikkim Proclaimed as a Treasure by Rig 'dzin rgod kyi ldem 'phru can', *Bulletin of Tibetology*, vol. 39, no. 1, pp. 31–53.

Brown, P. (1934 [1917]). *Tours in Sikhim and the Darjeeling District*, Calcutta: W. Newman & Co.

Chapman, F.S. (1945). *Memoirs of a Mountaineer: Helvellyn to Hamalaya, Lhasa: The Holy City*, London: Reprint Society.

Chettri, M. (2017). 'Chungthang: An Emerging Urban Landscape in Sikkim', *The Newsletter*, vol. 77, pp. 38–39.

Cüppers, C. and P.K. Sørensen (1998). *A Collection of Tibetan Proverbs and Sayings: Gems of Tibetan Wisdom and Wit*, Stuttgart: Franz Steiner Verlag.

Deroche, M.-H. (2013). 'History of the Forgotten Mother-Monastery of the rNying ma School: dPal ri Monastery in the Tibetan "Valley of the Emperors"', *Bulletin of Tibetology*, vol. 49, no. 1, pp. 77–111.

Dundas, L.o.Z. (1923). *Lands of the Thunderbolt: Sikhim, Chumbi, and Bhutan*, London: Constable and Co., Ltd.

Dyhrenfurth, G.O. (1942). *Himalaya-Fahrt: Unsere Expedition 1930*, Zürich: Orell Füssli.

Dyhrenfurth, H. (1931). *Memsahb im Himalaja*, Leipzig: Verlag Deutsche Buchwerkstätten GmbH.

Edgar, J.W. (1874). *A Visit to Sikhim and the Thibetan Frontier in October, November, and December, 1873*, Calcutta: Bengal Secretariat Press.

Ehrhard, F.-K. (2003). 'Kaḥ thog pa bSod nams rgyal mtshan (1466-1540) and His Activities in Sikkim and Bhutan', *Bulletin of Tibetology*, vol. 39, no. 2, pp. 9–26.

Ehrhard, F.-K. (2005). 'The mNga' bdag Family and Their Tradition of Rig 'dzin zhig po gling pa (1524–1583) in Sikkim', *Bulletin of Tibetology*, vol. 41, no. 2, pp. 11–30.

Ehrhard, F.-K. (2007). 'Kaḥ thog pa Bsod nams rgyal mtshan (1466–1540) and the Foundation of O rgyan rtse mo in Spa gro'. In J. Ardussi and F. Pommaret, eds., *Bhutan: Traditions and Changes*, London/Boston: Brill's Tibetan Studies Library, pp. 73–95.

Ehrhard, F.-K. (2008). '"Turning the Wheel of the Dharma in Zhing sa Va lung": The dPal ri sprul skus (17th to 20th Centuries)', *Bulletin of Tibetology*, vol. 44, nos. 1–2, pp. 5–30.

Ehrhard, F.-K. (2009). 'The Lineage of the 'Ba'-ra-ba bKa'-brgyud-pa School as Depicted on a Thangka and in "Golden Rosary" Texts', *Münchner Beiträge zur Völkerkunde*, vol. 13, pp. 179–209.

Ehrhard, F.-K. (2013a). 'Concepts of Religious Space in Southern Mustang: The Foundation of the Monastery sKu-tshab gter-lnga'. In F.-K. Ehrhard, ed., *Buddhism in Tibet & the Himalayas: Tests and Traditions*, Kathmandu: Vajra Publications, pp. 218–228.

Ehrhard, F.-K. (2013b). 'Political and Ritual Aspects of the Search for Himalayan Sacred Lands'. In F.-K. Ehrhard, ed., *Buddhism in Tibet & the Himalayas: Tests and Traditions*, Kathmandu: Vajra Publications, pp. 363–378.

Ehrhard, F.-K. (2015). 'Glimpses of the Sixth Dalai Bla ma: Contemporary Accounts from the Years 1702 to 1706'. In O. Czaja and G. Hazod, eds., *The Illuminating Mirror: Tibetan Studies in Honour of Per K. Sørensen on the Occasion of His 65th Birthday*, Wiesbaden: Reichert Verlag, pp. 131–154.

Erschbamer, M. (2013). 'The 'Ba' ra ba Teachings Reach the Hidden Land of 'Bras mo ljongs: Mahāsiddha dKon mchog rgyal mtshan (1601-1687) and the Taming of Demons in Chungthang', *Bulletin of Tibetology*, vol. 49, no. 2, pp. 25–33.

Erschbamer, M. (2015). '"Wild and Lawless Area"? Monastic Institutions in the Lachen Valley (North Sikkim, India)', *Bulletin of Tibetology*, vol. 51, nos. 1–2, pp. 47–70.

Erschbamer, M. (2017). *The 'Ba'-ra-ba bKa'-brgyud-pa: Historical and Contemporary Studies*, Wien: Arbeitskreis für Tibetische und Buddhistische Studien.

Erschbamer, M. (2018). 'Tibetan Troops Fighting the "Enemy of Buddhist Doctrine" (*bstan dgra*): The Invasions of the Gorkhas as Witnessed by Two Tibetan Masters of the Barawa ('Ba' ra ba) Tradition', *Cahiers d'Extrême-Asie*, vol. 27, pp. 121–137.

Erschbamer, M. (2019). 'Taming of Supernatural Entities and Animal Sacrifice. The Synthesis of Tibetan Buddhism and Local Shamanistic Traditions in Northern Sikkim (India)', *Études mongoles et sibériennes, centrasiatiques et tibétaines* (online), vol. 50, pp. 1–21, DOI: 10.4000/emscat.3915.

Freshfield, D.W. (1903). *Round Kangchenjunga: A Narrative of Mountain Travel and Exploration*, London: Edward Arnold.

Freshfield, D.W. (1904). 'The Roads to Tibet', *The Geographical Journal*, vol. 23, no. 1, pp. 79–91.

Gawler, J.C. (1873). *Sikkim: With Hints on Mountain and Jungle Warfare*, London: E. Stanford.

Gerner, M. (2007). *Chakzampa Thangtong Gyelpo: Architect, Philosopher and Iron Chain Bridge Builder*, Thimphu: Centre for Bhutan Studies.

Gurung, B. (2019). '13 Villages Marooned: Mantam Footbridge, Road Washed Away', *Sikkim Express*, 19 June.

Gyatso, T. (2005). 'A Short Biography of Four Tibetan Lamas and Their Activities in Sikkim', *Bulletin of Tibetology*, vol. 41, no. 2, pp. 49–76.

Hooker, J.D. (1854). *Himalayan Journals*, vol. II, London: John Murray.

Jackson, D.P. (2003). *A Saint in Seattle: The Life of the Tibetan Mystic Dezhung Rinpoche*, Boston: Wisdom Publications.

Kalmus, M. (2015). 'Remarks on Selected Bridges of Thangtong Gyalpo', *Journal of Comparative Cultural Studies in Architecture*, vol. 8, pp. 20–32.

Kellas, A.M. (1913). 'A Fourth Visit to the Sikkim Himalaya, with Ascent of the Kangchenjhau', *The Alpine Journal*, vol. 27, no. 200, pp. 125–153.

Kumagai, S. (2014). 'History and Current Situation of the Sa skya pa School in Bhutan'. In S. Kumagai, ed., *Bhutanese Buddhism and Its Culture*, Kathmandu: Vajra Books, pp. 127–139.

Macaulay, C. (1885). *Report of a Mission to Sikkim and the Tibetan Frontier: With a Memorandum of Our Relations with Tibet*, Calcutta: Bengal Secretariat Press.

Macdonald, D. (1943 [1930]). *Touring in Sikkim and Tibet*, Calcutta: Thacker, Spink & Co.

Maki, A. (2011). 'Pema Lingpa', *Treasury of Lives*, accessed 5 June 2023 at http://treasuryoflives.org/biographies/view/Pema-Lingpa/3000.

Markham, C.R. (1876). *Narratives of the Mission of George Bogle and of the Journey of Thomas Manning to Lhasa*, London: Trübner & Co.

McKay, A. (1997). *Tibet and the British Raj: The Frontier Cadre, 1904–1947*, Richmond: Curzon Press.

McKay, A. (2009/2010). '"A Difficult Country, a Hostile Chief, and a Still More Hostile Minister": The Anglo-Sikkim War of 1861', *Bulletin of Tibetology*, vol. 45, no. 2; vol. 46, no. 1, pp. 31–48.

McKay, A. (2012). 'The British Invasion of Tibet, 1903–04,' *Inner Asia*, vol. 14, no. 1, pp. 5–25.

Mullard, S. (2011a). 'Constructing the Maṇḍala: The State Formation of Sikkim and the Rise of a National Historical Narrative'. In A. Balikci-Denjongpa and A. McKay, eds., *Buddhist Himalaya: Studies in Religion, History and Culture*, vol. II: The Sikkim Papers, Gangtok: Namgyal Institute of Tibetology, pp. 53–62.

Mullard, S. (2011b). *Opening the Hidden Land: State Formation and the Construction of Sikkimese History*, Leiden: Brill.

Mullard, S. (2012). 'Tibetan and Sikkimese Relations: Preliminary Remarks on the Gam pa Disputes and the Gam pa-Sikkim Agreement of 1867'. In R. Vitali, ed., *Studies on the History and Literature of Tibet and the Himalaya*, Kathmandu: Vajra Publications, pp. 143–156.

Mullard, S. (2014). 'Sikkim and the Sino-Nepalese War of 1788–1792: A Communiqué from Bǎo tài to the Sikkimese Commander Yug Phyogs thub', *Revue d'Etudes Tibétaines*, vol. 29, pp. 29–37.

Mullard, S. and H. Wongchuk (2010). *Royal Records: A Catalogue of the Sikkimese Palace Archive*, Andiast: IITBS.

O'Connor, W.F. (1900). *Routes in Sikkim*, Calcutta: Office of the Superintendent of Government Printing.

Phuntsho, K. (2013). *The History of Bhutan*, Noida: Random House India.

Richardus, P. (1989). 'Selected Tibetan Proverbs', *The Tibet Journal*, vol. 14, no. 3, pp. 55–71.

Roaf, R. (2001). 'Sikkim, 1936: Climbing with Marco Pallis, Freddy Spencer Chapman and others, in the Zemu Valley', *The Alpine Journal*, vol. 106, no. 350, pp. 173–180.

Samuel, G. (1993). *Civilized Shamans: Buddhism in Tibetan Societies*, Washington: Smithsonian Inst. Press.

Schaeffer, K.R. (2013). 'Building Iron Bridges: Tangtong Gyelpo'. In K.R. Schaeffer, M.T. Kapstein and G. Tuttle, eds., *Sources of Tibetan Tradition*, New York: Columbia University Press, p. 485.

Singh, A.K.J. (1988). *Himalayan Triangle: A Historical Survey of British India's Relations with Tibet, Sikkim and Bhutan 1765–1950*, London: The British Library.

Sørensen, P.K. and G. Hazod (2007). *Rulers on the Celestial Plain: Ecclesiastic and Secular Hegemony in Medieval Tibet. A Study of Tshal Gung-thang*, Wien: Verlag der Österreichischen Akademie der Wissenschaften.

Stearns, C. (2007). *King of the Empty Plain: The Tibetan Iron Bridge Builder Tangtong Gyalpo*, Boston: Snow Lion Publications.

Steinmann, B. (1998). 'Territoire et frontières politiques, royaume et divinités montagnardes: l'usage des stéréotypes dans la construction d'une identité nationale (Sikkim)'. In A.M. Blondeau, ed., *Tibetan Mountain Deities, Their Cults and Representations*, Wien: Verlag der Österreichischen Akademie der Wissenschaften, pp. 145–158.

Steinmann, B. (2004). 'Sur la tendance aux métaphores visuelles: aller voir lHa btsun chen po au Sikkim', *Bulletin of Tibetology*, vol. 40, no. 1, pp. 69–92.

Temple, R. (1887). *Journals Kept in Hyderabad, Kashmir, Sikkim, and Nepal*, vol. 2, London: W.H. Allen & Co.

Valentine, J.H. (2016). 'Introduction to and Translation of *The Garland of Light: Lives of the Masters of the Northern Treasure Tradition*', *Revue d'Etudes Tibétaines*, vol. 39, pp. 133–165.

Vandenhelsken, M. (2006). 'Tibetan Masters and the Formation of the Sacred Site of Tashiding', *Bulletin of Tibetology*, vol. 42, nos. 1–2, pp. 65–92.

Vandenhelsken, M. (2008). 'Narrations about a Yogī in Sikkim', *Bulletin of Tibetology*, vol. 44, nos. 1–2, pp. 31–60.

Waddell, L.A. (1900). *Among the Himalayas*, Westminster: Archibald Constable and Co.

Walcott, S.M. (2010). 'Bordering the Eastern Himalaya: Boundaries, Passes, Power Contestations', *Geopolitics*, vol. 15, pp. 62–81.

White, J.C. (1909). *Sikhim and Bhutan: Twenty-one Years on the North-East Frontier 1887–1908*, New York: Longmans, Green & Co.

Younghusband, F.E. (1910). *India and Tibet*, London: John Murray.

Younghusband, F.E. (1921). *The Heart of Nature: Or the Quest for Natural Beauty*, London: John Murray.

10 A Manual for Teaching Dzongkha as a Foreign Language

Lungtaen Gyatso

Background

Dzongkha is the national language of Bhutan, native to eight western districts out of the twenty districts in the country. Besides serving as the language of governance, it functions as the lingua franca of Bhutan, helping to overcome language barriers among people from different linguistic backgrounds. It holds a significant place in Bhutanese culture. However, due to the absence of a regulated system of Dzongkha orthography in the country, various spellings for certain words have emerged organically. As a result, mastering Dzongkha is sometimes considered challenging. To address this issue, the Dzongkha Development Commission, chaired by the prime minister, established the National Committee of Dzongkha Language Experts. This committee was tasked with standardizing and developing Dzongkha orthography and grammar.

Furthermore, in an attempt to preserve and promote the language, Dzongkha is mandated as a compulsory subject in schools and colleges. Given its crucial role in communication within Bhutan, many expatriates employed by various international organizations in the country have shown a keen interest in learning Dzongkha. While it is essential for Bhutan to facilitate this learning, the absence of a structured approach to teaching Dzongkha as a second or foreign language, along with a lack of specialized teaching resources for instructing non-native speakers in the use of Dzongkha, present a significant obstacle.

In the absence of these resources, teaching Dzongkha to non-native speakers remains challenging due to the differing linguistic needs and proficiency levels between native and non-native learners. Native speakers, being familiar with the language's intricacies, can readily engage in grammatical exercises and language accuracy drills. Conversely, non-native speakers must begin from the basics, lacking any prior knowledge of the target language.

Consequently, to facilitate the learning of Dzongkha for non-native speakers, a dedicated manual titled 'A Manual for Teaching Dzongkha as a Foreign Language' has been developed. This manual aims to bridge the gap and provide an effective pathway for non-native speakers to acquire proficiency in the Dzongkha language.

Dzongkha is an expressive language, which means it is highly 'contextual' or, more accurately, 'situational' in nature. The Dzongkha verbs ཡོད་ /yö/ and འདུག་ /du/ encompass the existential, locational and attributive meanings akin to the English verb 'to be'. These verbs are used in a locational sense to indicate the subject's position, in an existential context to denote the availability or presence of a person or object, and in an attributive context to ascribe a quality to someone or something.[1]

Moreover, the verb ཡོད་ /yö/ denotes an intimate, pre-acquired knowledge at the moment of speaking, while འདུག་ /du/ conveys newly acquired knowledge, through senses (sight, smell, etc.). However, native speakers employ these verbs seamlessly, so the need to know the subtle difference never arises. Yet, when taught to non-native speakers, such terms require explanation, demanding a level of scientific and linguistic articulation attainable only through linguistic training. Consequently, teaching a language to non-native speakers necessitates a higher degree of ingenuity and linguistic expertise compared to what is typically required for a native audience.

Linguistic identity

In 1812, the famous linguist Wilhelm von Humboldt wrote that the difference between nations is most clearly manifest in their languages. In 1856, August Pott wrote that language is the key trait defining nationhood. In 1987, Emil Cioran wrote that we do not really reside in a country, but in our language. Our true fatherland, he said, was

1 Tshering and van Driem (2019: 114).

> nothing else than our mother tongue. Most of our thoughts and much of our identity are language-mediated and depend directly on our language. Our native language is where we grew up and how we came to know and understand the world. Our mother tongue is our mind's conceptual homeland.[1]

In a small and landlocked nation like Bhutan, wedged between two huge countries, India to the south and China to the north, the significance of Bhutanese identity as a sovereign state is magnified. Today, identity markers may vary across nations and eras. While some nations might view their economy and military power as identity markers, others may prioritize cultural values and ideology. For Bhutan, culture and its associated values form the cornerstone of identity. In this context, language, as an important aspect of culture, assumes immense importance in defining linguistic identity.

The government of Bhutan is concerned about the challenges Dzongkha faces in the context of the global prominence of English, driven by the internet, mainstream media and various social media platforms. In response, the College of Language and Culture Studies (CLCS) is tasked with nurturing and promoting the Dzongkha language. The CLCS offers in-depth courses encompassing language, culture, Buddhism and history to Bhutanese students.

Of late, the CLCS has realized the importance of reaching out to those who are beyond the mainstream Dzongkha teaching and learning framework. There is a demand to learn Dzongkha by non-native speakers and expatriates within the country. It was realized that in order to teach Dzongkha as a second language in a systematic way, it was first necessary to develop a teachers' manual to guide how to teach the language. To address this, the CLCS undertook the initiative to develop a manual for teaching Dzongkha to non-native speakers. This initiative is aimed at equipping teachers with a scientific and structured approach to teaching the language.

1 van Driem (2015: 61).

Manual overview

After more than six years of dedicated and intensive collaborative efforts involving lecturers from the CLCS, led by Lopen Lungtaen Gyatso and Françoise Robin,[1] the manual has now reached its final form. This manual has been meticulously designed to provide a step-by-step introduction to conversational Dzongkha. It is based on the method elaborated and tested at the Institut National des Langues et Civilisations Orientales (INALCO) for teaching spoken Tibetan.

The manual consists of eighteen lessons that encompass carefully selected grammatical elements and essential vocabularies necessary for day-to-day conversations. Its content is structured progressively, allowing each new piece of knowledge to build upon the previous one, facilitating incremental and cumulative learning. Moreover, the manual follows a very strict discipline of introducing only one concept or word at a time. This methodology enhances comprehensibility, ensuring that learners can grasp the material effortlessly.

Additionally, the manual provides ample learning opportunities within classroom settings, fostering interactions through pair, group and class activities. The objective is to create a social environment that encourages the use of Dzongkha in the classroom. This approach is founded on the belief that learners achieve fluency when the classroom atmosphere supports meaningful interaction. As noted by LaPrairie, '… the most effective way to learn a second/foreign language is by using it purposefully for the creation of meaning'.[2]

Because 'A Manual for Teaching Dzongkha as a Foreign Language' caters to non-native speakers aiming to acquire fundamental spoken Dzongkha communication skills, it predominantly emphasizes exercises in listening and speaking. In instances requiring auditory aid, audio recordings will be provided to assist learners in acquainting themselves with Dzongkha pronunciation. Additionally, to enhance the acquisition of precise pronunciation, transcriptions with roman letters are also provided.

---

1 A trained language expert in teaching the Tibetan language to non-native speakers at the INALCO, Paris, France.

2 La Prairie (2014: 26).

Course structure

Dzongkha is a subject integral to the curriculum of schools and monastic institutions in Bhutan. In schools, Dzongkha holds the status of a mandatory subject spanning all grade levels. The journey of teaching Dzongkha commences with some introductory texts for a couple of years before they are introduced to the two core Chökê (Chos sked: classical literary Tibetan language) grammar texts: *Sumchupa* (*Gsum chu pa*) and *Tagkyijugpa* (*Rtags kyi 'jug pa*), both authored by Thönmi Sambhota (Thon mi sam bho ta) in the seventh century CE. *Sumchupa* primarily focuses on the cases[1] and parts of speech, while *Tagkyijugpa* centers around verbs, tenses and gerunds.

For the non-native speakers, however, none of these language texts can be used as ready-made materials as the need for and level and objective of learning the language are different. In the light of these considerations, the framework behind the manual has been meticulously developed.

The manual starts with a brief introduction to consonants and vowels in general and in particular the tone registers and basic consonant phonemes, basic vowel sounds, diphthongs and nasal vowels. Different exercises are designed to enable learners to understand various sounds, with a particular focus on distinguishing between high and low tones, aspirated and non-aspirated sounds, retroflex and dental articulations, and nasal and non-nasal sounds.

Subsequently, the manual acquaints learners with the basic orthographic characters within words, providing an orientation to the structural framework of Dzongkha words. Once learners are familiarized with sounds, tones and selected essential vocabularies, they are introduced to the first lesson. Each lesson encompasses a specific theme, grammar objectives and a detailed explanation of relevant grammar aspects and essential vocabularies crucial for the lessons.

In addition, each lesson has two types of exercises: 'class activities' conducted within the classroom environment, involving both the teacher and peers, and 'home exercises' for independent practice at home. Consis-

---

1 First is nominative case, second is accusative case, third is agentive case, fourth is dative case, fifth is ablative case, sixth is possessive case, seventh is locative case and eighth is vocative case.

Table 10.1: Consonants

ཀ་kā	ཁ་khā	ག་ga	ང་nga
ཅ་chā	ཆ་chhā	ཇ་ja	ཉ་nya
ཏ་tā	ཐ་thā	ད་ da	ན་na
པ་pā	ཕ་phā or fā	བ་ba	མ་ma
ཙ་tsā	ཚ་tshā	ཛ་dza	ཝ་wa
ཞ་zha	ཟ་za	འ་a	ཡ་ya
ར་ra	ལ་la	ཤ་shā	ས་sā
ཧ་hā	ཨ་ā		

Table 10.2: Vowel diacritic signs

◌ི i	◌ུ u	◌ེ e	◌ོ o

tently, lessons provide essential vocabularies, followed by commonplace conversations like greetings, pleasantries and felicitations. These conversations are then followed by an introduction to basic grammar pertinent to the dialogue exercises.

Throughout the course, numerous class activities tailored for enhancing listening comprehension and oral expressions are integrated. The course ensures adequate engagement of learners during class activities while also promoting independent self-study at home.

Ucen script

Wangdi states, 'Dzongkha uses the same Ucen Script used for writing Classical Tibetan. Ucen "head-serifed" is one of the two scripts [...], the other being Umê "Un Head-serifed"'.[1] There are thirty consonants and a set of four vowels.

1 Wangdi (2015: 3).

The interplay of consonants produces a spectrum exceeding forty-nine consonant sounds, while the amalgamation of the four vowels with consonants gives rise to over thirty-four vowel sounds, encompassing diphthongs and elongated vowels. According to Dorjee, 'Dzongkha has 83 phonemes, 49 consonants, 34 vowels, which include 10 vowels with contrast in length and nasalization'.[1]

In congruence with several Tibetic languages, Dzongkha employs tonal distinctions. Two tones predominate: a high tone and a low tone.

Characteristics of Dzongkha orthography

The orthography of Dzongkha, along with Tibetan, exhibits a relatively complex structure. A particular word could have a maximum of eight different characters.[2] Notably, most of the letters within a word are unpronounced, which makes the orthography even more complex. In addition, Dzongkha uses a distinct writing style called '*mingtha*', wherein a suffix is directly appended to the postscript or post postscript by attaching it to the main letter. This style contrasts with the conventional Tibetan writing form. For example, words such as དཀརཔོ། བུམོ། ཡོདཔ། are written as དཀར་པོ། བུ་མོ། ཡོད་པ།.

Lesson one

Lesson one commences by introducing personal pronouns, question markers and some foundational vocabularies.[3] It also delves into the grammatical concepts of the essential copula 'is', denoted by 'ཨིན་' /ī:/ (to be, are).

---

1 Dorjee (2011: 8).

2 Prescript, superscript, postscript, post postscript, subscript, subjoined, radical or the main letter, and a vowel.

3 And, and then, by the way, he, Kuzu Zangpola, house, me/I, in/towards, not to be/ am not/are not/is not, she, to be/am/are/is, question marker, to go, too/as well, where, who, you.

Grammar aspect

Given that Dzongkha adheres to the SOV (subject-object-verb) sentence structure, the verb assumes its position at the end of the sentence, while the subject takes the initial place. For instance, 'nga Tshering /ī:/', denotes 'I am Tshering'. The negative rendition of 'ཨིན་' /ī/ is 'མེན་' /men/, as in 'nga tshēring men', conveying 'I am not Tshering'.

Question construction

When constructing a question employing a question word (such as 'who', 'what', etc.), the suffix སྨོ་ /-mo/ is usually added at the end, substituting ཨིན་ /ī:/. For example, ཁྱོད་ག་སྨོ་ /chhȫ ga:-mo/ translates to 'Who [are] you?'

In the case of an open-ended question (without a question word), the interrogative form of ཨིན་ /ī:/ becomes ཨིན་ན་ /īna/. For instance, 'ཁྱོད་རྡོ་རྗེ་ཨིན་ན་' /chhȫ dorji īna/ signifies 'Are you Dorji?'

The interro-negative structure མེན་ men/ transforms into མེན་ན་ /men-na/. For example, 'འཇམ་དབྱངས་མེན་ན་' /jamyang men-na/ denotes '(Are you) not Jamyang?'

Following the presentation of the grammatical aspects of the lesson, including personal pronouns, some basic words and question markers, various forms of class exercises are introduced. Learners are actively put through these exercises, undergoing a comprehensive process. This involves reading and grasping the intended meanings, followed by multiple listening exercises to further reinforce their understanding.

Lesson two

The theme of lesson two is 'family', while its grammatical focus is on the genitive case marker གི་ /gi/. The lesson starts with a curated collection of vocabularies provided in Dzongkha script, alongside transcriptions and corresponding English meanings.

Grammar aspect

In this context, Dzongkha incorporates the genitive case marker གི་ /-gi/ (GEN) between the possessor and the possessed. While the spoken form of the genitive marker གི་ /-gi/ remains consistent, its written representation exhibits variation in Dzongkha script as both ཀྱི་ and གྱི་ are attested. For instance, ཁྱོད་ཀྱི་བུ་ /chhö-gi bu/ conveys 'your son' (literally: you – GEN – son).

The genitive case is introduced through family relationships, employing a family tree and kinship examples. For instance, ཚེ་རིང་ རྡོ་རྗེ་གི་བུ་ཨིན། /tshering dorji-gi bu /ĩ:/ translates to 'Tshering is Dorji's son'. Similarly, སངས་རྒྱས་བདེ་ཆེན་གྱི་ཚ་བོ་ཨིན། /sangay dechen-gi tshao /ĩ:/ signifies 'Sangay is Dechen's nephew'.

Listening and oral exercises

At the outset of the lesson, listening, comprehension and oral expression exercises based on the family tree are provided, accompanied by audio resources.

Lesson three

The theme of lesson three revolves around 'occupation and preferences', while the grammatical objectives encompass the 'negative marker for verbs', and the usage of 'preferences' (like).

Grammar aspect

In Dzongkha, the case marker ལུ་ /-lu/ usually follows the object of affection, preference or liking (or disliking), although it can be omitted. The negative marker for verbs in the present/future tense is མི་ /mi-/.

The morpheme མི་ /-mi/ nominalizes the verb, and functions as an agent. It comes from the noun མི་ /mi/ 'person', and when applied to a verb, it can be translated as, 'the person who…'. For instance: འགྱོ་མི་ /jo-mi/ 'the person who goes', or དགའ་མི་ /ga-mi/ 'the person who likes'. It is also used in the expression ཟེར་མི་ /ze-mi/ 'that which is called' (literally, 'which calls itself'). For example: འབའ་ཐང་ཟེར་མི་ག་ཅི་སྨོ་ /bathang ze-mi gachimo/ 'What is it that is called bathang (archery range)?'

Instead of using དེ་འབདཝ་ད་ /debäuda/ 'but', one can use མ་པ་(འདི་) /mapa (di)/ '(but actually)'. For instance: བསོད་ནམས་ལུ་མི་དགའ། མ་པ་འདི་ཁོ་ངའི་ཕོ་ཀྲུམ་ཨིན། /sonam lu mi ga. Mapa (di) kho ngai phogem /ĩ:/ 'I don't like Sonam. But actually, he is my brother'.

Preferences

བཀྲ་ཤིས་ཐབ་ཚངཔ་ཨིན། ཁོ་བཞེས་སྒོ་ལུ་དགའ། /tashi thaptshap /ī: kho zhego lu ga/ 'Tashi is a cook. He likes food'.

བསོད་ནམས་བླམ་ཨིན། ཁོ་ཆོས་ལུ་དགའ། /Sonam lam /ī: kho choe-lu ga/ 'Sonam is a Lam. He likes spirituality'.

Lesson four

The central theme of this lesson focuses on 'numbers and counting', while the grammatical objective centers around the locative and possessive copula ཡོད་ /yö/.

Grammar aspect

Apart from ཨིན་ /ī:/, another crucial copula in Dzongkha is ཡོད་ /yö/. It conveys various meanings, primarily encompassing possession (to have) and location (to be situated somewhere). Hence, ཡོད་ /yö/ can signify 'I/you/he/she/we/they have' or 'I/you/he/she/we/they am/are/is (somewhere)'. The negative form of ཡོད་ /yö/ is མེད་ /me/.

To form a question, ག་ /ga is added after ཡོད་ /yö/, such as ཡོད་ག་ /yöga/, meaning '(Do you) have?', '(Does he) have?', 'Are (you somewhere)?', or 'Are (they somewhere)?'

After establishing existence, location or ownership, if further questions arise with question words (what, who, where, etc.), the interrogative form of ཡོད་ /yö/ becomes ཡོདཔ་མོ་ /yöp mo/. For instance, ག་དེམ་ཅིག་ཡོདཔ་མོ། /gademchi yöp mo/, means 'How many do [you] have?'.

When ཡོད་ /yö/ takes on the meaning of possession ('to have'), the owner is indicated by the possessive case marker, ལུ་ /-lu/, immediately following it. Thus, 'I have money' in Dzongkha is expressed as ང་ལུ་ཏི་རུ་ཡོད། /nga-lu tiru yö/, which literally means 'I-to money have'.

Location is also indicated by the locative case marker ལུ་ /-lu/, identical to the possessive case marker, placed immediately after the location. Therefore, 'He is in Thimphu' in Dzongkha is rendered as ཁོ་ཐིམ་ཕུ་ལུ་ཡོད། /kho thimphu-lu yö/, meaning 'He Thimphu-at to be (located)'. In some set expressions, /-lu/ is replaced by ཁར་ /-kha/ as in གཡུས་ཁར་ /ikha/ 'in the village', or ནང་ /na:/ as in རྫོང་ཁ་ནང་ /dzongkha-na:/ 'in Dzongkha'.

Lesson five

The central theme of this lesson focuses on 'house and furniture' and the grammatical objective centers around postpositions.

Grammar aspect

In Dzongkha, prepositions (like under, outside, in, etc.) are actually postpositions because they come after the nouns they modify. They are often accompanied by the genitive case marker གི་ /-gi/, which is optional with polysyllabic compounds. They are followed by the locative case marker ལུ་ /-lu/ (meaning 'at', 'in', indicated as LOC here) or by the affix ཁར་ /-kha/ (literally meaning 'on the surface' or 'at the edge'). For instance: སྐུ་པར་གྱི་བོ་ལོགས་ཁར་ /kupa-gi bolo kha/ 'Next to the picture' (literally, at the side of the picture, picture-GEN side-LOC); ཉལ་ཁྱིམ་གྱི་ནང་ལུ་ /nyä chhim-gi na:-lu/ 'In the bedroom' (literally, bedroom-GEN inside-LOC).

In Dzongkha, indefinite plurals are not marked (similar to English: 'one friend'→'friends'). However, definite plurals are indicated by the suffix ཚུ་ /-tshu/. For instance: འབྱུ་གཞོང་གི་འོག་ལུ་ཀ་ལ་ཛམ་ཚུ་ཡོད། /chhu zhong-gi wo: lu kala dzam-tshu yö/ 'Under the sink are the aluminum pots'.

Lesson six

The main theme of this lesson focuses on 'in the kitchen' and the grammatical objective centers around the testimonial existential copula འདུག་ /du/.

Grammar aspect

Much like ཡོད་ /yö/, འདུག་ /du/ is used to express the presence or existence of something ('there is…'), as well as possession ('to have') and location. While ཡོད་ /yö/ indicates pre-acquired, intimate knowledge at the moment of speaking, འདུག་ /du/ signifies new knowledge acquired through the senses (sight, smell, etc.). The difference between ཡོད་ /yö/ and འདུག་ /du/ is akin to the difference between ཨིན་ /ī:/ and ཨིན་མས་ /ī:mä/.

The negative form of འདུག་ /du/ is མིན་འདུག་ /min-du/, sometimes pronounced as /mi-nu/. The interrogative form of འདུག་ /du/ is འདུག་ག་ /du-ga/. For instance: ག་ཏེ་འདུག་ག /gate duga/ 'Where is [it]?'

The interro-negative form of འདུག་ག་ /du-ga/ is མིན་འདུག་ག /min-du-ga/ or མིན་འདུག་མོ། /min-du-mo/ when seeking confirmation. For example: ཨ་ཕ་མིན་འདུག་མོ། /apha min-du-mo/ 'It is not there, right?'

The semi-interrogative ཡ་ /-ya/ indicates seeking confirmation. For instance: ཨ་ཕ་འདུག་ཡ། /apha du-ya/ 'It is there, right?' Note that ཡ་ཡ་ /yaya/ is also a casual way to agree, or to conclude a conversation, similar to saying 'OK' in English, especially during phone conversations.

Lesson seven

The main theme of this lesson revolves around 'food and daily activities', and the grammatical objective is focused on the present tense.

Grammar aspect

Dzongkha is a 'contextual' or, more accurately, a 'situational' language. It lacks traditional conjugation. Instead, auxiliaries encode the mode of access to information, with the main ones being intimate, personal and ingrained knowledge compared to newly acquired and updated knowledge. These distinctions have already been seen in the case of the essential and existential copulas: ཨིན་ /ĩ:/ and ཡོད་ /yö/ convey intimate, personal and ingrained knowledge, while ཨིན་མས་ /ĩmä/ and འདུག་ /du/ respectively convey newly acquired, updated knowledge, often acquired through the senses. This differentiation also extends to the present tense and between the progressive and habitual present.

Positive statement forms in Dzongkha are as follows: (V + དོ་ /-do/, V + དེས་ /-de/, V + ཕུ་ཨིན་ /-p-in/, V + ཕུ་ཨིན་མས་ /-p-in-mä/).

For intimate knowledge, undergoing process: Verb + དོ་ /-do/. For example: ང་ལྟོ་ཟ་དོ་ /nga to za-do/ 'I am eating'. This mode is preferred for first person present progressive.

For no intimate knowledge, instant or close past witnessing of an undergoing process: Verb + དེས་ /-de/. For example: ཁོ་ལྟོ་ཟ་དེས་ /kho to za-de/ 'He is eating'. This mode is not associated with first person statements.

For intimate knowledge, habitual process (as opposed to undergoing process): inflected verb + ཨིན་ /ĩ:/. Inflected verb' (V') refers to the root with an added suffix, such as ཕུ་ /-u/ or མ་ /-m/ or པ་ /-p/, depending on the verb's spelling. Broadly speaking, verbs whose coda has no consonant sound must add ཝུ་ /-u/. For instance: ཟ་ /za/ becomes ཟཝུ་ /zau/ 'to eat', and འབད་ /bä/ becomes འབདཝུ་ /bäu/ 'to do'. Verb stems ending in /-ng/ become /-m/. For example, འཐུང་ /thung/ becomes འཐུངམ་ /thum/ 'to drink'. Verb stems ending in /-m/ and /-p/ are not affected, but verbs ending in /p/ see their spelling modified. For example, སླབ་ /lap/ remains /lap/ but the inflected stem is spelled (སླབཔ་), or ཤ་ཟཝུ་ཨིན་ /shazau- /ĩ:/ '[I/He/She/They] eat meat'. This is the preferred mode for first person and for people of whom the speaker has an intimate knowledge (friends, relatives).

For updated knowledge based on instant or previous witnessing: inflected verb V' + མས་ /-mä/. For example: ཁོ་ཤ་ཟཝུ་མས། /kho sha zau-mä/ 'He eats meat [I have just discovered it]'. It is associated with the third person and not associated with first person statements, except for verbs expressing feelings.

Lesson eight

The theme of the lesson is 'at the market', and the grammar objective is the imperative form.

Grammar aspect

The imperative can be formed by adding the morpheme ཤིག་ /-sh/ to the verb. For example, བཞེས་ཤིག་ /zhe-sh/ means 'Please have it' (honorific), and ལྟ་ཤིག་ /ta-sh/ means 'Look'. Only verbs that describe voluntary actions, actions that the agent can choose to do or not to do, can take an imperative morpheme. As a consequence, such verbs as 'to like', 'to recover' and 'to remember' cannot be followed by such imperative morphemes. The negative imperative, or prohibitive, is created by adding མ་ /ma-/ before the verb stem, which is then optionally followed by མས་ /-mä/. For instance, མ་ལྟ་མས། /ma-ta-mä/ means 'Don't look'.

The suffix བ་ /wa/ is a rhetoric question asked to oneself in powerless situations. For example: ག་ཅི་འབད་བ། /gachi bä-wa/ 'What could I do?' (subtext: there is nothing to do); similarly, ག་ཏེ་འགྱོ་བ། /gate jo-wa/ 'Where could I go?' (I have nowhere to go).

The suffix ལོ་ /-lo/ indicates reported speech and is used to convey a quotation said in a casual manner. For instance, མི་ཉོ་ལོ་ /mi-nyo-lo/ translates to ‘He/she says he/she won’t buy’.

Reported speech can also be formed by specifying the name of the speaker, followed by གིས་ /-gi/ to mark the agent (in this case, the speaker), then quoting the phrase, and concluding the quotation with either ཟེར་སླབ་མས་ /ze lap-mä/, ཟེརཝ་མས་ /zeu-mä/ or ཟེར་སླབ་དེས་ /ze lap-de/, which all mean ‘is saying, has just said’. For example, ཁོ་མི་ཉོ་ཟེརཝ་མས། /kho- mi-nyo zeu-mä:/ conveys ‘He says he won’t buy’. This method is considered a less casual form of reported speech compared to using ལོ་ /lo/.

The suffix ནི་ /ni/ functions as a nominalizer, transforming a verb into a noun, and indicates the act of doing, the actuality of doing, often rendered in English by a gerund. For example, ལྟ་ནི་ /ta-ni/ ‘looking’, translates to ‘looking’, ‘the act of looking’, as seen in the dialogue ལྟ་ནི་རྐྱངམ་ཅིག་ཨིན། / ta-ni chãmchi ĩ:/, which means ‘I am just looking’ (literally, ‘it is only the fact of looking’).

This suffix falls within the same category as མི་ /-mi/, which also nominalizes verbs and emphasizes the agent, the ‘doer’. For example, ལྟ་མི་ /ta-mi/ denotes ‘the looker, the watcher, the person who looks, or the spectator’. This nominalizer མི་ /-mi/ also forms objects and abstract entities (‘that which…’). For example, ཟེར་མི་ /ze-mi/ signifies ‘That which is called’.

The ergative case marker གིས་ /-gi/ is added after the noun phrase that functions as an agent (subject) of a transitive verb. For instance, ཕྱི་གླིངཔ་གིས་རྫོང་ཁ་མི་ཤེས། /pchhilip-gi dzongkha mi she/, translates to ‘Foreigners don’t speak Dzongkha’. In Dzongkha, the use of an ergative case marker is optional, especially in the context of present and future tenses.

Lesson nine

The theme of the lesson is ‘planning a trip’, and the grammar objective is the future tense.

Grammar aspect

The plain future tense can be formed by adding ནི་ /ni/ or ནི་ཨིན་ /ni-ĩ:/ to the verb. For example: འགྱོ་ནི་ཨིན། /jo-ni-ĩ:/ ‘[I] will go’.

To create a negative future tense, you would add མི་ /mi-/ before the verb. For instance, ཞག་བཞི་མི་སྡོད་ /zhazhi mi-dö/ translates to '[I] will not stay four days'.

The interrogative future for the second person is created by adding ནི་ཨིན་ན་ /-ni-ina/ to the verb stem. For example, སྡོད་ནི་ཨིན་ན་ /dö-ni-ina/ translates to 'Will [you] stay?', or 'Would [you] like to stay?'

Also, it's worth mentioning that there's a shorter version which involves using the verb stem followed by the abbreviated formula ནི་ན་ /-nna/. For instance, ཁྱོད་ཨ་ན་སྡོདནི་ན་ /chhö ana dö-nna/ means 'Will you stay here?' and དཔེ་ཆ་བལྟནི་ན་ /pechha ta-nna/ means 'Would you like to study?'

When the question includes a question word ('what', etc.), the suffix ནི་སྨོ་ /-ni-mo/ is often preferred. For example: ག་ཏེ་སྡོད་ནི་སྨོ་ /gate dö-ni mo/ 'Where will [you] stay?'

The interro-negative question is formed by adding ཡ། /ya/ to the negative form: མི་ + V + ཡ /mi-V-ya/. For instance, ཞག་བཞི་མི་སྡོད་ཡ། /zha zhi mi-dö-ya/ means 'Won't [we, you] stay for four days?'

Lesson ten

The theme of this lesson is 'nature and scenery', and the grammar objective is the adjectives.

Grammar aspect

When a statement is based on assimilated or intimate opinion, the adjectival predicate is formed by placing the adjective before ཨིན་ /ĩ:/ for affirmative statements, and using ཨིན་ན་ /ina/ for interrogative and མེན་ན་ /menna/ for negative statements. For example, ཐག་རིངམོ་ཨིན་ /tharim ĩ:/ translates to 'It is far', indicating that the speaker has personal knowledge of this fact.

When a statement is based on a newly acquired, updated opinion that comes from previous or current sensory perception (such as vision, sound, smell, etc.), the adjectival predicate Adj. + ཨིན་མས་ /ĩn-mä/ is used for affirmative statements. For interrogative statements ཨིན་མས་སྨོ་ /ĩn-mä-mo/ is used, and for negative statements མེན་མས་ /men-mä/ is used.

For instance, ཐུང་ཀུ་མེན་མས། /thungku men-mä/ translates to 'It is not short', and implies that the speaker has just discovered this updated information through their senses.

In Dzongkha, the structure Adj. + ཨིན་མས་ /ĩn-mä/ can be further shortened based on the suffix letter of the adjective, specifically, the structure Adj. + མས་ /-mä/ or Adj. + པས་ /-pä/ depending on the suffix letter of the adjective. Also note that the interrogative form Adj. + ཨིན་མས་སྨོ་ / ĩn-mä-mo/ can also be shortened to Adj. + མས་སྨོ་ /-mä-mo/. This allows for more flexibility and variation in constructing sentences while maintaining the same underlying grammar.

In Dzongkha, to express a newly formed opinion based on an experience or sensation, the structure Adj. + འདུག་ /du/ can be used. This structure indicates that the speaker's judgement is influenced by a recent firsthand encounter. The interrogative form is formed by adding འདུག་ག་ /du-ga/, while the negative form is either མིན་འདུག་ /min-du/ or its colloquial version མིན་នུ་ /mi-nu/. For example: བདེ་ཏོག་ཏོ་འདུག /deto:to du/ 'It is comfortable' (I have just felt the comfort), and ལམ་ལེགས་ཤོམ་མིན་འདུག /lam le:shom mi-nu/ 'The road is not good' (I have just experienced the road condition).

Adjectives can function as verbs and auxiliaries can be added to them. Verb-Adj. + པས་ /-pä/ or མས་ /-mä/ expresses a newly formed opinion based on a perception. It is similar in meaning to Adj. + ཨིན་མས་ /ĩn-mä/. For example: བདེ་བས་ /de-wä/ 'It is comfortable' (I can feel the comfort); ལེགས་ཤོམ་མས་ /le:shom-mä/ 'It is good' (I evaluate it based on a visual perception for instance). The interrogative form is Verb-Adj. + བས་ག་ /-wä-ga/. For example: བདེ་བས་ག /de-wä-ga/ 'Is it comfortable?' (answer: བདེ་བས་ /de-wä/ It is comfortable).

Superlative

The superlative in Dzongkha is formed by adding the suffix ཤོས་ /-sho/ to the root adjective. For example: སྦོམ་ /bom/ 'big' → སྦོམ་ཤོས་ /bom-sho/ 'biggest'.

Note that adjectives ending in /-m/ form their superlative in /-ngsho/, dropping the 'm'. For example: རིངམོ་ /rim/ 'long'; 'tall' → རིང་ཤོས་ /ring-sho/ 'longest/tallest'.

When the syllables 'mo' and 'pa' are suffixed to the root adjective, 'm' is dropped and 'sho' added.

Moreover, a few adjectives have an irregular superlative form: འཇའ་རིསམོ་ /jarim/ 'beautiful' → འཇའ་རིསམོ་དྲག་ཤོས་ /jarim dra-sho/ 'the most beautiful'; ལེ་ཤ་ /le:sha/ 'many' → མང་ཤོས་ /mang-sho/ 'most numerous', 'most', 'maximum'; ཨ་ཙི་ཅིག་ /atsichi/ 'few', 'a little' → ཉུང་ཤོས་ /nyung-sho/

'least', 'minimum'; ལེགས་ཤོམ་ /le:shom/ 'good' → ལེགས་ཤོས་ /le:sho/ or དྲག་ཤོས་ /dra-sho/ 'best'.[1]

Please note that དྲག་ཤོས་ can be abbreviated into དྲགོས་ in writing only; however, it is still pronounced /dra-sho/.

Comparative

To compare two entities, you can use either the morpheme བས་ /-wa/ or ལས་ /-lä/, placed after the basis of comparison. For example: ཁོ་ལས་ཁྱོད་དྲག /kho-lä chhö dra/ 'You are better than him', or ཁོ་བས་ཁྱོད་དྲག /kho-wa chhö dra/ 'You are better than him'.

Similar to other adjectival clauses, the verb ending will be modified based on how the opinion expressed has been formed (whether it's based on ingrained opinion, updated opinion, etc.). As a consequence, one might come across sentences like ཁོ་ལས་ཁྱོད་དྲགཔ་ཨིན། /kho-lä chhö drap-ĩn/, which means 'You are better than him', considering the specific way the opinion was acquired.

The adjectival verb can be modified when the statement conveys a newly acquired opinion, for example, ཁོ་བས་ཁྱོད་དྲག་པས་ /kho-wa chhö dra-pä/, 'You are better than him' (I have just found it out).

For complex adjectives, the copula འདུག་ /du/ can also be employed in comparisons when discovering a new property. For instance, when finding that one fruit is tastier than another, one can say: ཨ་ནི་ཤིང་འབྲས་བས་ཨ་ཕི་ཞིམ་ཏོག་ཏོ་འདུག /ani shingdrä-wa aphi zhimto:to dug/, 'This fruit is tastier than that one' (I discovered it now); ཨ་ནི་ཤིང་འབྲས་བས་ཨ་ཕི་ཞིམ་ཏོག་ཏོ་ཨིན་མས། /ani shingdrä-wa aphi zhim to: to ĩn-mä/, 'This fruit is tastier than that one' (I discovered it now); or ཨ་ནི་ཤིང་འབྲས་བས་ཨ་ཕི་ཞིམ་ཏོག་ཏོ་མས། /ani shingdrä-wa aphi zhim to: to-mä/, 'This fruit is tastier than that one' (I discovered it now).

In Dzongkha, it's important to note that only superiority comparison (expressing 'more than') exists, and there is no direct way to convey inferiority comparison (expressing 'less than'). For example, the sentence 'The black box is less heavy than the white one' would be expressed in Dzongkha as 'the white box is heavier than the black one' སྒྲོམ་དཀརཔོ་ལས་སྒྲོམ་

1 Note that དྲག་ཤོས་ also means 'knighted' and is in theory used only for people knighted by the king; however, today, it is a term of address used loosely to show respect to officials.

ནག་པ་ལྗིད་ཡང་། /dõm kãp lä dõm nãp ji yang/ or 'the black box is lighter than the white one' སྒྲོམ་ནག་པ་ལས་སྒྲོམ་དཀརཔོ་ལྗིད་ཅི། /dõm nãp lä kãp ji chi/.

Rather, quite: རང་ /-ra/

When used after an adjective, the affix རང་ /ra/ conveys the meaning of 'rather/quite'. When combined with a negative verb, it conveys the meaning of 'not quite'. For example: ཁོ་ད་ལྟོ་ཆུང་ཀུ་རང་ཨིན། /kho dato chhungku ra ĩ:/ 'He is rather/quite young'. Similarly, ལམ་འདི་མགྱོགས་པ་རང་བཟོ་ནི་ཨིན་མས། / lam di joba-ra zo-ni-ĩn-mä/ means 'This road will be repaired rather soon'.

Lesson eleven

The theme of this lesson is 'religious life', and the grammar objective is the past tense.

Grammar aspect

Aorist testimonial past

Dzongkha distinguishes between various types of past tenses. This lesson introduces 'aorist testimonial past', which closely resembles the English preterit and implies that the speaker has directly witnessed the action taking place. To form this tense, either ཡི་ /-yi/ or ཅི་ /-chi/ is added to the past verb stem, depending on the spelling of the verb. While ཡི་ /yi/ is the more common choice, verbs ending with the suffix letter པ་ and བ་ /-p/b/ change their stem to ཅི་ /chi/. This past tense is widely used when the speaker has personally witnessed the action. For example: ལཱ་འབད་ཡི་ / la: bä-yi/ 'worked' (all persons), and པར་བཏབ་ཅི་ /pa: tap-chi/ 'took a picture' (all persons).

The negative form is constructed by adding མ + V /ma-/ to the verb. For example, མ་སླབ་ /ma-lap/ translates to '[I/you/he/she/we/they] did not talk/speak'.

The interrogative is formed by adding ག་ /-ga/ at the end of the past verb group. This often involves either V + ཡི་ག་ /-yi-ga/ or V + ཅི་ག་ /-chi-ga/. For example: ཁོ་ལུ་སླབ་ཅི་ག /kho-lu lap-chi-ga/ 'Did [you] talk to him?' The use of ག་ /-ga/ can be omitted when the question already includes a question word. For example, ཁོ་ལུ་ག་ཅི་སླབ་ཅི། /kho-lu gachi lap-chi/ means

'What did you tell him?', and ཁོ་ལུ་ནམ་སླབ་ཅི། /kho-lu nam lab-chi/ signifies 'When did you tell him?'

Ergative case marker

Dzongkha, like most languages of the Tibetic family, as well as Basque, is an 'ergative' language. This linguistic structure signifies that it indicates the agent (the subject) of a transitive verb by attaching a case marker known as the 'ergative'. This ergative marker is denoted as གིས་ /-gi/ and shares a homophonic relationship with the genitive marker གི་ /-gi/. It is usually omitted in the present and future tenses but is often indicated in the past tense. The ergative marker serves the purpose of distinguishing between the agent and the patient in a sentence. For example, ཁོ་གིས་ང་ལུ་སླབ་ཅི། /kho-gi nga-lu lap-chi/ translates to 'He told me', vs. ང་གིས་ཁོ་ལུ་སླབ་ཅི། /nga-gi kho-lu lap-chi/ which means 'I told him'.

The mood particle: བོ /-bo/

The mood particle བོ /-bo/ is positioned after a verb and indicates a sense of surprise, doubt or reproach. For instance: མ་ཤེས་བོ་ /ma-she-bo/ 'What, you did not know?'

Relator: པར་ /-pa/ or བར་ /-wa/

The relator པར་ /-pa/ or བར་ /-wa/ serves the purpose of connecting two verbs in a way that signifies an objective (to do something, to do something else). It is placed between two verbs, with the second verb often being related to a motion verb (such as to go, to come, to run, etc.). There are two forms: Verb + པར་ /pa/ + Motion verb or Verb + བར་ /wa/ + Motion verb. This construction is often translated as 'to' in English. For example, སྤོས་བཏེག་པར་འོང་ཡི་ /pö tek-pa-wõ:-yi/ translates to 'I came to light incense'. Similarly, ལྟོ་ཟ་བར་འོང་ཡི་ /to za-wa-wõ:-yi/ means 'I came to eat food'.

Lesson twelve

The lesson's theme revolves around 'harvesting', while the grammar objective focuses on the 'inferential past: when'.

Grammar aspect

Inferential past

In the context of the inferential past, the auxiliary ནུག་ /-nu/ is used, differing from ཡི་ /-yi/ or ཅི་ /-chi/, and is used for past events where the speaker has seen the result, but not the process. For instance, ལོ་ཆོག་གཏང་ཚར་ནུག /lochho ta-tsha-nu/ signifies that the annual ritual is completed. In this scenario, the speaker was not present during the ritual but noticed its completion upon reaching the location. The negative form is མིན་ནུག་ /-mi-nu/, and the interrogative form is མིན་ནུག་ག་ /-mi-nu-ga/. For example, ཐིམ་ཕུ་ལུ་ས་གཡོམ་བརྒྱབ་ཅི། /thimphu-lu sayöm chap-chi/ indicates 'There was an earthquake in Thimphu' (as personally witnessed). Conversely, ཐིམ་ཕུ་ལུ་ས་གཡོམ་བརྒྱབ་ནུག /thimphu-lu sayöm chap-nu/ conveys 'There was an earthquake in Thimphu' (as evidenced by viewing the wreckage upon returning to Thimphu).

Completion

It is common in Dzongkha to specify whether an action has been completed. The completion verb ཚར་ /tsha/, which literally means 'to finish', is added to the initial verb to indicate the action's full completion. For example, ཁོང་ཚུ་གིས་ལོ་ཆོག་གཏང་ཚར་ཡི། /khong-tshu-gi lochho tang-tsha-yi/ denotes 'They have conducted the annual ritual', conveying the idea that the ritual has been successfully completed. The verb ཚར་ /tsha/ also sometimes bears the meaning of the English adverb 'already' as in 'They have already conducted the ritual'.

Adverbs

Adverbs are formed by adding སྦེ་ /-be/ to adjectives, which is akin to the English '-ly' construction. For instance, ལེགས་ཤོམ་སྦེ་ /le:shom-be/ translates to 'Well, nicely, in a good way', or འཇམ་ཏོག་ཏོ་སྦེ་ /jam to:to-be/ signifies 'easily'. Note that སྦེ་ /-be/ can also act as a linking morpheme between two verbs, the former indicating a means for doing the latter, which means the first verb indicates the means by which the second verb is accomplished.

For example, ང་ཀར་བདའ་སྦེ་འོང་ནི་ཨིན། /nga ka da-be wõ:-ni-ĩn/ translates to 'I will come by car', where 'drive a car + /be/' indicates the means of coming.

Temporal clauses

Temporal clauses in Dzongkha convey concepts of 'when' and 'as soon as' by adding a specific formula after the verb. To indicate 'when', the formula is an inflected verb V'+ད་ལུ་ /-dalu/, and for 'as soon as', it is inflected verb V' + ཅིག་ /-chi/. For example, ང་ལྷོད་པ་ད་ལུ་ཁོ་སོང་ཡི། /nga lhöp-dalu khosõ:-yi/ means 'When I arrived, he left'. Similarly, ང་ལྷོད་པ་ཅིག་ཁོ་སོང་ཡི། /nga lhöp-chi kho sõ:-yi/ translates to 'As soon as I arrived, he left'.

When the inflected verb is followed by ཅིག་ཨིན་ /-chi-ĩ:/, it conveys the meaning of 'to have just finished'. For example, ལོ་ཆོག་གཏང་ཚརཝ་ཅིག་ཨིན། / lochho tang-tshau-chi-ĩ:/ means '[I/We] have just finished conducting the annual ritual'.

Lesson thirteen

The theme of the lesson is 'weather', and the grammar objective is expressing uncertainty (epistemic) in the future using the conditional tense.

Grammar aspect

Uncertainty in the future

A simple way to express uncertainty in the future is by adding གཅིག་འབདན་ /chibän/ meaning 'maybe', 'might' or 'perhaps' to a future clause. For example, མོ་ནངས་པ་གཅིག་འབདན་ལཱ་འབད་ནི་མས། /mo nã:pa chibän la: bä-ni-mä/ translates to 'She might work tomorrow'. Similarly, མོ་ནངས་པ་གཅིག་འབདན་ལཱ་འབད་འོང་། /mo nã:pa chibän la: bä-wõ:/ could be understood as 'Maybe she will work tomorrow, she may work tomorrow'.

The negative form is indicated in the following manner: མི་ + V +དོ་འོང་ /mi-V-do-wõ:/ or མི་ + V + ནི་འོང་ /mi-V-ni- wõ:/. The inclusion of གཅིག་འབདན་ /chibän/ is optional. For instance, མོ་ནངས་པ་ (གཅིག་འབདན་) ལཱ་མི་འབད་དོ་འོང་ /mo nã:ba (chibän) la: mi-bä-do-wõ:/ can be interpreted as 'Maybe she won't work tomorrow', or མོ་ནངས་པ་ (གཅིག་འབདན་) ལཱ་མི་འབད་ནི་འོང་ /mo nã:ba (chibän) la: mi-bä-ni-wõ:/ could be understood as 'Maybe she won't work tomorrow'.

Another method of expressing uncertainty in Dzongkha is through the construction V + ནི་བཟུམ་ (གཅིག་) འདུག /V+ni-zum-(chi-) du/ or V + ནི་བཟུམ་ (གཅིག་) ཡོད་ /V+ni-zum-(chi-) yö/, which translates to 'there is a likeness of'. In this structure, བཟུམ་ /zum/ means 'likeliness', 'similarity'. The former is used when someone perceives an indication of the likeliness of an upcoming event, often through sight but also involving other senses. On the other hand, the latter structure is founded on prior knowledge and deductive reasoning. For instance, ཁོ་གི་ཨ་ལུ་མགྱོགས་པར་དྲག་ནི་བཟུམ་འདུག /kho-gi alu jopa drani-zum du/ means 'It looks like his child will recover soon' (I focus on having discovered elements that make me think that the child may soon recover). Similarly, there is ཁོ་གི་ཨ་ལུ་མགྱོགས་པར་དྲག་ནི་བཟུམ་ཡོད་ /kho-gi alu jopa drani-zum yö/ which translates to 'It looks like his child will recover soon (I deduct it from previously known elements, not from a recent discovery).

The negative form is V+ ནི་བཟུམ་ (གཅིག་) མི་འདུག་ /ni-zum-(chi-) min-du/ (or its variant mi-nu/). V+ ནི་བཟུམ་ (གཅིག་) མེད་ /ni-zum-(chi-)me/ is also possible when one bases one's assumption on deduction. For example: ཁོ་གི་ཨ་ལུ་མགྱོགས་པར་དྲག་ནི་བཟུམ་མི་འདུག /kho-gi alu jopa drani-zum min-du/ 'It does not look like his child will recover soon' (I have just seen the child, he looked like he was in pain), or ཁོ་གི་ཨ་ལུ་མགྱོགས་པར་དྲག་ནི་བཟུམ་མེད། /kho-gi alu jopa drani-zum me/ 'It looks like his child will not recover soon' (I have not seen the child, but I have heard bad report from doctors, nurses, friends, etc.).

Uncertainty can also be expressed in interrogative and interro-negative stances, but གཅིག་འབད་ is not used in this case. For example: མོ་ནངས་པ་ལཱ་འབད་འོང་ག /mo nã:pa la: bä-ong-ga/ 'Will she work tomorrow?' or ཁོ་གི་ཨ་ལུ་མགྱོགས་པར་དྲག་ནི་བཟུམ་མི་འདུག་ག /kho-gi alu jopa drani-zum min-du ga/ 'Doesn't it look like his child will recover soon?'

Conditional

Dzongkha distinguishes between two types of conditionals: present conditionals ('If you come tomorrow, call me', 'If I were him, I would go') and past conditionals ('If it rained this morning, then I will not have to water the plants', 'If we had called the doctor yesterday, he would have been cured'). In Dzongkha, these two types of conditional clauses primarily differ in the verbal group of the protasis, which is the first part of the conditional clause that sets the condition. This part is introduced by 'if' in English.

There are two significant differences between conditional clauses in English and in Dzongkha. In English, the protasis might come either first or second ('If the baby cries call me' = 'Call me if the baby cries'). However, in Dzongkha, the protasis 'If the baby cries' (in this case) always comes first. Furthermore, the conditional marker 'if' in English appears at the beginning of the protasis and precedes the verb, whereas in Dzongkha, the conditional marker is integrated within the verb, and is positioned at the end of the protasis ('The baby cries – if').

Present conditional

In the case of a copula (ཨིན་ /ĩ:/ or ཡོད་ /yö/), the protasis or the first part of the conditional clause ends with ཨིན་པ་ཅིན་ /ĩn-pa-chän/ or ཨིནན་ /ĩ:n/ or ཡོད་པ་ཅིན་ /yö-pa-chän/ or ཡོདན་ /yön/. For example: ཞལ་འཛོམས་ནང་(ལུ)མི་ལེ་ཤ་ཡོད་པ་ཅིན་ང་མི་སྡོད། /zhändzom nã:-(lu) mi le:sha yö-pa-chän nga mi-dö/ 'If there are many people at the meeting, I won't stay; ཞལ་འཛོམས་ནང་(ལུ་)མི་ལེ་ཤ་ཡོདན་ང་མི་སྡོད། /zhändzom nã:-lu mi le:sha yön nga mi-dö/ 'If there are many people at the meeting, I won't stay'; or ཁོ་ཁྱོད་ཀྱི་ཆ་རོགས་ཨིན་པ་ཅིན་ཁྱོད་དང་གཅིག་ཁར་འཁྲིད་ཤོག / kho chhö-gi chharo ĩn-pa-chän chhöda chikha khi-sh/ 'If he's your friend, bring him along'.

With negative statements in the protasis, མིན་པ་ཅིན་ /men-pa-chän/ or མིནན་ /menn/ or མེད་པ་ཅིན་ /me-pa-chän/ or མེདན་ /men/ are used. For example: ཞལ་འཛོམས་ནང་(ལུ)མི་ལེ་ཤ་མེད་པ་ཅིན་ང་འགྱོ་ནི་ཨིན། /zhändzom nã:-(lu) mi le:sha me-pa-chän nga jo-ni-ĩ:/ 'If there aren't many people at the meeting, I will go'; or ཁོ་ཁྱོད་ཀྱི་ཆ་རོགས་མིན་པ་ཅིན་ཁྱོད་དང་གཅིག་ཁར་མ་འཁྲིད་ཤོག /kho chhö-gi chharo men-pa-chän chhöda chikha ma-khi-sh/ 'If he's not your friend, don't take him along'.

In the case of a lexical verb (i.e. any verb except copulas ཨིན་ /ĩ:/ and ཡོད་ /yö/), the protasis end is V + པ་ (or བ) ཅིན་ /V + pa-chän/; negative is མ་ + V + པ་ (or བ་) ཅིན་ /ma-V-pa-chän/. For example: ད་རེས་ཁོ་དང་འཕྱད་པ་ཅིན་ཨ་ནི་འབྱིན། /dare kho da pchhä-pa-chän ani bjin/ 'If you see him today, give (him) this'; ཁོ་མེས་མེད་བཙོ་བ་ཅིན་ཁོ་ལུ་ཉན་ཁ་མ་བཏབ། /kho meme cho-wa-chän kho-lu nyänkhu ma-tap/ 'If he makes fun of you, don't pay attention to him'; or ད་རེས་ཁོ་དང་མ་འཕྱད་པ་ཅིན་ང་ལུ་འཁྲུལ་འཕྲིན་གཏང་། /dare kho da ma-pchhä-pa chän nga-lu drüthrin tang/ 'If you don't meet him today, give me a call'.

Past conditional

The conditional clause ends with the verb stem in the past, followed by the inflected stem V' + ཡིན་པ་ཅན་ /-in-pa-chän/ or V + ཡོད་པ་ཅན་ /-yö-pa-chän/ or V + ཡོདན་ /-yön/ (or the negative equivalent), or other forms of past. For instance: ཁ་ཙ་ཆརཔ་བརྒྱབ་བརྒྱབཔ་ཡིན་པ་ཅན་ད་རི་མེ་ཏོག་ལུ་ཆུ་བླུགས་མི་དགོ /khatsa chha:p chap-chap in-pa-chän dari meto-lu chhu lu mi-go/ 'If it rained yesterday, I will not have to water the plants today'; ཁ་ཙ་ཆརཔ་མ་བརྒྱབཔ་ཡིན་པ་ཅན་ད་རིས་མེ་ཏོག་ལུ་ཆུ་བླུགས་དགོ /khatsa chha:p ma:-chap-pa-in-pa-chän dari meto-lu chhu lu go/ 'If it has not rained yesterday, I need to water the plants today'; ཁ་ཙ་ཆརཔ་བརྒྱབ་བརྒྱབབ་མིན་པ་ཅན་ད་རི་མེ་ཏོག་ལུ་ཆུ་བླུགས་དགོ /khatsa chha:p chap-chap min-pa-chän dari meto-lu chhu lu go/ 'If it did not rain yesterday, then I need to water the plants today'; ཁྱོད་ད་རི་དྲོ་པ་སྨན་ཟ་ཟཝ་ཡིན་པ་ཅན་ཕྱི་རུ་ཁམས་དྲག་འོང་། /chhö dari dropa män za-zau-in-pa-chän pchhiru kham dra-wõ:/ 'If you have taken your medicine this morning, you will feel better by this evening'; ཁྱོད་ད་རི་དྲོ་པ་སྨན་ཟ་ཡོད་པ་ཅན་ཕྱི་རུ་ཁམས་དྲག་འོང་། /chhö dari dropa män za-yö-pa-chän pchhiru kham dra-wõ:/ 'If you have taken your medicine this morning, you will feel better by this evening'; ཁྱོད་ད་རི་དྲོ་པ་སྨན་ཟ་ཟཝ་མིན་པ་ཅན་ཕྱི་རུ་ཁམས་ཡང་མི་དྲགཔ་འོང་། /chhö dari dropa män za-zau-men-ba-chän pchhiru kham-ya mi-drap-wõ:/ 'If you have not taken your medicine this morning, you may not feel better even by this evening'; or ཁྱོད་ད་རིས་དྲོ་པ་སྨན་མ་ཟཝ་ཡིན་པ་ཅན་ཕྱི་རུ་ཁམས་ཡང་མི་དྲགཔ་འོང་། /chhö dari dropa män ma:-za-zau-in-pa-chän pchhiru kham ya-mi-drap-wõ:/ 'If you have not taken your medicine this morning, you may not feel better even by this evening'.

Lesson fourteen

The theme of the lesson is 'sharing experience', and the grammar objective is expressing past uncertainty.

Grammar aspect

Uncertainty in the past

Similar to the future tense, expressing uncertainty about an event in the past can be done in diverse ways. However, this lesson focuses on explaining only the main methods.

Just like in the future tense, the suffix འོང་། /-wõ:/ is used. It indicates that the hypothesis arises from a mental process like deduction. This lesson, based on the two types of pasts explained in lessons eleven (aorist) and twelve (inferential), introduces two specific sentence structures for this purpose:

1. Verb + inflected verb V' + འོང་། /-wõ:/. For example: མོ་ཧེ་མ་ལྷོད་ལྷོདཔ་འོང་། /mo hema lhö-lhöp-wõ:/ 'She must have been [here] before'. If the uncertainty has just been discovered to the speaker's mind, then མས་ /-mä/ can be added to the end of the sentence, for example, མོ་ཧེ་མ་ལྷོད་ཡོདཔ་འོང་མས། /mo hema lhö-yöp-wõ:-mä/ '[From what I have just seen or heard], she must have been [here] before'. The negative form is verb + inflected verb stem + མི་འོང་། /-mi-wong/.
2. Verb + ཡོདཔ་འོང་། /-yöp-wong/. For example: མོ་ཧེ་མ་ལྷོད་ཡོདཔ་འོང་། /mo hema lhö yöp-wong/ 'She must have been [here] before'. The negative form is མ་ /ma/ + inflected verb stem + འོང་ /-wõ:/, for example, མོ་ཧེ་མ་མ་ལྷོདཔ་འོང་། /mo hema ma lhöp- wong/ 'She must not have been [here] before'.

The auxiliary epistemic marker བཟུམ་ /-zum/ (literally 'like', 'as if') can also be used in the past. It indicates that the assumption is based on the speaker's senses (usually, sight), and not on a mental process (deduction). The structure is: V + inflected verb V' + བཟུམ་ཡོད་ /-zum-yö/ (and other related copulas). For example: མོ་འགྱོ་འགྱོཝ་བཟུམ་ཡོད། /mo jo-jou-zum-yö/ 'It seems like she must have gone'.

The negative form is constructed as follows: མ་ + inflected verb V' + བཟུམ་ཡོད་ /ma-V'-zum-yö/. For example: མོ་མ་འགྱོཝ་བཟུམ་ཡོད་ /mo ma-jou-zum-yö/ 'It seems she may not have gone'.

The negative particle can also affect the main, final verb: མོ་འགྱོ་འགྱོཝ་བཟུམ་མེད་ /mo jo-jou-zum-me/ 'It does not seem she has gone'.

The addition of མནོ་ /no/ 'to think', after an epistemic past statement, implies that the initial assumption of the speaker was wrong. For example: མོ་ཧེ་མ་ལྷོད་ལྷོདཔ་འོང་མནོ་ཡི། /mo hema lhö-lhöp-wõ: no-yi/ 'I thought she had been [here] before' (actually, I realize now that this was not the case).

Lesson fifteen

The theme of the lesson is 'at the doctor's', and the grammar objectives are 'duration, commitment, non-controllable actions'.

Grammar aspect

Duration

In Dzongkha, when expressing the long duration of an action (as opposed to instant duration) a specific verb construction is used, inflected verb V' + Verb + ས་ /-sa/, followed by the necessary auxiliaries as seen in the following examples: མགུ་ཏོག་ཟུག་བརྒྱབ་བརྒྱབ་ས་ཡོད། /guto zu chap-chap-sa-yö/ 'I've been having a headache' (indicating the duration of the headache over some time); མོ་སྐེདཔ་ནཝ་ན་ས་ཨིན། /mo kep nau-na-sa-in/ 'She has a backache now' (emphasizing the ongoing nature of the backache that I am aware of).

The negative forms ས་མེད་/-sa-me/ and ས་མིན་ /-sa-men/ are seldom used, but the interrogative form is fine: ཁོ་སྨན་ཟཝ་ཟ་ས་ཨིན་མས་ག /kho män zau-za-sa-in-mä-ga/ 'Is he continuously taking medicine?' or 'Is he is consistently on medication?'

The verb སྡོད་ /dö/ 'to stay' often accompanies ས་ in the above constructions. For example: ཕོཝ་ནཝ་ན་ས་སྡོདཔ་མས། /phou nau-sa-döp-mä/ means '(My) stomach keeps hurting'. Similarly, ཁ་ཙ་ཆང་འཐུངམ་འཐུང་ས་སྡོད་ཡི། /khatsa chhang thum-thung-sa-dö-yi/ 'I kept on drinking alcohol yesterday', indicating continuous drinking throughout the day.

The commitment morpheme: གེ་ /-ge/

The morpheme གེ་ /-ge/ following a verb stem conveys several meanings. First, it can mean the same as 'let's' in English, urging a group of people to engage in a collective action. For instance, ངལ་འཚོ་གེ་ /ngätsho-ge/ means 'Let's take a rest', and ལྷ་ཁང་མཇལ་བར་འགྱོ་གེ་ /Lhakhang jä-wa-jo-ge/ translates to 'Let's go to the temple'.

Secondly, it can suggest a voluntary decision taken by the speaker or their group to undertake an action, often to fulfill a requirement, similar to the English phrase 'let me'. In such instances, the personal pronouns 'I' or 'we' are often used. For example, ང་འབྱིན་གེ་ /nga bjin-ge/ translates to 'Let me give'.

When followed by མས་ /-mä/ or གེ་མས་ /-ge-mä/, it implies that the speaker is reconfirming their statement or emphasizing their willingness to carry out the action. For example, ང་ནངས་པ་འབྱིན་གེ་མས་ /nga nã:pa bjin-ge-mä/ translates to 'Let me give [it] tomorrow', with an added sense of confirmation or determination.

Lesson sixteen

The theme of the lesson is, 'A spoilt child argues with his mother', and the grammar objectives are 'cause and consequence'.

Grammar aspect

Causal clause

A causal clause (because…) in Dzongkha is always placed in the first position of the sentence and is then followed by its consequence ('Because she is my friend, I trust her'). In English, any order is possible ('I trust her because she is my friend'). The causal clause is constructed as follows: inflected verb V' + ལས /-lä/. The morpheme ལས /lä/ originally means 'from'. For example: མོ་ཁ་ཙ་ལྷོདཔ་ལས་ ད་རིས་གཉེར་ཚང་ཉོ་དགོ་པས། /mo khatsa lhöp-lä dari nyertshang nyo go-pä/ 'Because she arrived yesterday, I must buy some goods today'; ཁྱོད་ངེའི་ཨ་ལུ་ཨིནམ་ལས་ང་ཁྱོད་ལུ་དགའ། /chhö ngei alu ĩm-lä nga chhö-lu ga/ 'I love you because you are my child'; ང་ནངས་པ་འགྱོ་ནི་ཨིནམ་ལས་ ད་རིས་ཨ་ནི་ལཱ་འདི་ ཐར་རི་བ་རི་འབད་ཚར་དགོ་པས། /nga nã:pa jo-ni-ĩm-lä dari ani la: di thäri bari bä-tsha-go-pä/ 'I must absolutely finish this work today because I am leaving tomorrow'; མོ་ལུ་ཏི་རུ་མེདཔ་ལས་གཉེར་ཚང་ཉོ་མི་ཚུགས། /mo-lu tiru mep-lä nyertshang nyo mi-tshu:/ 'Because she does not have money, she cannot buy goods'; སློབ་དཔོན་མ་ལྷོདཔ་ལས་ང་བཅས་ངལ་འཚོ་སྡོད་ནི་ཨིན། /löpe:n ma-lhöp-lä nga chä ngä-tsho-dö-ni-ĩ:/ 'Because the teacher has not arrived, we are resting'; ངེའི་མགྱོནམ་ད་ལྟོ་མ་ལྷོདཔ་ལས་ང་ཁྱིམ་ན་སྒུག་དགོ་པས། /nyei: gyöm da-to ma-lhöp-lä nga chhim-na gu-go-bä/ 'I must wait at home because my guests are not here yet'.

Immediate past and future

To have just done something is constructed as follows: V + ཚརཝ་ཅིག་ཨིན་ /-tshau-chi-ĩ:/. For example: ཧོན་ཚོད་ཉོ་ཚརཝ་ཅིག་ཨིན། /höntshö nyo tshau-chi-ĩ:/

'I have just bought vegetables'; or སྒོ་བསྡམས་ཚརཝ་ཅིག་ཨིན་མས། /go-dam-tshau-chi-in-mä/ 'Oh, it [literally the door] is just closed!'

If a time indication in the past is given, ཚརཝ་ /tshau/ is not necessary and the formula becomes inflected verb V' + ཅིག་ཨིན་ /-chi-ĩ:/. For example: ད་རིས་དྲོ་བ་ཧོན་ཚོད་ཉོཝ་ཅིག་ཨིན། /dari dropa höntshö nyou-chi-ĩ:/ 'I have just bought vegetables this morning'.

When no past time indication is given, inflected verb V' + ཅིག་ཨིན་/ -chi-ĩ:/ can also mean 'to have just begun doing an action', and in that case, ཚརཝ /tshau/ is not used. For example: ཡི་གུ་འབྲིཝ་ཅིག་ཨིན། /yigu driu-chi-ĩ:/ 'I am currently writing a letter', 'I am in the process of writing a letter'.

As for 'to be about to do something', it is expressed using the following construction: V + ནི་འབདཝ་ཅིག་ཨིན་ /-nibäu-chi-ĩ:/ or V + ནི་འབད་དེས་ /-ni-bä-de/. For example: ལྟོ་ཟ་ནི་འབདཝ་ཅིག་ཨིན། /to za-ni bäu-chi-ĩ:/ 'I am just about to eat'; ལྟོ་ཟ་ནི་འབད་དེས། /to za-ni bä-de/; སྒོ་བསྡམ་ནི་འབདཝ་ཅིག་ཨིན་མས། /go-dam-ni bäu-chi-in-mä/ 'Doors are about to be closed'; or ནདཔ་སྨན་ཁང་ལུ་བསྐྱལ་ནི་འབད་དེས། /näp mänkhang-lu kä-ni-bä-de/ 'The patient is about to be taken to the hospital'.

Lesson seventeen

The theme of the lesson is 'obligations and wishes', and the grammar objective is 'nominalizer'.

Grammar aspect

Expressing one's needs and wishes

There is no direct equivalent in Dzongkha for the English verb 'to want'. To ask, 'Would you like some tea?' one would use a polite formula: ཇ་འཐུང་ནི་ན། /ja thung-nna/ 'Will you have tea?' The verb དགོ་ནི་ /go-ni/ 'to need' can also be used in less formal situations: ག་ཅི་དགོ་ག /gachi go-ga/ 'What do you need?'

To express an intention in the future, one can use the structure V + དགོ་མནོ་ /go-no/ 'To think one must…'. For example: དྲུང་འཚོ་འབད་དགོ་མནོཝ་མས། /drungtsho bä-go-nou-mä/ 'I want/I intend to be a doctor' (literally, 'I am thinking of doing doctor'). If the urge or wish to do something is very strong, one can emphasize it by reduplicating the intended action and inserting རང /ra:/ 'itself' as follows: ང་ཏི་རུ་ཐོབ་རང་ཐོབ་དགོ། /nga tiru thop-ra: thop-go/ 'I must absolutely get [my] money [by any means]', ང་ལྷ་འདི་འབད་རང་འབད་དགོ། /nga la: di bä-ra: bä-go/ 'I must work [at any cost]', or 'I really want to do this work'. Note that, in the past and future, དགོ། /go/ is often associated with ཐོན་ /thön/ 'to come out, to compel', and in such cases, it is inflected, resulting in the form དགོཔ་ཐོན་ /gop-thön/. For example: ན་ཧིང་ཅ་ལ་འདི་དགོཔ་ཐོན་སོང་ཡི། དེ་འབདཝ་ད་ དུས་ཅི་མི་དགོ་པས། སང་ཕོད་དགོཔ་ཐོན་འོང་། /nahing chala di gop-thön-sõ:-yi debäuda duchi mi go-pä sangphö gop-thön-wõ:/ 'Last year I wanted/needed this thing. But I don't want/need it this year. Next year, I may need it'.

Nominalizing particles

Many nouns are created in Dzongkha by adding a nominalizing morpheme to a verb. The main nominalizing morphemes are ནི་ /-ni/, མི་ /-mi/ and ས་ /-sa/. The first one, ནི་ /-ni/, transforms a verb into an object or an abstraction in the present tense, representing 'the fact of doing something'. For example: ང་དྲང་དཔོན་འབད་ནི་གི་མནོ་བསམ་མེད། /nga drangpön bä-ni-gi nosam me/ 'I do not consider being a lawyer' (literally, 'I do not have a thought of doing/being/becoming a lawyer'); ང་གནས་སྐོར་འགྱོ་ནི་ལུ་དགའ། /ngan äkor jo-ni-luga/ 'I enjoy going on pilgrimage' (literally, 'I enjoy the fact of going on pilgrimage'); or ཨ་མི་རི་ཀ་ལུ་སློབ་སྦྱོང་འབད་ནི་འདི་ཟད་འགྲོ་སྦོམ་ཨིན། /america-lu lopjong bä-ni di zädro bom ĩ:/ 'Studying in the USA is expensive' (literally, 'The fact of studying in the USA is great spending').

The second one, མི་ /-mi/, creates an agent (the person who…). It is used in all tenses. The nominalized verb comes after the nouns it refers to. For example: ཀི་དེབ་ཉོ་མི་ག་སྨོ། /kidep nyo-mi ga:-mo/ 'Who will buy books?' or 'Who buys books?' or 'Who bought books?' or 'Who is the buyer of the book?' (here, ཀི་དེབ་ /kidep/ 'the book' comes first, followed by ཉོ་མི་ 'the buyer'); ཁ་ཙ་འགྱོ་མི་ག་སྨོ། /khatsa jo-mi ga:-mo/ 'Who is the one who went yesterday?' = 'Who went yesterday?'; ད་རིས་འགྱོ་མི་ག་སྨོ། /dari jo-mi ga:-mo/ 'Who is the one who goes today?' = 'Who goes today?'; ནངས་པ་འགྱོ་མི་ག་སྨོ། / nã:pa jo-mi ga:-mo/ 'Who is the one who will go tomorrow?' = 'Who will go tomorrow?'

In addition, མི་ /-mi/ serves to create objects of transitive verbs (the thing which…), in present and past tense. In that case, the nominalized verb is placed *before* the noun it refers to. For example: ཁྱོད་ཀྱིས་ཉོ་མི་ཀི་དེབ་ག

དེ་སྨོ། /chhö-ki nyo-mi kidep gade-mo/ 'Which are the books you bought?' (here, ཉོ་མི་ 'who-bought' before ཀི་དེབ་ /kidep/ 'book'); ད་ལྟོ་སླབ་མི་གློ་འདི་གལ་ཆེ་དྲག་ཨིན། /dato lapmi lo gä chhedra ĩ:/ 'What I am telling you now is important'.

For an object in the future tense ('the thing which will...') ནི་ /-ni/ is used. For example: ཁྱོད་ཀྱིས་ཉོ་ནི་ཀི་དེབ་འདི་ག་ཅི་སྨོ། /chhö-gi nyo-ni kidep gachi-mo/ 'What is the book that you want to buy?' or 'What book do you want to buy?'; ནངས་པ་སླབ་ནི་གློ་འདི་གལ་ཆེ་དྲག་ཨིན། /nã:pa lap-ni lo gä chhedra ĩ:/ 'What I will tell you tomorrow is important'.

The third nominalizing morpheme, ས /-sa/, transforms a verb into the place where the action took, takes or will take place ('the place where...'). This nominalizer is used for every tense. For example: ན་ཧིང་ང་བཅས་གཉིས་འཕྱད་ས་ཨ་ན་ཨིན། /nahing ngachä nyi pchhä-sa ana ĩ:/ 'This is the place where the two of us met last year'; དུས་རྒྱུན་ང་བཅས་གཉིས་འཕྱད་ས་ཨ་ན་ཨིན། /düjün ngachä nyi pchhä-sa ana ĩ:/ 'This is the place where the two of us usually meet'; སང་ཕོད་ང་བཅས་གཉིས་འཕྱད་ས་ཨ་ན་ཨིན། /sangphö ngachä nyi pchhä-sa ana ĩ:/ 'The place where the two of us will meet next year is this one'.

Lesson eighteen

The theme of the lesson is 'Festivals and time', and the grammar objective is 'temporal clauses (after, before).

Grammar aspect

ཞིམ་ལས། */-zhimlä/*

This temporal verb marker is used after a verb to mean 'after'. For example: དཔྱང་ཞིམ་ལས་ /pchang-zhim lä/ 'After hanging', or similarly, བླམ་ལུ་ཕྱག་འཚལ་ཞིམ་ལས་སྙན་དར་ཕུལ་ཡི། /lam-lu pchha tshä-zhimlä nyända phül-yi/ 'After prostrating to the *lam*, I offered money'.

To express anteriority in a temporal clause ('before + verb'), the construction is as follows: མ་ + V + པའི་ཧེ་མ་ /ma-V-pai-hema/. Depending on the spelling and pronunciation of the verb, པའི་ /pai/ can be replaced by བའི་ /wai/. For example: མ་དཔྱང་པའི་ཧེ་མ་ /ma-pchang-pai-hema/ 'Before hanging'; or གསུངས་ཆོག་མ་གནང་བའི་ཧེ་མ། /sungchhö ma-nang-wai-hema/ 'Before performing a ritual'.

Note that neither ཞིནམ་ལས་ /-zhimlä/ nor ཧེ་མ་ /hema/ can follow ཨིན་ /ĩ:/ or ཡོད་ /yö/. To express a statement such as 'After being a doctor', or 'Before having money', one has to use lexical verbs like 'to become' (འབད་) (literally, 'to do') instead of 'to be', or 'to obtain' (ཐོབ་) instead of 'to have'. For example: ཁོ་དྲུང་འཚོ་འབད་ཞིནམ་ལས་དགེ་སློང་འབད་ཡི། /kho drungtsho bä-zhimlä gelong bä-yi/ 'After becoming a doctor, he became a monk'; ང་ལཱ་གཡོག་ཐོབ་ཞིནམ་ལས་ཕྱི་རྒྱལ་ཁབ་ལུ་འགྱོ་ཚུགས་ཅི། /nga layo thop-zhimlä pchhi gäkhap-lu jo tshu:chi/ 'After I got a job, I was able to travel abroad'; ང་ལཱ་གཡོག་མ་ཐོབ་པའི་ཧེ་མ་ཕྱི་རྒྱལ་ཁབ་ལུ་འགྱོ་མ་ཚུགས། /nga la:yo ma-thop-pai hema pchhi gäkhap-lu jo ma-tshu / 'Before I got a job, I could not go abroad'.

When the nominalizing particle ནི་ /-ni/ is followed by ཡོད་ /-yö/, it means 'things to be (done)…', as in མཇལ་ནི་ཡོད་ /jä-ni-yö/ '(There is something) to be seen/to see'. For example: ག་ཅི་འབད་ནི་ཡོད་ག /gachi bä-ni-yö-ga/ 'What is to be done?', or ག་ཅི་ཡང་འབད་ནི་མེད། /gachi ya: bä-ni-me/ 'There is nothing to be done'.

Conclusion

Teaching Dzongkha as a foreign language is in its infancy in Bhutan. Because it is a maiden attempt, it will undoubtedly be a learning experience and face numerous challenges along the way. In the process of developing this manual, the authors have realized how difficult it is to present a language to learners in the most sensible and intelligible manner. Unlike native speakers, learners will ask every possible question as to 'why and how' for every word and linguistic nuance.

However, during the process of developing the manual, Françoise Robin asked a volley of practical questions that would not have naturally arisen in the minds of native speakers, who take many things for granted. These questions prompted a thorough examination of the language, offering insights into how non-native speakers perceive it. Keeping this perspective in mind, they diligently worked to ensure that this manual addresses the majority of challenges anticipated in teaching Dzongkha as a second language.

Bibliography

Dorjee, K. (2011). *Dzongkha Segment and Tones: A Phonological Investigation* (PhD dissertation, the English and Foreign Languages University, Hyderabad, India).

La Prairie, M. (2014). *A Case Study of English-Medium Education in Bhutan* (PhD dissertation, Institute of Education, University of London).

Nado, L. (1982). 'The Development of Language in Bhutan, *Journal of the International Association of Buddhist Studies*, vol. 5, no. 2, pp. 95–100.

Tshering, K. and G. van Driem (2019). *The Grammar of Dzongkha Revised and Expanded with a Guide to Roman Dzongkha and to Phonological Dzongkha (4th ed.)*, Santa Barbara: Himalayan Linguistics, University of California.

van Driem, G. (1994). 'Language Policy in Bhutan'. In M. Aris and M. Hutt, eds., *Bhutan: Aspects of Culture and Development*, Gartmore: Kiscadale Publications, pp. 87–105.

van Driem, G. (1998). *Dzongkha*, Leiden: The School of Asian, African, and Amerindian Studies.

van Driem, G. (2015). 'Language Identity in Bhutan', *The Druk Journal*, vol. 1, no. 1.

Wangdi, P. (2005). 'Dzongkha Evolves', *Kuensel*, 7 September.

Wangdi, P. (2015). 'Language Policy & Planning in Bhutan', the Dzongkha Development Commission, accessed at https://www.dzongkha.gov.bt/en/article/papers

Wangdi, P., S. Dorji, D. Gyaltshen and L. Gyatso, eds. (2006). *English-Dzongkha Dictionary*, Thimphu: Dzongkha Development Authority.

11 What Does 'Being Educated' Mean? Analysis of the Bhutanese Education Discourse

Akiko Ueda

Introduction

Maximizing people's happiness is the goal of the Bhutanese government's development effort. The policy of Gross National Happiness (GNH) states that people's happiness is more important than economic growth. The policy environment is geared towards balancing the material and spiritual dimensions of people's lives, and the education sector together with others is expected to implement this vision. However, in the country's educational institutions, this effort is not without challenges. A senior college lecturer stated to the author that 'the balance of the elements of the 3Hs of education is emphasized, but when we teach, we tend to focus on Head and Hands elements more and to overlook the Heart element' (personal communication, 17 March 2015). The '3Hs' stand for 'Head', which corresponds to knowledge, 'Hands', relating to skills, and 'Heart', referring to attitude, perspectives, ethics and values. The immediate questions are why has it been formulated, and what are the difficulties in balancing the 3Hs? A close investigation of the issue leads to the much broader and more fundamental questions of what is education and what is it for?

This study attempts to answer these questions by analyzing the discourse on education at three levels from a development studies perspective. The first is the global level, in which so-called mainstream and alternative development frames of thinking emerge, contest, merge and sometimes dissipate. The second is Bhutan's national policy level, which states that people's happiness is the government's main concern.[1] In the GNH policy, economic development is not suppressed but is viewed as

1 See Thinley (1998, 2005).

the means to increase people's happiness. The third level is the grassroots, that of teachers and students in Bhutan. At this level, the various views on education and the purpose of education emerge, and the way these aspects relate to people's lives provides insight into people's perceptions of life and values. Education is a useful and important means to realize a good life, and, at the same time, it has value in itself. The data used in this study was collected in twelve schools and colleges during fieldwork conducted from 2018 to 2019 in Bhutan.

Discourse on education in the global development arena

The discussion on education in the global development arena has taken three main approaches: the human capital approach, the human rights-based approach and the human capability approach.[2] Firstly, the human capital approach sees the human being as one of the inputs into the economy. In this approach, therefore, the purpose of education is to equip individuals to produce goods and services efficiently and thereby contribute to the economy. At the individual level, it means access to income and employment. It is often described as the economic-instrumentalist approach.[3] Secondly, the human rights-based approach views education as a fundamental right to all human beings. It finds intrinsic value in education.[4] This aspect is significantly different from the human capital approach. The human rights-based approach, however, does not specify the contents of education. The third approach, the human capability approach, highlights the role of education in enabling each individual's potential and talent to flourish. Manion and Menashy point out that the capability approach is 'multi-dimensional and comprehensive, accounting for both intrinsic and economic as well as non-economic-instrumentalist roles that education can and does play'.[5]

---

2 Manion and Menashy (2013); Boutilier (2019).

3 Robeyns (2006).

4 Manion and Menashy (2013).

5 Manion and Menashy (2013: 218).

Each of these three approaches seem distinct. However, interpretations of the human rights-based approach and capability approach allow them to be positioned in a similar way to the human capital approach. Access to better income and employment is part of basic human rights, and education can provide a means to it. In this respect, the human-rights-based approach is similar to the human capital approach. This is especially so because the human rights-based approach does not specify the contents of education and recognizes its intrinsic value. From this perspective, any kind of education has value. The capability approach talks about freedom and the flourishing of individual potential and talent. This can include economic freedom and nurturing individual potential to generate income.

In the current practice in the global development arena, the World Bank is the largest provider of funds and expertise to the education sector in the world and has promoted education based on its economic-utilitarian values.[6] This itself is evidence that the human capital approach has been dominant in development practices, but this point can also be established from the relation between poverty and education. Poverty reduction is still a central concern of the global community, and education has been identified as a core strategy to fight against poverty.[7] As far as education is viewed from the poverty perspective, and as far as poverty is defined in terms of income and employment, it is natural that education should focus on creating human capital. If poverty (and development) were to be defined differently, it would change the definition of education. In this current global climate, the human capacity approach is the mainstream in the education sector, because the poverty-education nexus is strong, and poverty is primarily defined from a material point of view. The other two approaches can be interpreted in a similar manner.

If poverty and development were defined not only according to income, employment and economic growth but in combination with other elements, what would they look like? Bhutan is one such country that defines development differently from many other countries in the world. In Bhutan, development is seen as an increase in people's happiness, which is not exclusively determined by individual income. The next section

6 Manion and Menashy (2013).

7 Tarabini (2010).

looks into Bhutan's Gross National Happiness policy and examines how education is defined in that policy framework.

Bhutan's official view on the role and definition of education

Gross National Happiness (GNH): Bhutan's development goal

The Bhutanese government states that the country's development goal is to enhance people's happiness.[8] The concept of GNH was coined by the fourth king of Bhutan, Jigme Singye Wangchuck, in the 1970s. Kinley Dorji narrates the official debut of the concept.[9] According to him, it occurred in 1979, when a group of Indian journalists interviewed the fourth king at the airport in Mumbai, India. The king was on his way back from Havana, where he had attended a Non-Aligned Movement Summit. Although India is a neighboring country to Bhutan, the domestic situation of Bhutan was not very well-known in India at that time. One of the journalists asked, 'We do not know anything about Bhutan. What is your Gross National Product?'. The king answered, 'We do not believe in Gross National Product because Gross National Happiness is more important'. It made a captivating headline.

Bhutan's constitution clearly states, 'The States shall strive to promote those conditions that will enable the pursuit of Gross National Happiness' (Article 9, Section 2).[10] In terms of policy, GNH has four pillars: (1) sustainable and equitable socioeconomic development; (2) preservation and promotion of culture; (3) conservation and sustainable utilization and management of the environment; and (4) promotion of good governance.[11] A set of indicators for GNH has been formulated to monitor the progress in terms of people's happiness. The GNH Index has nine domains,[12]

---

8 Planning Commission (1999).

9 Dorji (2008).

10 Royal Government of Bhutan (2008).

11 Gross National Happiness Commission (2013: 3).

12 The nine domains are psychological wellbeing, health, time use and balance, education, cultural diversity and resilience, good governance, community vitality, ecological diversity and resilience, and living standard.

which are considered to have significant impacts on Bhutanese people's perception of happiness. The GNH Policy Screening Tool is designed to ensure that each government policy is aligned with the goal of Gross National Happiness.

The concept of GNH has also drawn attention from the international community. In 2011, the General Assembly of the United Nations adopted a resolution to undertake steps that give more importance to people's happiness and wellbeing.[13] The International Day of Happiness is observed on 20 March, and *The World Happiness Report* has been published annually since 2012.[14] Eight international conferences on GNH have been held so far.

The concept of GNH is a proposal to pursue an alternative model of development. It expresses that the Bhutanese people's common sense does not accord with the mainstream development model and demonstrates the priorities that are generally considered important by the Bhutanese people. A message of concern regarding the tendency to encourage excessive consumption was also expressed in a lecture by Queen Mother Ashi Dorji Wangmo Wangchuck in 2004.[15]

The happiness that is stated in the policy and generally experienced by the Bhutanese people might be slightly different from what those outside Bhutan would imagine. For most people outside Bhutan, happiness is a momentary feeling that arises when something positive happens, or when one enjoys something. People, therefore, tend to seek happiness and try to obtain it as if it were an object like a piece of chocolate. In Bhutan, happiness is not something to strive towards directly. Dasho Karma Ura, the president of the Centre for Bhutan Studies, explains:

> Relationships, or shared situations, are where happiness spontaneously arises—you are not looking for happiness, but it comes out when relationships improve. Relationships are fundamental to happiness. When the quality and the direction of relationships improve, you feel happier. We can have better relations, not necessarily when we have

---

13 UN (2011).

14 UN (2012).

15 Wangchuck (2004).

> more money, more goods or better houses, but especially when we have better motivations and intentions—that heals you. [...] happiness is really a by-product of improving relationships; it is wrong to focus all the time on objective conditions as giving you happiness.[16]

Relationships in this context are interpreted not only as human-to-human relationships but also as those between humans and the natural environment. Happiness, therefore, should not be sought directly: as relationships are improved, happiness naturally arises. Karma Ura notes that one can 'understand development ultimately as improvement in the relational capacity of people'. 'Relationship' is the keyword of happiness, and when happiness is the ultimate goal, the progress of the human being, both individually and collectively, is in the improvement of the capacity to deal with all forms of relationships.

Educating for GNH and the review of official education documents

Under the above understanding of happiness, the education sector has been aligning education policy with GNH. This alignment has been actively pursued particularly since the late 2000s. In 2010, the government started the Educating for GNH (EGNH) initiative, which, together with the *Education Blueprint 2014-2024*,[17] has formed the primary national framework to operationalize GNH in the education sector.[18] As part of this initiative, the government has produced supplementary materials and held several workshops for teachers, researchers and education practitioners both in and outside of the country. These provide rich materials on the official discourse on GNH education. This section examines this official discourse to establish what education means in Bhutan.

In 2007, the then Secretary of Education issued a letter to all school principals in Bhutan. He highlighted '*Sem Go Choep Zo Ni* (*sems go chodp bzo ni*) [enabling children to use their mind and heart to positive

16 Ura (2008).

17 Ministry of Education (2014).

18 Tshomo (2016).

ends, for themselves, their families, and the country] as the most important elements of the quality of education which His Majesty, the Fourth King, commanded whenever our teachers had an audience with His Majesty'.[19] '*Sem Go Choep Zo Ni*' is a concept that was repeatedly used by the fourth king of Bhutan. 'Positive ends' in this context means compassion – being kind and good to others.[20] Education here signifies being kind and compassionate to oneself, others and the country. The level of knowledge, skills or certificates are not mentioned, as the focus is on the individual's mindset. The letter from the secretary sought to remind all school principals in the country of the purpose of education.

The emphasis on the development of children's minds can be traced back to the late 1980s when people started to increasingly experience the negative impacts of modernization such as violence and disrespect towards the elderly.[21] It was expressed in policies that promoted holistic and values-based education in 'a move away from exam-oriented and academic studies as the sole purpose of school education to an emphasis on the overall development of the child'.[22]

The emphasis on values-based education continues and seems to have become even stronger under the Educating for GNH initiative. In 2009, an official document titled *A Proposal for GNH Value Education in Schools* was published. It was written by Dasho Karma Ura, the country's leading intellectual and the president of the Centre for Bhutan and GNH Studies, a government research institute, and has become the basis of values education in schools.

In this document, emphasis is placed on consideration for others and cultivating a caring mind. It states that objects of a caring consciousness should go beyond the people one knows to include literally everyone in the world. One should cultivate a mind of caring and helping that extends beyond oneself and one's friends and relatives.[23] This is because, according

19 Ministry of Education (2007: Annexure II).

20 This is according to an explanation provided by a lecturer at an education college in Bhutan. Personal correspondence on 26 September 2019.

21 Ueda (2003).

22 Ueda (2003: 126).

23 Ura (2009: 4).

to the document, a person's welfare and happiness cannot be created by themself alone: they also depend on the community and society. This is a view based on the recognition of 'profound interdependencies'.[24] This point resonates with the view that happiness is a by-product of improving relationships, as mentioned above. Both views highlight the importance of good relationships that are underpinned by helpfulness and a caring mindset. The document states, 'commitment to values that restrict our narrow interest to a reasonable degree on the one hand, and commitment to values that affirm welfare of all on the other, is important'.[25]

The emphasis on compassion and interdependency reflects the influence of Buddhist teachings. It should also be understood in the context of the social situation in which the older generations and the education authority feel that young people are increasingly becoming narrow minded and behaving in a selfish manner. The document points out the need to include techniques and training on ways to increase young people's motivation to be compassionate and broad minded.[26]

One of the most eloquent thinkers and speakers on GNH, former prime minister Jigme Y. Thinley, began the task of establishing the direction of GNH society and defining the role of education. He stated in his keynote speech at the Educating for GNH Conference in 2009, 'the greed, materialism, and consumerist fallacy have turned us into mindless economic animals, and are destroying the planet'. He argued that the solution to the challenges in energy, food, poverty, resource degradation, water shortage and climate change 'requires nothing less than a change of consciousness and hence of lifestyle. Education is the key'.[27] To fully implement GNH and to realize the shared vision and goals of happiness, he stated, there is no more effective, comprehensive and far-reaching way than to infuse the 'education system fully and properly with the humane and ecological principles and values of Gross National Happiness'.[28]

---

24 Ura (2009: 4).

25 Ura (2009: 4).

26 Ura (2009: 12).

27 Ministry of Education (2010: 13).

28 Ministry of Education (2010: 13).

He tasks education with the role of being 'the glue that holds the whole enterprise' of GNH together.

> If we are ignorant of the natural world, how can we effectively protect it? If we don't know that smoking, junk food, and physical inactivity are unhealthy, how can we have a healthy citizenry? If we are ignorant of politics and national issues, how can we cast an informed vote? If we are ignorant of the extraordinary teachings of Guru Rinpoche, Zhabdrung Ngawang Namgyal, and other great masters who taught and practised right here in Bhutan, how can we appreciate our legacy, embody our own culture, and serve the world?[29]

Education is not only to instill a compassionate and helpful mindset; it also plays a pivotal role in the entire GNH initiative. Mind, skills and knowledge must be combined to fully realize the GNH society.

At the same time, the official discourse highlights another dimension of education: the employment and economic gain of each individual. An executive order from the prime minister's office issued in August 2006 touches on this aspect:

> The Royal Government has felt an important and urgent need to reform the education system in order to improve the existing quality of education. The need has become even more expedient in light of the new political changes taking place in the country and the long cherished desire of the Royal Government to provide a [*sic*] gainful employment to all Bhutanese.[30]

The official discourse does not dismiss the economic instrumentalist dimension of education, nor does GNH policy. It clearly states that students should be prepared for employment and a stable means of earning a living.

The GNH vision, however, goes further. The holistic role of education is emphasized, which is clear from the official statements cited above. Education is the 'glue' to bind all the elements of GNH. At the same time,

---

29 Ministry of Education (2010: 14–15).

30 Ministry of Education (2007: Annexure I).

education is a vessel to inculcate the Bhutanese values that the government wants students to cultivate and maintain as members of a society in which each individual's happiness depends on that of other members and the natural environment.

The official discourse on education under the GNH policy identifies education's three main roles: (1) to inculcate Bhutanese values among students, (2) to play a pivotal role in the overall GNH initiative, and (3) to equip students to access employment and a stable source of income. What follows introduces the discourse among students and teachers about what education means. Two main ideas about education are illustrated: being helpful to others and being successful economically and socially. These two views sometimes compete and at other times work in harmony. Before introducing the contents of the discourse, the fieldwork methodology is presented.

Fieldwork methodology

The fieldwork was conducted in two phases. The first was in September 2018, and the second in February 2019. Twelve schools and colleges were visited, and in each location, focus group discussions were held with teachers/lecturers and students separately. The location of the schools and colleges cover ten out of the twenty districts in Bhutan, mainly in the western and the southern parts of the country.[31] Eighty-three teachers/lecturers and 140 students (Grade 6 and above) participated in the focus group discussions,[32] where topics included what and how students learn in schools, why children come to school and what constitutes an educated person and a successful person. The discussions were recorded and later transcribed. Information about the contexts of views and opinions expressed in the discussion and the general environment of the school was

31 The ten districts are Thimphu, Paro, Chukha, Punakha, Trongsa, Dagana, Tsirang, Sarpang, Samtse and Haa.

32 For the teachers, fifty-seven percent of the participants were male and forty-three percent were female. As for the students, fifty-five percent were male, and forty-five percent were female.

gathered from teachers and lecturers who were sometimes present in the focus groups.

The selection of participants was dependent on a contact person and the willingness of the principle of each school and college. The gender of the participants was well-balanced, and the specialties of teachers were diverse. The focus group discussions were held in an available room in the school, typically a meeting room or a library. Most conversations were in English. As the medium of instruction in the education institutions was English, both teachers and students did not seem to have much difficulty in expressing themselves. However, participants were also informed that they could speak in their own language if it was easier.

As each visit was for the purpose of engaging in focus group discussions, the participants may have felt that the situation was somewhat formal. Though the focus group discussions were mostly quite lively, the fieldwork data which appears in the following sections should be understood in the context of this environment.

Students' and teachers' views on education

This section is divided into two parts: students' and teachers' understanding about what students learn in schools in Bhutan, and their perceptions of the differences between an educated person and a successful person. The information from the field shows that these two topics are intimately related. Each discourse also illustrates competing ideas and dilemmas among teachers and students.

What students learn in schools in Bhutan

At school, the students study subjects according to their levels, including mathematics, science, English, Dzongkha and social studies. Apart from these subjects, many students and teachers point out life skills and values education as part of what students learn in schools. According to them, life skills include how to cope with stress, decision-making skills, problem-solving skills, cooperation skills and teamwork, as well as critical thinking. Some of these are 'infused within the lessons'. In addition to teaching life skills as a regular part of the curriculum, each school also has a special week at the beginning of the academic year called 'value week'. Meditation and mindfulness training are also pointed out by both students and teachers as part of what students learn in school. Each lesson starts with a silent period of a minute or two, in which students are to focus their consciousness on their breath and count as they breathe in and out. One teacher explained that it was an effective way to nurture concentration.

Two students identified what they learn in school, as follows: one said, 'We learn that we need to respect others', immediately followed by another student, who added, 'We should not bully others. We should not fight others'. Respect for others was also highlighted in another school. One student said, 'we learn how to appreciate others. Your opinions are not [the] only [ones that] … matters [*sic*]. Others' opinions may also matter'. Students in six schools and colleges out of the twelve pointed out that respecting others is an important value they learned.

Other values they learn include *Driglam Namzha* (*sgrig lam rnam gzhag*), the traditional Bhutanese etiquettes, social protocols and self-discipline. GNH values are also taught in regular content lessons making a connection with a relevant GNH value. One teacher gave an example of how to relate textbook contents to GNH values.

> When you try to teach the student about the biology topic about animals, insects. So first of all we try to share with them about the cultural context, Bhutanese context. Which means if you try to kill insects, it is a sin. And then try to tell them how to kill animals and also in a way how to save these animals. Because when you try to kill animals, it is a sin. And in that perspective we can thread a narrative in relation to the cultural context. Otherwise, students will, the moment they see the insects, they will have this feeling of killing the animals without thinking of the sin of killing the animals. This is a simple example, but we have so many other examples that we can relate to.

Another teacher gave an example of a GNH value. He said that awareness has changed the way of presenting an example in a mathematics textbook.

> I think over the years when the curriculum is reformed; the developers are keeping in mind the GNH values. I got a little interested with one

> type of question in mathematics. When we were students, there were questions like, "there were ten birds on a tree. A hunter came, shot, and three birds fell down. How many birds flew away?" So there we can see a killing concept. So now they have reformed and made in a saving way. That is one interesting way. We also try to incorporate that way. For keeping positive values. So whenever we frame questions, we keep that concept in mind. That is saving is one of the GNH values in Bhutan.

Striking a balance among Head, Hands and Heart (3Hs) seems to be a concern of some of the teachers. One science teacher stated:

> For example, when we do the experiments in science subjects, we make sure we take care of the three domains: scientific knowledge, the scientific value, the scientific skill. The simplest example, as soon as we enter the lab, we tell them that you will be assessed on these three domains. The scientific skill, we need to give them an example of how you hold the apparatus. For example, if the child holds an apparatus like this, this is not the proper way. […] And the scientific value is, for example, when they use the chemicals, some students tend to open the spirit lamp. They keep it open. Then that time we used to mend that. We have to close it, [otherwise] it will evaporate. And the other classes which coming after, won't have enough spirit in the lamp. So you are having some value that you need to preserve for the future. So through this we make sure [of] this.

Even in the answers in which the word, '3Hs', was not used, in all the focus group discussions the teachers seemed to be aware of these different elements of education. Balancing different aspects in education, however, is not always easy. Many teachers expressed their dilemma in balancing the teaching on knowledge on the one hand and other elements such as skills and values on the other. This was stated explicitly in focus groups at six out of the twelve schools and colleges. One teacher's statement captures the situation well.

> I think we have a holistic way of bringing up our students. […] However, having said that, I think the truth, the fact here in Bhutan is ultimately *we judge the student based on the marks they scored.* So that remains a fact. And then that fact, students know that. So most of the students they say, "Uh, I may not be able to make a living out of games. I may not be able to make a living by music and dances and all". So most of the students, I think, they are focusing on academics. (Emphasis added.)

In Bhutan, academic marks, especially those obtained in the common examinations at the end of grades ten and twelve, are very important as admission to the next level of education is determined by the examination results. Just before the examination day, the students go to temples to pray for good performance in the exam, and long queues in front of major temples are reported in the national media. The announcements of exam results capture the headlines of national newspapers and are reported on TV. This is the same phenomenon as reported by Ueda twenty years ago.[33] The difference is that students today face tougher competition to be admitted to the next level of education and to get their desired job, as there are more students in the education system.[34]

Teachers are required by the education policy to inculcate GNH values and, at the same time, they also recognize how important exam marks are for the future career of each student. Another teacher expresses it thus:

> As per the education blueprint we have, I think by the end, we should have GNH graduates. Which means that [a] particular graduate should not only have content knowledge in him. Should also be having some ethical values, universal values, not only the content knowledge.

Students speak about their side of this same story, and similar views were voiced in six out of the twelve schools and colleges. One student expressed her feeling about an excessive emphasis on exam results.

---

33 Ueda (2003).

34 The number of students in all the educational institutions in the country in 2017 was twice that in 1997 (Central Statistical Organization 1999; National Statistics Bureau 2018).

> I guess from my point of view, the examination is not checking what we have learned. They're just checking what we have memorized from the textbook [gestures of agreement amongst participants]. Examinations in Bhutan, I don't think it's helping us to be a better person in the future. They are just checking what we have memorized.

Another student distinguishes memory from intelligence.

> Usually, the exam deals with our memory power. You have memorized everything. It doesn't check our intelligence. I think it just checks our memory power. Whatever we can memorize. It doesn't check our intelligence. Maybe in math or physics, it tests our intelligence. But other subjects like history, geography and English and Dzongkha and so forth, we have to deal with the memory power.

Both teachers' and students' statements point out the ineffectiveness of examinations as a means to check what they have truly learned and to monitor the progress of learning things that will be useful in future, and express doubt about evaluating students' performance only via paper-based exams.

Reflecting on their days in schools, college students agree that the examinations were primarily to get good marks and did not help in the long run. One student in college states:

> We don't need examination. Because when it comes to the examination, we are only taught for just passing the examination. Actually, what we should be doing is that we should be taught for a lifetime. And education which can last for a lifetime.

A college lecturer agrees that schools are not balancing teaching between the 3Hs. He says, 'the problem is that at the end of the term or at the end of the year, they set a question just to test on one of the Hs, cognitive'.

A lecturer at another college points out that the heart element of the 3Hs is missing in college education. At schools, this is mostly attributed to the need to achieve high marks in examinations. In contrast, at the college level where most of the students will seek a job after graduation, the lecturer points out that the reason the heart element is missing is that people's minds are driven mainly by economic benefits. He states:

> I think we are missing this compassion. In Buddhism, we talk a lot about compassion, but in practice, I think we are missing that. And to just chip in at this tertiary level, I think it will be difficult for us. Because this compassion, this business was there when Lord Buddha was there. And okay, three thousand years back. [...] I think this compassion or happiness all it was there. But because of the economic drive people have forgotten. Now people are [thinking] all the time how I can make more money? And I was talking to my students. So, you want money? So, you want a post? Who pays a high salary and less work. Where in the world is this type of position [...]? You want high salary, no work. It cannot happen. Starting from sweeping the floor or picking paper, if you have positive attitude then you'll be happy. But if you are forced to do and all that, if you have a negative [...]. It's all to do with attitude.

Students learn values and life skills at school in addition to curriculum contents. This seems to embody education under the GNH policy. The importance of striking a balance among various elements of education is recognized by teachers and students. However, the exam marks which reflect cognitive knowledge are very important for each student's ability to obtain employment, and this poses a dilemma to teachers and students. The students recognize that examinations are designed to test only part of the education they receive, and they distinguish the knowledge from skills and values using different sets of words, such as memory and intelligence, or memory that lasts only till the exams end and education that lasts for a lifetime.

The way the students differentiate various learning contents is intimately related to the images of 'an educated person' and 'a successful person' held by both teachers and students. The next section examines these ideas closely.

'An educated person' vs. 'a successful person'

The debate over 'an educated person' and 'a successful person' emerged in response to the question about the reasons to study at school. It was almost unanimous among the students that one of the main reasons to attend school was to get a good job. One student answered, 'To be a successful person we have to come to school and study hard'. When asked to define 'a successful person', she answered that it means getting a good job and earning money. 'In a village, we cannot earn so much money. That is a problem', she said. Many students confirmed that their parents want them to go to school and to get a good job. A good job in their minds is a government officer, and this idea was expressed by both students and teachers in ten of the schools and colleges where focus group discussions took place. One teacher explains,

> A farmer is a low-income earner. And then a person wears a *gho* [*go*; Bhutanese men's dress], makes his *lagay* [*lag rgyan*; white cuffs worn with *gho*], and then goes to the office, is a more and respected highly honored man in Bhutan. That's the primary reason why parents send their children. And they also say it from their mouth. Directly say that don't you want to be a *Dasho* [*drag shos*; a superior one]? That's the primary reason why the students study hard.

This vision of being successful concords with Ueda's description of the situation in 1997.[35] At the top of 'the ladder of success', there is *dasho* wearing a red *kabney* (*bkab ne*; a ceremonial scarf worn by men on formal occasions), whose contribution to the country is recognized by the king. Many students in 1997 answered that they wanted to be a doctor, an engineer or a civil servant.[36] The fieldwork for the present study conducted twenty years later suggests this trend is still alive and strong. Since a doctor and an engineer embody a vision of a successful person for the majority, students want to enter the science stream at grades 11 and 12. As a result, other streams such as arts and commerce are entered into because of poor exams marks, and not by choice. One student said, 'those who

---

35 Ueda (2003).

36 A doctor and an engineer in this context work in the government sector.

study well will do better in life. Those who attain good marks will have a better chance of living a wealthy life'.

However, few participants displayed a derogative attitude toward those who did not study in school. Instead, they point out the good qualities of those people. One student gave the example of a man in his village whom he describes as 'the most valuable person'.

> I have an old man in my village called […] Ap Dolay. I feel he's been considered as the most valuable person in my village though he is not literate. […] he is such a person that he reaches to every home where there is in need of help. So he actually understands the need of that particular person. He is sensible enough that he values the necessity that is being caught by the neighbors. And he is also sensible that he is able to manage with the surroundings that actually surround him. So for this particular reason, we all in my village consider him to be the most valuable person.

The student also added that this is an example of an educated person.

One college lecturer said that he does not consider himself as an educated person, despite his high qualifications. He said that an educated person should have compassion, warm-heartedness and generosity. He also pointed out an aspect of an educated person from day-to-day life.

> Here I am taking tobacco. My teacher didn't teach me to take. I know it is not good for health, but I cannot deal without it. And drinking alcohol, that is another thing. So from these aspects, I don't consider myself educated.

A college student talked about the difference between an educated person and a literate person.

> Being literate means anyone who can read and write, probably. Educated means probably a person who has lots of values in it so they can use in their lifetime. An educated person not only means about living in academic but the person who has considered a lot of value and morals they can use in their life.

Another college student expressed a similar point.

> An educated person is not only a person who writes and reads a text. But a person who is actually sensitive enough, who is actually brave enough to accept the surrounding. So, we feel that in our country, in our society as of Bhutan, people having all those features are considered to be more valuable than a person who is actually literate. A person acquiring degree, certificates, or PhD certificate are sometimes not valued as that person who didn't even acquire primary level of studies. So, we feel that the person who is actually having more ethics, more values, more […] mindful [of their] surrounding[s] is considered more valuable than a person who is actually literate.

The above view was also shared by a student from a central school:

> Some people think that only those who can read and write are educated. But from my point, I think it is right that those who can read and write are educated. But if they don't have values, then reading and writing is useless. So I think those who have good values in their lives and those who give others in a good way. Those who show others a good path, they are educated.

The similar way of distinguishing an educated (or valuable) person from a literate person (or one with a higher education certificate) was expressed in eight schools and colleges out of the twelve.

In another central school, a student responded that an 'educated person means someone who is very kind, compassionate, and someone who can understand others and try to help others'. Another student in the same school said,

> An educated person is a person who can reflect the humanity of today's world. Not only literate. Sometimes we have people who are just literate, who are filled with ego. They are expert in one thing. Those people are just literate; they are not educated. Because they do not have value their ego just burns within themselves.

In these answers, we can find the influence of Buddhist teaching, which tells that reducing one's 'ego' is important. Ego in this context is selfish thinking, prioritizing one's own benefits over others. Selfish thinking and behavior is a source of suffering in Buddhist teaching.[37] It might give momentary happiness, but it does not last for long. Rather, it brings more suffering and misery. Long-lasting true happiness in the Buddhist context comes from a mind that cares about others, a compassionate mind. 'Their ego just burns … within themselves' in the above statement indicates that self-centered thinking is active in their minds.

Others also support this kind of view. Another student said,

> An educated person is those who have trained their mind or those who have educated value mind. Because all of my friends are saying that an educated person are those who are having a kind or compassionate mind. But to have that, […] firstly they should train their mind. Because our mind is like a king. Because as soon as our mind order any duties, our body will do. So the main purpose of our life is to become a good person or to track the right path. Don't involving[38] in negative activities. So for that we should train our mind, educate our minds. So that's the educated person.

Buddhism talks about working with one's mind.[39] Our mind, when it is not looked after, tends to stray, wandering through various thoughts and images, forgetting Buddhism's ultimate truth: the empty nature of everything. What the student meant by 'train the mind' is to get out from self-centered thinking and always to remember the importance of helping others. When people in Bhutan speak about the importance of helping others, they do not always refer to the Buddhist principles. The positive value of prioritizing others over one's own interest seems to be part of the social norm and goes without a particular reference.

'Being educated' does not preclude being in school, studying and gaining a certificate. However, there is a clear distinction between learning

---

37 Kongtrul and Waxman (2016); Kongtrul (2018).

38 This means, 'Don't get involved'.

39 Mingyur (2008; 2010).

in school and being educated. A person can achieve good marks in the exams and hold a certificate, but that does not necessarily mean they are educated. This is a point on which the majority of interviewees agree.

From the statements presented above, the following conclusions can be drawn. Firstly, in schools today in Bhutan, the curriculum encompasses the core subjects as well as life skills and values education. These correspond to the Head, Hands and Heart of the 3Hs. The policy of educating for GNH is implemented in this way. The GNH values are inculcated both during 'values week' in school and during subject lessons in which teachers make connections. The examinations, which are exclusively about subjects such as mathematics and English, however, pose a dilemma. Both teachers and students recognized that pursuing further education and job opportunities are largely determined by exam results. In this sense, skills and values have secondary importance. It was widely recognized, however, that from a broader perspective, skills and values are important for their lives. Secondly, there is a clear distinction between their images of 'a successful person' and 'an educated person'. It was largely accepted by the interviewees that a successful person is someone who has a higher education certificate and a job in a government office, someone who will become a '*dasho*' in the long run. On the other hand, an educated person is someone who has values, is helpful and compassionate and can think in someone else's shoes. Many responded that what they aim to become is an educated person rather than a successful person, as an ultimate model of a good human being. In this sense, the dilemma between exam results and being a good human being is somewhat resolved. To be more precise, the dilemma is felt only temporarily when the examination becomes an immediate concern, but from a broader perspective, people understand which direction they should head towards to become a better human being.

Conclusion

This study has examined what education means at three levels: global development discourse, Bhutan's national policy, and at the grassroots level (teachers/lectures and students in schools and colleges in Bhutan). In the global development discourse, the view that education is designed to provide a means to access employment is dominant. Though this has been criticized as an economic-utilitarian approach, other voices that emphasize the intrinsic value of education are still weak and lack appeal in the global discourse in which the greatest concern is poverty reduction.

The Bhutanese government has stated since the 1970s that its development goal is not economic growth but enhancing people's happiness. Under the policy of GNH, the government's approach to education is distinct from the dominant global discourse. Under the policy of 'educating for GNH', education has been given two roles. It must glue together all the elements of GNH, and, at the same time, it must inculcate the values of GNH.

Under this policy, values education and life skills are emphasized. However, at the same time, the key examinations, especially at the end of grades 10 and 12, are understood to determine the future of each student. If one wants to be 'successful' in terms of career, one needs to achieve higher marks in these examinations. This will lead to economic gain and social respect to a certain extent. What was remarkable, however, in the discussion among the students and teachers/lecturers was that they distinguished 'a successful person' from 'an educated person'. The majority of them responded that what they strive for ultimately is to become an educated person, who is compassionate and helpful to people in need and can think in another person's shoes. One student said that knowledge and skills without values are useless. The globally dominant view that education is to provide the means to access employment opportunities is equivalent to the model of a successful person in the Bhutanese grassroots discourse, and this is not what people in Bhutan set as their ultimate goal as a human being. School education in Bhutan seems to provide opportunities to become both successful and educated, though opportunities to become educated are not exclusively in the domain of schools.

An important element that produces these differences between global discourse and the grassroots level in Bhutan seems firstly to be based on government policy. At the global level, poverty reduction is the biggest concern, and it is defined almost exclusively from an economic point of view. For the Bhutanese government, the ultimate policy goal is to increase people's happiness. These differences give different roles to education. Secondly, the cultural and social background of Bhutan plays a role in defining education. Buddhism teaches one to be helpful to others and to reduce one's ego and warns against excessive consumption. In the Buddhist view, an accomplished person is one who has attained enlightenment. This is a vision that is very different from being successful economically and socially. The students and teachers in Bhutan in this study hold these two visions, and nurturing one's ability to achieve in both areas is the role of education in Bhutan.

Acknowledgements

This study is part of the research project, Education Values for a Sustainable Society, which is funded by the Toyota Foundation (project number D17-R-0362). The author would like to express gratitude to the members of the project, Dr. Kezang Sherab (Paro College of Education, Royal University of Bhutan) and Dr. Matthew Schuelka (University of Birmingham, UK) for useful exchanges during fieldwork.

Bibliography

Boutilier, S. (2019). 'Growing up Malala: Is Today's Educated Girl Tomorrow's Neoliberal Woman?' *Journal of International Development*, vol. 32, no. 2, pp. 186–206. DOI: 10.1002/jiid.3442.

Central Statistical Organization, Ministry of Planning, Royal Government of Bhutan (1999). *Statistical Yearbook of Bhutan 1997*, Thimphu: Royal Government of Bhutan.

Dorji, K. (2008). 'Policy of Happiness', *Himal*, August, accessed on 3 November 2019 at http://old.himalmag.com/component/content/article/825-policy-of-happiness.html

Gross National Happiness Commission (2013). *Eleventh Five Year Plan, Volume 1: Main Document 2013-2018*, Thimphu: Gross National Happiness Commission, Royal Government of Bhutan.

Kongtrul, D. (2018). *Training in Tenderness: Buddhist Teachings on Tsewa, the Radical Openness of Heart That Can Change the World*, Boulder: Shambhala.

Kongtrul, D. and J. Waxman (2016). *The Intelligent Heart: A Guide to the Compassionate Life*, Boulder: Shambhala.

Manion, C. and F. Menashy (2013). 'The Prospects and Challenges of Reforming the World Bank's Approach to Gender and Education: Exploring the Value of the Capability Policy Model in the Gambia', *Journal of Human Development and Capabilities*, vol. 14, no. 2, pp. 214–240.

Mingyur, Y. (2008). *The Joy of Living: Unlocking the Secret and Science of Happiness*, London: Random House.

Mingyur, Y. (2010). *The Joyful Wisdom: Embracing Change and Finding Freedom*, London: Random House.

Ministry of Education, Royal Government of Bhutan (2007). *26th Education Policy Guidelines and Instructions*, Thimphu: Royal Government of Bhutan.

Ministry of Education, Royal Government of Bhutan (2010). *Proceedings: Educating for Gross National Happiness Workshop*, 7–12 December 2009, Thimphu: Royal Government of Bhutan.

Ministry of Education, Royal Government of Bhutan (2014). *Education Blueprint 2014–2024*, Thimphu: Royal Government of Bhutan.

National Statistics Bureau, Royal Government of Bhutan (2018). *Statistical Yearbook of Bhutan 2018*, Thimphu: Royal Government of Bhutan.

Planning Commission, Royal Government of Bhutan (1999). *Bhutan 2020: A Vision for Peace, Prosperity and Happiness*, Thimphu: Royal Government of Bhutan.

Robeyns, I. (2006). 'Three Models of Education: Rights, Capabilities and Human Capital', *Theory and Research in Education*, vol. 4, no. 1, pp. 69–84.

Royal Government of Bhutan (2008). *The Constitution of the Kingdom of Bhutan*, Thimphu: Royal Government of Bhutan.

Tarabini, A. (2010). 'Education and Poverty in the Global Development Agenda: Emergence, Evolution and Consolidation', *International Journal of Educational Development*, vol. 30, pp. 204–212.

Thinley, J.Y. (1998). 'Value and Development: "Gross National Happiness"', keynote speech delivered at the Millennium Meeting for Asia and the Pacific, 30 October–1 November 1998, Seoul, Republic of Korea.

Thinley, J.Y. (2005). 'The Philosophy of GNH', statement delivered at the UNDP Asia Regional Conference, 30 April 2005, Bangkok, Thailand.

Tshomo, P. (2016). 'Conditions of Happiness: Bhutan's Educating for Gross National Happiness Initiative and the Capability Approach'. In M.J. Schuelka and T.W. Maxwell, eds., *Education in Bhutan: Culture, Schooling and Gross National Happiness*, Singapore: Springer.

Ueda, A. (2003). *Culture and Modernisation: From the Perspectives of Young People in Bhutan*, Thimphu: Centre for Bhutan Studies.

UN (2011). General Assembly Resolution A/RES/65/309.

UN (2012). General Assembly Resolution A/RES/66/281.

Ura, K. (2008). 'Understanding the Development Philosophy of Gross National Happiness', interview by Bhutan Broadcasting Service with Dasho Karma Ura, unpublished transcript.

Ura, K. (2009). *A Proposal for GNH Value Education in Schools*, Thimphu: Gross National Happiness Commission, Royal Government of Bhutan.

Wangchuck, A.D.W. (2004). 'Lay Buddhism in Contemporary Bhutan', lecture given on 7 October 2004 at Bukkyo University, Kyoto, Japan.

Part III
Law and Politics

12 Feudal Tyranny and Democratic Shangri-la: Sikkim's and Bhutan's Contemporary Public Narratives on Medieval and Pre-Modern Law[1]

Miguel Álvarez Ortega

Introduction: Sikkim, Bhutan, and the muddy business of (legal) comparison

'Comparing' is not only one of the major causes of psychological malaise as touted by the blooming business of self-help literature ('you are unique, do not compare yourself to others!'), but a significant philosophical issue with complex epistemological ramifications in the humanities and social sciences. The notion of cultural incommensurability, in which each sociocultural entity is a unique cadre providing values and meanings within its own boundaries and therefore is incomparable to others, has inhabited Western literature at least since nineteenth century European

1 My gratitude goes to Anna Balikci-Denjongpa and Mélanie Vandenhelsken for bringing my attention to Sikkimese customary law and generously making varied sources available; Saul Mullard for his discussion and inputs on early Sikkimese legal documents; Michael Peil and Michaela Windischgraetz for sharing their information on the JSK Law School and the Punakha Code; and Tashi Chopel for the access to the BA program in political science and sociology of Sherubtse College. I also appreciate the comments made by the reviewers of this paper. Needleless to say, any inaccuracies and flaws remain my sole responsibility.

This paper is part of the research conducted within the project 'Philosophical Foundations of the Legal-Political Realm in the Tibeto-sphere' (Grant-in-Aid for Scientific Research (C): 22K01112) of the Japanese Society for the Promotion of Science.

nationalism, and it seems to reappear cyclically opposing different forms of universalism, as in the case of communitarian and postmodern movements in vogue in the late 1990s.

In the case of political and legal studies, the questioning of the possibilities and functions of comparison has affected the very consideration of disciplines, namely comparative law. Projects dedicated to comparing either whole legal systems or specific elements or institutions thereof have often been criticized as a sheer, let us say, arbitrary juxtaposition lacking any scientific systematicity or justification and have even been reduced to something of a collector's hobby.[2] As a response, it is now assumed that legal comparison is a cross-cutting enterprise defined by a plurality of ends. This entails that, beyond claims of presumed similarities, each comparative project needs to explicitly justify both the election of its object (entities to be compared) and its end (practical, theoretical, and so forth).[3]

Regarding the compared objects, shared properties and characteristics must coexist along with diverging ones in order to avoid a sheer realization of identity on one extreme, and the confirmation of unrelatability beyond the inclusion in super categories, on the other.[4] In this regard, Sikkim and Bhutan are not only neighbors that once shared a blurred contact zone,[5] but also entities that have presented both clear sociohistorical similarities and dissimilarities since their inception as political entities, as explained in the introduction to this volume.

As for the end of the legal comparison, the focus is put on the ideological narratives concerning the medieval and pre-modern legal past contemporarily developed by institutional bodies, and native scholarship and higher education. It is, therefore, not intended as a study of legal history

---

2 Ewald (1995: 1961); Valcke (2004: 714).

3 This has typically been phrased as a functional approach as a reaction to juxtaposition (Siems 2014: 33ff).

4 Ferreira de Almeida (2018: 39–44).

5 Balikci has argued that there are important shared religious and linguistic elements behind claims that the 'neighbouring valleys, now belonging to three different countries—Chumbi to China, Ha to Bhutan, and Sikkim to India—were perhaps once populated by a somewhat homogenised Lhopo population' (2008: 73); see also Mullard (2010).

itself but of the self-(re)presentation of the medieval and pre-modern legal past within the public spheres of these political entities. In what follows, I shall lay out a brief summary of the scholarly research on the legal past as an introductory background for the discourses of the branches of government, local intellectuals, universities and other higher education institutions. The study of each country is thus first presented separately, inviting one to question and ponder common prima facie assumptions, namely the identification of a narrative of disruption with the legal past in the case of Sikkim and one of continuity in the case of Bhutan.

The final goal, addressed in the concluding section, is to compare and try to understand the discourses of these two countries as strategical answers to contemporary challenges related to nation-building and legal efficacy in a globalized context. In this regard, considering the assumed 'odious' character of comparative enterprises[6] and the understandable suspicion raised by a foreign perspective,[7] it is probably appropriate to clarify that this study prefers a descriptive or explicative approach, excluding any prescriptive or evaluative pretensions on the self-representations of each country considered both individually and comparatively.

Sikkim: a narrative of democratic disruption?

Sikkim's medieval and pre-modern law: an overview

If Sikkim's historiography is still generally considered to be in its infancy, especially regarding the foundational seventeenth century,[8] it is more so the case regarding its legal history. Nevertheless, thanks to the archival and scholarly efforts of S. Mullard, H. Wongchuk, P. Choeden Namgyal and A. McKay, many historical sources have been catalogued and made

6 Traditionally, John Lydgate (ca. 1440) is attributed with the quote, later employed by Cervantes and Shakespeare, that 'Odyous of olde been comparisonis. And of comparisonis engendyrd is haterede'.

7 The appearance of Said's *Orientalism* (1978) raised the awareness of the ideological connotations and perils of the alien – namely Western colonial – view on Middle Eastern and Asian cultures.

8 Mullard (2011: 5).

available for research, including texts with clear legal and political content and significance.[9]

Among them, the *Lho mon gtsong gsum* agreement, an oath of unification and allegiance to the first king signed by representatives (ministers, leaders) of the three historical Sikkimese ethnicities (Bhutia, Lepcha and Limbu), is commonly identified as the earliest legal document (1663).[10] The text, which uses a variety of Tibetan Buddhist legitimizing elements (e.g. invocation of deities or Guru Rinpoche), bears primordial political significance and is usually conferred a foundational meaning. However, whether it did actually represent a peaceful political start ex novo or was rather a peace treaty after a war period is currently an object of debate.[11]

An earlier source, the *La sogs rgyal rabs* (1657), basically a royal chronicle narrating the origins of the Sikkimese royal family in Kham Minyag and its establishment in the territory subduing local clans, also contains important references to legal and political notions. The text recounts how, upon the arrival of Chogyal Phuntsog Namgyal in 1642,

> The royal law was enacted and many great celebrations took place;
> The Great Drum of the Dual Legal System was sounded there.

---

9 In November 2008 the Namgyal Institute of Tibetology received an important part of the royal collection, mostly dealing with pre-colonial issues, held at the Art and Cultural Trust of Sikkim from Prince Wangchuk Namgyal. Following the unsuccessful attempts of A. Holmes and K. Dorje, Saul Mullard and Hissey Wongchuk managed to present an organized catalogue comprising legal documents, international and domestic agreements, and letters dating from 1663 to 1875 (Mullard and Wongchuk 2010). Subsequently, the Sikkim Palace Archive Digitisation Project, directed by Pema Choeden Namgyal and academically coordinated by Alex McKay, started to focus on the 1875–1975 period. Its material was made accessible by the British Library in the summer of 2020 (https://eap.bl.uk/project/EAP880/search). See McKay (2017).

10 Mullard corrected the previously assumed date of 1641, still quoted in some sources, as we shall see below. Only a negative of the text from the twentieth century has survived (Mullard 2011: 140). The text is part of the Royal Records catalogue (P.D. 1.2/001). An edited version may be found in Mullard (2011: 240–245).

11 Mullard (2011: 145).

> The domains of religion and politics were [thus] constituted [and he] was established as lord of all.[12]

The fragment contains well-known legal concepts incorporated from the Tibetan tradition, in which the drum represents one of the emblems associated with the proclamation of the law as well as the capacity to summon assemblies (with the imagery of its beating sound),[13] while the 'dual legal system' refers to the secular and religious normative spheres.[14] Below, the text also alludes to a council (*'dun ma*) where representatives of the kingdom gathered with the Lepchas with the aim of explaining individual property rights (*rang 'og bdag thob pho*) and the master-servant relationship, so that 'the lineages of lords and servants [would] benefit the local customs like a flowing river'.[15]

These references take place in a royal chronicle, which implies that either their legal formalization took place in different text(s) to which the chronicle does not directly refer or that the chronicle stands as a proof that the notions were orally formulated and then assumed as part of the legal tradition. In this regard, British political officer in the 'North-East Frontier' (Sikkim, Bhutan and southeast Tibet), J. Claude White, presented in the late nineteenth century an English rendition of the *Sixteen-Laws Code* as allegedly the oldest Sikkimese legal code, stating it was an adaptation of ancient laws by Tibetan Desi (i.e., regent) Sangye Gyatso (b. 1653, d. 1705), along with a compilation of oral customs on marriage.[16] While

---

12 *rgyal khrims mnga' gsol dga' ston brgya chen mdzad/ gnas 'di lugs gnyis khrims kyi rnga chen sgrogs/ bstan srid sde btsugs kun gyi rje bor bkod/* (folio 9). I used Mullard's critical edition of the text (2011: 221), though the translation is mine.

13 Fitzherbert (2017: 7); Pirie (2018).

14 On the concept of '*khrims gnyis*' (two laws) see Pirie (2017).

15 *dpon g.yog rigs brgyud chu mo'i rgyun ltar gnas lar rgyar phan/* (folio 10). Mullard (2011: 222).

16 The sixteen sections are as follows: (1) General rules to be followed in time of war; (2) For those who are being defeated and cannot fight; (3) For officers and government servants; (4) Law of evidence; (5) Grave offences; (6) Fines inflicted for offences in order to make people remember; (7) Law of imprisonment; (8) For offenders who refuse to come in, an orderly has to be sent expressly to enquire about the case; (9) Murder; (10) Bloodshed; (11) Oaths required for those who are false and avaricious; (12) Theft; (13) Disputes between near relatives, between man and wife, and between neighbors who have things in

there exists epistolary proof that the second *chogyal*, Tensung Namgyal (b. 1644, d. 1699?), asked the Tibetan regent for guidance on the introduction of a legal code, so far no scholarly study has provided evidence that White's manuscript implemented the *desi*'s advice, or that it belonged to the seventeenth century, or that its content was legally enforced.[17]

In Mullard and Wongchuk's introduction to the *Catalogue of the Sikkimese Palace Archive*, an 1876 legal document, which Mullard refers to as the *15-Clause Domestic Settlement* (PD 9.5/027), is regarded as the most important law code for Sikkim attested so far. It contains core elements defining a legal-political system, such as the prominence of the aristocracy; the relationship of lords and lamas with their taxpayers; the importance of inter-ethnic harmony; descriptions of legal procedures where community-based (elders) arbitration coexists with the right to appeal to the *chogyal* in major cases; and religious obligations, such as the performance of Vajrayāna rituals in case of conflict.[18] Interestingly, it resorts to expressions aiming at presenting itself in line with the primordial *Lho mon gtsong gsum*.[19]

In general, the collection of documents, largely understudied, allows the observation of a hereditary landed aristocracy whose consent is sought and laid down in oaths and agreements by a king, landowner of the whole

---

common; (14) Taking another's wife, or adultery; (15) Law of contract; (16) For uncivilized people. They were first published in *The Gazetteer of Sikkim* (Risley 1894: 46–56) and later in White (1909: 311–321). According to F. Pirie, the text is a reproduction of the *khrims yig zhal lce bcu drug*, a legal code dating from the Phagmodrupa period inspired by imperial motifs (Pirie 2013: 236–240).

17 Mullard (2011: 152, 162). Regent Sangye Gyatso is a relevant figure in Tibetan legal history, credited with the drafting of the *Guidelines for Government Officials* (Cüppers 2007). The surviving letter is the regent's response to the Sikkimese king: *'Bras ljongs bstan srung rnam rgyal gyis sde srid sangs rgyas rgya mtshor khrims skor dogs sel/ gcod zhu ba* (Question(s) by Tensung Namgyal of 'Bras ljongs [Sikkim] to Desi Sangye Gyatso for Removing Doubts about Law). Van der Kuijp (1999: 270).

18 See a synopsis at Mullard and Wongchuk (2010: 230–231); the whole text is transcribed, translated and analyzed in Mullard (2017).

19 Mullard interprets the allusions as a 'clever trick' to state a basis for nationalism and create a clear division between native Sikkimese Buddhists and the ever-increasing population of Nepalese immigrants at the end of the nineteenth century. Mullard (2017: 26–27, 30).

kingdom only formally; the roles of officials and representatives of the king in the administration of justice; and a taxation system with documents from the mid-eighteenth century onwards.[20]

As for customary law, besides the well-known problems related to its dating (surely orality does not equal remote origins), current scholarship has not yet produced a systematic or historical overview but has focused instead on particular contemporary issues. These mainly relate to traditional forms of marriage and inheritance and the institution of Dzumsa, a self-governing body operating on customary law in the Bhutia communities of Lachen and Lachung that originated in the first half of the nineteenth century.[21]

Portrayals from the branches of government

The contemporary legal and political frame that constitutes the present watchtower from which the legal past of Sikkim is observed is the result of a series of sociopolitical transformations since the late 1940s that turned the country first into an Associate State of India and finally into a State of the Indian Union in the mid-1970s.[22] This situated Sikkim within the complex legal web of a peculiar asymmetrical federal political regime. Like the rest of the Indian states (with the exception of Jammu and Kashmir until August 2019), Sikkim does not have a constitution, the epitome of a legal instrument expressing national idiosyncrasy. However, it does possess its own bodies for the three branches of government with the capacity to both make decisions (more or less limited according to body and subject, since powers are distributed and shared with that of the union under Title XI of the Constitution) and develop their own discourse on its historical law. For the purposes of this research, it is also important to note that Sikkim's contemporary institutional setup is not entirely novel, continuing relevant traits from its pre-merger configuration.

---

20 See Mullard and Wongchuk (2010: esp. 4–11, 15, 31).

21 See, among others, Bourdet-Sabatier (2004); Bashin (2012: 8, 16, 23–41); Dukpa et al. (2019: 161, 167–168).

22 For a constitutional overview since the country's inception up to the transition period see Hecker (1970: 9–21).

The legislature

Sikkim commenced its legislative journey with the formation of political parties[23] and the formal creation (1951) and promulgation (1953) of the State Council, operating under a parity formula establishing an equal distribution of seats between the Bhutia-Lepcha and the Nepalese communities.[24] The chamber underwent different reformations, keeping its parity principle and incorporating representatives of the sangha and Scheduled Castes (1958, 1966). A series of reformations adopted in the early and mid-1970s made Sikkim first an associate state, with a seat in the Council of States (Rajya Sabha) and one seat in the House of the People (Lok Sabha) elected by members of the Sikkim Assembly, and following the abolition of the monarchy, a full-fledged State in the Union.[25] Article

---

23 See Kharga (2019) on the development of political parties in Sikkim.

24 The Proclamation of His Highness the Maharaja of Sikkim of 23 March 1954 provided that: 'Subject to the assent of the Maharaja, the State Council shall have power to enact law for peace, good order, and good government of Sikkim. Provided that the State Council shall not, without the previous sanction of the Maharaja, make or take into consideration any law affecting any matter hereinafter defined as a reserved subject' (Clause 13). The chamber assumed powers on the so-called 'transferred subjects': 'I. Education. 2. Public Health. 3. Excise. 4. Press and Publicity. 5. Transport. 6. Bazaars. 7. Forests. 8. Public Works' (Clause 21). All references to Sikkimese legal texts are taken from the collection contained in Sharma and Sharma (1998).

25 The entire process was too complex to be fully accounted for here. Academic references will be provided below in the section on higher education and local scholarship. The main legal milestones are the following. After an episode of political turmoil, the Tripartite Agreement of 8 May 1973 was signed stating the basis for a democratic constitutional regime for Sikkim, including 'a system of elections based on adult suffrage which will give equitable representation to all sections of the people on the basis of the principle of one man one vote' for an assembly elected every four years. The Government of Sikkim Bill implementing the Tripartite Agreement was introduced in July 1974, containing controversial references to the relationship with India. Political agitation increased. The assembly passed a resolution requesting representation of Sikkim in the Indian Parliament, which resulted in the enactment of the 35th Amendment of the Constitution of India making Sikkim an associate state. The 38th Amendment of the Indian Constitution incorporated Sikkim as its twenty-second state. The act established the Tenth Schedule, according to which the representative of the House of the People shall be chosen by direct election of the constituency of Sikkim (Article 4).

371F of the Indian Constitution enabled the Sikkimese Assembly to reserve seats for certain social groups or sectors, so from the Second Assembly onwards, the Representation of the People (amendment) Act of 1979 abolished the reserved seats for Sikkimese-Nepalese and distributed the thirty-two seats as follows: twelve for members of two specific Scheduled Tribes (Bhutia – now including other Tibetoid groups such as Sherpa and Yolmo – and Lepcha); two for Scheduled Castes; one for the sangha (Buddhist monastics); and the remaining seventeen were declared general seats.

Sikkim's legislature, which has been conferred relevant powers,[26] is arguably the branch of government that has shown the least interest in the medieval and pre-modern legal past of the country. However, it presents itself as a continuation rather than a clear-cut rupture with pre-merger institutions. Thus, in 2003, the legislative assembly secretariat published a booklet entitled *Sikkim Legislative Assembly: Retrospect and Perspective- An Overview*, which traces the history of the institution to the aristocratic advisory council operating in the late nineteenth century, although it does not contain any scholarly or legal references.[27] A similar narrative was employed in a book on the evolution of the legislative system commissioned to Rajiva Shanker Shresta, which dedicates a section to the State Council and other late pre-merger institutions, like the Lhade Mede (described by the author as a religious council despite including both lamas and laymen), and includes legal documents from the early 1970s.[28]

26 The powers conferred to the Sikkim Legislative Assembly in exclusivity are enumerated in List-II in Schedule Seven of the Indian Constitution, comprising sixty-one matters, such as police and public order, local government, public health, communications, agriculture, social welfare and elections to the State Legislature subject to any law made by the parliament. List-I contains 100 items on which the union has exclusive legislative power such as defense, foreign affairs, citizenship, transport, currency, foreign trade, banking and census. There is a third list (List-III) of fifty-two concurrent topics on which both the union and the state have powers, like marriage, education, contracts and unions. The fact that the parliament prevails over the state legislatures in case of a jurisdictional conflict and that it also monopolizes the legislative power on residuary (i.e. non-mentioned) subjects shows the centralizing character of the federal Indian regime.

27 Sikkim Legislative Assembly Secretariat (2003: 1).

28 Shresta (2005: esp. section IV, 'Looking Back').

The judiciary

When the annexation took place, Sikkim already had a court system and a functioning High Court, which was established in 1955 by the High Court of the Judicature (Jurisdiction and Power) Proclamation of the King.[29] It was conferred final authority in all matters, civil and criminal, subject to the exercise of the royal prerogative of mercy (Article 6); it also had the power, supervised by the king, to classify all courts of Sikkim for the purposes of jurisdiction, appeal and revisions (Article 7). The Government of Sikkim Act made no special reference to the High Court but established that 'All judges shall be independent in the exercise of their judicial functions and subject only to this Act and the laws' (Article 31). Post-merger constitutional Article 371F granted institutional continuation to both the High Court of Sikkim (Section i) and the rest of the courts, subject to the provisions of the constitution.

The High Court of Sikkim has not itself produced any monograph on the legal history of the country, but its members have had the chance to express their views mainly in the court's online site as well as in a book published in 2017 by the recently created Museum of the High Court. Former judge Justice A. P. Subba, in his online *Historical Perspective of the Sikkim Judiciary*, presents the following overview of the legal past with no reference to specific laws, legal documents or scholarly quotations:

> The King who was popularly known as "the Chogyal" was the fountainhead of justice. King's [*sic*] words were the laws. Under the then administrative set up there was no place for an independent judiciary. The judicial procedure being followed then was very simple and free from legal technicalities. The Courts were dispensing substantive justice based on the principle of justice, equity and good conscience. Lawyers were not allowed to appear in Court.

---

29 The king also retained his prerogative to set up a special tribunal for the review of any case, civil or criminal. The Royal Proclamation was published in *Sikkim Darbar Gazette Extraordinary* on 17 April 1955. See the *Sikkim Code*, vol. 2, pp. 82–83. An analogous body called the Chief Court of Sikkim functioned previously (1923–1953).

> The available records do not throw much light into the remote past. It can, however, be gathered from these records that the administration of justice in Sikkim in the last century was being carried out by the Feudal Landlords (Adda Courts), Jongpons (District Officers), Pipons (Headmen) and Mandals with the Chogyal at the top.[30]

The same justice, currently chairman of the High Court Museum, is author of the 'Foreword', along with Justice Meenakshi Madan Rai and Justice Bhaskar Raj Pradhan, to the *Judicial History of Sikkim*, compiled by advocate Miss Yanchen Doma Gyatso and published by the museum. They welcome the publication as a 'milestone' for the access to the past legal history, so far 'confined to the memories of the elderly and in scattered records, [...] lost in the mist of antiquity'.[31] The book, created with the cooperation of the Namgyal Institute of Tibetology, contains a collection of historical legal texts, a reproduction of diverse legal documents, and both a summary and a detailed chronology of the judicial history, and ends with a series of pictures with their corresponding captions which represent traditional systems of justice and abolished punishments.

The first and oldest legal text presented in the book is the *Lo-men-Tshong sum* (*sic*), which they date to 1641, followed by the treaties signed with the British since the beginning of the nineteenth century. An English rendition of the *16-laws* is also presented later below along with legal documents from the twentieth century. Their overview of the history of the judiciary also starts with the *16-laws*,[32] followed by general references to feudal Adda Courts (presided by *kazis*, lamas and *thikadars*) being progressively conferred judicial power by the king, 'magistrate, monarch and high priest all in one'. Then the book gives a detailed account of the different legal configurations of the judiciary from 1906 leading to the reorganization of the courts implementing a gradual introduction of the

30 Subba (n.d.), consulted 1 February 2019.

31 High Court of Sikkim Museum (2017: 5–6).

32 The chronology presented follows that included in White (1909: 311), dating it to 914 BC, then rewritten in 1182 by Sakya Pandita and then by Desi Sangye Gyatso (b. 1653). See High Court of Sikkim Museum (2017: 44).

'principle of independent judiciary' (1973) and, finally, the abolition of the institution of *chogyal* in 1975.[33]

As mentioned, the last part of the book contains a series of illustrations of old institutions, some surviving, like the Dzumsa, a customary conflict-solving mechanism which 'exists from time immemorial';[34] some abolished, like the '*kuruwa*', a type of unpaid forced labor practiced by landowners and allegedly the royal family until 1947.[35] Interestingly, the very last references are to cruel punishments from the *16-laws*, such as being thrown from a cliff or having the hands cut off, which the publication claims were still practiced until the end of the monarchy in the twentieth century. Nevertheless, though the text mentions the existence of 'few available evidence' for such barbarous penalties, no legal or scholarly source is quoted.[36]

---

33 In 1906 the Adda Courts had their jurisdiction and powers limited and defined. The main landmarks mentioned are: 1910–1911 (creation of the Court of Political Officer [British subjects; criminal] and Indian Panchayat [for British, civil]); 1916 (Sikkim Chief Court came into existence as appeal for Adda Courts); 1923 (introduction of Courts of Munsiff); 1927–1928 (existence of fifty-seven Adda Courts); 1948 (abolition of Adda Courts and creation of Panchayat Tribunal in every state); 1950 (Honorary Court Rules framed); 1955 (High Court of Judicature (Jurisdiction of Powers) Proclamation). High Court of Sikkim Museum (2017: 46–50).

34 High Court of Sikkim Museum (2017: 135). This contradicts the anthropological studies quoted above situating its origins in the nineteenth century. The Sikkim Panchayat Amendment Act (1995, 2001) recognized its statutory status: 'the existing system of the traditional institutions of Dzumsa practiced in the two villages of the Lachen and Lachung in north district of the state shall continue to exist in accordance with the traditional and customary laws of the Dzumsas. Notwithstanding other provisions of the Sikkim Panchayat Act, the traditional institutions of the Dzumsas existing in the villages of Lachen and Lachung shall exercise the power and functions as provided under the Act in addition to the powers and functions exercised by them under the existing traditional and customary law'.

35 In Notifications No. 3590-4089/G (1946) and No. 4816/G (M) (1947) the king ordered the abolition of forced labor. See Rose (1978: 215 ff); Tran (2012: 7–11); Upadhyay (2017: 118).

36 The only reference made is to the official banning of whipping in 1922 (High Court of Sikkim Museum 2017: 180–181).

The executive

One the greatest impacts of the merger was logically on the executive and the head of the state. Sikkim had been ruled since its inception by the Namgyal dynasty for over three-hundred years uninterruptedly, except for the periods of partial Bhutanese and Gurkha occupations. The 1974 Government Act situated a chief executive at the head of the administration to be nominated by the Government of India and appointed by the *chogyal*, and entrusted a council of ministers appointed by the *chogyal* with all administrative duties derived from the powers assigned to the assembly (Chapters IV and V). After the abolition of the Buddhist monarchy and subsequent merger in 1975, the President of India succeeded the king as the head of state and Sikkim's executive powers came under the federal two-tier scheme of the Indian Union.[37] This means that Sikkim State's executive is not directly elected by its citizens, but directed by a governor[38] appointed by the President of India who appoints the chief minister (counting on the support of the majority in the Legislative Assembly) and the other members of the Council of Ministers.

Despite being the branch of government most dependent on the Indian administration and most representative of the new political frame, the executive has also had its chances and ways to express its vision of Sikkim's legal history. Particularly, the Law Department commenced in the early 1980s a project to codify Sikkimese law under the title 'Sikkim Old Laws: the Sikkim Codes', which was developed in six volumes.[39] The first volume was published in 1984 and covered the period 1975–1982,

---

37 Part B in the Tenth Schedule specifies the responsibilities of the Government of India (2) and the exercise of certain powers by the president in Sikkim. For an overview of Sikkim's state government, see Sengupta (1985); for a focus on decentralization, see Chhetri (2012).

38 Article 371F section (g) of the constitution confers to the Governor of Sikkim a 'special responsibility for peace and for an equitable arrangement for ensuring the social and economic advancement of different sections of the population of Sikkim'.

39 The codes are widely available online at the sites of the Government of Sikkim (https://www.sikkim.gov.in/portal/portal/StatePortal/UsefulLinks/OldDocuments) and of the High Court of Sikkim (http://highcourtofsikkim.nic.in/hcs/old-laws), among others.

while the last volume encompasses 1998–2001. The mainly practical purpose of the compilation is expressed in the preface to the first code by Justice A.M. Bhattacharjee, who comments that though 'legislative enactments were scanty and could be counted on fingers' in pre-merger Sikkim, annexation brought a huge increase in legal production and case-law.[40]

Volume II is the most relevant for this study, since it covers the oldest period in the collection. In his presentation, B.R. Pradhan, law secretary to the Government of Sikkim and person in charge of the publication, refers to the difficulties in identifying laws prior to 1950, when they started to be published in the Sikkim Darbar Gazette.[41] The preface, written by Shri Vepa P. Sarathi, contains interesting reflections on the legal traditions of the world and their codifying efforts, from the Romans to the French, also passing by the Hindus and the British.[42] No reference is made to Buddhist or Tibetan traditions in that matter. He solemnly concludes:

> The law is now known. How much of it should be amended is for the policy makers. Much of the existing law, however, should not be tampered with, because it has the protection of Article 371 F of the Constitution. Any change should be slow. All change is not always progressive.[43]

The oldest legal document contained in the code is a notice by Political Officer J.C. White dated 2 January 1897, which relates to a transfer of land by Bhutias and Lepchas. There is no allusion to the *15-Clause Domestic Settlement* (1876) or earlier texts.

Other efforts of the Law Department were aimed at the 'ascertainment and codification of Customary Laws and Usages' of the Nepali, Lepcha, Bhutia and Sherpa communities, which lead to the appearance of draft

---

40 Bhattacharjee (1984: iv).

41 'The laws promulgated or made prior to 1950 were not published in any form that we may understand by the term "publication" in these days. They were published in small sheets of paper under the signature of the officers in the then Sikkim Government Press but never in a compiled form' (Pradhan 1991: i).

42 Senior advocate of the Supreme Court of India and later advocate general for the State of Sikkim and chairman (Sarathi 1991: iv).

43 Sarathi (1991: vii).

reports regarding the later three in 2002.[44] Such measures are taken in the context of certain legal domains (mainly inheritance and marriage) being excluded from general Indian legislation in the case of Scheduled Tribes.[45]

Local scholarship and higher education

Local – broadly speaking – academic literature has only tangentially touched on Sikkim's legal history. The only book-length publication on the legal system operating in Sikkim, which also includes a brief history of the judiciary, is volume 18 of the Criminal Justice of India Series dedicated to the twenty-second Indian State. It does not address ancient laws, yet provides a detailed account of the legal origin and current functioning of Sikkimese institutions involved in penal jurisdiction.[46] As stated above, studies on customary law take a contemporary approach, touching only marginally on history in brief introductory remarks.[47]

Apart from that, in general, we find two broad types of scholarly publications that contain references to the legal past. On the one hand, we find sociopolitical and anthropological studies of ethnic groups and relations, such as those conducted by A.C. Sinha or more recently by Gurung.[48] On the other hand, there are accounts of the process of merging

---

44 Subsequent (annual) reports of the Law Commission indicate the enterprise of tracing and revising such customary laws under the Indian Constitution is still an ongoing project.

45 See sub-section (1) of the Hindu Succession Act and sub-section (1) of the Hindu Marriage Act.

46 Banerjea (2005).

47 For local studies on the Dzumsa, see Chhetri (2013), Tamang (2015: 70–72) and Thapa (2017); on marriage and inheritance, see Rai (2016: 128–137) and Bhutia (2017).

48 A.C. Sinha is considered an expert on Himalayan studies and the politics of the Eastern Himalayas. His works (Sinha 1975, 1984 and 2008) explore the topic of what he calls 'frontier feudalism' in Sikkim. His later books take a more active political stand defending the idea of a greater Nepal (Sinha 2018, 2019). Suresh Kumar Gurung teaches at Sikkim University. Gurung (2011), focusing more on contemporary ethnic dynamics, has been widely criticized in Vandenhelsken (2012).

with the Indian Union, written by historians such as P.R. Rao,[49] and notable figures who were an active part of the accession process, like L.B. Basnet and B.S. Das.[50]

All these studies tend to share a certain narrative that presents annexation as a means to conquer democracy and put an end to a feudal, oppressive and theocratical regime.[51] They typically start with an introductory overview of Sikkim's political history from its origins, and include treaties and agreements with the British, the influence of whom is usually regarded as positive in terms of progress and democratization, but they generally refrain from referring to specific Sikkimese laws and legal documents prior to the 1950s.[52] Allusions to the *Lho Mon Gtsong gsum* by a few scholars stand as a solitary exception.[53] Only Upadhyay's recent work on peasants' resistance makes regular use of legal material, mostly related to land and taxation; again, relevant general legal instruments like the fifteen-clause domestic settlement are omitted.[54]

The place of Sikkimese legal history in higher education is marginal and more relevant in non-legal university degrees. Indian universities have a varying degree of autonomy in their design of courses and academic programs, and the Bar Council of India has established certain rules and

---

49 See Rao (1972, 1978). P. Raghunada Rao was professor of history at the University of Venkatesvara, Tirupati.

50 Lal Bahadur Basnet, a Nepalese-Sikkimese who formed the Sikkim Janata Party, was deputy speaker of the Sikkim Legislative Assembly from 1979 to 1984. His *Sikkim: A Short Political History* (1974) is still quoted profusely by local scholars. Indian diplomat Brajbir Saran Das served as chief administrative officer in Sikkim from 9 April 1973 until 23 July 1974. Das (1983) combines his personal reflections on the merger process with a historical frame.

51 Datta-Ray (1984/2013; a publication frowned upon by the Indian authorities written by an Indian journalist present during the merger) and Duff (2015; focusing on the royal family's perspective) present a different perspective and a more complex narrative contextualized in the power politics of the Cold War, though their works hardly dedicate any space to the older history of the country.

52 This topic and idea are also contained in a book recently published by Rajiv Rai, PhD in international relations from Sikkim University (Rai 2015).

53 Sinha (2008: 47); Das (1983: 5).

54 Upadhyay (2017).

limitations in this regard.[55] They prescribe that university syllabi need to be comparable to those of the leading universities in India and provide a list of compulsory subjects – the content of which is not determined – while giving freedom to create other subjects not included in the list.

The first law school to operate in Sikkim is the Sikkim Government Law College, founded in 1980 and affiliated with North Bengal University[56] until 2008, when it became associated with the newly created Sikkim University.[57] The latter also offers several law programs and degrees coordinated by the Law Department, which belongs to the School of Social Sciences. The structure (courses, units and reading lists) of the five-year law program offered in these two institutions is practically the same, with minor variations in the order by which the subjects are taught. Historical content is mainly addressed in three subjects, History I to III, the last one dedicated to constitutional and legal history. Historical issues are also touched upon in Political Science and Jurisprudence. The scope and perspective of these courses is clearly pan-Indian, while the theoretical background combines Western (mainly Anglo-Saxon) and Hindu elements and sources.[58] The only law subjects covering specific Sikkimese legislation are Environmental Law and Land Law and Housing

---

55 The Bar Council of India by resolution no. 110/2008 approved the Rules on Standards of Legal Education and Recognition of Degrees, usually known as 'BCI Education Rules, 2008'. The first regulation dates to 1965. Schedule II. 2. University's responsibility: 'A University is free to design its academic program under LL.B. and LL.B. Honours course as well as program under the integrated degree program in Bachelor degree component as well as the LL.B. component with or / and without Honours course. However, LL.B. courses shall include the courses as stipulated under this schedule'.

56 North Bengal University is a state university established by an Act of the Legislature of West Bengal in 1962.

57 The University of Sikkim is a central university established by an act of parliament (the Sikkim University Act 2006 No. 10 of 2007), and is under the purview of the Department of Higher Education in the Union Human Resource Development Ministry.

58 For example, H. Hart and J. L. Austin are studied alongside 'Hindu Jurisprudence' (LAW-UG-C501); Machiavelli, Hobbes, Locke and Bentham, alongside the Laws of Manu and Kautilya's Arthashastra (LAW-UG-C505). Also, LAW-UG-E201: Sociology – I covers marriage and family systems pertaining to the Hindu, Muslim and Christian traditions, but not Buddhist or tribal.

Laws of Sikkim.[59] There is also a course on Eastern Himalayan studies, which assimilates Sikkim to other Himalayan enclaves and focuses on social, economic and environmental issues, but not on their legal or political aspects.[60]

Students are more likely to acquire a foundation in the political and legal history of Sikkim in other programs, like political science, history or anthropology.[61] The most complete degree for those specifically interested in such issues is arguably Bhutia studies, encompassing political, cultural, linguistic and religious aspects of Sikkimese history from a Tibetan, so to say, rather than Indian perspective.[62]

Bhutan: a narrative of Buddhist continuation?

Bhutan's medieval and pre-modern law: an overview

Historiographical research on Bhutan possesses a longer trajectory compared to that of Sikkim, dating back to the 1970s.[63] In this regard, the

---

59 LAW-UG-C906: Environmental Law. Unit III: Wild Life Protection (specific reference to Sikkim); LAW-UG-CX02: Land Law and Housing Laws of Sikkim (its oldest legal reference is a notice dated 2 January 1897 titled 'Relating to Transfer of Land by Bhutias and Lepchas').

There is also a mention of the amendment of the constitution and Sikkim's special status in LAW-UG-E401: Political Science – IV: Indian Constitution and Government.

60 LAW-UG-CX04. The Law Department of the University of Sikkim does not offer any information for this course in its syllabus; the heading reads: LAW-UG-X04: Eastern Himalayan Studies/Human Rights/Public Administration/Gender.

61 Post-grad course POL-PG-E405 Government and Politics in Sikkim; undergrad course HIS-UG-C502 History of Sikkim; post-grad courses HIS-PG-E303 History of Sikkim (the only to mention an ancient legal instrument like the Lho-Mon-Tsong-Sum); ANT-PG-O304 Anthropology of North East India – Unit IV: Anthropology of Sikkim People, Culture, Religion, Identity and Development.

62 The syllabus, written in English and Bhutia, includes courses like: BHU-UG-C401 Ethnology and Genealogy: A historical study of Sikkimese rulers and Bhutia community; BHU-UG-C402 Religious History of Sikkim (Ethnology and Genealogy: A historical studies of dissemination of Buddhism Sikkim; early middle and later spread); BHU-UG-C601 A Brief Political History of Sikkim.

63 Michael Aris, who tutored the children of Bhutan's king in the late 60s and early 70s and later became a SOAS and Oxford scholar, is usually regarded as the pioneer in this regard.

converging interest of historians and Buddhologists in a country established and functioning as a Vajrayāna theocracy up to the early twentieth century has enabled the relatively early identification of legal instruments and notions as part of non-legal research projects.[64] Even so, as specialist in contemporary Bhutanese law R. Whitecross stresses, most of the archival research is still to be conducted and pre-modern Bhutanese law remains insufficiently studied and understood.[65] Currently, there is no published catalogue of historical legal documents. The Bhutan National Legal Institute (founded in 2007) only holds a small collection of contemporary books, journals, magazines and research publications related to judiciary praxis. Although the National Library and Archives of Bhutan (founded in 1967) possesses a Choekey (Classical Tibetan) database of more than 130,000 entries on history, religion and culture, it has not yet arranged a specific collection dedicated to legal texts and manuscripts.[66]

An important step in enabling the study of Bhutan's old laws is the very recent (2019) translation and introduction by M. Windischgraetz and Rinzin Wangdi of a mid-seventeenth century legal code. It is preserved in a slate inscription in Punakha, is traditionally attributed to Bhutan's founder Zhabdrung Ngawang Namgyal (b. 1594, d. 1651)[67] and considered to be the first general legal instrument to rule the incipient Himalayan

---

64 E.g.: White (1909: 301–310); Aris (1979: XX–XXIII, 229, 262–263; the main legal text was included in a microfilm and later appeared in printed publications); Aris (1994: 36–37); Imaeda (1986: 55–60); Pommaret (1997: 198–200).

65 Simoni and Whitecross (2004: 170); Whitecross (2017: 87–97).

66 The digitization of documents is part of the broader DANIDA project between the National Library of Bhutan and the Royal Library of Denmark, which started in 1996. In 2002, the National Library website (www.library.gov.bt) was launched. According to Professor Sørensen, involved in the project: 'By now, the entire collection of indigenous books and manuscripts at the library and many collections throughout the country have been inventoried; during our work on location we have traced a good number of rare texts' (Hazod 2015: XX). For an overview of the history of the library, see extensively Shaw (2013).

67 Both dating and authorship remain disputed. It is well-known that the Zhabdrung's death was occulted for fifty years. Ardussi has argued either 1651 (2009: xix) or 1652 (2016), while Windischgraetz establishes a range up to 1708 (Windischgraetz 2019: 10–11). It could of course be the case that the code was composed much earlier than the inscription.

country.[68] The text has been characterized mainly as an 'Administrative code' inspired both by the ideology and structure of the Tibetan Empire, although it also contains some rules and duties for commoners (whose legal affairs are considered by the authors to be have been mostly regulated by oral customary law), principally related to taxation.[69] Thus we find the notions of law as a Golden Yoke (gser gyi gnya' shing), the Dual – lay and religious – System of Government (in varied expressions such as lugs gnyis kyi, bstan srid, and chos srid), reference to the lawgiver as a *chos rgyal* (dharma king) associated with Songtsen Gampo, and allusions to the five precepts and the sixteen pure laws of conduct.[70] The Zhabdrung is also attributed with the composition of an earlier monastic code (bca' yig, 1614) for his monasteries[71] and the development of rules of etiquette for

68 Some texts also refer to *srgis rnam gzhag* (regulation of order) as a primary legal frame established by the Zhabdrung. It is unclear if this is an allusion to the Punakha Code, to monastic regulations or to any possible earlier 'lay' legal instrument (Aris 2009: 130–131, 167; Windischgraetz 2019: 11–12).

69 Windischgraetz identifies as the main administrative model the *Section on Law and State*: a chapter on Tibetan imperial law and administration by Pawo Tsuglag Threngwa (dpa' bo gtsug lag phreng ba, b. 1503/04, d. 1566) found a mid-sixteenth century text entitled *mkhas pa'i dga' ston* (*A Scholars' Feast*) (Windischgraetz 2019: 14). According to her division of the code in paragraphs, their content could be summarized as follows: 1–3: ideological legitimation (golden yoke, benefitting sentient beings, Songtsen Gampo); 4: six laws of the great incarnate king; 5–7: administrative positions and duties; 8: respect of monastic rules of the Drukpa school; 9: importance of knowledge and craftsmanship; 10: lawsuits; 11: five precepts and sixteen pure laws as the essence of law; 12: duties of officials; 13: duties of commoners; 14: administration of Dzong khan; 15–22: administrative positions, duties and structure (including 19: decision of lawsuits); 23: lawsuits fees and punishment principles; 24–25: duties of religious persons; 26: duties of store-keepers; 27–29: sixteen pure rules of human conduct; 30–32: rules for commoners (taxes, economic compensation, prohibition of foreigners, funeral rites); 33: general request of compliance with the code (Windischgraetz and Wangdi 2019: 25–40).

70 See paragraphs 6, 8 and 20. On the dual system in Bhutan, see Ardussi (2005).

71 The code was composed in 1614 for the Ralung Monastery (Tibet) and then implemented in the Cheri Monastery (Bhutan) in 1620 (Imaeda 1986: 65; Aris 1979: 215).

officials and public events (*driglam namzha*) that would be extended in the twentieth century to the whole population as a national ethos.[72]

The 1729 bka' khrims, the other located medieval legal code, was translated by M. Aris in 1979 and later included in his *Sources for the History of Bhutan* (1986, 2009).[73] The text was commissioned by the tenth Druk Desi Mipham Wangpo (b. 1709, d. 1738) and included in a historical work entitled *Lho'i chos 'byung* (*Dharma History of the Southlands,* 1731–1759). This code, longer in length, is also dedicated to matters of public administration. According to Aris' division, the first part explains the principles of 'theocratic rule' employing the common Tibetan Buddhist tropes mentioned above, followed by two extensive sections on the duties of rulers and ministers, and the duties of government officials. Cüppers has found parallelisms in a Tibetan document titled *Guidelines for Government Officials* drafted in 1681 by the fifth Dalai Lama's regent, Desi Sangye Gyatso.[74] Ardussi notes that Mipham Wangpo states that his composition draws from earlier material, namely a Bhutanese law code issued by the first Druk Desi Tenzin Drukgye (b. 1591, d. 1656); and also, that a biography of the fourth Desi Tenzin Rabgye (b. 1638, d. 1698) attributes the Zhabdrung with the composition of a code entitled *A Clear Mirror of the Dual System* (*lugs gnyis kyi bka' khrims gtsang ma'i me long*). These have not yet been found.[75]

The succeeding periods are considered less productive from a legal point of view. Leaving aside taxation measures and minor penal reforms, and despite the relevance of the establishment of the hereditary monarchy in 1907 by means of an agreement (*genja* or *bagen*) signed by the state

72 For the relationship between these two elements, see: Aris (2009: 167, n. 35); Phuntsho (2015); Phuntsho (2004: 572–573). For its contemporary efficacy and criticism, see Whitecross (2017b).

73 Aris (2009: 122–168). A summarized translation can be found in Appendix I, 'The Laws of Bhutan', in White (1909: 301–310).

74 The whole Tibetan title reads: *Glang dor gsal bar slon pa'i drang thig dwangs shel me long nyer gcig pa*. See extensively Cüppers (2007). Whitecross also suggests similarities with other Tibetan works like the *Lde'u Chronicles* and the aforementioned *A Scholars' Feast* (Whitecross 2017a: 95).

75 Ardussi (2009: XV).

councilors, high lamas and officials, and supported by the British[76], there were no significant legal innovations until the appearance of the Supreme Law Code (Thrimzhung Chenmo, 1953–1959), marking the beginning of the modern legal era in Bhutan.[77]

Portrayals from the branches of government

The contemporary institutional design of the kingdom of Bhutan is the result of a series of reforms starting in the late 1950s and leading up to the Constitution of 2008, which self-describes the regime as a 'Democratic Constitutional Monarchy' respecting the separation of powers.[78]

The king and the legislature

The figure of the king (Druk Gyalpo) is largely transformed through devolution and mainly exercises a symbolic or representative role as head of state, embodying the union of Chhoe-sid-nyi (dual system of dharma and politics).[79] However, he still holds notable political functions called 'royal prerogatives', such as granting amnesty or, more importantly, commanding bills and other measures to be introduced in parliament.[80] He is actually part of the parliament under Article 10 of the Constitution. The

76 Signed in Punakha on 17 December 1907 presided by the Zhabdrung's seal (White 1909: 224–230; Aris 1994: 94–98).

77 Whitecross (2017a: 98–100). The Nationality Act of 1958, ending servitude and slavery, was also a milestone in this phase. On the Thrimzhung Chenmo, see Whitecross (2004).

78 For a summary on 'constitutional' developments in Bhutan, see Hecker (1970: 22–32); a lauditory work on Bhutan's top-down and peaceful democratic transition is Gallenkamp (2012). See also Miele (2017).

79 Articles 1.2, 1.3, 2.1, 2.2 of the Constitution of Bhutan.

80 2.16. 'The Druk Gyalpo, in exercise of His Royal Prerogatives, may: (a) Award titles, decorations, dar for Lhengye and Nyi-Kyelma in accordance with tradition and custom; (b) Grant citizenship, land kidu and other kidus; (c) Grant amnesty, pardon and reduction of sentences; (d) Command Bills and other measures to be introduced in Parliament; and (e) Exercise powers relating to matters which are not provided for under this Constitution or other laws'. The king is also in charge of formally appointing most official positions under Article 2.10.

present and first constitutional king, Jigme Khesar Namgyel Wangchuck,[81] declared,

> Many hundreds of years ago, Zhabdrung Ngawang Namgyal unified the nation, established the dual system and laid the foundations on which a unique Bhutan was born. This new nation was then further strengthened over the course of history by fifty-four Desis and generations of Bhutanese. The last hundred years, the Wangchuck dynasty further strengthened the foundations laid by the Zhabdrung and handed over a special Nation to our People in 2008. All of this was possible because our People have lived as one small family, true to the ideals of the Zhabdrung and the foundations of a unique and special Bhutanese identity.[82]

Besides the king, the legislature consists of two representative chambers, the National Council and the National Assembly. The National Council is the upper house, mainly composed of members directly elected from each of the twenty *dzongkhags* (districts).[83] Its website contains a list of Bhutanese acts displayed in alphabetical order, the earliest being the Thrimzhung Chenmo (1953) and the Nationality Act (1958).[84] There is no account or reference to older or 'historical' legal instruments, though such may be found in articles appearing in *NC Reflections*, the periodical publication of the National Council mainly aimed at rendering law-making and constitutional issues accessible to citizens. Namely, Justice Kuenlay Tshering (Supreme Court), in a series of articles on the constitution and the legal system, resorts to the tropes of the origin of the legal system in the Zhabdrung's code, the Buddhist inspiration of law and politics (lha chos dge ba bcu [Ten virtuous acts] and mi chos gtsang ma bcu drug [Sixteen deeds of social piety]) and the continuation represented in the monarchy,

---

81 The fifth king of Bhutan accessed the throne upon the abdication of his father Jigme Singye Wangchuck, responsible for the democratic transition, in 2006 and was formally crowned on 6 November 2008.

82 Namgyal Wangchuck (2012).

83 Article 11 of the Constitution of Bhutan.

84 https://www.nationalcouncil.bt/en/business/acts

even suggesting that both the rule of law and democracy may be traced back to the very inception of the country and progressively enhanced by the kings.[85] Thus, these papers, manifestly more informative than scholarly in nature, create a narrative in which the distant legal past is tainted with contemporary notions of law and justice and is linked with a legal present allegedly dharma-based by the constitutionalization of the dual system and Buddhism as the spiritual heritage of Bhutan.

The lower house, firstly established in 1953 and constitutionalized in 2008, is called the National Assembly and is composed of up to forty-seven members who are directly elected by the citizens of constituencies within each *dzongkhag*.[86] The annual publication of the National Assembly is called *The Legislative Journal*, described as a 'high quality publication bringing in analytical views, opinions and reflections from a broad section of democratic, legislative and legal fraternity'.[87] Legal history does not seem, so far, a prominent topic, but when addressed, it is with a similar angle to the above seen rhetoric. The arrival of Guru Rinpoche and the Zhabdrung is characterized as 'miraculous', bringing Buddhism, and law and peace, respectively.[88] The link with the present is again stated:

> He [the Zhabdrung] brought peace, security and stability to the country by establishing a strong and dynamic administrative system and by codifying a set of strict but fair and just laws of such enduring values based on the Buddhist tradition that they have formed the framework for the present judicial system of Bhutan.[89]

The National Assembly possesses a library holding newspapers, government publications, acts of the Kingdom of Bhutan and legislative books,

85 Tshering (2009a: esp. 23; 2009b: 32; 2010: 6).

86 Article 12 of the Constitution. On the history of the chamber, see Mathou (2000: 237 ff).

87 *Terms of Reference. Legislative Journal and Editorial Board*, online at http://www.nab.gov.bt/assets/uploads/docs/download/2017/Terms_of_Reference_of_LJ_and_Board.pdf

88 Om and Dema (2017: 1–2); Dorji (2017: 6).

89 Dorji (2017: 8).

among other material, but it does not have a collection dedicated to legal or political history.[90]

The executive

Article 20 of the Bhutanese Constitution establishes that the executive power is vested upon the Lhengye Zhungtshog, consisting of the ministers and the prime minister, who is the head of the government and is elected by the people every five years. In the current ministerial composition, there is no ministry of justice (such functions are assumed by the Royal Court of Justice); while the Ministry of Home and Cultural Affairs does not include legal matters among its publications.[91] Neither are there any references to 'old laws' in the website of the cabinet.[92]

The judiciary

Bhutan's judiciary, composed of the Supreme Court, the High Court, the Dzongkhag Courts, and any other courts that may be established, is collectively referred to as The Royal Court of Justice.[93] The judiciary offers a wider and more technical array of publications compared to the other branches of government, ranging from annual reports and speeches, to papers and specialized books. In its online collection of *Acts and Rules*, the earliest act listed is the Thrimzhung Chenmo,[94] while its entry 'Introduction to the Bhutanese Legal System' traces its origins back to the Zhabdrung, though it is actually the Thrimzhung Chenmo that is regarded as the 'first comprehensive codified law code, [...] the basis

90 See the only introductory entry on the library at http://www.nab.gov.bt/en/library/introduction. The library is a recent project, still developing. On this issue, see Dem (2013).

91 These include themes related mainly to architecture and environmental issues. (http://www.mohca.gov.bt/index.php/publications-2/)

92 https://www.cabinet.gov.bt/the-cabinet/functions-of-the-cabinet/

93 Article 21 of the Constitution of Bhutan.

94 http://www.judiciary.gov.bt/index.php/Welcome/get_pages?id=4

for all the subsequent laws enacted in Bhutan'.[95] Foremost among the materials published by the judiciary are the articles and books written by two prominent judicial figures who were members of the Constitution Drafting Committee: Sonam Tobgye and Lungten Dubgyur.[96] Though they do not focus on legal history, their publications on contemporary legal issues rely on the same notion of Bhutan as a dharma democracy dating back to the seventeenth century and defended by Kuenlay Tshering. Thus, Sonam Tobgye sustains that Bhutan 'has always expounded the rule of law', which he associates with the Buddhist concept of '*uppeka*', and describes the Zhabdrung's code and regime as a federal system enshrining the separation of powers.[97] At times, his consideration of historical and philosophical influences also encompasses wider Indian elements such as Garuda Purana, Tak Shastra (*sic*) or Paninian Grammar, though Buddhism is still regarded as the main influence.[98] This idea may be observed in

---

95 The description goes as follows: 'Zhabdrung Ngawang Namgyal promulgated the first set of Bhutanese laws and codification of these laws was completed in 1652 [...]. The Code was based closely on Buddhist principles and addressed the violation of both temporal and spiritual laws. These laws contain specific reference to the ten pious acts, known as Lhachoe Gyewa Chu and the sixteen virtuous acts of social piety, referred to as the Michoe Tsangma Chudrug'. http://www.judiciary.gov.bt/index.php/Welcome/get_pages?id=2

96 The Honorable Lyonpo Sonam Tobgye is former chief justice of both the High Court (1991–2009) and the Supreme Court (2010–2014). He was the chairman of the Constitution Drafting Committee. He also served as chief advisor to the interim government from 28 April to 27 July 2013. 'Chief Justice of Supreme Court retires', 15 November 2014 (https://thebhutanese.bt/chief-justice-of-supreme-court-retires/).

Lyonpo Lungten Dubgyur pursued postgraduate studies in information technology law and intellectual property law at the Edinburgh Law School. He has participated in drafting several laws, such as the Direct and Indirect Taxation Act of Bhutan. Before joining his current position as High Court judge, he served as judge of the Paro District Court.

97 He also argues that 'The Constitution of Bhutan is the culmination of the constitutional culture that existed in Bhutan since 1907' (Tobgye 2014a: 3–4; 2014b: 6). At the same time, he considers the Bhutanese legal system to have a long traditional background based not only on the Zhabdrung's code but on what he calls Buddhist natural law (Tobgye 2013: 10).

98 The author mentions 'Tsema Namdruel or Tak Shastra', which is most probably a misguided reference to Indian Logics. Tsema Namdruel seems to be *Tshad ma*

Lungten Dubgyur's interpretation of criminal judicial procedure in the light of Karma Lingpa's Bardo Thodrel (*sic*), suggesting that certain elements pre-date their Western equivalents.[99] The best example, however, of the dharma democracy construct is the institution of kingship: the alleged elective legitimacy of the first king would make him a Mahāsammata,[100] while the notion of constitutional monarchy, rather than a freshly imported idea, would find its roots in the consideration of Bhutanese kings as dharma rajas (*chos rgyal*).[101]

These statements endorsed by the judiciary, though garnished with both Western and Buddhist philosophical references, are not supported by any sort of textual analysis or historiographical research.

Local scholarship and higher education

Legal history is not a predominant topic among Bhutanese scholars. There is no monographic and systematic approach to the origins and development of legal sources and institutions in the country. We do find, though, references to such topics in either general and political history books or in publications on contemporary legal issues.[102]

Among historians, authors writing in classical Tibetan, like Phuntso Wangdu, typically adopt a traditional or local scholastic take focusing on the reception of Indian and Tibetan culture and the description of lay and religious lineages. Wangdu's recent *'brug gi rgyal rabs* contains scarce

---

rnam 'grel (i.e. Dharmakīrti's *Pramāṇavārttika*), while Tak Shastra appears to be a corrupted form of *tarkaśāstra* (Tobgye n.d.1: 5).

99 Dubgyur (2003). See Whitecross (2009: 208 ff) for a critical assessment of the recent use of Buddhist iconography in the trial system.

100 The *Aggañña Sutta* narrates the mythical origin of the world and mankind, and relates the election of the first king, Mahāsammata, as a means to protect against violations of the recently acquired property of rice fields. Its primary political significance is still highly controversial, ranging from contractualist readings (Sharma 1996: 49; Rogers Macy 1979: 48) to religious apolitical approaches (Collins 1983: 387). The historical invocations of this figure with varied purposes are addressed in Collins and Huxley (1996).

101 Tobgye (2014c: 3, 37).

102 For an overview of Bhutanese scholarship with an emphasis on history and anthropology, see Pommaret (2002) and Penjore (2013).

legal references to Ngawang Namgyal establishing the dual system (*lugs gnyis kyi khrims*) or to the first Desi Tenzin Drukgye uniting 'previous royal law' (*sngon gyi rgyal khrims*) with the 'pure proper customs of religious laws' (*chos khrims gtsang ma'i srol bzang*).[103]

A prevalently modern approach may be found in works written in English by Western-educated scholars. Young political scientist Kezang Wangchuk stands as a rara avis, proposing a reading of the *genja*, the founding agreement establishing the Bhutanese monarchy, in Hobbesian terms.[104] Sonam Kinga dedicates one section of his *Polity, Kingship and Democracy. A Biography of the Bhutanese State* (2009) to 'Kathrim - codification of Laws'.[105] Drawing almost exclusively from Aris (1986), he presents the 1729 Code as both the first written formalization of previous functioning laws, and the first political treatise published in Bhutan.[106] He also strives to legitimize both the Zhabdrung and the first king as well as their actions following the Buddhist models of Mahāsammata and the Cakravartin, employing an undisguised religious language.[107] A more tempered and descriptive tone is used by Karma Phuntsho, first Bhutanese doctor by Oxford University, who states in his *History of Bhutan* that the monastic code of etiquette (*cha yig*) composed by the Zhabdrung,

> became the core of the religious law and ecclesiastical rules and regulations in his new state. Zhabdrung's secular law, following the

---

103 Wangdu (2007: 26–28, 83).

104 Wangchuk (2015).

105 Kinga (2009: 95–101). Dasho Sonam Kinga obtained a BA in English from Sherubtse College (Bhutan) and a MA and a PhD in Area Studies from Kyoto University. He served as deputy chairperson to the National Council between 2008 and 2013. https://www.nationalcouncil.bt/en/content/former-members; https://www.pearsoncollege.ca/alumnus-dasho-dr-sonam-kinga-awarded-red-scarf-by-his-majesty-the-king-of-bhutan/

106 Sonam Kinga's work, written before Ardussi reedited Aris' *Sources for the History of Bhutan*, seems to somehow imply that the code carved in Punakha and the 1729 Code are the same text (Kinga 2009: 101).

107 Kinga (2009: 19–30). He writes 'Zhabdrung Rinpoche was a Boddhisattva, he was the embodiment of the militant Buddha of Compassion called Lokesvara. Unleashing violent means for territorial defence and expansion with a Boddhisattva mind however, was nothing anti-dharmic' (Kinga 2009: 23).

> example of Songtsen Gampo's legal codes, was based on 'the sixteen pure laws of man' [...] and 'the ten virtuous laws of gods' [...]. However, no separate legal document seems to have been written until 1729 and the law was enforced through unwritten understanding and through edicts, ordinances and regulations on the behaviour of officers, taxation, etc. [...] His dual system was partially styled on Tibetan precedents of hereditary religious families, including the Gya establishment in Ralung.[108]

Regarding legal scholarship, allusions to Bhutan's legal history are even scarcer and more succinct. As an example, the already mentioned Justice Lungten Dubgyur's 2015 book on Bhutan's recent constitutionalism, edited by Queensland Magistrate Annette M. Hennessey, only provides a laconic reference to the Zhabdrung's establishment of the Dual System and enactment of the Chayig Chhenmo drawing from ecclesiastical law.[109] The first chapter of the book, however, in line with his publications in the Royal Court of Bhutan, is fully dedicated to associating contemporary constitutional legitimacy with the Buddhist myth of the first king, who is presented as a champion of democracy, equality and redistributive justice.[110]

Higher education is a relatively recent phenomenon in Bhutan,[111] especially regarding law and legal practice. Traditionally, legal operators would acquire a monastic education, or just be locally legitimized regardless of their formal instruction. Only since the late twentieth century have they started to receive institutional training, typically in India. The Jigme Singye Wangchuck School of Law (JSW Law) started operating in July 2017. Created by a royal charter, the law school is considered an 'autonomous tertiary educational institution', and so it falls outside the

108 Phuntsho (2013: 874–875).

109 Dubgyur (2015: 31).

110 Most of the chapter is a commentary to *Aggañña Sutta* in order to conclude that: 'The Constitution of Bhutan places a sacrosanct role of our monarchs. It pivots our foundation of society particularly based upon the legal order of *Mangpo Kurwai Gyalpo* [Mahāsammata]. It is based on voluntarism, elective and democratic process' (Dubgyur 2015: 13).

111 The first college officially recognized was Sherubtse College, founded by Jesuit W. Mackey. In 2003 it was incorporated into the Royal University of Bhutan.

scope of ordinary university regulation and the comprehensive structure of the Royal University of Bhutan.[112] This has meant that the school has enjoyed great freedom in designing its curricula and syllabi.[113] In this regard, international assistance and participation should not be overlooked. United States law firm White & Case, as well as both American (namely, Stanford and George Washington University) and European (namely the University of Vienna) universities have contributed in different ways to the funding and development of the law school; so has the Indian Government, whose model of legal education has served as an inspiration.[114]

The only current operating program is a five-year undergraduate degree in law (LL.B.). Bhutan Legal History (eighteen units) is a first-year compulsory subject, split into an English and a Dzongkha module.[115] The English module, designed by Prof. Windischgraetz, takes an Indo-Tibetan Buddhist approach, starting with an overview of ancient Indian law and society and law at the time of the Buddha, followed by the development of law in Tibet from the imperial era up to the Phagmodrupa period. Then, specific Bhutanese sources are addressed, focusing on the Zhabdrung Code as the only written sample, while exploring varied regulatory topics developed orally (e.g., punishment; mediation and dispute settlement; marriage and divorce; taxes and corvée labor).[116] The Dzongkha module focuses on legal history from the time of the first king onwards. Students are also exposed to Buddhist logic and debate, as well as to a subject

112 The law school is bound by Bhutan's 'Bhutan Qualifications Framework. Point of Reference and Tertiary Education Qualifications in Bhutan' (BQF, 2012) and its 'Tertiary Education Policy' (TEP; Ministry of Education 2010). Neither document refers to required subjects or contents for specific degrees.

113 Under the Statutes for the Law School (2016), the Governing Council approves the curriculum and module descriptors, while the Academic Council approves individual syllabi.

114 Davis (2018: 28–31). Considering the people involved in the project, the president of the school is Princess Sonam Dechan Wangchuck, a Stanford graduate and LL.M. graduate of Harvard Law School; and the vice dean is Prof. Michael Peil, Doctor of Law by Cornell University and former associate dean for international programs at Washington University School of Law.

115 The whole structure of subjects (curriculum) is available online at: https://www.jswlaw.bt/academics/coursework-2/curriculum/

116 Syllabus kindly provided by Prof. Windischgraetz.

exploring the relationship between law and religion.[117] A second year course on jurisprudence and statutory interpretation, taught by Dr. Stefan Hammer and Tenzin Leewan, addresses common trends in Western legal thought, such as natural law and legal positivism, but contextualizes them in Bhutan.[118]

The BA in Political Science and Sociology program offered by Sherubtse College also tackles legal history issues in its module titled Political History of Bhutan (PBT101). Providing an outline that starts from the eighth century, the only explicit approach to pre-modern law takes place in a section on legal codification during the Zhabdrung's unification period.[119]

There are also legal courses offered by non-university institutions, the paradigm being the National Legal Course for Judicial Service Personnel.[120] This course takes a Buddhist traditional and linguistic angle (qualification in legal Dzongkha stands as a major need),[121] including, alongside modern Bhutanese Law, subjects such as Pramana (Logic), while leaving out legal history considerations.[122] The Bhutan National

---

117 Year 3: Tsema (Buddhist logic and debate) (eighteen units); Year 3: Law, Religion & Culture.

118 The syllabus reads: 'The entire course will be taught in the Bhutanese context, wherever possible, the examples from Bhutan will be used. For instance, the historic Genja of 1907 will be the basis to teach Hobbes' Theory of Social Contract'. LAW 203. Syllabus kindly provided by Prof. Peil.

119 PBT101: Political History of Bhutan is a first-year course. Specifically, Unit I (Ancient and medieval Bhutan), section 5.1.3. Establishment of Dual System-The Dharma and Desids, Administration and Codification of Laws. The reading list does not provide any primary sources; Kinga (2009) and Phuntsho (2013) are given as major secondary sources.

120 The National Legal course is also taken by aspiring *jabmis*, recently professionalized traditional legal intermediaries (Whitecross 2007).

121 Simoni (2003).

122 The curriculum includes Dzongkha and Buddhist classical language courses, Madhyamaka and the study of texts such as *A Guide to Bodhisattva's way*. As explained in the education and research section of the judiciary website: 'National Legal Course is established for pre-service and in-service training of the Judicial Service Personnel to meet the human resource requirements of the Judiciary. The Courses ensures pre-service and continuing legal education with special emphasis on ethics, morality and traditional values. There are two levels

Legal Institute, operating since 2011 and devoted to 'continuing judicial and legal education', also assumes research and publishing as part of its aims. Its publication, *Bhutan Law Review*, though, has not yet published any paper on pre-constitutional law.[123]

Conclusions: feudal tyranny vs democratic Shangri-la

Conventionalism (or constructivism) is a long-accepted component of national history, up to the point that such provocative terms as Hobsbawm's invention or Anderson's imagination are now commonplace. This means that countries are typically assumed to move within a wide space of options and possibilities when presenting their history, in this case, their legal history. This conventionalism encourages enquiring into the choices made before other potential alternatives, and the reasons behind them.

In this paper, the main section titles were phrased as interrogations in order to open up for questioning the assumed representations of Sikkim's past in terms of disruption and Bhutan's past in terms of continuity with their own respective histories. In this regard, we have seen how Sikkim's institutions generally tend to show a lack of interest in pre-1970s law, and when old or founding laws are addressed, they are presented in an unfavorable light, as a dark retrograde past that needs to be left behind. Within this logic, the remaining customary laws and institutions are preserved according to the Anglo-Indian category of Scheduled Tribes, i.e., in terms of their belonging to societies in a different state of evolution compared to the main society, not based upon the historical or 'national' respectability of such elements. Even more explicitly, local scholars (none of whom are legal historians) share a certain narrative focused on merger as a means to conquer democracy and put an end to a feudal, oppressive and theocratical regime. There are, therefore, distinctive elements con-

of entry: 1. Two years course after completion of Class XII for Bench Clerk; and 2. 18 months course after completion of LLB degree for lawyers' (http://www.judiciary.gov.bt/publication/course.php). See Tobgye (n.d.2: 8–10).

123 There are currently seven volumes published (from 2013 to 2017), the last one in Dzongkha. They are all available online at: http://www.bnli.bt/index.php/resources-2/publication/

firming a common narrative of rupture with the past. Bhutan seems also to persistently corroborate the idea of an unbroken line that links its contemporary frame with its very inception. Bhutanese political bodies, educational institutions and scholars typically take the Zhabdrung as the founding father and his code as the foundational law, the Buddhist philosophy and influence of which would clearly manifest in contemporary law.

At the same time, these narratives are neither monolithic nor impermeable to possible alternative representations. The emblem of the State Government of Sikkim, the Kham-sum-Wangdu, traditionally used by the ruling Namgyal dynasty, is filled with Buddhist iconography. Sikkim's legislature and judiciary admit a pre-merger origin and a progressive modernization, which excludes a radical break, while the current reservation of seats at the Sikkimese Assembly for Bhutias and Lepchas is not only associable with the last *chogyal's* parity formula for the State Council but with the very seventeenth century foundational *Lho mon gtsong gsum*. Similarly, there are instances of Bhutanese institutions and officials referring to the fairly recent Thrimzhung Chenmo (1953) as the first 'comprehensive codified law code' from which the current system evolved. The monarchic transformation at the turn of the twentieth century or even the democratic transition of 2008 may easily be interpreted as discontinuing events, yet they are not locally presented in that light. An illustrative example in this regard is the lack of monastic seats in the allegedly continuist Buddhist-inspired Bhutanese legislature, while there is a seat reserved for the Buddhist sangha in the supposedly breaking modern and lay Legislative Assembly of Sikkim.

In this regard, Sikkim's and Bhutan's narratives may be interpreted as diverging strategies to deal with different political scenarios and social compositions: a 'Nepalized' Sikkim within the Indian Union, which seems to 'need' a story of democratic rupture; versus an independent, still 'Vajrayāna-centered', yet highly transformed Bhutan, which seems to 'need' a flowing national story rooted in the distant past. These interests may explain the radical and extremely opposed depictions of what most probably was, *mutatis mutandis*, a fairly similar medieval legal-political scenario: Sikkim as a cruel feudal theocracy and Bhutan as a democratic Shangri-la. Besides the clear anachronisms, and despite these contrasts,

Sikkim and Bhutan share important elements in their approach to legal history. Scholarly specialized research is meagre and overwhelmingly foreign, while legal history occupies a marginal place in Sikkimese higher education and is only very recently, and with the significant support of foreign scholars, a part of Bhutanese college education. In the case of Sikkim, the lack of interest in old legislation might have a partial prosaic explanation in Article 371 F of the Indian Constitution requiring explicit abrogation for pre-merger laws.[124] However, this legitimizing invocation of old laws without the support of serious textual and historical scholarship shared by both countries[125] raises interesting questions regarding the notion, perception and use of law in traditional Buddhist Himalayas, an issue that falls beyond the scope of this paper.

Sikkim and Bhutan are no longer isolated Himalayan kingdoms, but multi-ethnic political entities striving to efficaciously navigate a globalized world while preserving a sense of identity. In a sense, they face the same dilemmas and issues encountered by European and American countries in the era of nation-building and legal codification, when the tensions between traditional or national identity, on the one hand, and democratic change and commercial fluidity, on the other, characterized legal debates and draftings. In such a context, Western governments, lawyers and scholars undertook a highly functional and pragmatic approach, representing traditional elements as modern and 'rational' or laying a patina of long-rooted traditionalism over modern imported elements: what Whitecross calls the 'Buddhicization' of Bhutanese law, which refers to the presentation of contemporary mostly Anglo-Indian based law as drawing from ancient Buddhist elements, on the one hand;[126] or the legitimation of the contested and controversial reservation of legislative seats for two Tibeto-Burman ethno-linguistic groups and Buddhist monastics in Sikkim based on British categories such as Scheduled Tribes and on the modern Western discourse of protection of minorities and indigenous peoples

124 This was noticed early on, e.g., regarding the orders of the *chogyal* (Bhattacharjee 1978).

125 In the case of Sikkim, the use ceased upon merger with India.

126 Whitecross (2009: esp. 208–211; 2013: 139).

instead of on historical arguments, on the other[127] – both seem to follow the very same strategies.

Bibliography

Acharya, C. (1995). 'Guru Padmasamhbhava's Contribution: The Genesis of Buddhism in Sikkim', *Bulletin of Tibetology*, vol. 31, no. 1, pp. 19–24.

Ardussi, J. (2005). 'Formation of the State of Bhutan ('Brug gzhung) in the 17th Century and its Tibetan Antecedents'. In C. Cüppers, ed., *Proceedings of the Seminar on the Relationship Between Religion and State (chos srid zung 'brel) in Traditional Tibet: Lumbini 4-7 March 2000*, Lumbini: Lumbini International Research Institute, pp. 10–32.

Ardussi, J. (2009). 'Introduction'. In M. Aris, ed., *Sources for the History of Bhutan*, New Delhi: Motilal Banarsidass.

Ardussi, J. (2011). 'Sikkim and Bhutan in the Crosscurrents of 17th and 18th Century Tibetan History'. In A. McKay and A. Balikci-Denjongpa, eds., *Buddhist Himalaya: Studies in Religion, History and Culture. Proceedings of the Golden Jubilee Conference of the Namgyal Institute of Tibetology, Gangtok. 2008. Volume II. The Sikkim Papers*, Gangtok: Namgyal Institute of Tibetology, pp. 29–42.

Ardussi, J. (2016). 'The Traditional Institutions of Governance in Bhutan Before 1907 and Their Modification with the Coming of the Monarchy', *The Druk Journal. A Journal of Thought and Ideas*, accessed at http://drukjournal.bt/the-traditioonal-institutions-of-governance-in-bhutan-before-1907-and-their-modification-with-the-coming-of-he-monarchy/

Aris, M. (1979). *Bhutan. The Early History of a Himalayan Kingdom*, Warminster: Aris & Phillips.

Aris, M. (1994). 'Conflict and Conciliation in Traditional Bhutan'. In M. Hutt, ed., *Bhutan: Perspectives on Conflict and Dissent*, Gartmore: Kiscadale, pp. 21–42.

Aris, M. (2005). *The Raven Crown: The Origins of Buddhist Monarchy in Bhutan*, London: Serindia Publications.

Aris, M. (2009). *Sources for the History of Bhutan*, New Delhi: Motilal Banarsidass.

Aris, M. (2010). *Hidden Treasures & Secret Lives*, London/New York: Routledge.

Arora, V. (2006). 'Roots and the Route of Secularism in Sikkim', *Economic and Political Weekly*, vol. 41, no. 38, pp. 4063–4071.

Balikci, A. (2008). *Lamas, Shamans and Ancestors: Village Religion in Sikkim*, Boston: Brill.

Banerjea, D. (2005). *Criminal Justice India Series. Volume 18. Sikkim*, Kolkata: Allied Publishers.

127 See the discussions in Arora (2006) and Subha (2013).

Bashin, V. (2012). 'Social Organization, Continuity and Change: The Case of the Bhutias of Lachen and Lachung of North Sikkim', *Journal of Biodiversity*, vol. 3, no. 1, pp. 1–43.

Basnet, L.B. (1974). *Sikkim: A Short Political History*, New Delhi: S. Chand.

Bhattacharjee, A.M. (1978). 'Law of Sikkim. Orders of the Former Ruler', *Sikkim Law Journal*, vol. 2, no. 19, pp. 1–6.

Bhattacharjee, A.M. (1984). 'Foreword'. In Law Department, Government of Sikkim, ed., *The Sikkim Code. Volume I*, Gangtok: The Gangtok Press.

Bhutia, R.T. (2017): 'Legal Rights of Sikkimese Women', *International Journal of Recent Scientific Research*, vol. 8, no. 12, pp. 22110–22114.

Bourder-Sabatier, S. (2004). 'The Dzumsa of Lachen: An Example of a Sikkimese Political Institution', *Bulletin of Tibetology*, vol. 40, no. 1, pp. 92–104.

Central Intelligence Agency (2019). 'South Asia. Bhutan', *The World Factbook*, accessed at https://www.cia.gov/library/publications/the-world-factbook/geos/bt.html.

Chhetri, D.P. (2012). *Decentralised Governance and Development in India with Special Reference to Sikkim*, New Delhi: Mittal Publications.

Chhetri, D.P. (2013). 'Preserving Cultural Identity through Tribal Self-Governance: The Case of Lachenpa and Lachungpa Tribes of Sikkim Himalaya (India)', *American International Journal of Research in Humanities, Arts and Social Sciences*, vol. 3, no. 1, pp. 23–28.

Collins, S. (1993). 'The Discourse on What is Primary (*Aggañña Sutta*)', *Journal of Indian Philosophy*, vol. 21, no. 4, pp. 301–393.

Collins, S. and A. Huxley (1996). 'The Post-Canonical Adventures of Mahāsammata', *Journal of Indian Philosophy*, vol. 24, no. 6, pp. 623–648.

Das, B.S. (1983). *The Sikkim Saga*, New Delhi: Vikas.

Datta-Ray, S.K. (1984). *Smash & Grab. Annexation of Sikkim*, Delhi: Vikas. (2013 edition published by Tranquebar Press.)

David, R. (1964). *Les grands systèmes de droit contemporains*, Paris: Dalloz.

Dem, T. (2013). 'Library and Archive. For the Love of the World', *The Legislative Journal*, vol. 1, pp. 65–66.

Dorji, K. (2017). 'The Founding and Construction of the Nation State of Bhutan: A Tribute to the Triple Gem of Bhutan', *The Legislative Journal 2016*, vol. 3, pp. 6–17.

Dubgyur, L. (2003). 'The Influence of Buddhism on Bhutanese Trial System', paper presented at a seminar titled 'Nalanda: Interface with Buddhism and Environment, Thimphu, Bhutan', accessed at http://www.judiciary.gov.bt/publication/buddhism.pdf

Dubgyur, L. (2015). *The Wheel of Laws: An Insight into the Origin of Buddhist Kingship, Constitution and Judicial Independence in Bhutan*, Thimphu: Royal Court of Justice, High Court of Bhutan.

Duff, A. (2018). *Sikkim: Requiem for a Himalayan Kingdom*, Edinburgh: Birlinn Limited.

Dukpa, R., D. Joshi and R.A. Boelens (2019). 'Contesting Hydropower Dams in the Eastern Himalaya: The Cultural Politics of Identity, Territory and Self-Governance Institutions in Sikkim, India', *Water*, vol. 11, no. 46, pp. 1–23.

Evans, R. (2010). 'The Perils of Being a Borderland People: On the Lhotshampas of Bhutan', *Contemporary South Asia*, vol. 18, no. 1, pp. 25–42.

Ewald, W. (1995). 'Comparative Jurisprudence (Part I). What Was It Like to Try a Rat?', *University of Pennsylvania Law Review*, vol. 143, no. 6, pp. 1889–2150.

Ferreira de Almeida, C. and J. Morais (2018). *Introducción Al Derecho Comparado*, Santiago de Chile: Ediciones Olejnik.

Fitzherbert, G.S. (2017). 'Law and the Gesar Epic', *Cahiers d'Extrême-Asie*, vol. 26, no. 1, pp. 61–86.

Gallenkamp, M. (2012). 'When Agency Triumphs Over Structure: Conceptualizing Bhutan's Unique Transition to Democracy', *Heidelberg Papers in South Asian and Comparative Politics*, vol. 68, pp. 1–21.

Gurung, S.K. (2011). *Sikkim. Ethnicity and Political Dynamics. A Triadic Perspective*, Delhi: Kunal Books.

Gyatso, J. (1993). 'The Logic of Legitimation in the Tibetan Treasure Tradition', *History of Religions*, vol. 33, no. 2, pp. 97–134.

Hazod, G. (2015). 'Interview with Per K. Sørensen'. In O. Czaja and G. Hazod, eds., *The Illuminating Mirror: Tibetan Studies in Honour of Per K. Sørensen on the Occasion of His 65th Birthday*, Wiesbaden: Dr. Ludwig Reichert Verlag.

Hecker, H. (1970). *Sikkim Und Bhutan; Die Verfassungsgeschichtliche Und Politische Entwicklung Der Indischen Himalaya-Protektorate*, Hamburg and Frankfurt/M.: Forschungsstelle Für Völkerrecht.

Hutt, M. (2005). *Unbecoming Citizens: Culture, Nationhood, and the Flight of Refugees from Bhutan*, New Delhi/Oxford: Oxford University Press.

Imaeda, Y. (1986). 'Le Code de Lois (bka' khrims)'. In *Histoire médiévale du Bhoutan: établissement et évolution de la théocratie des 'Brug pa* (PhD dissertation, Pierre and Marie Curie University), pp. 55–60.

Jansen, B. (2015). *The Monastery Rules: Buddhist Monastic Organization in Pre-Modern Tibet* (PhD dissertation, Leiden University).

Jha, P.K. (1985). *History of Sikkim, 1817–1904: Analysis of British Policy and Activities*, Calcutta: O.P.S. Publishers.

Kharga, M. (2019). 'The Role of Political Parties in Sikkim's Democratic Transition', *International Journal of Research in Social Sciences*, vol. 9, no. 3, pp. 62–78.

Kinga, S. (2009). *Polity, Kingship, and Democracy: A Biography of the Bhutanese State*, Thimphu: Ministry of Education, Royal Government of Bhutan.

Law, D.S. (2018). 'Isolation and Globalization: The Dawn of Legal Education in Bhutan', *Yonsei Law Journal*, vol. 9, pp. 1–35.

Macy, J. (1979). 'Dependent Co-Arising: The Distinctiveness of Buddhist Ethics', *The Journal of Religious Ethics*, vol. 7, no. 1, pp. 38–52.

Marshall, J.G. (2004). *Britain and Tibet 1765-1947: A Select Annotated Bibliography of British Relations with Tibet and the Himalayan States Including Nepal, Sikkim and Bhutan* (1st ed.), London: Routledge.

Mathou, T. (2000). 'The Politics of Bhutan: Change in Continuity', *Journal of Bhutan Studies*, vol. 2, no. 2, pp. 228–262, accessed at www.bhutanstudies.com/pages/journal/2.2_folder/contents.html

McKay, A. (2009, 2010). 'A Difficult Country, a Hostile Chief, and a Still More Hostile Minister: The Anglo-Sikkim War of 1861', *Bulletin of Tibetology*, vol. 45, no. 2; vol. 46, no. 1, pp. 31–49.

McKay, A. (2017). 'The Sikkim Palace Archive Digitisation Project', *The Newsletter*, vol. 76 (Spring), International Institute for Asian Studies, accessed at https://iias.asia/the-newsletter/article/sikkim-palace-archive-digitisation-project

Miele, M. (2017). 'Isolamento ed interdipendenza, tradizione ed impermanenza. Note sul percorso costituzionale del Bhutan', *Annuario Di Diritto Comparato E Di Studi Legislativi*, vol. VIII, pp. 381–404.

Mullard, S. (2010). 'Editorial Introduction: Along the Crossroads of Bhutan and Sikkim', *Bulletin of Tibetology*, Special Issue, vol. 45, no. 2; vol. 46, no. 1, pp. 5–10.

Mullard, S. (2017). 'Regulating Sikkimese Society: The Fifteen-Clause Domestic Settlement (nang 'dum) of 1876'. In S. Mullard and J. Bischof, eds., *Social Regulation: Case Studies from Tibetan History*, Leiden/Boston: Brill, pp. 10–48.

Mullard, S. and H. Wongcuk (2010). *Royal Records: A Catalogue of the Sikkimese Palace Archive*, Andiast: International Institute for Tibetan and Buddhist Studies.

Namgyal Wangchuck, J.K. (2012). 'His Majesty the King's National Day Address to the Nation'. In *Thus Spoke the King. Speeches by His Majesty Jigme Khesar Namgyel Wangchuck, King of Bhutan*, 17 December, accessed at http://no.dou.bt/2012/12/17/kings-speech-national-day-2/

Om, K. and R. Dema (2017). 'The Legacy Still Continues with the Birth of Gyalsey', *The Legislative Journal 2016*, vol. 3, pp. 1–5.

Pattanaik, S. (1998). 'Ethnic Identity, Conflict and Nation Building in Bhutan', *Strategic Analysis*, vol. 22, no. 4, pp. 635–654.

Penjore, D. (2013). 'The State of Anthropology in Bhutan', *Asian and African Area Studies*, vol. 12, no. 2, pp. 147–156.

Phuntsho, K. (2004). 'Echoes of Ancient Ethos: Reflections on Some Popular Bhutanese Social Themes'. In K. Ura and S. Wangdi, eds., *The Spider and the Piglet: Proceedings of the First International Seminar on Bhutan Studies*, Thimphu: Centre for Bhutan Studies, pp. 564–579.

Phuntsho, K. (2013). *The History of Bhutan*, India: Random House.

Phuntsho, K. (2015). 'Driglam Namzha: Bhutan's Code of Etiquette', *Kuensel*, 16 August, accessed at http://www.kuenselonline.com/driglam-namzha-bhutans-code-of-etiquette/

Phuntso Wangdi, D. (2007). *Brug gi rgyal rabs*, Thimphu: National Library and Archives of Bhutan.

Pirie, F. (2013). 'Law and Religion in Historic Tibet'. In F. von Benda-Beckmann, K. von Benda-Beckmann, M. Ramstedt and B. Turner, eds., *Religion in Disputes*, New York: Palgrave Macmillan, pp. 231–247.

Pirie, F. (2017). 'Which "Two Laws"? The Concept of trimnyi (khrims gnyis) in Medieval Tibet', *Cahiers d'Extrême-Asie*, vol. 26, pp. 41–60.

Pirie, F. (2018). 'The Drum of the Law: Symbol of Shamanic Power, Warfare, or Justice?', *Tibetan Law*, 24 July, accessed at http://tibetanlaw.org/node/56.

Pommaret, F. (1997). 'The Birth of a Nation'. In F. Pommaret and C. Schicklgruber, eds., *Bhutan: Mountain-Fortress of the Gods*, London/Vienna: Serindia Publications – Museum für Völkerkunde Wien, pp. 179–208.

Pommaret, F. (2000). 'Recent Bhutanese Scholarship in History and Anthropology', *Journal of Bhutan Studies*, vol. 3, no. 2, pp. 139–163.

Pradhan, A.M. (1991). 'Preface'. In Law Department, Government of Sikkim, ed., *The Sikkim Code. Volume II*, Gangtok: The Gangtok Press, pp. i–iii.

Rai, R. (2015). *The State in the Colonial Periphery - A Study on Sikkim's Relation with Great Britain*, Gurgaon: Partridge.

Rai, S. (2016). *Property Inheritance Laws of Women in Tribal Societies: A Case Study of Sikkim* (PhD dissertation, Sikkim University).

Rao, P.R. (1972). *India and Sikkim, 1814-1970*, New Delhi: Sterling Publishers.

Rao, P.R. (1978). *Sikkim: The Story of Its Integration with India*, New Delhi: Cosmo.

Risley, H.H. (1894). *The Gazetteer of Sikhim*, Calcutta: Bengal Secretariat Press.

Rose, L.E. (1978). 'Modernizing a Traditional Administrative System: Sikkim 1890-1973'. In J.F. Fisher, ed., *Himalayan Anthropology: The Indo-Tibetan Interface*, The Hague/Paris: Mouton Publishers.

Sarathi, V.P. (1991). 'Foreword'. In Law Department, Government Of Sikkim, ed., *The Sikkim Code. Volume II*, Gangtok: The Gangtok Press, pp. iii–vi.

Scott, D., ed. (2011). *Handbook of India's International Relations* (1st ed.), London: Routledge.

Sengupta, N. (1985). *State Government and Politics: Sikkim*, New Delhi: Sterling Publishers.

Sharma, R.S. (1996). *Aspects of Political Ideas and Institutions in Ancient India*, Delhi: Motidal Barnasidass.

Sharma, S.K. and U. Sharma (1998). *Documents on Sikkim and Bhutan*, New Delhi: Anmol Publications.

Shaw, F. (2013). *Conserving Our Heritage: Evolution of the National Library of Bhutan*, Bhutan: The National Library & Archives of Bhutan.

Shresta, R.S. (2005). *Sikkim: Three Decades towards Democracy. Evolution of the Legislative System*, Gangtok: Sikkim Legislative Assembly Secretariat.

Siems, M. (2018). *Comparative Law* (2nd ed), United Kingdom: Cambridge University Press.

Sikkim Legislative Assembly Secretariat (2003). *Sikkim Legislative Assembly: Retrospect and Perspective- An Overview*, Gangtok: Sikkim Legislative Assembly Secretariat.

Simoni, A. (2003). 'A Language for Rules, Another for Symbols: Linguistic Pluralism and Interpretation of Statutes in the Kingdom of Bhutan', *Journal of Bhutan Studies*, vol. 8, pp. 29–53.

Simoni, A. and R.W. Whitecross (2007). 'Gross National Happiness and the Heavenly Stream of Justice: Modernization and Dispute Resolution in the Kingdom of Bhutan', *American Journal of Comparative Law*, vol. 55, no. 1, pp. 165–196.

Sinha, A.C. (2001). *Himalayan Kingdom Bhutan: Tradition, Transition, and Transformation*, New Delhi: Indus Pub.

Sinha, A.C. (2008). *Sikkim: Feudal and Democratic*, New Delhi: Indus Pub. Co.

Sonam Tobgye, L. (2013). 'Address by the Hon'ble Chief Justice of Bhutan, Lyonpo Sonam Tobgye at the "International Conference on Buddhists Laws" in Sarnath, Varanasi, India. 15th-16th February 2013', *Royal Court of Bhutan. Speeches by Hon'ble Lyonpo Sonam Tobgye*, accessed at http://www.judiciary.gov.bt/publication/CJSS.pdf

Sonam Tobgye, L. (2014a). 'Law and Law Making. In *Royal Court of Bhutan, Articles by Hon'ble Lyonpo Sonam Tobgye*, accessed at http://www.judiciary.gov.bt/publication/law1.pdf

Sonam Tobgye, L. (2014b). 'Making of the Constitution of the Kingdom of Bhutan'. In *Royal Court of Bhutan, Articles by Hon'ble Lyonpo Sonam Tobgye*, accessed at http://www.judiciary.gov.bt/publication/constitution1.pdf

Sonam Tobgye, L. (n.d.1). 'Sentinel of Democracy – The Bar (Mumbai 28th February)'. In *Royal Court of Bhutan. Speeches by Hon'ble Lyonpo Sonam Tobgye, Chief Justice of Bhutan*, accessed at http://www.judiciary.gov.bt/publication/SENTINEL%20OF%20DEMOCRACY%20%20Mumbai.pdf

Sonam Tobgye, L. (n.d.2). 'Education System in Bhutan – Past, Present and Future a Reflection'. In *Royal Court of Bhutan. Articles By Hon'ble Lyonpo Sonam Tobgye, Chief Justice Of Bhutan*, accessed at http://www.judiciary.gov.bt/publication/educationCJB.pdf

Steinmetz, G. (2004). 'Odious Comparisons: Incommensurability, the Case Study, and "Small N's" in Sociology', *Sociological Theory*, vol. 22, no. 3, pp. 371–400.

Subba, A.P. (n.d.). *Historical Perspective of the Sikkim Judiciary*, Gangtok: High Court of Sikkim, accessed at http://highcourtofsikkim.nic.in/JudicialHistory

Subha, T.B. (2013). 'Making Sikkim more Inclusive: An Insider's View of the Role of Committees and Commissions'. In U. Skoda, K.B. Nielsen and M. Fibiger, eds., *Navigating Social Exclusion and Inclusion in Contemporary India and Beyond: Structures, Agents, Practices*, London/New York/Delhi: Anthem Press, pp. 135–149.

Tamang, G.M. (2015). *Indigenous Methods of Conflict Resolution in Sikkim: A Study of the Dzumsa* (M Phil. dissertation, Sikkim University).

Thapa, S. and S.A. Sachdeva (2017). 'The Institution of Dzumsa in North Sikkim: A Sociological Understanding Sandhy', *Sociological Bulletin*, vol. 66, no. 2, pp. 212–222.

Tobgye, S. (2014). *The Constitution of Bhutan: Principles and Philosophies*, Bhutan: Royal Court of Bhutan, accessed at http://www.judiciary.gov.bt/index.php/Welcome/get_pages?id=49%20&cat=10

Tran, H. (2012). 'Chogyal's Sikkim: Tax, Land & Clan Politics', *Independent Study Project (ISP) Collection 1446*, accessed at https://digitalcollections.sit.edu/isp_collection/1446

Tshering, K. (2009a). 'Rule of Law in Bhutan', *NC Reflections*, vol. 1, pp. 31–35.

Tshering, K. (2009b). 'Salient Features of the Constitution of the Kingdom of Bhutan', *NC Reflections*, vol. 1, pp. 18–27.

Tshering, K. (2010). 'Legislation - Formulation, Application and Interpretation', *NC Reflections*, vol. 2, pp. 6–10.

Tshewang, P., K.P. Tashi, C. Butters and S.K. Saetreng (1995). *The Treasure Revealer of Bhutan: Pemalingpa, the Terma Tradition and Its Critics*, Kathmandu: EMR Publishing House.

Turin, M. (2012). 'Results From the Linguistic Survey of Sikkim: Mother Tongues in Education'. In A. McKay and A. Balikci-Denjongpa, eds., *Buddhist Himalaya: Studies in Religion, History and Culture, Volume II*, pp. 127–142.

Valcke, C. (2004). 'Comparative Law as Comparative Jurisprudence - The Comparability of Legal Systems', *American Journal of Comparative Law*, vol. LII, no. 3, pp. 713–740.

Vandenhelsken, M. (2009). 'Reification of Ethnicity in Sikkim: "Tribalism" in Progress', *Bulletin of Tibetology*, vol. 45, no. 2; vol. 46, no. 1, pp. 161–194.

Vandenhelsken, M. (2012). 'Book Review: *Suresh Kumar Gurung, Sikkim. Ethnicity and Political Dynamics. A Triadic Perspective*, Delhi: Kunal Books, 2011', *Bulletin of Tibetology*, vol. 47, no. 1, pp. 1–12.

Wangchuk, K. (2015). 'A Hobbesian Look into the Genja (Contract) of 1907', accessed at https://www.academia.edu/12895932/A_Hobbesian_Look_into_the_Genja_Contract_of_1907

Whitecross, R.W. (2004). 'The Thrimzhung Chenmo and the Emergence of the Contemporary Bhutanese Legal System'. In K. Ura and S. Kinga, eds., *The Spider and the Piglet: Collected Papers on Bhutanese Society*, Thimphu: Centre of Bhutan Studies, pp. 355–379.

Whitecross, R.W. (2007). 'Changing the Contours of the Legal Landscape: The Jabmi Act 2003'. In J. Ardussi and F. Pommaret, eds., *Bhutan: Traditions and Changes*, Leiden/Boston: Brill, pp. 159–170.

Whitecross, R.W. (2009). 'Keeping the Stream of Justice Clear and Pure: The Buddhicization of Bhutanese Law'. In F. von Benda-Beckmann, K. von Benda-Beckmann and A. Griffiths, eds., *The Power of Law in a Transnational World: Anthropological Enquiries*, New York/Oxford: Berghahn Books, pp. 199–215.

Whitecross, R.W. (2013). 'Separating Religion and Politics? Buddhism and the Bhutanese Constitution'. In S. Khilnani, ed., *Constitutionalism in South Asia*, Oxford: Oxford University Press, pp. 116–144.

Whitecross, R.W. (2017a). '"Like a Pot without a Handle": Law, Meaning and Practice in Medieval Bhutan', *Cahiers D'Extrême-Asie*, vol. 26, no. 1, pp. 87–103.

Whitecross, R.W. (2017b). 'Law, "Tradition" and Legitimacy: Contesting Driglam Namzha'. In J. Schmidt, ed., *Development Challenges in Bhutan. Contemporary South Asian Studies*, Cham: Springer International Publishing, pp. 115–134.

Windischgraetz, M. (2019). 'Circumstances and Content'. In M. Windischgraetz and R. Wangdi, *The Black-Slate Edict of Punakha Dzong. A Legal Code Attributed to Zhabs-drung Ngag-dbang rnam-rgyal, the Founder of Bhutan*, Timphu: JSW Law Publishing Series, pp. 9–24.

Windischgraetz, M. and R. Wangdi (2019). *The Black-Slate Edict of Punakha Dzong. A Legal Code Attributed to Zhabs-drung Ngag-dbang rnam-rgyal, the Founder of Bhutan*, Timphu: JSW Law Publishing Series.

13 'Ranked' Sacrificial Offerings: Reconstructing Bhutan's Historical Public Service Through New Textual and Ethnographic Sources

Dendup Chophel

Introduction

Beginning with the founders of Bhutanese studies like Michael Aris, John Ardussi, Yoshiro Imaeda and Françoise Pommaret, the formation of the Bhutanese state and its historical public service[1] has been studied in varying detail by modern Bhutanese scholars writing in English, most prominent among them Dasho Karma Ura, Dasho Sonam Kinga and Karma Phuntsho.[2] This chapter, through a combined methodology of historiography and ethnography, discusses the provenance and nature of the Bhutanese state bureaucracy that has come to be the stuff of medieval romanticism, which was nonetheless tempered with a sense of duty and honor, though some state officials were naturally more (or less) zealous than others in their functioning.

The overriding creed of the courtiers and attendants, who formed the state bureaucracy at the time, was firstly to serve the lord, secondly to perceive the adversity of people and thirdly to pursue their own interests.[3]

---

1 By 'historical public service', I refer to the system of civil administration introduced by the Zhabdrung, the prototype of which was firmly established by the time of his death in 1651. During the course of the reign of the third king, Jigme Dorji Wangchuck ('jigs med rdo rje dbang phyug, r. 1952–1972), this system was extensively reformed by bifurcating the civil service from the court service.

2 See Ura (1995, 1996, 2004, 2023); Kinga (2009); and Phuntsho (2013).

3 Ura (1996: 16).

The *Ballad of Pemi Tshewang Tashi* (*pad ma'i tshe dbang bkra shis*[4]; hereafter *Ballad*), in this regard, is a highly emotive and eloquent source of information on the inner functioning of the courts of the powerful *desis* (*sde srid*, historical civil rulers) and their regional overlords (*dpon slob*). As the seat of administration was the *dzong* (*rdzong*, fortified castles divided between monastic and civic usage reflecting the state's dual imperatives), abstinence from leading the life of a normal lay person was a necessary prerequisite for all officials.[5] This practice can be interpreted as preserving the moral integrity and superiority of the state officials who cut themselves off from at least one possible source of corruption that leading a family life with all its obligations and imperatives can bring. Lay officials in office appropriated the image of an accomplished monk by taking at least preliminary vows.[6] It is not farfetched to argue that the usage of maroon and yellow robes by historical officials was a part of this scheme, which is now a formalized system of state honors.

Boys who were barely in their teens would be sent as *tozeys*[7] (*lto gzan*). The ritual of getting them admitted to the court would entail presenting themselves before the lord. As soon as they were in audience, they had to perform the three customary prostrations. Then, in the presence of their guardians, they would have to offer a cane of *araa*[8] (*a rag*) and a silver coin known as *betam* (*bal kram*) in front of the throne as a token of their formal registration as junior functionaries.[9]

---

4 I have attempted to give the definition of all Bhutanese words and expressions in the body of the chapter or as footnotes. However, some of them are colloquial in nature without standardized orthography. When I reproduced them in the chapter, I did so unaltered from the original text, which I have used as the basis of my analysis. I have given common Romanized spellings of all proper nouns, and on their first appearance, have given the Wylie transliteration in parenthesis. Where necessary, the Romanized nouns have been pluralized as for English words, for example, Drukpas. Where I have made a direct quote, I have retained the original orthographic convention.

5 Schwerk (2019: 24).

6 Aris (1979: 262–263).

7 Literally meaning recipient of food, they were fresh recruits who apprenticed with senior courtiers.

8 Local liquor.

9 Ura (1996: 26).

More often than not, admittance to the court was based on hereditary obligations.[10] Entitlements for new recruits included all the necessary paraphernalia of a court servant like swords (*dpa' rtags*) and scarves (*bkab ne*), all of which had to be returned upon their death in a custom called *ro-du* (*ro 'du*). Following the *Choeje Drukpai driglam namzha* (*chos rje 'brug pa'i sgrig lam rnam gzhag*[11]), all recruits had to start at the very bottom of the ladder, spending several years doing the most menial jobs in the court before being noticed. Even after the establishment of the hereditary Wangchuck dynasty, this noble tradition was preserved. At least in their preparatory years, even the heirs apparent had to serve as menial attendants before assuming higher responsibilities.[12] This was to not only instill a sense of untiring dedication to the task at hand and the dignity of labor, but also to ensure the instinct of survival so crucial to rising up through the ranks. One consolation for the rigorously tested apprentices was the knowledge that the system was based on meritocracy, and as long as they had the right attitude, there could be hope for continued ascendency.[13] Thus, the defining features of a functionary became the inexhaustible qualities of diligence, strength and tact.

As the protagonist of the *Ballad* demonstrates, struggle and sacrifice defined a person's existence in the courts. In the decadent two centuries

---

10 The state depended on households to provide militia, corvée labor and occasionally, monks. For a discussion on the recruitment of militia (*dpa mdzangs pa*), see Chophel (2011).

11 The code of conduct of the glorious Drukpa order that includes everything from general court etiquette to moral righteousness (Whitecross 2017). Dasho Passang Wangdi (in a public talk on 21 June 2013) mentioned that a big part of apprenticeship in court was learning the protocols of serving and attending to the kings.

12 Gongsar Ugyen Wangchuck, for example, had to transport at least two loads of tough oak on his back per day with other attendants in Thimphu Lungtenphu and Samarzingkha, in addition to serving as *changarp* (*phyag sgarp*, personal attendant to a lord; Pema Tshewang 1994: 513). Similarly, Ura (1995) reports Prince Jigme Dorji Wangchuk's impeccable service as a junior attendant in his father's court.

13 In this regard, one might examine the rise of Jigme Namgyal who hailed from a remote area but who through sheer diligence saw a meteoric rise through the court hierarchy. For details, see Tshewang (1994: 479–505). Because his career started from the lowest rung as customary, he was mistaken by a British officer, Ashley Eden, to be of 'low extraction' even though he belonged to an ancient religious nobility (Aris 1998: 72). For a comparison on the commensality and

following the passing away of the state's founder, Zhabdrung Ngawang Namgyal (zhabs drung ngag dbang rnam rgyal, b. 1594, d. 1651), power struggles between rival factions became rife.[14] Since the Bhutanese state was a 'theocratic republic', power was in principle open to all those who pursued it, and in fact, this was for the most part true.[15] Thus, ruthless competition for supremacy ensued in which regional overlords competed among themselves for state resources and positions. Given the general risk and hardship entailed by court life in those days, there was indeed a celebration and appreciation of the good that power could bring.

Both a sense of control and gloom[16] pervaded the atmosphere in the *dzongs* at the time. It is not surprising that in the *Ballad*, courtiers are likened to the hundreds of furry yaks and the thousands of furless yaks of the rich nomadic herders awaiting their imminent slaughter.[17] Chamberlain Tshewang Tashi, who was a senior official in the Wangdue Phodrang Dzong (dbang 'dus pho brang rdzong), laments his condition in the following verses implying that he was still susceptible to bouts of unbridled sentiments typical among lowly courtiers.

> In the fortress of Wangdue Dzong
>
> I, my mother's Pemi Tshewang Tashi,
>
> Though my body appertains to that of a Lord
>
> My mind still belongs to that of a gaarp [*sgar pa*].[18]

However, despite the sense of personal grievance and deprivation, the commitment to the cause of the theocratic state was beyond reproach.

---

starting level of historical Bhutanese officials to their Tibetan counterparts whose induction depended upon their family's social stature, see Travers (2011).

14 On the extent of the issues that had beset the system, see Chophel (2014).

15 Kinga (2009).

16 A popular phrase, *sgar pa'i thrue nang*, expresses the complex mentality of the court retainers who were very emotional due to prolonged deprivations experienced while serving under difficult circumstances.

17 Ura (1996: 3).

18 Ura (1996: 4). All translations of the *Ballad* included in this chapter are from Ura (1996), unless otherwise stated.

Throughout Bhutan's protracted factional history, the lords and their men had been able to unite against a common enemy no matter how bitterly divided they were among themselves. As a result, Bhutan successfully fended off all aggressions from both the north and the south.[19] When the call of duty arrived, the emotional chamberlain is quick to put behind all vicissitudes and rise to the call.

> The command of *Dzongpon* Angdruk Nim -
>
> To dismiss it, is as dear as gold,
>
> To carry it out, is as heavy as hills.[20]

He obeys his lord despite his personal premonition of imminent doom and misgivings about the soundness of his lord's judgement.

Against this background of the chivalrous, and sometimes frivolous (even capricious) lords and their courtiers, this chapter will now attempt to systematically delineate the origin and nature of the Bhutanese state, and the *dzong* bureaucracy that emerged as a result. Towards this end, existing materials from various sources will be systematically organized and discussed. Thereafter, a ritual manuscript will be analyzed. Even though much of this information has already been presented in various scattered sources, most ostensibly in the secular chronicles of the country, it may be noted here that this important subject deserves to be treated in a more nuanced and consolidated way on its own.

---

19 Mathou (2000). The Bhutanese fended off several Tibetan invasions and were dragged into at least two territorial wars with the mighty British army. Internally, the Bhutanese state had to overcome the numerous challenges mounted by the group of five *lams* (Schwerk 2019: 24). Though the modest Bhutanese attributed their success to the protective deities, even these adversaries grudgingly admired the fighting qualities and resilience of the Bhutanese in their respective records.

20 Ura (1996: 5). This verse is a variation on a famous Bhutanese saying, *dbang chen dpon gyi bka' rgya/ 'bag na ri bas lci/ 'bor na gser bas phangs/*.

The foundation of the Bhutanese state

Through a process of consolidating territories previously under the sway of petty local chieftains, the Zhabdrung laid the foundation of the Bhutanese state. In the process, he had to overcome numerous obstacles mounted by both local and foreign opponents. However, he was firmly supported by both human and non-human inhabitants of the Bhutanese land, over the entirety of which he ruled.[21] This process is fairly well documented, so we will instead now focus on the formation of the Palden Druk Zhung (dpal ldan 'brug gzhung) or the 'Government of the Glorious Drukpa'. This formation took place through four processes: the promulgation of the founding seal of the well-known Nga Chudruma (nga cu drug ma) in 1622; the proclamation of the founding of the government in 1626; the establishment of the capital at Punakha with the completion of the *dzong* construction in 1639; and the recognition of the Bhutanese government by neighboring countries in 1640.[22]

The theoretical structure of governance of the Bhutanese state seems to have evolved gradually out of the precedents at hand and the temporary arrangements of the Zhabdrung and his small entourage.[23]

> Initially it was perhaps something of a clone of the situation of Ralung, i.e. a monastic *gdan-sa* with a few officials and a network of patrons and properties. Other than personal attendants and his Tibetan teacher *Lha-dbang Blo-gros*, whom he appointed to serve as the chief monastic preceptor, the principal officer known for certain to have been appointed by *Zhabs-drung* was his Bhutanese patron *bsTan-'dzin 'Brug-rgyas* (1591-1566), who was delegated the responsibilities of civil administration.[24]

One of the main tasks of the formation of the state was bringing the country under the laws of the Choesid Zungdrel (chos srid zung 'brel),

---

21 Kinga (2009).

22 Kinga (2009: 57).

23 In this regard, Mathou (2000: 240) affirms that 'pragmatism and a predilection for gradualism has been its guiding principles'.

24 Ardussi (2004: 15).

which was accomplished through the application of the *chayig* (*bca'yig*), which in turn was first developed as in-house rules for the clergy but later expanded to include all the citizens.[25] In 1729, the tenth Je Khenpo Tenzin Chogyal (bstan 'dzing Chos rgyal, r. 1755–1762), persuaded by the tenth Desi Mipham Wangpo (mi pham dbang po, r. 1729–1736), wrote the *Kathrim* (*bka'khrims*) for the country of Bhutan in which he mentions that he relied upon the draft laws of Songtsen Gampo (srong btsan sgam po), Thri Ralpachen (khri ral pa can), the Zhabdrung and Desi Tenzin Drugye (also known as Desi Umze, sde srid dbu mdzad), implying that civil laws were already in place during the time of the Zhabdrung and his immediate successor.[26] The Zhabdrung had brought the country under the dual system of the religious law, which 'tightens like a silken knot',[27] and the secular law, which 'becomes heavier like a golden yoke'.[28]

The theoretical foundations of the Zhabdrung's new ecclesiastic state are presented in elaborate detail by his biographer, Tsang Khenchen (gtsang mkhan chen, b. 1610, d. 1684), himself a refugee Karmapa monk. Even though the Bhutanese state was supposed to be a natural successor to the Sakya and Phag-mo-gru-pa models,[29] in fact there were significant differences in the actual organization.

> An important difference was that Zhabdrung was an independent entity. Unlike the figurehead Imperial Preceptor or Di shi of Sakya, his spiritual rule did not depend on an external Mongol protector. No military strongman granted him authority in Bhutan in the way that the Mongol Gushri Khan did for the 5th Dalai Lama. Nor did the Chinese emperor play-act a "lama-patron" role in the guise of Manjushri as happened in Qing Dynasty Tibet. Bhutanese support for the Zhabdrung accrued gradually during his lifetime, in part by willing patronage and in part by conquest and expulsion of rival lamas.[30]

---

25 Phuntsho (2013: 257).

26 Aris (1986: 123); Windischgraetz and Wangdi (2019).

27 *chos khrims dar gyi mdud pa/*

28 *rgyal khrims gser gyi gnya'shing/*

29 For example, see Phuntsho (2013: 208).

30 Ardussi (2004: 17).

Comparing the aforementioned text with its Tibetan equivalent,[31] Cuppers writes:

> The Bhutanese text gives the ordinance that the officials should investigate and see whether all people are living in happiness, and that there is no poverty or injustice to be found in the country. This kind of investigation is not of interest in the Tibetan case […]. Here, the officials are enjoined to investigate whether there is any blame or harm done to the government. The shift of focus from the "happiness" of the people to the "protection" of the good name of the government is an underlying tone in the text of Tibet.[32]

Comparing the same texts, Windischgraetz and Wangdi claim that 'In fact, the ranks of administration in Lho-mon kha-bzhi were quite different from those mentioned in the *mKhas pa'i dga' ston*. Most of the positions mentioned in Tibetan imperial law did not exist in Bhutan'.[33] Windischgraetz and Wangdi translated and analyzed the earliest summary description of the functions of state ministers, which can be found on the slate inscriptions of Punakha, and which was installed by the thirteenth Desi Sherab Wangchuck (shes rab dbang phyug, r. 1744–1763).

Initially the Drukpa order was sustained purely through voluntary patronage called *wangyon* (*dbang yon*). The Portuguese missionary Estevao Cacella who visited the Zhabdrung in 1627 attests to this in his report.[34] However, as the state grew in scope and size, there was a need to establish a timely and reliable revenue base, which could only be guaranteed through a minimalist taxation structure. In this regard, the enthronement records of Zhabdrung Thugtruel Jigme Dragpa I (thugs sprul 'jigs med grags pa, b. 1725, d. 1761) provides enlightening evidence of the tax structure, which developed from the rudimentary structure that was enforced from the Zhabdrung's time onwards. The record also shows why

31 The Guidelines for Government Officials written in the year 1681 by the regent (*sde srid*) Sangs rgyas rgya mtsho.

32 Cuppers (2007: 50).

33 Windischgraetz and Wangdi (2019: 17).

34 Baillie (1999: 19–20).

territorial conquest was a big preoccupation. In an attempt to minimize the tax burden on its own people (residents of *lho-kha-bzhi*), the Bhutanese government made imperial forays into foreign land and thus commanded substantial tithes and other obligatory revenues from the far-flung lands of Ladakh, Nepal, Sikkim, Chumbi and Ma-'gor (India?)..., and in particular those belonging to the senior and junior ministers of Cooch Behar and other kingdoms of Kamarupa in India.[35]

The main tax unit was a household called *threlpa* (*khral-pa*) though there were other households who paid half the tax obligation of a *threlpa*. There were still others who worked for the *dzong* or fulfilled other such roles in lieu of tax.[36] On the other hand, there were special nobilities like *zhengo* (*zhal ngo*) who were exempted from any kind of tax. The households paid their taxes in kind (*rlon khral*) or in cash (*skam khral*), even though the former was more lucrative for the state. All these taxpayers either dealt directly with the *dzong* or in case of particularly large districts, they were obligated to sub-district administrators called *drungpa* (*drung pa*).[37] It may be noted that while western districts reported directly to the Punakha Dzong, the capital fortress, there was an additional level of hierarchy for the other districts, which reported first to the regional capitals –Trongsa in the east, Dagana in the south, and Paro for the southwestern districts. Based on the record, John Ardussi and Karma Ura estimate Bhutan's tax-paying households (*mi-khyim*) in 1747 at 27,223, with 217,784 tax obliged people.[38]

The Bhutanese state clearly stood on a considerable reserve of revenue in addition to the corvée labor at its disposal. So, what were its main

35 Ardussi and Ura (2000: 47).

36 *Zurpa* (*zur pa*), *ponger* (*dpon sger*), *drapa* (*grwa pa*), *zhinyer* (*gzhis gnyer*), *zakhen* (*rdza mkhan*); while the first in this list is a half-tax unit family, the rest are the servant class families who stayed close to the *dzong* and served particular masters. The last in the list belongs to the family of pot makers, an occupation that was considered lowly in the traditional society (see Barth 2018).

37 See Ura (2023: 182–188) for a detailed discussion on the division of the country under some forty-eight *dungpas* in 1746 and some 126 of them by the time of the second king who abolished most of these jurisdictions to restructure tax administration and reduce the burden on the people.

38 Ardussi and Ura (2000: 56).

responsibilities? The most obvious ones were of course the provision of external security, and internal law and order. But the Bhutanese government was founded on the principle of Choesid Zungdrel under which the secular administration (*srid*) was to provide patronage to the religious community embodied in the Palden Drukpa Rinpoche (dpal ldan 'brug pa rin po che), while the latter ensured the spiritual services (for the benefit of all sentient beings) that was one of the principal preoccupations in a society founded on religious orthodoxy.

Origin and nature of the state bureaucracy

The Bhutanese state grew organically with the growing influence of its founder. By the end of the founder's life, it had guaranteed the resources it needed to survive. Ensuring its continuity was the administration of a functioning bureaucracy. When the Zhabdrung began his quest to build the Bhutanese state, he only had the services of a few reliable men, most of whom came with him from Tibet. Thus, the Portuguese missionaries referred to Umze Tenzin Drugye as 'the whole government of the king' (referring to the Zhabdrung).[39]

By the time he passed away in 1651, the Zhabdrung had already put in place the foundation of an administrative framework and a system of governance for the political structure and civil organization, which came to dominate Bhutan until the major administrative reorganization during the reign of the third king. In his own days, the religious and political rules coalesced into a natural union in his own person. The office of the Zhabdrung was known as the *tse* (*tse*) or 'apex' and immediately under him were the branches of 'inner' ecclesiastical affairs headed temporarily by Drung Damcho Gyaltshen (drung dam chos rgyal mtsan) and 'outer' secular administration headed by Desi Umze until his death.[40] The Zhabdrung appointed a host of monastic and civil officials, but we will return to this in a little while.

The prototype of the machinery of governance was fully developed by the time of the Zhabdrung's death. So, three months after his death, Desi

39 Baillie (1999: 23).

40 Phuntsho (2013: 257).

Umze held the first council of the government of Bhutan during which he took the opportunity to announce that he and Drung Damcho Gyaltshen, or any other person appointed under the seal of the Zhabdrung in case of their inability to do so, would hold the reins of the state for an indefinite period until the emergence of Zhabdrung Rinpoche from his 'meditation', which was thought plausible because his death was kept secret at the time, and it continued to remain so for more than half a century afterwards.

Before we proceed further, it may be educative to look at the very first instance of the formation of a bureaucratic system in Buddhist history because the Bhutanese state was by all admissions based on Buddhist origins. Buddhism emerged as a minimalist doctrine that strictly discouraged excesses and indulgences. So, the Lord Buddha led a hermitic life with his close followers. However, as his teachings soon attracted large followings, the Buddha devised numerous sets of regulations which are contained in the Vinaya corpus of Buddhist scriptures. One of the earliest developments in the institutionalization of Buddhism was the founding of the rainy season retreat, and with that, many communal needs became evident, the most apparent being a common meeting hall (*upasthana sala*). Sukumar Dutt[41] points out one example when a Brahman named Ghokamukha, being eager to make a donation to the sangha, was advised by a monk named Udena to build a meeting hall for the Sangha at Pataliputra. Other buildings soon began to appear, strewn over the grounds of the settlement. All of these structures were the collective property of the sangha. Thus, for the first time in the history of Buddhism, the development of an administration was necessary.[42]

Much like the early Buddhist administration, the Zhabdrung's humble circle of supporters soon branched out into a systematic and sophisticated network of officials and court functionaries. When Desi Umze held the first council, the following officials composed the cabinet or council (*lhan rgyas gzhung tshogs*): Tenzin Drukdra (btsan 'dzin 'brug sgra) as the

---

41 Cited in Prebish (1974: 6–8).

42 For a comparison with the formation of the Tibetan models of state administration, see Travers (2011: 156), who extensively reviewed the modern studies on this subject, prime among them being the works of Luciano Petech and Melvyn Goldstein.

chila (*spyi la*) of Paro, Mingyur Tenpa (mi 'gyur bstan pa) as the *chila* of Trongsa and Tenpa Thinley (bstan pa 'phrin las) as the *chila* of Dagana. The title *chila*, which meant a regional monk overlord, was in later periods replaced by the alternative compound *penlop* (*dpon slob*). The three *dzongpons* (*rdzong dpon*, governor) of Punakha, Thimphu and Wangdue were also part of this council. They were respectively Pekar Rabgye (pad dkar rab rgyas), Aou Tshering (a'u tshe-ring) and Namkha Rinchen (nam mkha' rin chen). There was another important official in this council, Druk Namgyal ('brug rnam rgyal), who was the *zhung dronyer* (*gzhung mgron gnyer*) or the state's chief of protocol. Later, two other officials, the *zhung kalyon* (*gzhung bka' blon*, functionally a chief of advisors) and *debi zimpon* (*sde pa'i gzims dpon*, *desi's* chamberlain) were included in this circle to make it a council of nine people. These position holders were the top echelon in the hierarchy of officials after the *desi* and were considered as ministers of the state with matching entitlements from state resources in cash, kind and staff.

As most early office holders were monks, lay officials later appropriated the robe and other accessories of the monk officials with the additional paraphernalia of a silver-scabbard sword, which then became the formal regalia of these ministerial post holders and their decorated subordinates. From available historical sources,[43] as well as through a comparison with the equivalent dress code of the *lopen zhibs* (*slob dpon bzhi pa*),[44] it seems most likely that the official *kabney* (*bkab ne*) of the *lhengye* was red (maroon) *bura* (*'bu ras*, Endi silk) with five folds at the shoulder (*lnga bkal*). From the time of the third king when ministers as we know them now were first appointed, the color of *kabney* for ministers was a distinctive orange corresponding with the orange robe of the *lams* (*bla ma*) in the monastic body. They were entitled to the form of address

---

43 There are several pictures of Trongsa *penlop* Ugyen Wangchuck with his fellow *penlops* and other deputies from which a fair inference on the type of *kabney* (color coded scarves won by Bhutanese on formal occasions) can be made.

44 The four principal abbots of the various ecclesiastical departments, *rdo rje slob dpon* (Vajracharya division and second in command to Je Khenpo), *dbyangs pa'i slob dpon* (liturgical division), *mtshan nyid slob dpon* (metaphysics and logic division) and *sgra pa'i slob dpon* (lexicographical division) were ministerial rank holders in the monastic hierarchy.

of Mi-je (mi rje, equivalent to His Excellency) and thus, were the veritable 'lords of the *dzong*'.

Below the *zhung lhengyes* (*gzhung lhan rgyas*), there were chief secretarial officers referred to collectively as *zhung nyikem* (*gzhung gnyis skal ma*) with positions such as secretary of the treasury, *nyerchen* (*gnyer chen*), the chief of protocol (*mgron gnyer*) of *dzongs* other than Punakha, and the chamberlains (*gzims dpon*) to the *penlops* and *dzongpons* of the three major *dzongs*. From the list of the officers under Wangdue Phodrang Dzong, one of the three central *dzongs*, that is given in the investiture records of Zhabdrung Jigme Dragpa (zhabs drung 'jid med drags pa, b. 1724, d. 1761), we can clearly see that there was a *dronyer* (*mgron gnyer*) and *nyerchen* (*gnyer chen*) in Wangdue Phodrang. As can be corroborated from the *Ballad*, the *zimpon* to the Wangdue Dzongpon, one of the three principal *dzongpons*, was also a *nyikem* ranked officer. Thus, in each of the three principal *dzongs* plus the regional power centers of Paro, Trongsa and Dagana, there were at least three principal secretaries of *nyikem* rank. *Dzongpons* of all other minor *dzongs* were also of the rank of *nyikem*. *Nyikem*, as the compound suggests, were entitled to twice the share of government resources that their deputies, *chibzhoem* (*chibs bzhon pa*), received as emoluments. Together with the customary sword, the *nyikems* wore red *kabney* (*'bu ras dmar pa*) with ordinary folds like a commoner. They formed the *dpon kha* or secondary echelon of officials in the *dzong* below the *lhengye* rank. They were entitled to the honorific *dasho* (*drag shos*), which has now been formalized as a system of state honor granted as a royal prerogative by the king.

Next in the hierarchy of state officers were the *chibzhoems* or 'mounted officers'. The most frugal use of state resources was highly advocated by the laws of the country (as can be attested from the *Kathrim* of the tenth *desi*). Therefore, obtaining a riding horse at state expense for such purposes as travel between the two capitals (*gzhung gdan sa phan tsun*) was a rare privilege. As a result, the managerial staff were called the mounted officers or *chibzhoem*. This type of official included such managerial staff as *gorab* (*sgo rab*, gate controller), *shanyer* (*sha gnyer*, meat master), *tapon* (*rta dpon*, stable master), *tsanyer* (*tsa gnyer*, fodder master), *banyer* (*ba-gnyer*, cattle master), *drungpa* (*drung pa*, sub-district controller) and *dzongzungpa* (*rdzong bzung pa*, master of satellite fortresses). As part of their official dress code, they wore ordinary white *kabney* with or without frills, and were entitled to the same swords as the former two categories of higher officials. However, because of their lesser material means, their sword had only a partial silver scabbard. The rest of the multi-segmented sheath was covered with an assortment of lacquered pelts or stingray skin, which nonetheless makes an aesthetic sword albeit less valuable.

At the lowest rung of the ladder, the rank and file consisted of menial servants and orderlies under the *nyikems* and *chibzhoems*. This class of lowly functionaries was also ranked, by one classification in terms of the quantity and quality of free meals to which they were entitled from the common mess or *soethab* (*gsol thab*). This appears to be reflected in the titles of servants.[45] *Tshogs-thob*, as their title implies, were authorized to receive all meals at state expense. The syllables *dkar-'dra-ma* may be an error for *dkar-dro-ma*, indicating their entitlement to 'white food', a term interpreted to mean high grade rice. These lowly functionaries were not entitled to any regalia but some of them could wear functional short or mid-length swords (*dpa' rtags rbed dum* and *ring min thung min*) because of the nature of their responsibilities like running state errands in vulnerable areas. Apart from the functional swords, there was a considerable variation in the swords used by this class of official orderlies, one of them being the *zang-shen chem* (*zangs shan canm*), or the copper-scabbard swords, which were of the same length as the swords of the officials in the higher echelon.

This multiplicity of functionaries at the lowest rung (at least those who were in immediate service of the lords) was what constituted the class of *boe garps* (*'bod sgar pa*) or *zingarps* (*gzim sgar pa*). They were the most numerous amongst the rank and file of the *dzong* bureaucracy. As mentioned in the introduction of this chapter, the state service was in principle egalitarian and if a capable person at this level demonstrated the requisite dedication, he could certainly hope to rise up through the ranks.

In the courts of the hereditary kings, there was a vast array of permanent retainers. In *The Hero with a Thousand Eyes*, speaking through the first-person narrator, Dasho Karma Ura[46] stated that in the court of the second king (jigs med dbang phyug, b. 1902, d. 1952),

45 Ardussi and Ura (2000: 45).

46 Ura (1995: 22).

> there were over a hundred and fifty Changarps (*chang sgarp*, butlers, valets, conveyors of orders or men in waiting), five or so Kadreps (*bka' bgres-pa*, conversation companions), forty Changdaps (*chang mda'-pa*, security detail), fifteen Chazhumis (*phyag zhu mi*, personal aides), a hundred or so Zingarps (*gzim sgarp*, menial task force), twenty silver smiths, twenty stable men or liveries/syces (*a drung*-s), five cooks in the common kitchen and three chefs (*gsol gyog*) in His Majesty's kitchen.

Today in Bhutan, there is a preoccupation with the mode of address to government officials and persons of exalted social standings. So, what lessons can we draw from the practice and forms of address in the historical courts? *Dasho* (*drag shos*) is today used as a generic address to all people of consequence in society. At least one source suggests that this honorific title was in use during the time of Namkha Gyeltshen (b. 1475, d. 1530), the reincarnation of Choje Barawa (b. 1310, d. 1391), whose biography written in the sixteenth century says that when Choje Barawa came to Bhutan, Dasho Jangsarwa, the *spyi-dpon* of southern Paro, became his patron.[47]

Although it would be tempting to thus surmise that *dasho* was used as an honorific address from ancient times, it certainly seems misplaced, for in enumerating thousands of court officials, the record of the enthronement of Zhabdrung Jigme Dragpa, or in fact any other literary and historical works, do not mention this form of address.[48] Instead, the officials are addressed by their positional title, thus for example, if one Sangay (a person) became *dronyer* (a position), he would be addressed as Dronyer Sangay and if he retires from the *dzong* in this post without further promotion, he would be called Dronyer Drep Sangay (mgron gnyer bgres pa gsangs rgyas), literally meaning former or ex-*dronyer* Sangay. However, the practice nowadays is to address almost all officials as *dasho*, and in

47 Ura (2004: 99).

48 Ardussi and Ura (2000: 45). However, it seems probable that although it was not used as an official title, it was used as a respectful address to the lords and their high officials as can be seen in the historical *Ballad* where the chamberlain addresses his 'lord' as *drag shos* in personal conversation, though in public, he uses the more formal title *poen* (*dpon*; Ura 1996: 15).

the case of senior officials, this certainly is always the case. Thus, if the same Sangay is holding the post of a *drungchen* (*drung chen*, secretary), the highest position in today's civil service, he is not called Drungchen Sangay, but is called Dasho Sangay, which besides many other things, creates confusion as to the actual position of an official which could not have arisen previously. In any case, once this type of trend is introduced, then every official feels entitled to such forms of address.

Then there were the people who did odd jobs in the *dzongs* who were not state employees and thus were not entitled to meals from the mess. Some of them have already been discussed under the various types of citizens in the previous section of this chapter. Some of them were called *dro-rgyar thob-pa* (morning tea entitled), *lto-gzan bkyus-ma* (lowly food recipient), *bza' pa* (a serf class), *gzhis-gnyer* (unattested position) or *gzhung dpon-sger* (bonded servants to senior officials). They were all various classes of bonded servants with varying degrees of responsibility. Their positions were hereditary, and some of their ancestors were brought as war captives or were bought in slave trades even though such practices were increasingly discouraged under the new state.

In the tax administration of the country, *dzong* officials were assisted by minor tax collectors called *drungpa*, who according to the aforementioned record of enthronement, were responsible for looking after sub-districts whose tax-paying households exceeded eighty in number. Forty-eight *drungpas* are individually named in the record indicating that there were as many such officials in the country. As the immediate intermediary between the government and the people, there was a semi-elected official called *gup* (*rga po*) whose duty it was to look after all matters concerning the tax-paying sub-districts in the country, which numbered about 140. While most of the traditional official positions have today been replaced, the post of *gup* still continues with the same regalia, mode of address and responsibilities.[49] Ura provides a detailed analysis on the variations in sub-regional administration between western and eastern Bhutan, where

49 Ardussi and Ura (2000: 50). Another post that continues as a royal sinecure is that of the *penlop* (cf. Aris 1976: 630). See Ura (2023) for a discussion on the rationale and process of structural reforms during the early period of the Wangchuck dynasty.

a number of old positions seemed to have been retained and incorporated into the state structure, whereas most positions in the west were new and expedient innovations.[50]

The enthronement record of 1747 lists a total of 1,149 state officials and functionaries. The record also makes mention of twenty *nyikems* and 160 *chibzhoems* for Punakha and Tashichhodzong, although it could very well be that these numbers were in fact for the whole country, which the record mixed up, or perhaps there is a present misreading of this record from more than 200 years ago.[51] A perhaps better reading, in any case more realistic data, is given by Aris (1979), who writes:

> In the account of the 13th *sDe-srid*'s virtuous achievements we learn (on f.93b) that on his retirement in 1763 after 14 years of rule, there were 679 lay government servants. These were divided into six ranks starting with 14 "ordinary" officers entitled to double salaries-in-kind (*gzhung-gi nyis-skal bkyus-ma*; in present vernacular, *'nyikem'*). Below them stood 90 officials entitled to a government horse (*rta-thob*; *chibs bzhon* in the honorific), and so on down to the sixth rank of "common servitors" (*lto-gzan dkyus-ma*), 280 in number.[52]

It may be an opportune moment here to mention that while the basic structure of the state was already in place by 1651, the internal administration of the country on a nationwide basis was regularized during the reign of Minjur Tenpa as the third *desi*.[53] It may also be noted here that the code of conduct of the bureaucracy was enshrined in the *Kathrim* and the officials were thus obliged to comply with the code. As the body responsible for enforcing the law of the country, they were required to maintain the highest standard of integrity and conduct.[54] Bhutanese people in general

---

50 Ura (2023: 182–188).

51 Ardussi and Ura (2000: 44).

52 Aris (1979), as cited in Phuntsho (2013: 262–263).

53 Kinga (2009: 92).

54 Aris (1982: 13) argues that the 'quasi-monastic style of government militated against the formation of heritable wealth or power'. As individual wealth accumulation was systematically disincentivized, the risk of corruption was reduced.

were god-fearing people, and as these officials discharged their functions in the *dzong* overseen by the protective deities of the country, we have ample historical evidence that the officials tried to adhere to the basic tenet of Buddhism of being honest under all circumstances, failing which they would have had to make rites of atonement which was a difficult process and thus, the best course was to refrain from wrong-doing in the first place.

In any case, even if some dubious officials were inclined to disregard the unseen code, the *Kathrim* gives specific guidelines concerning the conduct and entitlement of the rulers and governors.[55] The *Kathrim* acted as today's equivalent of the civil service act because its intended purpose was to provide a framework of civil administration of which the main arbiter was the state bureaucracy. Thus, state officials were required to establish good relations with the people. Upon appointment, *dronyers*, *dzongpons* and *penlops* had to first report on the merits and demerits of the government under their jurisdiction. They also had to give a report on expenditure incurred for rituals and prayer ceremonies, as well as lawsuits tried by them. The meritorious had to be rewarded by receiving appointments to government positions, but those who claimed credit for doing good and blamed others for doing evil were not to be given government powers.[56] *Dzongpons* and *dronyers* had to eat meals together in the kitchen. All *dzongpons* and *jadrungs* (*rgya drung*, ambassadorial officials) were entitled to 'white rations' or high-grade rice. When they traveled to try lawsuits, they were not allowed to take more than three or four attendants. Second class government officials were entitled to two attendants and one groom while junior officials were entitled to one attendant and groom each. No official could accept more than a single jar of alcohol from each litigant.[57]

At the beginning, appointment of high state officials was a straightforward case of choosing the most able from the ranks of the monastic body. However, a layer of complication was added when this tradition was replaced with the introduction of lay officials in state service. Here it is profitable to look at the career of the first lay *desi* of the country,

---

55 Windischgraetz and Wangdi (2019).

56 Aris (1986: 145).

57 Aris (1986: 149).

the infamous eighth Desi Druk Rabgay (*'brug rab rgyas*, r. 1707–1719).[58] From Sinmo (*srin mo*) in Wang (*wang*), the valley of Thimphu from where most state and monk officials originated, Druk Rabgay started out as a Choje Drukpai *garto* (*chos rje 'brug pa'i sgar lto*, court servitor of the Drukpa lordship) and steadily rose through the ranks to become the *shanyer* (abattoir in-charge) of Gasa (mgar sa), *zhung dronyer* and then *dzongpon* of Thimphu before eventually becoming the first lay *desi*.[59] Joining the Choje Drukpai *garto* was often not a matter of choice as it was obligatory for all tax paying households to send a man from each generation to serve in the court, so sons succeeded father in the *dzongs* as *garto*. However, the question of promotion generally depended on one's merit and dedication to the service unless one was an immediate relative of some high ministerial official in which case favoritism was known to occur in senior level appointments.

Though appointment at junior levels (in most cases up to the level of *chibzhoem*) could be made and endorsed by the *penlops* or *dzongpons*, appointments and endorsements of *nyikem* and higher officials needed the approval of the *lhengye zhungtshog* and the *desi* though nomination could be made by the respective lords of the *dzongs*. This was certainly the theory of recruitment, promotion and appointment of officials until the reign of Jigme Namgyal as the *penlop* of Trongsa. He emerged as a strongman in Bhutan, and *dzongs* under his jurisdiction – which comprised the whole of eastern Bhutan – gained relative autonomy from the central government in Punakha. As a result of one of his many successful interventions at the center, the *desi* in Punakha cancelled the four bags of coins that the Trongsa Penlop paid annually to the government. He was also bestowed the full prerogative to appoint all senior officials under his jurisdiction.[60] Apart from the financial gain, this prerogative almost certainly sealed the unchallenged ascendency of the Trongsa Penlop as he could then appoint men of his choice to any position he saw fit without any intervention or oversight from the center.

58 Phuntsho (2013: 307).

59 Tshewang (1994: 290).

60 Phuntsho (2013: 438).

To conclude this section, we will look at one of the main state ceremonies, which was a major preoccupation in a theocratic state. The *zhugdral* ceremony (*bzhugs gral phun sum tshogs pa*) is an interesting consideration here because this is an occasion where officials were seated according to their relative positions, the senior-most occupying the most advantageous seat in the assembly hall and so on, until the junior-most would have difficulty finding even a place to squat in state ceremonies.[61] The *chibdral* (*chibs gral*) procession[62] is another important ceremony of the state. The performance of this ceremony is recorded in some detail in the *Ballad*, but a more elaborate detail can be found in the historical novel set in the time of the second king when the traditions of the theocracy were rehabilitated and reinforced. In this account, a 300 strong contingent of men and horses form the *chibdral* procession at the entrance of Punakha Dzong for the king who was on his periodic visit to the ancient capital.[63]

The significance of the role of ceremonies in a theocratic state is a foregone conclusion, one that hardly needs reiterating here. The significance of the role of state officials as organizers of and participants in these ceremonies, however, can hardly be stressed enough. This concludes our theoretical and contextual discussion of the state bureaucracy, and we now proceed to new evidence on the nature and functions of the state administration and the society of this period of Bhutanese history. It may be reiterated here that consolidated accounts of civil administration are difficult to find, if they exist at all. This fact is not just limited to Bhutan, but is also an issue across neighboring Tibet and the Himalayas.[64] Therefore, a complete reconstruction of the historical bureaucracy, which takes into account its origin, structure and functions, can only be done when we juxtapose textual evidence with oral resources, which come in two forms. Firstly, we can access such resources from folk rituals of this period, and

---

61 For details of this ceremony, see Penjore (2011). In this paper, the institutionalization of ceremonies (*rten 'brel btsi ni*) is shown as an integral part of state formation, especially in the case of ecclesiastical states.

62 For a detailed discussion of the theory and practice of the ceremony, see Rigzin (2011).

63 Ura (1995: 133–135).

64 Travers (2011); Jansen (2018).

secondly, we still have former courtiers with memory of the old system before the major reforms of the 1950s. In the following section, a detailed treatment of one such source is made.

Analysis of the text of *Dralha*

In this section, a two-pronged approach of textual reading and ethnographic observation is taken. Before we start this section, it is opportune to reflect on the assertions of Ardussi and Ura who argued that 'The origin and protocol of the traditional Bhutanese civil service is a subject of great interest, yet poorly documented for nearly centuries'.[65] This chapter argues that even though this might very well be the case, various oral sources from this period survive to this day that provide an equally intriguing, though fossilized, account of the Bhutanese state, bureaucracy and society. The source material used in this section is the ritual text (*mgo btsem*) of the ancient martial festival called *loju* (*blo 'gyur*) discussed in detail in my preliminary analysis of the text and the festival.[66] I have argued that the origin of the festival (and its ritual verses containing a long passage on the theme of this present chapter) is in historical Bhutan, and is at least as old as the Punakha *domchoe* (*sgrub mchod*), which was instituted as a ritual celebration of the Zhabdrung's victory over the Tibetans during his struggle to establish the Bhutanese state.[67] Stoller argued that cultural memory can be found in commemorative rituals, where 'the past is, as it were, sedimented in the body'.[68] So, genealogically and semantically studying such rituals as a sedimented repository of cultural and social facts allows us to reconstruct lost or incomplete social facts, like that of the historical bureaucracy and perceptions of it by ordinary village folks in their folk idioms.

---

65 Ardussi and Ura (2000: 43).

66 Dendup (2011).

67 Chophel (2011: 101); Schwerk (2019: 23). A detailed discussion of 'King's New Year' (rgyal-po lo-gsar) held in Punakha and its role in instituting the Bhutanese state is a subject of Aris's (1976) paper.

68 Stoller (1997: 59).

To begin with, the text contains the following ten chapters:

Chapter 1. The Birth of the *Dralha*

Chapter 2. *Dralha's* Lineage: The Glorious Palden Drukpa

Chapter 3. Conjugal of Tonden Phajo (*stong ldan pha-jo*) and Sonam Pelden (*bsod nams dpal sgron*): The Founding of the State of Bhutan in Puna Dewachen gi Phodrang (*spungs thang bde ba chen po'i pho brang*)

Chapter 4. The Making of Wine Offering

Chapter 5. Preparation of Meat Offering and Dismembering a Carcass

Chapter 6. Offering of Flour (Cereal) With Butter

Chapter 7. Invitation of the High Birth *Pawo* (*dpa'bo*) and Preparation of Ritual Cakes

Chapter 8. Propitiation of *Dralha*

Chapter 9. Arrival of *Dralha* and Description

Chapter 10. Introduction and Praise of *Dralha*: Subjugation of the Malevolent Spirit

Our interest here concerns the fifth chapter. While no actual slaughter takes place, in keeping with the mood of the martial ritual invoking a warrior deity (*dgra lha*), a (symbolic) killing of a yak takes place, after which it is dismembered and various parts of its carcass are offered as meat offering (*sku skal phul*) to the deities and high officials, and as meat share (*shag skal byin*) for the common functionaries and various stereotyped characters of the society.[69]

This region of Bhutan practiced elements of agropastoralism where rice cultivation and cattle herding coexisted in a household economy. In analyzing the bond between the people and their animals in the Himalayas,

---

69 *che sa sku skal phul/ chung sa shag skal byin/*

Levine calls it a 'multifaceted interdependence'.[70] She draws upon a review of anthropological studies on human-cattle relations, and says:

> Those accounts highlighted the centrality of cattle across the cultural landscape, their place in local cosmologies, and the role cattle played in social transactions and status ranking. They also highlighted the affection that men displayed toward their animals and their seeming reluctance to slaughter them.[71]

Even though limited animal slaughters took place in these societies for both dietary and ritual purposes, Buddhist influence generally sought to subvert animal sacrifice rituals (*dmar mchod*) and replace them with alternative offerings like dough effigies,[72] or as in this case, by mere verbal recreation. It may be remembered that Buddhism itself accommodated the inevitability of certain types of violence,[73] especially ritual forms. In fact, 'magical warfare'[74] or ritual slaughter was used as an effective alternative to real violence. Mathou claimed that 'because the use of violence has been channeled by religious practice through tantric rituals, peace has become a system of government used by the civil administration known as the "Peaceful" [*zhiwey zhung-yog*]'.[75]

In his paper titled 'Dismemberment and Sharing of Game Meat […]', Huber (2019) extensively reviews the relevant literature on such practices in some Tibetan and Himalayan communities.[76] In one instance, Macdonald described a process he calls 'creative dismemberment', by which a certain Sherpa community claims that their clans (*rus*) are named according to the part of the carcass that they seized.[77] Such a dismemberment process

70 Levine (2019).

71 Evans-Pritchard (1940); Herskovits (1926) as cited in Levine (2019: 9).

72 Bentley (2009/2010: 148); Olschak (1965: 98, 166) as cited in Erschbamer (2019: 11).

73 Zimmermann (2006).

74 Schwerk (2019).

75 Mathou (2000: 232).

76 Huber (2019).

77 Macdonald (1980) as cited in Huber (2019: 17).

also appears in the origin myth of a small southwestern Bhutanese community.[78] What is of more relevance to my analysis is what Huber calls 'symbolic differentiation', which is 'always associated with defining identity or rank in relation to an animal's body'.[79] Clarifying further, he writes, 'To my present knowledge, it is only evident in mythological and hagiographical narratives written in Tibetan language. Its logic entails that specific parts of a wild animal's carcass are allotted to persons with a distinct social identity – and who are sometimes even identified after the portion they receive – or the nature and order of the body parts is indexed to some form of social ranking'. He calls this differentiation an example of allotment of 'ranked' shares. However, while there are striking parallels between Huber's classification and the case in this chapter, there are also certain differences. For example, such dismemberment – which Huber affirms is called '*sha bgo stangs*' in the wider region – is according to 'an ideal division into "eighteen portions of a carcass" (*sha lhu bco brgyad*)'. He specifically maintains that apart from these major cuts of the bovine carcass, the 'fringes of belly hair, horns, sinews, hide and an internal organ (*nang cha*)' are not considered part of such schematic divisions. However, in our case, the exact opposite is true. In the Bhutanese case, there is no attempt to achieve the ideal cut of eighteen equal portions, but on the contrary, the portions ritually shared consist of exactly those very body parts that are discounted in the accounts surveyed by Huber.

Like the long oral *Ballad of Pemi Tshewang Tashi*, which originated in the Shaa (shar) region famed for the eloquence of its people, the verse of the *dralha* is also in beautiful oral poetry. The sequence of the butchering begins with a search party scouting for appropriate sacrificial animals fit for purpose as an offering to the *dralha*. The party first describes the three types of meat animals that cannot be considered for their various perceived deformities and unpalatable habits. They are the stinking *rwa chung*[80] (goat), the *o kha dhu ru phag pa* (pig) with filthy habits, and the

78 Dorji (2013).

79 Huber (2019: 14).

80 Here it should be noted that the manuscript is a verbatim transcription of an oral narrative in vernacular Dzongkha idioms. The text precedes the recent standardization of Dzongkha orthography. The spellings occurring in this section

deformed *tsa li bya pod* (rooster). On the other hand, the animals that can be considered are large bovines like the 'pristine' *gangs gi lha gyag zer po* (yak), the 'graceful' *glang chung dpal gdong* (a particular breed of bull) and the 'fat' *gyang dkar lug po* (lamb). So, with this list, the search party is provisioned respectively by the *chang gnyer* (wine butler), *mang gnyer* (officer in-charge of butter) and *sha gnyer* (in-charge of abattoir), who solicits the *desi* (addressed as *sde srid mi dbang rgyal po*) to issue a writ[81] to the highlanders to identify a befitting meat animal from the approved list provided. An auspicious yak is chosen for the sacrifice, and it is tied with a *gnag thag* (yak wool rope) and led to *gdan sa khra mo* (the luxuriant palace) by a *khra chung can ma* (referring to a highlander with their distinctive sartorial identity) from the front and a *tsho ma sgar pa* (a court servant) who musters from the back. Upon reaching the *gdan sa*, the yak is first ritually purified by sanctified water (*khrus chu*) poured on its head and then tied to a post and slaughtered. Then the 'ranked' offering is made. This whole process is evocative of the logic and functioning of the *dzong* administration and the sometimes-arbitrary imposition of orders on the citizens using 'poetic license', as Huber also affirms, to 'achieve a particular symmetry or set of allusions'.[82]

Then begins the elaborate offering of meat portions to the various designated recipients, numbering forty-six in total. The recipients can be roughly categorized into five groups based on certain real or arbitrary similarities between the forty-six anatomical parts and their putative correspondence to functions of the office, or particular characters and qualities associated with the office holder, or a member of the society or a pantheon of deities, each of whom can grant a particular favorable outcome. Thus, as indicated in detail in Table 13.1 in the addendum to this chapter, the recipients are deities/bodhisattvas (six), monastic officials (five), civil officials (fifteen), junior civil functionaries (six) and stereotyped societal characters (fourteen) who can also partake of

---

of the chapter are as they occur in the manuscript.

81 *bka' shog ri rgyal 'dra cig bzhengs/*

82 Huber (2019: 15).

any public resource distribution ceremony even if they were allocated inferior portions.[83]

As it is in Tibet and the wider Himalayan communities, the offering (*sku skal phul*) or allocation/share (*shag skal byin*) of body parts roughly corresponds to the relative importance of the person or the object of offering: the best portions, or portions that are perceived to signify certain ritual significance, are reserved for the significant receivers while some inferior portions like the bladder (holding urine and thus signifying lust) are allotted to putatively frivolous characters. This serves mainly as a form of ridicule of the role and nature of some of these stereotypical characters in the society like *zam 'dod chags can* (lustful women), *mi ngan rnams* (bad people), *pha rgan rgas* (elderly men), *aa khu brog pa* (highland nomads), etc. However, like the *sbyin bdag bzang po* (generous patron), these representative characters also have a significance to the state, either as its supporters or beneficiaries.

The specific details of the ritual correspondence of the 'ranked' shares and the bureaucratic and societal positions of the receivers is given in Table 13.1 in the addendum to this chapter. Even though the perimeter of such a poetic symmetry between butchered body parts and state functionaries cannot accommodate a full enumeration of the hierarchy of the state, what is demonstrated amply is the common people's impressions of the state, and their real or imagined relation to it. One may be tempted to point out the incompleteness or inaccuracy of these narratives, but we must not forget that these are largely figurative renditions by common folks, who cannot be expected even contemporaneously to be able to accurately or exhaustively represent a governing structure. Significantly, these embedded folk memories have far outlived the state itself, which has undergone various iterations since then, most of which are not formally or customarily documented or memorialized.

---

83 According to Pommaret (2009: 60), 'These resources could be, amongst others, stones, timber, paper, ink, cheese, butter, textiles and vegetable dyes. A kind of redistribution of the wealth took place through rituals or other functions as we can understand from the *bkang gso* ritual at Orgyan chos gling where there is a display of wealth and the prosperity…'

Conclusion: continuity and departures from the historical bureaucracy

The historical officialdom (*poenkha*) is the predecessor of the current civil service under the Royal Civil Service Commission (RCSC) of Bhutan. This metamorphosis is described by Ura as follows:

> In the tax reforms initiated by the second King and completed early in the reign of the third King, the traditional posts, of which a large number were linked to collection, storage and disbursement of in-kind taxes, were abolished. Thus, the number of traditional posts of *Nyikem* and *Chibzhoem* in the Dzongkhag (modern administrative district) was reduced, while new posts in the centre proliferated extensively in accordance with the demands of centralized planning and aid mobilization. The generic rank of *Chibzhoem* disappeared altogether.[84]

With these reforms, one important change that took place was in relation to the role of citizens. From being patrons (*sbyin bdag*) of the state,[85] sometimes reluctantly so and with much inconvenience, under the Wangchuck dynasty – particularly from the time of the third king – the people have become the primary beneficiary of the developmental state's largesse. The reforms introduced new modes of revenue generation and largely relieved the citizens of all their responsibilities towards the upkeep of the state.

In the traditional bureaucracy, hierarchy was kept to a minimum and all dedicated and meritorious servants could hope to achieve higher positions. There were only two types of *kabney* in use then, the red and white, although the red could be stylized and worn differently to distinguish the *lhengye* from the *nyikem*. Under the new and expanded system, there is a proliferation in the classification of civil servants. There is also a growing trend to seek professional distinctions.

However, even as excesses are naturally bad, it must be said that upholding the best of the traditional system, with its 'ranked' privileges, is an integral part of the country's statecraft. Phuntsho claims that 'as the civil service replaced medieval officialdom and its officers became

84 Ura (2004: 103).

85 Kinga (2009: 74).

the immediate point of call for the citizens, the prestige and benefits of working as a civil servant increased and this subsequently changed the expectation of most young people […]. [T]he post of a Dasho or a high-ranking official became a much desired ambition in life'.[86] While some might perceive this point with misgivings, this in fact shows a positive preoccupation that has systemic benefits. Globally, public service is a profession that abounds with titles and decorations. Frey corroborates this when he argues that 'in the public sector, more awards are supplied […]. [T]he special generosity to state servants stems from the relative modesty of public sector salaries when compared to the private sector'.[87]

This chapter, based on primary, secondary and ethnographic sources, has delineated the institutionalization of the Bhutanese state, a process that included the creation of various privy and public offices, differentiated actors, and standardized processes. While the sparse primary textual evidence enables the enumeration of particular offices and their holders, including their codes of conduct and privileges, it is in folk literature that we actually see how the people perceived them. It is also in this literature that we get a glimpse of how the common folk were able to engage and negotiate with the system. Through sacrifices and perseverance, many of them were also able to become a part of the system, thus making it receptive to their particular needs and interests. It is perhaps this reciprocity that enabled both these parties to endure to this day under the patronage of an overarching dynastic polity.

86 Phuntsho (2013: 569).

87 Frey (2005).

Addendum

Table 13.1: Ritual/poetic correspondence between 'ranked' shares, and the recipients' official and societal positions

Body part	Translation	Recipient	Category	Rationale
mar ro chen dbus kyi rnam shes	life force	*dorji chang*	deity	for the enlightenment of the departed soul
srog lus dbang thang	essence of body, spirit and 'field of power'	*dkon mchog gsum*	deity	to pursue the path of dharma
dmar po khrag gyi spal thag	blood vein	*yidam lha*	deity	for quintessential benefits of the path
brang khog tshil lu	fatty cut of the chest	*dpa' bo mkha' 'gro*	deity	for instant fruition of actions
glo ba gangs ri dkar po	the mountainous heap of lungs	the four *slob dpon*	monastic official	maintaining purity of the dharma
mtho sar bkal ba'i bya la	the elevated hump	*lha dbang sde pa*	civil official	for greater authority in bringing peace to the southern gorge (*lho rong*)
raa ba gyas raa gyon raa	pair of horns	*spyi la*	civil official	to defend the religious state
rna cog gyas gyon	pair of ears	*gzim dpon*	civil official	maintaining greater awareness
gyang kho sha yi bang mdzod	?	*gzim dpon nang ma*	civil official	maintaining prosperity of the treasury
grod pa'i log gi gong ma	?	*gong ser gzim dpon?*	civil official	for eloquence of speech
mig gtog gyas gyon	pair of eyeballs	*sku tshab*	civil official	for broadening of vision
grod pa'i log gi mtshe ra	?	*gnyer chen/ ngyer gyog*	civil official	maintaining sufficient food stock
lce ru tog med pa	boneless tongue	*chos gnas dmang* (priests)	monastic official	for effortless recitation
glo ba'i ltag gi dung cung	esophagus	*graa tshang dbu mdzad*	monastic official	for throatful chanting
gong 'dril mar gyi dung chung	?	*sha gnyer*	civil official	for granting of a more generous meat share
pho ba dzing gi skal pa	tripe	*gsol dpon/gsol gyog*	civil official	for consummate food preparation

Body part	Translation	Recipient	Category	Rationale
tsig pa'i log gi tsig chen	prime spare rib	*rta dpon*	civil official	for command of horses and transport
dung snying sha yi zur cung	heart	*yul lha*	deity	to maintain community order
mgu tog	head	*dgra lha*	deity	appeasing the warrior deity
klag pa'i log gi 'od tshil	fat in the hoof?	*bskang brgyud pa*	monastic official	?
sgal tshig nyi shu rtsa brgyad	28? vertebrae bones	*btsi pa'i slob dpon*	monastic official	for keeping astrological tabs
khal mi rda ga rdog go	kidney	*bzo rig slob dpon*	civil functionary	for intricate carving
rgyu ma log gi btag tshil	fat in the tail joint?	*tshems bzo*	civil functionary	kaleidoscopic embroidery
rgyod pa'i log gi che chum	?	*brag wa dza mo* and *mi tsam to can*	societal character	?
rgyod pa'i log gi sbrang tshang	?	*dar dkar rnams* and *sbrang bcom mi*	societal character	harvesting honey as a livelihood?
rgyu ma na ra nu ru	unruly intestines	*chang chu aa lo*	societal character	for sloppy consumption
rgyu ma nang gi dur dur	content of the intestines	*dam nyams dgra ba*	societal character	to incapacitate enemies?
chin po dza ri smug po	liver	*bshan pa*	civil functionary	for butchering a carcass
chin pa'i log gi khris pa	pancreas?	*mi nad gzhi can*	societal character	to overcome diseases
glo ba'i bar gyi bar bcad	?	*aar dpon*	civil official	to keep miscreants (*aar mkhan*) at bay?
bya la 'gu gi dam spu	strand of hair on the hump?	*dpral thal rnams*	societal character	to cover baldness?
rakang pa'i bar gi bar sha	meat between the legs (probably rump cut)?	*gros dpon*	civil official	for balanced decision making
rtsi ba gyas gyon gnyis	two rib sides	*sbyin bdga bzang po*	societal character	for prosperity of the generous patrons
lgang phu chu yi brkyal pa	bladder	*zam 'dod chags can*	societal character	to satiate lust and ensure progeny

Body part	Translation	Recipient	Category	Rationale
rdo rje rtsa ba'i pags ko	hide around the genital?	*rdzong zhong za mo* and *sman chu bu mo*	societal character	to scratch wherever it itches
rkang pa'i bar gyi zam cung	?	*mi ngan rnams*	societal character	?
mjug ma 'og gi tshum tshum	anus (closing/ opening below the tail)?	*sgo ra dpon*	civil official	to control entry
mjug ma dar gi phod go	the tail-end hair	*rtogs ldan sgar pa*	societal character	to explore with gaiety like the wagging tail
ko ba'i la pa le pa	patches of hide?	*ko kred rnams*	civil functionary	to earn livelihood from leather work
spu rtsi nyi shu rtsa brgyad	the fur/hair	*aa khu brog pa*	societal character	to weave colored shawls to keep away summer rains in the highland
ru to ko ltab bzhi	four limbs	*pha rgan rgas*	societal character	to supplement the health of elderly bodies
rkang pa'i log gi rmig cum	the hooves	*bang chen rnams*	civil official	to aid movement while on law enforcement expeditions
rting ma'i rtsa yi rag rog	sundry ankle sinews and bones?	*thab dpon*	civil functionary	for disposal?
sna pa gyas gyong gnyis	two nostrils?	*spyi dpon* and *las tshan*	civil functionary	for augmented awareness
so yi dung so dkar mo	the white tooth enamel	*dpa' rtsal rnams*	civil official	to bite into enemies
klog mi nang gi dung cung?	the wind pipe?	*rigs bzang dpa bo*	societal character	to conduct propitiation ritual (*lha gsol*)

Bibliography

Primary sources (*Chos skad* and *rdzong kha)*

CBS (2008). *Gong sa 'jigs med rnam rgyal gyi rtogs brjod dpa' bo'i gang rgyangs bzhugs so*, Thimphu: Centre for Bhutan Studies.

DDC (1999). *Pha jo 'brug sgom zhig po'i rnam thar thugs rje'i chu rgyun*, Thimphu: Dzongkha Development Commission.

Drag shos sangs rgyas rdo rje (1999). *Dpal ldan 'brug pa rin po che zhabs drung ngag dbang rnam rgyal gyi rnam thar*, Thimphu: Dzongkha Development Commission.

Drag shos shes rab mtha' yes (2008). *'Brug gi bstan srid chags rabs*, Gelephu: Sherab Lhamo Publication.

Kun bzang phrin las, ed. (n.d.). *Gzim dpon pad ma'i tshe dbang bkra shis*, Thimphu: KMT Printers and Publishers.

Slob dpon gnag mdog (1986). *'Brug dkar po: 'brug rgyal khab kyi chos srid ngas stangs*, Tharpaling: Author.

Slob dpon pad ma tshe dbang (1994). *'Brug gyi rgyal rabs/ 'brug gsal ba'i sgron me*, Thimphu: Jamyang Lhundrup.

Secondary sources

Ardussi, J. (2004). 'Formation of the Bhutanese State (*'brug gzhung*) in the 17th Century and Its Tibetan Antecedents', *Journal of Bhutan Studies*, vol. 11 (Winter), pp. 10–32.

Ardussi, J. and K. Ura (2000). 'Population and Governance in Mid-18th Century Bhutan, as Revealed in the Enthronement Record of *Thugs-sprul* Jigs med grags pa I (1725-1761)', *Journal for Bhutan Studies*, vol. 2, no. 2 (Summer), pp. 36–78.

Aris, M. (1976). 'The Admonition of the Thunderbolt Cannonball and Its Place in the Bhutanese New Year Festival', *Bulletin of the School of Oriental and African Studies*, vol. 39, no. 3, pp. 601–635.

Aris, M. (1979). *Bhutan: The Early History of a Himalayan Kingdom*, Warminster: Aris & Philips.

Aris, M. (1982). *Views of Medieval Bhutan: The Diary and Drawings of Samuel Davis 1783*, London/Washington D.C.: Serindia Publications and Smithsonian Institution Press.

Aris, M. (1986). *Sources for the History of Bhutan*, Wein: zu beziehen von.

Aris, M. (1994). 'Conflict and Conciliation in Traditional Bhutan'. In M. Hutt, ed., *Bhutan: Perspectives on Conflict and Dissent*, Scotland: Paul Strachan - Kiscadale Ltd., p. 24.

Aris, M. (1998). *The Raven Crown: The Origins of the Buddhist Monarchy in Bhutan*, Chicago: Serindia Publications.

Baillie, L.M. (1999). 'Father Estevao Cacella's Report on Bhutan in 1627', *Journal of Bhutan Studies*, vol. 1, no 1. (Autumn), pp. 1–35.

Barth, F. (2018). 'Power and Compliance in Rural Bhutanese Society', *Journal of Bhutan Studies*, vol. 38 (Summer), pp. 46–64.

Chophel, D. (2011). 'Invoking a Warrior Deity: A Preliminary Study of *Lo-ju*', *The Journal for Bhutan Studies*, vol. 25 (Winter), pp. 82–120.

Chophel, D. (2012). 'Animal Wellbeing: The Concept and Practice of Tsethar in Bhutan'. In K. Ura and D. Chophel, eds., *Buddhism Without Borders*: *Proceedings of the International Conference on Globalized Buddhism*, Thimphu: Centre for Bhutan Studies, pp. 97–114.

Chophel, D. and D. Khandu (2014). '*Byis pa'i dpa'bo*: The Dance of Youthful Heroes'. In S. Kumagai, ed., *Bhutanese Buddhism and Its Culture*, Kathmandu: Vajra Publications, pp. 207–220.

Cüppers, C. (2007). 'Bstan 'dzin chos rgyal's Bhutan Legal Code of 1729 in Comparison With sde srid sangs rgyas rgya mtsho's Guidelines for Government Officials'. In J.A. Ardussi and F. Pommaret, eds., *Bhutan: Change and Tradition*, Leiden/Boston: Brill, pp. 28–45.

Dargye, Y. (2001). *History of Drukpa Kagyud School in Bhutan* (12th to 17th Century A.D.), Thimphu: self-published.

Dargye, Y. and P.K. Sorensen, with G. Tshering (2008). *Play of the Omniscient: Life and Work of Jamgon Ngwang Gyaltshen* (17th to 18th Century), Thimphu: National Library of Bhutan.

Dorji, C.T. (1997). *The Blue Annals of Bhutan*, New Delhi: Vikas Publishing Limited.

Dorji, S. (2008). *The Biography of Zhabdrung Ngawang Namgyel*, Phuentsholing: KMT Publishing House.

Dorji, T. (2013). 'An Ox for Talang: Appeasing the Guardian Deity and Renewing Community Pact', unpublished working paper.

Erschbamer, M. (2019). 'Taming of Supernatural Entities and Animal Sacrifice: The Synthesis of Tibetan Buddhism and Local Shamanistic Traditions in Northern Sikkim (India)', *Études mongoles et sibériennes, centrasiatiques et tibétaines*, vol. 50, https://doi.org/10.4000/emscat.3915

Frey, B.S. (2005). *Knight Fever: Towards an Economics of Awards*, CESIFO Working Paper no. 1468, http://www.cesifo.org/DocDL/cesifo1_wp1468.pdf

Huber, T. (2019). 'Dismemberment and Sharing of Game Meat by Pastoralist Hunters on the Tibetan Plateau', *Études mongoles et sibériennes, centrasiatiques et tibétaines*, vol. 50, https://doi.org/10.4000/emscat.3969

Imaeda, Y. (2013). *The Successors of Zhabdrung Ngawang Namgyel: Hereditary Heirs and Reincarnations*, Thimphu: Riyang Books.

Jansen, B. (2018). *The Monastery Rules*: *Buddhist Monastic Organization in Pre-Modern Tibet*, Oakland: University of California Press.

Kinga, K. (2009). *Polity, Kingship and Democracy: A Biography of the Bhutanese State*, Thimphu: Ministry of Education.

Levine, N.E. (2019). 'A Multifaceted Interdependence: Tibetan Pastoralists and Their Animals', *Études mongoles et ibériennes, centrasiatiques et tibétaines*, vol. 50. https://doi.org/10.4000/emscat.3822

Macdonald, A.W. (1980). 'Creative Dismemberment among the Tamang and Sherpas of Nepal'. In M. Aris and Aung San Suu Kyi, eds., *Tibetan Studies in Honour of Hugh Richardson*, Warminster: Aris & Phillips, pp. 199–208.

Mathou, T. (2000). 'The Politics of Bhutan: Change in Continuity', *Journal of Bhutan Studies*, vol. 2, no. 2 (Winter), pp. 250–262.

Penjore, D. (2011). 'Rows of Auspicious Seats: The Role of bzhugs gral phun sum tshogs pa'i rten 'brel Ritual in the Founding of the First Bhutanese State in the 17th Century', *Journal of Bhutan Studies*, vol. 24 (Summer), pp. 1–42.

Phuntsho, K. (2013). *The History of Bhutan*, Noida: Random House India.

Pommaret, F. (2009). 'Alliances and Power in Central Bhutan: A Narrative of Religion, Prestige and Wealth (mid 19th-mid 20th centuries)', *Bulletin of Tibetology*, vol. 45, no. 2, pp. 49–66.

Prebish, C.S. (1974). *Buddhist Monastic Discipline: The Sanskrit Pratimoksa Sutras of the Mahasamghikas and Mulasarvastivadins* (First Indian reprint 1996), Delhi: Motilal Banarsidass.

RAPA (n.d). *Punakha Drubchen and Tshechu*, Thimphu: Royal Academy of Performing Arts.

Rapten, P. (2001). 'Patang: The Symbols of Heroes', *Journal of Bhutan Studies*, vol. 5, pp. 94–112.

Rigzin, K. (2011). 'Chibdral: A Traditional Bhutanese Welcome Ceremony', *Journal of Bhutan Studies*, vol. 24 (Summer), pp. 43–54.

Schwerk, D. (2019). 'Drawing Lines in a Mandala: A Sketch of Boundaries Between Religion and Politics in Bhutan', *Working Paper Series of the HCAS 'Multiple Secularities – Beyond the West, Beyond Modernities'*, vol. 12, Leipzig University, https://doi.org/10.36730/2020.1.msbwbm.12

Sewala Trulku Ngawang Pekar (n.d.). *The Introductory Biography of the Hereditary Prince Incarnation* (*The First Zhabdrung, Ngawang Namgyel*) (ed. S. Dorji, 2004), Thimphu: Centre for Bhutan Studies.

Stoller, P. (1997). *Sensuous Scholarship*, Philadelphia: University of Pennsylvania Press.

Tashi, T. (2008). *Mysteries of the Raven Crown: The Inner, Outer and Secret Coronations*, Thimphu: Bhutan Observer.

Travers, A. (2011). 'The Careers of the Noble Officials of the Ganden Phodrang (1895-1959): Organisation and Hereditary Divisions Within the Service of State', *Revue d''etudes tib'etaines* (RET), vol. 21, pp. 155–174.

Tshewang, P. (n.d.). *A Brief History of the First Hereditary King of Bhutan*, unpublished manuscript.

Ura, K. (1995). *The Hero with a Thousand Eyes: A Historical Novel* (fifth reprint: 2011), Thimphu: Author.

Ura, K. (1996). *The Ballad of Pemi Tshewang Tashi: A Wind Borne Feather*, Thimphu: self-published.

Ura, K. (2004). 'Regalia of Distinction of the Civil Service'. In *Deities, Archers and Planners: In the Era of Decentralization* (Collection of papers), Thimphu.

Ura, K. (2012). 'Massive Rice Offering in Wangdue Phodrang in Zhabdrung Rinpoche's Time', *Journal of Bhutan Studies*, vol. 27 (Winter), pp. 1–14.

Ura, K. (2023). *Bhutan: The Unremembered Nation*, vol. 2, New York: Oxford University Press.

Whitecross, R.W. (2017). 'Law, "Tradition" and Legitimacy: Contesting Driglam Namzha'. In J.D. Schmidt, ed., *Development Challenges in Bhutan: Perspectives on Inequality and Gross National Happiness*, Cham: Springer Verlag, pp. 115–134.

Windischgraetz, M. and R. Wangdi (2019). *The Black-Slate Edict of Punakha Dzong*, Thimphu: JSW Law Publishing Series.

Zimmermann, M. (2006). 'Only a Fool Becomes a King: Buddhist Stances on Punishment'. In M. Zimmermann with the assistance of C.H. Ho and P. Pierce, eds., *Buddhism and Violence*, Lumbini: Lumbini International Research Institute, pp. 213–242.

14 Law, Rights and Childhood: United Nations Convention on the Rights of the Child and Its Implementation in Bhutan

Richard W. Whitecross

> In Bhutan, family systems have always been strongly maintained. Children are well taken care of by a society which accords them high importance.[1]

International conventions and how they are perceived and understood by policy and lawmakers and how the principles set out in the conventions are translated into official policy and law remain an under researched area in Bhutanese studies focusing on contemporary Bhutan. More importantly, from wider legal, human rights and development perspectives, looking critically at the reception and role of the conventions in Bhutan illustrates the complex interaction between a range of competing normativities from which valuable lessons can be learned. Whilst research suggests that implementation or the resistance to implementation of aspects of international conventions highlight underlying paradoxes in the wider international human rights agenda, the focus of this chapter is on the following question: How does ratifying an international convention influence policy and legal development in the ratifying state? Bhutan,

1 Royal Government of Bhutan (1999: 4). This paper draws on fieldwork notes gathered during various periods of research conducted in Bhutan between 2000 and 2004. These are augmented by further email exchanges and more recently virtual discussions with Bhutanese lawyers and civil society leaders. In addition, further legal research has been undertaken as part of a wider research project on the role of the Convention on the Rights of the Child in South Asia. The opinions expressed are those of the author only.

often overlooked in academic literature, offers a range of insights into how states engage with international conventions. Through an analysis of Bhutan's ratification of the United Nations Convention on the Rights of the Child (hereafter UNCRC), this paper, which complements and extends Alvarez Ortega's chapter, argues that the constitution and the new political framework it created have been critical in this process of constructive engagement and have embedded in policy and lawmaking a new approach to international conventions and human rights in Bhutan.

According to the Initial State Report to the Committee on the Rights of the Child submitted by Bhutan in April 1999, all Bhutanese children are 'considered an important target group of all integrated development programmes', and the 'rights and interests of children are safeguarded by many provisions of different Acts'.[2] Located between India and China, Bhutan has undergone major social and economic changes in the last seventy years, notably the introduction of state sponsored education, increasing rural–urban migration and a rise in non-agricultural occupations. These changes have taken place against the political and constitutional transformation of the country with a gradual move from direct royal rule to the introduction of parliamentary democracy following the enactment of the Bhutanese Constitution in 2008.

The UNCRC was signed by Bhutan on 4 June 1990 as tensions between the Bhutanese authorities and Lhotshampa settlers in southern Bhutan flared up. By signing the UNCRC, Bhutan expressed its intention to comply with the treaty. However, an expression of intent in itself is not binding. Bhutan went further and ratified the UNCRC on 1 August 1990. By ratifying the UNCRC Bhutan was committing that it would deal with the UNCRC according to its own national procedures. Ratification therefore is important both for demonstrating the willingness to implement the UNCRC, and for the spotlight it then brings to bear on the existing national policy and legal frameworks of the ratifying state.

The UNCRC 1989 presents a particular vision of children and childhood. This chapter argues that the 2008 Constitution marks a major juncture in the preparation and enactment of legislation and policies more aligned to the UNCRC's vision for children and their rights in

2 Royal Government of Bhutan (1999a: 5).

Bhutan. Merry, writing on the Convention on the Elimination of all forms of Discrimination Against Women (CEDAW), describes it and other international conventions, including the UNCRC, as 'law without sanctions'.[3] Although the CEDAW reporting process, as Merry notes, lacks the power to 'punish, it does *important cultural work* by articulating principles in a formal and public setting and demonstrating how they apply to the country under scrutiny' (emphasis added).[4] It is this '*cultural work*' that is the focus of the discussion below. This chapter presents the first legal anthropological analysis of the three state reports submitted by the Bhutanese authorities and the formal responses, called 'concluding observations', of the Committee of the UNCRC to those reports. Building on Merry's approach, the state party reports and presentations made by the Bhutanese governments and the concluding observations between 1999 and 2017 are analyzed. It is argued that with the Third State Party Report submitted in 2014, six years after the enactment of the 2008 Constitution, we see a remarkable and significant transformation in the approach of the Bhutanese authorities to the reporting process. Article 9 of the 2008 Constitution sets out the 'Principles of State Policy' to be applied by Bhutanese governments. Article 9, Section 3 of the Constitution states 'the State shall endeavour to create a civil society free of oppression, discrimination and violence, based on the rule of law, protection of human rights and dignity, and to ensure the fundamental rights and freedoms of the people'.[5] This transformation reveals the 'cultural work' of transforming policy and lawmaking as evidenced by the substantial increase in substantive legislation and policy developments set out in the 'Third State Report' submitted in October 2014.

This chapter sets out the broad context of international conventions and the emerging focus on human rights law in Bhutan in the 1990s. It then outlines the main framework of the Convention on the Rights of the Child, and the importance of the state reports and review function of the UN committee. It then critically examines the three rounds of reporting and committee hearings since Bhutan submitted its first state report in

---

3 Merry (2003: 943).

4 Merry (2003: 943).

5 Constitution of Bhutan, 2008, Article 9, Section 3, p. 18.

1999. From this examination it is argued that we can detect a cultural shift in the approach to the UNCRC, reflected by the level of engagement with the UNCRC principles in the state reports prepared and submitted by the Bhutanese government. More specifically, through the examination of the three state reports, we can identify major legislative and policy developments that support the incorporation and implementation of the UNCRC in Bhutanese law and policy making. It is this unnoticed, yet remarkable, change that reveals the symbiotic relationship between the 'cultural work' of the UNCRC and the 2008 Constitution of Bhutan.

Turning a spotlight on Bhutan: international conventions and human rights

Bhutan's admission to the United Nations in 1971 was perhaps the most significant achievement in terms of marking its independence and sovereignty. The 1950s and 1960s witnessed the steady transformation of Bhutan with the introduction of a formal education system and the development of a recognizable civil service. The third king introduced through the National Assembly a consolidating legal text, the *Thrimzhung Chenmo*, in 1957 which outlined state law for a range of legal issues from property ownership and marriage to criminal law. However, the late 1980s and early 1990s was a troubled period for Bhutan.[6] The widely reported exodus of approximately 100,000 Nepalis from primarily southern Bhutan to refugee camps in eastern Nepal brought Bhutan under scrutiny from a range of international organizations, notably Amnesty International, the International Committee of the Red Cross and the UNHCR, who expressed grave concerns over the treatment of political prisoners and suspected terrorists and other human rights abuses.[7] Prior to the international crisis, moves to break Bhutan's isolation from the international political scene began with the cultivation of relations in the South Asia region when Bhutan joined the Colombo Plan in 1962 and SAARC in 1985.

As already mentioned, Bhutan became a signatory to the UNCRC at the point where international attention was focusing on human rights issues

---

6 Hutt (1994); Long (2019); Mathou (1998); Thinley (1994).

7 Amnesty International (1994); UNHCR (2002).

in Bhutan. A major series of structural reforms of the legal system in part in response to the external criticism were instigated under the supervision of former Chief Justice Lyonpo Sonam Tobgye, for example, the formal training of judges and the improvement of the criminal justice system and the preparation of a new Civil and Criminal Procedure (2002) and Penal Code (2004). In turn, the same chief justice chaired the Constitutional Drafting Committee responsible for the 2008 Constitution.

Merry argues that 'the process of ratification, preparing reports, and presenting and discussing reports fosters new cultural understandings'.[8] For a legal anthropologist, this prompts a range of questions. How do these 'new cultural understandings' reach the domestic, private level? How do these 'new cultural understandings' fostered through the exchanges between international bodies, advisers and Bhutanese officials filter down and become socially meaningful in the complex quotidian networks of relationships? What new local meanings arise from these encounters and how do they translate into material, as well as symbolic, resources of power and influence? This paper cannot address all of these questions; however, it will focus on the 'new cultural understandings' that informed policy makers and legislators. Even before the first 'concluding observations' from the UN committee issued in 2001, aspects of this process were beginning to be evident in the late 1990s in Bhutan. A prominent aspect of the reforms mentioned above that began in the mid and late 1990s was the emphasis on the introduction of formal legal education for lawyers and judges, funded by various international NGOs, notably Danida. In the early 2000s, young lawyers educated in India engaged in civic education sessions with young people and villagers about their rights and obligations as part of a conscious move to educate the public.[9] Although this approach was top down and focused on duties and responsibilities, as much as it did on rights, it was an important step towards creating new, local understandings of the role of laws and policy in everyday life.[10]

---

8 Merry (2003: 943).

9 From interviews and discussions gathered during fieldwork (2003–2004).

10 E.g. Youth Development Fund (2004).

The UNCRC: the framework

The United Nations Convention on the Rights of the Child represents the culmination of the International Decade of the Child (1979–89).[11] The UNCRC is the most widely ratified human rights convention with 196 countries as State Parties as of October 2015. Bhutan joined the UN in 1971 and was amongst the first signatories to the UNCRC in 1990. The UNCRC consists of forty-two articles that set out children's rights and how governments should work together to make them available to all children.[12] Under the terms of the UNCRC, governments are required to meet children's basic needs and help them reach their full potential. Central to this obligation on the state is the acknowledgment that every child has fundamental rights.[13]

The UNCRC is, arguably, the most comprehensive international human rights instrument to date, for civil, political, economic, social and cultural rights are all prescribed in a framework that recognizes the role of parents and legal guardians in developing the child. Although most rights automatically accrue to the child, there is a clear recognition of the evolving role of the child in decisions affecting them – as the child matures, the child is expected to participate in the decision-making processes. Whilst the UNCRC complements rights enshrined in other instruments, e.g., the right to education, it does more than codify existing

---

11 In 2000, two optional protocols were added to the UNCRC. One asks governments to ensure children under the age of eighteen are not forcibly recruited into their armed forces. The second calls on states to prohibit child prostitution, child pornography and the sale of children into slavery. These have now been ratified by more than 120 states. A third optional protocol was added in 2011. This enables children whose rights have been violated to complain directly to the UN Committee on the Rights of the Child.

12 The full UNCRC has fifty-four articles in total. Articles 43–54 focus on how adults and governments should work together to ensure children are able to enjoy all their rights.

13 These include the right to:

- Life, survival and development
- Protection from violence, abuse or neglect
- An education that enables children to fulfil their potential
- Be raised by, or have a relationship with, their parents
- Express their opinions and be listened to.

law: it can be argued that the UNCRC and its committee represent a new peak of the UN era of international human rights law. Why? Because the committee oversees its implementation by actively involving all relevant UN agencies and receiving alternative reports from local NGOs. Finally, the committee works closely with UNICEF and takes a strong stance, as we shall see, on many issues affecting children in the reporting state. In this case, Bhutan.

Finally, when the committee drafts its concluding observations, it must take the best interests of the child (Art. 3) and the principle of non-discrimination (Art. 2) as underpinning the realization of the rights set out in the UNCRC. Unlike other reporting systems, the committee of the UNCRC requires that governments publish the reports and disseminate the observations of the committee. The emphasis on transparency was reflected in an important policy framing document issued by the Bhutanese government in 1999 entitled *Bhutan 2020: A Vision of Peace, Prosperity and Happiness*. However, more significantly, the 2008 Constitution explicitly makes the right to information a fundamental right in Article 7, Section 3. Importantly, the committee's approach is one of consolidation – it regards itself as working alongside developing internal state systems for monitoring and realizing children's rights. This is a crucial part of the process of 'cultural work' referred to by Merry and central to the underlying argument of this chapter.

The Initial State Report: 1999 and the legal framework

> There is no child abuse here – we aren't like the west.[14]

The Initial State Report submitted by Bhutan to the UN Committee on the Rights of the Child (the Committee) was submitted in April 1999, only nine months after a *kasho* (royal decree) issued by the fourth king, Jigme Singye Wangchuck, on 10 June 1998 devolved full executive power from the king to an elected cabinet.[15] In its conclusion, it states that 'one can see that there are many areas of the Convention not translated into

14 Interview with a civil servant, Thimphu, Bhutan F/N, 31 August 2004.

15 Mathou (1999).

law. This is due to the fact that problems in those areas have not emerged in Bhutan'.[16] Indeed, during fieldwork discussions with Bhutanese lawyers and officials there was a commonly expressed view that many of the problems addressed by the UNCRC simply did not exist in Bhutan.[17] They stressed, as illustrated below, an image of Bhutanese society as possessing a coherent, homogenous value system that safeguards all Bhutanese children.

At the time of the 1999 Initial State Report, the legal framework of Bhutan covered some, but not all, of the articles of the UNCRC. Amendments to the Marriage Act 1980 sought to address Article 9 on the separation of parents by providing for the maintenance and wellbeing of children in the event of their parents divorcing. Similarly, the Rape Act 1993 incorporated articles 19 and 34, the right to protection from violence and from sexual exploitation respectively. The Committee on the Rights of the Child published its 'Concluding Observations' on the Initial State Report on 9 July 2001. In it, the Committee observed that:

> While noting various legislative measures already taken or proposed with respect to child rights [...], the Committee is concerned that they do not reflect a comprehensive rights-based approach to the implementation of the Convention.[18]

The Initial State Report submitted by the Bhutanese authorities presented a positive view of children in Bhutan, stressing the importance of shared social values, respect for religion and 'traditional' family structures that protect children. The Initial State Report states as follows:

> The primary concern of Bhutanese parents has always been the welfare of their children. Children, too, respect their parents. Bhutanese are traditional people. Respect for the religion and culture and respect for parents, teachers and elders are not only taught at home and at school but are also seen in practice. It is these values that have moulded in

16 Royal Government of Bhutan (1999: 39).

17 Various periods of fieldwork were conducted between 2000 and 2004.

18 Committee UNCRC (2001: para. 12).

> Bhutan a society which is less familiar with social problems that are prevalent elsewhere in the world.[19]

This statement echoes the National Assembly resolution approving the Sixth Five Year Plan that stated:

> The wellbeing and security of the country depends on the strength of its culture, traditions and value systems. Therefore, every effort must be made to foster the unfailing faith, love and respect for the country's traditional values and institutions that have provided the basis and ensured the security and sovereignty of the nation while giving it a distinct national identity.[20]

The Committee noted that 'nevertheless, it is concerned that traditional attitudes towards children in society at large may limit' the exercise of their rights 'especially within the family'.[21] The image of Bhutanese society and culture as a static, bounded, homogenized space in which rights discourse already existed in a local form, often reflecting religious principles and social values, was challenged by the Committee. This challenge was illustrated by concerns for children of the Lhotshampa minority:

> [The Committee is] concerned about the impact on children of reports of discrimination against individuals belonging to the Lhotshampas. In particular, it is concerned about reports: that these children face de facto discrimination in access to education and other services and on the basis of status, activities, or opinions of their parents, or relatives.[22]

The 'Concluding Observations' of the Committee make it clear that it viewed the reference to 'traditional values' as an attempt to deflect or contain any critical reflection on the treatment of children and the varying levels of inability to resist, challenge and, above all, alter their social

---

19 Royal Government of Bhutan (19991: 11).

20 National Assembly, 65th Session, June 1987, Resolution No.18.

21 Committee UNCRC (2001: para. 32)

22 Committee UNCRC (2001: para. 30).

realities. Therefore, the Committee is explicit in setting out its concerns that children were unable to exercise their rights within the family. Furthermore, the Committee highlighted the lack of data by which to monitor policies designed to implement the UNCRC. In particular, the absence of disaggregated data in respect of ethnic groups, ill-treatment of children, disabled children from poor households and child labor were among the main areas identified. The focus on data is significant. It underscores the importance for reliable and verifiable information to underpin claims set out in the Initial State Report. This concern for data is a common feature of the 'Concluding Observations' and it is one that can present a reporting state with a range of challenges. Within the Bhutanese context, it was an important lesson that international bodies require tangible information that often was not at the time routinely gathered.

In part, the approach of the Bhutanese authorities was to argue that existing legislation adequately provides protection and that there is no need for an explicitly rights-based approach. The Initial State Report stated, 'Laws are framed and adopted by the National Assembly which is comprised of the representatives of the people'.[23] From earlier archival research on the annual debates in the National Assembly, there is little indication of any meaningful awareness of, or engagement with, human rights and the UNCRC among the elected representatives. This has however changed – the 2008 Constitution consciously sets out its provisions based on terms of the UN Convention on Human Rights as well as the UNCRC, for example, Article 9, Section 3, discussed earlier. The Committee's 'Concluding Observations' set out in the section on 'Family environment and alternative care' the following recommendations:

a. conduct a study to assess the nature and extent of ill-treatment of children […];

b. take legislative measures to prohibit all forms of physical and mental violence, including corporal punishment and sexual abuse of children in the family, schools and in institutions;

---

23 Royal Government of Bhutan (1999a: para. 183).

c. carry out public education campaigns about the negative consequences of ill-treatment of children;

d. establish effective procedures and mechanisms to receive, monitor and investigate complaints, including intervention where necessary;

e. prosecute instances of ill-treatment, ensuring that the abused child is not victimised in legal proceedings;

f. train teachers, law enforcement officials, care workers, judges and health professionals in the identification, reporting and management of ill-treatment cases.[24]

These recommendations were further developed by concern over the insufficient information on children working, notably in the urban areas as waiters, bus attendants, *doma* (betel nut quid) sellers and domestic workers. A study was conducted by UNICEF among children; however, this is not publicly available. Some additional legislative steps were taken following the 'Concluding Observations' – notably regarding trafficking and a redefinition of sexual assault on minors in the Penal Code 2004.

The Second State Party Report 2007

Six years after the 'Concluding Observations to the Initial State Report' issued in 2001, Bhutan submitted its second periodic report in July 2007. There is a tangible difference in its presentation, the level of detail and discussion provided. The detailed articles identified specific articles of the UNCRC and set out how they were addressed within the Bhutanese context. It is noticeable that the Second State Party Report uses nine clear headings that reflect the higher-level themes of the UNCRC 1989. The third section explicitly addresses the General Principles of the UNCRC, non-discrimination (Art. 2), best interests of the child (Art. 3), the right to life, survival and development (Art. 6) and respect for the views of the child (Art. 12). Article 6 was one area that was, as noted above, absent from the Initial State Report. Reading the Second State Report, in the tone and level of engagement with the UNCRC and its language, we see

24 Committee UNCRC (2001: para. 41).

recognition of 'emerging issues' such as child labor, and domestic abuse being acknowledged.[25] There is a recognition that a major challenge for the report is the limited data on many of the issues that fall under the UNCRC.[26] There is even reference to the draft constitution which includes 'provisions concerning the best interests of the child'.[27]

However, in June 2008 the Committee issued a list of fourteen issues for clarification by the Bhutanese authorities. In August 2008, full written responses to the fourteen points were submitted for consideration by the Committee. Among the issues raised were clarification over which sections of the Penal Code had been amended to address children in conflict with the law, and which 'articles of the Civil and the Criminal Procedure Codes have been amended to include provisions for children (citing main relevant sections and articles)'.[28] Similar concerns were expressed in relation to domestic violence and child abuse, and the Bhutanese refugees settled in camps in Nepal. Reflecting the wider concern of the UNCRC Committee to promote awareness of human rights, Issue 9 requests:

> Please indicate what kind of human rights training have been organized and which professional groups have been targeted, and if these trainings are systematic and ongoing. Indicate if education on the Convention on the Rights of the Child has been integrated in the school system.[29]

Part two of the list notes that to address these issues it required information on new bills being prepared or enacted legislation. In addition, it required information on new institutions or organizations created to support the implementation of the UNCRC, as well as newly implemented policies, programs and projects. Part three set out a major request for missing data. The final section set out a preliminary list of fifteen major issues (not contained in part one) that the Committee 'may take up during the dialogue with the State Party. They do not require written answers. This

---

25 Royal Government of Bhutan (2007: para. 81).

26 Royal Government of Bhutan (2007: para. 101).

27 Royal Government of Bhutan (2007: para. 80).

28 UNCRC (2008: 1).

29 UNCRC (2008: 2).

list is not exhaustive as other issues might be raised in the course of the dialogue'. Of these the first four focused on the ratification, harmonization, coordination and monitoring of the implementation of the UNCRC. The remaining ten dealt with a range of questions about inequalities with three explicitly touching on ethnic minority rights.

In his 'Opening Statement to the Committee' on 22 September 2008, Lyonpo Thakur S Powdyel highlighted the coming into force two months earlier on 8 July 2008 of the first written Constitution of the Kingdom of Bhutan. Although reference is made to the refugee issue, the opening speech was careful to not focus on ethnicity. Issued on 8 October 2008, the Committee's 'Concluding Observations' positively commented on 'the adoption of the Constitution on 18 July 2008 and the inclusion of child rights specific provisions therein'.[30] Further comments welcome the child related changes to the Penal Code and Civil and Criminal Procedure Code, Labour and Employment Act 2007, and the establishment in 2007 of the Women and Child Protection Unit. In regard to the implementation of the UNCRC, the Committee emphasized the need for improved data on health, education, vulnerable groups, violence, child labor and exploitation. The Committee noted 'with satisfaction that the State party has translated the Committee's previous recommendations into Bhutanese and disseminated them among government officials and the media'. This was, however, caveated by the Committee adding that 'the Convention has not been translated into local languages and integrated into the school curriculum'. This is a practical challenge given that the majority of local languages are not written and serves as a reminder that the Committee itself may be unfamiliar with the complexities such requests present.

There remained higher level concerns that were raised in the 2001 'Concluding Observations' around non-discrimination, and the duties on the state under articles 3 and 12 to promote the 'best interests of the child' and 'respecting the views of the child'. It is worth putting these comments into the broader context that the majority of state parties to the UNCRC struggle with the implementation of both of these duties. The Committee further noted that there remained a lack of a clear definition

---

30 UNCRC (2008: para. 3(a)).

of a 'child' in Bhutanese national legislation.[31] Finally, it urged Bhutan to ratify the Optional Protocols on the sale of children, child prostitution and pornography and involvement of children in armed conflict.

The Second State Party Report and representations made to the UN Committee on the CRC were substantially more developed and nuanced in their approach to the UNCRC. However, key issues remained unaddressed. 'The Committee reiterates its concern…' is the strongest language the report uses and it emphasizes those aspects that the Committee requires to see legislative and policy initiatives, notably to 'adopt a comprehensive children's code which incorporates the principles and provisions of the Convention […] the State party [should] ensure that the draft Child Care and Protection Act is harmonised with the Convention […] and encourages its speedy adoption'.[32] The Committee wanted to see a fuller range of legislative and policy ('programmatic') measures introduced by Bhutan to implement, in the national law and policies, the UNCRC. The Third State Report submitted in 2016 demonstrates the work undertaken to address these concerns.

The Third State Report:[33] embedding and extending the UNCRC

The political transformation of Bhutan in 2008 and the democracy it established cannot be underestimated. As commented on above, the Committee noted in its 'Concluding Observations' in 2008 with 'appreciation […] the adoption of the Constitution on 18 July 2008' and its 'inclusion of a child rights specific provision'.[34] This transformation is reflected in the Third State Party report submitted by the Bhutanese authorities in September 2016. The report covers the third to fifth periodic report due by the Bhutanese authorities. This reflects the 'challenges in the finalisation of the report' due to the preparations for second national elections held in

31 UNCRC, Concluding Observations (2008: para. 23).

32 UNCRC, Concluding Observations (2008: para. 6).

33 Technically the report is the combined third to fifth reports for Bhutan.

34 UNCRC (2008: 3(a)).

2013.[35] The 2016 Report highlights that following the recommendations made in 2008, Bhutan ratified two 'Optional Protocols' on the sale of children, child prostitution and child pornography and involvement of children in armed conflicts in 2009. In the following year, Bhutan signed the Convention on the Rights of People with Disabilities. The 2016 Report sets out a broader discussion of major new laws and policies that apply to children in Bhutan.

The discussion of the legislative and policy changes is framed by the 2008 Constitution in which 'rights of children are enshrined'. Three sections of the Constitution are specifically discussed: Article 9(15) and (16) on the right to education and free education and Article 9(18) on protecting children from 'discrimination and exploitation'. Building on these articles, two 'milestones in the strengthening of the legal framework for the care and protection of children' were introduced. The first was the Child Care and Protection Act 2011. This act was in draft form for some time and was previously mentioned in the initial and second reports submitted in 1999 and 2008. The report clearly sets out how the Child Care and Protection Act 2011 addresses concerns over the lack of a consistent definition of a child across different acts and asserts that individuals below eighteen will be treated as children in line with the UNCRC.

The second act was the Child Adoption Act 2012. When the act was being drafted, 'reference was made to the Hague Convention on Protection of Children and Co-operation in respect of intercountry adoption' with primary consideration being given to the 'best interest' under Article 3 of the UNCRC. Of significance is the establishment of the National Commission for Women and Children (NCWC) to monitor domestic adoptions 'until the child' turns eighteen.[36] The creation of the NCWC as an independent monitoring body addresses earlier recommendations made by the UNCRC Committee in their 'Concluding Observations'. In addition, the NCWC is responsible for the implementation of a third statute, the Domestic Violence Prevention Act, 2013. It reflects both a growing understanding of the reporting process and, it is argued, the cultural work of translating into local policies and practice the underlying approach to

35 Royal Government of Bhutan (2016: para. 1).

36 Royal Government of Bhutan (2016: para. 9).

the UNCRC. Earlier concluding observations recommended improving coordination between government and non-government organizations, particularly as the UN Committee encouraged the development of more non-government, or civil society, organizations. The report noted that the NCWC coordinated with the Royal Bhutan Police district level measures to provide women and children with protection, whilst working with emerging civil society organizations to provide other necessary services. Finally, the NCWC coordinated work with the Bhutan National Legal Institute to strengthen the justice process, though detail of what was done is lacking. The impact of the NCWC was made possible only by putting in place the necessary infrastructure and local adoption and incorporation of the ideas and principles of the UNCRC. In turn, this became possible as the officials became familiar with and internalized those principles, reflecting the importance of the 'cultural work' of the UNCRC.

Prior to the discussion between the Bhutanese delegation and the UN Committee, the latter issued a list of eleven points that it required further information on and twenty-two requests for data and statistics. The Bhutanese response was submitted in May 2017. Following the 'constructive dialogue', the UN Committee issued its 'Concluding Observations' in July 2017. It 'notes with appreciation the legislative, institutional and policy measures adopted to implement the Convention'. In particular, the Committee highlighted the 2011 Child Care and Protection Act, 2012 Child Adoption Act and the development of the National Plan of Action for Child Protection as part of the eleventh Five Year Plan (2013–18). The recognition of the significant legislative changes and wider policy framework reflects the approach adopted by the first two governments, elected in 2008 and 2013 respectively, to address the 'Concluding Observations' made in 2008.

The tone of the 'Concluding Observations' was positive; however, the Committee went on to make a range of recommendations. It noted for example concerns that the minimum age of marriage for girls in the Marriage Act 1980 was different from that for boys. Indeed, there was a need to revise the Marriage Act 1980 in line with the 2011 Child Care and Protection Act. Similarly, concerns were raised about aspects of the Penal Code 2004, for example Article 109 to bring it into line with a range of recent statutes prohibiting the use of corporal punishment.[37] This focus on ensuring that Bhutanese legislation is consistent in its approach marks a change in the approach and focus of the UN Committee in its review. There is an acknowledgment of the major changes introduced to implement in Bhutanese national laws the principles of the UNCRC. The Committee is acting as a critical friend, noting inconsistencies and making recommendations, rather than 'reiterating' concerns. Indeed, the Committee 'commends' the Bhutanese authorities for the 'measures taken to address violence against children, such as the first national study of violence against children in Bhutan, undertaken between 2013 and 2016'.[38] This was balanced by 'concerns over high rates of violence and abuse experienced by children'.[39] Reflecting new and emerging areas of concern the Committee approved of the adoption of the second National Adaptation Programme of Action to reduce climate change whilst recommending that the state increase children's awareness of and preparedness for climate change.[40]

Reading the 'Concluding Observations' to the Third State Report, there is a distinct change in approach and tone. The Committee recognized the transformation presented by the third report and the actions undertaken by the Bhutanese authorities to address the recommendations of the previous 'Concluding Observations'. However, one point requires our attention: the focus on building resilience and preparedness for climate change. Certainly, this is a global concern. Yet there is another reason for focusing on resilience. Under the Constitution of Bhutan it is a principle of state policy 'to promote those conditions that will enable the pursuit of Gross National Happiness' (Art. 9(2)). In the work undertaken by the Centre for Bhutan Studies to develop the Gross National Happiness (GNH) Index, one of the nine domains of GNH is ecological diversity and resilience.[41] The third report, building on emerging ideas about GNH, and its reception

37 Child Care and Protection Act 2011, Child Adoption Act 2012, and Domestic Violence Act 2013.

38 UNCRC, Concluding Observations (2017: para. 23).

39 UNCRC, Concluding Observations (2017: para. 23).

40 UNCRC, Concluding Observations (2017: para. 36, 36(b)).

41 Ura et al. (2011).

by the UN Committee shows a major transformation in the Bhutanese engagement with and understanding of the UNCRC. The development of the GNH Index, as well as the local and international discussions about GNH, have enabled the cultural work required to transform non-local, higher-level ideas and reframe them in local terms.

Discussion and concluding observations

> The future of the nation lies in the hands of the younger generation. (H.M. Jigme Singye Wangchuck)[42]

Bhutan 2020: A Vision for Peace, Prosperity, and Happiness, describes the legal system of Bhutan as 'founded on the teachings of Buddhism' and states that the 'absence of a colonial history prevented the introduction of alien systems of law and justice [...] although, in more recent times, several principles and procedures of Western jurisprudence, especially with regards to criminal justice, have been absorbed'.[43] There was a notable lack of reference to human rights and to the UN Conventions (CEDAW and UNCRC) ratified by Bhutan. The creation in the late 1990s of various child orientated organizations (e.g., Youth Development Fund) and highly publicized meetings focusing on a range of issues (including juvenile delinquency and child abuse),[44] together with the UNICEF sponsored Year of the Child 2004, undoubtedly raised awareness of children's rights. However, as demonstrated above there remained barriers to implementing and more significantly, 'translating' the principles of the UNCRC into Bhutanese legislation and policy.

As Merry argues, it is essential to examine and consider the process of translation of transnational ideas of human rights in local settings, in this case, Bhutan.[45] A major factor in the promotion of human rights, including those of the child, is the vernacularization of human rights.

---

42 The quotation is from a speech by the current king, Jigme Singye Wangchuck, cited in *Bhutan 2020* (Royal Government of Bhutan 1999b: ii).

43 Royal Government of Bhutan (1999b: 81).

44 Choden (2004, 2005).

45 Merry (2003, 2006).

The principles set out in the UNCRC are universal, setting a minimum standard that accommodates cultural differences. The ability to tailor the principles of the children's rights into the Bhutanese context requires them to be resonant with the existing local cultural framework. The key to understanding this process in Bhutan is the process of creating and debating the draft constitution and its ratification on 18 July 2008. The period of almost seven years between September 2001 and 18 July 2008 marks a remarkable watershed in Bhutanese legal and political thought. We cannot and should not underestimate the transformation in thought and ideas that the 2008 Constitution ushered in.

This chapter, through a high-level review of the approach adopted by Bhutan, as a State Party to the UN Convention on the Rights of the Child, provides new insights into this transformation. The emphasis on tradition and the hesitancy to directly engage with the principles of the UNCRC in the initial report reflect a defensive, guarded approach following and during a period of intense international scrutiny. The 'Concluding Observations', the first the Bhutanese authorities had received, were clear and touched on sensitive issues. The Second State Report revealed that lessons were learned from the Initial State Report and it directly sought to address the UNCRC principles. However, the Committee made similar recommendations whilst welcoming the constitution and its child focused provisions. It is the Third State Report that presented a range of new enacted legislation and policy developments. Of course, it would be reasonable to argue that the legislation and policy initiatives were delayed due to limited resources and the focus on the constitution. However, the constitution and the new parliamentary framework appears to have created an improved forum for developing and finalizing legislation and for policy initiatives. I argue that it goes beyond the infrastructure established by the 2008 Constitution. Rather, the process of preparing and approving the draft constitution facilitated the 'cultural work' necessary for the translation and vernacularization of the principles of the UNCRC.

There are several reasons for this transformation. With the development of legal education there is increased familiarity with human rights discourse and the principles of the UNCRC that in turn transform local understandings. The move to a new parliamentary structure has created legislative time to develop, debate and enact new acts. And, finally, the development of the theoretical underpinning of the concept of Gross National Happiness, particularly the nine domains and their indicators, have made it possible to map the principles set out in the UNCRC onto a local approach that helps to assess the impact of policy and new laws. This mapping is not restricted to the GNH domain of 'good governance'. The UNCRC with its focus on the wellbeing and best interests of the child[46] maps across all nine domains: health, education, living standards, psychological wellbeing, ecological diversity and resilience, community vitality, cultural diversity, good governance and time use. Perhaps we can see, through the work to develop the GNH Index, a convergence that enables Bhutan to incorporate and extend its implementation of the UNCRC based on its own approach aligned to its national laws.

46 See Footnote 5.

Bibliography

Amnesty International (1994) 'Bhutan: Forcible Exile', ASA14/004/1994.

Choden, K. (2004). 'Child Abuse: A Bhutanese Perspective', *Kuensel*, vol. 19, no. 34, p. 5.

Choden, K. (2005). 'Discussing Violence Against Children', *Kuensel*, vol. 20, no. 17, p. 5.

International Committee of the Red Cross (1997) *Bhutan: Visits to Security Detainees*, news release 97/42, 10 October.

Mathou, T. (1999). 'Bhutan: Political Reform in a Buddhist Monarchy', *Journal of Bhutan Studies*, vol. 1 no. 1, pp. 114–145.

Mathou, T. (2000). 'The Politics of Bhutan: Change in Continuity', *Journal of Bhutan Studies*, vol. 2, no. 2, pp. 228–262.

Merry, S.E. (2003) 'Constructing a Global Law - Violence Against Women and the Human Rights System', *Law and Social Inquiry*, vol. 28, no. 4, pp. 941–977.

Merry, S.E. (2006). 'Transnational Human Rights and Local Activism: Mapping the Middle', *American Anthropologist*, vol. 108, no. 1, pp. 38–51.

Royal Government of Bhutan (1999a). *Initial State Report of Bhutan*, 20 April.

Royal Government of Bhutan (1999b). *Bhutan 2020: A Vision of Peace, Prosperity and Happiness*, Thimphu: Planning Commission.

Tobgye, S. (2014). *The Constitution of Bhutan: Principles and Philosophies*, Bhutan: Royal Court of Bhutan.

United Nations High Commission for Refugees (2002). *UNHCR Statistical Yearbook.*

Ura, K. et al. (2011). *The Gross National Index – Happiness Index of Bhutan: Method and Illustrative Results*, Thimphu: Centre for Bhutan Studies.

Youth Development Fund (2004). 'Advocacy and Awareness Raising on Child Abuse and Youth Issues', *YDF* Newsletter, vol. 1, no. 5, p. 1.

Statues and Legislation

Child Adoption Act 2013

Child Care and Protection Act 2011

Constitution of Bhutan 2008

Domestic Violence Prevention Act 2013

Labour and Employment Act 2007

Marriage Act 1980

Penal Code 2004

15

Transforming Buddhist Kingship: From Chogyal to Maharaja

Alex McKay

In March 1935, Sir Tashi Namgyal, the eleventh monarch of Sikkim's Namgyal dynasty, became a patron of the Bengal Royal Flying Club.[1] Some six years later, his eldest son and heir, Crown Prince Kunzang Paljor, enlisted as a pilot officer in the Royal Indian Air Force, only to be killed when he crash-landed near Peshawar shortly before he was to be posted to active service in Burma.

Today we are accustomed to British royalty performing such duties – Prince Andrew flying in the Falklands War, Prince William flying with RAF Search and Rescue, and so on –but that Sikkimese royalty should take on such roles seems difficult to reconcile with our existing understanding of Buddhist models of kingship. Given that in the pre-colonial period the Namgyal dynasty had adhered to more traditional norms, it seems clear that the aerial associations of those Sikkimese royals derived from their encounter with the British colonial state and its imposition of new social models.

The British take-over of Sikkim in 1888–89 initiated a period of transformation for all sections of Sikkimese society. This involved the introduction of the structures of British Indian government and in the wider context an ideological transformation that overlaid a Tibetan Buddhist worldview with British Indian concepts of modernity. Within that framework of modernity was a new understanding of the appropriate role and duties of a ruling monarch. That understanding was based on models of European and particularly Victorian British royalty, but also

1 Sikkim Palace Archives (hereafter SPA), PA/MS/014, various correspondence.

the experience of dealing with India's maharajas, for the refiguring of the appropriate character and actions of Sikkim's *chogyals* was not simply a process of superimposing a British kingship model on Sikkim. Rather, it was a model developed by colonizers whose ideologies and understandings of the necessary trajectories for Sikkimese royalty were deeply rooted in their experience of dealing with Indian royalty.

The *chogyals* thus had to learn to take on the British Indian model of kingship, but while exercising their power under ultimate British authority, the *chogyals* were nonetheless able to retain elements of their traditional authority and role, and to find new spaces in which to centralize and consolidate their power. This was particularly the case in the religious sphere where the colonial power was, after the events of 1857–58 (the 'Indian Mutiny'), reluctant to intervene, and the *chogyals* were able to gain both unprecedented control over Sikkim's Buddhist structures and institutions, and to ensure the continuing patronage of the faith.

In what follows, we shall examine the processes of imposition, emulation and negotiation that transformed the Sikkimese form of Buddhist kingship during the first decades following the British takeover, in order to demonstrate how the earlier ideal of the *chos rgyal* (Tib. 'religious king') was reconfigured in the colonial period. Along with the records of the colonial state preserved in British and Indian National Archives, this work draws on the recently released Sikkim Palace Archives from the 1875–1975 period.[2]

*

We may speak of a general model of Buddhist kingship, one rooted in early Indic cosmologies that centralize and even sacralize kingship. That Indic model was expressed in texts that formulate the concept of *rajadharma* – the duty of kings.[3] Local cultural aspects and political realities then shape the final forms that the Buddhist model takes in any particular realm. The

---

2 These archives were digitalized in a project on which I was academic advisor, and in August 2017 the digital files were transferred to the British Library website (EAP880). The digitalization project was part of the Endangered Archives Programme funded by Arcadia and administered by the British Library, to whom my thanks are due.

3 On which see Derret (1976: 597–609).

Tibetan tradition – to very briefly summarize it – combined two concepts, the ideal of the *cakravartin*, a universal monarch pacifying the world by his Buddhist virtue,[4] and the Mahayana ideal of the bodhisattva who, on attaining enlightenment, vowed to continue to take earthly form until he had led all sentient beings to enlightenment. The Tibetans went further, identifying a specific bodhisattva, Avalokiteśvara (Tib. Chenrezi), with their ruler and his realm. So, we see in the *Mani Ka'bum* for example, that the first of the Yarlung dynasty 'Religious Kings', Songtsen Gampo, is specifically identified as an emanation of Chenrezi. With the institution of the incarnation system and the growing power and sanctity of the Dalai Lamas, they too came to be seen as emanations of Tibet's protective bodhisattva and as *cakravartins* leading the world to the path of Buddhist enlightenment.[5] (There was a certain logic to the idea of an enlightened bodhisattva emanating as a *cakravartin*, for they would thus be best placed to lead the world to enlightenment.)

The Buddhist ruler of Sikkim was clearly not of the status of a *cakravartin*. Sikkim was a small principality with a population of less than 60,000 according to the 1901 census.[6] In the regional pre-nation state system, Sikkim can be seen as having existed within a greater Tibetan 'Mandala state'. That was a typical political world in the pre-nation state era, when polities were defined by their centers not their borders, and sovereignties merged and even overlapped in broad frontier zones. At least in the Tibetan perspective, when Sikkim emerged in the mid-seventeenth

---

4 This *cakravartin* concept was expounded in the canonical fourth/fifth century *Abdhidharmakośa* ('Treasury of Higher Knowledge') by Vasubhandu, which was translated from the Sanskrit into Tibetan in the ninth century. Tibetans applied that *cakravartin* status retrospectively to the early 'Religious Kings' of the Yarlung dynasty.

5 We are increasingly well-informed about the Tibetan kingship tradition, not least thanks to the work of the 'Kingship and Religion' research group at Ludwig-Maximilians University in Munich. See, for example, the special edition of *Cahiers d'Extrême-Asie*, vol. 24, 2015, edited by Brandon Dotson, and in particular the articles by Doney (pp. 30–31) and Ishihama Yumiko (pp. 169–170). Also see Halkias (2013: 491–451) and Ramble (2006: 129–149).

6 *Sikkim State Gazetteer, Statistics 1901-02*, Calcutta, Government Press, 1902. A rough census in 1891 had indicated a Sikkim population of only 30,458; Risley (1894: 27).

century as a distinct state under a Buddhist king (who claimed descent from a Yarlung dynasty 'Religious King'), that state was a frontier principality within the Tibetan mandala and its ruler was (in theory) ultimately subject to Tibetan authority.

In practice, while Sikkim remained autonomous it had close links with Tibet. In the nineteenth century, for example, the *chogyals*' court spent the rainy seasons in the Chumbi valley, which was ultimately under Tibetan governance at that time. The *chogyals* and many aristocrats took Tibetan wives. The Tibetan government would occasionally intervene in Sikkimese affairs, even court affairs. In 1841, for example, when the aging seventh *chogyal* had not produced an heir, the Tibetan government funded and carried out recommended rituals and 'meritorious acts' to bring him a son and sent the necessary ritual items for the Sikkimese court to do the same.[7]

From the establishment of the Namgyal dynasty in the 1640s down to the so-called 'merger' with India in 1975, Sikkim's rulers held the Tibetan title *chos-rgyal*, meaning 'one who rules for the benefit of (the Buddhist) religion'. Unlike the Dalai Lamas, however the *chogyals* were not an incarnating, but a family lineage. But while not referred to as *cakravartins* (as far as I am aware), they were Buddhist kings, and their role was understood within Buddhist models of kingship: they ruled for the benefit of religion.

There were a number of parallels between Sikkimese and British ideals of their sovereign. As the *chogyals* claimed their lineage extended back to the Yarlung kings, so British royalty looked back to Alfred the Great of Wessex,[8] a ninth century ruler credited with paving the way for the unification of England. The entirely legendary King Arthur also played an important role in the construction of the British monarch as moral guardian and exemplifier of the gentlemanly and knightly virtues.

While not considered divine, the British monarch was still ideally envisaged as God's Regent and held the title of 'Defender of the Faith and Supreme Governor of the Church of England'. In the public sphere

---

7 *History of Sikkim* (1908: 64). This work was compiled on the orders of the Chogyal Thutob Namgyal and Gyalmo Yeshe Dolma and translated into English by Kazi Dawasamdup. It was privately printed in Gangtok and exists in various printings; I cite a copy in the possession of the author. A revised and edited retranslation of this work is now available; see bibliography for details.

8 Yorke (1999).

their role, at least from the Victorian era,[9] was envisaged as a duty to the people, meaning a particular concern with health, education and charitable works. They also retained the right to bestow all civil honors – peerages, knighthoods, and so on. Even if the British monarch no longer led troops in battle, they retained their position as head of the Armed Forces. So too did they remain 'the fount of justice', with judicial functions performed in the sovereign's name and their retaining of the 'prerogative of mercy' – to spare persons sentenced to death, for example.

The concerns, rights and duties of their monarch were considered by the British in India to be manifestly right and proper, and thus appropriate for indigenous rulers in states under British control. But having ruled parts of India for over a century before taking Sikkim, their ideas of kingship were shaped by that local experience.

India's kings did not see humility as a virtue. Mughal rulers and India's rajas and maharajas favored ostentatious visual displays of power and martial splendor, and to the extent possible directly ordered their kingdoms. Their personal control over internal and external affairs were considered part of their *rajadharma* and, at least in their youth, they frequently led their forces into battle. But they were also embedded in local religious society, with their presence essential to certain rituals and their patronage determining both the continuance and the development of religion(s) in their realm.

When the British took Sikkim and set out to remove the *chogyal* from the Tibetan orbit, they had no understanding of the difference between the kingship ideals of Buddhist Sikkim and those of Hindu/Muslim/Sikh India. Indeed, they never referred to the Choygal by that Tibetan title; he was initially termed the 'Raja' of Sikkim and increasingly from the late nineteenth century, as the 'Maharaja'. While this terminology was later a symbol of British Indian rather than Tibetan authority over Sikkim, it was probably initially no more than a lack of familiarity with Tibetan language and customs.[10]

---

9 Queen Victoria was Britain's first real constitutional monarch, a transformation which, as in Sikkim under the British, went hand in hand with the expansion of the state and the development of a centralized interventionist bureaucracy.

10 At the time of the first encounter between Sikkim and British India, when the two

From the time of their initial contact with Sikkim in the early nineteenth century, however, the British had found it difficult to deal directly with the *chogyal*. Even when he was not resident in Chumbi, which was his home for much of the year, he was both hard to contact and even harder to influence or draw into a binding agreement. Nor could the British isolate any other powerful individual with whom they might form such an alliance. That was not a situation that an expanding colonial power could allow to continue on their frontier.

But the British failed to understand that the *chogyal* was not only following Tibetan expectations that he would try to prevent European access to Tibet through his territory. They also failed to understand the implications of the Sikkimese belief that the *chogyal* was primarily a religious figure, one whose secular actions were ruled by his Buddhist role. As such he was expected to devote himself to religious practices – the ritual worship of lineage and state protectors, receiving visiting religious figures and their teachings, and so on, with his performance of these duties considered essential to the good fortune of the state. Unlike Hindu/Muslim/Sikh kings, the Buddhist *chogyal's* religious status, which placed him partly if not fully beyond the mundane world, meant that he was, ideally, expected to be above day-to-day politics. By not intervening in worldly affairs, he demonstrated his enlightened detachment. Non-intervention enhanced his religious stature and thus his power was actually the greater for his 'masterful inactivity'.

One result of this detachment from worldly affairs was that a series of 'strong men', both secular aristocrats and powerful lamas, tended to dominate Sikkim's domestic realm, and even that of foreign policy.[11] European observers, almost entirely ignorant of Tibetan Buddhist culture, regarded the influence of these 'strong men' as evidence of the *chogyals'*

---

allied against the Gurkhas in the 1814–15 Anglo-Nepal war, there were no Tibetan speakers in the East India Company's administration.

11 In the mid-nineteenth century for example, Sikkimese affairs were dominated by Tokhang Namgyal, (remembered as Pagla ['Mad'] Dewan: an epithet of uncertain origins). He was regarded by the British as hostile to their interests. By the 1880s, two men considered by the British as favorable to their interests, Kangsa Dewan and his brother the Phodong Lama, were the most prominent figures in the Sikkimese administration.

powerlessness. They assumed that the *chogyals* were weak rulers under the control of these 'strong men' and would relish British support for their position.[12]

I am not suggesting here that Sikkim's *chogyals* were an unbroken lineage of ideal Buddhist kings, following the textual models of the *cakravartin* or even of a *chos-rgyal*. There had been more prominent and interventionist *chogyals* in the past, notably the early *chogyals* in the period in which Sikkim was concerned to manifest a distinct identity separate from the Tibetan state. In the period with which I am concerned, however, from the mid-late nineteenth century onwards, Sikkimese in contact with the British framed the character and identity of their rulers in those ideal terms

There may be other explanations for their reticence and religious stature. The seventh Chogyal Tsugphud Namgyal (r. 1793–1863) increasingly withdrew from worldly affairs as he aged. His successor, the eighth Chogyal Sidkeong Namgyal (r. 1861/63–74) was a recognized incarnation of primarily religious orientation, while Thutob Namgyal (r. 1874–1914) took the *gaddhi* at the age of just fourteen. This period may thus be something of an anomaly and the apparently primarily religious orientation of the *chogyals* may be representative of those specific circumstances, and/or of elements of Sikkim's hierarchy agreeable to closer ties with Tibet. But it was from this period that the British derived their understanding of Sikkim and its royal system, and which thus provided the knowledge base for their transformation of that system.

*

During the nineteenth century, relations between Sikkim and British India had declined both as a result of misunderstandings over the status of Darjeeling,[13] and because of the Sikkimese reluctance to assist the British

12 The lack of a common language was a significant part of the British problem, with communications being in Hindi rather than English or Tibetan/Lepcha. In addition, the British official in charge of dealing with Sikkim in the 1840s and 1850s was the Darjeeling Superintendent Archibald Campbell, who was extremely hostile to Sikkim; on which see McKay (2016: 31–48).

13 On which see Namgyal (1966: 46–58).

in accessing the isolationist Tibetan state. In 1888–89 the British took over Sikkim, placed it under the authority of a political officer (or 'Resident'), and set about eliminating Tibetan influence there. They might simply have deposed the *chogyal* and installed a new local ruler as they did elsewhere in their empire, but such 'puppet-kings' required some degree of local legitimacy such as royal descent or established community leadership and there was no-one in Sikkim who would take up that chalice. The main local allies of the British politely declined even to appoint a local head to the advisory council the British created to serve under the political officer,[14] and none of the aristocrats or royal family members were prepared to challenge the right of the *chogyal* to rule Sikkim – for to challenge the Buddhist king of a Buddhist state was to challenge Buddhism itself.

In essence, the British were stuck with the *chogyal*. Unable to replace him as the local ruler, their only option was to transform his role and turn him into a modern monarch on the British Indian model. They firstly ordered then Chogyal Thutob Namgyal and his court to abandon the practice of rainy season migration to the Chumbi and to reside permanently in their Gangtok palace. That not only removed him from Tibetan influence but also began the reformulation of his position. In the British understanding, a king ruled his kingdom all year round. He might make occasional state visits to other realms, but his ideal place was on his throne in his palace. This principle of court residence was henceforth firmly established – never again would the *chogyals* cross the passes to Tibet. Even when the Chinese invaded in 1962 the *chogyal* held firm in his palace just as George VI remained in Windsor during World War Two.

The British then set to replacing culturally Tibetan administrative systems of land tenure, taxation and so on, with British Indian systems. Within two decades, Sikkim was entirely transformed, its administrative structures replicating those of British India and establishing, in line with British Indian forms of modernity, state responsibility for matters such as health, education and infrastructure that had formerly been under the authority of local landlords.

Sikkim was not annexed by British India, but it was initially controlled by the political officer stationed in Gangtok. He was supposed to administer

---

14 SPA, DA/AD/002/011-014, council meeting of 29 January 1893.

the state with the assistance of the *chogyal* and a council of leading men, but the first political officer, John Claude White, totally alienated the *chogyal*, and confined him to West Bengal for some years while White set about the transformation of Sikkim. In 1895 however, the Government of Bengal, over White's head, negotiated the *chogyal's* return to Gangtok and to the leadership of the advisory council.[15] From his first appearance in November that year, the *chogyal* began to manipulate council proceedings to regain at least some of his authority. The Sikkimese members fell in behind his lead,[16] and the council increasingly became the means by which the *chogyal* could articulate his desired vision of Sikkim's future.

White still enjoyed ultimate authority, but in the wider context the British wanted the *chogyal* to be an active ruler – his earlier inability to act decisively (whether because of his powerlessness, his personality or his cultural understanding of his role) had been a major part of the colonial state's difficulties in dealing with Sikkim. This was consistent with British policy in regard to the so-called 'Princely States'. In those realms, rulers who acknowledged British overlordship and cooperated with British interests were supported by British arms and were allowed considerable autonomy within their kingdoms, rather than being taken under the direct rule of the Government of India.

From July 1896, the *chogyal* was allowed to assist White in his judicial role,[17] and he soon gained the authority to judge all but the most serious cases.[18] He was allowed to regain power in that sphere because again, this was in line with British understandings of a king or a maharajah as the fount of justice in his state. When the *chogyal* began to pardon prisoners on state occasions, that too was acceptable as being a power maharajahs (and British monarchs) enjoyed.

---

15 This was apparently because White's treatment of the *chogyal* was common knowledge among Himalayan and perhaps wider royalty and was reflecting badly on the colonial power.

16 British Museum, *Charles Bell Sikkim and General notebook*, pp. 10–11, entry of 4 June 1909. His informant A-chuk Tsering advised Bell that the *chogyal* had informed the councillors that they had to agree with him in council and thus they were afraid to voice their own opinions.

17 SPA, DA/AD/002/075-076, council meeting of 20 July 1896.

18 SPA, DA/AD/002/097-098, council meeting of 10 March 1897.

In 1903–04, when the British invaded Tibet via Sikkim, both *chogyal* and people had no option but to assist the British. However reluctant, that assistance was rewarded. Thutob Namgyal was received with far greater honors than he had expected when he met the Prince of Wales and Viceroy Lord Minto in Calcutta around New Year of 1905–06. The effect of that reception was a revelation,[19] satisfying him that the British had accepted the role formerly held by Tibet: that of protector of Sikkim and the Namgyal dynasty. Thutob had completed a personal transformation from *chogyal* under the Tibetans to maharaja under the British, albeit that in the wider context of royal transformation he was a transitional and indeed reluctant figure.

As a result of ill-health, Thutob Namgyal's prominence declined in the years prior to his demise in February 1914. His last significant act was to lead the Sikkimese delegation to the 1911 Delhi Durbar. There, in recognition of his acceptance of Sikkim's transformation from a Tibetan to a British protectorate, he was knighted by the visiting king and Sikkim was made a fifteen-gun salute state, an award enhancing its status to equivalency with some of the leading Princely States.[20]

✳

Thutob Namgyal seems to have been an unenthusiastic convert to British models of state. Yet the benefits of Sikkim's development became increasingly obvious and there is no indication that he opposed the economic model introduced by the British, or the improvements in infrastructure, health and education that it brought. In apparent contrast to the more socially conservative elite classes in Tibet, their Sikkimese counterparts seem to have readily accepted such aspects of modernity. This was partly because of the greater Sikkimese exposure to Western education and the accessible example of Darjeeling, where empirical observation demonstrated its benefits. The modernization process was also abetted

---

19 *History of Sikkim* (1908: 132–134).

20 SPA, FA/BI/001/018, Government of India Foreign Office to the Chogyal, 12 December 1911. Only around twenty of more than 100 maharajas were entitled to more than a fifteen-gun salute.

by its being embedded in local culture through the 'Sikkimization' of personnel, however, and the addition of Sikkimese cultural characteristics to modern practices and structures: retaining traditional architecture, the deployment of Buddhist monks and rituals in hospital practice, and so on.[21] The initiative for these developments seems to have come from the Sikkimese elites and particularly the *chogyal*, who thus identified an area in which the colonial state was reluctant to impose itself.[22]

Thutob's son and successor Sidkeong Tulku was a recognized Buddhist incarnation and was initially destined for a monastic life, but with his elder brother Tshodag Namgyal preferring to remain in Tibet, the British selected Sidkeong to succeed to the throne. Sidkeong had a very different outlook to his father. Crucially, he had been educated by the British, who had set up schools in India such as Mayo College in order to educate, and to instill loyalty in, young Indian princes. The result was that in the twentieth century, virtually all important Indian royals were English-speaking, held a scientific worldview and allied their interests with those of the colonial power. They were thus loyal citizens of the empire, and Sidkeong Tulku was such a prince.[23]

After the British recognized him as heir to the Sikkim throne (*gaddi*) in 1899, they set out to shape him as a modern maharaja on the desired model. In 1900–01, White escorted Sidkeong on a tour of India, Burma and Ceylon that was clearly designed to impress the young man with the achievements of the British Empire and to introduce him to British Indian ruling society.[24]

The party stayed at some of the empire's great hotels, which, like his meetings with the viceroy or dining with ship captains, was a part of the

---

21 On which see McKay (2007: esp. 84–113).

22 For example, the *chogyal* was able to ensure that his new palace was rebuilt in the Tibetan style rather than the European style favored by political officer J.C. White: see SPA, DA/AD/002/107-108, council meeting of 6 April 1898; SPA, DA/AD/002/109-110, council meeting of 22 April 1898.

23 On Sidkeong Tulku, see McKay (2003: 27–52; 2021: esp. 196–241).

24 On which, see *Diaries of Chogyal Sidekeong Tulku. The 10th Chogyal of Sikkim Tour of Ceylon and India 1900*. (A copy of this unpublished typescript is held at the Namgyal Institute of Tibetology, Gangtok.)

process of learning European customs and the social behavior expected of a royal. They also stayed with local dignitaries, including Indian princes, and these too were lessons in British expectations for the young heir. In the palaces of India's maharajas, Sidkeong Tulku could imbibe lessons on such matters as court protocols, heritage preservation and presentation, or just how a ruler should ride an elephant.[25] He may also have observed that colonial overlordship was not monolithic, but could be manipulated to their advantage by local rulers as long as their essential loyalty to the Raj was unquestioned.

In 1908, Sidkeong Tulku was taken on a world tour, during which he studied at Oxford and was introduced to British society, not least to the king. In proposing this tour, he noted that, '[i]t will be necessary to adopt the European style of dress so as not to be conspicuous'. This was an important point in the wider context. The adoption of Western dress was a symbolic marker of an individual's acceptance of, and identification with, Western modernity. Sidkeong would, however, also take his monastic robes with him, and wear them when he met the thirteenth Dalai Lama in China. He was learning to move between two worlds.

In the wider context, the gradual development of such understandings of the 'Other' was characteristic of both sides of the colonial encounter. Considerable academic attention has been paid to the ways in which the colonial state compiled information concerning every aspect of the subject cultures and to the effects that knowledge-gathering process had on matters such as caste or national identity.[26] But rather less attention has been paid to the ways in which those subjected to the colonial regime learned to manipulate the systems and personalities to which they were subject. There was in fact considerable scope for negotiation and compromise particularly at a local level, for colonial power was fragmented and relied on intermediaries and supporters far more than on the threat or actuality of military force. We saw that the restoration of Chogyal Thutob Namgyal to the advisory council enabled him to negotiate concessions and ultimately to regain much of his stature (albeit in a modified form). With the support of the aristocrats who made up the council, he was able to influence the

25 *Diaries of Chogyal Sidekeong Tulku.*

26 Notably Bayley (1997).

decisions of the political officer at least in specific areas. Sidkeong Tulku similarly used his knowledge of the mentality and policies of the British to advance his position.

One example of this was his maneuvering to fulfil his desire to study at Oxford rather than at a London technical college as White favored. The British system of social classes and behavior appropriate to those classes would have been apparent to the prince from his tours of India and from his encounters with British royalty and imperial officials. Those codes of behavior were, after all, not entirely dissimilar to Sikkimese social structures and the nuances of their aristocratic interactions. Thus they were a tool he could use to achieve his own aims.

It was well-known that White hated his one-time friend W.F. 'Frank' O'Connor,[27] a Tibetan-speaking political officer with whom Sidkeong had travelled to Khamba Dzong in 1903 while interpreting for the Younghusband mission and again when O'Connor was escorting the Panchen Lama on his visit to India in 1905–06. There was a considerable social disparity between White, with his background in the Public Works Department, and O'Connor, an aristocratic officer from the much higher status Indian Army and a personal friend of the then Indian Foreign Minister, Louis (later Sir Louis) Dane. Sidkeong understood that O'Connor had far greater influence in the halls of power than did White. Sidkeong wrote asking O'Connor to speak to Sir Curzon Wylie at the India Office to arrange an educational program at Oxford rather than in London. He requested that O'Connor do so: 'without incurring displeasure to Mr White, I shall be ever so grateful if you can arrange this quietly. But whatever you do I do not wish Mr White to find out'. O'Connor obliged, and in due course Sidkeong informed White, 'I believe they have decided me to go to Oxford', as if he had no part in the decision.[28]

By the time he returned from Oxford it was clear that British India was prepared, in exchange for submission and loyalty, to eventually return full powers of local administration to the *chogyal*, for the British had no

---

27 On which enmity see, for example, McKay (1997: 36–38).

28 SPA CO/PS/001/019-022, Sidkeong Tulku to W.F. O'Connor, 25 October 1906; SPA, CO/PS/001/023-029 (quotation from 029), Sidkeong Tulku to J.C. White, 16 December 1906.

intention of taking Sikkim into British India. Sidkeong Tulku received a foretaste of the power he would inherit, being given charge of the departments of education, forestry and religious affairs (the latter a newly-created position).[29] In the education department, he was responsible for numerous initiatives, including the opening of a state-funded technical school in Gangtok in 1909,[30] and a school for the daughters of landlords in 1912.[31] These were just the kind of initiatives that the British thought suitable interventions by a modern monarch.

Sidkeong Tulku had satisfied the political officer that he was 'thoroughly pro-British'.[32] Indeed he joined the Royal Asiatic Society,[33] and even became a Freemason.[34] Yet Sidkeong did more than satisfy the British that he had learned and would govern Sikkim according to their desired model. Fundamental to the autonomy allowed to loyal monarchs was non-interference by the colonial state in local culture and particularly religion. The lessons of 1857/58 had been well learned.

Religion and culture consequently became an important social sphere outside colonial control, one in which traditional rulers and religious practitioners could exercise their authority. This is something rather neglected in the historiography of the colonial period – the extent to which local agents were able to reshape and reform their religious traditions (Buddhist, Hindu or even Bön)[35] in a world almost entirely outside the colonial sphere. Only if these agents crossed a line into the political world were the British concerned with them – the Tibetan polymath Gedun Choephal being a prime example,[36] but there were others.

29 *Administration Report of the Sikkim State for 1908-1909*, Calcutta, Government Press, 1909.

30 SPA, DA/AD/004/025, council meeting of 30 April 1909.

31 SPA, DA/AD/004/106, council meeting of 1 August 1912.

32 British Museum: Charles Bell collection, Sikkim and General notebook (p. 10), entry of 5 April 1909.

33 Jansen (2014: 604).

34 Chalon (1985: 205–206), cited in Wikipedia, *https://en.wikipedia.org/wiki/Alexandra_David-N%C3%A9el*; accessed 9 February 2018.

35 I discuss a number of these figures in McKay (2017: see for example, 182–183, 358–360 re: Khyung-sprul).

36 On whom see, Mengele (1999); also see Stoddard (1985).

While colonial records emphasize his role in education and forestry, wider reading reveals the impact Sidkeong Tulku had on Buddhism in Sikkim. He was influenced by the *Rimé* movement and his encounter with the Theravadin Buddhism of Burma and Ceylon (Sri Lanka) led him to imagine a wider unity of *all* Buddhists. He even appointed a Scotsman who had become a Theravadin monk in Ceylon (Silacara Bhikku, a.k.a. John McKechnie), as director of religious instruction in Sikkim's Buddhist schools,[37] and under Sidkeong's influence Sikkim became a center for Buddhist modernism.

Sidkeong also sought to eliminate a laxity of practice and morality in Sikkim's monasteries. Most notably, he composed a *chayik*, or set of monastic rules, applicable to all monasteries in his realm.[38] This *chayik* had one particularly significant aspect. It forbade monasteries from making important decisions without consulting him, formalizing the new position he had created for himself at the head of Sikkimese Buddhist structures.

This meant that when he inherited the throne, he would be – within the limits of colonial power – in full control of both the religious and secular structures in Sikkim. That was a position more centralized and more powerful than that of any of his predecessors. Alexandra David-Neel quoted him as telling her, 'Ah! If I was the Dalai Lama ... If I had the power to reform Buddhism!'[39] Sidkeong's *chayik* may be seen within that context: as an initiative that would enable him to emulate the authority of a Dalai Lama and empower him to reform Sikkimese, and perhaps wider, Buddhism.

Sidkeong, with his deep understanding of both cultures, can thus be seen to have been reformulating the model of kingship that he would inherit, transforming it into his own blend of British and Sikkimese royal formulations. The model demanded that the *chogyal* should no longer be a detached figure, existing on a spiritual plane above day-to-day government.

---

37 *Administration Report of the Sikkim State for 1914-1915*, Calcutta, Government Press, 1915.

38 On which see Jansen (2014: 604).

39 Alexandra David-Neel to her husband, from Kalimpong, 15 April 1912, translated from the original French by Dr. Anna Balikci-Denjongpa: correspondence held at the Namgyal Institute of Tibetology, Gangtok.

The *chogyal* should not just rule, but lead. And Sidkeong would lead not just in the secular realm, but also claim power in the spiritual domain, thus fulfilling the traditional role of the Buddhist king, advancing Buddhism. While also promoting the identity of Sikkim as a Buddhist state, he linked that Buddhism not only to the person of the *chogyal*, but to a higher loyalty to the British king-emperor, just as there had been a higher loyalty to the Tibetans in the pre-colonial period.

The outbreak of war in 1914 gave Sidkeong another opportunity to demonstrate his leadership. The Princely States of India had quickly joined the British cause. Sikkim, acknowledged as a state outside Indian frontiers, was theoretically free to avoid involvement. But Sidkeong understood that Sikkim's overlords – be they Tibetan or British – had the right to call on the state's assistance in times of war.

Sidkeong placed the resources of his state at the disposal of the British,[40] and gave a personal pledge of complete loyalty to the viceroy, assuring him, 'I hold an honorary commission in the Northern Bengal Mounted Rifles and I am ready to fight if I can thus best serve the King-Emperor'.[41] The incarnate lama and Buddhist monarch, ideally detached from worldly concerns, was now transformed into the British ideal of the Indian king, ready to lead the battle against the enemies of the British Empire.

*

Following Sidkeong Tulku's death after less than a year in office, his half-brother, Tashi Namgyal, succeeded him.[42] As a boy Tashi had had an English governess and then attended Mayo College. Instilled with the ideals of the empire, he too assured the British that they 'have none more loyal to them and their interests than myself. My personal services, and all my State stands for, is at their call'.[43]

---

40 SPA, MA/W1/001/019-023, council meeting of 13 August 1914. SPA, MA/W1/001/024, Chogyal to Political Officer Basil Gould, 7 August 1914.

41 SPA, MA/W1/001/026-027, Chogyal to viceroy, undated (August 1914).

42 *Administration Report of the Sikkim State for 1914-15*, Calcutta, Government Press, 1915.

43 SPA CO/OF/016/250-252, Chogyal to Charles Bell, 8 [?] February 1920.

Tashi Namgyal was initially given control of education, forestry and religious affairs, just as his predecessor had been. Then at his ceremonial installation in May 1916, the date fixed by the astrologers as the most auspicious, he was given additional responsibility for police, jails and income tax and excise. He was also given a billiard table, thought suitable as a coronation gift from the Government of India to a local ruler! The political officer recorded his assurance that the new *chogyal* would be 'a wise ruler, happily blending the old customs with such [W]estern ideas as are suitable for Sikkim'.[44]

In November 1919, Sikkim marked the Armistice with three days of 'peace prayers', public celebrations and the observance of the British tradition of two minutes of silence. The *chogyal* announced free treatment for any soldiers still suffering from wounds and they were subsequently freed from any requirement to provide free labor to landlords or the state.[45] The compassionate ruler was again on display.

Conclusion

Chogyal Thutob Namgyal was forced into the British Indian model of kingship. Detained for several years, his unquestioned stature among Sikkimese made his acquiescence essential to the colonial project. He was then able to use the advisory council to regain much of his stature, and while powerless to prevent Younghusband's mission from using his territory, ultimately benefitted in terms of British trust and consequent rewards.

Furthermore, the transition from Tibetan to British overlordship resulted in the centralization of power in Sikkim, with government structures on the modern nation-state model greatly strengthening the *chogyal's* position. No longer could aristocratic or monastic leaders contract freely with foreign powers or ignore royal command. The reformulated kingship model resulted in an engaged, rather than detached monarch.

44 *Administration Report of the Sikkim State for 1919-1920*, Calcutta, Government Press, 1920.

45 *Administration Report of the Sikkim State for 1919-1920*, Calcutta, Government Press, 1920.

Sidkeong Tulku loyally embraced the new kingship model in his brief reign. He made himself visible to his people, promoted modern health and education, and personally exercised authority in internal politics and diplomatic matters. But he was also able to use the new kingship model to fulfil the traditional duty of a Buddhist king to advance Buddhism, reforming its institutions and hosting Buddhist prelates and seekers. His successor, Chogyal Tashi Namgyal, carried on this patronage and presided over a florescence of temple and monastery building.[46] That was one of the activities expected of a Buddhist ruler and their patronage of such activities added greatly to their status and to their legacy.

Declarations of loyalty to the British empire by Sidkeong Tulku and later Tashi Namgyal were entirely sincere. We are reminded of Homi Bhaba's definition of the 'hybridized discourse' of the colonized, which is not repressive, but emancipatory.[47] The British had not threatened their religion and had actually increased their personal power in a state under a much stronger protection than Tibet had been able to offer. They had authored a transformation of Sikkimese kingship from the implicit to the explicit display of authority, from the decentralized to the centralized monarchy, and placed the state's religious structures under the personal control of the *chogyal*. He became, in effect, almost an absolute monarch, the representative of his realm and the commander of not only secular and religious forces, but also of the military.

The changes in the *chogyal's* position and role were not necessarily dramatic, indeed they might seem largely a product of modernization and economic growth rather than ideological transformation. Yet nineteenth

---

46 Following the British take-over of Sikkim, such activities were largely in abeyance for two decades. In 1890 there were forty-two monasteries in Sikkim, including one built that year. In 1900, another monastery was built, but in 1910 there were still just forty-three monasteries in Sikkim. Yet in the remaining thirty-seven years of British overlordship, there were twenty-four more monasteries built. This continued in the post-colonial period when Sikkim remained under the *chogyals*. Sikkim today has 111 monasteries (eighty Nyingma and twenty-eight Kargyu, with one monastery from each of the other three main Tibetan sects: Geluk, Sakya and Bön), meaning forty-four have been constructed in the seven-decade period from 1947 to date: figures from http://www.sikkimeccl.gov.in/History/AboutEccl.aspx, consulted 6 February 2018.

47 See Bhabha (2004).

century modernization in Europe had been associated with increasing secularization and in Sikkim – as in contemporary Mongolia and Tibet – European colonialism actually resulted in both religious and political power becoming increasingly centralized in the hands of a religious leader. It also resulted in the construction of modern expressions appropriate for the colonial era, of the traditional role of a Buddhist monarch: the protection and promotion of Buddhism.

Bibliography

Bayley, C.A. (1997). *Empire and Information: Intelligence Gathering and Social Communication in India, 1780–1870*, Cambridge: Cambridge University Press.

Bhabha, H.K. (2004). *The Location of Culture*, Oxford: Routledge.

Chalon, J. (1985). *Le Lumineux Destin d'Alexandra David-Néel*, Paris: Librairie académique Perrin.

Derrett, J.D. (1976). 'Rājadharma', *The Journal of Asian Studies*, vol. 35, no. 4, pp. 597–609.

Doney, L. (2015). 'Early Bodhisattva-Kingship in Tibet: The case of Tri Songdetsen', *Cahiers d'Extrême-Asie*, vol. 24, no. 30–31.

Halkias, G.T. (2013). 'The Enlightened Sovereign: Buddhism and Kingship in India and Tibet'. In S.M. Emmanuel, ed., *A Companion to Buddhist Philosophy*, Hoboken: Wiley-Blackwell, pp. 491–451.

Ishihama, Y. (2015). 'The Dalai Lama as the *cakravarti-rāja* as Manifested by the Bodhisattva Avalokiteśvara', *Cahiers d'Extrême-Asie*, vol. 24, pp. 169–170.

Jansen, B. (2014). 'The Monastic Guidelines (bCa' yig) by Sidkeong Tulku: Monasteries, Sex and Reform in Sikkim', *Journal of the Royal Asiatic Society*, vol. 24, no. 4, pp. 597–622.

McKay, A. (1997). *Tibet and the British Raj: The Frontier Cadre 1904-1947*, Richmond: Curzon Press.

McKay, A. (2003). '"That He May Take Due Pride in the Empire to Which He Belongs": The Education of Maharajah Kumar Sidkeon[g] Namgyal Tulku', *Bulletin of Tibetology*, vol. 39, no. 2, pp. 27–52.

McKay, A. (2007). *Footprints Remain: Biomedical Beginnings Across the Indo-Tibetan Frontier 1870-1970*, Amsterdam: University of Amsterdam/IIAS.

McKay, A. (2016). '"A Difficult Country, a Hostile Chief, and a Still More Hostile Minister": the Anglo-Sikkim War of 1861', *Bulletin of Tibetology*, vol. 41, no. 2, pp. 31–48.

McKay, A. (2017). *Kailas Histories: Renunciate Traditions and the Construction of Himalayan Sacred Geography*, Leiden: Brill.

McKay, A. (2021). *The Mandala Kingdom: A History of Buddhist Sikkim, 1815-1947*, Gangtok: Rachna books.

Mengele, I. (1999). *Gedun Choephel: A Biography of the 20th Century Tibetan Scholar*, Dharamsala: Library of Tibetan Works & Archives.

Namgyal, (Gyalmo) H.C. (1966). 'The Sikkimese Theory of Landholding and the Darjeeling Grant', *Bulletin of Tibetology*, vol. 3, no. 2, pp. 46–58.

Ramble, C. (2006). 'Sacral Kings and Divine Sovereigns: Principles of Tibetan Monarchy in Theory and Practice'. In D. Sneath, ed., *States of Mind: Power, Place and the Subject in Inner Asia,* Bellingham/Cambridge: Western Washington University, pp. 129–149.

Risley, H., ed. (1894). *The Gazetteer of Sikkim*, Calcutta: Bengal Secretariat Press.

Stoddard, S. (1985). *Le mendiant de l'Amdo* (Recherches sur la Haute Asie), Paris: Societe d'ethnographie.

Yorke, B. (1999). 'Alfred the Great: The Most Perfect Man in History?' *History Today*, vol. 49, accessed on 15 May 2019 at https://www.historytoday.com/archive/alfred-great-most-perfect-man-history

Primary source

History of Sikkim (1908): This work was compiled on the orders of the Chogyal Thutob Namgyal and Gyalmo Yeshe Dolma and translated into English by Kazi Dawasamdup. It was privately printed in Gangtok, and exists in various printings; I cite a copy in the possession of the author. A revised version of this work entitled *The Royal History of Sikkim. A Chronicle of the House of Namgyal: as narrated in Tibetan by Their Highnesses Chogyal Thutob Namgyal and Gyalmo Yeshe Dolma; based upon the Preliminary Translation by Kazi Dawasamdup*, corrected, supplemented and thoroughly revised by John Ardussi, Anna Balikci-Denjongpa and Per K. Sørensen was published by Serindia (Chicago) in 2021.

16

A Forgotten Extradition Accord Signed between British India and Tibet to Secure the Mon Region Bordering Assam in 1854[1]

Lobsang Tenpa

Introduction

This chapter will present a forgotten extradition accord signed by representatives of Tibet and British India in 1854 to secure the so-called Mon region bordering Assam. The Mon region is presently divided into the Tawang and West Kameng districts in the state of Arunachal Pradesh, India. Historically, the region was an important part of the wider Indo-Tibetan Buddhist cultural area due to the significant cultural and political roles played by its geopolitical situation and its dominant ethnic group, the Monpa. I begin with a short introduction of the region and then discuss some of the background and circumstances that led to the signing of the treaty. As the English version of the treaty has not yet surfaced, I present here an annotated translation and a facsimile of the Tibetan-language version. The extradition treaty was agreed upon after a series of conflicts that started in 1851, which almost led to a border war at the trijunction between British India, Bhutan and the Tibeto-Mon region.

Introduction to the Mon region: Tawang and West Kameng districts

Traditionally, the territory known as the Mon region (Mon Yul) has been understood by locals and Tibetans to comprise the two westernmost

1 I would like to express my gratitude to Prof. Dr. Tsering Shakya, Dr. Olaf Czaja and Dr. Lobsang Yangdon for their critical comments and editing of this article.

Figure 16.1: Map of the Mon region Source: Paul et al. (2018: 437).

districts of the modern state of Arunachal Pradesh, India: the districts of Tawang and West Kameng. Besides the Monpa, several other major Scheduled Tribes exist in the region: the Aka, Bugun (Khowa), Miji (Sajolong), Memba, Sartang and Sherdukpen. They are among the major twenty-five 'Scheduled Tribes' of the state and have had interactions with Tibet and India for centuries. The majority Monpa tribe, which comprises roughly ninety percent of the total population of 49,997 in Tawang and more than seventy percent of a total population of 87,013 in West Kameng,[2] has played a significant role in cross-cultural contact and activities in the region. Although various Scheduled Tribes in the Mon region speak different languages and belong to different ethnic groups, inhabitants of the region are often grouped under the single term 'Monpa' besides those aforementioned tribes. 'Mon pa' can thus refer either to a person living in the Mon region or someone of Mon ethnicity, regardless of their region. Tibetans and other northern highlanders use the words Mon and Monpa as blanket terms to designate a range of neighboring regions or people situated to the south. The ambiguity and relativity of the term thus pose challenges for researchers.

The transnational inconsistency of these terms can be observed today in Tibet and other Himalayan regions. Specific groups of indigenous peoples in Tawang and West Kameng, India, are now categorized as members of the Monpa 'Scheduled Tribe'. At the same time, the Moinba/Monba – the Chinese *pinyin* spelling for Monpa – are classified as one of the fifty-six ethnic groups of the People's Republic of China, living in the Tsona and Medog counties of Tibet.[3] Meanwhile, a tribe officially recorded as 'Memba' but denoting Monpa also currently lives in the districts of Shi-Yomi and Upper Siang in Arunachal Pradesh, on the opposite side of the border of Medog County, Tibet (China).

---

2 *2011 Census of India* (2014).

3 Since 1964, Moinba/Monba has been given ethnic minority status, but it is not clear if any law will be passed for them to become an official *minzu* (ethnicity/nationality). Moinba/Monba were first recorded in the 1982 population census of China at around 1,140 persons; thereafter the Moinba/Monba population increased considerably, having risen to 7,475 in 1990, 8,928 in 2000, and 10,561 in 2010 according to subsequent Chinese censuses. C.f. '2010 Population Census' released by 'National Bureau of Statistics of China' (www.stats.gov.cn).

In the Mon region in India, the Monpa tribe is categorized geographically into northern, central and southern branches, known as the Tawang Monpa, Dirang Monpa and Kalaktang Monpa, respectively. Members of these different Monpa sub-tribes or branches are not speakers of the same language but demonstrate considerable linguistic diversity. Members of the last two groups, the Monpa of Dirang and Kalaktang, are Tshangla (tshangs la) speakers, and the former, the Monpa of Tawang, are speakers of Tawang Moenke (mon skad), which is known to academics as Dakpa (dag pa).[4] Besides these languages, there are also Hrusso (i.e., the spoken languages of Aka and Miji), Bugun (Khowa), Puroik (Sulung), Chug/Lish and Sherdukpen.[5] Almost all of these languages are classified by linguists as belonging to the East Bodish language group within the family of Tibeto-Burman or Sino-Tibetan languages. As such, even the broadly defined category of Moenke/Monpa (the so-called language of Mon) by Monpa themselves and Tibetan speakers includes at least four to five distinct languages: the vernaculars of Tshangla, Dakpa (i.e., the Tawang Moenke), Chug/Lish-ke and Sartang-ke, as well as at least two Tibetan dialects.

The last two spoken dialects, which are closely related to the modern Tibetan language, are spoken in villages neighboring Tawang town, in the Mago-Thingbu Circle area, as well as in the Sengedzong-Nyukmadung regions in West Kameng. Although the spoken language of Mago-Thingbu and Sengedzong-Nyukmadung regions is known as the Brokpake ('brog pa skad/'brog skad) language,[6] it is spoken without any difference in Jora Dzong (in Tibet) as well as in the Merak-Sakteng regions in eastern Bhutan. Conversely, the spoken language of the nearby villages, particularly of the Shyo village of Tawang town, is closely related to the language spoken in Lhoka Prefecture in Tibet. Similarly, Tshangla and Dakpa are

---

4 See Andvik (2010) and Dzongkha Development Commission (2018) for more information on the Tshangla language; for the Dakpa language see Hyslop and Karma Tshering (2008) and van Driem (2007).

5 See Post et al. (2017) for more on these languages; also see Bodt (2020) and Bodt et al. (2015) for more on Chug/Lish and Miji; Lieberherr (2017) for Puroik (Sulung); and Jacquesson (2015) for Sherdukpen.

6 Dondrup (1993), van Driem (1991) and Dzongkha Development Commission (2016).

widely spoken across national borders. In Bhutan, Tshangla is known as Sharchokha (*shar phyogs kha*, 'eastern language'), while Dakpa is known as Dzalakha, and each is widely spoken in seven and two Bhutanese districts, respectively. In contrast, in Tibet, Dakpa is known as Moenke and is spoken in Lekpo-tso valley in the Tsona County, whereas Tshangla, known as Pemakho-ke (padma bkod skad), is the primary mother-tongue in Medog County in Nyingchi Prefecture. The same Tshangla is also spoken in the Mechukha, Manigong, etc. Circle areas in the newly formed Shi-Yomi district and Tuting Circle area of the Upper Siang district in the state of Arunachal Pradesh, India.[7]

Historically, due to the misconception about the Assamese plain areas bordering Bhutan and the Mon region as Holy Indian Buddhist sites by the people of Tibet and the Himalayan regions, the Mon region became an important pilgrimage and trade route until the early twentieth century. The region is mentioned in the writings of Tibetan historiographers from at least the late fifteenth century. That said, the founding of Tawang Monastery in 1681 under the patronage of the fifth Dalai Lama Ngawang Lobsang Gyatso (ngag dbang blo bzang rgya mtsho, b. 1617, d. 1681), as outlined in his edict, issued in 1680,[8] and the recognition of a local child as the sixth Dalai Lama Tshangyang Gyatso (tshangs dbyangs rgya mtsho, b. 1683, d. 1706) in 1697 further heightened the Tibetan profile of the region. Its importance for Tibetan authorities can be further appreciated in light of various other edicts issued by Lhasa policy-makers in the later periods, as in the case of the edict of 1731 issued by the regent (*sde srid*) Pholhane Sonam Topgey (pho lha nas bsod nams stobs rgyas, b. 1698, d. 1747) regarding Tawang Monastery,[9] the 1752 edict concerning the Berkhar (ber mkhar) family of the sixth Dalai Lama issued by the seventh Dalai Lama Kalsang Gyatso (bskal bzang rgya mtsho, b. 1708, d. 1757),[10] as well as in documents regarding the renovation of Tawang Monastery

---

7 Refer to notes 4, 5 and 6 above for further details.

8 See Aris (1980), Schwieger (2015: 66–67) and Tenpa (2018: 195–208) for the edict.

9 See further details in Tenpa (2018: 208–216).

10 See further details in Tenpa (2018: 180–186; 2015: 483–507).

conducted in 1810–11 by the fully ordained monk (*dge slong*) Lobsang Thapkhe (blo bzang thabs mkhas, b. 1772, d. 1827).[11]

Still, despite these important ties with the government in Central Tibet, the region seems to have enjoyed considerable autonomy in terms of administration during the aforementioned periods. This is evident in records of the activities of hereditary rulers in the region referred to as *jowo* (*jo bo*) or *babu* (*ba spu*),[12] who signed a number of agreements with British India in the mid-nineteenth century (without Tibetan interference).[13] These agreements were crucial in shaping the terms of rulers' subsequent engagement with British India and later also with the Union of Indian States.[14] Some of these treaties were renewed in 1853, both with and without oversight by Tibetan government representatives. The treaty that is the subject of this article relates to these agreements and is connected with the same sequence of events that gave rise to them. Nonetheless, it is a distinctive type of treaty, one which was arranged between British India and Tibet to secure the Tibeto-Mon border to the then North-East Frontier Province (i.e., present-day Assam).

The signing of the agreement

For several centuries, Tibetans used trade-routes passing through the Mon region or Bhutan to do business with trading partners in the plains area of the Ahom Kingdom and the Bengal region of India.[15] Frequent interactions on these routes led to diplomatic engagements. For instance,

11 See Blo bzang thab mkhas (1827), manuscript.

12 See *Rgyal rigs* (1986 [1728]) or *Mon chos 'byung* (1988 [1728]) for further details. Although both the texts are published under a different title, they contain the same historical developments of the Mon region.

13 Tenpa (2016).

14 See Tenpa (2014, 2016) for more details.

15 For more on the formation of different kingdoms within the Ahom Kingdom (1206–1823) and other smaller kingdoms, such as the Kachari Kingdom, and their place in the history of Assam, see Gait (1906). For more on the historical development of the Pala Kingdom (eighth to twelfth c.), Bengal Subah (1576–1757), the Bengal Presidency (1857–1912), and Bengal Province (1912–1947) see Paul (1939) and Bayly (1988).

in 1844 and 1853, four little-known treaties were signed between Tibet/Tibeto-Mon and British India officials.[16] In the midst of this period, a fully ordained monk (*dge slong*) Sherab Dakpa (shes rab grags pa, d. 1864) of Tawang Monastery[17] was appointed as a fortress commissioner (*rdzong dpon*) of the Taklung Dzong (stag lung rdzong) at the southern end of the Mon region. His appointment to the post is significant because the position was one of three main administrative positions in the Mon region and held a high degree of autonomy and responsibility in the old thirty-two-Tsho administrative system in place there.[18] The other two positions were those of fortress commissioner for the Dirang Dzong (sde rang rdzong) and Gyangkhar Dzong (rgyang mkhar rdzong) fortresses. Besides these positions, there existed hereditary chieftainships known as *dingpon* (*lding dpon*) or *shalngo* (*zhal ngo*).[19] As the position of commissioner was usually assigned for three years, Sherab Dakpa was probably appointed to the post sometime between 1849 and 1850. However, he may have taken up the position some years prior to this as well.

Whatever the case, in late 1851, Sherab Dakpa decided to overreach his authority by keeping the annual taxes collected under his jurisdiction and the revenue (*posa*) generated from the Assamese *duars* for himself and not send these on to the Lhasa-appointed ecclesiastical manager (*bla ngyer*) at Tawang Monastery.[20] These actions led to several conflicts within

---

16 Aitchison (1865); Tenpa (2016). Interactions along the trade route continued and several edicts were issued by the Tibetan cabinet (Kashak, *bka' shag*). One was in 1856 to reduce the heavy taxation by the Tsona rice-officials (Tsona Dre-Dubpa, mtsho sna 'bras sgrub pa) after a complaint was filed by the local trade association in 1845. Other treaties followed in 1859 and in 1888 which related to obligatory *corvée* labor services.

17 See the short biography of Sherab Dakpa (shes rab grags pa) in Tenpa (2016: 86–87).

18 See Tenpa (2018: 217–223, n. 604) and also Mizuno et al. (2015: 48–49).

19 Tenpa (2018).

20 See Tenpa (2016); Shakabpa (1986 [1976]: 19–20); Mackenzie (1884: 16). Partly based on Lamb (1966: 294–305), Petech (1973: 92, 170) briefly discusses the Mon border conflict (1852–1853) between British India and Tibet and provides further detailed information on Tibetan representatives present at the negotiation. This information proved helpful for reconstructing the full names of the Tibetan negotiators, mentioned in the biography of the eleventh Dalai Lama (236a–237a)

the region and beyond. As the controversy ended up leading to the death of various local people, Sherab Dakpa escaped to Assam and sought refuge in British India. Pursued by Tibeto-Mon militias, the monk's transgressions and subsequent exodus almost triggered a full-blown border conflict or a small-scale war between British India and the Tibeto-Mon region. This conflict was resolved diplomatically by the signing of several treaties related to the national border and trade and extradition accords between 1844 and 1854.[21]

Among those treaties is a document dating to the Wood-Tiger year (1854), currently only extant in Tibetan. The text is written in cursive (*khyugs*) script in fourteen lines, and with two extra lines as a heading, which seems to have been added later for the purpose of cataloging. The document measures forty-eight by fifty-four cm and is affixed with a single, black square seal. The condition of the document is good, but it needs restoration as it was written on plain handmade paper without any protective covering. Interestingly, rather than being formally signed by British India, the document notes in writing instead that it is an agreement reached between the 'Supreme [British East India] Company' and the Ganden Phodrang (dga' ldan pho brang), i.e., the Central Tibetan Government in Lhasa.[22]

---

and in the Chinese language source by Wen-tsung, c.f. *Ta-Ching li-ch'ao shih-lu* (50.8b–9a, 75.15b–16a, 89.38b–39a) and Petech (1973: 170, n. 2). Petech does not mention the signing of any agreements, however, despite stating that 'Shedra (bshad sgra) settled the affair to the full satisfaction of the Emperor, who granted him the extension to two generations of the heredity of his title of 2nd *taiji*, besides other rewards to his large staff' (Petech 1973: 170).

21 Since I have provided a detailed description of this incident elsewhere (Tenpa 2016), I offer here only a short summary of these events and how they influenced the signing of treaties between British India and Tibet.

22 Instead of recording English, the record of the East India Company in the document is worth noting, because officially, the British Empire started to rule India only after the 1857 mutiny, when native Indian soldiers rose against the East India Company.

The amended and facsimile edition of the 1854 Treaty

ཤིང་སྟག་ [1854]

༄༅།། དགའ་ལྡན་ཕོ་བྲང་པ་ཆེན་པོ་དང་ཕྱི་གླིང་བཙས་ཀྱི་ས་མཚམས་བར་ལ་དགྲོག་ཤིང་[23] བྱེད་མི་བྱུང་ན་ཡར་ཕྱིར་དུ་རྩ་

འཛིན་བྱེད་རྒྱུའི་ཆོད་དོན་འདྲ་གཉིས་ངོ་མའི་འདྲ་ཤུས་

༡༽ བླ་མ་དཀོན་མཆོག་དང་ཆོས་སྐྱོང་སྲུངས་མ་[24] དམར་ནག་རྣམས་དཔང་དུ་གཙུག་ཏེ་སྔར་ལོ་དགའ་ལྡན་ཕོ་བྲང་ཆེན་པོ་

དང་ ཇེ་བཛུན་[25] ཀུམ་པ་ཏི་བཅས་དགའ་

༢༽ ཕྱོངས་ཤེས་གྲགས་[26] སྐོར་ཆོད་དོན་འཛོག་འགང་[27] མཛད་པ་ལྟར་ལ་ཕན་མཚུན་[28] གཉིས་ནས་ཚད་འཛིན་གྱི་གཅིག་ཕན།

གཅིག་ཐོག་[29]བྱེད་པ་མ་རྟོགས་[30] ཅིག་[31] གནོད་གཅིག་

༣༽ ཀྱེལ་[32] མེད་ན་ཡང་བར་དུ་འབྱུང་པོར་རྒྱུད་བསྐུལ་ལྟ་བུའི་མི་འདྲིས་ལབ་བྱུང་ཟེར་རྒྱུ་མེད་པའི་སྡིར་གཏམ་སྣ་ཚོགས་ཡར་

ཐོག་མར་ཐོག་[33] གྱི་ཕན་མཚུན་གཉིས་ཀ་དགོས་པའི་གནས་

༤༽ ཕྲན་བུ་ཕྱུར་པར་རྟེན་ཆུ་དཀར་པོའི་མདོར་སྟག་རྫོང་ང་འཕོད་[34] རྣམ་རྒྱལ་རྡོ་རྗེ་དང་བཀའ་འབྲེལ་བཤད་ཞབས་སྐྱིད་

སྟོད་པ་ཆེད་འཁྱོར་དང་ཏེ་སོ་སྤྲུ་རི་སྤྱིན་ཆེན་ས་ཧེབ་མར་རྟེང་

༥༽ ས་ཧེབ་ འཛགས་སམ་ས་ཧེབ་ཏག་ཏར་ས་ཧེབ་དང་སྡིར་གཏམ་སྐོར་ལ་འགྲོལ་མོལ་[35] བགྲིས་སྐབས་ཆོད་དོན་ལྟར་ལས་

---

23 Recte: དགྲུག་ཤིང་

24 Recte: སྲུང་མ་

25 Recte: བཙུན་

26 Abbr.: ཤེས་རབ་གྲགས་པ་

27 Recte: གང་

28 Recte: ཕན་ཚུན་

29 Recte: གཅིག་གྲོགས་

30 Recte: མ་གཏོགས་

31 Recte: གཅིག་

32 Recte: རྒྱལ་. The term སྐྱེལ་ could be applicable.

33 Recte: ཡར་ཐོགས་'མར་ཐོགས་

34 Also written without the prefix འ་, i.e. ང་ཕོད་.

35 Recte: གྲོལ་མོལ་

གསར་སྒྲོས་རིགས་མེད་པའི་ཚང་མ་བད་སྟན་[36] གསལ་དྭངས་བྱུང་ཅིང་

༦༽ ཕྱིན་ཆད་མཛད་སྒོའི་ཐད་འགའ་[37] ལྷན་པོ་བྲང་པ་ཆེན་པོ་དང་རྗེ་བརྩུན་ཀུམ་པ་ཎི་བཅས་ཐུགས་སེམས་ཆུ་དང་འོ་མ་ལྟར་ཆགས་བཞུགས་བཞིན་པར་བར་དུ་དཀྲུག་ཤིང་བྱེད་མི་དགའ་ཁོངས་

༧༽ ནས་བྱུང་ན་འཛིན་བཟུང་གི་སྟག་རྫོང་དུ་རྫོང་བཟའ་[38] བྱུང་བསྟུན་རྩ་འཛིན་ཡན་སོང་མེད་པ་བྱེད་རྒྱུ་དང་ཀུམ་པ་ཎི་མི་ཁོངས་ཨ་ཙུར་སོགས་ནས་དཀྲུག་ཤིག་[39] བྱེད་མི་བྱུང་ན་འཛིན་

༨༽ བཟུང་གི་ཏེ་སེ་སྒྲུ་རིའི་སྐྱིན་ཆིག་ས་ཉེབ་དུ་རྫོང་བཟའ་[40] བྱས་རྗེས་ཁྲུབ་འདོམས་ཡན་པོར་མ་གྱུར་བ་བྱེད་རྒྱུ་བཅས་ ཕྱིན་

ཆད་པན་མཚུན་[41] དགོང་པ་[42] དྭངས་ཆེད་དུ་ད་ལམ་ཆུ་སླང་ཟླ་༡༢ ཚེས་༡༥

༩༽ ཉིན་ཚོད་དོན་ཞག་[43] པ་འདི་དང་སྔོན་དུ་འཛོག་གནང་མཛད་པའི་ཚོད་དོན་ལྟར་ལ་ཚད་ཟུངས་[44] ཞུ་རྒྱུ་ཞུས་པ་དང་། འདི་ལས་འགལ་བའི་ངན་གཡོའི་རིགས་སུ་ཐད་ནས་ཞུས་ཆེ་

༡༠༽ བླ་མ་དཀོན་མཆོག་དང་། ཆོས་སྐྱོང་བསྲུངས་མའི་[45] བདེན་ཚོགས་བྱེད་སྟེ་[46] སུ་ཡིན་ཐོག་ཏུ་སྨྱུར་དུ་རྩལ་[47] དུ་གསོལ་ཞུ་

རྒྱུའི་སྟག་རྫོང་ང་པོད་རྣམ་རྒྱལ་རྡོ་རྗེ་དང་བཀའ་བློན་བཤད་

༡༡༽ ཞབས་ཅན་གྱི་རྟགས་ཏེ་སེ་སྒྲུ་རིའི་སྐྱིན་ཆིག་ས་ཉེབ་མར་རྟིང་ས་ཉེབ་འཛགས་སམ་ས་ཉེབ་རྟག་རྟར་ས་ཉེབ་བཅས་ལྷན་སྐོར་གྱི་རྟགས། ཚོད་དོན་ཡིག[48]

༡༢༽ གོ་ངོ་མ་དང་ཚིག་ཤུས་ཀྱི་དམ་འབེབས་[49] བྱས་ཤིང་སྟག ཟླ་ཚེས་ལ།།

---

36 Recte: སྤྲེད་བསྟན་
37 Recte: དགའ་
38 Recte: རྫོང་བདའ་.
39 Recte: དཀྲུག་ཤིང་
40 Recte: རྫོང་བདའ་.
41 Recte: པན་ཚུན་
42 Recte: དགོངས་
43 Recte: གཞག་
44 Recte: ཚད་བཟུང་
45 Recte: སྲུང་མ་
46 Recte: དེ་
47 Recte: སྐྱལ་
48 Recte: ཡི་
49 Recte: ཕེབས་

Photo 16.1: Facsimile Tibetan copy of the 1854 Extradition Treaty

An annotated translation of the 1854 Treaty[50]

[*Title*:] Wood-Tiger Year [1854]: [This is] an exact copy [of one of the] two original versions of the extradition accord outlining what is to be done in cases when a person should happen to stir up trouble at the border between the Great Ganden Phodrang (dga' ldan pho brang) [i.e., the Government of Tibet] and the Foreign World [i.e., the British East India Company].

[*Narratio*:] In line with the resolution[51] which was entered into last year between the Great Ganden Phodrang and the Venerable [British East

50 The pattern of this translation follows Schwieger (2015: 4–5), who notes that almost every Tibetan document is divided into 'three major parts: the *protocol*, the *context*, and the *eschatocol* or the *closing protocol* (…) In the *context*, which is the main part of the document, we often find *publicatio*, *inscriptio*, *narratio*, *dispositio*, and *sanctio*. (…) (T)he *publicatio* (or *promulgatio)* (…) contains the notification to the public, the *inscriptio* identifies the addressee. The *narratio* then informs us about the preliminary events leading up to the issuance of the particular document. (…) (T)he *dispositio* contains the legal act. Finally, the *sanctio* warns against violating the decree and may set out the punishments for such violations in more or less precise terms'.

51 The term *chod don* is translated as 'resolution, decision' in several Tibetan-English dictionaries. However, in the Tibetan-Tibetan-Chinese dictionary (Bod rgya tshig mdzod chen mo: 824), the political interpretation of the term is downgraded, and

India] Company with the *Guru*, the [Three] Rarity,[52] and the red and black Dharma Protectors established as witnesses,[53] which concerns the Ganden Phodrang (dga' [ldan pho brang]) subject, Sherab Dakpa (shes [rab] grags [pa]), both [parties] are encouraged to limit themselves to only benefiting one another, to being nothing but friendly with one another instead of there being a situation between them where one of them is the winner and the other the loser. Nonetheless, various baseless rumors, not knowing who had spoken that but rather being blamed on a demon instigation, have gone back-and-forth between both parties and have been an object of doubt and concern.

Therefore [in early 1854], to minimize these problems, Ngaphoe Namgyal Dorjee of Takdzong (stag rdzong[54] nga phod rnam rgyal rdo rje)[55] and Kyitoepa (skyid stod pa)[56] who was acting on the instructions

---

it is defined simply as a settlement of a dispute, for example, *rtsod gzhi 'dum 'grig gi don gnad*, i.e. 'the principal points of reconciling a dispute'. In the same dictionary, the term *chod don* is glossed as *kha mchu 'grig pa'i kha chad yig cha*, i.e. 'the document [outlining] the agreements arranged in a legal case'.

52 In Sanskrit: *triratna* refers to the Buddha, dharma and sangha, which is commonly translated as the Three Jewels.

53 See Heller (1992) for further details about the various wrathful Dharma Protectors or guardian spirits connected with the Tibetan state. Moreover, the red and black Dharma Protectors are generally understood to be the two primary protector deities of the Central Tibetan Government, i.e. Nechung/Pehar and Palden Lhamo.

54 It is not clear why Takdzong (stag rdzong) is written before the family name 'Nga phod'. It might be that Namgyal Dorjee temporarily took over the position of the fortress commissioner (*rdzong dpon*) of Taklung Dzong (stag lung rdzong) or that his family was related to the Staklung Kagyu (stag lung bka' rgyud pa) school.

55 Ngaphoe Namgyal Dorjee (nga phod rnam rgyal rdo rje) is none other than the unnamed 'son of Nga phod' (nga phod *sras*), as recorded in the biography of the eleventh Dalai Lama (Petech 1973: 99). Based on the biography of the eleventh Dalai Lama, Petech notes that he 'was appointed *mi-dpon* in 1849 and appears with that title in 1852 and in 1853, when the emperor granted him the peacock feather; he was appointed *lha-gnyer* in 1854'. Namgyal Dorjee was with Kyitoepa (skyid stod pa) in 1854 in Tezpur, Assam, to meet the British Indian officials and to represent Lhasa at the highest level. He might be the great-grandfather or great-great uncle of Ngaphoe Ngawang Jigme (nga phod ngag dbang 'jig med, b. 1910, d. 2009). See Petech (1973: 99–104) for further details about the 'Nga phod' family.

56 Kyitoepa (skyid stod pa) who is described as a kind of 'deputy for the Minister, Shedra (bshad [sgra]; bka' 'brel bshad zhabs)' is Kyitoepa Dorjee Dondup

of the [Minister] Shedra zhabdrung (bshad [sgra] zhabs [drung]), came specifically to the confluence of the Chukarpo River and had a discussion with Gyanchand Singh Sahib from Tezpur, Martin Sahib, Jackson Sahib, and Doctor Sahib about these rumors, during which time nothing new was decided upon beyond [what was already in] the agreement and all things hidden and revealed were completely clarified.

[*Dispositio*:] Henceforth, if there should happen to be a subject from the Ganden Phodrang (dga' [ldan pho brang]) who instigates provocation in a functional capacity between the Great Ganden Phodrang (dga' ldan pho brang) and the Venerable [East India] Company, who in heart and mind [i.e. in their relationship] have become joined like water and milk, they will be arrested, extradited to Taklung Dzong (stag lung rdzong), and detained accordingly, without fundamental freedom of movement. [Similarly,] if there happens to be a subject from the [East India] Company, such as an atsara (a tsa ra, ācārya, i.e., an Indian) who provokes trouble, he will be arrested and sent/brought back to the stronghold of Gyanchand Sahib of Tezpur, and thereafter will not be left free to his own devices.

[*Sanctio*:] Henceforth, in order to make the underlying intention [of the arrangement] between the parties clear/transparent, it was requested that parties adhere to the [terms] of the agreement recently settled on the fifteenth day of the twelfth month of the Water Ox year [i.e., 1854]

(skyid stod rdo rje don grub). Petech (1973: 91–92) states that 'in 1853 he was a phokpon (*phog-dpon* [seventh rank]) and again accompanied Shedra, this time to Tawang (rta dbang)'. Petech further states that Dorjee Dondup became a cabinet minister or *kalon* (*bka' blon*) around 1858. Tenpa (2016: 85, n. 33; 88) argues however that the two unnamed Tibetan officials in the Tibetan copy of the 1853 treaty are Kyitoepa Lhaden Chime (skyid stod pa lha lden 'chi med) and Shedra Wangchuk Gyalpo (bshad sgra dbang phyug rgyal po). Although the family lineage of Kyitoepa is said to have been broken in the early twentieth century, the family estate continued. This famous estate, known as the Kyitoepa school (skyid stod pa slob grwa), was a school run by Chinese Kuomintang representatives in Lhasa from 1933–1949, where Chinese language was taught to Tibetans. For further details about the Kyitoepa family, see Petech (1973: 91–92). Kalon Shedra (bka' blon bshad sgra) here refers to the famous Shedra Wangchuk Gyalpo (bshad sgra dbang phyug rgyal po, d. 1864), who took the name of Shedra after marrying Shedra Dondup Dorjee's (bshad sgra don grub rdo rje) daughter. He quickly rose to the position of *kalon* (*bka' blon*) and ruled Tibet for some time after consolidating power. See Petech (1973: 165–180).

and the agreement previously entered into [as well]. However, when someone makes appeals in a deceitful sort of way that contradict [these agreements], it is requested that, whoever it may be, should be handed over immediately, with the Guru, [Three] Rarity, and Dharma Protectors gathered together in truth [as witnesses].

[*Eschatocol*:] The seal of Ngaphoe Namgyal Dorjee of Takdzong and Kadrel Shazhab (bka' brel bshad zhabs).[57] The [seal] represents together Gyanchand Sahib of Tezpur, Martin Sahib, Jackson Sahib and Doctor Sahib.[58] [This] was copied from the exact words of the original agreement document and firmly established on the date in the Wood-Tiger [year, 1854].[59]

Closing remarks on the treaty

It is possible that this agreement could be the first extradition treaty ever signed between British India, represented by the British East India Company, and Tibet. One of several interesting points in the treaty is the authors' use of the term 'foreign world' (*phyi gling*) and 'Supreme or Venerable Company' (*rje btsun kum pa ni*) to refer to the British East India Company and, by extension, India, in place of simply using the Tibetan term for the country (i.e., rgya gar/dkar). Indian officials' names are also recorded alongside those of English representatives. This implies that the Tibetan officials were fully aware with whom they were having a diplomatic relationship and with whom they were concluding a treaty. The document also mentions the existence of previous treaties entered

---

57 See notes 52, 53 and 54 for further information about these two signatories.

58 A seal signifying the Tibetan representatives can be seen at the end of the document. See the next note.

59 This black, square seal contains three columns of *'phags pa* script with double rim lines. A symbol of a sun on top of a crescent moon is marked at the top middle of the seal. The script is difficult to decipher, but I have roughly identified the columns as follows: col. 1. *phun po ta la*; col. 2. *tshogs so*; col. 3. *bkra shis so*. Schuh (1981: 17) notes that several versions of this kind of seal exist, all of which closely resemble each other and were used by the Tibetan cabinet (*bka' shag*) from 1728. This seal may have been carried and used by Ngaphoe (nga phod) and Kyitoepa (skyid stod pa) to represent the cabinet minister Shedra (bshad sgra).

into between Tibetan and British Indian representatives. These treaties may refer to the 1844, 1852 and 1853 agreements, but this is neither clearly nor categorically stated. The treaty under review accords with the clauses of those other agreements, with this new one emphasizing that pre-existing relationships between the two powers ought to be maintained and not damaged. While it seeks to secure the border regions safely, the agreement also allows any individual who tries to disrupt the relationship and cause disturbances in the border regions to be extradited to the relevant authorities and forbids culprits from roaming freely on opposite sides of the border.

Although the symbol representing British India is mentioned, a seal is not visible on the document. However, the seal signifying the Tibetan representatives can be seen at the end of the document. It is mentioned in the last line of the text that it was copied from an original, probably a Tibetan copy (which may well be lying safely in Lhasa). Still, it is not fully clear whether the treaty was translated from the as-yet-undiscovered English version or was copied directly from a text written in Tibetan. Even though we know that an English copy of the 1844 and 1853 agreements exists,[60] the original English copy is definitely not published in any of Aitchison's fourteen volumes of collected treaties. As the exact English copy of the treaty has not been found, I argue that the publication of such documents and the choices made regarding their contents, whether they be in Tibetan or English, is selective.[61] For example, Shakabpa recorded a supplementary treaty reached between British India and Tibet on the first day of the third month of 1853.[62] This treaty, which is related to the treaties of 1844, contains only Tibetan officials' names, and the document does not record the names of any of the local Monpa chieftains involved, which can be found conversely in the English version of the agreement.

Similarly, Aitchison's collection of treaties from 1844 and 1853 only records the names of Monpa elites and British Indian officials and not those of Tibetan officials, with whom British Indian officials reached agreements. Unpublished copies of treaties hopefully still exist in the India

60 Aitchison (1938); Tenpa (2016).

61 Tenpa (2016: 90).

62 Shakabpa (1976; 2010: 592).

Office Records (IOR), London, or in the National Archives of India (NAI), New Delhi. As Tibet is currently under the Chinese administration, the legal aspect of this translated treaty cannot be ignored because Schweiger raised the legal authentication of those documents of pre-colonized Tibet.[63] Sørensen, however, argued that '[Schweiger]'s selection of rare historical documents no doubt is chosen with a view to verifying that Tibet was part of China'.[64] The importance of those documents and their contents, hence, cannot be ruled out because theoretically and legally the country is still considered an occupied nation.[65]

Bibliography

Tibetan language sources

Aris, M., ed. (1986 [1728]). *Rgyal rigs. Sa skyong rgyal po'i gdung khungs dang 'bangs kyi mi rabs chad tshul nges par gsal ba'i sgron me* (short title: *Rgyal rigs 'byung khungs gsal ba'i sgron me*, author Ngag dbang [byar bande Wagindra]) (The Lamp Which Illuminates with Certainty the Origins of Generations of 'Earth-Protecting' Kings and the Manner in Which Generations of Subjects Came into Being Is Contained). In *Sources for the History of Bhutan*, Vienna/Wien: Arbeitskreis fur Tibetische und Buddhistische Studien, pp. 11–85.

Blo bzang thabs mkhas (b.ca.1787–d.ca.1827). *Rta dbang grwa tshang gi gtsug lag khang rten dang brten pa bcas legs bcos rab gnas dang chos rgyun sbyor 'jags gnang skor gyi byung ba brjod pa'I dkar chag* (*Rta dbang sdod ring sgra tshangs la 'byor 'jags byas pa dnag/ gtsug lag khang gsar gzheng legs gso dnag/ rab gnasur jee sgrubs pa chen po 'dren zhus bskor byi dkar chags*). Copy of a cursive manuscript of 49 ff (*dbu can* ms, 25 x 8 cm) from the private collection of Michael Aris (1980).

Bod rgya tshig mdzod chen mo (Tibetan-Tibetan-Chinese Dictionary) (1993). Beijing: Mi rigs dpe skrun khang.

Mkhas grub rgya mtsho'i rnam thar (n.d.). *Lhar bcas skye rgu'i gtsug nor 'phags chen phyag na padmo rje btsun ngag dbang bskal bzang bstan pa'i sgron me mkhas grub rgya mtsho'i dpal bzang po'i rnam par thar pa ngo mtshar lha'i rol myong byangs can rgyud du bsnan pa'i tam+bura.* The biography of the eleventh Dalai Lama Mkhas grub rgya mtsho (b. 1838, d. 1856) compiled by Blo bzang 'phrin las rnam rgyal, 267 ff.

63 Schweiger (2015).

64 Soerensen (2015: 282).

65 Walt van Praag (1987).

Mon chos 'byung (1988 [1728]). 'Rje 'bangs rnams kyi rigs rus kyi 'byung khungs gsal ba'i sgron me'. In Nga phod ngag dbang 'jigs med, ed., *Bod kyi lo rgyus rig gnas dpyad gzhi'i rgyu cha bdams bsgrigs* (Selected Research Materials for Tibetan History and Culture, vol. 10), Beijing: Mi rigs dpe skrun khang, pp. 87–130.

Western-language sources

Aitchison, C.U. (1865). *A Collection of Treaties, Engagements and Sanads: Relating to India and Neighbouring Countries*, 13 vols. (Reprinting and republishing of the last edition in 1929 [1938], vol. XIV, p. 90.)

Andvik, E. (2010). *A Tshangla Grammar*, Leiden: Brill.

Bayly, C. (1988). *Indian Society and the Making of the British Empire*, Cambridge: Cambridge University Press.

Bodt, T. (2020). *Grammar of Duhumbi (Chugpa), Languages of the Greater Himalayan Region, Vol. 23*, Leiden: Brill.

Bodt, T. and I. Lieberherr (2015). 'First Notes on the Phonology and Classification of the Bangru Language of India', *Linguistics of the Tibeto-Burman Area*, vol. 38, no. 1, pp. 66–123.

Census of India (2014). *Census of India 2011 Arunachal Pradesh, Series 13 Part XII-A, (Tawang and West Kameng) Village and Town Directory*, Itanagar: Director of Census Operations, Arunachal Pradesh.

Dondrup, R. (1993). *Brokeh Language Guide*, Itanagar: Director of Research, Arunachal Pradesh Government.

Dzongkha Development Commission (2016). *Dzongkha-Brokat Bi-lingual Language Book*, Bhutan: Dzongkha Development Commission.

Dzongkha Development Commission (2018). *Tshanglhai Drayang: A Tshangla-Dzongkha-English Lexicon*, Bhutan: Dzongkha Development Commission.

Gait, E. (1996). *A History of Assam*, Calcutta: Thacker, Spink and Co.

Heller, A. (1992). 'Historic and Iconographic Aspects of the Protective Deities Srung-ma dmar-nag'. In I. Shōren and Y. Zuihō, eds., *Tibetan Studies: Proceedings of the Fifth Seminar of the International Association for Tibetan Studies, Narita 1989*, vol. 2, Tokyo: Naritasan Shinshoji, pp. 479–492.

Hyslop, G. and T. Karma (2008). 'Preliminary Notes on Dakpa (Tawang Monpa)'. In S. Morey and M. Post, eds., *North East Indian Linguistics*, vol. 2, New Delhi: Cambridge University Press India, pp. 1–22.

Jacquesson, F. (2015). *An Introduction to Sherdukpen Language*, Bochum: Brockmeyer.

Lamb, A. (1996). *The McMahon Line: A Study in the Relations between India, China and Tibet, 1904 to 1914, I, II*, London: Routledge & Kegan Paul.

Lieberherr, I. (2017). *A Grammar of Bulu Puroik* (PhD dissertation, University of Bern).

Mackenzie, A. (1884). *History of the Relations of the Government with the Hill Tribes of the North-East Frontier* (reprint: [1995]. *The North-East Frontier of India*, Delhi: Mittal Publ.).

Mizuno, K. and L. Tenpa (2015). *Himalayan Nature and Tibetan Buddhist Culture in Arunachal Pradesh: A Study of Monpa*, Tokyo/Heidelberg: Springer.

Mon chos 'byung (1988 [1728]). 'Rje 'bangs rnams kyi rigs rus kyi 'byung khungs gsal ba'i sgron me'. In Nga phod ngag dbang 'jigs med, ed., *Bod kyi lo rgyus rig gnas dpyad gzhi'i rgyu cha bdams bsgrigs* (Selected Research Materials for Tibetan History and Culture, vol. 10), Beijing: Mi rigs dpe skrun khang, pp. 87–130.

Paul, A. et al. (2018). 'Phenological Characteristics of Rhododendron Species in Temperate Mixed Broad-leaved Forests of Arunachal Himalaya, India', *Journal of Forest and Environmental Science*, vol. 34, no. 6, pp. 435–450.

Paul, P.L. (1939). *The Early History of Bengal*, Calcutta: The Indian Research Institute.

Petech, L. (1973). *Aristocracy and Government of Tibet: 1729-1859*, Roma: IIMEO.

Post, M. and R. Burling (2017). 'The Tibeto-Burman Languages of Northeastern India'. In G. Thurgood and R.J. LaPolla, eds., *The Sino-Tibetan Languages*, London/New York: Routledge, pp. 213–242.

Schuh, D. (1981). *Grundlagen Tibetischer Siegelkunde. Eine Untersuchung über Tibetische Siegelaufschriften in 'Phags pa Schrift*, St. Augustin: VGH Wissenschaftsverlag.

Schwieger, P. (2015). *The Dalai Lama and the Emperor of China: A Political History of the Tibetan Institution of Reincarnation*, New York: Columbia University Press.

Shakabpa, W.D. (1986 [1976]). *Bod kyi srid don rgyal rabs, Vol. 2*, Dharamsala: Tibetan Cultural Press.

Shakabpa, W.D. (2010). *One Hundred Thousand Moons: An Advanced Political History of Tibet* (trans. D.F. Maher), Leiden/Boston: Brill.

Sørensen, P.K. (2015). 'Book Review: *The Dalai Lama and the Emperor of China: A Political History of the Tibetan Institution of Reincarnation, 2015*', *Cahiers d'Extrême-Asie*, vol. 24, pp. 281–283.

Tenpa, L. (1991). *Skad rigs ma 'draw ba'i dbye zhib thengs dang pa'i snyan zhu / Report on the first Linguistic Survey of Bhutan*, Thimphu: Dzongkha Development Commission Royal Government of Bhutan.

Tenpa, L. (2014). 'The Centenary of the McMahon Line (1914-2014) and the Status of Monyul until 1951-2', *The Tibet Journal*, vol. 39, no. 2 (Autumn/Winter), pp. 41–86.

Tenpa, L. (2015). 'Peripheral Elites of the Eastern Himalayas: The "Maternal Uncle Lord of Ber mkhar" of Tawang'. In O. Czaja and G. Hazod, eds., *The Illuminating Mirror: Tibetan Studies in Honour of Per K. Sørensen on the Occasion of his 65th Birthday*, Wiesbaden: Dr. Ludwig Reichert Verlag, pp. 485–509.

Tenpa, L. (2016). 'Notes on the (Tibeto-) Mon and Sherdukpen Treaties with British India in the 19th century', *The Tibet Journal*, vol. 41, no. 2 (Autumn/Winter), pp. 73–101.

Tenpa, L. (2018). *An Early History of the Mon Region (India) and Its Relationship with Tibet and Bhutan*, Dharamsala: Library of Tibetan Works and Archives.

van Driem, G. (2007). 'Dzala and Dakpa Form a Coherent Subgroup Within East Bodish, and Some Related Thoughts'. In R. Bielmeier and F. Haller, eds., *Linguistics of the Himalayas and Beyond*, Berlin: Mouton de Gruyter, pp. 71–84.

Walt van Praag, M.C. (1987). *The Status of Tibet: History, Rights, and Prospects in International Law*, London: Westview Publications.

Index

Subjects

Person's Names

Geographical/Area Names

Ethnicity Groups

Dialects/Languages/Language Groups

www.ingramcontent.com/pod-product-compliance
Lightning Source LLC
Chambersburg PA
CBHW072038020426
42334CB00017B/1311
* 9 7 8 1 9 2 0 8 5 0 2 4 1 *